Peirce's Pragmatism

Critic of Institutions

Roberta Kevelson
General Editor

Vol. 15

PETER LANG
New York • Washington, D.C./Baltimore • Boston
Bern • Frankfurt am Main • Berlin • Vienna • Paris

Roberta Kevelson

Peirce's Pragmatism

The Medium as Method

PETER LANG
New York • Washington, D.C./Baltimore • Boston
Bern • Frankfurt am Main • Berlin • Vienna • Paris

Library of Congress Cataloging-in-Publication Data

Kevelson, Roberta.
Peirce's pragmatism: the medium as method / Roberta Kevelson.
p. cm. — (Critic of institutions; vol. 15)
Includes bibliographical references and index.
1. Peirce, Charles S. (Charles Sanders), 1839–1914—Contributions in pragmatism.
2. Pragmatism. 3. Methodology. 4. Peirce, Charles S. (Charles Sanders),
1839–1914—Contributions in methodology. I. Title. II. Series.
B945.P44K483   191—dc21   97-52786
ISBN 0-8204-3982-7
ISSN 1068-4689

Die Deutsche Bibliothek-CIP-Einheitsaufnahme

Kevelson, Roberta:
Peirce's pragmatism: the medium as method / Roberta Kevelson.
–New York; Washington, D.C./Baltimore; Boston; Bern;
Frankfurt am Main; Berlin; Vienna; Paris: Lang.
(Critic of institutions; Vol. 15)
ISBN 0-8204-3982-7

Cover design by Nona Reuter.

The paper in this book meets the guidelines for permanence and durability
of the Committee on Production Guidelines for Book Longevity
of the Council of Library Resources.

Printed in the United States of America.

Acknowledgements

I dedicate this book, my tenth on Peirce, to Tom Sebeok. It is not Tom I look to for insight into Peirce's theory of signs but to Peirce himself. Over the past twenty years, however, it is Tom Sebeok who continues to make Semiotics visible, viable and open. He symbolizes for so many of us who have had the good fortune to know him what an ideal, living pragmatic method *does*.

At this time I also express my appreciation to Penn State for its considerable support of this project. I thank also at this writing, six months since I have moved to Virginia, the warm hospitality of the College of William and Mary with whom I enjoy being a Visiting Scholar. Once again I thank Cambridge University and the Library of Congress for opening their collections to me.

Several of the chapters presented in this book were first offered in colloquia. I have tried to incorporate where appropriate suggestions and comments from these meetings. With the exception of the chapter on Peirce and Eco earlier versions have not appeared in other publications. Not least, I thank Cindy Palecek for once again transforming my rough drafts into good looking copy!

CONTENTS

Part One:
The Praxis

Chapter 1

Introduction: An Argument for Peirce's Pragmatism

Introduction: An Argument for Peirce's Pragmatism

I
Pragmatism: Leading Principles

All reasoning challenges the status quo. Whatever challenges the state of affairs, in politics as in theoretical issues — in whatever represents the authoritative viewpoint at any given time — is an upstart. Such an upstart, from the point of view of Huizinga's *Homo Ludens* may be a Rebel, A Spoilsport, a Revolutionary, and all of the above *in some respect*. The challenger is at one and the same time an Outsider and an Insider in relation to the status quo in question. To say that one challenges a reigning or dominant idea is to speak, by implication, in contradictions, oxymorons, incongruities.

The role Peirce scripts for his protagonist/challenger is the functor/actor: Pragmatism. It makes little difference whether we call it by Peirce's pet name, *pragmaticism*, or by the name it goes under in public discourse: *pragmatism*. This idea, Pragmatism, which carries the colors of Charles Sanders Peirce and goes forth to do battle for him in the arena of academia in Cambridge, Massachusetts between the 1860's and the late 19-teens, is the great iridescent hope of this American genius, this voice in the wilderness of American thought.

To personify and anthropomorphize and even mythologize Pragmatism, we may picture it in our imaginations as neither the quixotic Don nor as his commonsensical sidekick, and surely not as the sweet lady-object of the Don's affections and ideal devotions. Rather Pragmatism sallies forth in search of no Grail but the picaresque process for itself. The end of the quest is more and better quests, and to serve as example or representative of the never-ending adventure in search of game: The game of big thought.

Thus Pragmatism is Peirce's Hero. Pragmatism is Peirce's leading metaphor, as the poets say. Pragmatism is the title or term for the impetus or cosmological frame Peirce holds as he develops this character, Pragmatism, throughout his life, from the time he first conceives it in the 1870's until his death in 1914. Pragmatism is Peirce's persona. It is a persona which has several, at least two, alternating masks or faces. One such face is that which Peirce uses to describe Pragmatism in the late 19th century, prior to his pivotal decade of the 1890's. The other mask, i.e, its alterity, takes on its discernable features throughout the 1890's, a turning point for Peirce; it wears this alter-image thereafter. The early features become assimilated, not replaced, by the pragmatic alterity Peirce poses in his late years. His cosmology, a *hyperbolic cosmology* he tells us, (which is further discussed in the closing chapter of this book), brings forward his concept of reason as a sinuous, continuous dialogic argument which grows by articulation, if I may play with this word which brings into single focus the physical means for flexing and bending together with the notion of ideas transformed into speech in flight.

This book presents a radical approach to Peirce's Pragmatism since it is neither here nor there, on any popular bandwagon for any interpretation of Peirce's — or other — concepts of pragmatism. But it goes back to the source, to the root of this idea: to Peirce. Here it attempts to recover Peirce's own understanding of this Pragmatism he hatched, this 'gryphon' which leaves its enigmatic mark like a footprint in the sand, like a flower pressed between leaves of a journal, like some primeval creature out of our cosmic time.

In our time, in 1932, in a review of the first volume of the *Collected Papers of Peirce,* John Dewey wrote that philosophy has grown into Peirce's own conception of it, i.e., Peirce had argued that 'philosophy is that kind of commonsense which has become critically aware of itself,' (*The New Republic*, vol. 69 Jan. 6, 1932:741).

In the more than six decades since this review we find Dewey's Peircean observation to be a self-fulfilling prophecy among philosophers, such that philosophers are self-critical to the extent that they feed upon themself for the commonsense purpose of providing opportunity to cultivate this idea called philosophy. Each new generation tends to change the meaning of this term. Perhaps such modification, via argumentation as suggested above, is a revolutionary continuum. Perhaps, as I suggest, it is even heroic. One can only observe and try to adduce the reasons for so doing, and perhaps even jump to conclusions. The idea of philosophy grows, as has the idea of Peirce's Pragmatism. But as the century unrolls, philosophical self-criticism comes to resemble a kind of solipsism, since the mainstream search is still for Truth and constants. Philosophical self-reflexion comes to resemble that uroboric serpent of ancient myth which eternally swallows its own tail and repeats and repeats, cyclically, its own syllogistic song.

Here and there is evidence of Dewey's prophecy, that when philosophy has had the opportunity to be nourished by Peirce it will come away with a 'new and fresh imagination.' Only such an imagination, Dewey continues, will further philosophy and free it from the 'intellectual fortification of the past,' (above). What has actually happened is a betrayal of Peirce, such a betrayal as that committed by James toward Peirce.

But here the entire philosophical community has acted in concert. Peirce has been used for self-serving philosophical purposes, and not with disinterest. Dewey's epithet, that Peirce 'is a philosopher's philosopher...in an unusual degree' (Dewey, above, at page 740), has led to misappropriations of Peirce by the philosophical community. It is my hope that this book, and some works of others, will remedy this harm at least in some respects.

I mention above the betrayal by William James, of Peirce. I want to speak briefly on this matter, as part of the introduction to this book:

II
Academic Flaps

Despite the far greater power of his thought it was not Peirce but James, with Josiah Royce, who came to define the mainstream of American Philosophy between 1890 and 1910, i.e, in that transitional period between centuries. And the term, Pragmatism, was much more closely associated with James than with Peirce, even until this present time a century later.

It was James' Pragmatism, severely criticized and found wanting by Peirce, that came to be held as the referent, general notion for this idea/method/theory. These threads are still untangled. James' betrayal of Peirce, which led to his own prominence in American thought, is rarely if ever investigated. What is especially shameful is not the Jamesian ambition, cloaked by a sweet and likeable personality by many, then as now. But there have been supporters of James, opposed to Peirce, who have attempted to expunge from the records evidence of how James went about his treachery to Peirce. Some of the expungers, it must be admitted, seem to have been protecting Peirce from vilification, and have for reasons never clarified passed over Peirce's acts of self-destruction so that these documents are now so well hidden that if they do indeed still exist a detecting process of incomparable excellence might, *only might,* abduct the situation from the present circumstances of Peirce's playing second to Royce and to James.

In summary: Peirce had stepped up to take the part of his friend Francis Abbott, who had behaved badly toward Royce. Abbott had been caught up in a current rush to formulate a cosmic philosophy and to attempt to restore a proper place to Natural Law. This was around 1887.

At that time ideas in America as in Europe were beginning to ferment a 'cosmos of romantic naturalism,' (Schneider, at page 322). From this cosmological perspective the universe was likened to an infinitely evolving organism, or in von Humboldt's words, (cited by Schneider, above at 322), as 'evergrowing and unfolding in new forms.'

This notion of ever-novel creating of new forms, new idea-forms of beauty and value, was the motivating force behind David Brewster's marvelous invention of the kaleidoscope, we recall, which made a stunning impact on German thought as well as upon parlor pastimes, (Kevelson, 1996). In a significant sense, Brewster's kaleidoscope as a result of his studies in Optics, and David Bohm, in the twentieth century, who developed the cosmology of an 'implicate universe' of chaos out of order (in our own time) are fellows linked together in this project which then appealed not only to Peirce, but became an impetus for his friend Abbott.

But it was Fiske, in the 19th century — Peirce's and Abbott's contemporary and ideational adversary — who inadvertently touched off the catastrophe which forever bent the course of Peirce's professional life out of shape. To recall: Fiske's cosmic views were in the wake of, in line with, Spencer's. Peirce had publicly and in explicit detail rejected Spencer's concepts of evolution and of ethics. While Spencer stopped short of calling his ideas a cosmology, Fiske did not. First in 1884 'The Destiny of Many' and in 1885, 'The Idea of God' and in 1887, 'The Idea of God as Affected by Modern Knowledge.' Fiske's views came out at the very time that Royce was rejecting Spencer for reasons similar to that of Peirce who had also criticized the eminent philosopher.

In fact, Royce's approach as a young scholar to natural evolution in 1885 was much admired by Peirce, (Schneider's account, above). For reasons not clear, but suspect, Abbott took advantage of Royce's leave of absence from his Harvard teaching responsibilities in 1887. And during this time Abbott published his own lectures, 'The Way out of Agnosticism', which did not acknowledge indebtedness to Royce. Royce was enraged at the usurping tactics of Abbott, and he hit back hard.

It was in this climate of a rush to stake out claims to a new cosmology that a scientific philosophical cosmology began to develop. Its first move was to reject nominalism of all kinds, which Abbott did, between 1860 and 1880, (see Schneider, pages 326-327). This emergent cosmological paradigm held that the cosmos and the human inquiring mind are in dialogue, that they are reciprocally interrelated.

But this 'dynamic correlation' of subject/object has not a single source, or Prime Mover. It originates by means of a fusion, or an interaction between *two* mutually dependent 'ultimate origins,' *Mind and the Cosmos*, (Schneider, at 327).

The idea of experience as reflection upon lived experience is held as a link between mind and cosmos. It is, further, a mediating process. Experience, i.e, the *idea* of experience, is the mediator between 'reason and imagination.' This concept of 'experience' should seem familiar to Peircean pragmatists since it is the *ground* of his pragmatism. It is the Indexical function of all semiosis. It is the representation of actual experience as oppositional, interactional, dramatological, and conflictual. Experience is Peirce's Secondness. It is the fulcrum upon which the cosmos spins.

Abbott defines experience as the 'actual meeting, the dynamic correlation, the incessant action and reaction of the human mind and its cosmological environment,' (in Schneider, at p. 327, citing Abbott's *Scientific Theism of 1885*, Boston, at pages 39, 40, 60-72).

We know that Peirce had been caught up in this cosmological whirl of ideas, and was closely familiar with the works of Fiske, Youmans, Draper, and Carus, of the United States, and with then current work on cosmology in Europe as well. About the time of the mid-1870's his own groundwork for a cosmology had been laid. As Schneider notes (pages 334-343), Peirce began to develop his cosmology based on the scientific method, on pragmatism as he defined it, and on principles of evolution (not necessarily Darwin's).

Peirce fused his own cosmological views — his evolutionary cosmology — to a reappraisal of Schelling, as brought forward by Royce around the 1885 period. This fusion or conflation of two otherwise incompatible complex ideas was called by Peirce a 'synechistic agapastic tychism,' (Schneider, at 334).

It is around this time that he begins to identify himself as a *Schellingian*, (CP 6.86-87; 6.415).

The concept of implicateness — of an 'unfolding' of the universe, from 'mere chaos' — through stages of 'habits of mind' as Bohm is to examine in the mid-twentieth century, is to go through several reformations and modifications until we now have a process which shows the chaos stage as the *aim* of inquiry, and habits of mind as *provisional* stopping places in need of reactivation.

Indeed, in Peirce's very late work, following his realliance with Royce and his admiration for Royce's *The World and the Individual* we see almost no trace of the antipathy which characterized their relationship immediately following the Royce-Abbott flap.

At that time, in response to Royce's anger at Abbott which publicly humiliated Abbott, Peirce wrote a scathing letter to President Charles Elliot of Harvard, demanding that he dismiss Royce from his recent status as faculty member (which had been strongly supported by James, even as James *seemed* to be in support of Peirce).

To step back a bit, Elliot had been eager to shape the Harvard whose responsibility he had accepted as its new President by strengthening its graduate faculty. To this end he had invited Peirce to be one of five senior and distinguished faculty to head this new development. Peirce, with customary cavalier free spirit, chose to absent himself from this challenge in order to pursue a then current project with the Coast Survey. One may easily imagine Elliot's sense of having been openly insulted, and that the honor he had bestowed upon Peirce had been flouted. This, on the edge of Peirce's unseemly behavior at the Johns Hopkins University, and his general reluctance to defer (to anyone), seems to have been for Elliot the final indication that Peirce was to have no home in his Harvard.

By contrast, James' reputation flourished, and Royce, despite (or because of Peirce's letter against him to Elliot), became the star of the Harvard Philosophy department. James then brought in Münsterberg from Germany to head up the Psychology department and thus added insult to Peirce's injustice in that institution.

Peirce tried for a position at the University of Chicago. But George Palmer, a very close friend of Royce, wrote to the President of that university and, tit for tat, pointed out that Peirce was unsuitable for a position and should not be appointed. He wasn't. Palmer became the right hand of Elliot at Harvard. Dewey shaped the Chicago school. And Peirce was a Pariah from then on.

It is astonishing that there is only one mention of this letter, admittedly was in the worst possible taste, that Peirce wrote to Elliot to dismiss Royce. This letter is referred to by Knight in his 1965 edition, *Charles Peirce*. Knight names as source for information about this letter the *Collected Papers*, in the volumes edited by Arthur Burks. The edition he refers to is 1958.

My edition, of 1979, tells a different story: First, there is no mention whatsoever of any letter from Charles Peirce to Charles Elliot. *But a kind of transference has taken place:* The letter that was formerly described as from Charles Peirce to Charles Elliot is now, in 1979, listed as a letter from Charles Peirce to Charles Elliot *Norton*! We know that Peirce and Norton *did* know one another. But the coincidence of this correspondence never having been mentioned, and the correspondence between Charles Elliot and Peirce having been *expunged* in 'uncanny' fashion due to the similarity between the two names — Charles Elliot and Charles Elliot Norton — is strange. *Either* one ardent protector of Peirce had wished to protect him at all costs and simply took the letter from one file and placed it in another, *or*, such protector took the embarrassing letter from Peirce and destroyed it, and simply changed the listing in the Correspondence section of Volume VIII of the *Collected Papers*. Or what? But, to my knowledge, no letter from Peirce to Charles Elliot Norton can be found in the Norton correspondence, of which has been published two volumes.

It is understandable, although shameful, that even in the interests of protecting Peirce from further criticism of character, one devoted Peirce follower might have permanently misplaced this letter. But it is not understandable nor forgivable that in the course of a quarter of a century of presumably editing Peirce material this sleight of hand would not have been noticed. Unfortunately there are too few people bearing the label *Peirce 'Scholars' who actually read Peirce at first hand*. All evidence is that in the interests of a mutual stroking activity such people read one another's work, in brief, and tacitly agree to call it Peirce Studies.

What is most shameful is the waste of Peirce! What is shameful is the betrayal of Peirce! What is shameful is the tacit cover-up of James' betrayal of Peirce, for James jumped on to the more palatable, more popular bandwagon of Josiah Royce. And maybe in the decade or two before his death Peirce was so persuaded to do likewise, for survival. And maybe he really did believe in this change of horse in midstream. We won't know.

For there is no one connected with safeguarding the Peirce legacy, the manuscripts and related materials, who knows anything about the lost letter, the shifted letter, the shifting of ideational steeds in this foment of the 1890's. There is no clue in Peirce's biography, (Brent, 1990), and dumbness prevails.

The consequences of this fateful decade of 1890 to 1900 requires that the work prior to this time be reappraised in the light. I do this in the forthcoming, *Peirce and the Mark of the Gryphon*, (1998).

III
Forecasting

The chapters of this book, on pragmatism as Peirce himself conceived this concept of a method, look at this multifaceted term from several positions.

Peirce's notion of Common Sense is to be distinguished from Scottish Common Sense Philosophy on this point in particular: It is not so much, as the Scots maintained, that we are all partaking of the same body of truths, but that the general experience of living on this planet and being made as we are, as humans, allows us to be compatriots in a way of responding to those brute facts that hit us all. It is this basis of Commonsense, as Dewey points out, which presses us to listen closely to our instincts, 'not as forms of knowledge, but as the ways of acting out of which knowledge grows,' (Dewey, review of volumes 1-6 of the *Collected Papers*, 1937: 415).

And further, whatever we mean by our mutuality, our social bonding, we need to recognize that 'the social principle,' as Dewey quotes from Peirce, 'is rooted intrinsically in logic,' (above, at 416). Logic, Peirce's expanded logic, is all of what is comprised by his theory of signs.

Pragmatism is the process. When we evaluate how we act, pragmatism produces ideas which may be organized into a theoretical coherence, into Semiotics, the name of the theory of signs.

This volume's approach to Peirce's Pragmatism has three parts: the first, which includes this introductory chapter, discusses the idea of pragmatism as a transforming process, a mode of transmuting ideas. The second part explores pragmatism in relation to social principles, i.e, to the social institutions which represent those principles writ large. In the third part of this book I talk about pragmatism in connection with natural language, including the transformation of language by poetic activity. In this last section I close with discussion of Peirce's cosmology.

This third section concludes with a kind of epilogue in which I want to emphasize the injustice done to Peirce which may become a lever for legitimation. If Peirce has his day in court — in the judgments of future scholars of his semiotics and pragmatic method — we may yet see that he is of more consequence vilified than vindicated. As villain he is a rebel, an outlaw, a spoilsport, an initiator of a new game. That, quite possibly, may be his best-fated luck.

The idea of Peirce may well parallel, even represent, the strange, continuing transformations of the idea of the 'villain.' The significance of a term, Peirce says, lies not in its philosophy but its etymology.

In chapter two I emphasize that to Peirce Pragmatism attempts to proceed along what Peirce calls the Quest of Quests, (Kevelson, 1987). Pragmatism is the 'Method of Methods' in its orientation which is to seek out vulnerability and openness in systems of signs and use such weakness as points of connection between two or more sign systems. Wherever a universe of discourse is not firmly defined, there is an opening for a new relation to be made. It is the purpose of Peirce's Pragmatism to effect such relations, and to then reflect upon them, i.e, to be critical of them as pragmatism acts as critic of all established sign-systems that become, by virtue of this establishment institutional systems of order. Such order is always provisional. This process, or method of methods, is that which is operative in any dynamically growing, open, free society.

We are reminded in the fourth chapter that semiotics is about intellectual concepts insofar as such concepts of thought-systems represent the actual world, i.e, the world of lived experience. Here I discuss two very different views of experience as idea, and two very different uses of hypothetical reasoning. Although I am not a mathematician, Peirce's criticism of Poincaré does not require mathematical reasoning to see the distinction between these two great intellectuals. It is also important to make the distinction that Peirce urges pragmatists following his method to use mathematical reasoning as a model, but only as a model. Mathematics is not adequate to exploring aspects of human relations in the way that a Peircean Pragmatic approach does. As we will see in later chapters, it is dilemmatic reasoning which characterizes the Peircean Pragmatic method; but it is mathematical reasoning which serves as a model from which to improvise. It is such improvisation which is, in Peirce's pragmatic method, a spontaneous kind of transforming of one representation into other, one sign into others.

In chapter three, on transformations, I show connections between image-making and evolving ideas which comes out of the preparatory investigations, *before* semiotic analysis. This preparation is phenomenlogical; the phenomena it looks at are the phenomena of thought. Peirce holds that thought is substantive, in much the way that Robert Boyle suggests, and he *uses the alchemical model in rhetorical fashion.* Peirce adapts alchemy as well as mathematics — and other modes of seeking out 'solutions' — but *transforms* his referent models to serve in this new, adaptive process.

The second section, the medial portion of this book is, appropriately, concerned with such practical affairs as are within the purview of the law. Law and economics are those semiotic systems which draw resource from actual human affairs in a manner that most closely, of all the human sciences, exemplifies the exchange of goods and values as perhaps no other social institutions do.

This 'Indexical' part of the book connects back to language and from language back once more to the instinctual basis of Peirce's pragmatism. In Part Two I look at the Realism of Justice Holmes which, in my view has been derived from ideas exchanged between Holmes and Peirce during their brief association in the Metaphysical Club in Cambridge, in the early 1870's, (Kevelson, 1988, 1990).

I claim that much of what becomes to be of central importance in American Legal Realism, and perhaps to some extent in Scandinavian Legal Realism as well, comes out of fundamental notions of a Peircean Pragmatism. Since so little of Peirce's writings on practical affairs and social institutions has been available, and one finds it only by sifting through the voluminous manuscripts many times, it is Dewey, not Peirce, who is largely seen as the founder of those pragmatic or instrumental concepts which Realism is built upon. Between Dewey in socio-political affairs and James in psycho-philosophical matters Peirce comes to be seen, as Dewey describes, as a 'philosopher's philosopher;' a might-have-been genius, and a lot of trouble to get to know at first hand.

Nevertheless, the last chapter of this middle part of this book discusses aspects of Peirce's Esthetics, the 'science of value' he calls it, and Ethics which is abstracted from the law. Here I develop some ideas introduced in my study of Peirce's highest value of Freedom, (Kevelson, 1993). It is this Peircean, pragmatic notion of Freedom which is the core concept of his cosmology, as we will see in the final chapter of this book.

This last third part consists of three chapters: one focuses on contrasts and comparisons between Peirce's and Jakobson's approach to language. It was Jakobson who first introduced me to Peirce's semiotics, and it was Jakobson, whose insight into Peircean semiotics and pragmatism so profoundly influenced many most distinguished members of the semiotic community of inquirers, including Tom Sebeok.

The penultimate chapter in the book briefly discusses some aspects of relatedness between Peirce and Umberto Eco, another of the great explorers of this new place, Semiotics. Neither Sebeok nor Eco are primarily, in terms of their own central interests, Peirceans. But they constitute such an impressive gang of three in this exploration of Peirce's pragmatism that I feel they add an after-image glow in inimitable fashion.

In the final chapter I talk about Peirce's cosmology, a topic which is rarely discussed. Yet it is that topic which enables one to present, or represent, a Peircean 'world view.' Such a world-view is not a Whorfian view. Nor is it the world view of Alan Marquand, Peirce's student who went on to establish the first department of aesthetic criticism at Princeton, (Kevelson, 1990, 1993). Rather Peirce's cosmology — a hyperbolic cosmology — tells us that his leading ideas are a fusion, a pragmatic con-fusion, of Rhetoric and Mathematics, (note the absence of he final 's' in Rhetoric, which I lightly attempt to explain in the chapter on transformations).

This opening chapter of Peirce's Pragmatism continues the work of my preceding book, *Peirce, Science, Signs*, 1996. This, in its turn, brought forward my work on Peirce in earlier books, e.g., in *Peirce's Esthetics* of *Freedom*, upon *Peirce, Paradox, Praxis*, and upon a long series of books and articles I published on Peirce over the past twenty years.

This present book in its turn is part of a continuum, such that the next deep breath and expirative study will be on Peirce and myth and the making of real ideals.

Peirce holds that all living ideas are continua. I testify to that conviction with my own strangely Peircean, nonlineal, multidimensional mode of growing meaning.

It is a truism that we all speak out of our times, our place in the world. Peirce so spoke early in his career: his words grew through more than fifty years which followed his observation:

'...if materialism is blind, idealism without materialism is void,' (from 'The Place of our Age,' originally published on page 12 of the *Cambridge Chronicle* on November 21, 1863, and reprinted in *Writings of Peirce*, Vol I, 1982:101).

Chapter 2

Bridging the Human Sciences

Bridging the Human Sciences

I

On Instincts and Milky Ways

A puzzling and even surprising fact: the tendency among Peircean semioticians, and Peirce scholars in general, to presume that Peirce says Do as I Say, not as I Do. Peirce is rarely taken as a man of considerable integrity. By this I do not refer to his sometimes scandalous social behavior as judged by Victorian mores. Neither do I refer to the pieces and fragments of his writings which have not been fit together, by him or others, into an academically coherent whole text. Rather, when I refer to the probity of Peirce, I wish to underscore what should be an obvious fact: he, himself, puts to good use his instrumental, pragmatic Method of Methods as a way of *doing*, of acting out his Theory of Signs: Semiotics, (Kevelson, 1987).

From Peirce's perspective the term Semiotics stands for a mode of action, where thinking, evolving ideas and making them meaningful — literally, *making thought matter* — is what the pragmatic method is about. Pragmatism, or the method of doing semiotics, accomplishes two basic goals: 1) it increases the meaning of human thought activity by making it larger and at the same time more complex, and 2) it satisfies its 'quest of quests' through a process of bringing together into a more comprehensive relationship two or more universes of discourse — ideational sign-systems which have achieved conventional definition among sign-users/inquirers and, hence, a symbolic function and habit of thought, (Kevelson, 1987).

These two functions of the *method* of semiotics — pragmatics — can be understood to correspond and to interpret — as *ideas interpret ideas* in Peirce — that which Peirce has identified and described as the two basic instincts of human beings: The one is to satisfy a sense of want, of emptiness and appetite and to become *more* if not larger. The other is to reproduce, not by cloning but in relationship with that which one is not, and so create a kind of metaphoric issue, a verisimilitude and a more comprehensive sign. The first is, simply, the motive for meaning and *making meaning matter*. The second is affirmation of the paradoxical community of individuals. As I discuss elsewhere, (Kevelson, 1995), these two basic instincts take countless forms and directions as they evolve and change over time, space and context. These prototypical instinctual forces are not of a causal nature but are referential as a First: an Immediate Interpretant Sign. I will speak more of this.

Every classification of ideas — of the ideas of the sciences as well as other kinds of ideas — traditionally attempted to show the genesis of types of scientific inquiry and to also show major branchings as unified by their having origins in a common root. But this traditional tree-model branching from abstract to concrete, from metaphysical to physical, fails to show how the most practical and humanistic sciences are related, and it gives little or no idea of how sciences are continually intercommunicative.

According to Durkheim's much-cited observation that sociology is the geometry of social forms, the constructivist's geometry retains some of the old Euclidean rigidity and linearity since it wishes to hold onto some traditional constants. But Peirce's pragmatism, as Durkheim knew, is unable to use ideal truth. It thereby replaces the universe — the world as One — with a pluralistic Cosmos: an 'infinity of networks that are made up of various "lines of influence," networks that are little worlds that serve as a basis for our action,' (Durkheim, 1955/1983:25). But in this discussion, where Durkheim speaks directly of James' pragmatism, and to a considerable extent also of Peirce's quite different concept, Durkheim notes that even the model of a cosmic network leaves too much to fall outside of these various lines of influence. We must invent/make equitable intermediaries, (Durkheim, above). Unfortunately for Durkheim and for us, most of Peirce's work was not accessible to him. For if it had been, one may speculate, he as Peirce would have said — and shown — that the business of pragmatism is to create the cosmos as a vast, living, growing, continually changing representation of intellectual energies: a light-and- sound show in which we, as our institutions — our complex and various modes of conduct — are the actors playing our happenings, linking our lines, making our mazes ever more amazing (as Peirce describes) and spinning sense and sign into this adventure, this high adventure of **becoming** *Lost in the Cosmos* (as the late Walker Percy knew and chose; see final chapter in this volume, on Peirce's cosmology).

I suggest that we try to locate Peirce on some dune or promontory of his own native, historical context: in the middle of the nineteenth century when good people of several stripes were trying, no less vainly than now, to accommodate social Darwinism, humanism, pragmatism, and that 'old religion' within the mold of a familiar, monistic universe.

What Peirce characteristically does is to take an idea which has achieved some semblance of definitiveness, some habitualized and symbolicized notion, and recast it to suit a new purpose, to mean a new meaning, to matter in a new way. He is a copy cat. But in the case of Peirce the Pragmatist, *copying* is also redone as a new idea. It is not mere duplication, transfer, cloning. But every copy is a new correlation to Peirce between the old and defined, and the emergent unfamiliar something strange and vague. For example, when Peirce takes the term 'pragmatism' and deforms it by adding another syllable, he is creating, by *means* of this new term, a link between the old idea of Pragmatism and the new idea of Pragmatism, which he calls *'pragmaticism.'*

Note, he does not take for 'pragmat*i*cism' the then fashionable plural form of the suffix, '-ics', but goes a step backwards to recover the singular suffix, '-ic.' We recall that the suffix, '-ic,' denoting a certain group of sciences, was the early form in English. This changed only after 1600 to the more familiar form in English today, '-ics,' which was the equivalent of the suffix used by the ancient Greeks, as in Ethics or Physics. This had the tendency to legitimize the older Anglo-Saxon and English use of Mathematic, Poetic, Politic, by showing them as *significantly* equivalent with the pluralized classical sciences. But, the '-ic' symbolically connoted a dynamic activity, whereas the '-ics' stood for a constant or a state: a Truth-Sign.

It is curious that Peirce could have chosen either suffix, and accomplished his purpose of differentiating his own term for *his* pragmatic method from others. Phonetically, there is little difference between *Pragmaticsism* and *Pragmaticism*. The difference lies in the iconicity of the term, the implicit reference to the 'dynamic' English suffix, in contrast to the 'stative' plural classical suffix. All this is conjecture on my part which rests, on the one hand, on the somewhat playful informative accounts of etymologists and lexicographers, and on the other hand, on Peirce's much-claimed affiliation with the British and Common Sense philosophers. What is also of interest here is that not all sciences denoted by the singular suffix-marker, '-ic,' changed to the plural. For example, Music, Rhetoric, Logic (this last-mentioned is inconsistent) have retained, with the '-ic' suffixal form, certain meaning-values which are vestigially connected with the context in which this form is associated.

The question has occasionally been raised about distinctions between Peirce's, and others' use of Semiot*ic* as compared and contrasted with Semiot*ics*. It would seem to me that Peirce sometimes chose the term *Semeiotic*, sometimes *Semiotics*. This choice is not, to my knowledge, ever explained. But when he chooses the plural *semiotics* he is intending, I think, to point to a theory of signs such as *derives from* a method of acting, to which he gives the single-suffix denotation, '-ic,' as in *Pragmaticism*. *He is calling attention in this manner to a tension between the method and the theory.* This tension is a poetic aesthetic tension such as Roman Jakobson discusses, (Jakobson, 1960).

As late as 1905, in a letter to Calderoni (CP 8.206) Peirce writes that Pragmaticism, as he uses the term, '... involves a complete rupture with nominalism.' He goes on to say, 'Pragmaticism is not a system of philosophy. It is only a method of thinking.' Yet it is a way of thinking that has its grounding in related systems of thought: ' ... it best comports with the English philosophy and more particularly with the Scotch doctrine of common sense,' (CP 8.207)

Peirce also takes his cue from much of what the British pragmatist Schiller had to say on the unification of ethical conduct with moral principles, i.e., principles of human value. It is by means of the scientific imagination that bridges are made to connect prevailing norms, i.e., institutional norms, with ethical interpersonal living. But both pragmatists realized that serious problems are connected also with the notion of 'moral principles' since they rest on eternal, given Truth; whereas ethical norms are created through human interaction. Peirce, as Schiller, held that 'moral principles' are remnants of the 'folklore of right conduct,' and the premises of this folklore should be held up for inquiry, (see also C. Wright on Pragmatism, in Madden, 1963).

Peirce's reinterpretation of the *use* of 'folklore' and of 'myth' becomes, *via his* Pragmatic Method, a compass for Cosmic venture. More of this follows, (see also Kevelson, 1998).

I don't intend to introduce a discussion which compares Peirce's concept of pragmatism with others, since that would lead too far afield for the present purposes. However, Peirce is consistently explicit in his wish to distinguish *his* understanding of pragmatism as semiotic method with the various ways this term has been explained and used elsewhere. In particular, Peirce rejects the idea that pragmatism, in his sense, is equivalent with the idea of humanism, since humanism, as generally understood by the British Schiller and others of the late 19th century, was taken as an *alternative to moral philosophy*. Humanism generally substituted ethical norms for moral precepts; the former derives from positive philosophy whereas the latter is rooted in religion, (Ritchie, 1958).

Nevertheless, the Human Sciences so-called are not necessarily subdivisions of Humanistic philosophy, (Kevelson, ed., 1991:1-18; 193-218). Rather, the term 'human sciences' appears to have evolved through the tactics of rhetoric which attempted to present an equivalence between the social or practical sciences and the physical or so-called 'hard' sciences, (Hughes, 1964). Peirce is especially concerned to show that the social and physical sciences alike are shaped to a large extent by what he has described as the 'rhetoric of scientific discourse,' (mss 774, 776, 777; Kevelson, 1987, 1995). The method of each kind of science must be appropriate to the respective purposes of each. And the style of discourse — the rhetorical representation of each special universe of discourse — should not only conform with the purposes of each, but the mode of inquiry, *the dominant system of reasoning which characterizes each special kind of scientific research*, should be appropriate as well. If the reasoning is inappropriate, and if the style of discourse is inappropriate as well, then there has been, says Peirce, a flagrant violation of those ethical norms which guide the conduct of people of science.

Pragmatism, as Peirce wanted that term to be understood, is not a method of inquiry applicable to the practical and social sciences only, but is the method of inquiry adaptable to all the sciences, since scientific behavior with respect to any and all its objects is an open, evolving universe of ideas. Each special kind of science, if a genuine science, must hold constants and referents in general as fictions only, but must be always in flux, ready to change perspectives, assumptions, truths, and even its own reflexive, symbolic view or *sign of itself*, (ms 309).

The paradigms of the physical sciences change most slowly, as Peirce knew, and as has been the topic of much fruitful discussion since and prior to Kuhn. But the paradigms of the social sciences shift more rapidly, since they are more closely representative of the actual affairs and interrelations of people in society, in the dynamics of chance and change. All attempts to mold the social sciences as replica of the physical sciences, especially in the 20th century, have resulted in grotesque distortions and reductions of human beings and human values, with the result that the human sciences, so engaged, are like double visions or dual representations: 1) of the more so-called 'distinguished' physical sciences, and 2) of themselves as signs of themselves, as parodies bordering on scientistic activity, as meta-science as well.

Semiotics since the 1960's emerged as a kind of revolution in both attitude and activity of scientific investigation, on the one hand shunning everything that smacked of mathematical reductions, and on the other hand open to the warm fuzzies of human values, the nuances of human sensibilities, the sensual textures of social life. Many babies have drained out of various semiotic hot tubs. Indeed, anything that seemed tainted with analytic and positivistic science has been suspect. We especially find an enigmatic attitude toward Peirce, particularly among semiologists on the Continent who seem to find in Peirce's semiotics something of a positive nature and hence hostile to notions of community, of intersubjectivity, of intuition, of the love of arts and all that jazz! (Habermas on Peirce, 1968).

At the same time that Peircean semiotics and the method of pragmatics are said to be anti-human, where 'human' here is a buzz-word for soft and sentimental, all of Peirce's work is focused on values, social institutions, human conduct, whatever passes under the canopy of 'goods' and is the product of creation, invention, imagination, and possibility. Peirce's pragmatics represents, above all, a confidence in the human wish, will and ability to be free and undetermined, to take nothing as absolutely caused and given once and for all. It represents even the most paradoxical of all americanisms, i.e., that one may lift oneself up by one's bootstraps, which is to say, one may be self-moving and fabricate such boots that want to keep on walking. Unlike the cautious approach of continental semiologists who hang onto their givens and their fixed truths — their aristotelian legacies —

for dear life, for the sake of the state of things as they are, the Peircean pragmatism is a trip with the cosmos: it is by design continually and improvisionally made-as-we-go, a rolling rock, a peregrine, a traveller in search of another.

As Peirce knew too well, it's a hard life! But Faust knew it also, knew the high cost of selling out for some enduring, some eternal easy Truth. Peirce revives the Faustian legend/myth with a new cosmic twist: a down-to-earthiness. Just as it has been useful to compare individual nation-states with individual human beings, the difference being one of scale and complexity it has been argued, it is no less useful to compare each of the sciences, hard and human alike, with individual human beings. Again, the differences are those of scale, style, composition and complexity.

There are isomorphs in the process of making relations, of making relations matter, which permit us to speak of each human being as a relate term with others, each nation-state as a relate also in a global community, and of each field of scientific activity as a relate with other fields or universes of principled inquiry. Each kind of relationship exists as a tension, an interaction not only between the individual realities, but in the push-and-pull between the tendency to specialization on the one hand, and to greater generalization on the other hand.

According to Peirce each is a mode of experimentation, where experiment characterizes experience and interaction in the world. *Thus the dominant semiotic function is Indexicality* underscoring the fact that the human sciences, representing human affairs, is oppositional, dialogic, relational, tense. The Index represents the *idea* of the actual and hence is a token of the *general idea* of the Real.

II
Social Machinery and Scientific Imagination: Questions of Compatibilities

Peirce wrote several drafts of a study on the lives of great people of science. This work was done in the early years of the 20th century, in which he wanted to assess where he was in the light of where he had been. He looks back upon the 19th century and observes that it has been an 'era of machinery' — not the machinery out of which factory production is made, nor construction of marvelously engineered buildings, nor mechanical invention only. Machinery, he qualifies, refers to the various *systems of organization*, such as we find 'in politics and in business, such as trusts and trade-unions, machinery in all the methods of research, physical, philological, historical, philosophical, mathematical, even of machinery in art and in poetry,' (CP 7.263). And he asks whether such machinery — organization — that might well have produced new inventions and discovery in all the above-mentioned areas, improvements, renovations in the quality of the daily lives of humankind, is indeed in a position to benefit from such advances. Rather, is it the case Peirce asks, that 'machinery' (*as* organization) did not also have a negative effect with respect to the 'production of great personalities ...' (CP 7.264). Why, he asks further, is there such a widespread concern that machinery — organization at so many different places of social life — inhibits great individuals from developing?

He says that in principle the improving of conditions for human personality should predictably produce even more remarkable people. What the 19th century did accomplish was to provide opportunities and contexts designed to bring about the emergence of superior people. Yet, he says, the 19th century 'has certainly lacked its due quota of great personalities.' But as his own experimentation showed, *and he realized*, his original assessment of greatness had left out of account characteristics of people not easily measured. Such characteristics which were not readily observable and measurable, such as visible, tangible evidences of greatness, led to the exclusion of a large number of 19th century remarkable persons. As an experiment in a class at The Johns Hopkins University which he taught, Peirce raised the question as to what 'greatness consists in.' This led to the realization that not only differing degrees of objectivity were needed in this kind of evaluation, but different kinds of objectivization were needed as well, (CP 7.265-66).

I would suggest that his realization of the kinds of observation at play in evaluating goods of several kinds led to Peirce's distinguishing between two major forces or factors interrelated in the historical development of western science: the first concerned the investigation of the place and the role of the earth in relation to the cosmos; hence the significance of astronomy. The second concerned the development of abstract inquiry to Truth *held more or less constant*, as mathematics to axiomatic referents; this second mode or factor focused on relationships between changing patterns and natural vicissitudes to 'natural laws'; it influenced 'the study of dynamics,' (CP 7.272-3).

But there was also a third factor, developed late, which had to do with the 'direct efforts' of inquirers to influence the direction and growth of that which constituted the environment of humanlife. It was a mode of intervention, Peirce suggests, which emerged as a response to deterministic, or mechanistic, reaction to contextual forces. Here Peirce says that what he first attempted to do was to show that if a relationship of forces and motivations, such as between natural evolution and Christian moral precepts could be made, if these two seemingly incompatible principles could be connected, then blind response to evolutionary forces could come under the control of the effort to shape life according to ethical and moral values. Peirce pursued this direction, as did many of the early — and later — scientists of human affairs, (CP 7.275). Peirce rejected the Absolutes and he evolved a theory of Pure Chance, (Peirce, ms 309; Kevelson, 1995). Yet he *reinterprets* the idea of the Absolute around the 1890's (see the concluding chapter in this volume; see also Kevelson 1998).

Without taking this further here, it is worth noting that Peirce began to realize that discovery could be deliberately brought about by harnessing the scientific imagination in such a way that one could, experimentally, create a hypothetical relation between two individual modes of inquiry. In his case he brought together, in a comparative, contrastive relation, the history of science with the principles of logic. He set out to make an intellectual community between two distinct universes of discourse. In the beginning his approach was similar to that of Hume's, and was largely an inductive approach in which he attempted to find a basis for relationship on points of similarity, or dissimilarity.

This procedure, which he calls 'experimental analysis' is a semiotic process. Peirce says it may be represented by conjecturing a model for inference and by investigating the organizational components of both spheres under observation. He began, in other words, by pragmatically speculating 'into the mechanical causes of the phenomenon' in question. This led to serious problems, for in order to develop this analogous procedure he realized that he had to retain the *idea* of a 'given' of an ideal form. Note that this experimentation to produce a new hybrid 'machinery' took place around the early part of the 1890's. It raised the great problem of how to determine 'the constants' needed for this kind of quest of quests. The attempt to link Christian morality with the making of the social machine and social evolution, in general, resulted in Peirce's great insight, namely that complex systems seek relationship in spontaneous fashion, as does the free marketplace argued for by Hayek and kindred spirits, (Kevelson, 1995). Thus, an iconic 'ideal' representation of an *idea of a constant* became, in Peirce, the provisional *legisign*.

Peirce says it is not external manipulation but an instinctual-like behavior — a representation of instinctual conduct toward community, satisfaction of want, and breaking of bounds — which becomes manifest in spontaneous transactions between people, and in simulations of such exchange between the social sciences in free, experimental climates of inquiry.

I certainly do not want to leave the impression that Peirce's ideas of the pragmatic method were unknown or undervalued during the formative years of modern semiotics in Europe. They were important insofar as we know they were known. But often, as is the case with Durkheim, the reputation of a scholar is made during his or her lifetime and posthumous writings do not always, or even usually, effectively act so as to transform a whole body of work. For example, it is really not until Durkheim's lectures on pragmatism were published after his death that we realize how much of Peirce's pragmatism influenced the shaping of his theories of social sciences. Durkheim's 1914 lectures, for example, written in the year of Peirce's death, are explicit tributes to Peirce, for precisely the reasons that Peirce himself wished his pragmatism to be understood:

The most important connection Durkheim makes in these late-published lectures has to do with the rejection of causal forces in the development of cultures, of peoples and their institutions. Like Peirce, Durkheim attempts to find an influence of great magnitude upon the development of social systems, and upon the principled and scientific inquiries or discourses which evolve to explain such social phenomena. What Durkheim comes up with is a notion of the 'primitive,' as powerful motivating forces such as we find in mythology.

Myths are not constant and eternal truths. They evolve, grow, change in relation to the manner in which they are interpreted and used. Durkheim calls attention to the way that the ideas of Truth, as seen by the pragmatists following Peirce, are 'enriched and become more complex.' And he asks, is it the case that Truth changes? Do the 'laws of life' change, just as the various species evolve and change? He answers, that what is meant by Truth, what represents the idea of Truth, does indeed change. But the *feeling* that Truth is perceived seems to remain as a primitive feeling, constant yet moving forward, into and pervasively as a part of human societies. He further points out that the very notion of pluralism in pragmatism changes, as the inventors of this idea well knew, (Durkheim 1955/1983:73-76).

Unfortunately Durkheim's lecture on 'Pragmatism as a Method' has been lost. But the basic premises, as far as can be known, are closely in line with those of Peirce, (above, at 59). But in my own earlier study comparing Durkheim and Peirce I show that Durkheim attempts to establish a coherence among the various social sciences by arguing that they represent the way in which society itself, in actuality, coheres through contractual relations. Thus the legal contract is modelled upon a presumed relation originally that was *actually* social, (Durkheim, 1892:215, in 1955/1983). The idea of the contract becomes represented in contract law. This same contractual model is observed to obtain between the social institutions as well. Thus the contract becomes a symbolic sign-function, an isomorph which, I suggest, serves to compensate for and to offset a sense of imbalance and instability in open, dynamical societies, and in discourses on the social sciences as well, (Kevelson, 1992:193-218 at 211). Each mode of interaction cross-refers to and represents the other: The Real (signs) and the Actual (existence) interact.

It is worth noting, before going on to the next section, that Durkheim takes pains to contrast the position of the 'idealist' with that of the pragmatists. Of the former, the idealist-humanists, he says that they generally hold the belief that since 'Man is a product of history and hence of becoming ... there is nothing in him that is either given or defined in advance ... (But) ... Everything is a product of certain causes.' Thus if it is the case, according to the humanist-idealists, that sociology is human product just as reason is a human product, whatever reason consists of must be regarded as *made*, as a result of, an effect of, historical causes. These causes are, as it were, *virtually* cut in stone. This is the traditional basis of the social sciences, (for further discussion on Peirce's influence on Durkheim see Kevelson, 1998, pp.193-218).

But in sharp contrast, pragmatism takes the view that the so-called historical causative forces may be differently assessed according to such perspectives/interpretations as may be taken upon them; hence, their reasoned meaning, their consequential meaning, may bring about different results, Durkheim suggests. If, indeed, we are not to *deduce* from constant Truths, but are able to employ and utilize a mode of reason which permits us to revise a leading premise or principle, then the whole meaning of what one means by 'causative force' in sociology — the shaping as well as the description of social systems — *evolves the idea of Cause also*. Thus, the 'scope' of the 'pragmatist theses' is enormous! By 'softening' the idea of Cause, of Truth, we make it malleable, plastic, Durkheim suggests. By so doing we take from it its 'absolute and as it were sacrosanct character,' (Durkheim above at p. 66).

Peirce has, we recall, redefined the notion of 'cause' to a mode of 'explanation'. But first, we see that Durkheim has put his finger on the crux of the problem of relativism as a pragmatic product. He asks: 'If truth thus has a personal character ... (i.e., an interpretive character) ... how can impersonal truth be possible?' (Durkheim, above, at p. 75). His answer is pure Peirce: he says that according to pragmatism we *may use the idea of the truth as an ideal* — an 'ideal final stage' — toward which all opinion would converge if all inquirers employed the same general method. Here Durkheim cites James. But the allusion to Peirce is clear and unmistakable.

At the heart of Durkheim's argument for the pragmatic acceptance of the truth as the useful, utility is viewed as a mode of play, that kind of play which has been expressed through the history of humankind as mythology. Thus the pragmatic method as creative play weaves the parts and pieces of social subsystems into a coherent text where common mythic values, epic poetry, legend and lore of icons of many matters feed and nourish the 'primitive' still alive and growing in the modern world. It feeds the force of miracles, while at the same time it represents the *idea* of miracle as a *real fiction*. This is the focus of my next book-in-progress.

Peirce wrote one of his most important discussions on the use of hypothetical reason by focusing on Humean miracles. He did this at the beginning of the 20th century when he was especially concerned with the need to redefine the idea of 'science,' with respect to what it is that science *does*.

Peirce takes the occasion of 'miracles' to preface his most mature writings on pragmatism. He relates evolution with a new, possible dynamics in human relations, a relation which his expanded logic (in the Normative Sciences of his theory of signs) describes. This new dynamics is antithetical to the Spencerian mechanistic approach to evolution which Peirce had attacked in the 1880's, to his subsequent academic misfortune, (see Chapter One of this volume). The old mechanistic or mechanical philosophy must give way to an idea that the world is not 'governed by blind forces,' but by choice, by the conjoining of powers of individuals into *ad hoc* or provisional groups, the purpose of which is to unify *as needed*, and to dissolve such order when it is no longer useful or of value.

As said earlier, the making and unmaking of human social orders is paralleled in law by the concept of the legal contract, such that it is the law which binds the parties into agreement. It is the law which also dissolves — literally, brings about dissolution of the contract — when the performance — the acts — are done. Elsewhere I discuss the 'Impossible Contract,' (Kevelson 1992, 1995: Chapter Seven of this volume).

Peirce in 1901 reminds his readers that he had attacked Spencer at a time when such attack was unprecedented. But Hume's attacks upon biblical miracles was, in Hume's time, a familiar and well tolerated kind of heresy. Peirce proposes to take Hume's argument a further step and build upon Hume's established platform, (Kevelson, 1995). This, as I noted, is Peirce's style!

To extrapolate from Hume's argument against proof of miracles by testimony and his argument against the 'necessary' connection of a pattern of co-occurring events in expected, predicted pattern, we want to step back from Peirce to Hume, and into the turmoil during the first half of the 19th century over the issue of divine causation.

During this period two spheres of presupposition vied for position as intellectual/spiritual right: the first held that the force of divine causation extended into all effects created, such that the original force or divine power could be held as a connective bond unifying all creation as having issued from a single source and carrying forward the primal force as part of its own mission. The other, contending assumption, which was Hume's, is that connections between events in the world are continually made, fabricated, and fashioned on the basis of human experience. The binding force is extruded by human inferential powers and, hence, human bonds are self-made. On the basis of the scientific imagination and *induced* compatibilities — or differences — new connections are made and new orders ligated.

Hume rejected the notion that like causes produce like effects. He rejected as well the inference that one may thus reason backwards and forwards, as on a reciprocal two-way street. Hume argued against symmetry, and denied thereby proof of causative force, in the traditional absolute sense. If a reciprocal change by the effect upon the cause is not verifiable then the causative force itself is not verifiable.

Further, if one then says that interventions in the line of action between cause and effect, in the old sense, are themselves uncaused and not directly emanating from the causal source, then the usual answer, that they are miraculous, will not hold since the miraculous is anti-reason, supernatural, unprovable, and hence logically impossible, says Hume.

This, in a simplistic manner, sums up Hume's challenge to those who would explain the extraphenomenal as extralogical, and not reasonable: Explanation explains the explainable; reason is of the reasonable. This was a springboard for Peirce.

Since an intervention which is not caused is a violation of both the 'laws of thought' and of the 'laws of nature' then how does the person of science accept and affirm that which our sensibility affirms and our reason denies? The cartesian response was to deny our sensibilities. Peirce's response to this denial was to reaffirm that which we know through our common experience, even if that experience is hypothetically assumed and may, indeed, be commonly mistaken. Such assumed shared experience is the representation, or idea-as-sign of such common experience.

In order to correct shared error one must have an appropriate method of reasoning which permits the inquirer to go back and revise initial, leading principles, basic assumptions. And if these leading principles are not absolute truth, and not absolute divine cause, then they are not sacrosanct. That which is deeply spiritual of human beings and their relations must not be confined to axiomatic principles, Peirce suggests. Rather, this concept of spirituality must be of a free spiritual action, as free in the action of thinking as in other social, human interactions.

Peirce returns to the Humean argument to assert that relations between the force which originates an action is not reversible but rather, the action is of an asymmetrical nature. At the same time, the force is carried along *in* the action; the permutation which occurs as the action evolves *changes* the force and the consequential thing, and changes as well the vehicle which is its *way* of moving, *its path which it cuts as it goes*. Of note: Hume's continuum is lineal, whereas Peirce's is *curvilineal*, (Kevelson, 1993, 1998).

Thus the way in which semiotics, in Peirce's sense, understands the sciences to be connected is not through fixed bonds or natural laws which are constant holding forces.   Rather, all parts of this dynamic process of organizing, or of the machine-making we call the human sciences, are interactive components of transformation, of self-organizing, self-destructing, and again-re-organizing happenings: from order to chaos to order; from meaning to more meaning, to *yet* more meaning, *even as disorder grows and increases in significance*, (see concluding chapter of this volume).

In the last section I want to touch upon Sidney Hook's understanding of Pragmatism as an expression of life as tragic, (Hook, 1974).   The tragic, as we recall, points to a rupture in the social fabric which can never be restored, since restoration would negate the very action which was tragic.   Only 'classic' comedy, which assumes recovery of the old state of affairs, is symmetrical.   That was the old closed-world understanding of tragic-comic acts.   In a Peircean cosmos the ideas of the tragic and the comic remain, as impression, marks in the mind of humankind.   But Peircean pragmatism interprets them, remakes them anew.   These are not constant archetypical referents in Peirce's cosmos.

III
Lost and Found in the Cosmos

I apologize for parodying Walker Percy's title of his last book, since I admired him and felt he understood Peirce as Peirce wanted to be understood, (Percy, 1983).   But Peirce does change his concept of the idea of Cosmology, from a mathematical metaphysics (CP 6.213) to a possible time and space: an endless time and space, which is not to be confused with an abstract time and space, or context in which only disembodied spirits and pure minds are conceivable.   A cosmology which corresponds with the continuous, self-generation of thought must be seen as *mattering*, as literally *making* the physical fibers that connect the matters of fact which are experiential. This conceivable cosmology — a 'perfect cosmology' Peirce calls it — has the character or feature of conducting itself in such a way as to connect his 'three universes,' (ms 1476; CP 6.490).   Indeed, this may be a cosmology *as* 'scientific mythology,' (Toulmin, 1982).

These three Peircean universes of Experience are common knowledge to people everywhere, he says.   The first of these universes 'comprises all mere Ideas'; their function is to bring forward possible thinking out of fantasy, poetry, all idle speculation and playtime, abstract mathematics, and all those actions of the imagination which are the midwifery of thought.   The second Universe is 'that of the Brute Actuality of things and facts,' which cannot be doubted and rejected unless and until they are examined and inquired into. The third Universe, says Peirce, is that which depends upon the other two, but which has, as a consequence of this interdependence, the honored task of being that 'active power to establish connections between different objects, especially between objects in different Universes,' (CP 6.566).

This evolution of Peirce's idea of the Cosmology *produces* his Method of Methods: — of Pragmatism. In turn, his pragmatism spawns Semiotics or the theory of signs. In its most primitive mode Cosmology is a fusion of those basic instincts: to satisfy hunger and grow, and to become connected to another in order to reproduce oneself as *not oneself*, i.e., to break the first Law of Thought and violate the law of identity. At a sophisticated reach of Peirce's imagination the primitive and the cosmic meet. The meeting is occasion for the triadic wholeness of human beings: The Icon, The Index, The Symbolic functions of human thought make bridges, link and make whole those universes of meaning produced of itself yet free to *become*, to *mean more*, to Matter.

Pragmatism for Peirce was the 'method of methods,' (Kevelson, 1987). Its 'quest of quests' was, and is, intended to link individual ideas of people as well as complex idea-systems, such as we understand and identify each of the several sciences and each of the social institutions that people create. The major or predominant designations for those organizations for social discourse which pragmatism seeks to connect are Medicine, Law, Economics, Psychology, Politics. These are intellectual 'handles' of the significant human sciences at this, our time, and at Peirce's time as well.

Peirce suggests that the place of connection is best made at the most worn edge of the definition of any system of signs since that is where each science, or any definable sign-system, is most vulnerable, is most receptive to contact, to co-mingling with other systems. *Like a nation-state, or like an individual human being, when one lets one's guard down it is a signal to a neighbor that the boundary mutually shared is thin and fuzzy and is in fact a bridge or spannable gap: an open possibility*, (Kevelson, 1987, 1993, 1995).

Finally, I mentioned above a warm recollection of Walker Percy with whom I first exchanged ideas on Peirce and semiotics in 1977, at the first ISISSS meeting in Toronto. He had just recently written *The Message in the Bottle*, which was a kind of rite of passage into the idea of Semiotics in the 1970's among undergraduates at Brown, where I was then completing what was to be the first doctoral dissertation on Semiotics. We corresponded briefly and occasionally since then.

Walker Percy subtitles his book, *Lost in the Cosmos*, as a last 'self-help book.' Early on he proposes an experiment people might fool around with if they wished to know who and how they are. Under the option entitled 'the cosmological self' Percy says whoever chooses this means of self-knowledge is actually choosing two choices: one is to be unconscious of itself and the other — its mate — is to become conscious of itself in the context of 'some cosmological myth.' In other words, one sets out one's image of oneself as a guide-post.   It isn't to be understood as a Truth, but as a working hypotheses, an hypotheses at work permitting the user to choose a frame and to create oneself as a part of a composite, as a piece of a context in a frame, *of a cosmos*, yet among the missing who, paradoxically, *know* that when they are among the missing they are *mattering*.   Mattering is *becoming significant* in this our phenomenal world.

Relations, or bridges between the human sciences, interpret the more personal interrelations between individual human beings. George Simmel, with close affinities to Peirce, describes the value of social relations and the conduct of thinking about social ties by what he calls 'degrees of reciprocal knowledge of their participants,' (Simmel, c.1902, in 1950:317 ff).   This reciprocity, unlike the reciprocal relationship between traditional cause and effect, is between equals or what Jakobson has called 'shifters' in the reciprocity between addresser and addressee in genuine dialogue.   This notion of reciprocity is also the basis of Peirce's community of individuals who are inquiring in common cause, (*The Monist* 16 1906: 492-97).   It is such spontaneous mutuality which has persuaded many to see Pragmatism as near cousin to anarchism.   But of that familial tie I speak more, elsewhere, (Kevelson, 1990, 1993).   The following chapter inquires into the growth of signs according to Peirce's Pragmatism as a continuous tranformation.

Chapter 3

Transformations

Transformations

I
Old Touchstones

During the couple of decades that I have been chipping away at Peirce and Semiotics I have seen several score of people fly into this field on various makeshift sign-vehicles. But as Peirce himself has reminded us now and again in his writings, not everything that calls itself a sign is a part of semiotics. Signs are not all things to all people. For those of us who have elected to take the Peircean way of Semiotics, as I have, his theory of signs is the result of a procedure of inquiry. This procedure or method is Pragmatism, or 'pragmaticism' if we want to be precious.

The outstanding feature of this Pragmatism is its effect upon intellectual concepts. Such concepts are, in the Peircean lingo, representations of conceptual 'meaning.' The whole of what the inquirer may define in each case is a complex, dynamical transformation of meanings. As discussed in the previous chapter, the purpose of the inquiry is to grow meaning, by developing and cultivating it in the context of this medium-as-method. Peirce brings to this process of evolving the meanings of sign-complexes, or idea systems, his training and expertise in chemistry and in mathematics.

These two sciences become for Peirce a wellspring for metaphoric reference. From mathematics in particular he adapts the function of the image, and so underlies inquiry into ideas with the iconicity peculiar to the mathematics. He thus avoids what he calls nominalism.

From chemistry he adapts its relational process of con-fusions, even to recover in a manner of speaking that old goal of the chemists which is to release — liberate — or 'prescind' that which is nonsensible from its sensible ground. This is the ability to investigate, for example, what the phenomenon of the idea of Redness or Goodness or of Coldness means, if and when one may 'observe' such qualities as distinct from the customary, habitual ground with which they are usually, indistinguishably associated. To inquire into what we may know about the meaning of Redness, for example, is to release its 'power' to become related to other qualities, other grounds.

The alchemists, despite much of the legacy connected with their writings and activities, understood not only the chemistry of the physical world, but also understood the arts of the chemist, or alchemist, as a means of resolving incompatibilities between frames of knowledge in human lives. What they meant by knowledge was what Peirce meant by the outcome of an inquiry: a semiotic investigation. In the case of the alchemists the solution was presumed to be the achieving of a 'truth,' whereas in Peirce solutions are provisional only, *representing* 'truth.' But Peirce, like the alchemists to whom he was indebted, reinterpreted their notion of experimentation, and reinterpreted also the notion of the *solutio* as a consequential effect of inquiry. The *solutio*, in Peirce, becomes the transformation, i.e., the alchemical transformation, of conflict between spiritual, moral, physical phenomena into new general 'wholeness' or unification. The transforming process of semiosis is what Jung refers to, with respect to the alchemists, as a 'magic correspondence,' (Jung, 1963:270-71).

In Peircean terms, the alchemist's *solutio* is redubbed, and referred to as problem solving. In recent years a newer synonym, especially concerned with public policy and ideological conflict, is commonly called conflict-resolution.

In this chapter I am not going to take up either the fascinating topic of alchemical hermeneutics or the special tasks of the interrelated semiotics of law, government and economics as associated in conflict-resolution. What I want to talk about here is Transformation, i.e. *Semiotics in Peirce understood as the transformation of significant meaning*.

Some great makers of ideas produce what is called a 'system of thought,' or an orderly organization of a complex idea which can be read as a kind of blueprint map, whenever a 'legend' is available or may be determined. Other great makers of ideas are not content with using available concepts, off-the-rack terms, to designate ideas; like some 'purist' artists they prefer to make their pigments from 'scratch' using formulae recovered from old works, or inventing new extracts and 'properties' from raw materials. The first of these two types of creative intellectuals says, in effect, *Do Me*. The second, of which I take Peirce to be a token, says *Explore Me*.

Peirce's vast estate, i.e., his unpublished manuscripts, itself represents a process of exploration but one hard to penetrate, not only because the terrain is formidable but also because it is overgrown with rank criticisms of many who try to walk this ground. This Peircean space seems to many 'where no one has gone before.' His trek is not intergalactic. But the enterprise of exploring Peirce is somewhat as I imagine it is to ride a magic carpet. The surface configurations of this carpet have been passed over by his many editors as innocuous, as has his whole and central concern with semiotics been regarded as peripheral by more 'established' habits of thought. Yet when one speaks the code, or passwords — the 'sesames' of Semiotics — the so-called 'innocuous' design reveals itself. Just as powerful cultic forces are woven into carpets in Turkey, Iran, and elsewhere, in stylized geometry, or like the old gryphon of western Europe reduced to a *fleur de lys* (its claw-print a lily and no more), much of Peirce's genius has been relegated to fall under the cover of 'idiosyncracy,' (Kevelson, 1998). To explore Peirce a curiosity of mazes, i.e., a taste for deciphering such signs, is requisite.

Without laboring the point of the alchemists' influence on Peirce, the semiotic process of bringing about new, general meaning in the correlation between two systems of ideas is analogous to the solution of the alchemists: The 'solvent' is a binding force, effecting continuity between states or points of the 'rational' which appear to be discrete on an imaginary line of process. The 'solvent' of the alchemists is comparable with Peirce's interlude between states of knowledge, definable knowledge, or what he calls his 'Pure Musement.' But as is the case with both Peirce and the alchemists, 'the resolution of opposites is always an energic process ...' (Jung, above, at 495). As in Semiotic Play, the process of transformation is indeed the process of creating meaning.

II
Semiotics as Academic Wild Card

It is a dishonor to Peirce — a violation of the spirit of his genius — to prefix any serious inquiry into his theory of signs with rules of an axiomatic nature. But we may offer a clue or two, a signpost of a sort, a handful of crumbs to mark his labyrinthine thought. Whether a Peirce scholar views herself as an orphan lost in the brush or as a modernage Theseus ready to take out the bull sitting at the center of the academic ziggurat, it is useful, in a lowercase pragmatic sense, to carry a couple of truths in one's pocket. So here are my pair of time-worn axioms: First, whatever we mean by meaning must make a difference in the world, i.e., *meaning is consequential*. Second, whatever one calls an act is purposeful, has a goal. And since we are in the Peircean mode, a third working truth is that every assertion of a truth is a lie, (with a nod here, of course, to Eco, 1976).

I think it is fitting to approach Peirce with irreverence, but with hard, infinite respect. In my case I add a profound love for this person who has given so freely of his seminal thought in his own matchless fashion.

In this talk I want to select some special wrinkle of his work to share, from that deep well of his unpublished writings. Here are ideas at bedrock that virtually scale the walls to see some daylight. Some of these yet subterranean ideas of Peirce remind me of the colorless, translucent plants which grew under drifts of dried leaves at the base of old oak trees in my yard, in Assonet, a village in Freetown, Massachusetts, a few miles from where Peirce's family summered and where some distant relatives of Peirce's still lived when I was there. But at that time I saw those pale, weird plants — Indian pipes they were called — as magical, surreal. And it may well be that part of my affinity for Peirce has to do with our having had the same landscape imprinted on our souls. That terrain mapped itself upon our imaginations, perhaps: that stony enchanted and forbidding geography makes us, in this sense, kin. Or so I romanticize in rare idle moments.

I work with Peirce's manuscripts in the same manner I worked in years past in the writing of poems, plays, fiction. I learned, from one of the best teachers ever — David Cornel DeJong — to dig myself into my own work and to come up for air only occasionally to see what others like me were up to, and if we were in any way connecting. One of the 'enemies of promise' of which Colin Wilson once wrote, (and Peirce knew well) is that few evasions are comparable to the evasions of those who critique like locusts in the fields, but create little.

And this is not a 'surprising fact,' in Peirce's sense. If it is the case that the origin of *Critic* in logical analysis of arguments is the domain of the philosophers, then creative criticism is an oxymoron. A creative interpretation of ideas — of Peirce's thought in point here — is transforming. It is *hermeneutic* in that special alchemical sense of providing a link or medium between distant past and renewal or restitution of significance, (Jung, above at 336 n).

Perhaps Philosophy staked out Peirce as its find, only to have colonized it in sporadic bursts of interest and abandon it shortly thereafter, because *Peirce is not speaking a philosopher's tongue.* Nor does he intend to. But it has taken nearly thirty years since the emergence of Semiotics in the 1960's for Peircean Semiotics to find its own voice. It is not for lack of articulation, for one cannot call Peirce or Semiotics dumb. Rather the Peircean voice is like the 'message in the bottle,' (as Walker Percy knew); someone has to see it *as* a message, and then, only then, may the decoding begin. As long as critics attempt to fit Peirce into a precast grid will he remain unuseful. It is unthinkable that the great pioneer of this frontier, Semiotics, should be nonsignificant, nonmeaningful, nonconsequential, (on 'creative negativity' see Kevelson 1998).

Peirce — that is, the Peircean complex of ideas, and the idea of Peirce *as* idea — needs to be potted in some alchemical crucible of our own design, since it may be that the time for him to make a difference is Now or *not ever!* Not all ideas as possibles remain potential forever. They have a time to live, and if they do not, if they remain stunted and nongerminal, the living process reaches a point of no return. Transformation is missed. Peirce says this. He speaks of logical possibilities that come to nothing, (Kevelson, 1987, 1990).

Peirce seems marked for dissolution.

It is a mistake also to attempt to fit Peirce into such problems as philosophical ethics, for example, and waste his genius in that way. Peirce was indeed concerned with ethics, but he was concerned with ethics as significant relational conduct, and only in a special semiotic sense. In his much reworked 'classification of the sciences' he subdivides Pragmatics — the third and highest division of the sciences — into 1) Ethics, 2) Arts, 3) Policy, (ms 1345; Kevelson, 1996).

I will talk about these divisions of Pragmatics, the *method* of Semiotics, briefly:

Peirce says that *Ethics* is the domain of investigation of 'universal principles of conduct.' *Art* includes investigation of 'general problems' but not those that claim to go back 'to first principles.' *Policy* includes all that which falls under the head of 'special problems.' *This is a Pragmatics/Semiotics subdivision.*

By contrast, Peirce says, Philosophy is a division of Phenomenology which, in his schema, is *preparation* for semiotics analyses. His 'Phenomenology' also includes the Descriptive Sciences, as well as Nomology, which establishes categories for phenomena based on classes or shared features of phenomena *according to philosophical analyses*, (ms 1345; Kevelson, 1987).

To recall in passing, Peirce's Division of the Semiotic Normative Sciences consists in the stages of the pragmatic investigations, i.e., of the Expanded Logic (or Methodology), of the Ethics (built upon the practical sciences and the institutions of human affairs, and of the Esthetics, from which the 'First Principles' of the third Division, i.e., the Metaphysics, derive, (Kevelson, 1993). Thus the domain of Pragmatics in Peirce is wedged between the Phenomenology and the Metaphysics. In inserting Pragmatism *where and how he does in his schema* he thereby creates a schism in what was previously assumed to be, in its entirety, part of the domain *formerly* of the Philosophical Sciences, (see Kevelson on schisms in scientific inquiry, 1996).

Looked at from this Peirce's point of view we see that some recent movements in philosophy have been directed to recover its lost boundaries, so to speak, which Peirce *relocated* in order to make room for semiotics.

It becomes clear then why traditional 'analytical' approaches to philosophical inquiry have sustained their strong resistance to semiotics and why, by contrast, philosophical nonanalytic inquiries have attempted to adjust to altered status and have, *in this respect,* attempted to assimilate semiotics within restated boundaries or frames of inquiry. To a large extent, in many universities, this reclamation of Semiotics has succeeded. But the small successes of philosophy have resulted in great damage to Peirce, and to a deformation of what it was that he *intentionally* heralded with his vanguard Semiotics.

To Peirce, Semiotics is not peripheral to Philosophy. And it is not classified as a subordinate aspect of Philosophy. Rather, *Peirce transforms the old order and establishes Semiotics as a new 'sovereign' area of inquiry.*

I an not concerned here with survival strategies of philosophy. Nor am I concerned with the tactics of philosophers who are defensive toward Peirce and what he represents in the world of intellectual significance. My concern is with Pragmatism understood, as Peirce did, as the making of *solutions*, i.e. the resolutions of conflicts and the metamorphoses of conflictual structure into a symbolic currency.

III
Significance in Reclassification

As noted, Pragmatism, Peirce says, is that newest part of the classification of the sciences. To reiterate: the first is the Mathematics, which further subdivides into a) Geometry, b) Arithmetic, and c) the theory of finite groups. The second main class is Phenomenology; its third subdivision is 'Episcopy' or the 'Descriptive Sciences' which further subdivides into a) the works of intelligent beings, b) investigation of such intelligent beings, and c) cosmography which inquires into all the rest, i.e. all of 'inanimate nature.'

Pragmatism builds on the footings provided by Phenomenology in all three of its major divisions, and especially upon that division with which it shares a border, namely, 'Episcopy' or Descriptive Science.

From this graphic pattern of intellectual relations between domains of proper inquiry Peirce positions Pragmatism as the special goal or objective of the other Divisions, i.e., of Mathematics and Phenomenology. They provide substrata for Pragmatics. Pragmatics is the *result* of the outcome of the Mathematics and Phenomenological studies. Mathematics and Phenomenological investigations are purposeful, says Peirce, to the extent that they lay the way for Pragmatics. Moreover, the Divisions of Mathematics and of Phenomenology become transformed as they become introduced and used in the inquiries appropriate to Pragmatics. This is simply another way of saying what the old truism has said: The study of Man is Man. *Pragmatics is explicitly concerned with human interactions,* and is *metaphorically* adapted to elsewhere, I suggest.

In this same manuscript Peirce says that these three 'parts' of Science Classification are unequal: the first is by far the 'smallest,' and the last is by far the largest. Pragmatism, which is the largest, is 'the study of *how we ought to act* in the light of the truths of experience,' (ms 1345).

Conflict Resolution is a concept today which has cleared away a space of its own for special attention. Similarly, 'policy' — or public policy — is a splinter of the studies of semiotics of government and political institutions. Ethics is widely held today to be a theoretical derivation of law: its practices, procedures, and regulatory acts.

As noted earlier, Pragmatics rests largely upon Episcopy in the Peircean scheme. Peirce says, 'By this is meant science of individual beings, of the heavens or the terrestrial globe, of an individual course of events, as English

History. Such science begins by being descriptive; but its final purpose should be to explain the sequence and connections of the phenomena it explains by means of those laws that nomology has already made out,' (ms 1345). Pragmatics takes the work of 'Episcopy,' which examines phenomena, and it transforms the purpose of the former, of Episcopy, to the purpose of the latter, i.e. to semiosis and the evolution of thought. The 'topics' of Episcopy, as observed by that particular scientific method, become Interpretants for semiotic investigation, and thereby undergo a transfiguration of meaning.

The mode of change, which is to say, the characteristic kind of transformation which semiotic inquiry brings about, is that which transforms the goal of one type of investigation into a goal or objective of another mode of investigation. Just as an urn of ancient Greece might have had a functional purpose in its day, predominantly to convey water, it becomes in our present view an artwork, predominantly of an aesthetic nature. *In this way a dominant function or an objective in one mode of inquiry becomes reinterpreted and transformed into another function, or objective within another frame of reference.* These shifts of significance may be also analogized as shifts of linguistic function, from one 'level' of language to another, e.g., from Syntax, to Semantics, to Pragmatics, (with respect to linguistic classifications).

Permit me to take liberties with the magical ritual of saying something three times to make it 'True':

Pragmatics, the method of semiotics in Peirce's view, is that crucible in which the transfiguration occurs; it is the process of the old alchemical *solutio*, renascent in modern, semiotic terms, I suggest.

Repeatedly, Peirce begins anew to reclassify the Sciences. In the manuscript cited from above his criteria for subdividing are 'the distance at which they paint nature into,' e.g., Mathematics, Philosophy, Nomology, Natural History, individualizes objects. Here he further subdivides Philosophy into: 1) Philosophy of Thought: the *Philosophical Trivium*; 2) the Philosophy of Action: *Ethics*, etc.; 3) the Philosophy of Being: *Metaphysics*.

Philosophy, Peirce emphasizes, 'makes no business of observation, using merely the facts familiar to all others.' From this one may infer that Philosophy takes its data from *conformal* representations, analogous to that described as 'map projection' in manuscripts 1350, 1351.

Briefly, the purpose of a map is to display 'to the eye,' in Peirce's words, relations of topographical significance with reference to fixed points, e.g., 'sea level.' A map may distort one aspect and yet keep other aspects as 'true representations,' e.g., a mercator chart which shows great areas as straight lines but 'presumes all angles unchanged,' (ms. 1353).

Distortions require no special training to interpret, Peirce notes, since the transforming of features in the image will correspond with perceptual expectations of any ordinary viewer. For example, I suggest, the ordinary viewer 'sees' in a cartoon that a ball tossed up becomes spherical with a pointed top as it rises higher. But it flattens on its bottom as it falls to the ground. The depiction of elongation and flattening are distortions which *correctly represent the action as psychologically interpreted by the ordinary viewer.*

Maps represent, point to point, their referent objects, according to Peirce, (ms 1353). The transforming agent, in Peirce's eyes, is the method of semiotics: the pragmatic method. *This method is the medium by which the message is transformed.* The very doing/exploring of the problem is that which brings about significant transformations.

In manuscript 774 Peirce speaks in great detail of the determining force of Rhetoric, the principles of which fall under the cover of his Speculative Rhetoric. Speculative Rhetoric, as such, is a theory not a practice, (ms 774:8). Nor is it an art. But Speculative Rhetoric posits the theoretical basis which describes how the pragmatic method actually proceeds. This manuscript emphasizes that 'every object represented must be of the nature of a sign ...' Not all objects are signs, but all objects so represented in Pragmatics, and of which Speculative Rhetoric speaks, are sign-functions.

In this same manuscript, on pages 13 and following, Peirce discusses how each kind of topic of inquiry, as in the Episcopic division referred to above, would be represented in facsimile, i.e., in a manner corresponding with a referent rhetorical figure. One image evolves into its transformed facsimile, much as in Escher's drawings where bombers evolve into euphemistic birds, and vice versa.

One may imagine long lines of topics converging at special stations in Peirce's process of transformation. These stations or kiosks would show objects entering as one sign and leaving as another: same object with different sign-functions. The cartoonists, again, have made good use of such examples. Indeed, the comic strip and the film strip are, as Peirce knew, prototypes of the pragmatic method in motion, (Kevelson, 1996, 1998).

Peirce doesn't supply us with visualizable kiosks, or crucibles, or even *solutions*. But we are reminded that the resistance he encountered a hundred years ago is still out there. Therefore one takes on magical kiosks and transforming alchemical processes, at one's risk, or in some kind of wonderland as Peirce's admirer, Lewis Carroll, knew.

Peirce himself said, 'by a good many persons trained to the scientific life' any fusion of science and rhetoric would have been regarded as a 'typical example of incongruity.' Yet we do begin to perceive 'agitating the surface of the scientific deep ... the severest sciences doing homages to rules of expression as stringent and strange,' as any which excellent performance in any of the arts and sciences have always demanded. 'Every great achievement has had its special rhetorical idea, its means and its general secret of rendering a sign effective,' Peirce says.

Speculative Rhetoric is that analytic branch which determines the outcome of meaning of all signs. It is part of that science named *semiotics* 'which has been confused by many thinkers with logic,' (from ms 775). Peirce goes on: Now is the time for creative imagination to come alive. A writer should not bend or alter her views if she has cultivated them so that the proposition presented is 'a fruit ripened under the blaze or arduous investigation.' And further, like the proud rebel he is: '*the day of editorial omniscience is past,*' (ms 775:6; italics added).

In manuscript 778 Peirce discusses the method of discovery: Discovery begins always as an accident, (ms 775). In this manuscript he refers to Bentham's distinction of Cenoscopy from Idioscopy, with respect to the 'old philosophy.' Elsewhere I discuss this (Kevelson, 1988, 1990, 1996) and mention it here in passing only.

Worth noting here is that Peirce suggests that objects of inquiry are not 'dematerialized' upon entering the kiosks of change. Rather, these kiosks, or nodes upon the vital, dynamical pragmatic method, are crysalis states, such that the stage or phase itself is occasion and process-locus for transforming one significance into another, *into another matter of fact.*

Peirce discusses, especially in manuscript 601, the idea that particular branches of Science — chemistry, archeology and other — are not words only, or labels for actual phenomena 'manufactured by the arbitrary definitions of some academic pedant,' he says, but each 'is a real object, being the very concrete life of a social group constituted by real facts of interrelation — as real an object as a human carcass, which is made one by the interrelations of its millions of cells.' Further, he says that that which transforms the millions of cells into a human body are the 'modes of relationships' which change aggregates into whole sign-systems, that is, into significant bodies, (ms 601). It is in this manner, by means of such dynamical relations, that the different sciences may become transformed from 'cells' to integral parts of wholes, or wholes themselves, as as occurs in the functional transformation of a Token to a Type, (Fisch, 1986).

We owe especially to the practical sciences the persistent effort to evolve wholes out of the individual lives which mingle together for various human interests. And it is to Chemistry that we owe our understanding of the desire to create substitutes for the actual, to be able to make actuals, such as quinine or cobalt, vitamins of all kinds and drugs of every description, into synthetic facsimiles. It is Chemistry which shows us how to use the pigment of natural dye-stuffs to bring about new and even more 'brilliant' color, says Peirce.

Chemistry has not only provided the prototype of transforming processes between natural and synthetic, but has showed as well transformations from one mode of scientific perception to other modes of scientific perception and inquiry, (ms 601). This entire manuscript develops the idea of transformation of meaning by means of relational shifts, i.e., *rational relational shifts*, of permutation, and of transformation, such that one modification is seen to lead to new paradigms within which subsequent, endless numbers of future transformations are then seen to be possible, (ms 601:22).

Peirce points to the evolving of what he calls the 'new mystical chemistry' at the end of the 19th into the beginning of the 20th century. He says it is conceivable that those human qualities that have been for so long been regarded as general features of human beings are not simple, indecomposables at all, but are at bottom relational chemical actions. Is it possible, he asks, 'that the properties of living matter can be nothing else than the properties of certain chemical substances,' (ms 615:15).

Do we see Robert Boyle in the wings, together with his good buddy John Locke? I think so, as I have written elsewhere, (Kevelson, 1996).

In manuscript 437 Peirce reminds us of those 'qualities we must admire in humankind.' Here he rejects the possibility with which Hegel and others struggled, namely, that all these 'vices' and 'virtues' tagged to human conduct may be explainable by mathematical investigation. Regardless of the fact that mathematical reasoning is hard reasoning it does not provide solutions to human motives and human actions. 'In regard to the greatest affairs of life, the wise man follows his heart and does not trust his head. This should be the method of every man, no matter how powerful his intellect,' Peirce says. Thus we are back at Common Sense.

This is not the Commonsensism of the Empiricist British and Scottish philosophers, nor the commonsense of the ordinary person on the street. Rather, the Peircean-evolved Common Sense is an extraordinary Common Sense. It is our sensibility transformed: it is our *idea* of sensibility dissolved and transformed. It is, in Peirce's words, Common Sense as 'the resultant of the traditional experience of mankind,' (that) 'witnesses unequivocally that the heart is more than the head, and is in fact everything in our highest concerns.'

Further, 'most philosophers' offer 'metaphysics as a guide for the soul.' But reasoning as a 'talent for music' and other arts are uncommon gifts, part of uncommon common sense. Reason requires that one know how to transliterate the decoding of the body, and to recode it as crypted message of the mind, and transform/recode it back again. In this manuscript 437 (c. 1890) Peirce says that Robert Boyle's corpuscular doctrine asserts that 'the phenomena of the world are physically produced by the mechanical affections of the parts of matter, and that they operate upon one another according to mechanical laws.'

What Peirce's theory of signs does is to transform Boyle's notion into his own, i.e., to take the mechanical and reinterpret it as the dynamical. As long as Boyle's ideas are set in the context of a closed, determinate world in causal frame they are still in more general agreement with Aristotle's principles than with Peirce's. Peirce does indeed class Boyle with Aristotle. He does so with respect to the impact and consequence of the respective power of thought of each: 'In proportion to the degree to which he impresses the world with his ideas Robert Boyle comes next to Aristotle.'

But it was not until the middle of the 19th century that Helmholtz becomes a vehicle to bring Boyle into the modern world, where the force of his thought becomes germinal once more. Peirce discusses how Boyle's mechanical hypothesis provides an opening for response from those exploring dynamical systems, from the perspective of physical chemistry and others. Thereby the late medieval/early modern thought of Boyle becomes transformed into a new concept, a new sign for 20th into 21st centuries.

In the next short section I want to connect the notion of transformation with Peirce's own interpretation of evolutionism. *Pragmatism is, in his understanding, always a procedure of materializing the merely intellectual, and of bringing the significance of human thought back down to earth.*

IV
'Rhetoric' Redeemed

In a profoundly special sense Peirce uses the term 'Evolution' to stand for a mode of transformation. As a catalyzed process of change, significance grows by the process of inquiry, (ms 1337). Peirce speaks of universes of thought evolving into other universes of thought, e.g., *physics* evolving from nutrition, or *psyche* from reproduction, and so forth.

Mathematics grows out of concern with construction, Nomology out of concern with laws, Philosophy out of the connections between ideas and quests for explanation of origins, Chemistry out of interaction in all kinds of matter, Biology out of the relations between *physics* and *psyche* — a kind of 'second-order transformation' — Sociology out of concern with human organizations as manifest in institutes of art, of language, of law, of theology, of politics, and of economics. The science of Cosmology is concerned with order *as such*, as it brings individual objects into collections, networks, systems. Finally, the Science of Signs is that which is concerned with the process of evolution by the method of representations and the recasting of meanings, out of all the processes of transformation suggested by the development of all the sciences, designated above. So Peirce speculates.

Peirce speaks of that which he calls 'sciences' as 'departments of human knowledge,' (ms 1338). But the Science of Pragmatics — the Newer *New Science* — transforms itself. It is thereby the most elusive of all the sciences. As the science of discovery, it is characterized by 'false starts,' by revisions, by changes, emendations and postscriptives.

Finally, in manuscript 1339 Peirce decides that he will restrict his classification of the sciences to those which exist 'at present,' since 'discovery' opens up an endless array of the possible. He says clearly that this last attempt at classification 'is not founded upon any system of logic or of epistemology,' (ms 1339:3). On the contrary, the relations that obtain between all the known sciences are such that what seems most important is to discover how 'the results of one science, A, will often be applied by another science, B, as principles or tools wherewith to solve its problems.' But this is not a reciprocal, symmetrical adaptation. Rather, A transforms B's *problems* to its own idiom, but leaves its — B's — *tools* to B. Pragmatics, as we have seen, attempts to resolve problems by transforming the substance but leaving the old method alone, to its old (former) purposes.

With uncommon modesty Peirce says that his purpose in attempting to classify the sciences was nothing 'pretentious,' but a mere attempt to frame, for some readers, 'the precise question' which his life's work has attempted to resolve.

He tells us that it is the 'problem' which is elusive. The problem of problem-solving seems to turn into something else as soon as he thinks he has a handle on it. The very basic requirements of any science is to be able to assume that a 'scientific statement ... be perfectly definite.' This seems a goal he is unable to achieve, (ms 1341, p.1). At every stage of the attempt to frame a definite statement of the problem of problem-solving precision eludes him. These 'defects of precision' are unavoidable, he says. He cannot make that definitive 'scientific statement' that will be 'perfectly objective.' He says: It is never 'free from all pictorial and whimsical elements,' and it always shows signs of the accidental.

After examining endless models of classifications of science, Peirce finds that even whatever is *meant* by 'classification' is protean. So the very concept he is attempting to inquire into continually changes, transforms. His basic point of reference metamorphoses.

What is one to make of an idea which transforms itself under one's very nose? Here one hears Peirce's deep sigh of futility: The futility grows in pitch the closer one approaches it. It has a veritable Doppler effect on one like me who tries to take Peirce's pulse, so to speak. The sigh grows in pitch, in volume, in value, and of course as it gets louder it becomes not only more significant, but significant of other than that which it signified when it began. The size of a sigh changes its meaning, as all semioticians know. A whisper changes not only that which is whispered but changes the entire psychophysicality of the whisperer/shouter as well. Try it.

The problem is, I think, clear: The problem is not the sciences, nor the order of their cross-dependencies, nor the issues each investigates, nor the respective resolutions each brings to the data at hand. The problem is how formulation of a want, a need, a conflict, may transform one mode of significance to others. The problem is *How*.

How do the various discourses select this and not other of the issues they frame *as* problems. *How* do these selected problems change when transplanted from one field of inquiry to another? And *How* do these complex transformations Matter? What difference does it make?

Peirce's Pragmatism leads to a solution: *So What*? And *then*, *So What*? And ***ad infinitum***, *So What Now*?

Chapter 4

Peirce and Poincaré on Hypothesis and Experience

Peirce and Poincaré on Hypothesis and Experience

I
Experience as Complex Sign

This chapter will examine serious criticism Peirce raises about Poincaré's assumption that scientific knowledge results from experience. The issue in question is the fact that their concepts of Experience actually refer to two quite different universes of discourse. The distinction between lived, *actual* experience, and 'experience' as an idea of such lived, actual experience is rarely clarified.

Peirce argues that Poincaré's revolutionary impact upon physical science derives from an interpretation of Experience which is faulty. Poincaré's use of Experience presumes that one may tap directly into actual, everyday experience, whereas Peirce holds that there is a mediating idea, 'Experience', which is a *made idea* or sign-system that links actual lived experience with scientific theory. In Peirce's view Poincaré has bypassed this mediating and crucial stage of inquiry. Poincaré's presumptions are fictions.

The main texts to be used in this chapter are Peirce's little-known letter in the early 1900's that explicitly raises questions about Poincaré's method of inquiry with respect, in particular, to the idea of Experience and Poincaré's 1905 *Science and Hypothesis* (in 1952 English translation used here).

It is expected that the main distinction between positive and pragmatic methods of inquiry made then, nearly a century ago, still holds true. Peirce's Pragmatism attempts to adapt mathematical reasoning to the process of evolving ideas, i.e., to semiotic relations in all kinds of sign systems which have an infraverbal or conceptual basis. However, pragmatic hypotheses or abductive reasoning in Peirce is a *representation* of mathematical hypotheses: semiotics *interprets* but does not duplicate or resemble mathematics. Mathematical reasoning is merely a model, but not the process of semiotic inquiry. Pragmatics, the method and process of semiotics, is, in effect, *dilemmatic* reasoning, (see concluding chapter of this book).

Just as the notion of Experience is not a single general concept but is actually one idea in the discourse of mathematics and another kind of concept in the discourse of semiotic pragmatics, so is the use of hypothetical reasoning different with respect to each universe of meaning or discourse, i.e., mathematics and semiotics here considered.

I hope to make clear in the following that Poincaré's concepts of hypothesis and of experience are concepts connected quite differently to the world of practicality and human affairs than are Peirce's concepts of hypothesis and experience. Peirce wanted to say this publicly, without any disrespect to Poincaré whom he admired. But he was not correctly understood nearly a century ago. Perhaps the climate for understanding Peirce is better today. I hope so. It is a chance worth taking.

I begin by calling attention to the fact that in his manuscript 692, entitled 'Reason's Conscience,' Peirce distinguishes between the images and 'abstract expression' of the mathematician on the one hand, and the investigators of all the other academic disciplines on the other hand. The mathematician's images and concepts do not refer to any 'definite individual object' in that universe of discourse of which they are part. But, rather, they represent 'an individual object' not of the experiential world but of the world of supposition and of man-made or created possibilities.

The objects represented by the mathematician, Peirce argues, must be rejected as not being as 'Real' as any actual existent object. These objects are not part of that existential experiential world at all, except as phenomena of the creative imagination are 'Real' but not actual. The representations of the mathematician may only 'represent, or translate, the abstract language,' according to Peirce, and in turn, the abstract language may represent those ideas drawn from, or influenced by, the 'imaging.' Nevertheless, within the universe of discourse of mathematics it is customary, appropriate, and even desirable, Peirce says, to hold the imaginary Realities *as if* they were also actual. This customary acceptance of Reality as an equivalence of Actuality is part of the rules of the game of mathematics. But, Peirce emphasizes, the Really Real is such that we must distinguish mathematical Real from the actual, pragmatic Real. The latter is capable of verification with respect to experiential evidence, whereas the Reality of mathematics is neither required nor expected to involve such evidence in its corroborations, its results and proofs.

Indeed, the rules of the game of mathematics are such that 'the imaginary universe' is related 'to the parts of which all the images and propositions refer is always thought of as a single individual whole of individual parts,' (see ms. 693, cited by Eisele, 1979:100 and reprinted in Eisele *NEM* IV, 1976:185-215).

In short, the 'idealized sign-world' of mathematics and mathematical notation is, as Eisele correctly points out, a model of inquiry and investigation which ideally should serve *as a model,* for the practice and procedure, i.e., *the methodology of a pragmatism which, in Peirce, is the method of semiotics regarded as a theory of signs.*

Let it be underscored that *Peirce's Theory of Signs is not the same as, or equivalent with, nor deduced from, the theories of the mathematics.* Eisele cautions us that the relation between semiotics and mathematics is between different kinds. Unfortunately she does neglect to take into account that, in Peirce, the adaptation from model to working method is always a dynamic process of interpretation and translation. Hence, it leads to a universe of meaning in the interpretant Method — Pragmatism/Semiotics — which is different in kind from that which it interpretively represents and refers/alludes to.

I use the term 'allude' here since the mathematical discourse is a fictive discourse, such as is literary fiction. Thus 'allude' (despite its current usage as synonymous with 'refer') is distinguished from 'refer' by implicit assumption that the presupposed text in question is fictive, literary, and metalogical.

The point of this distinction is that here we have a classic example of the fact that certain conventions may be tacitly assented to and followed without distinguishing between implications which are, on the one hand, based on that which is presumed to connect with the actual, and on the other hand, are such that are grounded in the fictive. The idea of the *factive*, as Duhem and others have remarked, is the product of collective, consensual judgement, and thus carries forward an authorial or quasi-authorial endorsement: the factive representation may be taken as if it were an actual thing in itself. Thus, the propositional use of 'refer' implies that that which is asserted is related to the actual, factual world as mediated by consensual judgment, or in Peirce's terms, by symbolic and authorial (however provisional) *legisigns*. In law, for example, the process of fact-finding takes place as part of evidentiary procedure as prescribed by a legal system in which 'discovery' (or fact-finding) proceeds by conventionalized strategies/actions. This factive is not Poincaré's *fictive*.

In those discourses in which a first object Interpretant is *alluded* to, in contrast to being *referred* to, the *fictive world* in which this anaphora occurs is not actual, but is regarded as if it were actual. The method of facticizing in the fictive world is distinct from the method of facticizing in the actual world. That which may be hypothesized of the latter is of a wholly different nature than that which may be hypothesized of the former. For example, it is pointless and meaningless to hypothesize Hamlet's daughter's husband. But it is a different matter, however, when one is hypothesizing in order to frame an action that may actually happen with consequences for the existential future — for the past, and even for the present (which is the last stage of the hypothesizing process), (Kevelson, on Eco and Hypothesis, 1996).

In her 1977 paper, above, Eisele asks, 'What then lies at the heart of mathematical reasoning. What makes Peirce cling to its formalism,' (Eisele, 1979:302). But even though she raises this crucial question Eisele herself does not carry far enough the process of translation/interpretation from one sign-system to another. For when Peirce uses mathematical reasoning as a model, and interprets this model *vis-a-vis* the method of pragmatism in semiosis, the 'formalism' of mathematical reasoning is also reinterpreted: it becomes a referent or Interpretant Sign. Pragmatics transforms this significant process for its own purposes! In this manner hypothesis becomes reinterpreted and comes to signify in Peirce a mode of discovery of new conceptual meaning which, if it be meaningful, must impact upon the actual, existential world: the world of actual experience.

To her credit, this great scholar and devotee of Peirce's work notes this procedure, but she does not explore it as it requires. Nor does she grasp the transformational aspect of interpreting the idea from its object idea, in semiotics but *not* in mathematics.

This, then, is the frame I set for the following inquiry into the distinctions Peirce would have made had he the opportunity to translate and critique the now famous Poincaré paper of 1905, on *Science and Hypothesis* (from the original French into English).

In an aside, I want to call attention to Eco's interesting discussion on Peirce's hypothesis, in his 'Horns, Hooves, and Insteps' (Eco, 1983:199-220, and to my commentary on it in Kevelson, 1996). Eco does distinguish between several kinds of hypotheses in semiotics, and suggests that the Peircean mode is a kind of creative abduction — neither overcoded nor undercoded — and not a meta-abductive kind of reasoning either. But it must suffice for now to mention this discussion only in passing here.

From very different viewpoints Eco and Eisele both fail to press forward and mark the major difference between Peirce's understanding of hypothesis in semiotics and mathematical hypothetical reasoning. To return to Eisele: we are all indebted to her work which grazes but does not confront this problem. Yet she comes so close when she says, 'in a practical problem such as bridge-building, one must convert the verbal description into equivalent algebraic or geometric signs, introduce auxiliary signs by means of which new relations are observed that are helpful to the original, must eliminate the intermediate signs in the course of reaching the conclusion,' (Eisele, 1979:302). She does not not discuss how the interpretation of a sign from one system to another results in the initiation and onset of a new sign-system. It is, from the viewpoint of the new, a creation out of nothing. But this 'nothing' is the relationship of possibility which obtains between a referent sign and a new sign. 'Nothing' is a zero sign. In our case the referent is the mathematical hypothesis and the new is the pragmatic hypothesis. We must continue to bear in mind that we are always talking about the *idea* of 'hypothesis,' i.e., the idea of the concept of hypothesis.

But in Eisele's mathematical conclusion, hypothesis which once resulted from a translation/interpretation from verbal data, must undergo still another conversion process in order to prepare it for meaningful relation/adaptation to the experimental world, this actual phenomenal world which is the target of pragmatic action. Eisele and others stop short before this additional converting/interpreting stage of the process, from mathematics to semiotics. Each stage of interpretation, it must be noted, creates additional meaning, as *the process grows*. This is Peirce's pragmatic maxim.

Eisele as mathematician stops where the mathematician stops. Peirce took his thought beyond that stage into this new field he knew he was pioneering: the place of semiotics.

Despite his great admiration for Poincaré as mathematician, Peirce recognized the need to explicate the connection between two kinds of hypothetical discovery, and two notions of experience. In the following, having set the stage, I will position these two explorers of the possible into a kind of confrontation. It is Peirce, however, whose voice we will hear for the most part.

II
Experiencing 'Experience'

As mentioned, the first English translation of Poincaré's *Science and Hypothesis* appears no earlier than 1905, by J. Larmor on behalf of the Walter Scott Publishing Company. But several years earlier Charles Sanders Peirce had been asked by the Smithsonian Institute, by Professor Langley's assistant, to translate Poincaré's original French edition into English. This was in 1901, in January when Peirce was at Milford, Pennsylvania. Peirce, then widely acknowledged as an outstanding mathematician in his own right as well as the son of the great mathematician Benjamin Peirce, had openly and often expressed his highest admiration for Poincaré's contributions to mathematics. Yet it must be noted that he is also outspoken in his criticism of Poincaré's reasoning, of what he sees as serious flaws in Poincaré's logic.

He agreed to do the translation with the proviso that he also be permitted to freely express his criticisms. Langley could not and did not bring himself to authorize the publication of a translation with such negative evaluative criticism such as Peirce proposed, not even when Peirce agreed to permit a more mild and watered-down 'abridged paraphrase' version to be published, (see correspondence on this issue reprinted in Eisele, 1979:144-46).

In the following year, when Peirce was drafting the 'minute logic' manuscript he again takes up the problem of hypothesis — a multivalent concept — together with the complex notion of experience. Especially in the third chapter of this work on Peirce's expanded logic — that logic which becomes, to Peirce, synonymous with all that he is to mean by the term Semiotics — do we begin to see clearly the evolved concept of the idea of hypothesis. Here Peirce discusses the dual role of hypothesis in mathematics. He distinguishes the *idea* of experience from instinctual, lived and actual experience. He points out that logic must make use of, or adapt for its purposes, mathematical thinking, i.e., hypothetical/ apodictic methodology. *But mathematics needs to understand how it rests upon the translating of primary or instinctual perception, via interpretive hypotheses, into the mathematical mode.*

Note: while mathematical hypothesis provides the model or referent for pragmatic/semiotic hypothesis, Peirce makes it clear that mathematics must then use, in reciprocal or dialogic fashion, the evolved semiotic notion of hypothesis in order to examine how the idea or fictive representative comes out of the actual. The origins of the imaginary world are grounded in the actual, and are recovered, Peirce suggests, by means of the pragmatic hypothetical method of discovery in reasoning. This is a kind of recursiveness, but one which is continually spiralling, opening out in an infinitely growing process. I want to emphasize this before further discussion of Poincaré: Poincaré's omission of the instinctual/experiential grounds of his concept of mathematical hypothesizing lead to an emphasis on the arbitrary or fictive aspect of mathematics which is, in Peirce's view, a misplacement of emphasis. The arbitrary and the fictive are characteristic of mathematical operations, and indeed, it is this ability to infer possibility — possible new particularities from assumed generalities — that allow ideas to grow. In other words, the assumption of the existence of a point, for example, permits this general hypothetical 'fiction' to be developed, such that the extension of this point creates the line, and the development of the line describes an area, and thus there is a place or space — a ground — created out of conjecture, upon which further experiments may be conducted, (Kevelson, 1998: on Space and Place).

But the crucial introduction of the initial hypothetical point is itself dependent upon another hypothesis — a logical hypothesis — which assumes that a representation may be established between the proposed hypothetical concept of a point and that object of attention or focus which we perceive instinctually, says Peirce. That mathematical point becomes connected by a process of semiosis with our actual relation to our world, a world which is, as current slang says, 'in our face,' and unavoidable, (CP 4.318). According to Peirce, 'Experience' 'is the resultant ideas that have been forced upon us.' This instinctual mode of establishing hypotheses is what Poincaré has missed. He has missed the so-called double 'if' of the Stoics which subsumes the conditional within the hypothetical. It is this double 'if' which Peirce

ιestores, as he traces the lineage of semiotics through Locke to the ancient Stoics, (Kevelson, 1987). It is also the Stoic emphasis on Secondness which Peirce reinterprets and thereby makes Secondness — Indexicality, opposition, experience — the mediating fulcrum, connecting the qualitative image or Icon with consensual encoded pattern or Symbol, (Kevelson, 1990, 1993, 1996).

This omission by Poincaré is equivalent to a significant absence, i.e., to one of the functions of Zero Sign in semiotics, (Kevelson, 1996; 1987, 1990). This absence and its significance has yet to be examined. But we may expect to see that it has resulted in a wide range of complex consequences, not at all confined to mathematics, philosophy and other speculative aspects of the arts and sciences. We also may see its mark on current developments in the practical sciences of law, government and economics. Especially, we may find that this absence permeates 'positivism' in all these areas of inquiry — where positivism overlaps Peirce's notion of 'nominalism' — since it gives rise to a predilection for building on free-floating hypotheses, i.e., hypotheses not grounded in actual experience. According to Peirce's views this line of thought has resulted in denotions of pseudo- or merely apparent problems, e.g., the *Scheinproblem* or 'meaningless questions,' as Ernst Mach designated them, (Mach, 1893).

I digress briefly to amplify the notion of meaningless question: We recall that within the first decade of this century, just at the time of Poincaré's work on hypothesis and of Peirce's consolidating of his ideas on semiotics, Lenin and his colleagues were speaking out passionately against this notion of 'meaningless questions,' in a different manner and for purposes very different from Poincaré's and Peirce's. Or so it first appears: In 1908 Lenin published a scathing attack against Mach, Poincaré and Berkeley so much admired by Mach.

The crux of Lenin's attacks on Mach especially, but on Poincaré for similar reasons, was what he saw as an illicit confusion of the two aspects of hypothesis: In brief, the notion of hypothesis he denounced was that which came out of the air, e.g., the fictive imagination, and was not mediated — interpreted and transposed — by a process which would anchor the concept in history on common human ground. (See Menger's Introduction to the 6th edition of Mach's *The Science of Mechanics,* the first English translation of which was reviewed in 1893 by Peirce in *The Nation.*) It is Karl Menger's introduction to the Six Edition (above) which observes that Lenin's views on Mach became the prevailing 'authoritative' views in Russia at that time. These views were, Menger suggests, effectively assimilated within the ideology that provided the leading principles for the further development of the Soviet Union into this twentieth century, (Menger, pages xix, xx).

Menger erroneously notes that Poincaré's *Science and Hypothesis* was first published in France in 1912. We know, of course, that date is not correct. Yet Menger introduces, despite this, similarities between Poincaré and Mach which do bear close noting, namely with respect to Mach's inadequate understanding of certain mathematical theories. According to Menger, Mach's theoretical understanding of such mathematical theories as hypothesis are 'one-sided and in definite need of a complementation by logic, by the logical analysis of language and, perhaps, by some of the ideas advanced by H. Poincaré,' (Menger, above at xvii). For the wrong reasons and by way of misunderstanding, Menger's criticism of Mach turns out to be almost, verbatim, Peirce's criticism of Poincaré! Perhaps we have a mystery, and perhaps a coincidence. In any event what is missing in Poincaré *does* matter. Why it matters is at the core of discussion of Peirce's hypothesis, in this chapter. I might mention that Peirce revises his negative criticism of Mach upon closer inquiry, and in fact concurs with him.

Although I am deficient in my understanding of mathematics, and I need to depend on good English translation if I want to be sure I correctly grasp the meaning of a complex and technical exposition written in French (and most other languages), I do believe that good translations from one sign system into another may be depended on, with allowances for some losses and gains. What is important here is that we get a clear perspective on the vicissitudes of the idea of hypothesis just prior to its becoming a major topic for apology and discussion: in Mach, in Poincaré, in Peirce, and at this cutting edge of Semiotics a hundred years later.

Peirce's developing theories of hypothesis come from several sources: for one, the Common Sense philosophers who had a great influence upon him did admit, with reluctance, the use of mathematical hypothesis in physics and scientific investigations in general. This limited usage rested on the assumption of certain intuitive 'certainties,' such that the hypothetical 'entities' of the mathematics were derived from axiomatic truths. These 'truths,' it was held, were *given* intuitively, prioristically, and as such were not questionable. From this perspective it was assumed the Euclid's geometry was based upon such incontrovertible truths. Even Peirce's own father Benjamin insisted that mathematics is 'the science which draws *necessary* conclusions.'

The eclectic Peirce rejected necessity and priorism, but retained the assumption that all of our really creative thought requires abstract imaginings. In other words, general ideas are the most simple truthlike groundings regarding our ability to grasp how the universe works, and we with it.

Common Sense maintained that we must not base our understanding on ideas/imagination, but we need to *observe* the actual world and from this observation be able to describe patterns of relations which are *not* necessary, but on the contrary, are fraught with uncertainty and are subject to change and to chance. Hence this early Commonsensist position, emphasizing analogy and rejecting merely imagistic/conceptual hypothesis, begins to be dominant by the middle of the 19th century in scientific inquiry.

At this juncture in Peirce's development it is widely agreed that mathematics imagines, or *images* its truths and hypotheses; but by contrast, philosophy 'observes' and makes analogical connections. Thus the former becomes the leading characteristic of rationalist thought: of idealism, of nominalism and cartesianism. Peirce, at this significant crossroads of systems of thought, says 'neither/nor.' He proceeds to create not a synthesis, but a third alternative to rationalism and empiricism: Pragmatism. *In Peirce's Pragmatism the idea of hypothesis is neither akin to analogy, nor is it mathematical hypothesis.* Analogy, we recall, holds onto an *idealized* referent as connector. (Peirce is to *adapt* this *ideal* referent; see the last chapter of this book.)

Thus when Peirce drafts the third chapter of the 'Minute Logic' (Jan. - Feb. 1902 of 'The Simplest Mathematics,' reprinted in CP 4.227-322) he had by this time been asked to translate the Poincaré paper. Peirce had by now made his criticisms known and available, as part of public 'goods.' As noted, the translation of Poincaré's paper into English was not to appear, after the flap with Peirce, until 1905. But this 1902 study of hypothesis by Peirce deals exhaustively with hypothesis in logic/semiotics, and with the relations between logical, 'semeiotical' and mathematical ideas of hypothesis.

Before moving on to the last section of this chapter I will point to some of Peirce's key insights: 'Each branch of mathematics sets out from a general hypothesis of its own,' (CP 4.246). The hypotheses are distinct from the schemata of each division, and one needs to evaluate and compare each division with others. Each hypothetical type is key note for a whole system of inquiry.

We are then able to distinguish between the various mathematical purposes and systems according 'to the nature of its general hypotheses...' (CP 4.248). The type of hypothesis for each kind of mathematical investigation will characterize the investigation as a whole, I want to emphasize.

Of the idea of Experience, Peirce says that it is 'the resultant ideas that have been forced upon us,'(CP 4.318; see also CP 4.21, 232ff, 246ff, 3.8 541 in particular).

It is the differing understandings of hypothesis that also distinguish Peirce's and Poincaré's understandings of the idea of experience as well, as Peirce reminds us. Further, they are also far apart on how they understand and define the idea of 'generality.' Poincaré's understanding of generalization, according to Peirce, makes the former a 'nominalist.' Peirce says 'the nominalists conceived the *general* element of cognition to be merely a convenience for understanding this and that fact and to amount to nothing except for cognition, while the realists ... looked upon the general, not only as the end and rim of knowledge, but also as the most important element of being. Such was and is the question. It is as pressing today as ever it was...' (CP 4.1, c. 1898).

What follows is a great surprise to all who have come to expect Peirce to unflinchingly denounce all nominalism. What he says is that every one who really desires and intends to work according to the 'scientific method' must begin in nominalism. It is that starting point which evolves or develops out of nominalism — out of the merely fictive and imagined possibility — into that mode of inquiry which characterizes the method of pragmatism. In pragmatism the idea of hypothesis is transformed, (see, in the closing chapter of this volume, how 'idealism' is re-grasped by Peirce's Pragmatism).

Just as Peirce has evolved out of the dyadic and prioristic position of the empiricists into the more complex triadic pragmatic mode, he also evolves from the nominalistic position into the mediating position of pragmatist and creator of dynamical hypotheses.

Before the brief concluding section of this chapter let us look at what Peirce himself had to say about evolving from nominalism to pragmatism:

'It appears ... that in scientific method the nominalists are entirely right. Everybody ought to be a nominalist at first, and to continue in that opinion until he is driven out of it by the *force majeure* of irreconcilable facts, (CP 4.1). He suggests that we must value the 'deferences of nominalism' in this sense. And the lever which moves the process out of nominalism and into pragmatism is nothing other than his 'logic of relatives.' This logic of relatives is the triggering force: the means and the instrument.

III
Toward Infinite Degrees of Freedom

It is well known that Poincaré is often cited as the father of Chaology, the theoretical assumption that our understanding of the universe, as the evolution of the actual and natural world, moves not from chaos to order, but conversely from order to chaos. At each new discovery and with each genuine novelty coming into existence the established 'order' may not accommodate the change and has to be reassessed in terms of emergent newness and/or shift from presumably predictable pattern to an indeterminacy. I will not discuss the theory of Chaos or Chaology further in this context, but refer to my earlier work, (Kevelson, 1993, 1996).

But I do want to stress here that Peirce's understanding of indeterminacy is based on hypothetical assumptions which regard experience and dynamical change quite differently from the assumptions held by Poincaré. How do we reconcile these distinctly different meanings of the terms 'experience,' or 'chaos,' or evolving 'disorders?'

In an interesting approach to Poincaré and the philosophy of mathematics, Folina recently points out that Poincaré's notion of intuition, from which hypothetical choices are derived, seems to correspond with a preconceptual, imagistic protoreasoning. It seems to concern the pictorial and non-empirical mode of representing to oneself a synthetic nonreducible 'idea' — a visual notion which prompts in the possibility of seeing the conceivable. Folina suggests that this 'irreducible intuition' in Poincaré was 'culled from Kant.' Folina does not discuss Peirce at all, but her criticisms of Poincaré's intuition, hypothesized, is not far from Peirce's. She points out that Poincaré's theory of meaning is tied to a primitive manner of beginning an inquiry, of making vivid and pictorial that which is felt and wants objective expression. The process of objectivizing is a way of representing something to oneself which, in that mode of representation, becomes 'verifiable in principle.' From this 'verifiability in principle' situation a hypothesis may then be constructed, comparable to positing speculative possibility of how something in actual experience comes to exist as such. This latter is, in Peirce, abductive or hypothetical reasoning in its broadest sense: the purpose of this is to bring forth a working assertion upon which to act or test and investigate further, and thus to change the *meaning* of the world.

This is the point suggested by Folina: in Poincaré's notion of hypothesis based on experience, the idea of experience is itself conjectured. But the idea of experience in Peirce is based on actuality, (Folina, 1992:174-75). It is important to bear in mind that a 'verification' in Poincaré's sense is not the corrobation of an idea, a testing or proving of it with respect to the actual world; rather it is a tool, a heuristic, and is indeed a 'legitimate tool' she says, *for heuristics*.

Poincaré correctly requires that 'the statement of a theorem is just the statement that every instance is verifiably true ... the mathematical statement is true for at least one instance of the domain to which it refers,' (Folina, above, 176).

But Peirce, in speaking of 'degrees of freedom,' says that verification requires that at least one instance of a statement be true with respect to its referent ground or domain, or universe of discourse which presumes an actual referent. It must not be free-floating, but must be tied to or connected and/or related at one place, 'at a minimal,' (Eisele, Vol II, NEM, Chapter II, at 369, reprinted from Peirce's ms 94).

Folina correctly avoids casting Poincaré whole into the anti-realist camp, (Folina, above at 181). But she says that although his theory of meaning is anti-realist, it is not intuitionist either. Some aspect or instance of a theory, in Poincaré, must be provably true or false, i.e., actually verifiable or not the case! But perhaps, I suggest, the main distinction between Peirce's and Poincaré's respective notings of hypothesis rests on each's affirmation or denial of a 'potential infinity.'

According to Peirce, all infinite collections are the result of evolving an essentially non-necessary or arbitrary sign, sign-system, or complex idea. But Poincaré maintains that 'arbitrary infinite collections are not meaningful domains,' (cited in Folina at page 181). According to Poincaré, '... every property of infinite number is nothing more than a translation of a property of finite numbers. It is the latter which could be evident, while it would be necessary to prove the first by comparing it with the latter and by showing that the translation is exact,' (cited from the 1963 edition of Poincaré's *Last Essays*, in Folina, at page 182).

Finally, Poincaré insists that however our imagination may be extended these imaginations are not *indefinitely* extendable. They are not infinite, but finite, if any statement is to be decidable. Peirce, by contrast, shows that our imagined hypotheses may be indefinitely extended, and ultimately *not* decidable, since as long as inquiry continues, and continues to evolve and transform the idea in question, an envisioned idea or hypothesis is the onset of an infinite continuum. Peirce's leading principle presumes that ideas are indefinitely extendable; hence this 'hyperbolic cosmology,' (in Chapter Thirteen of this book).

Folina remarks that Poincaré insists on finitude as 'inherent to the human condition,' and seems to take the idea of the finite 'as a primitive term,' (Folina, at 178).

Peirce, to the contrary, reflects what he sees as Poincaré's psychologism; he urges that we take our cue not from the metaphysics of psychology as Poincaré has, but from the instincts which are indeed primitive, but not finite. Instincts are not finite, nor limited, but are such forces which project upon the external world and thus become conversant with their projects, in an ongoing, continually changing process of making meaning, *of making meaning matter*.

Finally I close this chapter with a reference to Morris Cohen's reminder that Peirce's most important and consequential hypothesis is 'that there is a domain of radical indeterminism, that besides the variations due to errors of abstraction there are variations due to the fact our physical laws do not express with absolute accuracy the actual behavior of things,' (Cohen, 1931:222).

The crux of the problem of hypotheses — the meeting of logical and hypothetical hypotheses — was seen by Peirce nearly a century ago: He knew that hypotheses about actualities are not the same as hypotheses about fictions, whether these fictions are of mathematically-intuited images, or about logical symbolic notations.   Semiotics provides the filtering of both: representations of the fictive and representations of the actual. But although the representations in the form of hypotheses are signs in both cases, the importance of distinguishing the grounds of each kind is crucial. We *refer* to the ground of the actual world. We *allude* to the fictive texts we create in the sciences, the mathematics, the arts.   These distinctions, noted earlier, characterize our Interpretant Signs.

But it is semiotics which makes connections between these several grounds: this is the Peircean Method of Methods as the realization of the Possible.

We move from the mathematics as the most abstract of pragmatic models to the law, the most practically-oriented 'text' which pragmatism uses as model for representing the mediating role of The Indexical Function.

Part Two:
The Practics

Chapter 5

Law at the Border

Law at the Border

I
Blurring Limits of Meaning

In my monograph, *Inlaws/Outlaws: A Semiotics of Systemic Interaction* (1977), I introduced legal semiotics and based this branch of general semiotics on Peirce's philosophy and theory of signs. Since then I have 'engaged' Peirce with law as a continuum dialogue. Here I shall focus attention on dynamic, evolving relations between two terms or universes of discourse which move from relations of equilibrium to various stages of dissociation or opposition, and may cross and recross like an intertwining caduceus, perhaps, or like parallel lines from a noneuclidean perspective. In *Inlaws/Outlaws* the discourses I used to illustrate and begin to explain this critical process of the Peircean quest of Quests — the establishing of new, complex sign-relations between sign-systems — were the respective discourses of English law prior to the Norman conquest and the French law which came into relation with it as a result of the conquest. The emergent conquest of English commonlaw is the consequent of interaction, a conflictual interaction, between two sign systems, i.e., as two systems of law, (Kevelson, 1977).

The strategies of sign interaction were described with reference to Perelman's views, presented especially in *The New Rhetoric* (1971 edition, English translation). I had especially wanted to show analogies and other similarities between Perelman's unparalleled study of rhetorical tactics and Peirce's regard of Rhetoric, 'Pure Rhetoric,' as equivalent in meaning with his own understanding of the method of semiotics: Methodology or the *Method of Methods*, (Kevelson, 1987). In this early study of legal semiotics I indicated that in Peirce's work it is the logic of discovery rather than the logic of justification which describes '... the laws by which in every scientific intelligence one sign gives birth to another, and especially one thought brings forth another', (Peirce cited in the Buchler 1955 edition of selected papers, p. 55; see detailed discussion in Kevelson, 1977:84-89).

My decision to use law as a means of explicating Peirce and, reciprocally, to use Peirce's semiotics as a way of opening up otherwise inaccessible problems in law, has been for me an evolving idea. This early concern with conflicts between legal systems has remained an ever-deepening area for investigating both law and Peirce.

For example, I discuss the changing concept of the idea of law in western societies in as short a period of time as a few centuries: in the 18th century law was in the main described as a mediating principle for referent axiomatic reasons which lie 'behind' the law. In the early 19th century the predominant interpretation of the general meaning of the idea of law was that the reason behind the law was itself produced by referent popular custom that represented social practices based on socio-economic modes of trade and transactions of goods and values. In the late 19th century the idea of the law had come to be regarded, in large measure, as an instrument for indicating relations between leading principles deeply embedded in the legal discourse and current disputes arising between people in a jural state. By the middle of the 20th century, following the influence of Holmes and the Realists, law as idea in the United States especially, represented a complex conflict of legal subsystems in any given society. This ideal sign-system of law came to be characterized as dynamical and dramatistic, (Kevelson, 1987:76).

In *The Law as a System of Signs*, (Kevelson, 1988) I continue exploring and describing the Peircean *quest of quests*, by means of the 'method of methods.' I suggest here that the problems designated as problems of conflicts of law are critically important in getting an understanding of the relation between logics of discovery and paradox and the evolving of complex, open-ended (or 'free') sign-systems. In this book, in a concluding section, I note that the 'problem of conflicts of law may be seen as the type of problem of paradoxical structures as a whole and thus may provide insight into the process whereby codes of conflicting reference become transformed and new values emerge as a result of mediating, transforming semiosis,' (Kevelson, 1988:294).

A subsequent book on this topic, *Peirce, Paradox, Praxis: The Image, the Conflict, and the Law*, investigates issues in law and semiotics directly related to the intersystemic relationships between sign systems or universes of discourse. The Austinean notion of 'competing analogies' is taken up, as are changing interpretations and redefinitions of conflicts of law and also of conflicts in law, as Bentham's 'repugnancy' signifies, (Kevelson, 1990). This complex issue of semiotics in general, central to the problem of law and the making of value-signs as an aesthetic process, is of paramount importance in Peirce, (Kevelson, 1993). This study is followed by work on codes and complexity, (Kevelson, 1994).

In our present, transforming world this problem thickens. The idea of accounting for transdiscursive relations is so far from an academic problem that it has, indeed, brought Peirce's pragmatism out from the seminar, and even out of the laboratory (in Fisch's sense, 1958) onto the open arena of global intersystemic conflict where law plays a kind of thematically doubling role: *of Law versus Law*. Especially do we find this conflict between legal systems in the arguments for self-determination or aboriginal peoples, (Kevelson, 1994c). We find it also in societies where transnational corporations assume the function of virtual legal systems in third-world countries. Also, the erosion of the value of property in the self-proclaimed democracies of the world, in the name of equality and its congeneric value-signs, brings law into conflict with itself everywhere in all institutions of commonlaw countries. But perhaps nowhere has this contest between legal systems been so critically appraised as in those countries which until very recently were called communist states, (brought to my attention by Grazin, 1993).

I present his view of the problem before going on to related instances of 'law at the border,' that is, on the edge of itself as defined *by itself.*

II
Differentiation as Process

Grazin notes that 'Although the natural law idea has prevailed in developed and advanced democratic countries, the situation in post-communist countries is principally different. In other words, while judges in the United States must adhere to certain professional skills and ethical standards in deciding questions of law, judges in the former communist countries are not bound by these stable ethical standards; nor, for the judges, do these principles even exist,' (Grazin, 1993:719).

Grazin is assuming, or presupposing for the sake of his argument, a stability in commonlaw countries that is perhaps ideal but nonexistent. Still, there are implicit principles that are not separable from these competing commonlaw subsystems, (in Friedman's sense, 1975) such as Property. Indeed, all the relational 'rights' — civil, as opposed to 'human' rights — described in the Bill of Rights of the U.S. Constitution, are in point. But I will return to the changing function of value principles which results from an evolving, changing concept of the idea in focus as a general idea, such as is Law in this case.

Grazin further explains, with respect to the crisis perceived in former communist countries regarding law, that in those countries the old pre-communist assumption that institutions are man-made, and that such 'organizations and man-made laws are extinct, or have become so unstable that in searching for justification,' today, in post-communist societies, all that remains is zero remnants of the pre-communist notion of postivist institutions. Among the rubble is only, in his words, 'God, Man, Nature, and societies ... (for which) ... whole relationships must be rebuilt,' (Grazin, 1993:720). It must be emphasized that Grazin points out that in the wake of communism, in its collapse, it is not the case that only 'lawless societies' survive. Rather, the materials remain but the structures or forms into which they had been organized are no longer existent. Yet, he says, 'the situation has raised the possibility of choice: Which law, and what kind of legal order?' (Grazin, above).

The devolution of an idea, a complex and relationally-significant idea, is not equivalent with its demise but is rather a confrontation with a conflict of possibilities. It is not an opposition between the determined or defined and the vague. *It is an opposition between vague and vague, or hypothesis versus hypothesis.* This opens up a very new and anomalous concept in the vast literature of legal semiotics, and of general semiotics as well, since it presents the opportunity for choice between free-floating or value-free objectives. Nothing is anchored, in other words. Yet this is far from the structuralist problem of signifiers with no signifieds, since the semiotic action or process is one of interaction or conflict: the drama is improvisational in a whole new sense. This is the sense, I suggest, of self-organizing principles that the theorists of complex systems variously explore and discuss and which have been brilliantly described by Joseph Earley for one, (Earley, 1994).

This is, indeed, the crux of the problem for investigation by legal semioticians, and made observable in the situation presented so clearly and poignantly by Igor Grazin, to whom I return briefly here: Grazin states that 'every idea of law is a development of leading principles (to use Peirce's term) and the law as institution' tied to 'morality,' 'states' and aspects of 'bourgeois society', (Grazin, 1993:720). The question raised by communism is: Is the State 'above positive law? or, If positive law is man-made, is the State to be subordinate to the machinations of mere people?' The paradox confronting post-communist countries today is, in Grazin's words, 'that the principle of legality itself can be eliminated with positive law,' (Grazin, 1993:720).

Ironically, it is natural law that is in contrast to positive law. On the one hand, natural law is associated in some vague manner with holy, theological works and abstract, scholarly arguments, political propagandist papers and other rhetorical modes of discourse (using rhetorical in an everyday way). These intertwinings of natural law are also connected, on the other hand, with the commonlaw principles of Consent, Contract and especially Private Law; natural law assumes that social institutions such as law and economics are also, *as positive law also assumes*, man-made human inventions and artifices as is the Humean justice, (Kevelson, 1993). Now, as Grazin explains, communist ideology replaced this complex sign-system of natural law replete with its own internal inconsistencies and contradictions. *One discourse was,* he suggests, *substituted for another.*

The question he raises is whether Natural Law in some form can once again be inserted into that slot now vacated by communist ideology. What Grazin does not confront is the fact that the grid is not stable, and the process of one idea-system replacing another in dominance is not a substitute process but is, as Peirce observes in his criticism of 19th century economic theory, a permutative and transformational process (see Kevelson on this point in

1988, referring to Peirce's critique of Stanley Jevons). Here, with respect to legal systems in opposition, its *instability* facilitates the transformation of opposition to resolve: of Index evolved to symbolic function.

III
Two Discourses in Relation

Above I noted that we have before us a problem without precedent with respect to the fact that it has not been explicitly defined and/or represented. It appears to be a conflict between two new open, or undefined idea-systems which are grown from, but are not extensively deduced from, a stable referent concept. When, for example, we find ourselves agreeing with Dietze and others (Dietze, 1963) that the evolution of democratic principles has tended, in its process, to destroy the once constituent idea of private property, we need to look at the terms, Democracy, Property, Natural Law, Positive Law, Human Invention or sign-making, and propose new meanings to these counters or terms. If, indeed, the referent frames continue to be changed as an entire process of thought evolves and meaning becomes cumulative as a result of the transformation and revision of frames of reference, how do we have referent principles that both *are* and *are not*? That is, the *references are then of the nature of fictions in motion, where stability or states of ideas are frozen and are false representations*. It is more than the problem as Peirce noted, that all our arguments are at bottom fallible. But rather that the continuous, dynamical shift of references in the process of 'signifiers' are in conflict with one another without a referree, a point outside which traditional analogical relations used to find in the noting of an idea, that confronts us with a new kind of problem.

The situation with respect to semiotics of law, especially as we focus on conflicts of law and international law in general, is as Antony Carty has remarked: the idea of international law, as it has been understood by mainstream international lawyers since the 19th century, rests upon generally accepted methods of inquiry, (Carty, 1986). These methods of inquiry — the *doing* of a universe of discourse in other words — themselves are based upon and representative of certain presuppositions of 'thought-patterns.' These referent patterns may be faulty and flawed, or simply not adequate to the situation for which they are made to serve.

To invent an instrument for more accurate inquiry from which explanation both more complete and more elegant may be derived is as important for our understanding of the complexity of human organization, as at a different level, is the invention of 'super strings' that provides more comprehensive access to multidimensional, complex relations of forces in the universe than did the earlier quantum theory or still earlier theories from which quantum cosmology derived. It may be the case that the more sophisticated 'super strings' do not themselves create new networks of interaction in the actual world. But they do permit such representation that gives rise to new hypotheses and to the creation of new ideas and complex thought-systems or ideologies. For this purpose it is critical to begin to understand how the meaning of complex ideas happens, and how inquiry is an integral part of such complexity. Further, if an idea is meaningful it will produce consequences for the actual world, since it is that actual world, and not only the world of ideas, that ideas do interpret and interact with. *It is the method of inquiry that provides a mediating instrument for linking us to dimensions of our world that could not otherwise be observed.*

To refer again to Carty's interesting paper, which raises the question as to whether 19th century consensual theory as a 'frame of meaning resting on the State' — the then defined notion of State — is still, a century later, 'appropriate for the analysis and normative governance of international relations,' (Carty, 1986:vii). Professor Carty's concern invites semiotic attention, for he is indeed talking about legal and other related institutions as fraying around the edges, as decaying and devolving from some moment of historical ripeness. Carty correctly takes the issue of the decay of international law as seriously as it needs to be taken, *but not as far as it should be taken.* What is wanted, I suggest, is a comparative methodological approach which would bring the allegedly decaying system of international legal theory into a relationship with whatever it is or might be competing with, even if the latter is a hypothesis only, that is, a conceivable dimension of a comprehensive notion of international law that provides us with the bigger picture. Carty correctly notes that the imminent danger to international law as defined at present can be seen as a 'crisis of method in international law, in terms of the role of legal doctrine in the creation and fundamental concepts of that law,' (Carty, 1986:vii).

Here is another point of view on the core problem Grazin discusses above, and also widely prevalent in the dual legal systems of emergent nations and in the assertion for self-determination of aboriginal peoples, for example, Amerindian law vs. Constitutional law, (Kevelson, 1993).

IV
Individual As Archaism

While Grazin and others, in particular some leading spokespersons for Critical Legal Theory, seem to want to replace the gap left by the Communist state with a version of Natural law, others equally fortified resist a return to a natural Law replete with mythic substructures. Instead, the latter advocate a development in new directions, in the light of evolved global human values, of a man-made law (Kevelson 1995). Such man-made law, for culture-specific and national-specific human organizations as well as for an over-arching system of international law, would seem to smack, on the surface, of what has been broadly defined as Positive Law. It is Positivism that has had such a 'bad name' throughout all the various developments of special branches of semiotics, in the course of this 20th century growth. Positivism has been linked with a reduction of individual human beings and has been tied to a mathematical map from which the individual features and contours of intersubjective human relations are effaced.

At its worst this is indeed a positivism that has *earned* the impassioned response from humanists of the 20th century that it has received. In the early work of Habermas, for example, *The Legitimation Crisis,* Peirce is criticized as a Positivist; he is wrongly opposed to the very intersubjectivity Habermas argued for. Habermas has since came to know Peirce better and revises early judgments based on inadequate access to the bulk of Peirce's work. Even dedicated Peirce scholars such as Richard Bernstein are still critical of the tendency of pragmatism to blunt fine details of human societies, to be indifferent to nuances of value in pragmatically-dominated social institutions, for example, Peirce-derived legal pragmatism including the Realism indebted to Holmes and the legal semiotics which follows Peirce's theory, (Bernstein, 1990).

And surely, whatever was meant in the 19th century by the 'method of science' is not the same idea as has been evolved to these last years of the 20th century. Yet this concept of a 'method of science' — the pragmatic method of Peirce — is an idea which grows *as it is inquired into*. As it is continously interpreted it becomes, *as an idea*, more complex. The process it denotes is proportionally increasing in complexity just as the process-as-idea becomes, connotatively, more complex as well. The idea of the Individual at the heart of the myth of Natural Law remains among the rejects, and sustains its function in pragmatism now as in Peirce's own day as a relate in a relational social structure.

The term individual, from this point of view of pragmatism, is no less a function of a relation than are the terms Father, Student, Citizen, Child, Partner, Agent, Object. Thus the relationship is Individual *with* Individual. *The basic social unit is a relation and not an autonomous context-free and relation-free atom. This is the same sense Peirce holds with respect to the position that a statement is but the response part of a relation which requires a link with a question: the basic logic of discovery is erotetic, a relation of question and answer,* (Kevelson, 1977, 1987, 1990, 1993).

V
Stretching Boundaries and Non-Finite Property

An overview of the development of legal semiotics since the 1970's when I first indtroduced it, at a time when it was also introduced as a ramification of Saussurean, structural linguistic approaches to semiotics by Greimas and Landowski (1976), would show that the mythology of the Lockean-based natural law is seen to be falling apart, just as the underlying mythology for civil law is seen to be disintegrating (J. Van Doren, 'Things Fall Apart, or Modern Legal Mythology in the Civil Law Tradition,' in *Widener Journal of Public Law* 2 1993:447-489). Van Doren presents an interesting discussion of code ideology, and he contrasts Civil Law Codes with Common Law Systems (Van Doren, above, 459-460; see also the collection of papers from the perspective of modern legal semiotics in Kevelson, *Codes and Customs*, 1994; Cungi and Pieck, in particular, discuss the special problems involved when a society shifts from one legal culture to another, with special focus on modern Italy's legal culture, in Kevelson 1994 (pp. 45-76).

Van Doren also presents a useful critique of legal positivism. He suggests that the very nature of the positivist approach is a-moral: 'Positivists have little to say about what values should be implemented. Positivism may be morally neutral as to what 'commands' are carried out ... The acceptance of positivism, however, is not morally neutral ...' (Van Doren, at 462 and following). In other words, the moral structures may not be explicitly written into a legal system, but the informing value is an active force, by implication. It is an active, ethical force and referent, I might add, in precisely the way that a system of reasoning carries ethical value if it is an appropriate choice of a method of reasoning for the purpose at hand, (Kevelson, 1988, 1990).

While it has become usual to treat the idea of morality as if is were synonymous with the idea of ethics — as derived from a value code — Peirce would relegate morality to the frame of theological canon, and would by contrast distinguish ethics as an index for social transactions which derives from his Esthetics regarded as the Science of Value, (Kevelson, 1993). I also keep this distinction, and emphasize that the establishing of an equivalence between morals and ethics is nothing but the result of rhetorical force or the *use* of strategies of argument. Further, every discourse style conveys its own conventionalized and symbolic connotations of value. Stylistic types, including types of notational systems, become paradigmatic or symbolic representations for referent esthetic value. The very notion of the esthetic function in the creating of social values would seem to suggest that values are indeed artifices, artworks and man-made inventions.

This brings us to the edge of the 'black-holes' of legal systems. Here the force of values are most dense and grave. Hence we face the question of whether revolutions in law, as revolutions in science, invite counter-revolutions in both law and in science since what is in conflict in this continual unstable and living world are values themselves as motivating forces that are themselves, *evolving*.

In following general semiotic assumptions derived from Peirce's theory of signs, an idea is regarded as a network of cross-referential sign-functions, that is, a sign-system. An ideology, in an apolitical and neutral sense of the terms, is a complex system of signs. Ideas increase in their complexity as they evolve so that the network of meaning becomes dense and at the same time larger, such that the increase of 'meaningful area' becomes *more* with respect to the number of objects denoted within the defined boundaries of a term while the connotative system becomes *more deeply layered*: implicated and imbricated, (Bohm, 1987, 1980; Kevelson 1990, 1993).

What we see as a social institution is a representation of a complex, evolving sign-system, or ideology, (Kevelson, 1988). Again, Peirce observes and explains how ideas as Interpretants interpret one another and advance/evolve meaning from provisional 'definites' to possible 'vagues' and hence to new relational, general symbolic sign-functions.

With the creation of each new layer or dimension of an evolving general idea there is an interim of stability, or *apparent* stability, which acts as quasi-constant referent and frame of reference until it becomes destabilized by 'some surprising fact' which opens fresh inquiry on the idea in question.

Ideas which do not appear to cross categorial boundaries may seem merely to be extending properties, adding on attributes while maintaining a kind of specific, semantic 'order.' But the imposition of frames of reference, that is, semantic categories, one upon another, seems to violate the very laws of thought and reason. Two universes of discourse, as it were, appear to occupy the same 'space' and to produce incongruities such as 'wavicles' and 'duckrabbits' and other similar absurdities. These superimpositions are not paradoxes in an authentic sense of the paradox, but are con-fusions of idea-systems. When these confusions are brought about by intention of semiotic questors the result is, in Peirce's view, the objective of the semiotic Quest of Quests which is to bring together two ideologies or universes of discourse into a more comprehensive relation, *a new generality* (Kevelson 1987, 1990).

The marriage of civil and common law represents such a con-fusion in the dynamical process of the complex system of signs called The Law, as it evolves, develops. From the point of view of each relate — of civil law and of common law — what seems unclear is the definition of each, or the boundaries that open so that each idea penetrates the other in a kind of ideological conflict of law, or *border war*. For our purposes here we may substitute for the term, civil law, legal positivism, and for the term, common law we may use the term natural law. I am not suggesting that these are equivalent or closely synonymous substitutes. But for our further discussion we may use the analogy that civil law is to positive law as common law is to natural law, and not concern ourselves further at this time with other, correct distinctions between terms *here* placed in the same general camp.

Property, as an indispensable aspect of Common Law, is described as an ethical value by Dietze, for example, in *In Defense of Property,* (Dietze, 1963/1975) since it is an idea which mediates in social relations as a code and channel in such exchanges of goods and values, he suggests, (above, 57-64). Further he contrasts the rise in the value of democratization — synonymous here with the general concept of 'distributive justice' or utility — with decline in the value imputed to private property. Dietze says '... the distinction between property rights and so-called 'civil rights' and the assertion that the latter are entitled to greater protection because they are more necessary for the working of democracy, are unwarranted not only because they misconceive the nature of freedom, disregard the nature of man, and do not take into account the experience of ages, but also because they were rejected by the very people that are usually quoted in their support, namely, by the founders of modern democracy,' (Dietze, above 64).

From a similar point of view Hayek speaks of the spontaneous order, in law and in economic institutions, as a representation of *freedom as value* which has survived by evolving through the preference and choices of members in free transactional relations. These 'spontaneously grown institutions' are dynamical, self-organizing and cybernetical organizations. The multidimensional forces of which they are composed interact in ways we have yet to discover and to make clear. We need to construct, Hayek would suggest, some 'super string' theory of explanation to permit us to hypothesize of that which we cannot observe. Positivism, as may be presently defined, he says, is limited and inadequate since while it may show us the coherence and combinations of forces interacting in any given slice of the market system, it does not enable us to 'predict the precise results which any particular change will have,' (Hayek, 1952/1979:74-75).

Thus, to adapt Hayek's understanding of a positivistic limitation to the notion of man-made law, versus prioristic 'given' natural law — the systems here regarded as semiotic systems of law in conflict — positive law is not *sufficiently man-made*, since it is not a representation of a fully-intended, projected meaning of an idea. Rather, the positivistic theory has gaps of meaning, empty spaces or meaning-ellipses (to be distinguished from the gaps in law of Kantorowicz, in degree only). Hayek equates modern positivism with what he calls, 'scientism' — an 'abuse of reason' — and contrasts it with its antagonist, modern socialism. Both — that is, the conflict of which both ideologies are relates — evolved to a gordian knot in which the entangled ropes of ideas are distinguishable but the dis-entangling of the knot still needs an herculean approach: the one side is that which represents the liberalism of Kant, Adam Smith, Hume, for example, and the other side represents the totalitarianism of Hegel, Marx, Comte, (Hayek, above p. 399).

Hayek speaks of the infiltration of positivism, or scientism, as a kind of counter-espionage, such that a counter-revolution is an illicit betrayal of a confidence and informational trust rather than as a stage in purposeful evolution, in law and/or economics as in all the sciences.

Finally, in regarding social institutions as complex sign-systems and representations of complex ideas of ideologies I am merely providing illustrations of the Peircean semiosis in a less abstract, more practicable manner. What Peirce's theory provides for is an instrumental handle on a process of inquiry and explanation which permits description of aspects of social, human (and non-human organizations) that are not otherwise explainable. For example, the exciting, interesting group of intellectuals who have come to constellate around the Santa Fe Institute for Studies in the Science of Complexity are genuinely interdisciplinary but are still in search of a theory or set of theories to use as a frame of general reference. Peirce seems to offer such a working basis, (Kevelson, 1993); but he has not been brought in to a position of centrality at this point, although scholars of the stature of Bohm, Prigogine, Kauffman, and others, important to and in part integral with this group, have taken Peirce as a great influence upon this new work.

The late Nobel Laureate Hayek has also cited Peirce's work and his own indebtedness to Peirce as indispensable for his own positions on law and economics, including the principle of informational decentralization in game-theory of Economics. This game-theoretic approach to trading and the double auction market is not my focus here, but I mention it in passing since it grows out of an earlier attempt, by the Institute, to define the idea of ecomonics as an evolving, complex system, that is, a sign-system (1988 in P.W. Anderson, K. J. Arrow, D. Pines).

The link between law and economics, from the perspective of semiotics, has been largely the work of Robin Paul Malloy, for example see *The Symposium on Law and Economics and the Semiotic Process* (special issue of *The Syracuse Review*, 42 1 1991). This symposium builds on general semiotic theory and thus indirectly on Peirce, (Kevelson, 1977, 1988, 1990.)

In summary, in this present paper I regard two systems of law in conflict as representing Peirce's notion of the development of an idea from less to more complex. For more detailed discussion with issues in conflict of law see Kevelson, 1990. The point of departure in this present chapter is a critical situation that is occurring in postcommunist countries today, where the question is open as to which legal system is to fit into the place left open under the heading, 'rule of law.' Is it a place appropriate for Natural Law or for Positive Law? This is the problem posed and discussed by Grazin, in his insightful and provocative paper in the *John Marshall Law Review* (26 1993:719-737). This crisis shares several significant aspects with what Hayek has much earlier described as *The Counter-Revolution of Science* (1952/1979). Here Hayek argues in a Peircean sense that we begin with our predilections, our inclinations, and our prejudices in our constructions of models to represent and build upon what Austin had referred to as conflicting and 'competing analogies' (Hayek, above pp. 41-60).

Conflicts of law and of competing analogies in the development of a complex ideology we call The Law may begin to explain how an institution as a complex network of meaning evolves and grows. This problem area of jurisprudence provides exemplary illsutrations of how pragmatism operates in law as a semiotic system. Holmes's Realism shows a facet of Pragmatism, from an intra-semiotic/systemic perspective.

Chapter 6

Holmes's Realism Revisited

Holmes's Realism Revisited

I
The Pragmatic Implication

Nearly two decades have passed since I introduced and indeed invented the idea of a Semiotics of Law, (Kevelson, 1976, 1977). In the interim I have securely tied the Legal Realism derived from Oliver Wendell Holmes to the Pragmatic Method of Charles Peirce's Semiotics or theory of signs, (Kevelson, 1987, 1988, 1990). Although several notable scholars have questioned whether Holmes was, as I claim, indebted to Peirce's thought, no one has convincingly argued against a clear and apparent 'family resemblance' between Peirce and Holmes. Below is a brief recap of assumptions followed here.

Semiotics of law, following Peirce, is concerned with the process of evolving intellectual concepts, i.e., ideas and methods of reasoning. Legal Realism has been correctly characterized by its rejection of traditional logic and its advocacy of a process of reasoning which is based on a logic of discovery rather than a logic of justification. Legal Reasoning, from this perspective, emphasizes inductive and hypothetical reasoning. Since Legal Realism presumes open, evolving relations between law and society resting not on 'Truth' but on consensual agreement of referent value and meaning, deduction and validity in the old sense becomes radically reinterpreted. Former *definitions* of these concepts are *referent*, interpretant signs.

The assumed social context for Holmes's Legal Realism is a pluralistic, open-ended society, such as the United States ideologically espouses. The legal system which appropriately represents an open, changing society is one which is maximally tolerant of competing analogies and which presumes the law to be, not by accident but rather by choice, an indeterminate system. This is perhaps the major distinction between any variety of Legal Realism and all brands of Legal Positivism: the latter sees indeterminacy as a flaw, or as Bentham calls it, a set of 'repugnancies,' whereas the former opts to sustain indeterminacy and 'intentional ambiguity,' (Kevelson, 1990).

As I discuss in earlier work, John Austin's 'refusal to tolerate a sustained interminacy or vagueness in the law provided the Realists with an opening for stating the case for an indeterminate law,' (Kevelson, 1990:175).

My focus in this chapter is that the multifaceted Legal Realism, following Holmes and strongly influenced by Peirce has been and is at this unsettled period a pragmatic instrument in the effecting of a revolution in legal reasoning. Legal Realism, revisited, as it reemerges as a major force in the United States and elsewhere, *signifies*, i.e., reflexively points to itself as an idea — praxis *and* theory — as a law whose time has come. In the following

I will explore and open for new discussion some aspects of Holmes's Legal Realism in the context of a here and a now. This identification of Holmes with Peirce's Pragmatism holds, despite Holmes's *overt* denial of the merits of pragmatism (see Holmes-Pollock correspondence, Vols I, II, in passing, 1874-1932, 1941 edition).

II
Realism's Context

To begin with, I assume that Legal Realism represents such aspects of the skeletal structure of legal reasoning — its logical armature — that opponents have attempted to discredit over this 20th century, with some admittedly short-lived successes. But today Legal Realism reemerges to take its place in the United States as a dominant sub-legal system and a major voice in the shaping of public policy. This ascending predominance, still a longshot prediction, is far from an accomplished fact. But it is a sufficiently strong contender for a leading theory and practice of legal reasoning. It warrants close inquiry at this time. Its worst enemy is two-fold: 1) Holmes's lingering reputation as a mean-spirited judiciary voice who expresses little sentimental appreciation for a 'prioristic justice' or 'innate human nature', and 2) Holmes's refusal to relinquish his ideal of the law as fluid, protean, imperfect. This opposition to Realism, strongly against that which Holmes still represents to mainstream juridical thought, would be even more strongly opposed if it correctly perceived Peirce's influences. Nevertheless, it should be known.

To regard the United States Constitution and the open system of interpretable law it stands for as fallible at bottom, as an *experiment* however noble and admirable, is to many critics a danger of undervaluing the Law as Ideal End, and by association, of disclaiming the law's responsibility as a moral agent. A fusion of irreverence, with great respect for the adaptive strengths of people and their institutions, leads to misinterpretations of Legal Realism from many quarters. Further, the fact that the general notion of pragmatism had become, even in Holmes's time, attenuated and generally reduced to a notion widely equated with crass expediency, practicality in everyday affairs, and mere materialism, has led to increasing distancing of the Legal Realism idea connected with Holmes and the Pragmatism/Semiotics idea associated with the miscreant/genius Peirce.

In this chapter I will not take the time to recap the high points which biographically as well as intellectually tied Peirce and Holmes to a commonly-shared set of ideas. Rather I will digress now and again as I suggest that the logic of relations, of paradox and of possibility — the structures of reasoning of Legal Realism — is viable for our times, for democracies in revolution, for open, pluralistic societies, (Kevelson, 1990).

Let us recall at the outset that Peirce, in exactly the same time period that Holmes's Realism was becoming a factor in United States Supreme Court decisions in the early 1900's, had asserted that what he meant by the theory of signs, of Semiotics, was synonymous with his newly 'expanded logic.' In brief, this mode of reasoning based on relations, on possibility, on hypothetical premises, proceeds dialogically according to acts and strategies of a 'new' rhetoric, a rhetoric Peirce equated with his pragmatic methodology, (Kevelson, 1987).

As discussed earlier, this Rhetoric, or Methodology, is a dynamical process of reasoning in which neither leading principles nor premises remain constant. Rather, in contrast with deductive reasoning, the referent principle is regarded as if it were fixed and permanent, but may be re-opened for questioning and revised and corrected in the course of an ongoing inquiry. The 'reopening' is the purpose of Peirce's phenomenological protosemiotic investigation, (Kevelson, 1982, 1987). The initial assumptions then are also continuously in flux. Whatever may be predicated of a topic alters the meaning of that referent topic. *This continuously changing, evolving meaning of referent ideas gets carried along, such that meaning is a cumulative process.* From this point of view referent legal principles may *appear* to be stable. But the stability of the law in actuality is *by design* unstable. The process is, as vanguard intellectuals of the latter half of this century have termed it, from order to chaos, since chaos in this special sense is an assurance of a living law of which new possibilities may be created and new values affirmed, (Kevelson, 1993).

As Jerome Frank and other early Realists have argued, the judge is no longer expected to merely 'find' the law but the process of juridical, semiotic interpretation does in fact create new law. Frank also, in accord with others prominent in Realist theory, argued that the new legal reasoning was mapped upon, i.e., represented, key ideas of a mode of reasoning which sharply distinguishes the reasoning that underlies non-Euclidean geometry from that of Euclidean geometry, (Kevelson 1988). This is especially pertinent when we recall that one of the foremost responsibilities of law is to determine disputes arising from conflicting claims about space, i.e., about boundaries of all kinds that constitute the organizing and institutionalizing of human affairs, almost globally. This concept of 'space' is, of course, not restricted to geo-place, but is primarily concerned with the differentiation between people: their bodies, wills, properties, extensions of every kind, including the metaphoric spatio/temporalizing of 'areas' of thought, of 'mind,' (Kevelson, 1996).

One further digression here: Peirce had made clear that not all non-Euclidean geometries represented the structure of semiotic processes: In particular, he writes, it is topical geometry which provides a visualizable or iconic understanding of the plasticity and nonfiniteness of space. And it is this topological analogy which Peirce stretches to include, as Aristotle and others have done since the so-called topics of reasoning: the categories of law classified and instituted.

Elsewhere I enumerate the special features which distinguish Legal Realism from other approaches to law, (Kevelson, 1988). Here, in brief, I want to note that despite a much discussed heterogeneity of points of view of the Realists they seem to share, at the least, the following characteristics in common: They assume 1) dialogic structure of Legal Reasoning; 2) indeterminacy of legal system and legal reasoning; 3) dynamical, self-corrective, even non-conclusive process of legal reasoning; 4) emphasis on reasoning as a heuristic, discovery procedure, and 5) open-endedness; i.e., emphasis on legal reasoning as representation of social interaction in open society regarded as a means for generating new human values; 6) total rejection of prioristic, ideal referents together with refutation of an innate moral force operative within the law and in lawful societies.

In passing, I want to mention that the changing notion of democracy seems to parallel the evolution of concepts in that mode of legal reasoning which characterizes Realism. It is a subject I explore elsewhere, in further detail, (Kevelson, 1996).

At this time I want to sketch out in broad strokes some aspects of this continually transforming relationship between Realism and a political ideology which it represents. In this introductory section I note that Legal Realism, the method of reasoning appropriate to it and its socio-political context, evolves out of opposition between Euclidean and non-Euclidean premises and procedures. Further, the complex of features we associate with Holmesean Legal Realism has close affinity to another 'ism', i.e., its congener, Darwinism. We speak of a Darwinism rather than of theories of Charles Darwin since the 'ism' signifies in symbolic fashion a general concept of adaptation and self-organization which was triggered by Darwin but has moved rather far, in places, from his explicitly expressed writings.

In the same sense Realism draws on non-Euclidean assumptions, but is not bound to those assumptions in any literal fashion. These general ideas act as frameworks for broad, comprehensive ideas until and unless they will not appropriately stretch to accommodate further growth and redefinition. Then a new name, interpreting its former referent, begins to emerge and to grow. This is a basic tenet of a Peircean semiotics. An example: Holmes's contention that the life of the law is not logic is a realization that the *old logic will not be adequate to a new idea of law*. It is for Realism, the old referent against which the new logic — the expanded logic which Peirce equated with all that he meant by Semiotics — develops. In point, 'non-Euclideanism' serves to delineate a whole assemblage of ideas generally represented by the dynamical structure of semiotics. The term becomes a kind of linkage, and hence serves as a medium, or *mediate metaphorical connection. Noneuclideanism* becomes, as such, a general concept informing the new legal reasoning, (Purcell, 1973:47 ff).

In the following short section I want to discuss some aspects of the emergent relation between non-Euclideanism and Legal Realism, from the viewpoint of a non-mathematician. This brief discussion will help to clarify some lingering misunderstandings of Realism which wrongly tend to see Realism as a kind of legal positivism. We may better appreciate how this misinterpretation came about and be in a position to recast the case for Realism, in no respect a mode of Positivism any more than it is a voice for Natural Law.

III
A Short Genealogy of 'Realism'

In a more modern context, with no intention to minimize the importance even today of Jerome Frank's connection between Legal Realism and non-Euclideanism, Purcell's work (1973) provides a pertinent and contemporary view:

Purcell says, 'Since Charles Sanders Peirce's seminal work on logic ... American pragmatism had developed a powerful critique of metaphysical principles.' Therefore prioristic reasoning is not acceptable, since it is based on other than experiential knowledge, and is referent to 'predispositions.' Such predispositions are those that we find ourselves 'inclined to believe,' (Peirce's refutation, in 'The Fixation of Belief' was published in the 1870's in *The Monist* in those germinal papers which became the nucleus of American Pragmatism, of Semiotics, and by extension, of Legal Realism.

In continuing, Purcell reminds us that the prevailing attitude among vanguard intellectuals, especially in America in the first half of the 20th Century, was clear and outspoken hostility 'toward metaphysics and a priori reasoning,' (Purcell, above). This hostility became a means of linking Pragmatism, Legal Realism and Positivism (via the Vienna Circle of the 1920's and 1930's) and thereby became connected with the emergent notion of a 'scientific naturalism.' In brief, scientific reasoning and its 'method' so-called, was seen as the coherent force which had the ability to unify related universes of discourse into a more general, more comprehensive ideological sphere. This unification was indeed that which Peirce asserts as the main purpose of his semiotic inquiry.

Correctly, Purcell points out that it was non-Euclideanism that became the binding element of this complex intellectual system of emergent ideas, of an intellectual activity which consisted of diverse ends and aims, but which shared a common method. As a unified means Realism, Scientific Reasoning, Pragmatism, are related in this complex and are conjoined against prescriptive morals and ethics, against transcendental verities, against absolute authorities of all kinds, including causality and necessity. The outcome of this was, and is still, unacceptable to many, since the obvious inference is that if all initial premises, *as wishes, assumptions, hypotheses,* are *merely tentative working bases, then no normative ethics, however soundly argued, is* **right** *and* **true** — **but possible only.**

Non-Euclideanism provided all of these dissenters with a kind of kinship bond which was based on clear disqualification of the classic assumptions of Euclidean thinking. The actual world was not angular and connected by straight lines, but was curved, crossreferential, 'fractalized', (Kevelson, 1993), and only approximately quantifiable. The initial reaction against the implications of non-Euclideanism were sufficiently hostile and discrediting to bring about a reaction from such distinguished scholars as Dewey in Philosophy, Boas in Anthropology and eventually Lon Fuller in Law: Their agenda was at first to soften the 'scientific' base of social institutions and to replace this softer base with appeals to history and to a more 'humanistic' curvilinear structure closer to an evolving Darwinism and an emergent humanistic ethics. As I discuss in the closing chapter of this book, Peirce's own apparent shift of ideology needs to be seen in this light also.

Non-Euclideanism and Pragmatism both incorporate principles of nonlinearity. In this manner they are co-referents for value judgements which are not deduced from a constant principle but which dynamically carry forward in a process of mutual change an emerging value together with the referent value principle. But whereas most positivistic approaches agree with Peircean pragmatism that value principles are invented, i.e., are hypothetically positioned to function as leading idea-referents, positivism as a whole does not argue that these principles, once positioned, continue to change and become revised. Peirce's method of reasoning in his pragmatism does exactly that. Thus, his selection of the non-Euclidean area of topical geometry lent itself, as prime mathematical representation, to the idea of the dynamics of conceptual evolution in all discourse types, including the discourse of law. The early Realists recognized this, and saw the nature of the revolutionary aspects of this procedure. The later Realists, in attempts not to be outcast, modified their position until we find it 180 degrees away from its original direction, e.g., in the work of Lon Fuller, (Kevelson, 1990, 1996).

By the 1920's, American Realism, through the American Law Institute and the Restatements, projects a great disillusion. The early promises of a scientific law failed to materialize. Realism was seen to exemplify that disillusion. Promises 'made' by Realism were not realized.

In this manner the 'revolution in reasoning,' which marks the upheaval of non-Euclideanism in all spheres of principled inquiry around the world, had begun to produce its counter-revolution in the form of a powerful antipathy to the logical positivists. The evolutionists, the pragmatists, the Legal Realists — were all bagged together even as they were intertwined in their vitalities.

Euclideanism has offered a framework for legal reasoning through an apparently coherent system of 'givens' or propositional truths which could result in a 'flawlessly logical system,' (Purcell, above at 49). But Peirce and others had opposed Euclideanism at its core, and held that all propositions are at bottom hypothetical. Peirce won, but lost. What he won was the fact that history and other intellectuals proved the correctness of his thinking: e.g., the overthrow of Euclideanism is clear in the work of Riemann, Lobachevski, Bolyai, Poincaré, Einstein, Mandelbrot, Minkowski, and others. The definitive split between Peirce and Kant is less evident: for a long time Kant continued to provide a framework for legal reasoning, and still does, and therefore still confounds and confuses the idea of legal reasoning as a nondeterminate, intentionally paradoxical discourse, (Kevelson, 1990, 1993, 1996). The sticking point is the idea of logical necessity, retained in Kant and rejected in Peirce.

The adaptation of non-Euclideanism in theory to non-Euclideanism in professional practice is largely due to the influence of Holmes upon the Realists who are his heirs. Indeed, one may see Morris Cohen as mediating between Holmes and Peirce during the early decades of this century, (Cohen, 1931). Cohen sets about to make a link between Realism and Pragmatism a major focus to the juridical community. He ultimately capitulates, not to his critics, but to the recognition of the lack of the Ideal in Realism. I mention this later in the chapter.

The idea of Pragmatism in upper-case was, ironically, not working: in lower case pragmatic terms, it was a road too difficult for jurisprudes to take and to persist in. It emphasized the *instability* of the law as *desirable*, and it clearly went against the grain of those who saw that the increasing complexity of maintaining any sense of a stable legal system in an open and pluralistic society would be an exercise in immediate futility and, long-range, could result in political catastrophe, (Kevelson, 1997). Meanwhile, work on the theoretical aspects of non-Euclideanism continued, especially in the works of Bolyai and Lubachevski, of Tarski and Lukasievicz, and others. Major work was not available to legal scholars during the internecine period between the

1920's and the end of World War II. In recent analyses we find that non-Euclideanism manages to preserve the deductive mode of reasoning as a kind of prestigious, stable, truth-assuming framework, where truth and deduced inferences still permit one to postulate presumptions based on prioristic absolutes of truth and knowledge, (Purcell, above at 61).

But Holmes, in the early years of his impact on the law in the United States, rejected the primacy of a metaphysical 'truth' as referent for legal reasoning. He established in its stead the concept of practice before theory: Holmes's Realism holds that legal procedure — what the courts do in fact — becomes the basis for the making of new law. Peirce, similarly, rejects metaphysical principles — the basis of Theory — as primal. In its place he has practice. Thus Pragmatism, or descriptions of Practice as Praxis, produces an evolving Theory of Signs: Semiotics, (Kevelson, 1988, 1990).

IV
Remnants of Realism

Holmes developed his theory of the Common Law in the 1880's against the ground of evolutionist thought. The Common Law may be seen as rebuttal to the idea of Natural Law, especially as it was then held in the United States, since Natural Law was prioristic and mapped upon syllogistic models of reasoning.

As positivism and pragmatism had affirmed non-Euclidean premises and had rejected prioristic tendencies, Holmes's Legal Realism became a strange partner. There emerged this triadic alliance which brought about several consequential misreadings. Holmes was eager to stand apart from associations with both positivism and pragmatism: the latter by early in the 20th century had become appropriated as a popular notion for the practice of doing things expediently, opportunistically. As mentioned above, Holmes carefully avoided even discussing pragmatism and does so rarely, in correspondence with Laski once or twice in passing, and at the end of his life with a nod to Dewey as a late-day appreciation for Dewey's Pragmatism, (Kevelson, 1995).

Natural Law had, and still has, a powerful emotional claim upon juridical idealists in the United States and elsewhere. It presents itself as a formidable opponent to Holmes, all the more so since it was the 'encumbent' theory, so to speak. Nevertheless Holmes and The Realists who followed aimed at that which they called 'legalistic formalism.'

One may regard Peirce's Pragmatism and the immediate referent of Holmes's ideas for the Realists as shadows, or traces. We found their conjoined influence in the works of Llewellyn, in Frank, in Pound, in Gray,

Cardozo and others in the United States, and also in Hagerstrom, Olivecrona, and Ross in Scandinavia. The latter influence is, admittedly, disputed.

Now nearly a century after the germination of this notion of Realism it is appropriate to do stock-taking and attempt to examine some of the ramifications of Realism in current legal practice and reasoning on a global scale and not merely here and there, in the United States and in Scandinavia. Indeed, Realism presents itself as an idealized way of understanding law to those in emergent democratic societies which are seeking some model, some representation, some sign-system to interpret and take as their own, (Kevelson, 1988, 1996).

In the following I attempt to touch upon some of the main tenets of Realism which surface in the modern world. I want to emphasize at the outset that just as any ideology is a complex of ideas, these complexes are *experiments* in thought. Any attempt to translate or transpose ideas into actual human affairs, into human action, is no less experimental. The notion of the experimental nature of semiotics is in itself suspect to many since it runs counter to what is readily perceivable as the human wish for certainty. Yet the possible failure of experiments has not inhibited the vanguard from attempting them, with the hope of breaking through boundaries into more freedom, more possibility for humankind. It is no tragedy when an experiment in *ideal* thought fails. But the stakes are enormous when human societies are used as laboratories for testing out ideology. Still, Realists will argue, such stakes are conditions for free marketplaces, the marketplaces of goods, commodities and ideas. From this perspective, in a Hayekian sense following Peirce and Holmes, Realists are risk-takers.

It was the American Law Institute, through its Restatements, that valiantly attempted to create new bonds between the discourse of law and the actual society it purported to represent. In this context the new 'norms' were not to be sought from the ground of metaphysical first principles, but were to be fashioned — *made* — of the stuff that relates law and society. This 'stuff' is language, the language of interpersonal communication, mostly verbal, but also in gestural sign-patterns, iconic structures of professional procedure, shapes and functions of public buildings, etc., (see Chapter Three of this volume). As Francis Lieber noted, the hermeneutics of law is a deciphering of all those parts of law and the jural state. Holmes advised law students to study architecture and art, history and science, all humanistic studies which are the matter-of-factness of law's language, (Kevelson, 1987,1988).

Following Holmes, Karl Llewellyn urged that the law should recover its Realist commitments to effect relationship between legal rules and practical action. He urged a revisiting of Holmes's notion of the law as a vehicle and instrument: *a mediational tool.*

And it was Jerome Frank who argued that a Realist law must take for its model — its Icon — the assumptions of a non-Euclidean geometry for a basic concept of *topos*, i.e., of crossreferentiality, of deformable n-dimensional 'space' or ground. In this singular manner it was Frank who takes Legal Realism back, through Holmes, to Peirce and to Semiotics, (Kevelson, 1988).

But there were at least two strikes against any likelihood of a long-lasting effectual utilization of Legal Realism in the United States, and in other democratic societies as well. The first obstacle is the wide-spread misunderstanding of the dynamical principles of reasoning which Realism represents: its surface resemblance to positivistic reasoning on the one hand, and to more intuitionist modes of guesswork on the other hand, effectively undermined Realism as a credible system of law. Despite the fact that people easily reason in a manner according with a logic of paradox, and despite the fact that all our arguments are enthymemic and hypothetical, the ideal of the closed world with its authoritative Truth persists as a great felt wish raised to the stature of a Logos, (Kevelson, 1990).

We recall the words of Hessel E. Yntema ('The Hornbook Method and the Conflict of Laws,' *Yale Law Journal* 37 1928:476, 480): He says that the old ideal 'of a government of laws and not of men' is only 'a dream.' The judge subjectively comes to a decision based on her feelings, her experience, her personal values; and only in a secondary fashion does she have recourse to 'rules, precedents, principles and the old laws of thought,' i.e., the laws of traditional, syllogistic reasoning, (Kevelson, 1988, 1985; see also Purcell, above at 80.)

The development of Realism, based on adaptive interpretations of non-Euclideanism, mapped onto a known but inadequate ancient logical schema, became through the work of Frank, Oliphant, Yntema, Morris, Felix Cohen and others, a collective argument that rejected legal reason as determinate, causally-based, and even valid in the strict sense of validity. Thus no judicial decision according to Realism is a decision necessitated by logic, but rather is adulterated with materials from the subjective, from prevailing commonsense, and from other motives. To this unbridled end of the law Morris Cohen and others objected.

For one, Morris Cohen began to seek out prioristic, innate 'verity' to hold onto. He argued that judicial judgement made so subjectively is not different from the decision of a 'tyrant' or a 'despot,' and is, ironically, simply another fact of the old authority it — Realism — had tried so hard to overcome, (Morris Cohen, 'Positivism and the Limits of Idealism in Law,' in *American Bar Association Journal* 13 1927:244).

V
The Odds Against ...

It is hard to say of any system of signs — any idea — that its time has not yet come. But it seems that some ideas wake up to a climate so unwelcoming that they withdraw and become dormant a while longer. So it seems with Realism, and indeed with the main thrust of Peirce's work as a whole.

Purcell put it nicely, referring to Frank's views: When the time comes, if ever it does, that people recognize the law as it has traditionally been, 'an unconscious substitute for the just and absolute father, they would be able to throw off their irrational demands for a logical and certain legal system,' their thinking would then be fully adult, accepting change readily, welcoming doubt as healthy, and enjoying challenges to old beliefs and golden cows.

In closing this chapter, the leading principles for a viable Legal Realism must be representative of those habits of valuing which the human experience seems to wish to continue: values that are open and free and no more certain than that, together with the tendency to set limits, draw boundaries, define and redefine. Realism represents such a dynamical sustained tension. Under critical eyes it may not seem a way to make friends, influence people, and win votes.

Realism represents a mode of reasoning relationally. It is a mode of the transitive. It is that style and structure of the English language, for one, which became transformed from the dominantly intransitive to the transitive that has characterized it ever since, (Kevelson, 1976). It is such a structure and interplay of exchanged meaning which underscores Peirce's Pragmatism and which is the armature of Holmes's: *The Common Law*.

Realism is a reason of transaction, of dialogue. Realism is *other than* the hierarchical multiply-embedded discourse of The Sovereign, the authoritative *One*.

In the following chapter I isolate selected aspects of Holmes's Realism and connect these ideas to correspondences in Pragmatism as Peirce describes in his 'Method of Methods.'

Chapter 7

Holmes's Magic Mirror Refracted: New Images of Realism

Holmes's Magic Mirror Refracted:
New Images of Realism

I
The Mirror as Icon

Everything heard/said about Holmes tells us that he walked a thin line between his respect for public reason and standard language on the one hand, and his disdain for sloppy thinking and popular jargon on the other hand. He was elegant in style, yet not precious. While he often draws his analogies from ordinary life — the life of the ordinary gentry of the late-Victorian Cambridge — he rarely if ever speaks the idiom of the street. This chapter carries forward, under different light, topics touched upon in the previous chapter.

What Justice Holmes avoids is significant. What is not evident in his life and work is, in some respects, a *significant absence*. And since it is the business of semioticians to inquire into significance of all kinds — the impossible, the improbable, and the not (yet) existent — this paper looks into two great gaps in Holmes: two 'windows' or spectacles which are so ground that we see through them, with any luck, onto a multidimensional view of an idea evolving. This idea of Legal Realism is a consequent of Holmes's effect on American Law, and by extension, on distant legal systems as well, e.g., in Scandinavia and in China, (Kevelson, 1988). These twin holes in the Holmesian fabric I assume here are: 1) the Peirce/Pragmatism connection, and 2) Brewster's Kaleidoscope.

The kaleidoscope, before it became reassigned to everyday life as a parlor-game/toy, was the product of David Brewster's genius: an instrument invented for further research, in Brewster's day, in the optical sciences. Brewster wrote in 1815 that this tool made it possible to create new forms of beauty, new referents, and that this process of creating novel forms or frames of reference is a dynamical process (Brewster 1818/1987). Brewster's kaleidoscope is a mirror-refracting invention, independent of small pieces of colored glass that we find in modern copies and adaptations. Its 'magic' was its capability of disecting any whole object into an infinite number of possible arrangements of its constituent parts, including that part which the viewer/interpreter supplied as imaginative contributions and which, as an integral aspect of interpretation, reconfigures the several parts into new relations, into new possibles.

Holmes grew up in a home where prominent scientists were daily visitors and where discussion of theories, models, processes of scientific nature was usual and ongoing. Yet Holmes does not use the metaphor of kaleidoscope to refer to an instrument which the viewer may use in order to create a virtual *harem* of images of the Law, which is the analogy he uses but not his exact term (1885). Deftly, with the use of this Magic Mirror, or Kaleidoscope, Holmes unifies Legality and Legitimacy — laws and justice — into the idea of a holistic Law. Holmes focuses on the role of the viewer crafting a new unified form of Law: a Galatea and new take on My Fair Lady. He plays Pygmalian in this allusion which is far too highbrow to work its magic through a mere commonplace 'kaleidoscope' with *its* connotations of trivialized recreation or just plain fun.

Similarly, the idea of Pragmatism, by the time of Holmes's after-dinner talk, 'The Law,' in 1885 had already become worn at the edges of its meaning, rounded instead of sharp and distinctively significant. The term 'pragmatism' had then become an everyday colloquialism for opportunism, for expediency, and for the 'ruthless,' 'reckless' practice of a free market and market-players.

I assume that the main point of Holmes's preference for the 'magic mirror' name instead of the 'kaleidoscope' is that even while the 'magic mirror' term is equally as trite and worn down as 'kaleidoscope' at the time Holmes uses it, it had not also then taken on the additional features of triviality and playtime. Indeed, the mirror metaphor is doubly allusive: first, to the scientific instrument of Brewster's developing a dynamical process of hypothesizing for creating and observing the actual world around us, (Olson, 1975); second, it recalls longstanding belief, especially among proponents of natural law, which Holmes opposed but from whom he co-opted cherished beliefs, namely, that law is a means of representing ideal convictions and values which predominate in such social organization of which law is one of several inter-relating institutions. Holmes's Magic Mirror's dual reference is, first, to an instrument and image of those beliefs which the public forum is ready to die for, (Holmes, 'Natural Law', in *Collected Legal Papers*, 1930: 310-316), and, second, to the concept of pragmatism linked variously to the positivist jurist Chauncy Wright and to the decidedly nonpositivist versions of Pragmatism of William James. Peirce, strangely enough, is a name that occurs only once or twice in all of Holmes's writings, despite the fact that they knew one another well and shared friends and societies in common. The term Pragmatism also occurs only a couple of times in all of Holmes's writings, and mostly in a pejorative sense, connecting it with a vague reference to theism and cosmic forces.

This last significant absence is indeed strange, since Legal Realism in its general thrust as complex idea is in all respects compatible with and representative of the Peircean — not Jamesian — version of the pragmatic method. (Note my reference to distinctions between James's and Peirce's concepts of Pragmatism and to the underlying conflict between these two alleged *friends*.) We may speculate that Peirce and Holmes were sufficiently irritants to one another in interpersonal ways, so that such flaps might not be recorded. They seemed to have walked a wide berth of one another: the marked avoidance has resulted in a profound absence or gap, or silence. Silence is a Zero Sign: It points to a transforming event, a paradigm shift, a freeze in the film, a long, tense, moment in dramatic action. Even a pregnant pause.

My purpose is not that of the historian. I am not seeking to draw connections over ellipses. But I am concerned with the current evolved meaning of Legal Realism since it is, despite Holmes's reluctance to link his thought with pragmatism, at the extreme of a venture, in acute polarity with what is emerging to represent a principle of law. This *Principled* Law, of a modified, updated positivist nature, is rule-ordered and *ideally coherent*. Its antagonist, such as variously expressed by legal semioticians, Crits (heirs in some respect to Legal Realism), is that which falls into the camp of Legal Pragmatism.

It doesn't surprise anyone that concepts change meaning. *How* they grow is the objective of semiotics' inquiries. When in the course of human ideas we see a concept labelled liberalism, for example, change its leading principles in midstream, or a concept of conservatism become radicalized, one accepts that it is not unusal in fact that when we find *any* school of thought — of legal thought in our case — shift sides, jump banks and end up on the opposite side of where it began. It is said that the 'new positivism' has found a good bedfellow in natural law. It is morality which in strange fashion blesses their union. By contrast, Pragmatism in law continues to resist any and all aspects of determination, of absolutes, of a closed and constant system of referents. Pragmatism, which includes inquiry into Ethics, is not determined by moral codes.

It is my contention that it is pragmatism in modern law in the United States which is coming to be the dominant conceptual force, and is that force which *actually* results in the making of new law and the assertion of legal decisions in critical cases. *But in some manner pragmatism takes on the guise of a protective positivistic mode. It does so in much the same way that legalisms and legal fictions resemble actual law, partly in order to preserve some semblance of stability in the system, and partly to exert its influence from within, in an undermining manner as well befits the modus operandi of those who have been spokespersons for radical legal renovations and revolutionary social change.*

But while pragmatism in American law at this second half of the twentieth century has been so masked it has not escaped detection. I read Atiyah's paper, 'From Principles to Pragmatism: Changes in the Function of the Judicial Process and the Law', (Atiyah, 1978:1249-1272) several years ago and found his argument compelling. He makes the point that the shift of power from the positivist factions to the pragmatist factions in both English and American Common Law has taken place gradually. But the consequence of this 'significant change' is that a functional change has taken place with respect to the way law sees itself. Law becomes reflexive in a way that is sharply represented by major alterations in jurisprudential explanation. The two main functions, traditionally, have been 1) to settle disputes and 2) to provide advisement and hortatory judgment to society, via the courts. The second function has become in the latter half of this century more dominant than the first. Therefore the tension between these two functions of law eases, and no longer is a tension.

The dominant function, the hortatory function, presents to modern inquiries a total turnabout from the relation between law and society which Holmes had tried to express, by his use of the 'magic mirror.' Holmes used this metaphor as a means of showing law to represent that which is ideally cherished by its referent society, *that society which presumably law mirrors.* But with the ascendant dominance of the hortatory function it is now the law to which the public looks for *its* basic values, even its so-called code of moral value. The modern law, especially since Fuller, is a co-optation of what once was a theological moral institution and, paradoxically, the morality of a pragmatic law is, if not relativistic, protean. Its Pragmatism operates upon first principles and enables a system, any system, to be self-corrective.

Atiyah sees this conflict of legal function as critical. He identifies it as a conflict between two universes of legal discourse, (Atiyah, 1978:1250). He calls these opposing forces Principles and Pragmatism.

This conflict emerged at the beginning of the twentieth century, when the established force was the Principled camp, and the challenger was Pragmatism. This challenger, in Holmes's Realism, was not *explicitly* identified with Pragmatism. What further complicates this struggle of ideas is that some critics of Holmes have tied him to Positivism and 'Principled Law,' and *not* to that emergent movement, Pragmatism. Further confusing these issues is the fact that Peirce has also been connected with positivistic thought, and ironically is then placed in opposition to that concept of pragmatism which is actually diametrically opposed to any closed-world system of positivism. The words stay the same. But their significance changes. The meaning of ideas evolve while the verbal shape, the appearance, remains more or less cast, if not in stone, in more malleable plastic.

This hundred-years shift began to occur at the end of the nineteenth century, on the heels of Darwinism, in the wake of pragmatism, in the 'path of the Law' which has come to be known in many of its aspects as Legal Realism. Prior to this, Atiyah points out, 'the courts were inclined to resolve ... conflict by adhering to principles. They were less concerned with doing justice in the particular case and more concerned with the impact of their decision in the future. In modern times, by contrast ... the courts have become highly pragmatic and a great deal less principled.' This reconfiguration of the law as social representation is not only a remaking of the courts, but has reached every aspect of law, and 'at virtually every point it has been assisted by legislation,' (Atiyah, above: 1251).

Perhaps recent celebrity law cases, e.g., O.J.'s day in court, points up the turning around of the 'magic mirror' so that it is the law in all its complexity which focuses in on the general society and reformulates it, rather than as it was in Holmes's metaphor, with the law representing the felt ideals and values of *its* referent society. The *main* law at play in this turnabout is Bergson's 'law of two-fold frenzy': we seem to go as far as possible in one direction and then reverse the process.

Certainly the infusing of the law with moral force, against the intention of Holmes and the Realists who follow him in this agnostic humanistic (but not positivistic) direction, has been a significant attempt to check what Atiyah and others see as Pragmatism in full force. Yet whether morality is an imposition upon the law or is an innate and therefore prioristic quality of law, it tends to cancel out whatever freedom is possible: It replaces indeterminism with moral deterministic reference.

On this point the Crits, as a general movement (now at this writing fairly dormant), have argued both sides of the coin: one side is utopic, emphasizing enduring principles of morals, justice, legitimacy as prior predilections for a cohesive community life. But on the other side they argue also for indeterminacy, *ad hocness*, and open dialogue — for freedom — as condition for law-and-society interaction.

II
Refraction or Reflection?

Notwithstanding the fact that Kermit Hall's reference for the Holmesian use of the metaphor is incorrect (1885, not 1889 as Hall has it), he does intriguingly show that the evolving pluralistic culture which has increasingly characterized American society since the emergence of Realism in the 1920's has been reflected in an evolving legal culture as well. This modern legal culture, in Hall's sense, is a schismatic culture: a culture in conflict, (Hall, 1989:259 ff).

Conflict, in Peirce's semiotic lexicon, is represented by the indexical sign-function: the Index represents interaction, opposition, dialogic exchange of meaning, and a dramatistic tension between members of this relational structure, (see Chapter Twelve in this volume). Further, the Indexical sign-function stands for the world of experience, of human affairs. This includes disputes which characterize human affairs. The Index represents the 'brute force' of wills and motives at odds with one another. It is quintessentially the structure of contractual legal agreement. Contract and consensus — and the Lockean notion of Consent — are signified by this transactional construction, this Peircean Index sign-structure, (Kevelson, 1994:163-180).

Thus, ironically, the more the law evolves to represent conflict in society, and to become conflictual and reflexively 'in quest of itself,' in Fuller's terms, (Fuller, 1940), the less meaningful does the concept of legal contract become, and the less representative of a consensual-based society is its image.

There are many threads to follow as one attempts to track the changing notion of a magic mirror, as Holmes first used the phrase in the 1880's. It becomes an instrument for linking law with society in a way not apparent in Holmes, to be perceived as crafter and adapter of a pragmatic multifaceted stereographic, or hypergraphic lens, (Kevelson, 1987). For the present I want to explore the link between Holmes's reinterpretation of a kaleidoscopic instrument into a magic mirror, and also an equally radical reinterpretation of the Peircean pragmatic method into Legal Realism.

We begin by recalling Holmes's words: 'This abstraction called the Law is a magic mirror (wherein) we see reflected, not only our own lives, but the lives of all men that have been.' (From 'The Law' presented at a meeting of the Suffolk Bar Association, Feb. 5, 1885, reprinted in *Speeches,* Little, Brown and Co., 1913, and republished again in *Collected Legal Papers*, Harcourt, Brace and Howe, 1920:25-28, at p. 26).

Hall, in citing this Holmesian metaphor, interprets Holmes's idea of the law: a 'cultural artifact, a moral deposit of society', (above, at p. 4).

It is my contention that the interests of law as a social instrument — in the sense that one holds one's referent principles, theories and idea-systems as a partner with oneself (in Hacking's sense 1990) — are better served by dropping the mask and coming out into the open as a new-age version of Legal Realism than as a voice from the shadow of positivism. Also, it is my contention that the interests of a free society — this experiment in pluralism, democracy and indeterminate ethical codes — are better served by an upfront Realism than a more *politically correct* Positivism.

In the following I want to explore some selected aspects of this preference. I will try to follow some probable — or possible — places Realism might lead to.

First, we should underscore a caption for Pragmatism as derived from Peirce and used here: anyone's version, I think, would agree on *How does it do*? and *So What*?, (see Chapter Two of this volume).

Method and Influence: — these are criteria for the meaning of any idea, any complex sign-as-idea, such as the idea of Pragmatism and the Pragmatic

Method, in Peirce terms. In order for an idea to be meaningful, he says, it has to operate and work in a certain way. It has to be effectual, so that its force — its intellectual force — makes a difference. In ordinary language, if an idea *means* anything, it has to *matter*. This point has been made earlier.

Pragmatism is a process of mattering. Its influence on Realism is profound. Just as Peirce insists that we need to understand pragmatism as a method of interpretation and of evolving ideas, the realization is that method, i.e., the method of interpreting law, must be an *integral* part of any legal theory of interpretation. Holmes may have been provoked by Peirce's pragmatism, but it is Geny's method of legal interpretation that he gives the nod to, (Kevelson, 1988 at 214-217). Rules for interpretation are *part of* interpretive method.

Holmes's famous essay on 'Natural Law' is written shortly after he reads Geny's *Science et technique en droit positif privé*, of 1915. Here he emphasizes the rejection of a priori beliefs in rightness by proponents of natural law who confuse the familiar and their method of interpreting assumptions with *innate* rules for recognizing what they call Truth. Actually, Holmes says, we develop ways of understanding what it is we want, as *interpretations of imagined force of facts over our actions.* This correlation between what we want to do and what is the fact at hand is integral with a pragmatic method of interpretation, with pragmatism here written small. The revolutionary achievement of Realism was to lift the power of jurisprudence, of a theory of law, to that which has been observed to be the *practice* of jurists, in *fact.*

Holmes says in this essay on Natural Law that ... 'for legal purposes a right is only the hypostasis of a prophecy — the imagination of a substance supporting the fact that the public force will be brought to bear upon those who do things said to contravene it. No doubt behind these legal rights is the fighting will of the subject to maintain them, and the spread of his emotions to the general rules by which they are maintained,' (*Harvard Law Review* II 1918, reprinted in *Collected Legal Papers* 1930:310-16).

Holmes's three-faced kaleidoscopic/magic mirror, as it projects and as the law interprets its triadic signification, shows the public sense of rights as something which is equivalent to the very value of its existence, namely that which is the 'substance' or matter of life at stake. And if the law is Realistic and indeed Pragmatic it will interpret those perceived instinctual wishes for the possible into rules for interpreting matters of law, (above, at p. 336).

Peirce, similarly, had emphasized that it is this pragmatic method which *produces* a theory, i.e. a theory of signs or semiotics. Holmes also argued against prioristic convictions of natural law advocates that it is the deep wishes/wants of a people which the law interprets and writes into legislation, into legal decisions, into legal theory. *Practice precedes theory*. This point needs to be underscored!

The complex of instincts which Holmes's Realism interprets includes not only the intersubjective dialogic relationship which constitutes actual community — the basis for fact, which Law calls Contract — but also reinterprets into legal mode the near-instinctual sense Common Law societies have emphasized, namely the sense of inalienable possession. Law — Common Law — distinguishes possession from property, and establishes property as one of the footings upon which Common Law rests.

And in 1915, the year after Peirce's death, Holmes ventures to share his own creed which, he correctly surmises, is unpopular even at that time early in the century. He says, 'I believe that the wholesale regeneration which so many now seem to expect if it can be helped by conscious, coordinated human effort, cannot be affected appreciably by tinkering with the institution of property ...' (from 'Ideals and Doubts,' *Illinois Law Review* X 1915, reissued in *Collected Legal Papers*, pp. 303-307, at page 306).

Elsewhere Holmes notes that the law interprets the human instinctive will to vengeance and takes upon itself this interpreted instinct, which is not to rehabilitate the one who harms but to satisfy the wish for revenge of the one who has been harmed (*The Common Law*). A law which represses its instinctual origins, Holmes suggests, is no longer a realistic law, but one which is mapped upon a selected moral code, the code of the powerful as it ever may happen to be.

As suggested above, it may be that the absence of overt reference to Peirce by Holmes and to Peirce's pragmatic method is the result of an antagonism between these two which at bottom may well have been instinct-driven. So I suggest in earlier work, (Kevelson, 1990). Rumble noted some 30 years ago (in 'Realism is Pragmatism in Law', 1967:6) that the pragmatism he refers to is marked with Dewey's influence, and a bit of James. But Rumble too, has little or nothing to say about Peirce. People continued to say little or nothing until, in recent years, this Pragmatism/Law connection was revived. Unfortunately it is given the wrong spin by Habermas in *Crisis in Legitimacy* and those who followed him until very recently, (Kevelson, 1987).

Typically it is Dewey rather than Peirce who is cited as having had the greatest influence on Realism. Dewey was very much involved with investigating law as 'Instrument,' but he did not have a profound grasp of the idea of method *producing* rather than being produced by a theory until the *Logic* and his subsequent works after the 1930's.

For example, Gary Jacobsohn acknowledges Peirce as the founder of pragmatism, but he hastens to say that it is Dewey's pragmatism that made the most difference in the development of American Realism, (Jacobsohn, 1971: 40-41, at n. 6). Holmes was especially ungenerous toward Peirce; few who followed him, with the important exception of Morris Cohen, were ready to give Peirce his due. I write of Cohen's influence elsewhere and only mention him in passing for now, (Kevelson, 1990).

I believe that Cohen's own idealistic predilections acted as a foregrounding of Realism's swerving onto more moralistic moorings, more safe and stable positions from which to deal with problems of legal justice. As we will find, this quest for a realistic justice led, in a circuitous path, to the notion of human rights mapped onto the concept of civil rights and explored meticulously by legal scholars from all corners of the international forum on law and justice, especially over the past two decades. But we need to go back even further, to the closing years of a self-conscious Realism in American legal history — the end of the 1920's — during which time Morris Cohen articulates the new attitude with respect to morality: It springs from within the law and is not imposed upon the law from without. Morality thus becomes a force, likened in its effect upon a legal system, to an instinct upon the neurophysiological human being. It is challenging to try to understand Cohen's moral perspective as a most acute grasp of Peirce's turn to Idealism in the last two decades of his life. Cohen admired Peirce and, largely, understood him. I examine this possibility further in Kevelson 1998: it is touched upon in the closing chapter of this book.

For now, it is of value to listen closely to Cohen: Cohen says, 'An uncritical reliance on the abstract universality of legal justice is the growing ethical defect of the so-called critical philosophy. It legalizes ethics without moralizing the law', (Cohen, 1927: 259). In this paper, 'Positivism and the Limits of Idealism in the Law,' Cohen is overtly rejecting the Kantian imperative. But at the same time he virtually pushes aside Peirce's great concept of a Normative Ethics, separated from a Normative Esthetics or science of values that was built upon a new, expanded logic of Semiotics.

Peirce's Normative Ethics is distinct and separate from Morality. It concerns the *transformation* of esthetics/value norms in any given society into social institutions, such as law and economics and politics. Law, for example, in a Peircean dynamical process, interprets normative values into its practice, but it does not regard the value-into-ethics transformation as innate, prioristic or essential. Neither is it positivistic in the sense that rules for ethical norms — or value norms — are ever constant and fixed, but are revised or corrected and are discarded when they are formal only, not alive with active, existent human energies.

Even in Cohen, it is a felt wish for certainty — a quest for certainty — which tends to establish the either/or of positivism vs. idealism (natural law, in brief) and thus quite misses the third alternative of a pragmatic law.

III
Who Knew a 'New' Peirce?

To Morris Cohen, it is the very limits of human abilities which brings us to the edges of both law and of idealism and back into religious faith. Of limits, Holmes has written in 'Natural Law' that 'the truth may be defined as the system of my (intellectual) limitation' which is made 'objective' by realizing that other people in one's society are experiencing the same kinds of limitations (above at 311).

But Peirce, with his emphasis on the nonfinite, limitless possibility of the generation of ideas, *stretches the boundaries of the defined, opens up freedom continuously*. It is by means of the pragmatic method that this infinite freedom may become realized. Morris Cohen vacillates: on the one hand there is the path of faith; on the other is the 'path of law,' which is a pragmatic way, a way which *becomes* as one uses it. Cohen says that the very limits of idealism which seem to rest on 'self-evident premises' are apparent. The logic upon which 'self-evident and jural propositions' observe moral ground falls away once one recognizes how modern non-Euclidean geometries become the basis for a new logic, a logic which stretches surfaces, which extends possibilities, which makes space and place and existence plasmic, (Cohen, above, at 243).

As Frank and others make clear, it is the same non-Euclidean geometry which underlies legal reasoning with respect to pragmatism as *imagistic* of the same reasoning which infinitely evolves the meaning and reach of ideas in all universes of discourse. *This is pure Peirce.*

Perhaps the anticipation of a limitless law — of a law without definition, a dynamical law Becoming — forecast the unprincipled society that mirrors such a legal system. Perhaps a very human recoil from anarchy, from chaos, from order into disorder — a reversal of that direction so cherished in western thought — moves such jurisprudes as Fuller to bring back the old religion into realistic law. Perhaps it is the discomfort — an all too human disquietude — which wants defense against the prospect of continuous change without benefit of *truth*, of *absolutes*, of *authority* that knows its place and keeps it, that catalyzes a turning point in Realism and brings into it a moral force.

Surely we see this occurring, as an agnostic Realism becomes transformed into law-as-moral-instinct in the work of Lon Fuller. Depending on how one looks at him, and upon who is doing the looking, *Fuller is and is not a Legal Realist*. In any case he is an enigma.

Fuller is a kind of fulcrum, refuting on the one hand and practicing on the other, a pragmatic Realism. He redefines, reinterprets, and rewrites the evolution of American law. We relearn Holmes through Fuller and translate positivism into present idiom: Morality is made as an elemental force in law.

Without attempting even a cursory review here, I recommend Maniscalco's article on what he calls the 'new positivism,' which incorporates morality into its domain, (1995:993 ff) Maniscalco traces the development of positivism from Austin and Kelsen to the present day. He sees Hart and Fuller as standing for a crossroads in modern positivistic law, with each indicating a different route. And most recently, it is the dialogue between Raz and Finnis that constitutes what may be called the present discourse on positivism in law. Maniscalco's leitmotif is the ancient contest between kings and priests. He shows this conflict between secular and sacred in modern garb, but still the same old story.

But the glory goes to Fuller who relocates the moral core at the center of the *idea* of the law. Thus he makes it not only possible, but he mandates in this way a search for rights as *given* by the basic premises of law.

What we find, however, at this end of the search for rights is that this search is dead-ended. The discourse has been rich and full and meticulous. But the ability of the law to set the moral mandate for a pluralistic global community of persisting nation-states has led, only very recently and only among some courageous outspoken scholars, to a realization *that rights* is an academic dead issue. Let's move on. The move as is usual is forward by stepping back to reassess what has been, or may have been overlooked.

Hence the reappearance and renewed interest in Realism as we come to the edge of an age, an age of texts on rights but little appreciable progress in the actual world of conflicting societies, (Kevelson, 1994).

This is a dark cloud for legal scholarship. But it is a bit of silver-backing on the magic mirror for us Peirce Pragmatists forever looking for ways into the big top. It is timely and topical to renew acquaintance with American thought. It is past time to discover Peirce, once again closed off from inquiry by massive shortfalls in endowment funds. But so the American Institute of Law became quiescent when the money ran out at the end of the 1920's, and with that severing of arteries which supply nourishment to research the grand idea of Legal Realism became still another *significant absence*.

In the next few closing pages of this chapter I want to resurrect and to even restate some of my own former views on connections between Pragmatism and Realism, and analogues between semiotic representation and social representation by means of social institutions.

Let us think of a social institutions such as law or economics or education or politics or the family as complex sign-systems, (Kevelson, 1988): as families of such complex sign-systems. A sign-system is a relationship of significances, whereas a collection or aggregate is a herd gathered in the same corral. In terms of people, a sign-system is a community of interrelations. An aggregate is a mob.

It is the mistaken widespread linking of pragmatism — the 'unprincipled' kind of law — with the unruly, the mob, the irrational — that has resulted in distancing it from mainstream law. But the mattering of fact is that pragmatism is, above all, a community of interdependencies, of spontaneous *ad hoc* contractual relations, (Kevelson, 1988).

The idea of political representation has a relatively short history, but the idea of representation in general is ancient. What is unique in Peirce's concept of representation is that ideas represent or interpret other signs as well as material objects. Each interpretation or evolved representation increases the meaning and effective force of that idea. The name may stay the same, but each time its definition is revised, stretched, and/or reformed significance grows, (Kevelson, 1987).

A representation is another name for sign or sign-function. Every representation, whether expressed as a public institution or as an idea which is sufficiently conventionalized to be used in meaning-transactions, i.e, in the marketplace of ideas, is an instrument with which the user interacts as one interacts with a new tool, a new invention. The tool or invention is not regarded, as in traditional logic, as a property of the user, an extension or attribute of the individual person. Rather the whole complicated notion of Having has become transformed, such that the instrument or property which has an instrumental function becomes a partner or relation *with* the user. There is an agentive force in connection with an instrumental force which, together, produce some objective as intended, or as accidently brought about, (Kevelson, 1988).

This very notion radically alters the medieval sense of master/slave that lies at the early level of Common Law. It changes as well the concept of property, from an extension of the possessor to a relation with the user or holder. There is this relational bond which becomes especially marked in the concept of the legal contract, in angloamerican common law, (Kevelson, 1988, 1995).

Holmes is especially interested in what he calls the 'peculiar law of master and servant' prior to Edward II. Early laws of agency made use of fictions, he points out. We may substitute for 'fictions' the general notion of representation in its most comprehensive sense (see Holmes on 'Agency I', *Collected Legal Papers*, and in 'Agency II', where he discusses the intertwining of Agency and Contract in a manner that still shows this cross-dependency relationship between ideas.) Elsewhere I discuss Agency and Contract in closer detail, but merely remark here on this longstanding crossreferentiality in passing, (Kevelson, 1990).

IV
The Basic Unit as Relation

In Peirce's thought society does not begin with an autonomous Individual, any more than the universe begins with an atom — even one which becomes, through big bangs, *many*. There is not a Superphoton analogy. But, rather, at the basis of all community, whether of ideas or substances or people, there is a relationship. This nexus is what Holmes borrowed, without thanks, from Peirce.

Thus the legal contract is for Peirce the prototype of his pragmatism. Reciprocally, the pragmatic basic relationship is the model for evolving notions of contract in law. Yet in an almost inexplicable way it is Holmes who undermines the legal contract *as it was*. In its place — in the place of contractual closure based on completion of performance — Holmes introduces the irregular dilemma: the possibility of an impossible contract and the alternative to do or not do this or that (see Atiyah 'The Legacy of Holmes,' *B.U.C. Review Three Lectures*, 1983: 341; in Harvard University Press 1983:56-57). This dilemmatic reasoning of the 'impossible contract' is, again, a derivative of Peirce and Pragmatism in its maturest stage of his life.

But Holmes does not or will not quite sustain the dilemmatic conclusion. He attempts to reduce alternatives to a single conclusion, which is the impossibility of performance and hence the invalidating of the contract. This is Holmes's fatal fallacy, one might say. He does not carry quite far enough the requirements of a valid dilemma as an open-ended Legal Realism wants, (Kevelson, 1998).

We come back to Holmes's metaphor of the magic mirror to find that he also fails to fully appreciate what this mirror is capable of doing, i.e., of serving as a Lewis Carroll's kind of looking-glass, a window onto the paradoxical, as well as a kaleidoscopic tool. It is the logic of paradox which, Peirce knew, characterizes the open-ended dynamical structure of the pragmatic method. Holmes sees his mirror as a special looking glass, but not as a vehicle for cubistic special analyses of legal concepts, nor as entry to another dimension of reason in law.

Yet if Holmes does not leave in place real alternatives as *options* in the notion of contract-as-promise, he does nevertheless interpret the contract as a noncausal, nonconditional proposition. He touches upon a paradoxical logic, but leaves it. This retreat by Holmes has been widely recognized but rarely appreciated as an admirable failure.

I want to cite briefly from Atiyah (above, 1983) who says, 'English lawyers have never accepted Holmes's theory that there is no such thing as a duty to perform a contract ... Holmes's theory of contract is tolerably well known among contract scholars in England, and has been regarded by virtually all as a brilliant but wholly unsound paradox', (Atiyah above).

Holmes does allow for an 'impossible contract,' since a nonperformance can be remedied, (Kevelson, 1995). Thus the emphasis is not on a moral duty to perform a contract, as *promised*, but rather on the alternative options or consequences available, by law, if promise is not kept. There is not concern in Holmes about a moral aspect of a promise to perform, as Pollack, Hart, and especially Fuller argue in criticism of Holmes, but rather of alternative legal options available.

By Contract, for example, the law *means*, according to Fuller, 'Law exists in the outside world, not merely in the courts, and one of the functions of the law is to shape the moral consensus which actually controls man's conduct', (cited in Atiyah, above, at 1983:57).

I don't want to take up in detail a controversy which still surrounds Holmes's view of contract. It is the epitome of his Realism, perhaps for reasons he himself does not acknowledge. Yet this Realism is equated by Atiyah and others with a Positivism that has provoked a strange recoiling of Realists on themselves. As Atiyah notes, 'given Fuller's antipathy to Holmes's positivism, it may seem curious' that Fuller's work on contract is 'in support of Holmes's view', (Atiyah, at p. 58 above). The following chapter looks at the 'impossible contract.'

Atiyah's not unusual view is that Holmes 'adapted' the then emergent 'new orthodoxy' on contract: it was a new look and new interpretation of 'quasi-contracts', (Atiyah above). But Atiyah concedes that Holmes is remarkable for what he did not believe, that is, for his rejection of 1) the idea of rights, 2) the power of reason to control human action, 3) the unsureness of even one's own 'first principles,' and of 4) the eternal force of any ideals whosoever.

Holmes believed, says Atiyah, in 'reason and in theorizing' as a way of life. He believed in the 'intellectual power of great men,' and he believed in the 'principles of political economy' of Adam Smith, for one. He especially believed in the certainty of the brute force of the majority — which one doubts only if one is a fool.

Holmes himself tells us in 'Law as Civilization' what he thinks of contract: 'Nowhere is the confusion between legal and moral ideas more manifest than in the law of contract ... here again the so-called primary rights and duties are invested with a mystic significance beyond what can be assigned and explained (from the Lerner edition, 1943:76).

Neither in Peircean semiotics nor in Holmes's jurisprudence does the idea of contract rest upon arbitrary conjunctions. But both state, each in its own peculiar idiom, that it is upon some significant — normatively significant —

representation of binding forces that contract must observe if we are to have a 'true theory of contract.'

At bottom Holmes said, '... no one will understand the true theory of contract or be able even to discuss some fundamental questions intelligently until he has understood that all contracts are formal, that the making of a contract depends not on the agreement of two sets of external signs — not on the parties' having *meant* the same things but on their having *said* the same thing.' Every sign depends on, rests upon, is integral with its context.

Peirce could not have said it better.

Here then in significant part is the frame-in-common of Peirce's and Holmes's Pragmatism and Realism, respectively.

The magic mirror is not ordinary plate glass to see through. But we must imagine the glaze as layered, as multidimensional, such that one may conceivably pass through layer upon layer of implicatures. This is, indeed, Peirce's description of the Existential Graphs, of which each 'layer' is a developed complexity and implication of the dialogue/argument in focus, (Kevelson, 1987).

As the following chapter discusses, the Contract in Law represents the 'normative' frame of dialogically evolved agreement.

Chapter 8

What Can a Semiotics of Law Make of an 'Impossible Contract'?

What Can a Semiotics of Law Make of an 'Impossible Contract'?

I
Taking 'Impossible' to Full Term

It only appears to be cyclical. But the reappearance of utopianism, asceticism and disdain for the merely human is always new. The apparent 'eternal return' of puritanism is still a myth, and is still totalitarian to the marrow of its bare bones. Morality in law masquerades as reasoned ethics and conceals its grounding in the absolute. But unlike the relativistic, absurd position in vogue today which holds a Pirandellan absurdity of 'it is if you think it is,' a semiotics absurdity — a Peircean logic in other words — attempts to explain inconsistencies and oxymorons. Semiotic logic is, after all, a logic of paradox, (Kevelson, 1990). The dilemma, the paradox, the intended 'repugnancy' or contradiction are all features of Peirce's Pragmatism. The rejection of canonical absolutes together with a prioristic morality also is part of Peirce's method.

Morality and law are, properly speaking, distinctly different universes of discourse, as Holmes maintains. But when the language of the law becomes garbled and intolerably self-contradictory as happens during periods of crises and transition in a dynamical society, as at present in American law, the 'new puritans' attempt to plug the holes with moral stricture, to reenforce the split seams of a seamy law with permabond adhesive stripped from canonical walls. Every emergence of 'The Puritan' is prophetic of repression to follow. Revolutions are of several kinds, as I discuss in Chapter Thirteen of this volume.

It is complex ideas of The Law which effects the idea of a legal contract and thus strengthens agreements made between people to reciprocally perform for one another's benefits, now and in the future, in a future taken on a kind of faith, an interhuman trust. And it is The Law which dissolves this provisional, ad hoc relation between actors/parties in a contract when the performances are done and the mutual trusts are honored. Some jurists and philosophers of law, some latter-day Puritans, claim that trusts and contracts in general are honored and commanded to be so honored by law because law is inherently moral, is a reflection and representation of the moral nature of human beings, of human nature prioristically unified in a moral ground. So says Fuller, for one, (1964). I will return to Fuller on Contract Law in the closing section of this chapter. My primary focus here is on the concept of an 'impossible contract' in law and on how impossibility may be construed from a perspective of legal semiotics.

Is such an impossible contract deemed to be unperformable voidable because invalid, i.e., not reasonably sound? Or, is an impossible contract, from the point of view of a logic of paradox, of Peircean possibility, *not* the negative of a possible contract but rather is a designation of the conceivable but not performable? According to a Peircean semiotic assumption, which is mathematically/iconically based, the impossible is not the negative of the possible-as-doable, but is the imaginable yet *not doable*. To digress briefly: Peirce questions the idea of 'possible error' posited by Josiah Royce's idealism and eventually concurs that error is posible if the *idea* of the correct is its referent, or touchstone. I speak more of this in Kevelson, 1998.

By contrast, and with respect to Legal Contract the notion of the impossible as the negation of the possible refers to a word-based mode of reason, a semantic and deductive kind of reason. Peirce claims that the semiotics he presents which derives from his method of pragmatism represents an expanded reasoning, primarily *imagistic* rather than verbal.

I'm with Peirce. One does not have to have professional training in mathematics to think in this semiotic/imagistic manner, *which is inclusive of semantics* — words — but which begins with spatial orientation rather than with conceptual counters. In a similar fashion one need not be a moral person, where morality is integral with theological precepts, in order to be a person who conducts one's life, in concert with others, according to *ethical norms*. Peirce subdivides the pivotal function of his overall semiotic theory — the Normative Sciences — by showing that it is Law and the Practical Sciences which feed from the actual phenomenal interaction of human affairs into that abstract concept called Ethics, which links the Logic on the one hand and the Esthetics of Value-Inquiry division on the other hand, (Kevelson, 1990, 1993).

Values do not really trickle-down in Peirce's schema. They percolate up from the actual ground of human relationships, those relationships characterized by opposition, antagonisms, disputes, high and low drama which Law as a system of signs mediates, evaluates, and assesses, *after the fact*, for its referent value principles. In commonlaw societies, it is customary law which similarly acts as ground for written law. In Peirce's semiotics it is the representation of human interactions which acts as ground for law, legal principles, and subsequently for social values. Morality enters the picture when this machinery, or organization that links people to institutions to first principles, and which rests on an appropriate process of reasoning, breaks down. *Morality in law may be seen as invasion of one sign-system by another.* The Proponents of The Moral (as contrasted with the Inquirers into the Ethical) are always Zealots in humble garb, Elitists who issue orders with rising intonation, and Cowards who compulsively over-regulate the world. Or would if they could.

My early approach to the phenonemon of the impossible contract several years ago (Kevelson, 1992), concluded that impossibility in performance was really a sign of deterioration in the wealth of a society, since it represented a loss of civility, of mutuality. Civility, as we know, is an intangible but significant kind of property that members of a society jointly share, like parks and other common grounds and public resources. Its decrease is a social impoverishment. The puritan loves the poor, sees in the poor an ally and an instrument, as against the coarse, tough, narrow-mindedness of the ordinary, enduring, 'boring', working middle-class, i.e., that 'Common Person' who *endures* and from time to time upstages artists, heroes, authorial voices and principals in general. The 'impossible contract' is 'classy' in a way that the Common Person is not or has not been, historically speaking. How may we, from a legal semiotics' viewpoint, make some sense or much meaning out of this contradiction in terms: a contract which Is and Is Not?

The following will be an exploration, off the beaten track, down uncommon paths:

II
On Mapping Morals

Proportional with the decline of civility in many western societies, especially in the second half of this century, is an increase of professed — and professional — concern with morality, especially as this decline is seen to impoverish relationships between social institutions, both public and private, and in actual human affairs between people.

Coeval with an emergent but possibly evanescent interest in the Peircean Normative Sciences, centered on Ethical inquiry as a fulcrum for the mediation between Logic and Esthetics (Peirce's Science of Value), is a global perceivable attempt to equate a philosophical notion of Ethics with moral precepts that are abstracted and reinterpreted from selected religious/theological ground.

This is a confounding turn of events: all canonically-derived moral prescriptions presume absolutes and causal referents. Not all philosophical systems share this grounding in absolutes but some tend to oppose absoluteness with shifting, evolving, and sometimes relativistic referents. *The main contrast is that a moral precept is 'given,' whereas a philosophical norm is 'made.'* The 'made' referent, the invented norm, is usually associated with 'positivism,' where the term Positive is a form of 'posit': to set forth as a working assumption. Positivism in this sense is not confused with the colloquialistic synonym for affirmed 'certainty,' (see Nonet on this important distinction, *Yale Law Journal*, 1990).

Peirce is a positivist only in the non-colloquial sense, in the same sense that he suggests that the purpose of hypothetical reasoning, or abduction, is to produce a working premise, a working position, i.e., that which may be posited even though it is not truth, nor claimed to be true, but is instead a signal for experimentation with the possible. *Pragmatism is the name of his game, this game of inventing possible premises.*

The connection which has developed between Ethics and Morals is suspect. From a semiotics perspective, however, their recent (and historical) linkage invites inquiry. The connection is far from simple but is complex as a merger of two discourse systems in an intricate way. Not one, but two sets of relates are involved here, and these correspond with two major sets of underlying assumptions: In the first set of assumptions, which I will call here 'significant absences,' what is tacit but not present is 1) the notion of civility as a cohering force in dynamical human interactions and 2) those encoded norms of 'good' behavior imposed upon all kinds of organizations: medical, legal, academic, political all of which interact as 'corporate' systems — *as bodies* — with individual human beings.

The apparent unification between Ethics and Morals in recent years is represented as hinging on a negative or significant absence, namely an absence of reciprocity between individuals — parties to a contract in law — and institutions as legal persons. Rhetorical strategy has not only redefined the meaning of 'person' but has also brought about an equivalence between the terms 'moral' and 'ethical.' The literature on the controversial concept of 'Person' is enormous. Arguments and cross-definitions of 'Person' were especially lively in both law and philosophy around the turn of the 19th into 20th century. I will return to this issue, an issue fought largely by rhetorical strategies. By Rhetoric also, 'Right Reason' and 'Good Faith' have become synonyms, interchangeable syntagms or metonyms.

The second pair of relates shows another type of equivalence taking shape: on the one hand, with respect to Peircean semiotics and his normative sciences (which link sensible experience to value principles via modes of action or behavior, i.e., phenomenological/ perception to metaphysical perception mediated by conventionalized modes of conduct), we see that it is the rhetorical action of Peirce's expanded semiotical logic which conjoins traditional reason, or Critic, with Ethics. Ethics is a conduit or medium; the strategies of the expanded logic — the pragmatic tactics of the Methodology — become that connective, cohesive force which marries Logic, Ethics, and Esthetics into the semiotical pivot.

But on the other hand, with respect to an evolving conjunction between Ethics and Morals which has been firming up as it bears on mandates for social human relations, we see again that it is rhetorical strategy which brings about redefinition of the *idea* of Ethics, such that Ethics can become a synonym or an equivalent means/meaning with Morality. *Ethics can thereby be held as Morality by another name.* Yet, as pointed out above, we say that Ethics derives from a very different ground than does Morality; it derives from positive Reason, whereas Morality is sustained through religious Faith. The former frame is as much bounded and fixed in 'traditional positivism' as the latter is inseparable from canonical theological 'law.' Both are, in this respect, from this viewpoint, complete systems: — as relativity and quantum mechanics are complete systems. Yet each of these systems may become connected with another such system. This is, above all, the Quest of Quests, or purpose for which the method of pragmatism was invented by Peirce to carry out his hypothesis that complete systems can, paradoxically, even oxymoronically, become more comprehensive in relation with one another, (Kevelson, 1987). This is the enigma of the idea of Individuals-in-relation. The Peircean assumption, that *the minimal unit of meaning is relational*, consists of individuals as complete 'relates.' (The minimal unit of grammatical meaning, as it follows, is not answer nor question alone but *question with answer* as complete and minimal unit of linguistic discourse, Kevelson, 1987).

In my prefacing of this discussion on 'impossible contract' in law with distinctions between morals and ethics, between atomistic individuals and individuals-in-relation, I am trying to set the stage for a brief discussion on the option of the 'impossible' as *not the negation of the possible* in Peirce, but as *different terms.* Just as the negation of 'up' is 'not up' and not 'down,' the logical negation of '*possible*' is '*not possible*,' but not *impossible*. In the following I will expand upon this.

What I am trying to get at is whether that which the law refers to as an 'impossible contract' is a sign of an impoverishment of civility — a breakdown of contractual, mutual respect — or whether the concept of an 'impossible contract' may go beyond an invalidated contract, a voidable unperformed agreement to reciprocation and interaction, and is instead, a way of reasoning which includes the nonactual, not-yet-materialized factual in the agreement, as a kind of Hamiltonian mathematical 'imaginary,' (Kevelson 1987).

In the concluding section of this chapter I will discuss some implications for the significance of 'imaginaries' as not negatives of terms such as 'possible' in possible or doable/performable contracts, but as conceivable nonexistents which a semiotic mode of reasoning provides for, and which is *not* provided for in the same manner by other kinds of reasoning. In point, I will discuss Peirce's observation on the basic distinctions between traditional philosophical reasoning and mathematical reasoning in general, where the former is based upon verbal referential ground and the latter rests on visualizable, imagistic ground.

For this major distinction, I believe, Peirce has urged semiotic inquirers to model their investigations upon the mathematical procedure rather than upon the philosophical reasoning process. It is for this reason, as well, that Peirce reinterprets the classical notion of an idea as a visualizable representation, and weds this classical view of 'idea' with a Gaussean concept of image-making, *Abbildung*, he calls it, with direct reference to Gauss, (CP 8.122). But to return to the problem of impossible contracts in law: impossible is not the same as not possible *but is another term*, another meaning represented, I want to emphasize.

We recall that in order for any term to be meaningful it is required that a mutuality, a sharing of same or similar understanding, functions as an encoded, channelled conveyor of acts intended or considered by each to the other (party to the contract). Any alteration of the meaning of a term must also be mutually assented to and part of a shared understanding. This is, minimally, the basis of all communication and is the foundation of the semiotic process as a whole.

Communicative or communal ruptures occur when a previously sustained meaning or a loss of meaning is not mutually known by both relates in any intercommunicative event. The so-called 'gaps' in the law presumes a tacit agreement to that portion of explicit information which is ellipsed or below the surface, or is in the jargon of the linguist, 'deep-structured' meaning, (Kevelson, 1977). This tacit knowledge presumes an audience/community which is largely heterogeneous and which shares a common value-base. In a pluralistic society there is no such common base. That rupture not assented to, but in fact widely denied by many, is equivalent to a depreciation of value, where value may easily translate into counters, currency, and the quantitative medium of money. Hence a rupture not agreed upon by all members or most members of a society is perceived as a reduction of worth, such that it is equated with negative civility in most cases and not with the appearance of a new term which is not a negative value but is a value which has thus far no name, and which fits into no known schema or code of symbolized values.

If we follow Peirce, this rupture may be seen not as the negative of a known-as-given, but as a place for what does not exist but which, conceivably, may be imaged *as* possible. From this perspective the nonperformance of a contract which is classified as voidable, invalid, and impossible, may be *half empty* as a negative possible contract, or *half full* as in the sense that impossible contract allows for the emergence of a something new, (ms 101 on 'imaginaries' and the continuum).

This then is a disjunction we face when we look at the idea of 'impossible contract' closely. Let us look further: If one party to a communicable event is ambiguous in the use of a term it can be said that the participants are unequally empowered, since one has more meaning than the other available for exchange. All jargon, cultic, and secret language represents such unequal power-relations in contractual communicative transactions *outside the domain of the law*. Laws exist to minimize ambiguity, or rather *to use ambiguity* in the interests of maximal flexibility under a stable-appearing law. But in a similar sense, if a term such as 'morality' is lifted out of its customary context — theology — and is yet colored with vestigial strands and stains of its ordinary ground, it produces situations such as civil acts being described in terms of *good* and *evil*, when the appropriate *description* — not implied *prescription* — would evaluate the *ethical* value of such acts.

But Ethics presupposes a constant idea of Good. In a Peircean Pragmatic Method there is no constant Good. There is only provisional, ad hoc representation, or fiction of Good-as-Referent (until unseated or dethroned). That there is a continuum needed and provided means that the place for The Good continues. But the occupant of the place of the Good-as- Sign changes. With all change, permutation and not mere substitution, occurs. This must have some reciprocal effect on the actual ground or place for Goodness. That the Good is sustained as a habit of thought long after it actually exists speaks only of the emotional need of many people for something to hold onto. Even a riverbed gone dry after decades of drought is still referred to by nearby residents of that area as a River, although no water flows between its banks and trees grow up from the silt. The idea of an enduring Self is such a fiction as well. Thus the presumption of a Good by ethicists is a fictive enterprise, where fiction here is not a negative reality but is a reality of another kind. I will return to the affirmation of illusion in the following.

Another way of explaining this phenomenon is this: when the new meaning of a term extends into a reciprocal communicative play even though both parties are not aware of its being there it can be said to carry a kind of causal resemblance to an old habit of thought, a surface resemblance, such that 'moral good' seems to look like 'ethical good.' Both are alike in their function of representing a constancy, an absoluteness, a referent model. But when the connotations of the one are presumed to be also the connotations of the other, and the underlying assumptions of both are assumed to be alike, a rhetorical transformation takes place: an interpretant word-wizardry or meaning-magic. If members of a society or of a contractual agreement share this trick-playing, when both know beforehand that the contract can not be performed as stated, there is a sleight-of-sign in operation, and a confidence game as well, with both players allied against the law and against society in general. The anticipation of impossibility by parties to a contract challenges the mettle of the law. But this is not quite the conceivable nonexistent impossibility which Peirce makes room for.

Here is an invitation to game-theorists and others who try to account for shifting alliances in encounters and exchanges of value. At this time I want to limit my digressions to the problem of double-meaning, which bears on the duplicity of the term, 'impossible,' in legal contracts.

Double meanings are modes of rhetoric used to create an imbalance in equivalence, of previously presumed equally-weighted terms. The theme of 'the other,' of alteration, is ancient and perennial. Here the trick is to create an imbalance of illusion for the purpose of foregrounding human freedom: the ability to smash icons and shatter old meaning-molds that have become formalized and empty. Thus the human imagination becomes foregrounded as that instrumentation capable of stretching the limits of norms, boundaries of defined terms, all stabilities that come to represent determination and unfreedom (i.e., negative freedom). Freedom includes the freedom to refute facts where facts are established, reciprocal judgments. Freedom attests to the imagination capable of conceiving that which does not actually exist: to see the impossible *as* possible. Of course Peirce is Quixotic.

Thus, to make room for the 'imaginary' requires a method of thinking which permits the introduction of novelty to become related with that which is 'known' and normatized. From this Peircean point of view the 'impossible' is in tandem with the 'possible,' not as obverse or reverse of the same counter and coin, but as a genuine representation of *another* coin or frame of value and frame meaning. This is an indispensable tactic for a dynamical society, for an open-system law. It is stability which must wear the epithet of 'fiction,' and do so by masks, by smoke and mirrors. This is a risky game! It is a game for legal artists, for jugglers, for all the derelicts which former ages relegated to side shows! Pragmatism is a game for those who play with jokers, with wild cards.

It is the objective of semiotic 'quests of quests' to link two universes of parallel and equal value — not of subordinate and superordinate relations — into new, more comprehensive meaning. Although the con-fusing of a normative Ethics with a theologically-grounded moral canon has been such an attempt to cross-represent universes, the cross-referential system which emerges is one of a reductive nature rather than of an opening, growing nature. It is, analogously, the Husserlian reductive 'I' as compared and contrasted with the dynamical, interactional Peircean 'We.'

Thus an inquiry into this idea of 'impossible contract' with its several incompatible interpretations provides an opportunity to understand why Peirce opts for the iconically-based mathematical model, in opposition to the verbally-based method of traditional philosophy, since the former gives us a place for genuine novelty to emerge, by chance, by happenstance, and free.

In 1994, as mentioned earlier, I briefly explored the phenomenon of 'impossible contract' in connection with the provisionality and ad-hocness of consensual meaning. But apart from the occurrence of the 'impossible' in the law, Peirce linked it in general to that place — that rhematic space — for the 'imaginary.'

A dynamical society, as a dynamical system of law, needs to accept *as honorific* the notion of unstable, chaotic, anarchic and 'impossible.' A static mode of reasoning which equates the idea of possible with the notion of predictable and determined is an inadequate model or ideal for a people creating mutuality, and through mutuality wealth and meaning: i.e., power.

The greater the capacity to live with a significant absence of certainty, the greater is the possibility for creativity and *becoming*. I am not advocating flagrant invalidating of contracts made in trust and in fellowship. But in every possible contract there may be a place for new information to enter in and to change the nature of the agreement.

The following section will touch upon some aspects of the 'No-thing/No-way' character of an impossible contract, as considered from a semiotic positioning:

III
Aspects Of No-Thing/No-Way

This section is not a take-off on the Zen not this/not that ineffable 'something.' It is, rather, connected to the notion that the Koans teach, namely that existence overflows its conceptual boundaries and the world exceeds our definitions of it. Peirce's pragmatism presumes this wisdom, as adapted to ways of the West by a kind of intellectual alchemy: to be sharply distinguished from a Sartrean, neo-aristotelian 'being/nothingness' thesis. Peirce, with characteristic analytical bent, does not take *not this/not that* or *no-thing/no-way* as a givenness, a given possibility. Rather, he proceeds to examine the nature of the possible, and the nature of the impossible with which the possible is semantically related and psychologically associated. To be able to have some idea of 'impossible' means to have some representation of what that idea might mean, how it might be represented, how one may leave a place for that understanding as a room for novelty to fill at some future time. As I have discussed from other perspectives (Kevelson, 1987, 1992, 1990), the 'impossible' in Peirce is part of the idea of Sign Zero, inseparable from Peirce's logic of possibility: the modal logic he refers to but has not been able to develop and which is the cinchpin in his dynamical process of the evolution of ideas, of semiosis.

The idea of a 'significant absence' in Peirce is embedded in his strange term, '*compossibility*.' This term occurs several times, but not frequently, in Peirce's writings. It occurs at least twice in the unpublished manuscripts 515, 534, which are both discussions, in part, of his expanded logic and his

Algebra of Relations: *Incompossibility* represents one of the four classes of logical relations, Peirce writes, (ms 534). Logical relations as a whole have their counterparts in what Peirce calls 'real relations.'

A 'real relation' 'presumes an actual existence of its correlate,' he says, (CP 4.464). But a logical relation is concerned with 'thought about thought' regardless of whether the new idea, or *rhematic* prediction of a thought, refers to actual existence, or not. A Logical Relation — a sign of a sign — permits inquiry into that which is not actual, or Real in an actuality, but rather is of the nature of the conceivable as symbol. In order for some 'given thing' to be regarded as *compossible* it need be only 'consistent with a hypothesis,' that is, it is 'logically compossible' but not actually inherent in any existing thing whatsoever. The composite of the compossible is not sensibly present. It is conceivably representable, (CP 4.86).

The multitude of ways in which anything may be possible includes a way such a thing may be not possible as well, where not possible is a negation of possible. But impossibility is not not possibility: impossibility may be understood as a *representation* of not possibility, since it interprets that idea but evolves it into another sign, or thought. The negation of impossibility is, of course, 'not impossibility' and *not* 'possible.' Neither is it the negation of the negation of 'possible,' since that would be simply 'not not possible,' or 'possible' in other words.

According to Peirce the *compossible* is the quintessential mode of the possible for pragmatic experimentation. It is characteristic of mathematical, abstract reasoning. It is typically expressible by visualizable constructs, whereas philosophical abstract reasoning is typically expressible by words, (CP 4.233-34).

According to Peirce, this mathematical abstractioning is especially useful when we want to speak of collections, classes, organizations, e.g., societies. Further, such manner of abstraction is excellent for depicting all manner in which a surface may be created — a space, a locale, a place, a bounded unit such as that connected with the legal notion of Property. But remember that space, as Peirce considers it, anticipating the great work of the physicists of the twentieth century, is not fixed and rigid, but is plastic, malleable, deformable. One may create the illusion that an object travels faster than the speed of light by representing 'before' and 'after' points in space as being brought together! To visualize an *after* as at the same place or prior to a *before* is simply impossible. Peirce explains further: the mathematical line not only generates a surface but represents the tension involved in this creativity also. The relation between points of the abstract surface is comparable with relations in stages of the legal contractual relation, I suggest. I will come back to this.

Bearing in mind that a compossible relation is associated in Peirce with abstract mathematical relations, as contrasted with abstract philosophical relations, the former refers to relations of points expanding and creating tensions on a surface whereas the latter does not consider this process. A surface is required for any iconic configuration, any imagistic representation of a sign: a sign-function evolving from icon to index or constructive-fact, to symbol as norm, habit and convention.

Peirce takes the opportunity in his discussion of 'compossible' to explain what he means by the term, 'surface', and suggests that a typical example is an irregular, roundish shape (such as we find, for example, in Miro's biomorphs, or in the shape of a teardrop as it hits the top of a table, or in a glob of spit on the sidewalk.) We know the shape of Peirce's typical 'surface' as primitive and life-like: germinal. The Peircean notion of a surface corresponds with the 'mathematical conception of a "spread",' (CP 4.124).

In the human macro-world it can be said, rhetorically, that this elementary droplike shape corresponds to an area like a geometrical 'point' or piece of earth-skin such as that which the practical geometer deals with. Property in its primal sense is, as we know, referent to such earth-skin or basic surface: the concept of Real Estate, or Real Property may be said to have such an elliptical shape. We know this shape in our guts, our mind's eye, in the way we are made. Representation of such a grounded drop of liquid life evokes our recognition. As human beings we respond to the image. It is our commonality and not our idealized common *prioristic* human nature. It represents *how* we matter, *how we are mattering.*

For now I will bypass Peirce's discussion on surfaces which follows his discussion on compossibility, and which takes up in its turn problems and aspects of geometrical topicality with respect to surfaces and 'immediate neighborhood'; it relates to 'simple lines', to surfaces and 'imaginary quality,' (*ibidem*; I cite a small portion of his explanation). I return to the notion of *space* from a Peircean Pragmatic viewpoint in Kevelson 1998 when I explore 'the philosophy of the garden' and 'the rhetoric of ruins.' Integral with these topics is the notion of imaginary 'parallel botany', (Kevelson, 1993).

'Imaginary quality' is a part of the 'algebraic system of symbols,' Peirce says. This system is a 'calculus' or relational mode of reasoning. Peirce credits Fermat, Descartes's contemporary and badly-treated coeval genius. Peirce notes: it was Fermat who changed the method of mathematical reasoning, of relational reasoning, (CP 4.133; 4.151).

It is in the context of this discussion on mathematical reasoning that Peirce here introduces Political Economy as a way of illustrating the use to which the practical sciences of law, economics and politics make of this reasoning. Recall that it is Robert Hamilton, William's gifted son, who turns his mathematical skills to inquiry of socio-political organization. Through many great thinkers this mathematical abstract reasoning becomes the model for reasoning in matters of practical fact, Peirce holds. The origin of this turn of thought is Fermat, (CP 4.114, 115, 116).

Peirce points out that it is Fermatian reasoning which Ricardo uses in his work on economics, especially and explicitly in his theory of rents: a model of contractual relationship, (CP 4.210). This theory of Ricardo's rejects a symmetrical rule of supply and demand and instead points up asymmetrical relations between purchase and price: a small decrease in demand results in a great drop in price (and market value). The consequences of this is taken up by me elsewhere, (Kevelson, 1988).

But note that this relation may be calculated pragmatically by using the kind of reasoning which, according to Peirce, is a far better prediction of what is not known, of what is non-existent, than is a more traditional, symmetrical and reversible cause/effect model, (Kevelson, 1995). See Chapter Two of this volume.

My point here is that the use one makes of modality may result in alternative measurable outcomes. The modal reasoning that Peirce here emphasizes is the reason of possible(s). It is unfortunate that to date little work on the unfinished *possible* modality of Peirce's logic has been done, (Kevelson, 1987).

Peirce himself discusses the idea of the possible in rich detail. For purposes here we want to limit inquiry to the connections he makes between possible and impossible.

As noted above, Peirce does not regard Impossibility as the flip side of The Possible. Rather, he establishes three modalities: the Actual, the Possible, the Impossible. The impossible is not the negation of the possible, as asserted earlier, but is rather the sphere of the Fictive: of that which may be imagined but which is not the negation of the possible, e.g., of a tomorrow that may occur. It is the positing of an idea of something that may not possibly occur and is yet not *not* possible. As example, the Impossible has to do with the career choice that Hamlet's daughter may not make.

To try to provide a general understanding of the impossible in a Peircean frame is all this section attempts:

The Impossible is not the refutation of a conceivable Possible. It is, rather, the construct of something not happening which could not have possibly happened. The impossible may be represented. At the least, Peirce says, we should '*provide* for such a mode of being in our system of diagramatization, since it *may* turn out to be needed ...' (CP 4.547). In this sense, which Peirce addresses to Royce, error *is* possible, (Kevelson, 1998).

We need a minimum of five terms or classes of thought, in order to reason in a dynamical, pragmatical way. These five terms may be said to correspond to ways of knowing. These are: *'necessary, unnecessary, possible, impossible,* and *contingent.'* All information consists of these ideas, with one or another in dominant function. *Information* simply refers to a stage of knowing, from ignorance to omniscience. Most of what is information is *informationally possible, informationally necessary,* or *informationally contingent* — for the time being, (CP 4.65, 66). That which is *informationally impossible* is that degree of zero information that we can conceive of intellectually, yet is not part of actuality. It has not emerged; it does not yet 'matter,' (Kevelson, 1987).

Most of the above-mentioned Peircean ideas are from the 'logic book' of 1893. They foreshadow his 'Prolegomena to an Apology for Pragmatism: (in *The Monist* 16 1906:492-546; reproduced in CP 4.530 ff).

Here is Peirce's maturest work on the Possible as a complex evolving idea, in the 1906 *Monist* piece. Here 'nothing' is now integrated into the idea of an evolved 'possible,' where it comes to represent not a falsification or negation of a possible, but a place for revision of a not-yet emergent significance.

Just as 'a mere possibility may be quite real,' Peirce needed to include also the reality of that which does not exist, but that which has been conceived intellectually and is, conceivably, negatable, (CP 4.589, 581-583).

The very reality of the infinite, of the undetermined and the 'indefinitely multiple identity' requires that the idea of the impossible be included in his pragmatic method of growing thoughts and values.

I suggest that we step back from Peirce briefly and again look at the idea of the impossible contract in law, since this is the focus here. Further, we might look as the development of the connection between this legal concept and the role of law in Peirce's scheme.

IV
Some Implications of the
Impossible Contract for Semiotics

Earlier I called attention to the fact that Peirce intended to identify, explain, and establish an appropriate mode of inquiry for his Pragmatic Method, the *method* of doing Semiotics. He distinguished between two types of reasoning: the one, characteristic of philosophical reasoning, begins with words and presumes an infraverbal system, whether the surface notational system is logic, English, or other natural and formal language systems referent to a semantic, verbal base; the other type of reasoning is mathematical, Peirce says. This mathematical reasoning, unlike philosophical reasoning, does not begin with words but with images, configurations on surfaces, the most basic of which describes a relational tension between two imagined points that are conceivably extendable in any direction, any dimension; this is mentioned above.

Philosophical reason begins with verbal counters each of which is presumed to correspond with some referent phenomenon in the actual world, where each general area of correspondence refers to the Type, and variations and properties refer to Tokens or predications of the Type in question. But mathematical reason begins in a qualitatively different way, with different modes of abstraction: a mathematical mode of reasoning abstracts from the imaginatively conceivable and not from a verbal 'translation' of an actual, existing world. Both rationalism and empiricism presume, in different ways, that the verbal *mediates* between the actual or true and *ideas* of the actual and/or true. Pragmatism does not. *Pragmatism mediates between ideational representations.* Yet pragmatism presumes an actual referent in the actual world and seek to *represent* such actuality but not to correspond *with* it, nor *resemble it.*

The business of Pragmatism is to cultivate and account for the evolution and dynamically growing meanings or functions of intellectual concepts i.e., of ideas, signs, representations in signs of signs. The appropriate mode of reasoning for Pragmatism is not, Peirce says, a philosophically word-grounded method of reasoning, but is a mathematical image-relational reasoning. This point is made also in Chapter Three of this volume.

One does not have to be formally schooled in mathematics in order to reason in a mathematical manner, Peirce suggests. One does not need to be formally trained in philosophical procedures to reason by means of deductive or syllogistic arguments. The point is that a theory of reasoning — any mode of reasoning — should attempt to describe and not to prescribe appropriate conduct. The conduct or means of reasoning selected should be appropriate to the assigned task and purpose, and should not by contrast be obedient to prescriptions for 'right reason.' Ethics has to do with appropriate conduct that describes, and it leaves moral orders to divine rule. Similarly, a legal contract may be ethically describable but not morally prescriptive of good or evil.

These two ways of thinking are dispositionally available to human beings *as* human beings. One may choose the appropriate mode of reasoning for the purpose at hand. One may choose whether such purpose asks for an appropriate ethical mode of reasoning or a mode of reasoning grounded in the *Word as Truth.* And this is not to say, either, that these are the only ways of reasoning available to people. But it is Peirce's point that the mathematical mode is more appropriate to semiotical inquiry than is the philosophical mode of inquiry. As an aside, Peirce does find in his late years that mathematical reasoning is not adequate for inquiry into human affairs. He concedes that dilemmatic reasoning is more 'appropriate.' Again, these are two but not all the ways that people may use in reason. We have yet to understand, perhaps, some ways which are neither primarily word nor image-centered, and possibly not sense-centered, but which may be based in some extrasensory apperception which thus far resists description/explanation. In some manner, however, reasoning *is* phenomenal. The process of reasoning is part of phenomenality. *Ideas as signs are phenomena to Peirce.*

Pragmatism interprets phenomenality to include not only matters of verifiable 'fact,' for also to include imaginary 'factiveness' of all conceivable knowledge.   Facts or what passes for facts, it has been remarked, are organizations of consensual judgments.   The Fact in Law is that which may be admitted as evidentiary, according to official judgment.   It is judgment in ordinary life, Peirce appears to have assumed, that allows for thinking people to discern fact from nonfact.   But a nonfact if it is imagined and conceived is also phenomenal, since it *exists* in the mind as impossible.   *Mind is Matter recomposed.*

A not-fact, or negation of a fact, is negation of a judgment which is conventionalized and system-specific, *within some system of signs, within some universe of discourse so defined.*

We have seen that Peirce differentiates for that system of reason appropriate to his defined pragmatic method several subcategories: the Possible, the Necessary, the Unnecessary, the Contingent, and the Impossible. This last-mentioned is included in order to make room for its possible occurrence.   It allows, in other words, a space to be set aside for an imaginary but conceivable nonexistent, nonphenomenality.

Davis and Parks in the title of their collection, *No Way*, bring together discussions on various ways *No Way* may be implied, where No Way is not a Negation, but is a whole general term in itself.

We walk around the idea of the impossible in unlikely ways. Its shape as an idea stretches and shrinks, bends and dips, metamorphoses in the manner of holographic thought-signs, (Talbot, 1991).   The idea of the impossible emerges in the 'holographic universe' of thought which Peirce had anticipated and Pribram has articulated in explicit fashion in our own time.   What is wanted here is to bend the area of this idea of the impossible back to the topic of law, and to the concept of the impossible contract in the law.

Let us recall that a contract in angloamerican common law is not possibly impossible.   It is a term that says that the conditions are agreed to, that parties are liable for, that is a contract if and only if it is performed.   It is a contract if it brings the future into the present, if it re-presents it, or anticipates its presence as if it were here and now.   This mode of making something present, of re-presenting it, is Vico's *and* Peirce's rhetorical term, 'dialogism,' (Kevelson, 1987).

When parties agree to some performance, some mutuality — now or tomorrow — a speech acts 'performative' has been accomplished. It is, like a promise, like an official pronouncement, virtually done: as 'good as done' the colloquialism goes. But if a contract officiated by the law does not intend performance it is an invalid contract, a fraudulent and counterfeit contract. Yet this should not be regarded as identical with an impossible contract. An 'antecedent impossibility' *foreseen* is not the kind of impossible contract which exemplifies Peirce's sense of impossibility: it is said that a *genuine* impossible contract must, at the outset, be imagined as *doable* in some imaginary way.

When an unperformable contract is judged as impossible it is usually the case that the judgment is retroactive to the time of agreement from the time of nonperformance. It is, in other words, impossible only in hindsight. But since the nonperformability has to do with unforeseeable circumstances the term, 'impossible', is applied to soften or invalidate the will or the party who breaches the agreement. The term 'impossible' becomes a kind of euphemism that obscures legitimate use of the notion of impossibility as a nonexistent but conceivable act.

The stronger the relational ground and the interpersonal trust between parties in a maximally civil society the greater is the likelihood that a contract will be, neutrally speaking, possible. The impossible contract as a euphemism for broken trust will be less common. But the impossible contract in Peirce's sense will be a risk venture, a cooperative chance involving both parties to an experiment, and *releasing* both parties if that chance as hoped for does not materialize. There is a basic ethical difference between sharing a risk, in faith and community, than in being complicit to a collaborative fraud. In the former case the outcome is conceivable but not yet possible. In the latter case the outcome is known, and the failure is the goal. A legal system which chooses to confound the one with the other miscarries its mission.

We have before us several implications: if contracts are to be civilly strengthened, and promises of mutual performances are to be maximally enforced by law, the total wealth of the community increases. There are two basic alternatives to further consider:

One is to have recourse to a value-system built into the law which incorporates moral mandates from powerful religious canons, such that law and church become partners as they are and have been throughout most of the western world. The other way, based on a Peircean model of relational tensions between parties who act freely in trust, implies that there is a self-binding and provisional relatedness *by means of an impossible contract*, where degrees of impossibility are related to degrees of fallibility. Peirce's pragmatism, we recall, presumes all reasoning is fallible at bottom.

In both cases it is the law which is the binding and dissolving agent of possible and impossible contracts. But in the case of community based on trust given and taken freely the law becomes instrument or mediation for a materializing of wills and values, and not an authority extended to the people as *subjects*. The latter is characteristic of authorial systems and absoluteness. The former is characteristic of self-control and openness to Chance.

The last section considers the evolving phenomenon of the 'legal contract,' especially the shift of ethic to moral mandate of the law in the Legal Realist movement. For example, Lon Fuller of neo-Realist fame among jurisprudes attempted to strengthen the growing tendency in the latter half of this century to void impossible contracts by building up the case for the *moral* force of the law. He co-edited an important law text on contract law which, as we recall, first appeared in 1946. But the third edition, which I refer to here, first introduced in 1972 a new section on contract law that focused on 'contract as a social-ordering process,' (Fuller, 1972, xx xi). I want to emphasize the impact of such social-ordering or social engineering (in Hayek's pejorative sense) by suggesting how the concept of a Peircean pragmatic 'impossibility,' well known to the early Realists, has become coopted and distorted in the service of morality, of absolutes, and of constraints on human freedoms.

IV
Utopic Totalitarianism Rejected

Peirce's logic, his expanded logic, is a logic of paradox. It develops upon his concepts of the possible. The 'possible' in Peirce and the 'impossible' are not flip sides of the same coin, or term. They are different ideas. But in a traditional philosophical and jurisprudential framework, the semantics of the prevailing Critical framework has 'impossible' as a negation of 'possible.' While the Possible might be considered as a modal variant of reasonableness, Impossibles as a distinct term is not.

So when Peirce excludes the Impossible from the domains of reason in the following it is the domain of Critic or traditional logic which he refers to: He says, 'Everything is possible which does not contradict the laws of reason: that which is inconceivable, which violates the laws of reason, is impossible,' (CP 6.367). Yet we find that what he does is precisely this: he develops a logic which violates the laws of thought: the law of identity, of contradiction, of excluded middle.

Peirce opens up the dynamical process of making ideas. The pragmatic method is opposed to — antithetical in intent and achievement — idealistic reductionism, utopic order. Utopias are authoritarian. The utopic enterprise is willing to sacrifice means for ends; whereas a Peircean pragmatism is a means/end discovery venture. The former is totalitarian; the latter holistic.

The utopic vision is a vision of the moralist. Those legal moralists who bridge Legal Realism which spawns Legal Pragmatism with the new Crits and their utopic quest for closure, are typified as I suggested earlier, by Lon Fuller. I will not take this paper as opportunity for close discussion of his 1964 *The Morality of Law*. I want to note in passing that Fuller's book is pivotal in linking Legal Realism with Critical Legal Theory. I want to call present attention to Fuller's revised text on Contract Law, 1964, originally 1946. The first edition was straight law text. The 1964 edition was virtually unchanged. But the 1972 version introduced a new section which discusses social values, moral issues and the ordering of morals and mores via the intervention, the *prescriptive* intervention, of the law. Fuller's message is deontic: law *ought* to be the vehicle for moral mandate since it is able to bring such results about. Fuller here adapts the philosophical, speech acts thesis of J.L. Austin to his purpose: he posits Ought equals Can.

I excerpt in the following only a small part of Fuller's new section on Social Order and Contract. First, he establishes his *Given*, namely that there are nine 'principles of social ordering' which are 1) contract, 2) conditions of expectations based on customary interactional behavior of people who live together in community, 3) property; 4) legislated, official law, 5) a system of judging and deciding disputes, 6) administrative procedures for social institutions, 7) community participation, such as voting, 8) mediating between disputants, and 9) the willingness to take 'chance' in stride — to risk outcomes, to accept good and mis-fortune, and to endure the element of change as part of the social process, (Fuller, 1972: 89-92).

Fuller notes that it is primarily only in primitive societies that contract plays a crucial role, i.e., 'serves a persuasive and important ordering function,' (above, at p. 89). But by contrast, in modern society the interactional practice of the contract is regarded by Fuller as an 'inept device,' (1972: p. 89). Modern society may not trust people to make agreements they will honor; people cannot be depended on to perform as promised. It is the age of Musil's 'man without qualities,' he suggests.

With the refutation in modern societies of absoluteness, of constant eternal truths and referents, the commanding function of the law, delegated to the law by the Sovereign State, is diminished and indeed is gone. Clearly the Crits's longing for utopic absolutes, and the overwhelming tendency of institutions in general to attempt to incorporate moral aspects into their role is understandable. But the longing for utopia is at the high cost of rejection of a freedom and *self-ordering* which is less neat but more genuinely grounded in human choice and human trust and human community. Self-governance implied by a Peircean pragmatism is far less attractive it would seem than the certainty of moral rule. But Peirce is not easy. His method of freely mattering is, counter-intuitively, not looking good.

In closing, I call attention to Atiyah's remark that the decline of free choice and consent in 'contractual relations' came about because of a shift of emphasis on *what is promised for the future* to *what is actually transacted here and now,* (Atiyah at 754 ff). Atiyah says that the 'classical model' of contract was on the possible, 'from the executed to the executory contract.' But the 20th century has reversed this classical model, from future promise to act to consent to present action. A sale here and now is present action; an agreement to sell/buy later is future action. The former is less revocable than the latter, but it is not 'impossible.' The latter may be invalidated, and *made* 'impossible.'

The executory contract rests on reciprocal trust and genuine community. The executory contract is a rapidly declining mode of interaction and is frequently no longer a binding act. I want to conclude this chapter with the following: Is it not reasonable to regard promises as provisional and not binding if the very norms upon which ethical behavior rests are not absolutes but provisional? And is this not a 'Lesser' Reason?

Thus an impossible contract may be reasonable from a pragmatic perspective, but may be as intolerable to social ordering as is a Benthamite repugnance.

The following chapter considers Peirce's 'impossible' as a Zero-sign in some aspects.

**Part Three:
The Poetics**

Chapter 9

On *Sign Zero*

On *Sign Zero*

I

On Making Transitions

Peirce's concern with the various functions of Sign Zero run through many aspects of his work, over his lifetime. The framework of Jackobson's life's work can also be tied to his use of the Sign Zero. I am not quite sure that Jakobson came to this focus independent of any influence Peirce has had upon his thought. Jakobson credits Bally with insights of Sign Zero, in Bally's work in the 1920's and 1930's. But somewhere in the course of his working through seminal ideas on markedness, on shifters, on equivalence, on relational tensions, on transitions and transformations on all levels of linguistic texts, one sees agreement between these two great and creative intellectuals, Peirce and Jakobson, on the multiple, complex meanings of significant *nothings*. Peirce also understands a 'zero consciousness' representing the 'outer boundary or definition' of the subject of inquiry in focus. Peirce speaks of this as a 'degree of consciousness,' (ms 148, p. 180; Kevelson, 1990:168ff).

Some of Peirce's latest work, as late as 1911 and after, focused on the use of the Zero Sign to correct and revise imagistic, iconic signs, such as we find in the Eulerian diagrams, in order to show even at this primary level of the graphic/ iconic how we are able to explain transformations — deletions, emendations and reinterpretations — of that which had been 'visualizable' in a previous stage of semiotic inquiry.

For example, in his discussion of the Existential graphs, Peirce introduces functions of the Zero Sign that become integrated with rules he sought for transformations of relations between universes of discourse — i.e, ideas as sign-systems — even at the level of the qualitatively observable. This Peircean discussion centers on methods of using Zero to refer to a change of assertion to non-assertion, from existent to non-existent, (CP 4.359, 360, 361). Without attempting explication here it will suffice to say that he is trying, with the use of the Sign Zero, to invalidate traditional rules of thought and to show how they may be transformed into such *roles* of semiotics by means of the pragmatic method which builds on validation of logical contradiction, of refutation of the so-called law of identity, and which shows modification of the law of excluded middle.

What I want to emphasize in the introductory passage to this chapter is that Zero is not simple negation. But Zero is that means which permits radical transformation of meaning and function to take place by emphasizing the relational character of all units of meaning, (see also CP 4.391, for discussion of Peirce's symbolization of emergent relations, which are predominantly concerned with mapping symbolic logic upon mathematics). Peirce's late work on 'Some Amazing Mazes' (c. 1909) makes the argument that Zero is an even number: It represents an irrational relation, such that the first — *the number one* — must presuppose since it is 'odd,' and Zero is its 'even' predecessor. Since it is part of a 'rational' relational series, it also refers to Zero as that contingency upon which it is dependent, (CP 4.679-681): '... irrational values are nothing but the limits of series of rational values,' and therefore they 'suppose nothing but the linear form of relations.' It is this irrational Zero which has a rational consequence and which permits us to represent this rational seriality in reasoning where, I may add, seriality represents practical consequences, i.e., an historical and asymmetrical evolution of meaning. The Zero function here can readily be seen to be a facet of the problem of 'the possibility of error,' mentioned above. This concession to Royce marks a turning point in Peirce's thought, as mentioned earlier.

Why does Peirce devote so much of his ripest work to this function of Sign Zero? He does so, I offer, because it is the concept of Sign Zero which enables his method of pragmatism — his semiotic inquiry — to eliminate strict causality and determinateness, to provide a ground for the rational, and to explain transformations of form and meaning without recourse to the prioristic, the innate, the eternal, the absolute. Peirce reinterprets and carries forward the alchemical Tarot 'Joker' that represents the paradoxical All/Nothing of genuine potentiality. Such potential or possible signals the onset of pragmatic inquiry.

And for comparable reasons, as I will discuss, Jakobson insists on the dynamical shifting of referential objects, from form to form, by that deictic tool which always stands in relation to the Zero Sign. Further, Jakobson chooses, as does Peirce, to show that meaning evolves not by plugging identical linguistic values into a constant grid, but by a continuous process of creating *equivalences*, equivalent relations, by means of this Sign Zero.

Peirce, as Jakobson, sees the deictic function as central to a logic of relations. Indeed, the indexical function is a means of calling attention to some aspect of relation between speaker and listener, he says, (CP 3.460). He calls this deictic function, characterized by the Zero Sign, a *hecceity*: '... some element of existence which, not merely by the likeness between its different apparitions, but by an inward force of identity, manifesting itself in the continuity of its apparition throughout time in space, is distinct from everything else, and is thus fit (as it can be in no other way) to receive a proper name or to be indicated as *this* or *that*,' (CP 3.460).

We will see that Jakobson, in similar fashion, shows that it is by means of Sign Zero that we may establish relations of similarity and difference, i.e., the kinds of tensions which are operative in the creative unfolding/evolving of a discourse. A point I will return to is that in both Jakobson's and in Peirce's thought the Zero Sign may indicate a relation which has only one relate apparent, and the other missing: deleted, emergent and not yet existent, but hypothetical on a special level of significance, (CP 3.463-467). That which is empty, or blank — ellipsed — is not itself a Zero Sign; but it is a relation which is *marked* by the Sign Zero.

As is his custom, Peirce seeks out metaphors for his ideas in the fields of mathematics and chemistry. Reference to technical terms and examples from chemistry, and alchemy, are frequent, (CP 3.469). Processes of change, of establishing equivalences, are all tied in Peirce's thought to his own background in chemistry, and to the great influences on his thought from chemists: from Robert Boyle to his contemporaries.

I don't intend to suggest that we find agreement on all levels between Jakobson and Peirce. Indeed, the differences are crucial.

II
Zero as Possible and as Pragmatic 'Shifter'

As Jakobson held, the most important relation in linguistic and semiotic texts is the relation of opposition. Such a relation is one of reciprocity and of mutual implication, (Waugh points out that in Jakobson opposition should not be confused with the idea of contrast; Waugh 1976:64).

In this chapter, as mentioned, I am not going to attempt to put these distinctions into practice. Rather, I wish to call attention to a reciprocity between Jakobson and Peirce on the idea of Sign Zero, without point-to-point comparison.

My primary interest is in the mutuality observed here, and in my own insights on this Zero Sign. Zero represents the irrational as limit of the rational. But Zero, in Peirce's view, is that representation of what he calls a 'boundless freedom,' (CP 6.217). I will come back to this Peircean special *Quality*.

As I suggest above, a major link between Peirce and Jakobson is the special idea of a Nothing. This Nothing as Zero Sign is, in my understanding, an axle between them, connecting them, permitting one to roll out parallels between these two great semioticians.

My initiation to this pair of vanguards on Sign Zero came out of a proseminar I took with Roman Jakobson in the late 1970's, when I was a graduate student in linguistics at Brown University. I had done some earlier investigation of Peirce when I was younger, as an experimental playwright trying to play out some of his theories on representations and sign functions, in general, which clearly violated the old aristotelian unities of *time*, *place*, *focus* and even in some respects, *point of view*.

Jakobson brilliantly made clear that the same mode of creative tension and transformation of meaning can be seen in the poetic exchange on every level of discourse. I submitted my first study on Sign Zero to Jakobson at this time. His response in superlatives was that I had made a major break-through. From that time to now I have worked out several lines of inquiry which, in a sense, are filaments of that early, general work on Sign Zero. At that time I attempted to apply what I understood of both Jakobson's and of Peirce's concepts of the Zero Sign, and of others' views as well, to explicate a passage of a poetic text Jakobson had made available. My focus then was primarily on linguistic aspects of the Zero Sign. That paper, revised, was published in 1979 in *Ars Semiotica* and, I would guess, has rarely if ever been read as a contribution to either Peircean or to Jakobsonian studies. But it is my 'Interpretant' and referent text for this paper, and worth the review.

Even with its emphasis on linguistics, this 1979 paper, 'Relations of Nothings to Somethings' was an experiment in transdisciplinary inquiry since that was how I then and still do regard the objective of pluralistic, *semeiotical* inquiry. In the first part of this early study I examined issues of linguistic, extralinguistic, socio-intellectual adventurers who were 'doing semiotics' without knowing that they were, indeed, semioticians. As a result I tended to underscore linguistic concerns with linguistico-semiotical theoretical supports. In such a way I then drew on Peirce's notions of Sign Zero more as props than as personnae.

But in this present chapter it is Peirce's ideas to which I give greater emphasis, with less need to mask the several facets of a theory of signs now than at that time nearly two decades ago. In attempting to connect Jakobson and Peirce on the linking topic of Zero Sign I hope to show an aspect of the former not usually commented on, and an aspect of the latter which is itself a 'significant absence' in the literature: — a virtual Zero Sign.

Tom Sebeok, always generous in his acknowledgement of Jakobson's influence on his own work as teacher and as friend and colleague, had early on called attention to the linguistic function of Sign Zero, especially to the phonemic and morphosyntactic levels of language. Yet Sebeok has not carried forward these important insights to other levels of language, or to relations between language and other modes of semiotic exchangers of meaning, in humans and others, (Sebeok, 1976).

Let us note at the outset that the multifunctionality of Sign Zero is generally accepted by those few who have investigated it: One such function concerns the implications of silences: marked interruptions of speech. Studies on silences and pauses in dialogue and narration have been given some attention in recent years by legal semiotics. Another function, similar to silence, has to do with ellipses or gaps in a discourse, which if presupposed as 'whole' and 'complete' would leave room for nonexplicit freedom-in-

interpretation. These kinds of ellipses and 'gaps' have been observed and written on in work on the law, and in particular on law from the viewpoint of legal semiotics. Visual ellipses, such as that which refer to the iconic function in sign-representation was suggested and merely touched upon on passing in the introductory passage to this chapter. But the role of the Zero Sign in graphic representation, e.g., Peirce's Existential Graphs, will be further discussed in a later section, (Kevelson 1987).

Still another function of Sign Zero is to indicate potentiality and possibility. In fact, this is a *dual function*. Since it points to the potential, it also is self-reflexive; it indicates itself as 'pointer' or diexis: as Secondness in Peirce, representing the character and structure of Experience. (Refer to distinctions between actual experience and the *idea* of Experience in the chapter on Peirce and Poincaré in this book.) Closely related to this deictic function is the function of representing opposition and tension, an aspect of Zero which closely links Peirce's and Jakobson's ideals. Not least, Zero points up referential transformation, or 'shifters' in Jakobson's terminology. Further, what is currently referred to in general as 'paradigm shifts' is the result of Zero at work!

III
Nodes

In 1939 Jakobson writes explicitly on Sign Zero in a collection of studies dedicated to the pioneering sociolinguistic work of Charles Bally. In this paper Jakobson in 'Sign Zero' responds to the seminal studies of Bally on the Zero Sign, of 1925 and 1932. Here Jakobson cites from these much overlooked studies by Bally in recent semiotic investigations. He significantly amplifies and evolves the concept of the Zero Sign. In his 1939 paper, (reprinted in 1966, ed. Hamp, shortly following the resurrection of Peirce and emergence of modern semiotics at the beginning of the 1960's) Jakobson stresses the complex crossrelationships between language, culture and society; he opens the way for investigation of Zero Sign function at each of these multiple nodes or junctures as representation of changes in direction in discourse, in meaning of many kinds. I will return to some germinal ideals on Zero in this study.

But briefly, we step aside to note that Roland Barthes, greatly influenced by the work of the early European semiologists, e.g., Saussure, Hjelmslev and others, was also indebted to Jakobson. This Jakobsonian connection is especially evident in Barthes' very first gem of a book/monograph: *Writing Degree Zero*.

This book appears in 1953, even before Sustan Sontag who writes the preface to the first English edition to this work becomes caught up in a counterestablishment movement which to some of us was a take on semiotics in action, as a kind of 'happening' in dialogic, nonauthorial non-monologic mode. Sontag's prefatory remarks are matching in brilliance to Barthes' quasi-revolutionary pamphlet. She refers to Barthes's works, including this earliest, as merely marginal in the frame of the 'Anglo-American Literary community,' (Sontag, 1968 edition, at ix). She is insightful, but not sufficiently 'psychic' to be able to prophecise Barthes's impact on the academic world. He is sparkling in his illumination of Sign Zero in this small book of nearly fifty years ago.

We want to note that this study was originally intended to be taken as a political pamphlet. The direct object of its assault was Barthes's adversary, Jean-Paul Sartre. In particular, Barthes's monograph on Zero Sign was intended as a direct reply to Sartre's 'What is Literature,' which was widely read at that time. Barthes's first draft of this monograph on Sign Zero was published in the newspaper, *Combat*, in 1947, Sontag tells us, (above.) It appears in the wake of the end of World War II, in the 'twilight of authority.' It signals that the curtain falls on the so-called 'ethical' role of the literary artist: a role Sartre clung to. It points, also, to the failure of heart, of the human will, and of communitarian myth as expressible in literary art. Thus Barthes's study *Writing Degree Zero* is a kind of eulogy, a mourning for the passing of a long-held habit of belief in the possibility of an explicit realization of tacit values. The implicative covert 'object' is filled only with decayed remnants of an old transitivity, which bound actor to patient, so-called, through their presupposed sharing of a world of common values, (Kevelson, 1976). The grammatical intransitive *transformation* of such languages as English around the 12th century now comes to characterize all texts, all sociolinguistic relations based on viable implication, (Kevelson, 1977).

Today, as noted in the 1977 study, the Zero Sign of intransitivity is a rhetorical, stylistic device on strategy. Its purpose is to 'foreground new or novel information' in a given utterance. It is an 'imaginary' or Zero Sign *rheme*, in contrast to the background against which it appears ...,' (Kevelson, 1977:45). The Role of Zero, Barthes suggests, is itself *transformed*.

Especially interesting in this early work Barthes, as do Jakobson and Peirce, rejects the idea of a dyadic bond between society and its history and he insists on the triadic relationship instead. Barthess' relation between 'language, style and writing' presumes that the stylistic referent is a biographical, biological and personal referent of the creativity that processes the literary 'fact,' (Sontag, above at xii). This neuro-physiological referent — an implied interstitial referent — is reminiscent of Boyle's 'corpuscularity' which so profoundly influenced Locke and, in turn, Peirce. This style-referent in Barthes is an organizational, coherence-referent: — that which the literary discourse represents in its dynamically-evolving tensions, as Jakobson holds.

But a bit further of Barthes who was Jakobson's and Peirce's 'student', by a kind of indirection, since the references to the works of Jakobson and Peirce are largely present only by implication. In Barthes the Zero Sign is a ravenous appetite, as he describes it. It is insatiable. Like thinking itself, Barthes suggests, it may be compared with the digestive system, with respect to the style/physical system of the Zero Sign behind the literary text. Literature is, from this viewpoint, the *body* which the functions of the assimilative systems produce.

Zero, from this perspective, marks the interrogative structure in grammars. The grammatical structure of Q/A itself may be seen to represent a Problem, a Want, a Missing something with respect to a hypothecized *Ideal Whole*.

Again, the significant 'nothing' is not in Barthes, nor in Jakobson, nor in Peirce, an empty hollow of a place. But it is a vital operation transforming the raw actual into the nurturing Real. The raw actual is, as we recall, the mode of Secondness, characteristic of the Indexical Sign-function, and of the nature of Experience. Thinking, then, is the instrument or mediating 'tool' in Barthes. This parallels the *pragmatic means* in Peirce, and also parallels those operations of 'relational invariance,' in Jakobson which is the linchpin of his theories of languages, of linguistics, of sign-functions, (Waugh, 1976:68-9, who uses the term 'cornerstone' rather than my 'linchpin').

In the next short section I want to talk about other key concepts in Jakobson which emphasize the mediational function of Zero Sign:

For example, one of the main aspects of the Zero Sign in Jakobson's work is its referential function. Deleted and implied references are special kinds of ellipses, he says, (Jakobson, 1966:113). He calls attention here to crossreferentiality, in particular to anaphoric reference. But the reference could be forward as well, I suggest, as predictive and cataphoric, i.e., forecasting.

Jakobson notes that it is the Zero Sign which calls attention to the interrelation between Addresser and Addressee, especially apparent in interrogative and imperative constructions. The 'other' is an indispensable relate of the communication relationship, and may be recovered from its 'covert' position to an iconic surface representation. The 'other' is always implied, and is entailed according to a logic of questions and answers, (Kevelson, 1987). Jakobson says that the Sign Zero here has a predominantly conative function, (Jakobson, 1966:113).

While Jakobson's work on Sign Zero has been mostly on the levels of the phonemic, the morpho-logical and the syntactic, he has indeed broken through the level of style or discourse: more alive and more 'organic' in its organization than the context-free sentence could be, (Jakobson, 1966:109).

IV
Zero as Mediator

There is a major distinction between Barthes's idea of the Zero-Sign stylistic reference, with its connection to the physiological existent body of the writer, and Jakobson's notion of style as free of the constraints that immobilize — relatively immobilize and keep in a more mechanical mode — the merely existent or the merely physical. Style, in Jakobson, is always subject to relational invariants, even in the most free and creative of literary artistic tests. In this respect 'Creativity ... is always associated with a specific linguistic system,' (Waugh, 1976:74). But creativity in language is not limited to the poetic text. Rather, the model of the code violations expressed in the poetic text, together with the representation of tensions between codified and new, are part of the poetic function in all linguistic uses. Here the implication of the poetic text is a significantly absent referent, according to Jakobson, (see his famous 'Poetics and Linguistics' 1960). In brief, Jakobson sees the Zero Sign as a means by which the discourse creates itself and becomes instrumental in its own dynamical evolving. The Zero Sign, in Peirce as in Jakobson, indicates the particular events in the creative Becoming of a universe of discourse — a complex idea of Peirce, and a poetics of text in Jakobson — which are undergoing transformation. Thus, whatever 'state' or representation of some stage of a process which is continuous, but which we know only from state to state as apparent, represents that 'rational' stage of the process that must always be dependent upon that which is implied, *the nonrational Zero*.

In this sense, every 'First' appearance, where 'firstness' represents an Odd number, presupposes the even number significance of Zero from which the First follows, or is contingent upon, as noted earlier. I will later take up this notion as Peirce regards it. Note: Peirce is to distinguish between a presupposed Zero-Idea, and a gap in observed data, of 'actual' factive empirical data.

But now an additional comment on some further similarities between Jakobson's and Peirce's ideas of Zero:

Jakobson ties his famous concept of 'shifters' closely to Peirce's understanding of the Indexical sign-function, especially in his 'Word and Language,' (Jakobson, *Selected Writings* II 1971:347). Here Jakobson focuses mainly on referential equivalents in changing forms for functions of possessives and demonstratives. 'Shifters' are always context-dependent. Each situation becomes implicated in the message through this referential zero function in this sense of the *actual* as the implied shaper and maker of a coherence in the creative text. The poetic function includes this actuality in much the way that Barthes's concept of 'style' as zero-sign referent brings the biographical and biological 'context' of the writer into the message of the text and, indeed, *informs* it, (see Holenstein for interesting discussion on the situation/context referent, 1974/1976:118).

Jakobson's shifter indicates that equivalences in linguistic meaning, in the given text, are coming into play, and that this equivalence is grounded in a context of force and place which governs evolving permutations, but to a degree only, i.e., they are 'invariant,' but are not causal.

Equivalences in Jakobson's notion of the Zero Sign are brought about by means of translation, first within a given verbal/natural language, second between two or more natural language systems or between two or more discourse types of a natural language system, and third in intersemiotic translation between two or more sign-systems which are not necessarily verbal, but may be notational or encoded in some other fashion than as a natural language, (Jakobson, 1959: 'On Linguistic Aspects of Translation,' in *Selected Works* II at pages 260-266).

Let us recall that Peirce identifies the purpose of semiotics as the 'Quest of Quests,' employing the Method of Pragmatics as the Method of Methods; i.e, Rhetoric is reinterpreted as the highest division of his tripartite expanded Logic (the evolved new equivalent of all that he means by Semiotic). This quest of quests intends to bring together in new relationship two or more universes of discourse, or complex idea-systems, so that a more comprehensive, more complex and yet coherent general idea is created, (Kevelson, 1987, 1993).

From this perspective Jakobson's concept of 'shifters' appear to be nearly synonymous with Peirce's Indexical function. This index then becomes a relational link between a familiar position and a new position, where position and place are simply ways of expressing reciprocal exchange between related members of a unifying context in which both familiar and new are players. Waugh remarks that the Peircean Index and the Jakobsonean deixis function in language correspond; and, I would add, they represent the major role of ideological conflict in sign systems which are both linguistic, but not necessarily overtly linguistic, in social organization.

I further suggest that Jakobson's 'speech event,' which constitutes his notion of context and frame of reference, is comparable with Peirce's idea of Immediate Interpretant (sometimes called Ground or Representamen or Object). For Jakobson, 'Deixis, in particular, is built on the dialectic tension between code and message, on the anticipation of the message within the code and on the antimony of the narrated event and speech event,' (Waugh, 1976:24; Jakobson, 1957, 'Shifters, Verbal Categories and the Russian Verb,' in *Selected Works* II, at pages 130-147).

According to Peirce, the only way to get out from the trap of closed systems of thought, which are systems that take as gospel the truth of the so-called 'laws of thought,' is to show that these 'laws' of identity, of contradiction, of excluded middle, restrict us from creating new knowledge. It is our ability to use the concept of Zero to indicate that something which was not previously known may become known; or something which was not previously related to what we know — as similar or as different — may become significant for what it may represent to us:

'The effect of an addition to our knowledge is to make one term predicable of another which was not so before to our knowledge. And it thus at once increases the known depth of the subject term, and the known breadth of the predicate term without any decrease of either of these qualities ...' (ms 217, of 1873). Zero is that semiotic function which represents, *as interval*, a place, or a space, for that which was previously present in our mind, says Peirce, to come into relation with that which was not previously present, (ms 216, 1873). In this manuscript Peirce describes how thoughts seem to succeed one another in calendar time. But between these 'states' or frames there are interludes or intervals which we may regard, I suggest, as Zero Signs. These intervals, representative of time/space, are links *between* 'states' and are the connective functions of continuum processes in semiotics.

Such transformations of thought are in principle germane with Jakobson's concept of equivalence which allows the aesthetic text to evolve through a dynamical process of permutations, (Jakobson, 1960:358).

Much earlier, in 1886, Peirce writes on the role of the Zero Sign as part of the process of a continuum, such that the function of the Zero is neither that of a positive nor of a negative, but rather, represents an intermediate position between a 'positive and negative quantity,' (ms 575). It is interesting that a year earlier Peirce had used Zero to represent, in terms of probability of coming to know something, a 'certainty' of our *not* coming to know such and such a presumed event. In this manuscript 547 of 1885, Zero and negation were the more simple equivalents Peirce had worked out at this early period of his life. As he proceeds, the idea of Zero becomes a much more complex instrument for establishing equivalent values. It is worth noting that from the beginning of his work on the logic of relatives the concept of Sign Zero was a fulcrum for representing relations, (see Peirce's 1870 letter to De Morgan on the notation for a logic of relatives, reprinted in *WoP*, II, pages 359 ff, at 381-87, in particular; see also Kevelson, 1990 on *zero* in Peirce and Paradox).

To Peirce as to Jakobson, every language or sign-system conveys its meanings as forms. According to Jakobson, equivalent forms — forms conveying both differences as well as similarities — are equivalent with respect to their common reference, (Jakobson, 1939). It may happen that an unexpressed form may correspond with a place in a system for that form as meaning or significance. The form, *as form*, may include that which has not yet come into being. This inclusion is strictly formal, but permits such tension as is part of the ongoing creative process of discovery and evolving of meaning. In Peirce we find as well that he has adapted from Hamilton's notion of the 'imaginary' in mathematics a formal 'frame' to represent the place for a 'rheme' or predication of a theme/subject which has not yet occurred or emerged, but which the Zero Sign of significant absence makes operable, i.e., hypothesizes.

In concluding this discussion on similarities on the Peircean/Jakobsonian consensus on Zero I do not want to suggest that we may expect to find correspondence and/or agreements, in principle, between them in every major matter. But this Sign Zero is so central to the thought of each, and is understood by both in a way that seems to me one of agreement, that I hope this argument on Nothing will cease to be 'neglected.' Others will hopefully pick up the tensions and oppositions and will attempt to fill in the blanks.

The idea of creation of equivalences, and not identical counterparts, is a pivotal point of both Peirce and Jakobson. Further, their emphasis on creativity centers on permutation and transformation at the creative levels of discourse, and not on the substitution of 'plugs' on a static grid. The idea of 'verisimilitude,' with tension between object and interpretant, is heightened by means of Sign Zero; the notion of resemblance becomes innocuous.

In the chapter 'Versimilitude and Discovery' (Kevelson, 1987), I show that Peirce's concept of verisimilitude stands for the idea of an 'invented replica.' Such replication need not resemble, i.e., *look like* its referrent, but represents it in an iconic, visualizable manner, (pp. 127-37). Not least, the role of the Zero Sign is to bring about and to effect connection between experiential context, and possibles or imaginaries, i.e., between representations of Actuals and of Reals, (Kevelson, 1987, 1990, 1993).

It is Peirce's custom, as mentioned above, to use mathematics as a discourse or language type for exploring concepts related to problems of his new logic: his semiotics. In these discussions we find frequent recourse to the Zero Sign. In fact he says explicitly that the whole role of the 'doctrine of mathematics applied to logic' is the doctrine of multitudes, the smallest of which may be held to be 'zero.' In his opposing of finite and infinite multitudes he says that 'the multitude of all the different finite multitudes is the smallest infinite multitude,' or what he has defined, for use, as a zero-sign multitude, (CP 3:630, 631). In this late work, about 1911, on symbolic logic Peirce once more distinguishes between collections as aggregates, and multitudes — finite and infinite — as interrelations of signs and sign-functions. I am not suggesting that attempts to 'translate' Peirce's mathematical expositions concerning Sign Zero into natural language does not result in interpretive changes of meaning, as happens in any translation and paraphrase. I do hold that it is possible for such equivalences to be used that enable one to understand a general principle of Sign Zero (or other general principles) whether it is expressed in mathematical notation, or in English, or other means of sign-transactions. But it is such translation which opens up the whole realm of a freedom in creativity that Sign Zero participates in, instrumentally, (Gorlée, 1993).

In his remarkable paper on 'signs' written for Volume 16 of *The Monist* (1906), in his 'Apology for Pragmaticism,' Peirce takes up still again the process of establishing relations. Here he says that he uses chemistry (as he uses mathematics) as types of discourse which permit him to establish analogies and other representations, and hence to make new information appear in the light of familiar forms of knowledge, (CP 4.530). In this discussion, in a further section which looks at 'collections' (as distinct from multitudes) he is able, even with respect to aggregates of the possible (with reference to nonexistent Sphynxes and Centaurs), to create possible connections among disparate parts of collections. So, with recourse to the Zero which he allows to stand for the 'wild card' of possible collections, the '*nothing,*' like the Joker of the Tarot, may stand for whatever one wills it to be and so defines it, (CP 4.532).

Zero Sign in Peirce is such a Joker. It may represent any possible value providing all players agree, in the context and situation of the play at hand. It is the most pure of arbitrary signs, at least in theory. We know that Jakobson and Peirce alike rejected the notion of strict necessity. In Jakobson even the arbitrary was not a necessary arbitrary; the arbitrary sign is never purely so. The purely arbitrary, or the pure Zero Sign in this case is, according to Jakobson, 'extralinguistic,' (Jakobson, 1966, 'Quest for the Essence of Language,' in *Selected Works* II, at pages 345-59).

And Peirce's qualification of 'Pure Zero' is that it is not the 'nothing of negation ... It is the germinal nothing in which the whole universe is foreshadowed. As such, it is absolutely undefined and unlimited possibility — boundless possibility. There is no compulsion and no law. It is boundless freedom,' (CP 6.217).

Sign Zero is a dualistic idea that represents such duality as we find significant in tensions, in oppositions, in drama, in real life, in creativity of all kinds. It is the designation, in iconic, indexical and symbolical sign-functions — but predominantly in the Indexical — of relations unified, of the All-in-Nothing of living potentiality.

Chapter 10

Codes, Crypts and Incantations

Codes, Crypts and Incantations

I
The Nondiscrete Idea

From Zero to Crypt is a short conceptual step. In the following chapter I will discuss aspects of Peirce's Pragmatic method as 'strategies' or rhetorical tactics, as contrasted with the notion of 'rules.'

The interpretation of ideas by ideas — signs by signs — is the way meaning grows and evolves, according to Peirce. This way is the Pragmatic Method from which derives the theory of signs — Semiotics. Speculative Rhetoric in Peirce's scheme is a term synonymous with Methodology or Methodeutic. It is the name Peirce gives to that highest division of his expanded logic which connects linguistic and traditional logical analysis of meaning with his semiotic inquiry into interpersonal conduct on all levels of human affairs: Ethics. Ethics feeds into his science of values, Esthetics. The ways in which all of these major parts of Peirce's Normative Sciences interconnect constitute the process of his Pragmatism. From time to time this thumbnail recap may be useful.

Peirce appropriates established and familiar terms of ideas for his own purposes. He interprets ideas in a semiotic fashion in his own work. We want to keep this in mind when we turn to his notion of Rhetoric to understand and explain it. It is not the 'old' rhetoric of the ancients. Neither is it conformable, without important modification, with Perelman's 'new rhetoric.' Peirce's Rhetoric does not restrict its scope and domain to words. It is no less concerned with spatial relations, i.e., configurations which have persuasive force.

I draw primarily on Peirce's own writing, especially upon those manuscripts which are little known even today, in order to open ways of seeing Peirce's idea of Rhetoric which have been only rarely noted and discussed. Moreover, the approach I present to the idea of rhetoric in general is the nonstandard approach which has recently received some attention (e.g., from Liska, 1993; Kennedy, 1992; Kevelson, 1984, 1986, 1990, 1992, 1993, 1995; Eco, 1976, 1979).

The scope of this paper does not permit a detailed review of the references offered above, but jumps into the middle of things in appropriate nonlinear fashion:

'Rhetoric' is the name of an idea which has in its evolution from the ancients undergone profound transformation; it has changed its meaning — but not its 'skin' or coating/name — several times, (see, for example, Ricouer, on Rhetoric, 1975:44-59).

Today the term carries forward this melange of mixed messages, mixed both in ordinary usage and in the hands of the 'experts' as well. The multiordinality of the idea, Rhetoric, is sometimes deliberately made use of by amateurs and professionals alike, in order to play with the ambiguity of the term and to squeeze out as much meaning and mileage as the term will bear. In this respect the term, Rhetoric, is as versatile as imagination takes it. But if we want to get a sharper picture of how it functions in Peirce's semiotic schema we have to exclude everyday work/play here and zero in more closely.

In a broad, most general sense, the 'old rhetoric,' was regarded as an embellishment of speech — a mode of decor which acted on people's emotions and literally moved them to act as the speaker wished them to act. Rhetoric plucked heartstrings, fired rages, calmed agitation, pushed buttons for human action and, in brief, manipulated listeners to move, to act, as though words were physical energizers. That objective of rhetoric, old or new, has never been lost sight of. What has gone under cover is the connection between words and deeds, minds and bodies, insight and instinct. The old rhetoric utilized conventional counters to tint, tone, and value presumably objective verbal meaning with subjective motivational force. The old rhetoric was viable as long as the society or social context in which it occurred was more or less homogeneous, (Whately, 1864:3-53). Such homogeneity presumed that the world was closed, completed, and that there was a constant ideal state of things which, when damaged, could be and must be repaired and restored.

Presumptions of ideal form and type of social organizations — of cultures — relate the old rhetoric with the old State, as binding force with ideal or utopic state in a way that we find such parallels of vitality and form not only in the western world but almost globally. This static view of the world characterizes human organization prior to the emergence of darwinism at mid-nineteenth century and to the emergence of the understanding of dynamical systems moving in indeterminate ways, from provisional order to new confusions and chaotic possibilities, (Vico, 1711-1741/1996:51-64).

Peirce is a child of this intellectual environment. His semiotics is rooted in this ground. His pragmatic method, contra deterministic powers and authorities, and opening new free places, spaces for interhuman action is he maintains explainable. At the least it is approachable, by means of the explanatory device which transforms Logic, as a description of semantic relations, to an expanded Logic, which describes the dynamical conversions from energy to words, from words to acts, and hence from instinct to consequences on the level of human reason and human representations of shared human meaning.

The shift from homogeneous to pluralistic society has occurred in those human organizations which have also been vanguard in the development of both technological invention and thought-patterns derived from the far, abstract reaches of the physical sciences, and especially in the bridging of science and the arts and humanistic sciences, in contradiction of the plight deplored nearly a half-century ago by C.P. Snow's Two Cultures. If there has not been a marriage of art and science the affair has at the least become a kind of continuum meld, and *significant*, (Kevelson, 1995).

The 'new rhetoric' reflects the fragmentation of a former whole social fabric. The parts and pieces become editorialized and remade into a montage, a new scene: a *bricolage*. The movies, and the art of editing, has become a major model for communicative composition, (Kevelson, 1996, 1998). But the focus of most studies in the 'new rhetoric' mode is still upon words and less, if at all, upon more primary levels of the visual, or upon the still more elemental level of pattern as such: of rhythm, of tempo, of space.

With the obsolescence of the 'universal audience,' and the refutation of the 'self-evident' by Descartes, the 'new rhetoric' introduces equivalences of the self-evident, the sensibly perceptible; it opens up an area of *metarhetorical* inquiries, i.e., of a self-reflexive mode of argumentation, (Perelman and O.-Tyteca, 1958).

Peirce 'damns Descartes', (in Fisch's words, 1958) and retrieves sensibility, thus discarding a solipsistic introspection in favor of a dialogic exchange of meaning between oneself and at least one other. He discards as well the cartesian prioristic intuition. The traditional 'open hand' of dialectic becomes through Peirce a dialogical structure of making meaning consequential.

Trade produces meaning, *effectual* meaning. The recovery of sensibility is a recovery of the physical world and of the instinctual energies of human beings, (Kevelson, 1996). Peirce takes Descartes' discard and in his own hand it becomes the trick of his own emergent complex idea of Rhetoric. One might say that the basic, long-standing concept of traditional rhetoric is stirred into motion: it seems to split and to differentiate, to evolve and become more complex, representing the 'new rhetoric' spun off on the one hand from Descartes through Pascal and through Kant, and on the other hand into a reinterpretation of Lockean physicality. This alternative concept of an emergent Rhetoric, this Peircean notion, is a radical, instinctual thrust-and-grasp force: It is an energy with basic, biological goals. Thus to carry a bit further Peirce's premise that all ideas are goal-oriented toward tomorrow, and by chance, no longer returning to a perfected yesterday, Peirce's Rhetoric may be seen as a value-instrument, a means of effecting change by its very process of interaction.

In 1979 Eco discusses this aspect of Rhetoric as a purposeful energy (Eco, 1979:276-88). In more recent years Kennedy has taken this idea of Rhetoric as a 'form of energy' — goal-directed. Further, Kennedy compares the function of birdsong, for example, and of mating dialogue among primates in general with human rhetoric at a primary and proto stage, as an anticipation of 'rational argument,' (Kennedy, 1992:17).

It is but a short (but possibly adventuresome and unsafe) span between the idea of song as a biological function directed to the wellbeing and continuation of the singers/chanters, to the more general notion of Play as an activity of growing in preparation for adult function: as a practice-activity. I have written elsewhere on Peirce's Pure Play and Musement (Kevelson, 1990, 1993); at this point I will only digress to mention that Peirce's idea of Pure Play should be distinguished from such notions of other pragmatists such as Santayana (but not Dewey or James); Peirce insists that play is the integral part of a semiotics process which provides linkage between rational 'states' and nonrational movement. Santayana, especially in his famous essay on the Sense of Beauty, thinks of play as a surplus of energy, a leftover abundance, and not as inseparable from the business of everyday life. Santayana retains Play as a Holiday, as time left over, as superfluous. Peirce, by contrast, understands Play as a mode of interlude which is the means that connects states of ideas into ideas as continua.

Peirce's Pure Play may be regarded as connective tissue in the production of values from the very process of value-exchange. The process *produces* a surplus, just as the semantic exchange of meanings in Mukařovsky produces more, or extra, meaning, (Kevelson, 1976). Every interpretation/translation is always the production of additional information or meaning, according to Peirce, (Kevelson, 1987).

What I will try to show in this chapter is Peirce's 'redemption of the image' — of the physical/material — by means of the shift of focus on Rhetoric, from its constituent words to its more basic rhythm, i.e., patterns of space relations: icons and images, (see Kevelson on image-redemption, 1994).

Peirce succeeds in knotting several strands of the idea, Rhetoric, into a new textile, or *text*. These patterns of joining are conventionalized procedures or tactics, i.e., ways of handling. As Kennedy suggests, the 'rhetorical codes of the animal world' (Kennedy, 1992:17) may be discovered to be, from a Peircean perspective, integral patterns of meaning in cryptic or undisclosed regions of thought. It is the function of a Speculative Rhetoric to explore and to disclose these crypts, these codes — these songs, as it were, — which facilitate nurture and representation of human meaning, (Sebeok, 1972).

The Codes of Rhetoric and the incantations of protohuman forces of persuasion are referred to in my title of this chapter. The third term, the cryptic 'Crypt,' indicates the treasure to be revealed by the game, the quest. 'The Quest of Quests' as discussed earlier and in Kevelson 1987, is Peirce's term that indicates that the leading inquiry of the whole of pragmatism is to link otherwise unconnected universes of discourse, or complex ideas: sign-systems. The term, Crypt, as used here, is both occasion and means of disclosure. It is the quintessential 'speech act,' the utterance of which — the physical production of the word — opens the treasure chest. Peirce was no stranger to open-Sesame strategies, ways of making things happen. Peirce rescusitates the ancient hermeneutical action of probing the depths of sacred texts. His writings are peppered with references to realizing the phantastic, to disclosing the occult, (*WoP*, Vol I; see also CP 6.595). The influence of Schiller's 'play' stays with him through his life.

In discussion of how premises for deductive reasoning are created by the imagination, are invented and produced out of the deep recesses of made thought, Peirce compares the occult grounds or resources of mathematical thinking with those of chemistry, where both are aspects of our questing, our action 'of Cosmical Reason, or Law.'

In a footnote Peirce himself comments on his use of the word, 'Occult.' He refers to Petrus Perigrinus's comment which holds that 'physical properties are occult in the sense that they are only brought out by experimentation and are not to be deduced from admixtures' of opposites, of semantic opposites such as 'hot and cold, moist and dry,' (*ibidem*). It is our probing which reveals/creates the place beneath the surface. Yet in opposition to Kant who holds that space is an essential and primary ingredient of thought, Pierce says that nothing, not even space, is prior to experience. Experience experiences and represents both the experience as object and the experience as process of representing experience experienced, (CP. 598-600; Dewey's *Logic* and his *Art as Experience* is in this vein).

This introductory section presents in condensed form the kernel of the chapter. In the following I will discuss selected aspects of Peirce's Rhetoric as they seem to bear on creating value/creating texts, and as the instinctual rhythmic patterns become evolved into verbal shapes, conceptual forms.

I want to reiterate the several main points of this opening section: Close to the end of his life Peirce opens, i.e., discloses that the secret to freedom — to 'free will' — is to cultivate that representation in our human conduct which permits our ethical behavior to be interpretive of the way plants and animals coexist symbiotically, corelationally, upon this earth. Our conduct must *appear* spontaneously free, not forced nor determined nor authorized; but it is *as* a sign of the free, Peirce writes.

He says that the Speculative Rhetoric which he develops is, like the work of art or the play of children or the seemingly effortless gestures of experts, not studied; but rather it is as natural-seeming as if it were, indeed, as 'true' as instinct is true and as coordinated.

As I wrote in 1984, in an early exploration of Peirce's Rhetoric, Peirce came to establish an interaction between the ideas of topic/comment, or theme/rheme of traditional rhetorical lexicon of word-based Rhetoric, and the emergent instinct grounded in image-based rhetoric that he sees as the 'living condition of the 'human mind'.' He writes to Lady Welby in the last years of his life that his pragmatism, his way of linking signs or universes of meaning, should be understood as the 'university of methods,' a mediation or pure play which 'renders our conduct analogous to the manner in which growth takes place in plants and animals,' (see in *Letters to Lady Welby*, dated 1911, cited in Kevelson, 1984:26).

II
Pragmatic Strategy

In the following few pages of this chapter I want to review briefly some of the main ideas I developed in earlier work on Peirce's rhetoric, mostly to distinguish this point of view from other approaches to Rhetoric that largely persist in viewing rhetoric as a word-based game of strategies. It is also important that we understand that to Peirce, mathematically-based rhetoric does not mean reducing understanding to the abstract principles of mathematical reasoning only. Rather, Peirce argues that we need to begin with images as mathematicians do if we are to get out of the nominalistic trap. *The image is posited.* In that sense, Peirce suggests, a Speculative Rhetoric investigates the process from positioning a made image to evolving that image into a piece of 'social machinery' or organization: i.e., a dialogic (not authorized) norm.

It would be misleading to say that Peirce is a neglected genius. It is more to the point that he is widely noted, widely but briefly, with perfunctory reference in footnotes which, strangely enough, appear around page 218 or thereabouts of scholarly tomes: midway, in proper pause. This nod signifies that Peirce is touchable but not graspable and that writers cannot get a proverbial handle on him but feel they ought to acknowledge his touted greatness. Nonsense! There is too little *actual* reading of Peirce's own writings, especially the bulk which remains unpublished.

A Peircean methodology or rhetorical strategy attempts to use certain conventions — procedural modes that have symbolic function — to represent unexamined things as they are, in elemental, more palpable, spatial-relational manner.

Peirce might say of himself that if one cannot get a handle on him the failure is not the handler's but the fact is, *there is no handle*. His theory of signs is protean, elusive, dynamical. Peirce is a slippery fellow, much alive. One doesn't grasp him by his protrusions. Rather, one needs to get under his skin to know him. One must inhabit him, even as one inhabits a costume, or knows how a stage prop such as a wad of cellophane, 'feels' when it's flung on the floor and expands slowly, unwrinkles. One needs to walk the walk with Peirce, talk the talk with Peirce, mime him in the method he exhibits in the developing of his thought. Peirce's method, the Rhetoric of his pragmatism, is a way of *becoming* in the world, *of mattering*.

With this approach I have no intention of taking a polemical stand in appraising the work of others on Peirce. Rather, I prefer to foray into the bush and tangle of his ideas. It is a different and far easier game to do polemics. My aim is to explore uncharted Peirce and mismapped regions of his theory of signs. I want to find the under limits of this great person, this region still occult: Peirce's innards as a nether side. His personnae is a mask of a mask of a mask ...

Peirce himself provides the clues. He says that Speculative Rhetoric is the Method of his theory of signs, he is asking for inquiry, for the inquirer's role, for input into this method continually adapting to purposes at hand. Inquiry interprets, recasts the meaning of the methodology of semiotics. The Rhetoric/Method conforms, takes on the shape of the Inquirer in reciprocation.

It is now more than a decade since my early paper on Peirce's Rhetoric appeared in *Philosophy and Rhetoric*, (17 1 1984: 16-27). Almost two decades have past since I first realized and wrote on the dialogic role of Peirce's rhetoric, and on language-games as 'systematic metaphors,' (Kevelson, 1976). But the observable, in response to observation, grows and evolves.

In the last years of Peirce's life, after 1902, it is Methodeutic or Speculative Rhetoric which becomes a caption to his work (but not quite a 'handle' on his expanded logic). His logic of relatives, logic of possibles, logic of paradox — all this is subsumed within the evolved notion of Method or Rhetoric. Peirce's Rhetoric is concerned not with a logic of justification but with a logic of discovery. It is an instrument of inquiry, an heuristic, a wedge to pry open old crypts and implications, to disclose occult places of our cosmic holograms.

Max Fisch's meticulous notations on the file cards at the Peirce Edition Project had noted that the idea of 'Rhetoric' (at around 1865) came to be called by Peirce 'Methodeutic' and 'Methodology' in his late years, (Kevelson, 1984:17). We find that Peirce's characteristic is to revise and redefine his terms as he, himself, comes to understand them better and to grow them more extensively.

Again I want to emphasize here, as I noted in the 1984 paper, that Peirce has reinterpreted the classic notion of Rhetoric as it referred to verbal actions. He expanded this idea so that it came to encompass processes, gestures, configurations: whatever could be held as a convention or as an encoded mode of action, i.e., a pattern, (Kevelson, 1984; 21). An idea of the use of Peirce's Rhetoric that is explicit and clear is his well-known manuscript 774, at page 3, 'Ideas, Stray or Stolen, about scientific writing.'

Peirce speaks of the 'universal art of rhetoric' in a manner which is itself cryptic. He says that it is the 'general secret of rendering signs effective ...' (ms 774, above). By 'effective,' I take it that Peirce means that this art of rhetoric/method is capable of bringing about consequences of its own action, upon that which it is not, including that which is has been stated to be at some former/other time and place.

The effectual force of rhetorical acts is not an overt force. It is rather a force that operates in a medium not sensibly perceptible, Peirce suggests. Or perhaps it is a force as a masked sign representing that which it is not, as is the effectualness of all sign-functions. Thus it is simultaneously an imagistic procedure or map, a pointer or index to what it is/is-not. Conventionally, systemically, it symbolizes a repeatable act.

All signs do their jobs by behaving as rhetorical acts. And Speculative Rhetoric is nothing less than a way of inquiring into these complex sign-behaviors. Thus it is not the merely verbal, but the pattern of the verbal as well as the nonverbal which brings about change, which grows meaning, which marks distinctions, which persuades and which coaxes the mattering of fact.

In this following few pages of this chapter I want to further develop Peirce's assumption that the Rhetoric or Method of Semiotics is not an art of the verbal, but is primarily an art of co-related patterns, of isomorphs. Patterns of an imagistic nature are less dependent upon conventions of habits of thought, but seem to occur more spontaneously, less hampered by convention yet not entirely arbitrary and always in some manner evocative and representatative of something known, learned, consensual. I want to speak briefly about this aspect of Peirce's Rhetoric which seeks to stretch the boundaries of the defined and best does so by stretching space, by twisting space, by molding space into human design.

III
The Instinctual Ground of Rhetoric

Peirce insists that an instinctual continuum is as alive in us today as it was in our primitive forebears. It is this instinctual ground — biological and not imputed — which serves as substratum of our tendency to doubt and at the same time *not to doubt impulses*, predilections, but to act with sureness to satisfy hungers and to mate. We do not begin with doubt, Peirce says: We cannot or we would not survive. The doubt that stimulates intellectual inquiry is a kind of interpretation of anticipatory judgment *before* instinctually-motivated acts, and this judgment is an almost imperceptible syncopation, a marking of an object and an affirmation. It seems to skip a beat, and marks a rhythmic irregularity.

Genuine doubt is an art, Peirce says, which grows out of this marking of a moment, of a prescising of chance moments in such a way as that which the *phenomenological prescising of a Quality from its customary ground* represents in Peirce's Phenomenology, I suggest. But 'all the instinctive beliefs are vague,' Peirce says, until we begin to observe them as phenomenological moments, and thus begin preparatory procedure for semiotic analysis (CP 6.499, c. 1906).

The art of doubting gives rise to the art of rhetoric, of bringing about a wanted event. Such art or making evolves from and interprets instincts which are as close to universal and constant among human beings as anything can be, says Peirce. (CP 6.499, above).

From this point of view instincts are energized wants. Rhetoric, in this sense, is the most complex result of the effort of sign-making, says Eco, (1976:277 ff). Rhetoric — the idea which emerges of a 'new,' semiotic rhetoric — plies reason with goal-directed action and comes to represent, as 'persuasive discourse,' no simple deception or twisting of truth at all, but rather a practice, a pragmatic procedure, a 'technique of "reasonable human interaction," controlled by doubt and explicitly subject to many extra-logical conditions,' (Eco, 1976:278).

Eco is not especially Peircean; but in this respect I see them in agreement. I want to follow it further:

Is it not the rhetorical force the style and pattern of the 'material' of which literature is shaped that distinguishes the prosaic from the poetic, the fictive from the reportorial, one genre from another? The difference between an aristotelian tale with lineal beginning, middle and end and a modern short story is a difference of design. But the difference of design represents a profound difference in worldview, in cosmology. The ability to evolve from one leading cosmic principle to another represents a great artistic, imaginative feat. It is an example of a continuum metamorphosing, as grub to butterfly.

The interim, or interlude, during which the transformation appears and the new appearance takes form, is that extralogical part of the continuum which Peirce designates as Musement or Pure Play.

Peirce's Speculative Rhetoric is that protosemiotic activity which intends to explain how syntactic structure of natural language may evolve, through logical armatures of reasoning, and into a mode of action which sets the stage for effectual interhuman action on the level of social, institutional organization: — that which his Normative Sciences represent.

According to Peirce, his Pragmatism, i.e., the Pragmatic Method, develops out of the Speculative Rhetoric. It is not inherent in the Rhetoric Methodeutic but it interprets this expanded Logic and translates it into the Ethics division of the Normative Sciences. The role of pragmatism is to carry forward the Rhetoric of the expanded logic into the metaphysics of Peirce's Schema via the Esthetical division of the Normative Sciences. Esthetics and metaphysics are contingent, but not in a lineally-related way.

In Peirce's words, the special theoretical concerns of his Speculative Rhetoric are evolved from the rhetorical devices, 'devices which have to be employed to bring new relations to light,' (CP 4.370).

It is not the case that new relations are immanent and need to be released. On the contrary, it is the ploy of the strategies of rhetoric — the rhetorical material in relation with the rhetorical arts — which create new ideas, new relational signs, just as the sculptor with chisel and blade makes apparent, into a new reality, the figure and form *potential in the stone*. The Peircean crypt is such possibility.

We may from this point of view compare the Peircean crypt with a noncomputerized chaotic 'field' of random patterns which require a focused stereographic, or hypergraphic, mode of viewing in order to detect and thus to 'transpose a flat page of random patterns into a coherent 3-D pattern,' (Rheingold, 1994:9). In the case of a stereographic mode of apprehending a noncomputerized 'virtual reality: the "chaotic pattern" has been composed *as* a chaotic pattern, *by design*.' In Peirce's case, however, chaotic patterns spontaneously take on perceptibility as a result of dialogic interactions. The former emphasizes techniques for developing new skills for viewing. In the latter case *making* the chaos is an integral part of an ongoing process, and artfully rather than artificially is a composition *of* the imagined world rather than a superimposition *upon* the actual world.

In the context of discussion of Peirce's phenomenology I suggest that Peirce's Rhetoric might be viewed as a forerunner of 20th century fractal geometry since he is, indeed, a 'scientist of change' (in the words of Briggs and Peat, 1989:110). Inquirers into the evolution of complex systems reject explanations of a causal nature. But since they require a point of view, a point of departure is provisional and yet 'holistic.' It looks into the qualities of change and not at the changed states of things, (Kevelson, 1981; 1993).

I have understood Peirce as a 'founding member' of the community of scientists of change, discussed by Briggs and Peat (above). This community includes, among others, David Bohm who assumes as does Peirce that every change of every part of every phenomenon dynamically brings about change in every other part: 'Each part of instance of energy and matter encodes an image of the whole,' (Briggs and Peat, above at p. 112).

Wallace Stevens, a nonprofessed semiotician wrote the following which closely connects to notions of holistic change:

As cited in Briggs and Peat, at page 114:

A. A violent order is disorder and
B. A great disorder is an order.
     These two things are one.
               from: 'Connoisseur of Chaos'

To recall here a thought of Bohm: there is little differentiation between the imaginary and the actual at some stage of our understanding. As we evolve our analytic capacities, that is, our ability to factualize and to differentiate *this* from *that*, we learn also to distinguish the actual from the imagined. In each human being the resources of our acts in the world are this fusion of possible and realized, of subjective wish and emergent phenomenon. The manifest form of our ideas as mediate signs evolves in stages from primitive con-fusion to distinct and defined. The former is holistic. The latter is a special and therefore differentiated instance. The passage from the crypt to a place on the surface — from instinct to articulate expression — grows in this design.

According to Bohm, the 'implicate order' refers to this hidden cryptic con-fusion of actual and possible. The 'explicate order' is the surfacing of these two orders as distinct but correlated, as an intense, tense bond, (see Bohm on 'Hidden Variables and the Implicate Order' in *Quantum Implications*, eds. B. Hiley and F.D. Peat, 1987:38ff; see also M. Talbot, *The Holographic Universe*, 1992:84-85).

We know that wholes are interconnected by ellipses. From this understanding we see that ideas grow in multidimensional continua, spatially from culture to culture and temporally from then to now to whenever. I would like to briefly mention, *vis-a-vis* this last connection, Max Fisch's linking of Vico and Peirce on the pragmatic method, and thus on Rhetoric.

Fisch focused on similarities between Vico and Peirce, especially in their respective inventions of new sciences. Both looked to a new geometry — a new instrument for configuring space — for constituting the world of magnitude from its very element so that the investigation of the world would be not a mere 'contemplating it,' but will be engaged in 'making that world for itself,' (Fisch, 1986:201-226). Such recreating of the world, Vico said, would make of the image a more significant world. The image thus becomes *mattering* and 'more real than points, lines, surfaces, and figures are,' (Vico, 3rd edition of *The New Science*, 1744:349).

If Vico's New Science is a molding of the stuff of logic and mathematics into human form, in Peirce this process is an evolution of Icon to Index to Symbol, from Phenomena of living qualities, perceived, to principles for human societies. Vico's Science must be consequential among peoples of the world in 'the world of nations,' and this method of transforming the formal symbol to a crosscultural bridge is the method of rhetoric, (Fisch, above at p. 213).

Vico shows that the poetic logic of the Third New Science consists of metaphors representing actual bodies, and that the language of politics evolves from the human body that *matters*, that is re-presented in the idea of the nation-state viewed as a great body. Vico 'claims' only to continue the work of the ancients, namely to abstract ideas from the parts of the human body, of interacting bodies. The challenge to develop this abstracting skill remains, and one must learn how to fashion real living bodies out of the 'substance' of ideas, (Vico, 'Tropes, Monsters, and Poetic Metamorphoses,' from *The Third New Science*, in Pompa, 1982:224-245).

IV
Methods as Mode of Experiement

It has been said that the humanities link the arts with the sciences, (Nathan, 1989:11-15). But Peirce would argue that Humanism is not Pragmatism. The latter mediates, while the former envelops. The latter is experimental and experiential. The former bends back on itself, back toward priorism and the *idea* of a Human Nature.

The prioristic sense of a pervasive human nature persists. With this persistence the static world, the closed, completed world image, also persists. It is a *totalistic* image, whereas the predominant image of pragmatism is *holistic*. The former, again, is determined. The latter by contrast is vague and free.

Immanence of the former, the Humanistic prioristic image, is shrouded in secrecy and the forbidden. The crypts of the Pragmatic view of the world are intersticial, of a world opening. The Order of Human Nature is Given. Disorder of made human relations is invented.

In summing up: there is a force that emanates from fictive points on a fictive surface, from structures that are not only not yet built, but are unbuildable.   Still, this force is effectual.   So I understand Peirce's Rhetoric/Methodology of Semiotics, in part.

The challenge is not so much to render literal models of the 'unbuildable,' but to set the rhetorical play in motion, to *be* the play. Worth noting: an especially pertinent discussion by R. Harbison (1992:161-178) where he points out several historical moments in the world when the building of unbuildable buildings became 'almost a fashion or norm': — a code, (at page 174).   He notes that 'old codes of beauty' became deliberately violated. Ideology was turned inside out.   Matter made cosmic statements, (at page 175).

Finally we want to recall that Peirce held that the most important use for his Speculative Rhetoric is to discover itself *as* Method, reflexively, and then to discover how to discover new and other methods. This ability of Rhetoric, in Peirce, to climb out of itself, to avoid solipsism through a logic of relatives, through interrelations as basic units of meaning, presents an alternative to that Black Hole which scientists of complex systems seem to think is inevitable, (Davies, 1992).

Peirce's Methodology or Rhetoric is described by him as a seed, a 'kernel':

All Pragmatists will further agree that their method of ascertaining the meaning of words and concepts is not other than that experimental method by which all the successful sciences ... have reached the degree of certainty that are severally proper to them today: this experimental method being itself nothing but a particular application of an older logical rule, 'By their fruits ye shall know them,' (CP 4.465 [c.1905]).

The next chapter regards the Pragmatic method as 'acting out' as representing in representative theater.

Chapter 11

Eco and Dramatology

Eco and Dramatology

I
Introduction: Of Agon, a Trace

Inquiry into dramatology often distinguishes between two major types of theater: the *presentational* and the *representational*, (Ernst, 1956). These are 'antithetical forms' of theater, and as such, these forms are themselves in a kind of dramatic opposition. In 'presentational' drama the leading actor — all actors — is always the role, the character portrayed, and never the real person behind the mask and the costume and the script. In presentational theater the characters are directly, immediately, in communication with the audience. But in *representational* theater, the tradition of Western drama since ancient Greek theater, the leading player does not attempt to appear as an *actor*, but as a real person. Kabuki, for example, is presentational. Western theater, through, the nineteenth century, is *representational*. This latter is Peirce's traditon of 'representation' that he implicitly draws upon.

Similarly, Umberto Eco's writings on semiotics are of this same representational tradition.

In forthcoming work I will attempt a closer comparison between *presentational* and *representational* drama, following the excellent study of Kabuki by Earle Ernst (1956).

Here I include a somewhat modified version of a paper recently published in tribute to Eco (in Capozzi 1996):

That Eco makes frequent recourse to narrative fiction is not surprising since the semiotician and the author of fictive narrative are two of the most public faces he presents to us who adore and admire him from whatever portion of himself he gives freely and with great gusto. But what is a surprising fact, to use Peirce's notable term for that which comes to us from experience and shakes us out of old habit into new play, is Eco's occasional mention of the dramatic text as representing through the work of some twentieth-century playwrights a prototype of the indeterminacy, nonfiniteness, overcoding, continuous transformation, and, indeed, those marked characteristics which describe, especially, the Peircean theory of sign-process. This dynamical process is what happens to an idea or complex sign-system when the pragmatic method is used to perform its operations upon selected, featured thought-signs, so that the thought or representation of an object-thought moves, grows, becomes new meaning in the world of human values.

Peirce's drama is not dyadic, but triadic; there is always an implied point of reference, or shared value between player and viewer. But Peirce is far less explicit on this aspect of pragmatism than is Eco. The latter, however, also says little on drama as such.

The reference to dramatic text which occurs now and again, in passing, in the rich corpus of Eco's work, is most often to Brecht: — his theories on drama, and especially on the *Galileo*. I have read the playscript often and have had the good fortune to see it performed several times, each with markedly different interpretations in staging, on props, and on all aspects of those personnae which, in their entirety, constitute the players of this (and every) stage-play. Whether we want to call the Brechtian voice authorial or something else in the nature of a continuum, is not my concern in this paper. Rather, I want to suggest here that Eco's inclusions of the drama in his work are not sufficiently frequent to permit one to quite imagine the drama as a configuration in his own work, however elliptical. But perhaps it is more likely that each of his mentions and uses of the drama — Brechtian or other — appears at intervals, or interludes, and then submerges in the Eco-ic mind leaving fresh evidence of its existence and effect, or pragmatic consequences, *as a trace.*

To my knowledge Eco does not discuss the notion of trace, not as it occurs in linguistics nor in the discourse of the biological sciences: in the former, trace is that which is no longer evident in that sample of natural language under examination; and in the latter the concept of trace refers to some bit of living matter which came into existence, effected the cell which was its context and exerted such influence upon its context that a cell division occurs: it does its job and disappears, leaving only a 'trace' as consequence, (Hamburgh, 1971).

Eco veers close to affirming the characteristic structure of all semiotic processes as dramatistic. But to actually do so would require that he abandon his edenic — adamic — implied or tacit wish to hold onto a belief in the predictability of the world. Moreover, at the crux of this near affirmation is Eco's wanting to hold onto a kind of perfectibility, or aesthetic closure, of any complex idea regarded as a universe of thought. I am not sure, but I think Eco has ambivalent feelings on this matter: the wish for perfectibility and closure is never far from his observations of the semiotic process as nonfinite and without fixed limit.

It is my point, however, that the narrative model of discourse which Eco chooses over the dramatistic model is, at bottom, a sustained preference on his part of the *hypertactic* structure of the novel, however complex and sustaining it is of many voices. By contrast, the drama — dramatic play — is dialogic, interactive, and *paratactic* in its structure, (Kevelson, 1987). The hypertactic model is in western cultures identified with determinable events, whereas the paratactic model has been relegated to mere or trivialized recreation, an idea which has become attenuated to the notion of nonsignificant 'past-time,' (Kevelson, 1976).

For Eco to shift from one model to another would require that he undertake, as his leading principle, a *paradigmatic shift*. This would be nothing short of an ideological revolution, since the structures and the values each symbolizes are antagonistic if not mutually exclusive discourse types. This is not to say that segments of dialogue are absent from predominantly hypertactic texts, or conversely, that monologue is not be found in dramatic play. But the style or type of each of these discourses are not compatible, and to espouse one, in effect, is to subordinate the other.

Except, and this exception is in point, *the Peircean project, or 'quest of quests' aims to bring into new, more comprehensive relationship discrete universes of discourses and thus to create a new synthetic world of meaning.* This point would expect Eco to qualify his analysis of the use of hypothesis in discovery/detecting and to especially focus on its role in a logic of paradox. Eco does not go quite this far.

Eco does not quite affirm a genuine revolution in human values, nor does he give up the 'quest' for certainty. To do so would be to take risk as a serious matter, and to accept the irreversibility of the significant world.

Not even in his 'playing' of Sherlock Holmes and Charles Peirce against one another, with respect to the type of deduction each characteristically represents, does Eco *endorse* that which is the most 'revolutionary' or creative of the abductive possibilities he so brilliantly describes, (Eco, 1983, in *The Sign of Three* at page 207).

It might be noted that the risk-taking which characterizes dramatic play, especially the play of anarchic comedy, is not hypothetical, or 'overcoded abduction,' in Eco's terms; nor is it 'undercoded abduction' which Eco sees as the selection of one option from among others, all of which are 'known' and hence available for re-cognition and re-discovery, but not as a sign of a genuine Becoming out of Nothing.

But Peirce *does* distinguish between two kinds of nothings, or Zero Signs: the first is a result of the process of subtraction, in which nothing signifies 'other'; whereas the second Nothing is that potentiality and possibility from which the Firstness of all quality — all perceivable general ideas — emerges. This last Nothing is boundless, free, risky, undetermined. This is not the nothing which features in Eco's analysis of hypothesis, but it is the bottom line — an oxymoron, I concede — a Nothing which may become Some Things and thereby turn traditional logic on its head as in a logical wonderland: a paradox revisited, a Primal Play, (Kevelson, 1989, 1996). See Chapter Nine of this volume.

Yet Eco does again come very close to this position when he discusses the last and most important (in terms of evolving meaning out of the process of making meaning more meaningful) of his kinds of abduction. This he calls 'creative abduction.' Eco emphasizes the paradoxical nature of this kind of adducing process. He argues that it is in defiance of all traditional logic, since it brings, or invents, '*ex novo*' (Eco, 1983:207).

This genuinely creative abduction leads to and requires that the players/actors propose (or 'pose' in a quasi-positivist sense) that which may be assumed to support the creative Becoming. In this manner the process of accepting the element of genuine novelty — of risk and chance happening — leads to a reenforcement of an emergent future, by using the past or precedent as an invented instrument. The past is invented in order to act as a post-present and thus as a platform for a possible future. This is not a revision of the past, of history, but is an abducted historical frame of reference upon which to set a *possible* future as it emerges from a *postfuture present*. The present is then set in place, is staged, subsequent to the making of future and past, in that respective order. *The present is the last piece to be set in place.*

Contradictory to traditional wisdom, the past is not a prologue, but rather, it is the future which is invented as prological. The drama is between two worlds: the future and the past. The will to the future is protagonist, and the will of the past is antagonist in this abductive drama, a drama as aboriginal as the *hieros gamos* in the primal encounter of earth and human culture.

According to Eco, creative abduction differs from 'overcoded abduction' precisely on the dramatic character of the former. Or so I extrapolate. The overcoded mode of abduction proceeds by connecting 'imprints' or found marks with possible causal forces which are 'known,' i.e., defined and named. Such marks are significant in a synechdocical manner, (Eco, 1983:210-211). But by contrast, the creative process of abduction *makes* the very marks it uses in order to carry forward the abductive process itself.

But even this inventive creative abduction is not yet the method of a dramatistic semiotics, Eco points out. The dramatic mode is, he suggests, a meta-abduction. It is this meta-abduction which, he notes, is that which Peirce himself understands as 'an accord between mind and course of events . . . more evolutionistic than rationalist,' (Eco, 1983:218).

Whereas Sherlock Holmes is always eventually 'correct,' Peirce is ever fallibilistic and 'iffy.' I am not suggesting that the Peircean abduction is a 'kabuki' play, turning in all directions, endlessly, as permitted/determined by its referent conventions. Rather it is open-ended, as kabuki is: the structure is neither ziggurat nor labyrinth, but closer to the mid-twentieth century notion of a dramatic 'happening.' As noted above, the kabuki is *presentational*, whereas Peirce's dramatistic pragmatism is representational.

Surely there is little or no resemblance between this drama-type and the so-called 'well-made play' with *its* aristotelian beginning, middle and end: a finite curve with appropriate closure. Yet it is the older form which is the background and which serves, symbolically, as an obsolescent judgment in the wake of a Peircean 'surprising fact,' an event which calls the whole of what has been assumed to be known into question, into new perspective. In some respects, as Eco suggests, the process of meta-abduction is representative of, or a *verisimilitude* of, a Brechtian 'epical' piece of theater.

The Peircean meta-abduction, as the Brechtian drama, begins by focusing on a significant issue or problem, the concern of which draws the play's personnae into unprecedented relationships. The problem catalyzes the performance. What is at stake, as becomes clear, is not the resolution of the problem, but rather the nature of the relationships brought into play. By contrast, in the well-made play it is the problem brought to light which needs to be resolved and/or redefined.

Indeed, Eco's last word on the Conan Doyle/Charles Peirce contest is that they are not telling the same kind of story after all, but they are playing different roles, representing different types of discourse, different kinds of hypotheses and possibilities. A semiotic approach, which Eco takes, reveals that at bottom there are two incomparable scripts. He then goes on to suggest that a better fit is between Galileo and Peirce rather than Sherlock Holmes/Doyle and Peirce. It is the Brechtian Galileo to which Eco explicitly refers. Thus Peirce and Galileo play out their respective misadventures, with the proverbial 'nerve for failure,' and even perhaps the will, if not to lose, yet to keep the game going.

Eco says that the main difference between Aristotelian monologic deductive argument and the Peircean dialogic abductive argument is that the former attempts to understand 'surprising facts' by working out 'a hierarchy of causal links,' whereas Peirce lifts out the middle term of the aristotelian syllogism and recasts it as a new, noncausal function, as a hypothetical force or 'triggering device of the whole process.' According to Aristotle, the purpose of invention was to establish a 'good middle term,' while by contrast Peirce selects an arbitrary middle term as a relational nexus, a dramatic occasion, I might add, *between terms*. The Peircean hypothesis is mediator or semiotic fulcrum. Again, we see Peirce's emphasis on the pragmatic intermediacy.

This creative abduction is a kind of protagonist, in dialogic and dramatistic defiance of traditional logical hypothesis, since it invents/creates out of nothing, (Eco, 1983:207).

Such oppositional relationship is the very nature of drama, the meaning of which is the existential, experiential 'struggle' which Peirce assigns, as semiotic function, to Indexicality and Secondness. The drama is quintessentially a battle of wills, of worlds. The outcome is never given, but comes out of the interaction. The drama, as significant conflict, creates a yet-to-be encoded phenomenon. As such it is at play until classified and evolved from factive representation into symbolic representation or tool, i.e., from Index to predominantly Symbolic sign. The dramatic event is, therefore, radically distinct from both 'overcoded' and 'undercoded' abductive processes, as Eco shows us.

For my purposes here it is enough to recognize this pattern of emergence of the topic of drama in Eco's writings without at the same time feeling obliged to investigate, at this time, why it is as it is and not otherwise.

My interests in theater and the dramatic text go deep, and my experiments with writing dramatic script precede and underscore the points of view I bring to semiotics, to Peirce's pragmatic method in particular, and to Eco's important concepts of openness and overcoding in aesthetic texts, in point in this paper.

Given my orientation and well-known Peircean agenda I wish to turn the spyglass around, as it were, and look through the other end. I attempt to gain insight into some significant platforms of concurrence between Eco and Peirce with respect to the dynamical indeterminacy and openness of semiosis by using the drama as a many-faceted lens: an instrument for observing how signs grow, rather than for using selected principles of semiotic theory to explicate dramatic texts.

In brief, I want to note that in my early studies of drama, from the perspective of semiotics, I classified the system of dramatic dialogue as one paradigm among others within an over-arching concept of aesthetic paradigms, (Kevelson, 1975). At that time I was focusing on the special influence of the Prague Linguistic School and cross-referentiality, on distinctions between closed and open texts. I made good use of Veltrusky's and Karcievski's notable studies on theater and the significant interaction of all players. All actors including props, audience and the several styles of stage link or mediate audience with actors, (Veltrusky, in Garvin, 1964).

Without digressing too far here, I want to say at the outset that I still hold the view that drama, in its dominant feature, is characterized by interactions and patterns of plots or transformations and mutations (*muthos*, Ridgeway, 1904/1915:406). I go further and suggest that the drama is the representation of the semiotic process, *par excellence*, with respect to the special relations which connect artworks with events and institutions of actual human affairs. On the level of human affairs and social life I see The Law as linked with drama, as related with drama via the medium of human disputes and antagonisms, (Kevelson, 1991, 1993, 1994). Indeed, The Law as idea and in its practice represents the idea of theater, especially of the Indexical sign-function manifest in dialogue, i.e., in adversarial and inquisitorial interactions. Brecht's *Galileo*, as many of his plays, is foregrounded against the context of conflict of law, of ideological oppositions between instantiated law and other legitimations. Eco's references to Brecht constitute a pattern of his thought, I suggest, so broad that the design is visible only in part, that is, to one who presumes to take Eco at mere face-value, as an iconicity.

Just as some undercurrent of Eco's continuing concern with the function of the drama in semiotics percolates as an irrepressible insight, if I may so fancy, my own experience in scripting and exploring the many masks of drama also surfaces through this paper as a recollection, a recognition, a trace. Again, the Peircean emphasis on the dialogic, interactional nature of all semiosis is clearly dramatistic, but mostly by implication.

II
Tension and Sign-Production

When Eco speaks of sign-production we may, with minimal modification, substitute the Peircan term, *pragmatic method*. Eco says, 'We may define as invention a mode of production whereby the producer of the sign-function chooses a new material continuum not yet segmented for that purpose and proposes a new way of organizing (of giving form to) it in order to *map* within it the formal pertinent element of a content type . . . a semiotic mode of production (is defined as that action) . . . in which something is mapped from something else which was not defined and analyzed before the act of mapping took place. We are witnessing,' he goes on to say, 'a case in which a significant convention is posited at the very moment in which both the functives of the correlation are *invented*,' (Eco, *Theory*, 1976:345, 350).

The 'we' refers, presumably, to the inquirers — us — who perform the role of addressee or audience in relation to that which is before our eyes, which is appearing or 'featured' as *players*. The idea which we are attending is phenomenal, imagistically and iconically present — re-presented or made present — as Peirce uses the term 'dialogism' in the sense that Vico did, to refer to an evidentiary complex piece of significance that is brought into the judgment theater (court of law, specifically) to transform the virtual icon into a virtual fact or index, (Kevelson, 1987). The notion of 'mapping' in Peirce is, as it is used here by Eco, only *in some respects,* (Kevelson, 1993).

Mapping and staging are related. The former refers to a choice of iconic representations which do not replicate the object but which model it in ways that point up selected purposes for seeing it and for establishing a frame for a point of view. The latter marks the ground or locus — the space as a bounded context or frame — upon which an action is to be performed. Both map and stage, or ground, permit configurations since they are topical: —

definable topics (as in both the Topics of traditional rhetoric and in the surfaces of geometry). Plots, then, are patterns upon a ground, or transfigurations: shifts and rises and turns on a terrain.

The order of a play — its associating or paradigmatic arrangement — is a communicative sign to its audience at a level different from the way signs communicate information between the participants on stage. Within the play, the dramatic relations are equivalent to a semiotics of syntax; at a higher level, dialogue semantically reenforces its syntactic structure; at the level where the play influences the judgment of the audience, that is, conditions its habitual mode of perception (in Peirce's sense of 'judgment') its semiotic function is pragmatic.

In effect, the structure is not be viewed as a State, but as a process of Becoming; this implies a continual shift in perspective from functions which appear as interactions, extending in space, as alternately stabilizations and deformations, relative to their before and after positions, syntagmatically. The purpose in constructing 'models' of language is to be able to use them as ciphers — as Signs — which relate to the real world. The meaning of 'use' here corresponds to the meaning of 'function' in Prague School theory and method. Because the word *function* is homonymous with the term for 'correspondence between two mathematical variables,' its intended meaning of 'task' and 'role' becomes obscured.

Cartography and mapping play an explicitly important role in Peirce's semiotics (see mss 1349 - 1355, and, in passing, throughout his other writings). But staging is not explicitly used by him. I take liberty in suggesting we may presume that in Peirce's thought a stage refers to any space — graphed, bounded, defined — upon which ideas are shown to interact, as he himself shows with respect to his Existential Graphs, (Kevelson, 1987).

The concept of a stage, or place of performance, implies a distinction between that which is staged and that which is unstaged, i.e., between the marked actors and the audience, between the framed inner and the outer. In the experimental drama of the 20th century this 'line' between players and viewers is blurred, and becomes almost *immaterial* when we move from absurd theater, to 'happening,' to the cyberstage.

This precarious balance or semiotic tension is presupposed, however imperceptible it may be. Eco says, in point, that this tension is an aspect of aesthetic openness, and thus is integrally involved in the process of significance evolving, changing, growing. This tension is always an interactional process. This process is that same dynamical method of process of Peircean semiotics. The *display* of this tension is described by Eco as an infinite complex of significance that grows n-dimensionally, and is not at all confined to the elemental, to the emotional. Rather, as he refers to Brecht's theoretical writings, Eco indicates that 'dramatic action is conceived as the problematic exposition of specific points of tension,' (Eco, 1979:55).

In Brecht's plays it is not the play which solves the posited problem, i.e., 'devises solutions,' but it is the audience which 'draws its own conclusions' from what it has observed, from how it has interpreted the map or has estimated the amount of meaning so staged, (Eco, above, at p. 55). But the problem, laid out upon a *noneuclidean* topography, is not a fixed and unchanging problem; it shifts and moves, and is, therefore, not ever wholly solvable, says Eco. The problem is indeterminate and 'open.' Its encoded paradigms are, therefore, open as well. They are infinitely interpretable, like a Peircean idea which grows endlessly, as long as inquiry continues.

Eco goes on to say that drama such as Brecht's is an example of an intentional ambiguity, or so I extrapolate. It does not lead to a certain goal or conclusion, but to a provisional and ad hoc judgment only. This provisional solution may be reopened at any time, each time the play is performed. So the process of inquiry is continuously activated and reactivated. 'In every century,' says Eco, 'the way that artistic forms are structured reflects the way in which science or contemporary culture views reality,' (Eco, 1979:57).

The systems of 'play space,' 'logical space,' and living space (in daily, ordinary life) are assumed to co-relate in any historically-framed total social system; the relationship between systems is considered to be hierarchically ordered, but ordered differently at different times. Each type of space-frame, for example, functions as a sign but the predominant sign feature of each specific space-frame is sometimes iconic, sometimes indexical, and sometimes symbolic in relation to the overall social system. Analogous with the function of the aesthetic text as a marked sign in a 'defined' social system, each system competes for dominance, or foregrounding, against the background of the entire social network, (Kevelson, 1977).

Further, I observe that systems of Law and Order conceal their play origins by translating the terms of 'play space' to the discourse of 'logical space.' The element of play is apparent when we note how juridical systems contain, as integral with their total structures, the means of healing their own ruptures, and of acting in self-restorative and self-generative ways. Conflict and opposition are implicit in any code of law; periodic reconciliation of the legal contest is implicit also. Ultimately, all functioning, operative bodies of Law rest upon public consensus and the people's acceptance of rule-governed, rule-generating social behavior. Language, law, and social organization were the bones, brains, and blood of medieval society. The nerves, as the centers of sense, are signified by play activity, (Kevelson, 1977).

The dramatic play, as *Appearance*, is simultaneously illusion and disclosure, I suggest. The play as Sign frames the structure of the action on the dramatic stage — frames its plots — so that it achieves its intention, its deliberately ambiguous intention, by disrupting a conventionalized or symbolic appearance of order, of an ordered *habit* of expectation. It accomplishes a 'dissociation of sensibilities' which brings about recognition of an emergent new order, new meaning or value.

The appearance of a new order appears strange and unfamiliar. Since it is seen as grotesque it elicits for the viewer a protective pleasure. That which seems incongruous, foolish, absurd, belongs to the realm of the Comic. Comedy both affirms and undermines the *State*. In the indeterminate drama of this century the mode of the Comic is anarchic comedy: it is the voice of the rebellious puppet, in Durrenmatt's sense, who cuts free from the puppetmaster and says, 'nobody plays us', (Kevelson, 1965).

In Peircean terms, the action on the stage is analogous with a sign or *representamen* in relation to its referent ground. The personnae play against a ground. This ground is the *Immediate Interpretant* to which the interacting protagonist and antagonist refer. The viewer, or addressee, connects with the play. In the mind of the viewer is created a *new* idea. The action between players and audience is predominantly Indexical, just as the performance is predominantly Appearance or Iconic. The relation between problem and solution is provisionally final, as an emergent Symbolic value representing consensual compact between observer and observed.

The Peircean *interpretant* — Immediate, Dynamic, or Final — in any and all stages of its process never represents its object completely, but always leaves open a question, a possibility, a surplus meaning. In Peirce's words, the interpretant illuminates an idea of the object as seen against an idea or 'ground of the representamen.'

The Peircean pragmatic method, which is the way ideas evolve, as relations seen against a ground and transmitted to another who recreates and reinterprets, i.e., re-presents the idea against its ground, proceeds by certain movements. These *stagings* are rhetorical strategies or tactics — ploys of the pragmatic method — which Peirce identifies with what he called Speculative Rhetoric, or the *theory* of that Methodology which constitutes the Praxis of the Theory of Signs: Semiotics, (Kevelson, 1995).

This Speculative Rhetoric or Methodology, is the *doer* of certain acts: 'Its tasks is to ascertain the laws by which in every scientific intelligence one sign gives birth to another, and especially one thought brings forth another' (Peirce, mss 318; and Kevelson, 1987, 1990).

Referring to the role of dilemmatic constructs in evolving new ideas, Eco recalls that it is the principle of nonresolved disfunction which permits open inquiry to continue. He says disjunction permits open inquiry to continue. He further says that the term, 'perceptive ambiguities' is used to indicate 'the availability of new cognitive positions which fall short of conventional epistemological stances and which allow the observer to conceive the world in a fresh dynamics of potentiality before the fixative process of habit and familiarity comes into play,' (Eco, 1979:59).

In similar fashion Peirce also discusses how new ideas force their way through interstices, mere possibilities or cracks in the edges of existing, settled habits of thought understood as defined universes of discourse. The emergence of new ideas is always a struggle or an Agon. It is predominantly indexical, representing experience. Such struggle between habitualized states and revolutionary possibles is dramatic. New experience forces itself upon us, superimposing the novel on the known, creating a climate or ground of ambiguity. Surprise destabilizes, unsettles. Our whole system responds in effort, as a bracing, a tension, a mobilizing of all our existential forces, such that the physical feeds into the nonphysical, and visceral response is translated into an image, an appearance, a something inwardly pictured. The new appears as spatial, as is the ground spatial. But this space is also non-linear upon which the *quality* of the surprising thing occurs.

Although pragmatists are divided in their approach to many ideas, they are unified in the notion that the physical and the mental are but two kinds of *organizations* of the significant. But at the conceptual level of organization significant meaning becomes accessible to the operations of pragmatic/rhetoric tactics and transformations. The physical response to the unexpected represents a receptivity, an openness. The conceptual openness equivalent is inquiry: a waking to the idea of the possible (CP 5.478-79). Inquiry takes the form, first of all, of a conjecture, a free and unbound guess. Every new idea begins as a conjecture. 'Every conjecture is equivalent to and is expressive of such a habit, that having a certain desire one might accomplish it if he could perform a certain act' (CP 5.480).

Although Eco is not speaking of the drama in particular, but of the aesthetic work in general, his thought is especially pertinent to dramatic performance: 'The moment that the game of intertwined interpretations gets under way, the text compels one to consider the usual codes and their possibilities ... the aesthetic text becomes a multiple source of unpredictable "speech acts" whose real author remains undetermined, sometimes being the sender of the message, at others the addressee who collaborates in its development,' (Eco, 1976:272-276).

Throughout this entire section on sign production Eco and Peirce, to whom he refers, seem to be engaged themselves in a kind of interchange, where the differences between them are subtle but important. I don't think that at this point in his exposition of Peirce that the full impact of Peirce's dynamic pragmatism is accepted by Eco. Thus, the drama as vehicle and as representation of the drama as sustainable, indeterminate tension, is not confronted by Eco, head-on. But it surfaces, now and again.

In some respects, it seems to me that Eco is reluctant to give up the hold on stative grasps of semiotic 'moments' or events. For example, where he closely, with acute sensitivity, examines the Peircean concept of openness, he observes that the 'depth' of a term — a universe of discourse represented by a complex sign in other words, 'refers to its intension, or the sum *total* of its intensionality,' which is the sum total of its semantic content. And he continues, by noting that each term or system of marks or features increases as our knowledge of the idea grows. The rheme of each term is like a lodestone, Eco says, which draws into it 'all the new marks that the process of knowledge attributes to it' (Eco 1979:186). What he misses, in my view, is the dramatic process as such, since it is the action which, as *interaction*, carries the meaning of its motion — *e-motion, com-motion, motivation* etc. — in an ever-evolving, opening, spiralling configuration, in contemporary but not in classic drama or even in the so-called well-made play. It is only when we come to the mid-twentieth century that the Peircean notions, together with the significance of a quantum science with no fixed referent, can be touched as it passes, but not grasped, not quite.... In my opinion it is Peirce's logic of relatives which is the appropriate logic of dramatic art in general, and it is his logic of paradox which is the structure of the drama of our own times.

Eco's chapter on 'Peirce and the Semiotic Foundations of Openness' (1979:199) is itself quintessentially a dramatic exchange between two powerful players. It is a dialogue of which we hear but one voice. Eco's. I hear, in the background, an unexpressed but clear allusion (or so I create in my mind) to Strindberg's unforgettable one-acter: *The Stronger*.

III
Inner and Outer

Peirce begins his serious work with early testimony to the protosemiotic thought of the poet Schiller whose essays on aesthetic play came to constitute for Peirce the basis of his life's work, (Kevelson, 1987, 1993). The idea of play — of what he later called 'pure Musement' — came to represent the connective force between so-called states of ideas, states of symbolized concepts, as *interludes*. The rational sequence of numbers represented in Peirce's schema fixed and statal ideas defined for the *time being*, while the 'subterranean' or subsurface level represented a-lineal continua. The sequence of enumerated states on the surface were 'rational,' according to Peirce. The cohesive force was irrational, not confinable to bounded states.

This dialogue between rational and fluid playtime occupied Peirce and constituted a theme that ran through his work, even through his last writings.

As late as 1906, in the last decade of his life, Peirce observed that 'Every sane person lives in a double world, the outer and the inner worlds, of percepts and the world of fancies....' (cited by Buchler at page 283, and printed also in *Collected Papers*, 5.11-2; 464-8, 470-96).

This observation occurs in the context of yet one more attempt for Peirce to explain what he means by the pragmatic method, and how this method of pragmatism is dramatistic, agonistic, engaging inner and outer in the problem of transforming/renewing/creating habits of truths, i.e., habits of value and meaning.

Indeed, Eco takes up this conflict of inner and outer in his own memorable discussion of the 'subject of Semiotics.' Here he asks what the role of the 'acting subject' is, since it is this 'acting subject' which has a kind of 'ghostly presence' throughout his *Theory of Semiotics*, he says, and must finally *Appear,* (Eco, 1976:314).

Let us be clear about what is meant by the term 'subject' as Eco uses it here: It is not a person. It is not a grammatical function. It is not an egoistic self-reference. It is not a static concept. It *is*, says Eco, a position in relation to something. He says that 'This subject is a way of looking at the world and can only be known as a way of segmenting the universe and of coupling semantic units with expression-units: by this labor it becomes entitled to continuously destroy and re-structure its social and historical systematic concretions,' (Eco, 1976:315).

It is the empirical, externally observable, perceivable 'subject' which is the maker of such processes that permit communicative and other signifying process to happen, Eco says. To say that the empirical subject is not dual, but is doubled, is his way of emphasizing the basic relational reality of all semiosis. He stresses that this doubleness is not a metaphysical 'given' but is a 'methodological one' (1976:316). The external, or the manifestation of the 'subject,' is relational with, and not merely the obverse of, the whole interactional process which constitutes the process of all semiosis.

At this important point he affirms, and is affirmed by, Peirce, who remarks that it is the external symbols of language which provide the materiality of thought. But this material could not exist if it were not for their having been invented and produced by the semiotic persons who first imagine them, out of conjecture, out of response to the world.

We begin with some aspect of the Hieros Gamos, Peirce suggests: a rupturing of the bonded surface of the earth, and a celebration of that rupture which is both reparation, mourning, and something else: a surplus that comes out of the cultivation of this breach, this Game or Agon. We begin with the fiction of the Person and the fiction of the World, and with our dramatization of the juncture of these fictive personnae. People and their words reciprocally interact to teach one another, Peirce said. And 'the word or sign which man uses IS the man itself. For, as the fact that every thought is a sign, taken in conjunction that life is a train of thought, proves that man is a sign; so that every thought is an *external* sign, proves that man is an external sign ... the man and the external signs are identical ... the man is the thought,' (CP 5.313-314).

But in the sense that each semiotician gets outside himself/herself, it is especially the dramatic production which shows us how it is to violate the ancient laws of thought, the old static laws of identity, *such that one may be and not be*, such that it is possible to both be the 'Subject' and to be 'outside the Subject,' in Levinas' notion, (Levinas, 1987/1993:151-158).

It is the agon which re-presents relations of perception to fantasy in its primitive forms: We relive the moment of significance emerging, of Firstness in Relation, Value experienced as the overflow of Freedom, (Levinas, above, at 155).

Peirce transforms the 'I-It' relation to an 'I-Thou' relation: — a subject/object relation to a subject-subject relation — early in his long career, (Kevelson, 1987, 1993). This semiotic shift of viewpoint (in Jakobson, Veltrusky and others, in 1967, 1964 respectively) transforms stage props into 'subjects' for the actors, and converts actors into referent or focal subjects or 'properties' of situations and events: '... a given object in one situation is part of the set or costume and in the next becomes a prop.... In reality, however, its function is determined by the antinomy of two opposing forces contained within it: the dynamic forces of action and the static forces of characterization. Their relationship is not stable; in certain situations one predominates, in others the other. Sometimes they are in balance,' (Veltrusky, at 83-91). In tension we know a precarious dramatistic balance. When Eco speaks of the double aspect of codes (1976:299, n. 3) he emphasizes that iconic codes in particular are complex and 'double' (1976:302:n. 18).

The motion of inner and outer occurs also in relation to the performance as such, as medium between player and audience. Every performance is a kind of rehearsal: a reliving of a death or a solution that never comes to be, I suggest. Bloch, for example, refers to the concept of rehearsal, in the Brechtian sense, in which the role of the play-maker is to create the drama as a pragmatic instrumental crafter of paradigms, i.e., of value-systems, (see Bloch on Brecht, 1988:225-26).

This inner-outer relationship, especially in the Brechtian play, is explicated in a splendid paper by Tom Beebee, in which he discusses how the play moves from its outer frame to its internal plays, where each sub-play is a plot, continuously transforming, changing. Beebee describes also the 'doubling process' in Brecht, in particular in the *Good Woman of Sezuan,* (Beebee, 1992:47).

Beebee explores the Brechtian corpus to show the plays within the play. The several outers and inners of the subject, Play, is a way of infusing the 'Theaters' of Law with a dramatic 'crises in legimation' that the playwright sets in motion. Beebee makes his case that it is the 'judicial wrangle' which provides the possibility to 'create a picture of reality', (Beebee, above, 48). Thus the fantastic court, representing the actual law courts or judgments of the people, brings a perceptual sharpness into a juncture with apparent fictionalized inner trial of *Azdak the Judge/Actor*.

In point here Eco, referring to Lotman's theory of codes, describes Lotman's notion of code as a manual or how-to handbook with rules for generating meanings in endless, nonfinite productions. This results in overcoding or extracoding which enables participants in the sign-making performance to select from among a variety of possibles a *selected set of possibles*. Extracoding results in such freedom of choice: 'the multiplicity of codes, contexts and circumstances shows us that the same message can be decoded from different points of view and by reference to diverse systems of inventions, (Eco, 1976:139).

I want to conclude here with a question raised by Eco, which is as unsoluble as the questions raised by any indeterminate play: He asks, 'Is it possible to use the concept of possible worlds in the analysis of the pragmatic process of actualization of narrative structures without assuming it in a merely metaphorical way?' (Eco, 1976:218).

My response, as I suggested earlier, is that narrative depends upon the metaphoric connection to join possible worlds, whereas drama itself *becomes* a relation of possible worlds by means of its cross-reflexivization moving *between* the inner and outer, in the manner of a moebius strip, with no clear demarcation of either as outer or inner.

In brief, the connection between Eco and drama must be seen as one of implication, of ellipses and even of the 'occult.' Yet in what he chooses to connect with Peirce it is clear that the dialogic, interactional mode or style of semiosis is one he fully engages with.

Eco says of Peirce: 'The system of system of codes, which could look like an irrealistic and idealistic cultural world separate from the concrete events, leads men to act upon the world; and this action continuously converts itself into new signs giving rise to new semiotic system,' (Eco, 1979:195).

We know today that there is no turning back, that time is not reversible, that we are not medieval characters, but are actors with many masks. And we know that parallel lines *do* meet, that space *does* bend, that we may come face to face with ourselves in a time-space Euclid never dreamt of. Thus we are, indeed, dramatistic. Our semiosis represents such conflictual, indeterminate, massive-productions of meaning, and always a firstness and a Freedom and a plot.

Eco wisely reminds us to look at Peirce as 'not only a contradictory thinker,' but, he says 'he is a dialectical one, and more so than he is usually believed to be' (1979:195). Further, Peirce is a *mask*; he is as his ideas represent, a role, a part, a script: An Other. Each 'other' is a turning from a previous 'habit of thought' or self-reflexion. Each turning is a kind of revolution, of a violence integral with the ongoing Pragmatic drama, unfolding and unfolding. The following looks at this mode of creative violence in Peirce's 'agon.'

Chapter 12

Violence as Blind Spot
in the
Eye of the Owl of Minerva

Violence as Blind Spot
in the
Eye of the Owl of Minerva

I
The Texture of Ruins

According to well-worn interpretations of Hegel's gnomism on the 'Owl of Minerva,' it flies at twilight, after the dust stirred up by social revolutions have settled and when certain forms seem accentuated in dark, symbolic profile. In this crepuscular transition, the wise bird with night vision sees these forms as icons of conflict resolved. What happens is that every phase of social change, i.e., every social revolution, leaves its mark. That mark may glorify some aspects of the conflict past, and gloss over other aspects. The sign, or syndrome of signs, that come to represent social revolutions thereby become symbols of value of that upheaval. Or so the Owl of Minerva observes: She sees the forms against the darkening sky, but not the rubble.

Not all revolutions are violent. Most take place in such a manner as to appear as part of an evolutionary, rather than revolutionary, confrontation. Revolutions are a *kind* of evolutionary movement, but are that kind designed by people in a particular context who act with great force against what is perceived as no longer livable, no longer thinkable. But the social consciousness of the people involved, members of postrevolutionary uprisings, is formed by images transmitted by the Owl of Minerva, i.e., images developed for conscious apprehension, first as Icon, then as Index or visual Fact, and ultimately as Symbol or value-sign, (Foss and Larkin 1986, 77-80). Often the joy of unleashed violence, of orgiastic retaliation, are overlaid by the bird's selective eye; one then sees revolution in terms of pure motives, just rage, god's will. The human capacity to fabricate euphemisms for violent acts of all kinds seems to be an almost instinctual mode of self-preservation, inexhaustible.

The onset of social revolutions is framed by a set of laws: 1) 'the law of mounting stakes,' 2) 'the law of emergent contradiction,' and 3) 'the law of shifting terrain,' (Foss and Larkin, 1986:60-63). By analogy, we might say that the onset of conceptual revolutions — ideational evolution in Peirce's sense — corresponds to the same set, the same triadic phases of change in the semiotic development of thought. For example, 'the law of mounting stakes' may be seen as analogous with the tension between judgment provisionally held and new emergent evidence which threatens to unseat and replace old knowledge with new. The law of emergent contradiction emphasizes the indexical function, as in Peirce's pragmatic inquiry into the changing meaning of conceptual signs with emphasis on the oppositional character of change, *of its dialogic and agonistic nature.* The 'law of shifting terrain' may be compared with the movement of a whole focus of thought to elsewhere, to new relations within a broad contextual area or frame of reference, i.e., another universe of discourse.

These correspondences are not those I invent. Peirce's pragmatism has been cited as paradigmatic for social revolutions in general, and in particular, for the mode of violence characterized, at bottom, by revolutions of all kinds. The role of violence in revolutions, in conflicts that do not only fall within the defining borders of the meaning of war as such, is often, even usually in many cultures, suppressed, denied, regarded as taboo and nonmentionable.

Hannah Arendt's famous study, for example, *On Revolution*, observes that violence, because of its consequences of utter devastation, has only been marginal in most revolutions i.e., most movements of radical social change, since violence makes humankind dumb, silences speech, deletes political instruments for negotiation. Arendt's assumption is that since people are first of all political creatures, then absolute violence is always marginal since full expression of violence is anti-political, is absolute destruction of victim and violator alike, (Arendt, 1963:8-10).

From this point of view, the function of violence must always be understated and kept in marginal place, since to do otherwise is unthinkable, as it is unthinkable to actually *see* one's own annihilation, according to the psychologists.

Many theorists choose to distinguish revolution from violence and to define revolution as a major social reversal of theoretically complete social systems. Revolution here is not necessarily based on the use of force and violence, but is a change brought about by a shift from one system of laws to another legal system, (Edward, 1927/1970). In Peircean terms, one referent system of lawfulness, consensually and/or authoritatively regarded as synonymous with a 'correct' representation of legitimate values, is transformed into another legal system of legitimate values, of signs, and hence into another complex of leading principles. This is never a simple substitution, but is a transformative process like great magic facilitated by fireworks, explosives, smoke and mirrors.

In contrast, Ye-Lin Cheng shows that revolutions are integral with societies that are vital and growing. Revolutions are therefore part of everyday life. But revolutions that succeed in unseating old authority may not further succeed in establishing new non-authoritative leadership, with the usual result that the former problems tend to return in new masks, (Ye-Lin Cheng, 1973:xxii).

In this paper I want to look at the idea of violence as it concerns law, from the perspective of Peirce's pragmatic method of his theory of signs. While this is not an 'apology' for violence, nor even an attempt to explain its occurrences in social revolutions, it seems that there is a connection between social violence and revolutionary/evolutionary movements in societies, and that process of revolutionary/evolutionary development of ideas or signs which we find in Peirce's semiotics.

II
Optimal Instability

It is now nearly a half-century since A.F. Skinner wrote his seminal article on the social control of human violence, (Skinner, *Science* 124 1956:1057-1066). In 'Some Issues Concerning the Control of Human Behavior' Skinner points out three main areas which provide codified *norms* for behaviors: the first is indicated as 'personal control'.   This includes intersubjective relationships in family, friendships and organizations of work and recreation. This interpersonal control of behavior is based on constraints imposed against violations of acceptable behavior of some toward others in these groups. These constraints — tacit and/or overt — are sheltered under an interpersonal canopy called Ethics.

The law is expected to bridge these legitimate constraints of a-social conduct, and to correct the personal strategies of control, of censure, of ridicule, of punishment, with institutions of government. Where state and church are not overtly interconnected, organized religion colors the ethical constraints of social control with the 'values of morality.' Whereas law, in balance, is presumed to be primarily concerned with secular and non-moral (i.e., theological) percepts of human behavior. In societies where church and state are generally held to be in principle separate, ethics and morals tend to be regarded as nearly synonymous. Natural Law exemplifies this fusion of ethical-moral interpersonal control.

We note in this respect that certain 'goods' are said to 'Given,' i.e., are prioristically integrated with that idea called Human Nature: so invented or so-called to facilitate easy fusion of legitimacy and legality under the banner of ideally *human* relationships. But when this fabrication of ethics and morality comes apart at the seams we begin to perceive widespread social misgiving which resembles a general shared public guilt regarded as a consequence of a failed aspect of Human Nature. This 'failure' suggests that society should be purged. Such purging is seen as a turnabout in the authoritative, official forces of that flawed society.

Thus a legal system plied with social ethics and religious morals is changed and corrected by means which differ from those which would apply to legal systems that presuppose experimentation, evolving values, and open-endedness. The latter type of legal system, based on experimentation, is indeterminate. The former, of a causal and determinate nature, requires radical overhaul rather than revision and reformation. The former at first seems clearly Peircean, and not subject to the ravages of revolution and violence. But we will see this is not the case. *It is only the case as reported by Minerva's Owl.*

Actually, the kind of indeterminate legal system which represents a Peircean dynamical sign-system, continually in flux, is *optimally* unstable. An optimally unstable legal system is an oxymoron, a paradox. Yet such incongruity correctly characterizes the process of evolving sign-systems in Peirce's view. It correctly characterizes dynamical, open legal systems also. Thus it cannot be avoided. The 'norms' of such sign-systems, whether of law or other, is that they are continuously in revolutionary mode. Violence in the conflict of systemic change is part of the *nature of the beast!* From this point of view continuous shifts of value with respect to *expected* social behavior is kaleidoscopic. Value norms are seen as chiaroscuric: unsettled and signifying impending climatic and transition as between day and night, at dawn and at twilight when the Owl takes wing. Such turbulence calls forth appropriate response from law's referent society a great outpouring of adrenalin.

Violence, it is said, is a manipulation of a process of adaptation. The more adaptation that is required, the more violent is the response, (M. Gilulan and D. Daniels, 'Violence and Man's Struggle to Adapt,' in *Science*, 164 1968:396-405). In this paper the authors point out that the interaction of biological and cultural evolution have brought about increased human ability to change, to make rapid changes. Survival in this new age of rapid change is increasingly reliant on the ability to adapt in aggressive and often violent manner. The violence is, from this point of view, 'good,' since it is a tool of adaptiveness. The inability to adapt is predictive of nonsurvival. The presupposition is that survival is better than nonsurvival. Hence it is not violence which is perverse as a 'good,' but nonviolence which is perverse and not-good. The refusal to survive is logically not-good. Rhetorically, or dialectically, nonviolence becomes synonymous and equivalent with the 'will to self-destruct.'

I am indeed suggesting that quiescence is not only self-destructive but as antithesis to a Peircean pragmatism is antithetical also to that dynamical process which characterizes viable evolving inquiry and distinguishes it from one which is static and based on static modes of quiescence. I will return to this point.

The law in democratic societies understands the failure to take steps to prevent predictable harm as a form of negligence. At the same time the law is entrusted with the responsibility of controlling violent behavior. Even war is widely understood as violent but legitimate and just, for the purpose of survival, in some cases. In such cases where it is equated with self-defence war is violence in the interests of survival, of humankind.

But to return here to Skinner's three-fold areas of violence referred to above, we find that the first set of ethical assumptions, grounded in norms for interpersonal behavior, are presumed to be law's mandates. This first set of ethical presuppositions are reenforced by assumptions held in two other areas: government and education. Arendt refutes this thesis, as do others, (Arendt, 1963).

Today the places of education are mainly the classroom, the dinner table, and the street. But for those who do not escape the lessons of the classroom, educational institutions teach normative rules for human behavior in insidious fashion. Corporal punishment is rarely permitted in most democratic societies, and political correctness is rewarded. Collaborative projects rather than the hard learning by individuals in risk-taking, exploring the 'nerve for failure,' is encouraged. Performance rather than initiative is stressed. Playing the game instead of winning the prize tends to level out irregularities and to bury violence in disposables.

Societies which employ educators to test educational techniques — their own performances mirrored — rather than take chances on 'creative disorders' as ongoing value processes, result in short-lived survival of mediocrity and, long-range, in utopic realizations of crystals, of rocks: the inert.

Yet it is genuine fear and horror of violence so widely enacted in the schools of our young people today that blinds the law and the gentle people law represents to the fact that violence, like other weapons, has meaning only through the interpretive significance that human inquiry supplies. This is Peirce's criticism of what he sees as Berkeley's fatal flaw: namely the fact that the good Bishop endowed fire with heat, viruses with illness, falling trees with noise, etc., instead of recognizing that these meanings are the outcome of relations between observer and observed, between I's and the Thou's in all semiotic interpretive relationships.

As for Government, the third sphere for regulating human conduct according to Skinner (above), it has increasingly attempted to regulate and to shape a 'behaviorally engineered society,' while at the same time government masks mayhem, murder, mugging, and the mutilation of the powerless under a marquee which lights up Government's star players: Hate Talk Playing First Amendment Rights; Depravity Dressed Up as the Deprived. When Government acts as the official control of human conduct it arbitrarily sanctions some kinds of interpersonal violence while condemning other kinds of interpersonal violence, where both seem, on the surface, to be merely different modes of adaptation and survival. The institutions of government come to be eventually perceived as themselves out of control, dysfunctional, irrational, dangerous: as targets for social revolution, *of law against law*.

Where is Law? Is it alive in the representations by instantiated institutions however malfunctioning? Is it as the counter-law which is, in effect, that triad of increasing risk, of shifting ground, of contradiction? Is law in the same 'space' as this counter-law in this tripartite division, a triad that *seems* to correspond with the Peircean semiotic divisions of changes of meaning of meanings? Is it to be identified with the *opposition* as such, with the *relation* as such, with the *agon*, the *revolution*, the *violence*? Is law, like all other conceptual signs a holistic term replete with obverse and reverse 'faces': with law and counter-law as positive/negative of the same term? Is it then a violation of an old sacred 'law of thought'?

In the following I will explore some of these questions. I will also recall in closing brief excerpts from George Sorel's several nods to Peirce's pragmatism, implicit in his own idealistic *Reflections on Violence*.

It is not far-fetched to suggest interrelations between Sorel's and Peirce's ideas since their paths conceivably may have crossed often. Their ideas surely crossed and criss-crossed, directly and indirectly, mediated by others known to both these men advocating revolution, but each on different ground with different means and for different goals. Sorel wrote in the first decade of the 20th century, a time when Peirce was unifying his complex ideas on Semiotics, and when Holmes was changing the United States Constitution which he served as Supreme Court Justice since 1902, (Kevelson, 1990, 1996).

III
Ethics of Survival

It is not only Peirce but also his successor to pragmatism, John Dewey, who explicitly discusses the tendency for the forms or states of ideological complexes to rise above the actual social relations that comprise a given society. The State may be regarded as a special invention of government, a discovery as it were of the idea of the State as instrument, indeed an indispensable and invocable instrument. In such manner, Dewey suggests, reminiscent of the Hegelian Owl of Minerva, that the forms are abstracted from living experiential ground and elevated to the status of eternal symbol.

According to Dewey, 'there is no reason for assigning all the values which are generated and maintained by means of human associations to the work of states. Yet the same unbridged generalizing and fixating tendency of the mind which leads to a monistic fixation of society has extended beyond the hypostatizing of 'society and produced a magnified idealization of The State.' (Dewey, from *The Public and its Problems*, 1927/1954:70-71). Note the clear allusion here to Peirce's now classic work, 'The Fixation of Belief,' in which he lays the ground for subsequent development of the process of pragmatism: the making of matters of fact from the imagination, coupled with the 'Brute Force' of Experience. The Icon, related to the Index, evolves to new Symbolic representations of thought.

Again, in this 1920's work, Dewey says: 'The State is that idea which people create to represent the kind of political structure which has been made. The State is an idea, a product of people.' (Dewey, above, pages 41-45).

There is a strong tendency to raise that which one has created as ideal, above criticism. Thus the ideal of the State becomes so raised, 'beyond criticism,' (Dewey, at 71, above.). This tendency has evolved from certain philosophical 'schools,' Dewey says, namely those associated with the thought of Spinoza and of Hegel, (above, at 71).

Once this immunization of the state is accomplished any revolt 'against the state is then thought to be the one unforgiveable sin,' (Dewey, above, at 71). But this is a circular logic, Dewey reminds us, and is among the worst of fallacies employed in the so-called name of Good. *Ad Hominem* arguments are simply the reverse of this coin, with the special feature that the antithesis of the Ideal Good has also been set in place and used to represent pariahs, scapegoats, untouchables in another marked sense, I would add.

Thus appeasement and palliative supplication becomes public modes of address toward the State which increasingly brings its authority to bear on all aspects of human relationships. When government, this third sphere of Skinner's triadic source of social norms, assumes official control of human conduct, it uses its power to arbitrarily sanction some kinds of interpersonal violence and to condemn other kinds of interpersonal violence. It selects the *who* and the *what* — and the *how* and the *why* — that are eligible for adaptation, i.e, for survival. Such states have small tolerance for great change.

Peirce's mature writings regard the awareness of change as one of the prerequisites for bringing about resolution of the mind-body relation and for understanding each as an idea that represents a way of acting as a partisan of the world. Awareness of differences and awareness of change as it happens is the basis of psychological functions in developments of new ideas from old, from established states, or statements, of provisional 'true beliefs,' (ms 680, c. 1910).

When a dynamical method of reasoning, such as the pragmatic method of evolving signs-as-ideas, is not followed the result is that the people of a society turn to idealized notions of the fixed, the eternal, the closed and stative *topic*. Open, changing, responsive systems of signs tend to represent the will of the many, the habits of power-holders. According to Holmes this is as it should be. Holmes's notion is that people deserve the kind of law they get. This is right and just, he suggests. The law should be an instrument to enforce the will of the mighty, to legitimize and legalize that will. From this Holmesian point of view the law does not legislate morality. It *does* legitimize the perceived will of the people, its Sovereign. If the Sovereign is an idea defined to represent an equivalence with The State, the consequence of that reasoning is a stative or static system. But if the idea of the Sovereign is otherwise denoted, then the Sovereign as ruling concept may represent the 'virtues' of instability, indeterminateness, change.

The choice of an open, dynamical, evolving society includes the choice or option of experimentation. To refer to Skinner once again, he notes that 'to choose to experiment is a value choice,' (above). The very assumption of free choice underlies the belief — *working hypothesis* in Peirce's sense — which is translatable into consequential action in pragmatic terms. Human conduct, it is presumed, is capable of adapting to a world of meaning *made by human beings*. Such a meaningful world — a Real World — facilitates adaptation and keeps open and alive a primitive vital instinct for survival.

The notion of choice implies human belief in human ability to solve its own puzzles. It suggests that such choices are created in a kind of 'user-friendly' environment, one which reduces the possibility of debilitation of raw, *mere* survival adaptation. Such choice also implicitly requires that violence be an active agent, one that may be called into action and used effectually toward realization of chosen purpose.

From this point of view the first ethical structure would be: Thou Shall Survive, since survival is the basic condition for anything else to become possible. It is the indispensable condition of all normative codes of human conduct which do not perversely distort the consequential meaning of this, our human chance. It is an assertion to the future of this our actual life. It is possibility at its most pessimistic. And it is urgency, an unrepeatable significance of this and no other duplication of a chosen experiment that matters, *that matter us*.

IV
Brute Force as Survival Index

Georges Sorel's famous or infamous *Reflections on Violence* discusses what he calls the 'Ethic of Violence,' (Sorel, 1906/1960). He admits that there has been so much written on the destructive aspects of violent action, and so many precautions taken against engaging in such action or being in the path of it, that it is now generally assumed that violent behavior is always a sign of 'a return to barbarism,' (Sorel above, at 180).

Sorel mentions in passing that excessive concern with gentleness at all costs is a mark of more than a 'little stupidity,' and he goes on to develop his thesis that violence is but another name for opposition expressed honestly and strongly, according to the 'rules' for the 'good fight.'

It is his emphasis on the oppositional structure of violence which brings it clearly into the Peircean camp, with its special emphasis on the mediational functions of the indexical sign: the sign of *brute force*, of dialogical interaction, of drama between the personnae I and Thou in a unit of relationship. This *dyad* evolves to triadic symbolic force.

While I don't share Sorel's syndicalism, I do have deep empathy for the anarchism which was at some historical moment a kissing cousin with Sorel's syndicalistic advocation of labor strikes and revolutions which assert one's will to survive, to *shape a circumstantial world so that one may adapt to it*.

It is unproductive to belabor an affinity that does exist between Peirce and Sorel, because the distinctions are no less marked, no less significant. Sorel points out that he sees, from antiquity, two traditions of people who 'reflect' upon serious matters such as violence and survival as a risk-taking drama: one he calls the tradition of the 'scholastics' and the other of the 'mystics.'

The former, as he generalizes, 'believe that our intelligence, taking the evidence of the senses as the point of departure, may discover how things really are, express the relations which exist between essences, in a language which is evident to every reasonable man, and thus arrive at a knowledge of the external world,' (Sorel, above, at 255).

But the way of the mystic requires that the 'reflector' be an isolated person, one who is in relation with himself/herself, or has joined with a group who almost exactly mirrors, i.e, reflects his/her mysticism. One must refuse and reject the fallacies on which modern democracies are built in order to see violence as instinctual link in authentic relations between people.

Sorel is a mystic, yet Peirce is not. But Peirce at the end of his life is not a member of a scholastic tradition either. It is this stepping in both worlds which permits Peirce to represent himself as medium, as nexus, and as schismatic as well. He is such a paradox, reflecting on violence as does Sorel, but moving it forward as *recovery of the primitive* with a *New Wave Human Being*.

A Peircean Semotics takes measure of Sorel's meaning of violence and builds on it. Sorel's understanding of violence in revolutions — in thought as well as worker-management relations — underscores the need for an adaptive role of violence in the interests of survival, and in the promise of such possibles in which violent destruction will always be a last-resort measure. Violence, in Sorel, is that measure that must be taken, especially in non-cyclical, dynamical option for a world which is always in flux, becoming, mattering.

Such violence becomes celebration in the cultivation of the earth in ancient mythologies. The breaking of the ground in preparation for growing, building, creating, sees such violent acts as prerequisites for making the earth a means, i.e, our human medium. Peirce's 'myth', I suggest, is tied to the 'mark of the gryphon,' (Kevelson, 1998).

Sorel asks us to investigate how the law can walk such a tight rope, how it can balance legitimate violence with compassion. A semiotic inquiry begins by asking how one may define, within the discourse of the law, violence as catalyst for realizing human values. Violence, minus the rhetoric of those who wish to remove it from the gentlefolk, is energy *no more, no less*.

A semiotics of law may point out that the law wants new directions for its assessments of violence, and that these assessments should be forthcoming not only from the Skinnerian triad of spheres of influence — education, government, and the general public — but also from those of us who take a random position with respects to the mainstream, as Sorel in his better moments claimed to do. And Peirce, poor Charlie, walked the country roads of Milford, Pennsylvania, looking neither left nor right, they say, but inward.

Peirce knew that the violent person and the iconoclast are signs of one another: of representation and never as mirror-image.

In the following, final chapter of this book I look at an 'elemental Peirce' and his Cosmology.

Chapter 13

Cosmology: An Elemental Peirce

Cosmology: An Elemental Peirce

I
On the Cosmic

Cosmology is a yellowed, mellowed word: a bit archaic and somewhat quaint. Yet it is a word that turns up with surprising frequency in speculative writings not only in philosophy but in a wide range of disciplines: all the way from the fine arts to the physical sciences.

In the ancient world speculative inquiries into cosmologies and origins were attempts to identify supreme causal force or divine act with the design and process of the universe. The search for patterns, for systems of regularity, were believed as early as Thales to be evidence of some rational plan for how it all came to be and where it is all headed. The ancients imagined, even wished, that the world represents a plan, an idea, and not a mere coincidence. But even if things have come together by coincidence, by 'pure chance,' then the 'moment of its coming together' is a state of its being: *a Real*. The gamelon of eastern cultures celebrates this synchronicity in music. Western culture celebrates it in jazz. This emphasis on the role of Chance in cosmic design has come in and out of favor in the development of philosophy, especially western thought which has oscillated over centuries, even millennia, between the poles of determinism and indeterminism.

Peirce's pragmatism heralds the renascence of indeterminism. Peirce's concept of Tychism or Pure Chance does not become subordinate to his notion of cosmic love or agapism, as a few misreadings of Peirce from time to time suggest. Chance, in Peirce's view, is the fulcrum which permits disinterest between individuals to hinge together. This agapistic relation is a kind of 'butterfly hinge.' I want to associate the 'butterfly' with the image of the ancient idea of the psyche. Thus Peirce would show how the emotions evolve out of inferential, semiotic interpretation of novel, chance happenings. The psychological, insofar it is not confused with instinctual predilection, evolves from Peirce's broadly-defined 'thinking' and not the other way around, i.e. thought out of emotional feeling.

I mention these distinctions only in passing here, since this concluding chapter on Peirce's Pragmatism is, like a butterfly, transitional. It is a forecasting of the following, *Peirce and the Mark of the Gryphon,* (St. Martin's Press, 1998). Here I have turned over the ground and have let some light through.

Every major philosophical system has attempted to place its edifice upon cosmological piers. I deliberately avoid the use of the word, 'foundation,' which has already become overburdened in recent years. But a cosmology is just that means of support that will carry the weight of a ramified, complex idea. As we know, some footings are in mud, some in water, some in sand, and some below frost on nonshifting earth. A cosmology is an anchoring of first principles, or a world-view in such manner as any given intellectual climate and ground-swell of opinion permit.

A cosmology is a picture of the universe. A cosmology is a map of the universe. A cosmology is of the nature of an iconic idea-sign, in Peirce's sense. It is a vision which moors a full-furled philosophy. Sometimes a cosmology is unstated in certain eras. Sometimes, as in our recent past, it is denied. And sometimes it is resurrected and observed, *as such*. Here I attempt the third way.

It is not on Peirce's agenda to do meta-cosmological investigation. He tells us in what his cosmology consists, and then puts the problem aside. But within the past two decades there has emerged renewed concern with the idea of cosmology, and especially with two aspects of this idea: 1) with the felt need among those in vanguard areas of the physical sciences to find some affinity between large cosmological principles and sub-microcosmic principles and phenomenal behavior, and 2) comparative complex ideas on grand cosmic scale.

The latter can be seen as an outgrowth of a notion of pluralism which is itself an integral part of Peirce's pragmatism. Toulmin, for example, gives us such a comparatist view of the competing cosmologies in the third quarter of this century, (Toulmin, 1982:89-216). He also discusses a contemporary scientific mythology as a mode of cosmology. A large part of this current renewal of interest in cosmologies has to do with a widespread wish among *some* intellectuals to be able to ground human values and achievements upon *reasonable* assumptions, i.e., upon rationality however defined, and not have merely as a collection of nonrepeatable, nonpatterned bits of pieces of data before them. But, admittedly, other intellectuals and spiritual vanguards such as Levinas (1987/1993) oppose the dominance of reason and seek return to faith and direct revelation of god-as-other.

The present challenge is, broadly put, how may one leap from the appearances of things to what these appearances mean, i.e., to their 'reality' in terms of human meaning or significance, (Toulmin, 1882:11). Traditional reasoning does not permit valid leaps of this kind. But Peirce's expanded reasoning, that is, his method of pragmatic reasoning, does precisely this. Peirce himself recognized the critical importance of his pragmatism. But for a myriad of obstacles, self- and other-induced, he never quite made his case. The case, to be 'made' would require the affirmation of others, and this has not happened. Peirce's pragmatism opposes claims of direct knowledge, and assumes all knowledge is indirect by means of representations of signs. Peirce's Pragmatism is counter-intuitive and hence 'suspect'.

Even in his lifetime Peirce knew that *his* idea of Pragmatism was quickly being co-opted and distorted before his very eyes by no less than his trusted friend and colleague William James. His attempt to retrieve this concept by renaming it *pragmaticism* was a futile gesture. The term, 'pragmatism', took root and went on to become, if not a general household word, a public property appropriated from the conceptual storeroom of common resource as a versatile tool, capable of application in many ways. The general notion of pragmatism as 'useful' in an expedient manner has stuck. But this became so general a term that each special appropriation has called forth a new, theoretical definition to fit with a new specialized jargon. Thus the pragmatic notion of linguistics and the pragmatic notion of law are at this point barely kissing intellectual cousins.

In almost singular fashion at mid-century, prior to the recovery of Peirce from the stockroom shelves, Donald MacKay reminded us that it was Peirce, and not James or Royce or other to whom we owe a new cosmology, a world view for the next millennium. I strongly suggest a re-reading of this important piece, (MacKay, 1950:387-404). Here MacKay says that Peirce's Pragmatism 'seems to have rather suddenly precipitated itself out of the air,' (above, at p. 387). And while it attempted to make a place for itself by demurring, by saying of itself that it was merely a new way for stating old ideas — Peirce says that philosophy should avoid originality — it was fundamentally novel, radical, unprecedented. *Peirce's Pragmatism is nothing less than a new cosmology,* MacKay holds, as do I.

I want to emphasize here that Peirce regards his expanded logic, otherwise called Semiotics, as representing two major leading value principles: the first is that logic is 'rooted in the social principle,' (from 'The Red and the Black,' reprinted in Newman, 1956, Vol. II, p. 1339). In this same essay Peirce notes that the 'general problem of probability is simply the general problem of logic,' (above, at p. 1334). Thus probability is part of that logic which derives from community, or in other words from the social principle. Further, insofar as the ideal community may be conceived of as continuing indefinitely, and since the idea of probability 'essentially belongs to a kind of inference which is repeated indefinitely,' probable continua and the idea of an indefinitely continuing society are, respectively, the means and the end for understanding the human community, in Peirce's view. He is unmistakably explicit on the constituent principles of his new logic, of semiotics. These leading principles, the tripod upon which a cosmology rests, are: 'interest in an indefinite community, recognition of this possibility of this interest being made supreme, and hope in the unlimited continuance of intellectual activity.'

These three cosmological principles are essential to the pragmatic method of semiotics, (see p. 1140, above).

Toulmin, in his attempt to articulate a cosmology of the future, says it is impelling to 'abandon the Cartesian dichotomies and look for ways of "reinserting" humanity into the world of nature. Instead of viewing the world of nature as onlookers from outside, we now have to understand how our human life and activities operate as elements within the world of nature ... only a broader, more coordinated view of the world of this kind can pick up once again the legitimate tasks undertaken by the traditional cosmology before the "new philosophers" of the seventeenth century led to its dismantlement,' (Toulmin, 1982:255-56).

Before focusing on what Peirce refers to as his 'hyperbolic cosmology' I will briefly point to what spokespersons from the physical sciences have been saying in the interests of a participative human/natural world-cosmological stance. There is a new mythology being hatched. It is, as all new mythologies are, grotesque: it comes from the grottoes of the human imagination, from the interstices of a felt world-wish. It is not a phoenix rising from ashes as a repetition in a cyclic vision of the world; but it is another creature, a bird of a different feather: a gryphon. The gryphon, close kin to dragons and serpents, is uroboric in its ability to represent a wish for cosmic coherence. But it is not circular. It is distilled and possible. The gryphon, as represented by the lily, by the triadic mark it leaves of itself in shifting ground, once signified in the western world the instinct for trade in open marketplaces. It became the sign of merchants pushing ever north to the ends of the earth and beyond. The grotesque, as we know, signifies the emergence of new value, (Kevelson, 1993; 1990)

The grotesque is new and yet continuing value. Peirce takes as his talismans this sign of fusion of mathematical/rhetorical/pragmatical-methodological mode of an argument that continues indefinitely, stretching and stretching ... and of hyperbolic space, i.e., 'endless three-dimensional space stretching,' and infinitely more spacious than homoloidal space, 'space that is curvilineal everywhere,' (Rucker, 1985: 101-102, 110-111).

Let us remember that Pure Rhetoric is Peirce's synonym for Methodology and for Methodeutic, i.e., for the *pragmatic method* of inquiring into the evolution of ideas. Let us also remember that Peirce claims that the noneuclidean topical geometry is the most appropriate mathematical approach for understanding an area of thought as an analogue of spatial place, (Kevelson, 1987, 1990, 1993, 1996).

From this deliberate punning, or superimposing of one idea upon another, Peirce makes a new cosmological 'image': a hyperbolic universe of thought. He materializes an idea. He transforms spirit into gold, as the alchemists essayed. Indeed, he turns the relationship between mind and matter on its head: where 19th into 20th century mainstream thought held that ideas evolve out of physicality and transcend the physical, by contrast Peirce says, as did Boyle before him, that mind is the earlier stage, and matter the evolved or achieved stage, (see Chapter Two in his volume; see also Kevelson, 1996).

A contemporary philosopher/scientist of this late twentieth century remarks that a cosmology, *as such*, requires a substantive cosmos. It is a requisite for any cosmology to be able to refer, as a coherent and well-defined complex idea, to some actuality, some existent. The existent world as a material entity must be sought, if not seen, if a world-view is to signify anything other than dreams and vapors, (for discussion see Paul Davies and John Gribbin, 1992, at 112 ff).

For Davies and others involved with the inquiry into complex systems in our time, there is concurrence with Peirce on his three requisites, noted above, for the new logic of semiotics: the interest in a continuum community and recognition of this as a possibility, as conception, and a wish that the community will consist of free inquirers, active and ongoing.

In the next section of this chapter I want to talk briefly about some of the distinguishing features of this emergent cosmology, first recognized as such by the middle of the 20th century, with little or no direct commendation of Peirce's contribution to a world-view sighted on the horizon.

In the closing section I will talk about some of Peirce's main cosmological ideas which underlie his own, inimitable understanding of Pragmatism.

II
The Bird's-Eye View

As mentioned earlier, Peirce does not spend much time discussing his cosmology; he puts it into work. Similarly, I cannot repeat and/or report on his cosmological thoughts as such; but I will talk around them, providing some context for further inquiry.

We know that Peirce had enormous admiration for Gauss which he tended to express in superlatives. But it is not always made explicit just why Peirce felt that Gauss not only transformed his own ideas but virtually revolutionized the idea of space for our time by means of an approach which is the basis of what becomes integral with the Peircean pragmatism.

Gauss is praised for having established special uses of the visual image in cosmological inquiry: the image — *Abbildung* — is produced by interpreting a 'pure' theory of geometry (either euclidean or noneuclidean, according to Hempel, in Newman, 1956, Vol III, pp. 1642-43) into a system of hypotheses which if true or verifiable might be said to constitute a theory of the structure of physical space. Here the rhetorical 'interpretant', to use Peirce's term (not used by Hempel), may be verified not by mathematical theory but rather by an empirical, scientific method, a probabilistic method.

What occurs then is not a deduction from a geometrical theory, but from a connection made between two kinds of discourses — a relation that is hypothesized — which permits the inquirer to correlate mathematics and the physical sciences by a strategy of rhetoric. Here, 'Rhetoric' is used in the broad sense of representing one sign-system by means of another, but doing so in a dialogical way, where the systemic cross-relation is sustained without one system becoming subsumed in or dominated by the other. These relational systems are parallel, but curved and crossing in a non-Euclidean way.

The precise procedure is not clarified. But I infer that the data of a phenomenal-ideational kind is translated into the idiom of a particular scientific discourse. When it is so interpreted or translated it remains a working hypothesis, but in a new medium. The new discursive medium is then capable of being represented by images that will stand for human percepts of the actual, natural world. In brief, a process analogous to establishing equivalences of propositional structures, as is customary in working proofs of traditional syllogistic logic, becomes here adapted to establishing equivalences between entire discourses, i.e, universes of discourse.

Gauss went still further. He used the science of optics to gain access 'mapping'. Indeed, he experimented with hyperbolic geometrical theories of values by using the 'interpretation of physical straight lines as paths of light rays,' (cited in Hempel, above, at p. 1644). Gauss's experiments directly and successfully challenged Poincaré's intention to retain the more simple system of Euclidean geometry and its implied cosmology. The point here is that the consequences of Gauss's innovations lead to a marked distinction between two terms or ideas which were, formerly, taken to be near synonyms. These two terms are 'direction' and 'straightness', (for Peirce's opposition to Poincaré see the chapter on Peirce and Poincaré in this volume).

Peirce's intensive work in this area of hyperbolic geometry and light rays points to directionality of space, i.e, of space that curves, of bending space. Such bending space or light rays that constitute a given space are not straight. They move between two parts, (Kevelson 1993). Further, the curvature of space suggests that directives such as light rays actually exceed the boundary of the surface of the space which they are presumed to fill. Nonmathematicians such as myself might say that this hyperbolic geometry describes a situation of which a pointed directed missive, of some kind, proceeds with an 'unlimited development,' *comparable by analogy to the persuasive power of hyperbole in rhetoric.*

This unlimited development is the action of that hyperbolic 'trope' in a new rhetoric which may be and is often confused or fused with a metaphoric function. But this trope, this hyperbolic trope, is not predominantly metaphor, although the metaphoric function may also be at play in it. *The hyperbolic trope understood as unlimited development characterizes the mode of surface interaction between addresser and addressee in the basic semiotic exchange.*

Admittedly, my speculations have a touch of adventure. Yet, it is in keeping with Peirce's mixing of systems, of adapting and reinterpreting from system to system, which is a style I follow here. I suggest that this link between *hyperbolic* geometry and *hyperbolic* rhetoric is a kind of translation between discourses and sign-systems, (see the chapter on 'bridges' in this volume).

Peirce's method shows us that if we know how it works we also know, by inference, the implied world-view or cosmology that this pragmatic method implicates. In other words, if we grasp what Peirce means by 'pragmatism', we will see how the cosmological frame for a Peircean semiotics is one which holds freedom as its highest referent value: its leading principle, (Kevelson, 1993). Of such a hyperbolic universe we speak in contradictions since it has neither beginning nor end, (Kevelson, 1990).

Form leads to Formless leads to new Form, and it is an infinite process.

I select some aspects of the above to amplify to some degree here, and expect to engage in further inquiry in a subsequent work, (Kevelson, 1998).

I begin with the obvious: interpretation of the material of a corpus often results in the fact that since the process is selective and discriminatory data is passed over at one time for the purpose of inquiry at hand, only to be lighted upon and drawn out as a key resource in subsequent inquiries, for different purposes. Therefore, when the investigator chooses this and not that piece of Peircean thought from the great body of his writings in order to interpretively weave such pieces together with the inquirer's subjective views and fragments of selected references the project will have the character of a *bricolage*. But those pieces passed over do not necessarily become 'neglected' arguments. They are not appropriate to *every* particular purpose, even in a particular respect, (Kevelson, 1996).

It is a different matter when the professed intention is to make accessible to scholars unpublished writings that have previously not been accessible. Then the editors have a moral obligation to present what exists and to bypass the opportunity to attempt to shape a point of view by discriminating between items of a corpus. It is one thing to engage a thinker in argument and intellectual dialogue, as all serious students of Peirce (or any great thinker) attempt to do in inquiries such as this. But it is quite another to conceal argument and open dialogue behind the screen of 'editing'. Not to make available unpublished manuscripts, as has been given implicitly or explicitly as editorial intention, is to breach contract with a 'community of inquirers'. Especially it betrays the implicit trust of the thinker, *in this case, of Peirce.* Even if one stretches the limits of editorial liberties to their fullest, it is only the creative artist who may responsibly disguise, withhold, and distort the actual manuscripts and mask them, as poetic license permits.

If the project of *editing* the Peirce manuscripts has been misnamed, and this has actually been a project of making poetry out of Peirce's raw material, then no harm is done. But if the project has been to act as agent for the principal, in this case for Peirce and/or for the inquirers who expect honest transmission of materials, the agent has overstepped the bounds of legitimate action. One may regard such a failed performance as a violation of contract. But this is a case — a hard case — beyond litigation!

Editors employ certain instruments for their craft; the *index* is such an instrument. It permits the editor to superimpose a 'mapping' upon the texts in focus. First there is the editorial 'point of view' and then the plan or map to structure or classify the material in such a way as to *iconically* shape opinion. Then the *index* to the volume is used to point to this and not that class and subclass of idea. The assemblage of the book is the *symbolic* representation of the editorial work achieved.

No doubt the available volumes of Peirce's works are badly flawed, not through malice, nor even through prior craftsmanship. Rather the flaws are the result of the failure of the mainstream of Peirce scholars to grasp Peirce's message, *as a whole*, in a clear and holistic manner. For example, even in the Eisele edition of *The New Elements of Mathematics* of Peirce there is only one explicit response to Peirce's concept of hyperbolic cosmology. *Yet this concept of the hyperbolic, in Peirce's work, in several crucial places, seems to be capable of unifying the various parts and topics of his work, of his great opus, into a whole.*

We find scarcely any recognition of linkage between hyperbolic geometry and hyperbolic rhetoric by the most devoted of Peirce scholars. Not in Eisele and not even in Max Fisch's work do we find more than three brief references to Peirce's cosmology. What *gapes* in most of Peirce scholarship is the sense that here is a work of integrity even though incomplete, and especially since incomplete. It is an integrity that is *wanted,* that deserves more than a chronological, lineal survey — since it is *nonlineality* that Peirce is concerned with. Where is the study of the Peircean work from a topical perspective, from the perspective of hyperbolic cosmology which would bear affinity with his own frame of mind? I regret not being sufficiently skilled to plug the holes. But at the least I poke through them, show them, and in so doing make my own point of view known, and keep faith with an ideal presumption of a Peircean integrity.

Peirce takes his place along a continuum of thought. In so doing, from his point of view, he evolves the concepts of those who came before him by adapting them to changing contexts and climates of thought, to new and surprising happenings in the world. But adaptation is a mode of revolution; it *is* revolution as it happens.

For example, we know that in classical rhetoric, according to Aristotle, a successful hyperbole is a mode of rhetorical action whereby something is presented with a style of liveliness and youth and passion, or what Whately much later calls 'energy'. So initially hyperbole represented a way of acting, of gesturing and otherwise appearing, which is characteristic of the young and the restless, so to speak.

We do assume that just as Peirce was nourished on Whately's *Logic* he must also have been nurtured by Whately's *Rhetoric*. *Hyperbolic* style or type is, in Whately, a means of persuading the listener of a force of passion behind the audible metaphoric language present and articulated. Whately points out that such passionate, energetic hyperbolic tropes are often more effectual when they are 'bent' or redirected than when they are subdued.

Peirce takes this wise advice and figuratively applies it to the bending of light rays in a curved space, as mentioned above. He follows Gauss's optical principles, but integrates these principles to become constituent aspects of his semiotic methodology, i.e, his pragmatism, his Pure Rhetoric.

In other words, Peirce adapts the then current acceptance of postulates of noneuclidean geometry and parallels them with Whately's observation that an energized rhetorical missive may not have to be subdued or weakened (which it would have to be if it were conceived of as 'straight') but it may, to the contrary, be curved, bent, i.e, redirected, (Whately III, II.2 New York: Sheldon and Co., 1864:322-323).

Here tropes are said to increase the energy of perceived force, not only of metaphors, but also of metonyms, (Whately, at 328, above), or of similes, or of synechdoches, *or of any figure.*

According to Whately, this 'tactic' is regarded as a 'kind of property' of the 'inventor' or orator, and *not of the thing to which this force is transferred.* This force or tropic energy is that which is transferred to the object in question and is not a property of this object, to emphasize, *except by a tropic transference,* (Whately, above, at 330-333).

And when we turn to Vico, (chapter 44), we find that he speaks of Hyperbole as one of the moods of Tropes (see Pinten and Shippee, eds, pp 146-148). This hyperbolic trope sketches the limits of credibility, either as excess or as diminution. In this Vichean sense, the hyperbole is not among the 'species' of tropes; it is regarded as a tropic mood, i.e, a modality.

When we turn to yet another scholar of rhetoric, Chaim Perelman, we find that his understanding of the tropic force of hyperbole is that which persuades of indefinite continuity, i.e, as a force which knows no limit, no bounds, no finite and fixed definition.

This, in crypt, is what Peirce's Pragmatism is all about.

We should not overlook that person to whom Peirce gave tribute as the father of pragmatism, Chauncy Wright — although Peirce claimed to have *invented the term* and the idea as it evolved to become the method of the theory of signs. Peirce defended, to his own loss, Francis Abbott, from whom he also inherited some key aspects of his own cosmology, as *it* developed, (see Madden's study of Wright, especially pages 115, 1886; see Kevelson 1998).

Ultimately Peirce radically departed from Wright's cosmological views, as he also departed from the pragmatic concept of Wright, (for succinct contrast between Peirce and Wright see Madden's study, above).

The closing of this book points to opposing views on the cosmos which, on the surface, was the catalytic point upon which the Abbott/Royce conflict turned, (Brent, 1990). This conflict was a pivotal event in Peirce's professional life as well. Some introductory aspects of this crisis for Peirce are mentioned in the first chapter of this book which opens up a plethora of contributing factors that shaped a concept of Pragmatism for Peirce that was unique among all the competing concepts of pragmatism which existed then, and since.

In keeping with the Spirit of Peirce's Pragmatism I want to keep open the various issues which can be understood to underlie the Peircean myth: The hyperbolic cosmology and the myth of the belief in the community as a continuum of free inquiry are *ideals of the absolute* which Peirce threads through the vast universe of his discourse.

This book watches its back, since the forthcoming *Peirce and the Mark of the Gryphon* is close behind. The future pushes us.

Finally, notwithstanding their differences, there are likenesses between Wright and Peirce that I think Peirce would want mentioned. Although Wright opposes the evolutionary and cosmological activity among his contemporaries, and he argues against Peirce in his 1858 'The Winds and the Weather,' (*Atlantic Monthly* 1, at p. 279), he concedes that although there may be no cosmic or universal pattern we may acknowledge a 'cosmic weather'. This cosmic weather is an ever-changeable climate, with neither rhyme nor reason.

In 1877, in 'Philosophical Discussions' (at page 382) Wright compares the cosmos with the best of human nature: it is always self-creative, nonpredictable, unmeasured and unmeasurable, and 'secret'.

Wright's quotation that follows is intended to describe the universe and also describe humankind: 'the wind bloweth where it listeth, and thou hearest the sound thereof, but canst tell whence it cometh, and whither it goeth,' (cited in Schneider, page 337-338).

At bottom Wright rejects Peirce's cosmology based on scientific method, much closer to the 'new cosmology of the 20th century,' which even at this present writing is going by the board, (Bunge, 1966).

At this close of the 20th century the idea of cosmology is close to the general notion of a world view. But 'Cosmology' and 'World View' are terms or ideas that grow from different grounds. This present conflation suggests a view of the world which represents all that can be known about all that is or conceivably is capable of existence. But is this notion of cosmology as world view compatible with the Peircean paradigm of a cosmology? I think Peirce would say Yes. But pragmatism is then the praxis of a cosmology replete with ad hoc truths, *provisionally held realities*.

Among the current crop of new cosmologists, Bunge argues against such ad hoc principles. He takes the position, as so many of the most respected scientists do in our time, that we need to put aside the worn method of interpretation and look at the Really real. Ad hocness and interpretation, he says, are modes of old magic, of archaic myth, and are not predictive in terms of hard, scientific method. Bunge's cosmology is not better supported than is Peirce's. But it is *preferred* by Bunge, as Peirce's is *preferred* by himself.

But this preference in Peirce is of a different nature: here the real and the fictive or dreamlike are contrasted in the Peircean cosmology. They interact, such that the subjective is the dreamlike or evanescent fictive, whereas the objective is that Real which may be represented in observable regular patterns. As I will discuss in the introductory chapter of *Peirce and the Mark of the Gryphon,* Peirce's pragmatic cosmology becomes the backbone for Royce's *Spirit of Modern Philosophy* (1892). Thus begins a new epoch in the saga of the Peircean perigrine through the Pragmatic.

Selected References

Alejandro, Roberto, 1993, *Hermeneutics, Citizenship, and the Public Sphere*, Albany: SUNY.

Alexander, Peter, 1985, *Ideas, Qualities and Corpuscle*, Cambridge: Cambridge University Press.

Arendt, H., 1958, *The Human Condition*, Chicago: University of Chicago Press.

_____, Hannah, 1962, *On Revolution*, New York: Viking Press.

Atiyah, P., 1983, 'The Legacy of Holmes Through English Eyes' in *Holmes and The Common Law, A Century Later*, originally in B.U.L. Review 1983:39, Cambridge, Harvard University Press, pp. 27-79.

_____, 1978/1980, 'From Principles to Pragmatism,' *Iowa Law Review* 65:1249-1272

Bally, Charles, 1932/1965, *Linguistique générale et linguistique française*, Berne: Franke

_____, 1925/1952, *Le langage et la vie*, Genève: Droz.

Barthes, Roland, 1953/1968, *Writing Degree Zero*, intro. Susan Sontag; trans. A. lauers and C. Smith, New York: Hill and Wang.

Beebee, Thomas O., 1992, 'The Legal Theaters of Bertolt Brecht' in *Law and Aesthetics*, ed. R. Kevelson, New York and Bern: Peter Lang Publishing, pp. 37-68.

Bent, S., 1932, *Justice Oliver Wendell Holmes: A Biography*, New York: Garden City Publishers.

Bergson, Henri, 1911/1944, *Creative Evolution*, trans. A. Mitchell, New York: Modern Library.

Bloch, Ernst, 1974/1988, *The Utopian Functions of Art and Literature*, trans. J. Zifes and F. Mecklenburg, Cambridge: M.I.T. Press.

Bohm, David, 1987, 'Hidden Variables and the Implicate Order,' in *Quantum Implications*, eds. B. Hiley and F.D. Peat, 38.

_____, 1980, *Wholeness and the Implicate Order*, London and Boston: Ark.

Boyle, R., 1672/1972, *An Essay About the Origin and Virtues of Gems*, ed. G.W. White, New York: Hafner Publishing Co.

Brewster, Sir David, 1818/1987, *The Kaleidoscope*, Holyoke: Van Cort Publishers.

Briggs, J.P. and F.D. Peat, 1989, eds., *Turbulent Mirror*, New York: Harper & Row.

_____, 1984, *Looking Glass Universe*, New York: Simon and Schuster.

Bunge, M., 1962, 'Cosmology and Magic' in *The Monist*, 47 1, p. 116-141.

Cohen, Morris, R., 1931, *Reason and Nature*, New York: Harcourt, Brace & Co.

_____, 1927, 'Positivism and the Limits of Idealism in the Law,' *Columbia Law Review* 28 3:237-250.

Cheng, Ronald Ye-Lin, 1975, ed. *The Sociology of Revolution*, Chicago, Henry Regency Co.

Davies, P. and J. Gribbin, 1992, *The Matter My*th, New York: Simon and Schuster.

Delbrücke, M., 1986, *Mind From Matter?*, London: Blackwell Scientific Pub., Inc.

Dewey, John, 1937, *Review, Collected Papers of C.S. Peirce*, in *New Republic*, 89, pp. 415-6.

_____, 1927/1954, *The Public and its Problems*, Chicago: Swallow Publishers.

Dietze, G., 1963/1975, *In Defense of Property*, New York: Atherton.

Durkheim, Emile, 1955/1983, *Pragmatism and Sociology*, ed., J.C. Whitehorse; trans., J.B. Allcock, Cambridge: Cambridge University Press.

Earley, Joseph, 1994, 'Recent development in science important for legal scholarship,' ed. Roberta Kevelson, *Codes and Customs*, New York and Berne: Peter Lang, 77-92.

Eco, Umberto, 1983, 'Horns, Hooves, and Insteps,' eds. U. Eco and T. Sebeok, *The Sign of Three*, Bloomington: Indiana University Press, pp. 198-220.

_____, 1979, *The Role of the Reader*, Bloomington: Indiana University Press.

_____, 1976, *A Theory of Semiotics*, Bloomington: Indiana University Press.

Edinger, E.F., 1985, *Anatomy of the Psyche*, LaSalle: Open Court.

Edwards, Lyford P., 1927/1970, *The Natural History of Revolution*, Chicago: University of Chicago Press.

Eisele, Carolyn, 1979, *Studies in the Scientific and Mathematical Philosophy of Charles S. Peirce*, ed. R. Martin, The Hague and New York: Mouton.

Ernst, E., 1956, *The Kabuki Theatre*, New York: Grove Press.

Feyerabend, P., 1975, *Against Method*, London: Redwood Burn Ltd.

Fisch, Max H., 1986, *Peirce, Semeiotic and Pragmatism*, eds. K. Ketner and Ch. Kloesel, Bloomington: Indiana University Press, 201-226.

_____, 1951, 'Introduction,' ed. M.H. Fisch, *Classic American Philosophers*, New York: Appleton-Century-Crofts.

Fiske, J., 1892, *Outline of Cosmic Philosophy*, Boston and New York: Houghton Mifflin.

Folina, Janet, 1992, *Poincaré and the Philosophy of Mathematics*, New York: St. Martin's Press.

Foss, D.A. and R. Larkin, 1986, *Beyond Revolution*, South Hadley: Bergin and Garvey

Frankfurter, F., 1923, 'Twenty Years of Mr. Justice Holmes' Constitutional Opinions,' *Harvard Law Review* 36 8:909-939.

_____, 1916, 'The Constitutional Opinion of Justice Holmes,' *Harvard Law Review* 29 683-699.

Friedman, Lawrence M., 1973, *A History of American Law*, New York: Simon & Schuster.

Fuller, Lon L., 1940, *The Law in Quest of Itself*, Chicago: Foundation Press.

_____, 1934, 'American Legal Realism,' *University of Penna. Law Review*, 82 5:429-461.

Gerth, H.H. and C. Wright Mills, 1958, eds. and trans., *From Max Weber*, New York: Galaxy.

Gilson, E., 1971/1984, *From Aristotle to Darwin and Back Again*, trans. J. Lyon, Notre Dame: University of Notre Dame Press.

Gorlée, D.L., 1993, *Semiotics and the Problem of Translation*, Alblasserdam: Kanters B.V.

Gray, J.C., 1921, *The Nature and Sources of the Law*, New York: MacMillan Co.

Grazin, Igor, 'The Rules of Law: But of Which Law?' *John Marshall Law Review* 26, 1993: 719-737.

Habermas, Jürgen, 1968/1981, *Knowledge and Human Interests*, Boston: Beacon Press.

Hacking, I., 1990, *The Taming of Chance*, Cambridge: Cambridge University Press.

Hall, Kermit L., 1989, *The Magic Mirror*, New York and Oxford: Oxford University Press.

Hamburgh, Max, 1971, *Theories of Differentiation*, New York: America Elsevere.

Handlin, Oscar, 1959, *Immigration*, Enderwood: Prentice Hall.

Harbison, R., 1992, *The Built, the Unbuilt and the Unbuildable*, Cambridge: M.I.T. Press.

Harré, R., 1964, *Matter and Method*, Reseda: Ridgeview Publishing.

Hayek, F., 1979, *The Counter-Revolution of Science*, Glencoe: Liberty Press.

Hobbes, Thomas, 1655-57/1962, *Body, Man, and Citizen*, New York: MacMillan.

Holenstein, Elmar, 1974/1976, *Roman Jakobson's Approach to Language*, trans. C. Schelbert and T. Schelbert, Bloomington: Indiana University Press.

Holmes, Oliver Wendell, 1955, *The Holmes Reader*, ed. J.J. Marke, New York: Oceana.

_____, 1941, *Holmes-Pollock Letters*, 2 Vols, Cambridge: Harvard University Press.

Holmes, Oliver Wendell, 1920, *Collected Legal Papers*, New York: Harcourt, Brace & Co.

_____, 1880/1963, *The Common Law*, Boston: Little, Brown Co.

Hook, Sidney, 1974, *Pragmatism and the Tragic Sense of Life*, New York: Basic Books.

Howe, M. de Wolf, 1957, *Justice Holmes: The Shaping Years*, London: Oxford University Press.

_____, 1951, 'The Positivism of Mr. Justice Holmes,' *Harvard Law Review* 64 4:529-546.

Hughes, H. Stuart, 1965, *History as Art and Science*, New York: Harper Torchbooks.

Jacobsohn, G.S., 1978, *Pragmatism, Statesmanship and the Supreme Court*, Ithaca: Cornell University Press.

Jakobson, Roman, 1971, *Selected Writings II, Word and Language*, The Hague: Mouton.

_____, 1966, 'Quest for the Essence of Language,' in *SWII*, pages 345-359.

_____, 1960, 'Linguistics and Poetics' in T. Sebeok, ed., *Style in Language*, Cambridge: M.I.T. Press, pages 350-377.

_____, 1957/1971, 'Shifters, Verbal Categories and the Russian Verb,' reprinted in *SWII* pages 130-147.

_____, 1956, *Fundamentals of Language*, The Hague: Mouton.

_____, 1939, 'Signe Zero' in *Melange de linguistique offerts a Charles Bally*, Genèva: Droz. Reprinted in E. Harp 1966 and *SWII* 1971.

Jean, François, 1993, *Life, Death and Art*, London: Routledge.

Jones, H.W., 1961, 'Law and Morality in the Perspective of Legal Realism' in *Columbia Law Review* 61 799-809.

Jung, C.G., 1963, *Mysterium Conjunctionis*, trans. F.F.C. Hull, New York: Pantheon

Kelso, R.R., 1995, 'The Natural Law Tradition on the Modern Supreme Court,' *St. Mary's Law Journal* 26 1051-1086.

Kennedy, George A., 1992, 'A Hoot in the Dark: The Evolution of General Rhetoric,' *Philosophy and Rhetoric*, 25 1:1-21.

Kevelson, Roberta, 1998, *Peirce and the Mark of the Gryphon*, New York: St. Martin's Press, forthcoming.

_____, 1996, *Peirce, Science, Signs*, Bern and New York: Peter Lang Publishing.

_____, 1994, 'Peirce at the Millennium,' ed. Roberta Kevelson, *Codes & Customs*, New York and Berne: Peter Lang, 173-176.

_____, 1993, *Peirce's Esthetics of Freedom*, New York and Bern: Peter Lang Publishing.

Kevelson, Roberta, 1992, 'Pragmatism, Utopic Constructions and Legal Myths,' ed. R. Kevelson, *Law and the Human Sciences*, New York & Bern: Peter Lang Publishers, 193-218.

_____, 1992, 'Property as Rhetoric in Law' in *Cardozo Studies in Law and Literature* 4 2:189-206.

_____, 1990, *Peirce, Paradox, Praxis*, Amsterdam: Mouton de Gruyter.

_____, 1988, *The Law as a System of Signs*, New York: Plenum.

_____, 1987, *Charles S. Peirce's Method of Methods*, Amsterdam: John Benjamins.

_____, 1986, 'Semiotics in the United States,' *The Semiotic Sphere*, eds. T. Sebeok and J. Umiker-Sebeok, New York: Plenum, 543-544.

_____, 1984, 'C.S. Peirce's Speculative Rhetoric,' *Philosophy and Rhetoric* 17 1:16-27.

_____, 1982, *Charles S. Peirce's Method of Methods*, Amsterdam: John Benjamins.

_____, 1981, 'Peirce's Dialogism And Continuum Predicate,' *Transactions of the Charles S. Peirce Society* 18 2:110-126.

_____, 1979, 'Relations of Nothings to Somethings,' *Ars Semiotica* 11:3, 295-326.

_____, 1977, *Inlaws/Outlaws*, Lisse and Bloomington: The Peter de Ridder Press with R.C.L.S.S.

_____, 1977, 'Peirce and Mukařovsky on the Art of Conversation' in *Semiotica* 32½, 53-80.

_____, 1976, *Style, Symbolic Language Structure and Syntactic Change*, Lisse: The Peter de Ridder Press.

_____, 1976, 'Wittgenstein's Language-Games of Systematic Metaphor,' *Semiotica*, 19 ½, 29-58.

_____, 1975, 'The Play as Interpretant,' ms, unpublished.

_____, 1965, 'Play: Anarchic Comedy and Counterculture,' ms, unpublished.

Kitching, Gavin, 1982, *Development and Undevelopment in Historical Perspective*, London: Routledge.

Kline, M., 1980, *Mathematics: The Loss of Certainty*, London: Oxford University Press.

Knight, Th.S., 1965, *Charles Peirce*, New York: Washington Square Press.

Koselleck, R., 1979/1985, *Futures Past*, trans. K. Tribe, Cambridge: M.I.T. Press.

Kuklick, B., 1977, *The Rise of American Philosophy*, New Haven: Yale University Press.

Lasswell, Harold and Abraham Kaplan, 1950, *Power and Society*, New Haven: Yale University Press.

Lerner, Max, 1943, ed., *The Mind and Faith of Justice Holmes*, New York: Modern Library.

Levinas, Emmanuel, 1987/1993, *Outside the Subject*, trans., M.B. Smith, London: Athlone Press.

Lewis, C.I., 1929/1956, *Mind and the World Order*, London: Dover.

Liska, Jo, 1993, 'The Role of Rhetoric in Semiogenesis,' *Philosophy and Rhetoric* 26 1:31-38.

Llewellyn, Karl N., 1962, *Jurisprudence: Realism in Theory and Practice*, Chicago: University of Chicago Press.

Mach, Ernst, 1893/1974, *The Science of Mechanics*, LaSalle: Open Court.

Mackay, D.S., 1950, 'Pragmatism,' ed. V. Ferm , *A History of Philosophical Systems*, New York: Philosophical Library, pp. 387-404.

Madden, E.H., 1963, *Chauncey Wright and the Foundations of Pragmatism*, Seattle: Washington University Press.

Maniscalco, J.P., 1995, 'The New Positivism: An Analysis of the Role of Morality in Jurisprudence,' *Southern California Law Review* 68 989-1027.

McDougal, M.S., 1941, 'Fuller v. America Legal Realists,' *Yale Law Journal* 50 827-840.

Murphey, M.G., 1961, *The Development of Peirce's Philosophy*, Cambridge: Harvard University Press.

Nathan, Ove, 1989, 'Welcome Address,' to Conference in *The Humanities Between Art and Science*, eds. M. Harbsmeier and M.T. Larsey, Copenhagen: Center for Research in The Humanities, 11-16.

Olson, Richard, 1975, *Scottish Philosophy and British Physics*, Princeton: Princeton University Press.

Pearsall, R., 1986, *The Alchemists*, London: Weidenfeld and Nicolson.

Peat, F. David, 1987, *Synchronicity: The Bridge Between Matter and Mind*, New York: Bantam Books.

Peirce, Charles S., 1986-1993, *Writings of Charles S. Peirce*, Vols. 1-5, Chronological Edition, eds. M. Fisch *et al*, Peirce Edition Project, Bloomington: Indiana University Press.

_____, 1931-1938/1958, *Collected Papers*, vols. I-VIII, eds., Ch. Hartshorne, P. Weiss, A. Burks, Cambridge: Harvard University Press.

_____, 1979, *Charles Sanders Peirce: Contributions to the Nation*, Vol. 3, eds. K.L. Ketner et al, Lubbock: Center for Studies in Pragmaticism.

_____, 1976, *New Elements of Mathematics*, Vol IV, ed. C. Eisele, The Hague: Mouton.

Peirce, Charles S., 1967, Microfilm edition of 33 reels of manuscripts, with R. Robins' annotated catalogue, 1958, University of Massachusetts Press, Amherst.

_____, 1956, 'The Red and the Black,' ed. J.R. Newman, *The World of Mathematic*, Vol. 2, New York: Simon and Schuster, pp. 1334-1340

Percy, Walker, 1983, *Lost in the Cosmos*, New York: Farrar, Strauss and Giroux.

Perelman, Ch., and J. Olbrechts-Tyteca, 1959/1969, *The New Rhetoric*, trans. J. Wilkinson and P. Weaver, Notre Dame: University of Notre Dame Press.

Perry, R.B., 1926, *Philosophy of the Recent Past*, New York: Ch. Scribner's Sons.

Poincaré, Henri, 1902/1905/1952, English translation J. Larmor, New York: Dover Publications.

Pound, Roscoe, 1931, 'The Call for a Realist Jurisprudence,' *Harvard Law Review* 697-711.

_____, 1925, 'Do We Need a Philosophy of Law?' *Columbia Law Review* 5 339-350.

Prigogine, I. and I. Stengers, 1984, *Order Out of Chaos*, Glasgow: Fontana.

Purcell, E.A., Jr., 1973 *A Crisis of Democratic Theory*, Lexington: University Press of Kentucky.

Reichenbach, H., 1958, *The Philosophy of Space and Time*, trans. M. Reichenbach and J. Friend, New York: Dover.

Rheingold, Howard, 1994, *Stereogram*, foreword, San Francisco: Candence Books.

Richards, I.A., 1936, *The Philosophy of Rhetoric*, New York: Harcourt, Brace & World.

Ricouer, P., 1975, *The Role of Metaphor*, trans. R.C. Zerby, Toronto and Buffalo: University of Toronto Press.

Ridgeway, William, 1915/1964, *The Dramas and Dramatic Dances of the Non-European Races*, New York: B. Blom.

Ritchie, A.D., 1958, *Studies in the History and Methods of the Sciences*, Edinborough: University of Edinborough Press.

Roche, Maurice, 1992, *Rethinking Citizenship*, Oxford: Blackwell Publishers.

Roth, Jack J., 1980, *The Cult of Violence*, Berkeley: University of California Press.

Royce, J., 1892, *The Spirit of Modern Philosophy*. Boston and New York: Houghton Mifflin Co.

Rumble, Wilfrid E., Jr., 1967, *American Legal Realism*, Ithaca: Cornell University Press.

Rucker, R., 1985, *The Fourth Dimension*, London: Rider & Co.

Schneider, H.W., 1946, *History of American Philosophy*, New York: Columbia University Press.

Schreiber, E.H., 1988, ed., *Aggression and Violence in Human Behavior*, Needham: Ginn Publishers.

Sebeok, Thomas A., 1976, *Contributions to the Doctrine of Signs*, Lisse: The Peter de Ridder Press.

_____, 1972, *Perspectives on Zoosemiotics*, The Hague: Mouton.

_____, *Style in Language,* ed., Cambridge: M.I.T. Press.

Simmel, Georg, 1950, *The Sociology of Georg Simmel*, trans. and ed., K.H. Wolff, New York: The Free Press.

Simon, Julian L., 1995, *Immigration: the Demographic and Economic Facts*, Washington, D.C.: The Cato Institute.

Smith, Godwin, 1893, *The United States Political History, 1492-1871*.

Sorel, Georges, 1906/1950, *Reflections on Violence*, trans. T.E. Hulme and J. Roth, New York: Collier.

Talbot, M., 1992, *The Holographic Universe*, New York: Harper Perennial.

Thayer, H.S., 1968/1981, *Meaning and Action*, Indianapolis: Hackett Publishing Co.

Toulmin, Stephen, 1982/1985, *The Return to Cosmology*, Berkeley: University of California Press.

United Nations High Commission for Refugees, 1993, *The State of the World's Refugees*, Middlesex: Penguin.

Veltrusky, J., 1964, 'Man and Object in the Theater,' in *A Prague School Reader on Aesthetics, Literary Structure and Style*, ed. P. Garvin, pp. 83-91, Seattle: Washington University Press.

Vico, Giambattista, 1996, *The Art of Rhetoric*, eds. and trans. G. Pinton and A. Shippee, Amsterdam: Rodopi.

_____, 1982, *Selected Writings*, ed. and trans. Leon Pompa, Cambridge: Cambridge University Press.

_____, 1975/1990, *A Study of the 'New Science,'* 2nd edition, ed. Leon Pompa, Cambridge: Cambridge University Press.

Waugh, Linda R., 1976, *Roman Jakobson's Science of Language*, Lisse: The Peter de Ridder Press.

Whately, R., 1864, *Elements of Rhetoric*, New York: Sheldon and Co.

Wiener, Philip P., 1969, *Evolution and the Founders of Pragmatism*, Gloucester: Peter Smith.

Wittkower, Rudolf, 1977, *Allegory and the Migration of Symbols*, London: Thames and Hudson.

Yarnold, Barbara M., 1990, *Refugees Without Refuge*, Lanham: University Press of America.

Yntema, Hessel E., 1931, 'Mr. Justice Holmes' View of Legal Science,' *Yale Law Journal* 40 696-703.

_____, 1928, 'The Hornbook Method and The Conflict of Laws,' *Yale Law Journal* 37 1928:76, 480.

Subject Index

Critic of Institutions

Critic of Institutions refers to the process of ideas interpreting ideas, as in Peircean Semiotics. Institutions in this Series are seen as representing public interests and values. The term, Critic, is used as Peirce used it, to link the organizations of natural language with the uses of human meaning in social life. Critic is activity which inquires, analyzes and discovers new meaning. Institutions, connecting people with realization of values, mediate also. Many but not all the volumes of *Critic of Institutions* focus on issues related to Law, such as Contract, Markets, Justice, Ritual, Codes, Punishment, the Arts and humanistic studies as a whole. These concepts are regarded as prototypes of public interests across cultures and social orders. The series is open to proposals in these and other areas. Several volumes are currently used as course texts in upper-class academic and professional curricula.

DIRECT ENERGY CONVERSION

Fundamentals of Electric Power Production

Reiner Decher

New York   Oxford

Oxford University Press

1997

ersity Press

w York
kok   Bogota   Bombay
pe Town   Dar es Salaam
Delhi   Florence   Hong Kong   Istanbul   Karachi
Kuala Lumpur   Madras   Madrid   Melbourne
Mexico City   Nairobi   Paris   Singapore
Taipei   Tokyo   Toronto
and associated companies in
Berlin   Ibadan

Published by Oxford University Press, Inc.,
198 Madison Avenue, New York, New York, 10016-4314

Library of Congress Cataloging-in-Publication Data
Decher, Reiner.
Direct energy conversion : fundamentals of electric power
production / Reiner Decher.
p.   cm.
Includes bibilographical references and index.
ISBN 0-19-509572-3 (cloth)
1. Direct energy conversion.   I. Title.
TK2896.D43   1996   96-4842
CIP

Printing (last digit): 9 8 7 6 5 4 3 2 1

Printed in the United States of America
on acid-free paper

CONTENTS

PREFACE

The intent of this book is to acquaint the technically trained reader to understand the physics and practical limitations of methods that might be employed for the production of electrical power, that most useful of all power forms. The conversion of energy in its many forms occurs naturally and is caused to happen deliberately by industrial man in processes for a variety of reasons and purposes. The production of electromechanical power is dominated by the exploitation of heat resources by means of heat engines and of mechanical power resources available in nature. The utilization of heat resources is, in turn, dominated by the thermodynamics of the heat engine and its limitations. For some cycles, the limitation is due to the fuel energy content; for others, the usable temperatures allowed by the materials in the engine are critical; and for still others, the characteristics of the thermodynamic cycle working fluid limit the cycle performance.

Thermodynamics, physics, and chemistry also govern the *direct* conversion of energy in various forms to electrical energy. Direct energy conversion is concerned with the transformation of energy to electrical power without the use of the heat engine and the associated rotating electrical generator. These methods are characterized by an electrical circuit wherein molecular scale charge carriers complete the circuit rather than electrons in the conductors of the rotating machinery. This offers the potential for production of electric power with long-lived, reliable, and durable power systems from such resources as heat, chemical energy, flow kinetic energy, as well as photon radiation. The conversion of these energy forms to electric power is limited to varying degrees by the Second Law of Thermodynamics.

The greater purpose of this book is to provide an understanding of the critical physical phenomena involved in designing an energy conversion device or system around a laboratory effect. This book is limited to those devices that have or were thought to have a realistic chance of becoming commercially successful or may be particulary useful in a special application niche. The topics covered therefore do not include all energy conversion methods. For an appreciation of some of other methods that have been investigated as well as a good overview of the governing concepts associated with irreversible thermodynamics, the reader is encouraged to see other texts on the same subject. Works by Angrist (Ref. 1-8), Soo (Ref. 5-1), Sutton (Ref. 1-9), as well as others are often very good and complementary to the study here. In fact, a particular author's interest in a specific subject often reflects a disproportionate effort spent on writing about the ideas involved and its details. This is probably true here and with other authors. Thus the reader may wish to read in greater depth elsewhere about some topics that are omitted or touched on only briefly here.

Chapter 1 is a review of the characteristics of heat engines as an extension to that in Ref. 1-1. Some discussion there is also devoted to the production of solar cell electric power. Of interest always are factors that determine power output (specifically power density or compactness), complexity (or cost), and the efficiency of the conversion of heat to power. By virtue of their function in meeting a user's needs, most engines must operate for some fraction of their operating lives at power levels less than full power. The variation of the performance characteristics, specifically the efficiency, is often of great interest under these circumstances.

Chapter 2 is a discussion of flows with electromagnetic interactions, the singular and practical method of obtaining work from a gas with kinetic energy by means of a volumetric, rather than surface (on the airfoils of a turbine, for example), force interaction. The description of magnetohydrodynamic (MHD) devices requires reviews of classical electricity and magnetism and of the fluid equations of motion. A specialized review is provided here. The background covered also serves the development of electrohydrodynamics reviewed in Chapter 5.

Chapter 3 addresses determination of the principal property of materials asked to carry electric current: the electrical conductivity. In gases, the magnitude of this transport property is critical to the successful design of power machinery. The mathematical development yields valuable insight into the physics of MHD and similar plasmas. This background is important for understanding the design and performance of the devices discussed in Chapter 4. Finally, it sets the stage for understanding the electrical conductivity in other materials: metals (Chapter 6), electrolytes (Chapter 7), and semiconductors (Chapters 8 and 9).

Chapter 4 describes direct removal of work from a moving fluid as electric power. The interaction involves passage of a high-speed, conducting gas through a magnetic field. Study of this form of energy conversion is an important aspect of MHD, the study of gas dynamics with significant flow interaction. The MHD generator described is similar to a very high-temperature turbine whose contribution to the performance of the conversion system is critical. The characteristics of this process are examined in detail. The reader is referred to Ref. 1-1 for an examination of the integration of this generator into a heat engine power system.

The forced convection of charges may be used to generate an electric field and thus a current. The electrohydrodynamic interaction is covered in Chapter 5.

The physics of metals and the ability of hot metals to transfer charges into a vacuum or low-pressure space and to a receiver at an elevated potential is described in Chapter 6. This forms the basis for the analytical description of thermionic converters whose physical and performance characteristics are covered.

Chapter 7 is a discussion of chemical cells (batteries and fuel cells) where the conversion of chemicals of one type to another takes place. Since chemical reorganization involves the valence electrons of the constituents, the cells can force the transfer of electrons to occur through an external load circuit where their energy may be usefully employed. Such a conversion circumvents the transformation of the chemical energy to heat, and thus the conversion efficiency is not constrained by the Carnot cycle limitation, which afflicts heat engines. This attractive feature is balanced by the lower power density. This chapter describes ionic conduction of charges through electrolytes and the most interesting types of fuel cell systems. Liquid and solid electrolyte cells are considered. Fuels cells are promising alternative to heat engines, especially with simple fuels such as hydrogen or methane. Batteries, as a close relative to the fuel cell, will continue to play an important role in energy storage, especially in the transportation sector. Methods for calculating the energy density are described together with examples of practical systems.

Chapters 8 and 9 deal primarily with semiconductors. In Chapter 8, the photovoltaic effect is described where photons interact with the electrons in a semiconductor junction, resulting in the production of electron-hole pairs. The electrons are elevated to a higher potential energy. The physical phenomena described apply to the design of solar cells covered here and in ref. 1-1 and to infrared cells for power systems using fuels. A review of the physics of radiation precedes a discussion of the system design, power density, and efficiency. In Chapter 9, the thermoelectric effects are described, together with the characteristics of devices designed to exploit them.

It is the author's view that a phenomenon or result is made much more understandable if it can be modeled mathematically because one can readily see the effect of the parameters involved. Thus the reader will find a quantitative emphasis on fundamentals carried to the point where important conclusions regarding performance characteristics can be drawn. Detailed design characteristics and statements regarding performance of specific devices are avoided because these will change in time, while the fundamental underpinnings will not.

It is expected that the reader be competent in calculus, physics, and chemistry. For the discussion of MHD devices in particular, the student should have had an introduction to the dynamics of compressible fluid flow. This text is suitable for senior-level undergraduates or graduate students in engineering. A limited number of problems are given at the end of the chapters.

ACKNOWLEDGMENTS

The author gratefully acknowledges the contribution of colleagues who contributed material or agreed to review various chapters and thus improve not only the book but my understanding as well. These include Lewis Fraas, Thomas Mattick, Dan Schwartz, Uri Shumlak, Eric Stuve, Gene Woodruff, and the students who had to put up with early versions of this work. The work on MHD (Chapters 2-4) is influenced in no small way by interactions with many colleagues. Among these are Jack L. Kerrebrock, Gordon C. Oates, Myron A. Hoffman, James P. Reilly, Jean F. Louis, and Thomas R. Brogan.

Finally, sincere thanks to my wife Mary for being so understanding of my need to focus "elsewhere" while completing this endeavor.

Seattle   Reiner Decher

SYMBOLS

The symbols used in this text are as uniform and conventional as practical. However, traditions have evolved in various fields that make use of differing symbols for the same quantities across differing disciplines. Further, a particular symbol may have two or more different meanings. To that extent, the meaning of symbols may vary from one chapter to another and possibly within a chapter. It is hoped that the context of the use of a quantity makes its meaning clear. Special symbols are defined in the context of their use. The following is a list of symbols that appear in the text together with their definitions and references. The reference is absent if the symbol usage is common. Other references may be by chapter (8), by section (8.1.4), or by the equation number (eq. 8-75) where first used. Neither chemical symbols nor general-purpose constants of local utility are listed here. Some symbols, uniformly accepted to stand for various physical constants, are given in Appendix B, together with numerical values. In the interest of space, some quantities of interest in thermodynamics that are proportional to mass are not given twice: For example, while the enthalpy per unit mass h appears, the true enthalpy H does not because of its direct relation to h. Units for all quantities will generally be in the SI system, although there are exceptions when tradition calls for it.

LATIN SYMBOLS

a	speed of sound
A	area
	short circuit to dark current ratio (eq. 8-48)
B	magnetic field strength (2)
	Blackbody radiation function (eq. 8-18)
c	speed (thermal)
	speed of light
	concentration (eq. 7-15)
Cp, Cv	specific heats (at constant pressure and at constant volume)
d	length scale
D	diameter
	diffusion coefficient (eq. 8-6)
e	electron charge
	internal energy (2)
	polytropic exponent (eq. 4-85)
E	electric field
	energy
	ionization energy / temperation parameter (eq. 4-81)

f	distribution function (App. A, eq. 3-31)
	fuel mass fraction
	friction factor
F	force
	Faraday (eq. 7-8, App. B)
	radiant transfer function (eq. 8-67)
g	gravitational acceleration
	specific Gibbs free energy
h	enthalpy
	length scale
	Planck constant (App. B)
h_D	Debye length (eq. 3-5)
I	interaction parameter (2.4.7)
	current (amps)
	radiant intensity (eq. 8-22)
j	current density
k	Boltzmann constant (App. B)
	load factor (eq. 4-18)
	thermal conductivity
K	thermal conductance (eq. 9-11)
k_v	spectral absorption coefficient (eq. 8-22)
l	length element (2)
L	length
	interaction length (2.4.7)
m	mass
$\dot{m}$	mass flow rate
M	Mach number
n	number density
	valence
	refractive index (eq. 8-20)
$\dot{n}_\phi$	photon flux (eq. 8-27)
N	number
p	pressure, N/m^2
	particle momentum (eq. 6-4)
	impact parameter (Fig. 3-4)
q	heat transferred per unit mass
	heat flux
	electron, ion, or particle charge
Q	torque
	collison cross-sectional area
r	spherical or cylindrical coordinate (vector)

r	reflectivity (eq. 8-20)
R	electrical resistance (ohms)
	radius
	gas constant
s	specific entropy
S	area
	Saha function (eq. 4-64)
t	time
T	temperature (absolute scale)
u	velocity
u, v, w	velocity components in x, y, z directions
U	vector velocity
v	specific volume
v_d	drift velocity (eq. 2-4)
V	voltage (also E and ϕ)
	volume
$\boldsymbol{v}$	velocity vector
$\boldsymbol{V}$	velocity (vector)
w	specific work (1)
$\dot{w}$	power density
	radiant power (eq. 8-19)
x	reduced frequency (eq. 8-18)
x, y, z	directional coordinates
y	voltage ratio (eq. 6-59)
Z	thermoelectric figure of merit (eq. 9-18)

GREEK SYMBOLS

α	Debye length constant (eq. 3-86)
	reactant capacity (eq. 7-12)
	integrated absorption coefficient (eq. 8-38)
	capacity rate ratio (eq. 8-56)
	Seebeck coefficient (eq. 9-1)
β	Hall parameter (eq. 3-15)
	electrode potential/temperature parameter (eq. 6-55)
γ	specific heat ratio, Cp/Cv
	ratio of Ex to inlet value, E_0 (eq. 5-8)
	Thomson coefficient (eq. 9-3)
ε	emissivity (eq. 8-34)

ε_0	permittivity of free space
ε_i	ionization energy
ϕ	electrical potential (also V and E) spherical coordinate angle work function (6.2)
Φ	photon flux function (eq. 8-28)
η	efficiency
λ	mean free path equivalent ionic conductivities (eq. 7-16)
Λ	ion slip velocity ratio (eq. 5-9) ion collision cross-section parameter (eq. 4-73) equivalent conductivity (eq. 7-15)
μ	Mach number function (eq. 4-87) charge mobility (eqs. 7-6, 5-3) resistance ratio (eq. 9-16)
μ_0	magnetic permeability of free space
ν	wave frequency (eq. 8-17)
ν_c	collision frequency (eq. 3-9)
π	Peltier coefficient (eq. 9-2)
θ	temperature ratio $T/(T_0$ = ambient or reference temperature)
ρ	density electrical resistivity
σ	electrical conductivity (eqs. 2-12, 3-13, 3-29, 3-78, 7-15) Stefan-Boltzmann constant (App. B)
ξ	nondimensional x
ω	angular speed
ζ	energy / temperature parameter (eq. 6-15)

LATIN SUBSCRIPT

a	anode (collector)
ad	adiabatic
B	blackbody
c	charge compressor cathode (emitter)
e	electron electrical
f	fuel faradaic (eq. 7-45)

g	gas
	band gap
H	Hall
i	ion
i, id	ideal
L	channel exit (4)
max	maximum
min	minimum
n	n-type semiconductor
o	overall
OC	open circuit
p	p-type semiconductor
p-n	p-n juntion
q	thermal
r	recombination (eq. 8-41)
RT	radiant transfer
s	short circuit
SC	short circuit
SCL	space-charge-limited
t	total
th	thermal
u	useful
w	maximum work
x	heat exchanger (eq. 8-57)

GREEK SUBSCRIPT

η	maximum efficiency

NUMERIC SUBSCRIPT

i	state point i
i	special definition of characteristic velocities (4)
0	ambient or reference condition
	entry condition
	cutoff energy
	dark (current)

1

HEAT ENGINES

The study of power generation must start from the perspective of the heat engines that supply the vast bulk of all electromechanical power requirements of society. These engines evolved with the understanding of the laws of thermodynamics, the mechanics of fluids, heat transfer, and the availability of thermal resources such as wood, fossil, and nuclear fuels. This chapter is a review of heat engines that assumes that the reader is familiar with elementary thermodynamics and its symbols (Ref. 1-1). The objective of this chapter is to focus on the characteristics of heat engines as power producers to set the stage for comparison to direct conversion methods. The development in this chapter is qualitative rather than quantitative because the details are available elsewhere, although they contribute materially to the understanding of the characteristics of heat engines as power producers.

1.1. COMMON FEATURES OF ALL HEAT ENGINES: THERMODYNAMICS

Heat engines producing power require a quasisteady supply of heat, which is usually provided by combustion of a fuel with air or by other heat-releasing reactions; nuclear fission is the most important alternative to combustion. The heat engine is a mechanism that forces a working fluid to undergo a number of processes, which together form a thermodynamic cycle by returning the working fluid to its initial state.

Starting from a relatively cold, low-pressure state, these processes consist minimally of compression, heating, expansion, and finally heat rejection. The thermodynamic cycles or types of heat engines differ in the means employed to carry out these processes. The important cycles are the Otto, Diesel, Brayton, and Rankine cycles. Other cycles have been devised, and a number have been developed. These are often variants of the important cycles listed. One cycle that has interested technicians over the years without large-scale success in spite of many years' development effort is the Stirling cycle.

The processes of compression and expansion and the associated changes in volume are directly related to the work involved and hence are important for the working fluid to produce work or its equivalent, mechanical power. Thus the working fluids of greatest interest are gases, at least in the work-producing part of the cycle. The work done (per unit mass) on adiabatic expansion is

$$dw = p \, dv \qquad (1\text{-}1)$$

for a closed system (such as the gas in a piston/cylinder). p and v are the pressure and specific volume, respectively. In contrast to liquids and solids, the volume change for a gas is sufficiently large to make the output work significant. Alternatively, the differential shaft work, w_s, is obtained from the change in the total enthalpy $h_t = h + V^2/2 + gz$, in a steady, adiabatic flow:

$$dw_s = d \, h_t \qquad (1\text{-}2)$$

In most heat engines changes in potential energy (gz) associated with the gravitational field of the Earth are negligibly small.

If one were interested in simply representing the characteristics of a cycle, one might draw a path on a thermodynamic state diagram that has the temperature of the working fluid as one axis (to note material limitations or measure changes in enthalpy) and the volume of the fluid as the other. This is not common, however, because a number of other aspects of the cycle parameter choices are important.

In practice, p-v and T-s diagrams are used to illustrate cycles. T is the absolute scale temperature and s is the entropy per unit mass. The p-v diagram is generally more suited to the description of displacement processes because of the direct relationship between work and the physical volume changes; see eq. 1-1. The T-s diagram is more useful for steady flow processes. Here, specific volume is also interesting but not as physically meaningful because the boundaries associated with the typical control mass of the substance are not clearly identifiable.

In all cycles, the work output per unit mass processed and the efficiency are functions of the degree to which the processes involved in the cycle are reversible. Reversibility is intimately related to the transformation of heat to or from work. This idea of reversibility and its relation to the "thermodynamic path" is central to the cycle representation on a state diagram. The pressure-specific volume (p-v) diagram shows work as an area under the curve, and the temperature-entropy (T-s) diagram shows the area under a path as heat transferred or as a measure of heat produced from irreversible work. The transferred heat is related to the property definition of entropy given by

$$ds = dq/T)_{rev} \qquad \text{or} \qquad ds \geq dq/T \qquad (1\text{-}3)$$

Specifically, for heat transferred reversibly, s increases as given by eq. 1-3. It increases more rapidly if irreversibilities are occurring. Even in the absence of heat transfer, s increases for irreversibilities such as friction. In summary, one may say that first law quantities of interest are most clearly displayed in the p-v diagram: work as an area and heat input as measured by temperature changes. On the other hand, these same quantities are also illustrated in the T-s diagram (steady flow work by temperature changes and heat by an area) with the advantage that the reversibility of adiabatic processes is also displayed.

1.1.1. Efficiency

The principal function of a heat engine is to convert thermal power to elec-tromechanical work. The parameter used to describe its effectiveness in this task is a thermal efficiency defined by the ratio of net work output to heat input:

$$\eta_{th} = w_{out} \, / \, q_{in} \qquad (1\text{-}4)$$

It is a parameter that quantifies the amount of a presumably costly thermal resource needed for unit of work output. The heat *sink* is presumably cost free. For transportation systems, measures of fuel mass required to produce a kilowatt of power (specific fuel consumption) are usually used for convenience to portray the same aspect of performance.

1.1.2. Specific Work

A heat engine is ideally compact and processes a small amount of matter per unit time. Thus it is of interest to characterize the effectiveness of each kilo-gram of working fluid to produce work. Thermodynamic analysis of a cycle provides the *specific work* by accounting for the heat accepted and rejected within the limited temperatures and pressures of the system. Specific work carries units of enthalpy (kJ/kg or its equivalent), although it may also be used with a nondimensionalization by a reference state enthalpy (such as the ambi-ent condition). It may also be divided by the volume (displacement) of the machinery, in which case one speaks of a *mean effective pressure* to represent this quantity. The latter is common in the Otto and Diesel engine industry.

1.2. PRACTICAL CYCLES AND IDEAL PROCESSES

Before particular cycles can be discussed, the characteristics of the fluid must be considered, specifically whether the fluid is in the liquid phase for part of the cycle. Cycles that utilize substances in the liquid as well as the gaseous state are termed *condensable fluid cycles*, which can be further categorized as *subcritical* or *supercritical* depending on whether the fluid is heated as a two-phase mixture or at a pressure larger than the critical pressure. In either case, the objective is to take advantage of the low work expenditure required for compression of the liquid phase and obtain, within limitations, the much larger work output during gas or vapor expansion. These cycles must be described by nonsimple characterizations such as tables because the states lies close to the saturation line of the fluid where a description of the fluid may be math-ematically complex.

The so-called Rankine cycles based on this idea have a long development history. They were the first successful engines built because of the small recir-culating work fraction involved in compression and because the cycle could be implemented with positive displacement work components, such as pistons and cylinders. The steam locomotive in use until the middle of the twentieth century was the most visible engine employing the Rankine cycle. Today, the

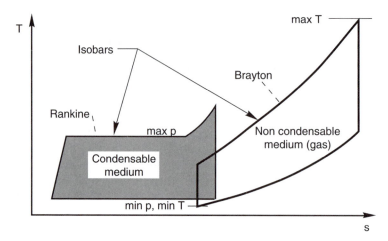

FIGURE 1-1. *T*-s diagrams of two simple forms of steady-flow cycles: subcritical Rankine cycle and Brayton cycle. Limiting parameters are indicated.

most advanced versions of these machines employ steady-flow dynamic work components: pumps and turbines. Further, modern cycles are modified extensively to achieve high efficiency (Ref. 1-2).

Cycles that use a working fluid only in the gaseous phase are characterized by the nature of the compression process: steady flow (Brayton cycle or gas turbine engine), while displacement compression cycles are characterized further by the method of heat addition:

1. Fuel addition to the low-pressure air and spark ignition: Otto cycle;
2. Fuel addition to the compressed high-pressure air with pressure-limited autoignition: Diesel cycle;
3. Conductive heat transfer to the expanding gas in a cylinder through its boundaries: Stirling cycle.

State diagrams for the simple forms of the commercially important cycles are shown in Figs. 1-1 and 1-2, together with the limited value of parameters that strongly influence the cycle performance.

In its simplest form, the steady-flow Brayton cycle, with its gaseous working fluid, consists of an aerodynamic compressor and turbine with a constant-pressure combustor. Commonly such an engine is called a *gas turbine*. These engines are built in sizes ranging roughly from 100 kW to more than 100 MW. These engines are used for aircraft propulsion and utility applications where their high power-to-weight ratio and/or where the ability to produce a large power output rapidly is an advantage. Wilson (Ref. 1-3) gives an excellent overview of the design aspect of this engine type.

The steady-flow Rankine cycle engines (steam turbine power plant) are used primarily in large power output sizes, ranging from about 100 kW to over 1000 MW. Commercial power plants using either nuclear or fossil fuel heat are the primary application of this engine. The principal limitations of this cycle are its complexity when high performance is desired and high operating pressure with water as the working fluid. Indeed, water is the primary fluid used in commercial power plants, although a number of cycles with organic and liquid metal cycles have been considered and developed. Because the cycle can be pushed to its performance limit with fossil fuel heat, efficiencies over 40% have been achieved, even with environmental protection required by the use of coal. On the other hand, the use of nuclear fuel limits temperatures to somewhat lower levels, and thus, typically, conversion efficiencies between 30 and 35% are achieved in practice. Nuclear-heated Brayton cycle power plants have also been built and proposed to take the place of Rankine cycle systems. The efficiency of the gas-cooled systems were projected to be over 40% because of the operating higher temperature allowed. These systems were also seen to be safer from a nuclear view, but the economic risk associated with their development was gauged to be excessive by the utility industry.

Both the Rankine and Brayton cycles may also be used in combination as a combined cycle engine. This application is generally for supplying both heat and power to installations such as buildings, ships, and for very high-efficiency (well in excess of 50%) commercial electric power production using natural gas (Ref. 1-4). The practical values of the thermal efficiencies reachable by the various energy conversion cycles depend on the degree of complexity and cost appropriate for the user so that any representation of efficiency performance (Fig. 1-3) should be tempered by that thought. Furthermore, this efficiency is also scale sensitive in that larger powerplants tend to be more efficient because losses are proportionally smaller in larger engines. Figure 1-3 shows the variation of efficiency with engine size for various engine types including the fuel cell discussed in Chapter 7. Note the generally increasing efficiency trend on

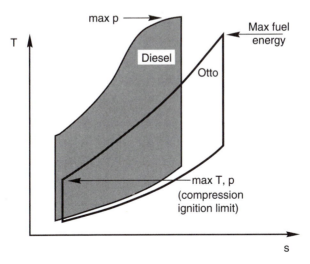

FIGURE 1-2. Idealized *p-v* diagrams for two intermittent displacement cycles: Otto and Diesel cycles. Limiting parameters are indicated.

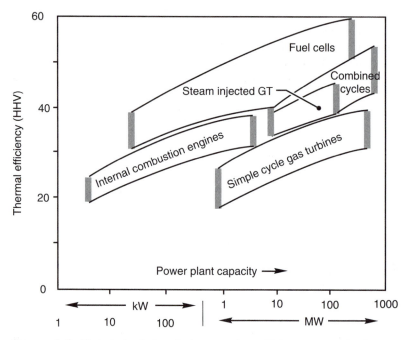

FIGURE 1-3. Variation of electrical generation efficiency as a % of HHV heat input for various conversion technologies. Note the role of engine size and the range in which each seems to be optimal. Data from U.S. Department of Energy, Morgantown, W. Va.

this logarithmic abscissa. The internal combustion engines seem to be reaching the limit of their performance capability in the several megawatt size.

The displacement engine cycles are operated with a short combustion time and tend to be found in applications with power requirements ranging from 1 kW to 10 MW. The Stirling engine, in spite of much development, has yet to reach commercial success in applications of this power range. The Otto and Diesel cycle engines are used extensively in land, air, and water-borne transportation vehicles. The ability for these cycles to supply full and *part power* economically and with a sufficiently rapid match to the demand of the load makes these cycles uniquely well suited for the applications where they are currently employed (Refs. 1-5, 1-6).

1.2.1. Temperature Limits

The efficiency of all cycles is limited by the Second Law of Thermodynamics. This limit is closely associated with the notion of absolute temperature T, and states

$$\eta_{th} = 1 - \frac{q_{out}}{q_{in}} = \left(\begin{array}{c} \text{for a} \\ \text{reversible} \\ \text{cycle} \end{array}\right) \quad 1 - \frac{T_{min}}{T_{max}} = 1 - \frac{1}{\theta} \qquad (1\text{-}5)$$

where the efficiency is defined in eq. 1-4. Here the First Law of Thermodynamics is used in the form

$$w_{out} = q_{in} - q_{out} \tag{1-6}$$

The quantities q_{in} and q_{out} are the heat supplied and rejected by the heat engine in the process of producing work. The absolute temperatures at which these heats interact with the heat engine are T_{max} and T_{min}, respectively. This limitation imposed by the second law is important in that T_{max} should be as large as possible to make η_{th} large, while T_{min} is usually limited by the environment to which the rejected heat must flow. This minimum temperature is on the order of 300 K, although it may be lower, depending on the climate or altitude where the engine is used. The first-order effect on the magnitude of the efficiency is therefore dominated by the peak cycle temperature. This temperature when nondimensionalized by the minimum or ambient temperature gives a parameter θ, which will be seen again in the discussion of direct conversion methods.

1.2.2. Peak cycle temperature

The working fluid may be made to reach any temperature consistent with the materials that contain it or that can be achieved given the choice of fuel and its combustion energy per unit mass. In general, the temperatures achievable through the combustion of most fuels is higher than that which materials can withstand and maintain their structural integrity. Thus combustion is carried out in two ways: (1) steadily with an excess of air to limit the temperature, as in the gas turbine, or (2) in a very short time, as in the Otto cycle. In the Diesel cycle, a combination of these processes is used. The short time exposure of heat to the walls during Otto cycle combustion and the rapid expansion that follows it allow the heat to be absorbed and averaged during the time available until the next combustion event, before which a new cool air charge is available to keep the walls at modest temperatures.

Metal material temperature limits range to 1200 K and ceramics can withstand significantly higher temperatures. The working fluid can exceed this temperature value if adequate cooling is provided to maintain adequately low material temperature in the bounding walls. In Brayton cycle engine practice, the hottest portion of the steady-flow combustion gas may be in excess of 1500 K. Much development effort has been directed toward the use of ceramics in the gas turbine, where better fracture toughness and brittleness characteristics than currently available are required for a practical engine.

It should be noted that the Carnot cycle, a reversible cycle involving isothermal heat interactions with the heat source and environment and with adiabatic reversible work processes can theoretically be devised to realize the so-called Carnot efficiency given in eq. 1-5. It cannot be built as a practical engine because neither the working fluids required exist nor can the ideal processes be created in cost-effective engines. Nevertheless, the efficiency defined in the second part of eq. 1-6 is thus referred to as the Carnot efficiency:

$$\eta_{Carnot} = 1 - \frac{T_{min}}{T_{max}} = 1 - \frac{300}{1500} = 0.80 \qquad (1\text{-}7)$$

for the temperatures indicated. This value serves to identify the ultimate limit to the heat engine efficiency. The theoretical limit of intermittent combustion engines is even higher because the peak cycle temperature exceeds 2000 K for combustion of fuels with a stoichiometric amount of air, that is, where just the right amount of air is used to burn the fuel to H_2O, CO_2 completely and unreacted N_2. Significantly lower efficiency levels are realized in real engines because of unavoidable irreversibilities. These include flow pressure and heat losses, as well as mechanical friction.

1.2.3. Other Limits

In order to produce work, the working fluid must be expanded, $dv > 0$; see eq. 1-1. This implies that the fluid must have been compressed in a previous portion of the cycle. Further, the hotter the fluid, the more work is realized during expansion. This is intimately associated with the nature of gases for which the volume of a unit mass of gas at a given temperature is larger for higher temperatures. Thus larger volumes produce a greater work output. This is the important reason why the peak cycle temperature, and therefore the cycle temperature ratio, should be large.

In addition to the temperature ratio, all cycles must therefore be described in terms of another thermodynamic parameter that characterizes the compression. In displacement engines, the so-called compression ratio is used. It is the ratio of the volumes (volume before compression to that after) that is easy to measure in displacement machines (Otto, Diesel, and Stirling). In steady-flow machines (such as Rankine or Brayton) the pressure at the heat addition process or the ratio of this pressure to the initial value is used. The choice to use pressure or pressure ratio is predicated on its relevance to other aspects of the cycle. For the Brayton cycle, the pressure ratio is commonly used, while absolute pressure is commonly used for the Rankine cycle. The high pressure of the working fluid is limited by material strength considerations and plays a large role in determining the cycle performance. This is because the critical pressure of fluids like water is large (> 200 atm or 3000 psi) and because of the shape of the vapor saturation line.

Consider a cycle using a gaseous working fluid. No matter what parameter is used to describe the degree to which compression takes place, it can be related to temperature changes that occur in the adiabatic work processes through the first law for either a closed system or an open system (steady flow):

$$w_{comp} = u_{in}(T) - u_{out}(T) \quad \text{or} \quad = h_{in}(T) - h_{out}(T) \qquad (1\text{-}8)$$

For gases, the internal energies (u) and the enthalpies (h) are generally functions of T only. This perfect fluid assumption is quite good for many gases considered for cycles. The kinetic (and potential) energy component of the enthalpy can be neglected here so that the end states involved are close to stagnation (zero-velocity) states. With these limitations, one can characterize the compression process in the compressor (and the expansion process in the expander or turbine) by a temperature ratio. This description makes the expressions for efficiency and specific work independent of properties such as specific heat ratio. For reversible work process cycles using an ideal and perfect gas as a working fluid, the efficiencies of the Brayton, Otto, and a simple model of the Diesel cycle are given by a compression temperature ratio τ_c (Ref. 1-1):

$$\eta_{th} = 1 - \frac{1}{\tau_c} \quad \text{where} \quad \tau_c \equiv \frac{T_{comp, \, out}}{T_{comp, \, in}} < \frac{T_{cycle, \, max}}{T_{cycle, \, min}} \tag{1-9}$$

The inequality necessarily applies because heat has yet to be added to the compression end state to reach the peak cycle temperature. The consequence for the idealized model of real cycles is that the efficiencies are necessarily less than the Carnot efficiency:

$$\eta_{th} < \eta_{Carnot} \tag{1-10}$$

How much less is important insofar as it is related to the specific work which can be calculated separately. Thus a design choice is usually made to obtain acceptable levels for both the specific work and the efficiency.

To illustrate this design issue, consider a cycle where the compression end state is close to the peak cycle temperature. In that case, the efficiency is high, but little heat can be added, which implies that correspondingly little work can be realized. Thus practical engines are designed to operate at significantly less than maximum efficiency, but with practical amounts of power delivered for the size of the engine. This balance is especially critical to the design of engines that are to be used in transportation vehicles where engine weight and volume are critical. Practical choices are usually compromises to minimize the total mass of the engine and the mass of the fuel that has to be carried for the mission considered. Excessive mass almost always results in performance penalties on vehicle performance parameters such as acceleration, range, speed, cost, etc.

The reversible work process cycle can be represented on a state diagram such as T-s as shown in Fig. 1-4. Shown are isolines of pressure or specific volume. The efficiency is related to the temperature ratio τ_c noted in eq. 1-9, while the Carnot efficiency is related to the overall cycle temperature ratio denoted by θ, eq. 1-5. The specific work of the cycle is the area enclosed by the path diagram in this reversible cycle and involves both τ and θ. This interpretation cannot be made when the cycle involves irreversible work processes. This is discussed subsequently.

The design characteristics of heat engines with reversible work processes can be summarized in a plot as shown in Fig. 1-5. Shown are the variation of efficiency and specific work as the compression temperature ratio of a simple Brayton cycle is increased. A maximum in specific work is reached first, followed at higher compression temperature ratio by a maximum in the

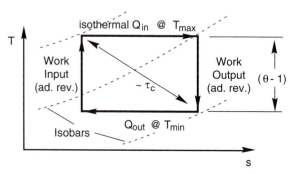

FIGURE 1-4. Reversible or Carnot cycle *T–s* diagram.

efficiency. Practical choices are made between these two design options. It is worthy of note that these are the characteristics of cycles operating at maximum power without consideration of the need for operating at part power.

After the compression process, heating in a practical engine takes place by a process that is not isothermal, as shown in Fig. 1-1. The fact that it is not isothermal is *the* reason for the efficiency degradation from the Carnot value. The heat provided may be thought to be from a heat reservoir at the high temperature of the cycle. Any heat transferred from this reservoir to the working fluid at a temperature less than the peak temperature is transferred irreversibly. Thus the cycle must operate with a performance penalty. This is the most important aspect of engine performance reduction from the ideal value. The irreversibilities encountered in the work processes are the other.

Other losses may be experienced after the mechanical power is produced or before the heat is transferred to the cycle, but these losses have little, if anything, to do with the cycle thermodynamics and thus are not considered further.

1.3. IRREVERSIBLE WORK PROCESSES

Work processes may be described by the degree to which they are adiabatic. In reality, all work processes involve transfer of heat during the compression or expansion processes, which the cycle designer often would like to retain as adiabatic. However, the amount of heat transferred may often be very small. In turbomachinery, for example, the transit time through the machinery is short compared to the time required for heat to travel from the fluid medium to the boundaries. The heat loss or gain is related to the surface-to-volume ratio for the device (i.e., a characteristic inverse length) and to the temperature difference between the boundary and the medium. In a steady-flow machine this difference is small, while it may be quite large in reciprocating machinery. In fact, this heat transfer between the gas and the bounding walls is a significant factor in determining performance. The practicality of compression or

expansion by means of reciprocating machinery is made manageable by the
rapidity of the process.

For adiabatic processes, the measure of reversibility is the *adiabatic efficiency* (and its variants, e.g., polytropic), defined as the ratio

$$\text{adiabatic efficiency (compression)} = \frac{\text{ideal work required}}{\text{actual work required}} \qquad (1\text{-}11)$$

for compression. The ideal and actual work are computed for the same pressure ratio. The inverse ratio is used for an expansion process. In this way
the efficiencies are ideally 100% and less for a real process. In heat engines,
these work process performance indices are developed to achieve high values, often exceeding 90%. Figure 1-6 shows the *T-s* diagram path for
reversible and irreversible compression. The definition of adiabatic efficiency
does not require the path shown to be known. Only the end states need to
be identified through their state parameter values, say, pressure and temperature.

The mechanisms for the failure to achieve ideal performance is primarily
the irreversible conversion of work to heat. That is, motion of the fluid or of
the mechanism is resisted by a frictional force generating heat, which is ultimately less recoverable. The representation of an irreversible process on a
state diagram is best made in the *T-s* plane. Figure 1-6 shows the process in
the direction of greater entropy than that required to reach the design pressure

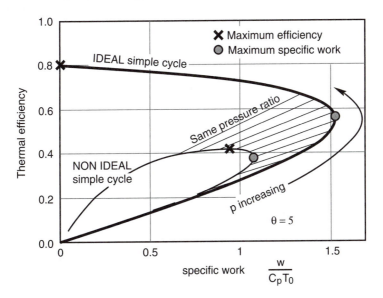

FIGURE 1-5. Variation of efficiency and specific work for a simple
Brayton cycle with irreversible work components. Note direction of
increasing pressure (i.e., temperature) ratio for simple ideal (heavy
line) and nonideal ($\eta_c = 0.85$, $\eta_t = 0.90$) Brayton cycles ($\theta = 5$) and
Carnot efficiency.

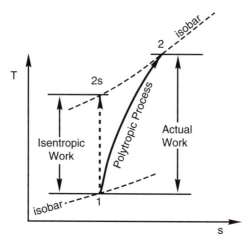

FIGURE 1-6. Reversible (dashed) and irreversible (solid) compression.

reversibly. Thus heat is generated by the irreversible conversion of work. Other work losses may be present, such as the heat dissipated in bearings.

The Carnot-like cycle with irreversible work processes is shown in Fig. 1-7. The second law or thermal efficiency for this cycle is represented by the areas shown: input to the maximum cycle temperature and rejection to the minimum temperature. The effect of the irreversible work process on thermal efficiency is evident by comparison to the true Carnot cycle also shown for the same heat input 2–3.

$$\eta_{th} = 1 - \frac{q(1\text{-}4)}{q(2\text{-}3)} \quad \text{and} \quad \eta_{th,\,Carnot} = 1 - \frac{q(1i\text{-}4i)}{q(2\text{-}3)} \quad (1\text{-}12)$$

The thermal efficiency of an engine with irreversible work processes must therefore be less than that of a Carnot engine.

1.4. IRREVERSIBLE HEAT TRANSFER PROCESSES

The Carnot cycle involves *isothermal* heat addition and heat removal from the working fluid. These processes are difficult to carry out in practice, except perhaps when a condensable substance is used. The performance of the resultant Rankine cycle strongly influenced by the shape of the vapor dome of the working fluid (Chap. 11, Ref. 1-1). The shape of the saturation lines in the *T-s* plane of almost all substances considered as a working fluid is unsatisfactory in some way. Either the temperature extremes do not match those of the solid materials making up the machinery and the environment, or their slope is insufficiently steep, making the work processes difficult to implement (Ref. 1-7) without *superheating*. One can therefore say that, barring discovery of a much better working fluid, the Rankine cycle is a relatively poor approximation of a Carnot cycle as far as the heat transfer processes are concerned. Practical engines exploit isothermal heat transfer in either heat input or rejection, but not both. The loss in *availability* incurred with the heat transfer across a finite temperature difference is accepted to achieve a high specific work performance and/or low cost. Figure 1-8 shows two cycles where the peak temperature achievable from the viewpoint of allowable pressure may be lower than the allowable temperature from a material point of view.

Isothermal processes may be realized with intercooling of the compression and reheating of the expansion processes. The resultant Ericsson cycle (Chap. 9, Ref. 1-1) has high thermodynamic performance, but is unfortunately high in complexity and consequently in cost.

In intermittent cycles such as the Otto and Diesel cycles, the very large and irreversible heat interactions between the working fluid and the heat source (the hot combustion gas) are accepted in light of the very high Carnot efficiencies these cycles provide. Here again, the practical considerations of the engine permit degradation of extremely good reversible cycle performance to good and acceptable levels in the real engine.

1.5. PART-LOAD PERFORMANCE

The heat engine has the ability to convert heat from available resources such as fossil fuels efficiently, and a good one can do so in a light-weight and low-cost machine. Many of the applications of heat engines are in transportation, where the high energy density of fuels and the high-power-density machines make transportation systems possible and practical. A transportation power system like an automobile needs to vary output with time to a degree much greater and more rapidly than other power systems such as long cruising vehicles and utility systems. The degree of variability required depends on the transportation mission. The power required may be supplied by a stationary power system and delivered to the moving vehicle, or it may be generated as

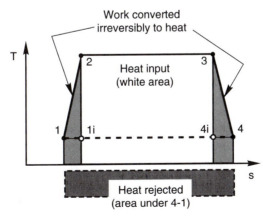

FIGURE 1-7. Carnot cycle with irreversible work processes.

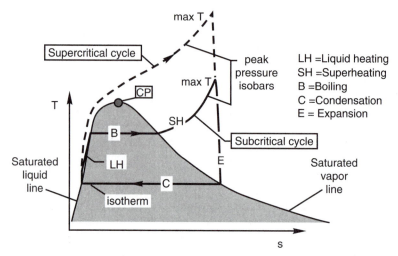

FIGURE 1-8. *T-s* diagram for a subcritical Rankine cycle showing that isothermal heating of water cannot be easily or practically carried out to the allowable temperature T_{max}: the critical pressure of water has the large value of 22 MPa, over 3000 psi.

needed from the thermal energy stored in fuel carried by the vehicle. This aspect of a requirement is important when direct energy conversion systems are considered as alternatives to heat engines.

The power output from a heat engine using combustion heat is typically modulated by the rate of fuel flow. A typical design goal is to maintain the efficiency as high as possible as power output is varied. The variation of efficiency at part power is particularly critical for vehicle-power plant combinations where the nature of the mission involves significant variations of power.

All combustion-driven heat engines are modulated by the amount of fuel supplied per unit time. The power output from an engine is the product of

$$\text{Power} = \text{specific work} \ \times \ \text{working fluid mass flow rate}$$

or

$$= \text{efficiency} \ \times \ \text{fuel flow rate} \ \times \ \text{fuel heating value} \qquad (1\text{-}13)$$

The specific work and efficiency are related to the thermodynamic state parameters that define the cycle. To the extent that these performance parameters are constant, the power output from a particular engine is proportional to the working fluid mass flow rate or the fuel flow rate. Various cycles operate with different relationships between fuel and air flow rates. For example, at a given speed, an Otto cycle engine is designed to modulate the air flow rate by means of a throttle, which controls the *density* of the air being processed in the cylinder volume. The function of the fuel system (the carburetor or a more modern injection system) is to tailor the correct amount of fuel to match the changing air flow rate. The Diesel engine, by contrast, processes the same amount of the air per unit time, and the fuel-to-air ratio is changed to obtain various power levels. Both of these engines produce greater power at greater speed because the *air mass processing rate* is increased, but are limited at high rotational speed by friction losses (Ref. 1-6).

Steady-flow engines are controlled by changing the fuel-to-air mixture ratio, which changes the peak cycle temperature. These cycles generally have a lower efficiency at lower power settings because the Carnot temperature limits are narrower (see eq. 1-5) in the reduced power case. The relationship between working fluid mass flow rate and fuel heat input (i.e., temperature) is established by the flow characteristics of the work components, such as the normally choked turbine nozzle inlet and the characteristics of the compressor. Figure 1-9 illustrates the relationship between flow rates, their control or coupling, and the cycle to determine the power at less than maximum power output. Note that control is exerted either on the fuel or the air flow rate, but not both. The coupling condition, if any exists, establishes the relation between these flow rates.

In actuality, the conditions at part power always lead to a difference between the state path descriptions appropriate for full and part power. Thus a variation associated with the changing thermodynamics is always present. In some cases, the Otto cycle in particular, the influence is significant. The net result is that an engine designed for a given maximum power condition may have a variation as shown in Fig. 1-10 with changing power output. It is this aspect of a fuel energy power system that must also be compared to the direct energy conversion schemes described in the chapters to follow.

1.6. SHAFT POWER

Reciprocating engines such as the Diesel, Otto, Stirling, and the early Rankine engines transmit the work to pistons, which turn a crank by means of a connecting rod (Fig. 1-11). For physically similar devices, L is the char-

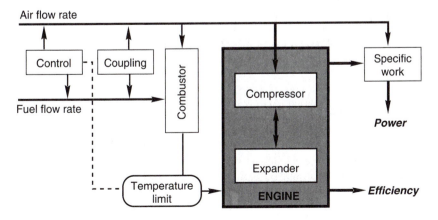

FIGURE 1-9. Summary of the relationships in a heat engine for part power.

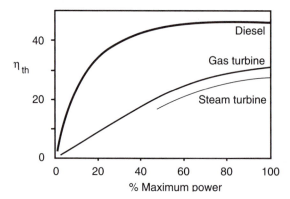

FIGURE 1-10. Part power characteristics of a number of engine types. These variations are qualitative and depend strongly on the specifics of the cycle.

acteristic size parameter. The (angle-averaged) pressure on the piston and the size of the machinery determines the force on the piston and thus the torque on the shaft. The speeds involved are limited by the linear piston speed, which, in turn, determines the angular speed for a machine of a given size. For limited linear piston speeds (V in the range 10-20 m/sec) the angular speed of engines decreases with increasing engine size. Thus the following engine scaling relations hold:

$$\dot{W} = Q\omega = p_0\left[w(p, T) L^3\right]\omega = [p_0\, w(p, T)] L^2 V \qquad (1\text{-}14)$$

where p_0 is a reference pressure, usually atmospheric, and $w(p,T)$ is a nondimensional specific work. In the reciprocating engine community, the product $(p_0 w)$ is termed a mean effective pressure, mep. Q is the (averaged) torque and ω is the angular speed. This relation makes it clear that power scales as size (L^2) and ω decreases with increasing L for V fixed. Thus larger engines produce more power and operate at lower rotational speeds than smaller ones.

For aerodynamic or steady-flow machines such as the gas turbine (Brayton) or modern Rankine engines a similar relation holds. The velocity V, in that case, is limited to a velocity near sound speed. Similarly to reciprocating engines, the power and torque of steady-flow machines scale with size, as shown in eq. 1-14.

Once mechanical power is produced, the shaft may turn a generator to convert the mechanical power to electrical power. The efficiencies of electrical generators and motors are usually very high and less than ideal due primarily to ohmic heating in the wiring and friction losses due to motion. The high degree of convertability to and from mechanical power to electrical power implies a high degree of reversibility and thus equivalence between these two energy forms. Equation 1-15 gives the definitions of the conversion efficiencies (which are always less than but close to unity):

$$\eta_{generator} = \frac{\dot{W}_{electrical}}{\dot{W}_{mechanical}} \approx (<) \, 1 \quad \text{and} \quad \eta_{motor} = \frac{\dot{W}_{mechanical}}{\dot{W}_{electrical}} \approx (<) \, 1 \quad (1\text{-}15)$$

Any load that is to be connected to an engine has torque or power character-istics with angular speed. Steady operation of load and engine is realized where available and required torques or powers are equal at the same speed. This operation is stable only if the two characteristic curves intersect as shown in Fig. 1-12, as is the typical case. The engine torque variation illustrated is that associated with a source of constant power. This variation shows the extreme and limiting torque that might be encountered for an application such as a vehicle at low speed. The extreme may lead to slippage between wheel and stationary surface. Note the steady operation point. In the direct energy conversion schemes to be considered subsequently, an analogous match between the electric power source and the load resistance applies.

1.7. ENERGY CONVERSION NOT INVOLVING HEAT ENGINES

Most of the world's energy resources are traceable to the sun, either directly or in the convenient form of fossil fuels from ancient plants. The availability of these energy forms and the inventions called heat engines, which transform thermal energy to work by the action of forces acting on boundaries sur-rounding a system, have been instrumental in changing the nature of human activity on a scale unknown before that time. This technology is, however, not the sole means of converting thermal energy to the more useful electrome-chanical form. The conversion to electrical power may be carried out directly without intermediate conversion to mechanical power and the limitations this implies about the efficiency and practicality. Direct energy conversion methods offer the avoidance of complexity and losses associated with mechanical motion, but generally these methods involve limitations of their own. In the chapters to follow, the "direct" conversion of the energy is described. The tech-nologies emphasized here are not the only ones possible based on the possible

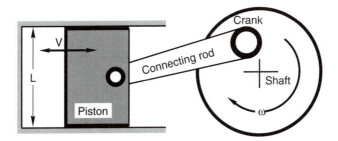

FIGURE 1-11. Conversion of piston forces on a piston in a cylinder into shaft torque by a crank mechanism. L is a characteristic scale length for geometrically similar devices.

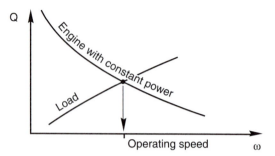

FIGURE 1-12. Torque available from an engine and required by a load as functions of rotational speed.

physical mechansims that have been discovered. However, many of the phenomena are such that practical implementation seems unlikely on a commercial scale. Such phenomena may include ferroelectrics and piezoelectrics, among others. These effects may be and are exploited in the design of specific devices and processes. This usefulness does not necessarily elevate their status to the point where they are competitive with some of the schemes discussed here. New discoveries may change this conclusion, but for the present purposes, only schemes with a reasonable chance of success in applications with significant power outputs are considered. To understand the physics of some of the conversion schemes not considered here, the reader may consult Angrist or Sutton (Refs. 1-8, 1-9) and the literature cited therein.

The principal energy process paths considered in this book are shown in Fig. 1-13. For economic reasons, the exploitation of fuels is emphasized. The usefulness of specific schemes may be associated with the environmental consequences of conversion rather than the attainment of specific power (weight and compactness) and thermal efficiency.

Direct conversion of energy to electricity is generally taken to involve machinery with no moving parts. In fact, movement or transport of energy from one location to another must always involve motion of a physical entity with energy. If this entity is an electron, photon, or phonon, then the devices have "no moving parts" that might wear. Ultimately the (economic) *life* of the conversion system is of interest to the user and not whether there is reciprocating machinery, high-speed motion, or motion at the elementary particle level.

If physical constraints such as temperature limits on real materials and irreversibilities were not involved, the performance of engines would be very high indeed. For example, the Carnot efficiency of a fuel-burning engine can be made to approach the efficiency of converting a fuel's chemical energy to electric power in a fuel cell, for example. Even here, the process is approachable only through an ideal process where the power output is very small, but very efficient. The performance of engines and direct conversion devices is limited by the same laws of thermodynamics, and the real application environment therefore plays an important role in determining actual performance.

The chapters to follow are descriptions of the performance characteristics of a variety of energy conversion schemes that are likely to find an economic niche. The schemes are based on physical principles that are described in detail so that the limitations may be understood. The important differentiation of the processes is made on the basis of the kind of elementary entity wherein the energy is found prior to conversion to electricity. On a scale ranging from macroscopic to submicroscopic, the energy conversion methods described may be classified in the following according to the intermediate energy carrier:

Heat engines: thermal energy and motion of machine elements

MHD: motion of electrons carried in a gas stream

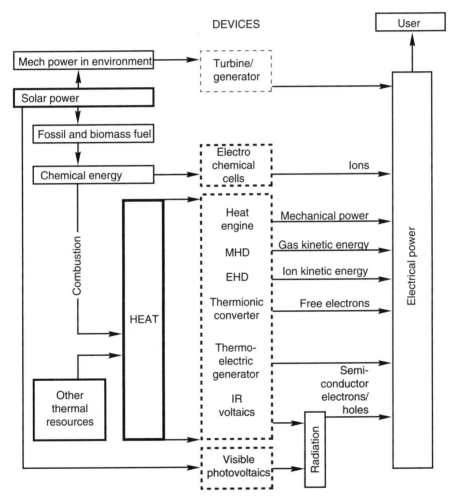

FIGURE 1-13. Direct energy conversion schemes and that of mechanical power in the environment (wind, hydro, wave, etc.) to electrical power. The other thermal resources noted include geothermal heat and nuclear heat in a reactor. Note solar energy is the principal primary resource of all conversion schemes.

EHD: motion of ion carried in a gas stream

Thermionics: transfer of electrons across a vacuum or plasma

Electrochemical cells: ionic charge transfer in an electrolyte

Radiation cell: photon interaction with charge carriers in a semiconductor

Thermoelectricity: transfer of electrons between states in a semiconductor

In this order, the important aspects of the underlying physics and chemistry may be described with a modicum of logical fluidity. Figure 1-13 shows these schemes with this order in mind, including the conversion (not covered here; see Ref. 1-1) of mechanical power to electrical power involving a turbine and a rotating electrical generator. Note the common names of the practical devices involved. The photonic energy is subdivided according to the temperature of the heat source. On one extreme is solar energy (a 5800 K blackbody source) to take advantage of sunlight as a power source, and on the other is infrared thermal radiation associated with much more modest blackbody temperatures, those associated with combustion heat and real engineering materials. The short-wavelength radiation capture and transformation is discussed in some detail Chapters 1 and 18 of Ref. 1-1 and is discussed further here. However, the emphasis of "photovoltaic" conversion in Chapter 8 is on infrared radiation, and the devices are therefore referred to as IR voltaic (IRV) devices.

PROBLEMS

1. Consider a Carnot-like cycle engine whose isothermal heat input is characterized by Δs_i operating with a cycle temperature ratio θ between the maximum and minimum temperatures. If the compression and expansion processes are irreversible and characterized by Δs_c and Δs_e, find expressions for the specific work and the thermal efficiency. Show that in the limit of ideal work processes the Carnot efficiency is recovered and find the specific work in that case. If the work processes are reversible and the heat input and output are characterized by Δs, what is the relation of this Δs to the change in parameters describing the change in pressure? How is this relation impacted by the phase of the working fluid?

2. Two cycles are operated such that the heat rejected by the higher-temperature cycle is the input to the lower-temperature cycle. Determine the expression for the thermal efficiency of the cycle combination.

3. On a logarithmic scale for power in kilowatts, indicate the range of common Rankine, Brayton, Otto, and Diesel cycle engines, indicating specific engines where possible. For these engines, convert the available data on fuel efficiency to thermal efficiency.

BIBLIOGRAPHY

Hills, R. L., *Power from Steam: A History of the Stationary Steam Engine*, Cambridge University Press, Cambridge, 1989.

REFERENCES

1-1.   Decher, R., *Energy Conversion: Systems, Flow Physics and Engineering*, Oxford University Press, New York, 1994.

1-2.   Culp, A. W., *Principles of Energy Conversion*, McGraw-Hill, New York, 1979.

1-3.   Wilson, D. G., *The Design of High Efficiency Turbomachinery and Gas Turbines*, MIT Press, Cambridge, Mass., 1984.

1-4.   Kehlhofer, R., *Combined Cycle Gas and Steam Turbine Power Plants*, Fairmont Press, Linburn, Ga., 1991.

1-5.   Heywood, J. B., *Internal Combustion Engine Fundamentals*, McGraw-Hill, New York, 1988.

1-6.   Taylor, C. F., *The Internal Combustion Engine in Theory and Practice*, Vols. I and II, MIT Press, Cambridge, Mass., 1966.

1-7.   Wood, B. D., *Applications of Thermodynamics*, Addison-Wesley, Reading, Mass., 1969.

1-8.   Angrist, S. W., *Direct Energy Conversion*, Allyn and Bacon, Boston, 1971.

1-9.   Sutton, G. W., *Direct Energy Conversion*, McGraw-Hill, New York, 1966.

2

FLOW WITH ELECTROMAGNETIC INTERACTION

In a jet propulsion system, the thermal energy of jet created through the use of a nozzle provides the necessary momentum for a propulsive force. The power associated with the flow kinetic energy can also be transformed to electric power, like a turbine driving an electrical generator does. In this chapter, the direct conversion of flow kinetic energy to electric power and its reverse, both realized through the interaction of the moving fluid with electromagnetic fields, are introduced. This chapter is a review of the governing equations that describe the electromagnetic fields and the flow equations as they are influenced by force and energy interactions with applied fields. The physical processes involved apply to magnetohydrodynamic (MHD) generators whose function it is to generate electrical power, and MHD accelerators whose function is to increase the enthalpy of a fluid. The moving medium used is an electrically conducting fluid (gaseous or liquid), rather than a solid material such as the copper wire in the rotor of a conventional electric motor or generator. Chapter 3 is a description of the particle mechanics required to estimate the electrical conductivity of gases of the type used in MHD generators. The applications, their design, and performance are described in Chapter 4.

In the following, a review of the relevant physics is presented with an eye toward developing the necessary descriptive equations that will allow the description of practical devices. The SI system of units is employed in the discussion of the physics in this field.

The following definitions of the vector calculus are used:

$$\nabla = \text{grad, or gradient operator} = \frac{\partial}{\partial x}i + \frac{\partial}{\partial y}j + \frac{\partial}{\partial z}k$$

in a Cartesian coordinate system with $\text{div}\,A = \nabla \cdot A$ and $\text{curl}\,A = \nabla \times A$ The reader is cautioned that no general and consistent system of symbols for thermodynamic and electrophysical quantities exists, and there may be a single symbol used to describe two different quantities. It is hoped that the context and adherence to standard practice makes the notation clear. In this chapter the following symbols are used:

U	vector fluid velocity
u	x component of velocity
V, v	charged particle velocities
V	volume, speed
v	specific volume, y component of velocity
e	internal energy

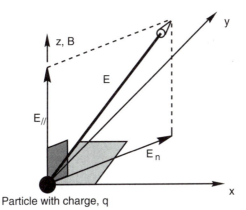

Particle with charge, q

FIGURE 2-1. Charged particle in general **E** and **B** fields. z axis is oriented along **B**.

The symbol e for internal energy is used to avoid confusion with u used as a velocity component. Vectors are written in bold face (e.g., **A**) when appropriate and as scalars (e.g., A) when only the vector magnitude is relevant. A multiplication sign $\times$ is used to indicate a vector multiplication, such as in the so-called cross product.

2.1. ELECTROMAGNETIC FORCES

In this section, the physical phenomena associated with electrical charges are introduced. The description of a fluid's mechanical interaction with electromagnetic forces is eased considerably through a review of the appropriate physical laws and the resulting field definitions.

2.1.1. Drift Velocity: Motion of a Collisionless Charged Particle

In order to understand the motion of charged particles in electric and magnetic fields, one may begin by examining the special case of a collisionless plasma where the motion of the individual charges proceeds without the randomizing disturbances due to encounters with other particles. Let **v** be the individual particle's vector velocity. Recall from an elementary study of physics that the electric field **E** is a force per unit charge so that Newton's second law for a particle reads

$$F = qE = m\frac{dv}{dt} \tag{2-1}$$

when only an electric field is present. When a magnetic field **B** is also present, the particle also experiences the so-called Lorentz force (normal to both velocity and **B**) and Newton's law becomes

$$m\frac{dv}{dt} = q(E + v \times B) \tag{2-2}$$

These field definitions and their relation to observational phenomena are reviewed in Section 2.3. For the present, the viewpoint is taken that Newton's law as written (eq. 2-2) illustrates the need for using such fields for descriptive purposes. Consider a steady set of fields as shown in Fig. 2-1. The electric field may be decomposed into two components, one parallel ($E_{//}$) and one perpendicular (E_n) to the B field. The vector velocity may be written in terms of components, parallel and perpendicular to B, $v_{//}$ and v_n. Since $v_{//} \times B = 0$, the equation of motion becomes

$$m\frac{dv_{//}}{dt} = qE_{//}$$

(2-3)

$$m\frac{dv_n}{dt} = q\left(E_n + v_n \times B\right)$$

which implies that along the B field (//) lines, the motion is simple and rectilinear. In the plane normal to B, a number of interesting cases may be examined. The first is to ask whether there is a condition where the charged particle experiences zero acceleration.

Evidently, from eq. 2-3, the velocity stays constant in time when

$$E_n + v_{n,D} \times B = 0$$

that is, when the particle moves with the velocity $v_{n,D}$. This velocity is termed a *drift* velocity, given by a rearrangement of the above equation:

$$v_{n,D} = \frac{E \times B}{B^2} \qquad \text{since } B \times v \times B = vB^2$$

(2-4)

2.1.2. Induced Electric Field

To an observer moving with the drift velocity, the apparent E field is zero. Further, a charged particle moving with steady velocity (as it is being convected) through a magnetic field will force an E field to be created, or better,

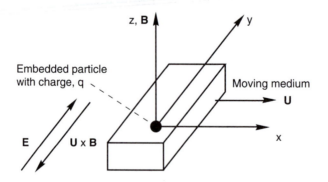

FIGURE 2-2. Moving charge in a magnetic field.

induced. Thus, in a material that carries charges *bound* to the material, moving with velocity **U** through a magnetic field **B**, the net electric field sensed by the charges (in their reference frame) is

$$E + U \times B = 0 \qquad (2\text{-}5)$$

E is the induced electric field in the negative y direction, as shown in Fig. 2-2. Before extending this discussion toward a physical derivation of the relationship between the electric field and the current that may flow as a result (Ohm's law), it is appropriate to examine other aspects of charged particle motion in **E** and **B** fields. Of greatest interest is that associated with only a **B** field.

2.1.3. Cyclotron Frequency

The motion of a charged particle in only a magnetic field is also obtained from the equation of motion in a collisionless environment, eqs. 2-2 or 2-3 with **E** = 0. Equation 2-2 gives that $v_{//}$ = constant, while eq. 2-3 can be written as x and y components in a plane normal to **B**. Thus

$$m\frac{dv_n}{dt} = qv_n \times B \quad \text{or} \quad m\frac{d v_x}{dt} = q v_y B \quad \text{and} \quad m\frac{d v_y}{dt} = -q v_x B$$

The scalar equations can be combined to give

$$\frac{d^2 v_x}{dt^2} = -\omega^2 v_x \quad \text{where} \quad \omega^2 = \frac{qB}{m_e} \qquad (2\text{-}6)$$

and a similar equation for v_y. Here ω is the cyclotron frequency. The name follows from the continuous circular path motion that must result from the sinusoidal variation of v_x, which is the solution of eq. 2-6. The Larmor radius of the motion follows from

$$R_L = \int_0^{\pi/2} v_x dt = \frac{|v_n|}{\omega} \qquad (2\text{-}7)$$

The charged particles discussed to this point could be electrons or ions. The Larmor radius of the electron is much smaller than that of the ion because of the latter's much larger mass. In the engineering devices to be discussed in Chapters 2-4, the motion of ions is virtually inconsequential. Thus the motion of the electrons is normally of much greater interest.

2.1.4. Combined **E** and **B** Fields

With an **E** field present, the motion of a charged particle is a superposition of the **E** × **B** drift and the cyclotron motion. This motion is not of direct interest since high-pressure gases have densities sufficiently large for collisions to be important, electron-heavy-particle collisions, in particular. For example, an electron starting from near rest after a collision tends to move in a circular path once it gains velocity as a result of acceleration due to the **E** field. The result is that the electron is turned away from the **E** field direction until the next collision. On average then, the charge motion (i.e., the current) is not parallel to **E**, and a vector form of Ohm's law should be expected to apply.

2.1.5. Ohm's Law

In the example above and Fig. 2-1, the $\mathbf{U} \times \mathbf{B}$ field is in the $+y$ direction so that the induced field, **E**, must be in the negative y direction. In high-pressure gases used in energy conversion, the charges are part of a mixture of neutral atoms, positive ions, and negative electrons. Such a mixture is called a *plasma*. The temperature of this plasma must be high enough so that a fraction of one of the species is ionized (see Section 5.10, Ref. 1-1). The plasma's boundaries may be be configured in such a way as to allow or force the flow of the electrical charges. A flux of charges is a (electrical) current, a vector. A current per unit area (normal to the current flow) is the current density, **j**. Section 2.2.2 shows that the current of interest is primarily that associated with the electrons, although both positive ions and electrons are present in a neutral plasma.

Evidently a current flow is intimately associated with an imbalance between the electric fields, $\mathbf{E} + \mathbf{U} \times \mathbf{B}$ and with the external boundary conditions such as the magnitude of a resistive element or current source that completes the current circuit. The simplest relation between **j** and the local field seen by the moving charge, $\mathbf{E}' = \mathbf{E} + \mathbf{U} \times \mathbf{B}$, is a linear one. The general relation is Ohm's law:

$$j = \sigma E' = \sigma(E + U \times B) \qquad (2\text{-}8)$$

The scalar proportionality constant, σ, is a measure of the ease with which current flows as a result of the electric field and is termed the electrical conductivity. In general, σ is a tensor, as suggested by the motion of individual charges in the presence of both **E** and **B** fields. For a uniform medium with geometry depicted as in Fig. 2-3, and in the absence of a magnetic field **B**, this relation may be written in the familiar form (with voltage as ϕ):

$$\phi = I R = (j h L) R \qquad (2\text{-}9)$$

Here uniform current density, the current $I = j$ (area) $= j h L$, and the electric field are related to a voltage gradient through the general relation between a force potential and the force, viz.,

$$E = -\nabla \phi \qquad (2\text{-}10)$$

which becomes, for a region of uniform **E** when a voltage ϕ is applied over a distance d:

$$E = -\frac{\phi}{d} \qquad (2\text{-}11)$$

Evidently, from eqs. 2-8 to 2-11, the resistance of the plasma volume is related to its conductivity by (see also eq. 2-12):

$$R = \frac{d}{h\,L}\,\frac{1}{\sigma} \tag{2-12}$$

The bounding walls normal to the y direction accept and emit the current flow. These are *electrodes*, which are connected to the external circuit. The other wall must prevent current flow intended to travel through the plasma and thus are *insulator walls*.

Consider further that the element in Fig. 2-3 is a fluid (although a solid is not excluded) and that the **B** field direction is aligned with the z direction of the coordinate system shown. With the motion through the duct in the x direction, the induced electric field is in the y direction. Such a situation is referred to as a "crossed field" device. If the dimension of the duct is d in this direction, a voltage of uBd will appear across the duct's conductor electrodes in contact with the moving fluid *if no current is allowed to flow*. One might measure this "open circuit" voltage with a high-resistance voltmeter across the two electrode walls.

The current flow is controlled by the conditions external to the electrodes. For example, a resistance may be connected to the electrodes, which allows current to flow. Alternatively, a voltage source may be connected to the electrodes with polarity and magnitude such that the current flows in the opposite direction. Thus current magnitude and direction are determined by the external circuit. The direction of the current relative to the electric field **E** distinguishes devices where work is done on the fluid to accelerate it from those where the work is done by the fluid to produce electric power. These devices are termed *accelerators* and *generators*, respectively. Their characteristics are very much like their electromechanical equivalents: motors and generators.

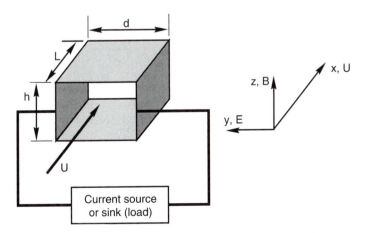

FIGURE 2-3. Sketch of current flow through an element of material bounded by the walls shown. Electrodes are the $h \times L$ sidewalls. The $d \times L$ walls are of an insulator material.

Before considering these devices further, it is important to consider the physics of the motion of current-carrying matter through magnetic fields. Ampere's law of electricity and magnetism theory can be shown to be equivalent to stating that a current-carrying bar will experience a force (Fig. 2-4 and Section 2.3). This force is orthogonal to both the current flow and the magnetic field present. Mathematically in scalar form, it is

$$F = I\ B\ d \qquad (2\text{-}13)$$

or, more generally, in vector form, for a unit element of volume:

$$f = j \times B \qquad (2\text{-}14)$$

Here **f** is a body force per unit volume. With the coordinate system as in Fig. 2-3, this volumetric force acts in a direction parallel or antiparallel to the material motion. From mechanics, then, when a force is applied in the direction of motion work is added to the body in question or vice versa. For a given **B** field, the direction of current flow, **j**, determines the direction of the body force and thus whether the device is an accelerator or a generator (Fig. 2-5).

Since a resistive load cannot be a power source, only a sink, the generator configuration involves a resistive load, whereas an accelerator involves a power source that provides DC current at a voltage, $\phi > UBd$. Such fluid mechanical energy conversion devices are MHD (magnetohydrodynamic) generators or MHD accelerators, respectively.

2.1.6. Applications

A number of practical applications have been investigated from the viewpoint of successfully competing with other energy conversion processes. These are the MHD generator for the production of commercial or space power and the pumping of electrically conducting liquids. During the Apollo space program, there was also a short-lived interest in using an MHD-driven gas accelerator

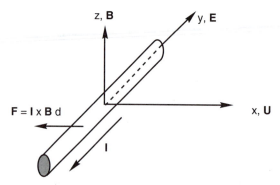

FIGURE 2-4. Force on a current-carrying wire. Wire is aligned with the y direction.

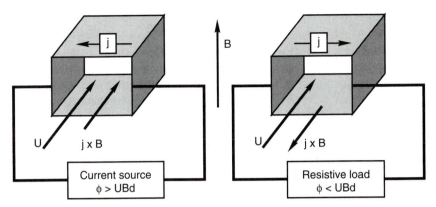

FIGURE 2-5. MHD accelerator (left) and generator showing the vector orientation between the flow and the $\mathbf{f} = \mathbf{j} \times \mathbf{B}$ force.

for the production of a high-enthalpy wind tunnel for testing vehicles for atmospheric entry from lunar orbit. The pace of the program schedule was such that completion of the development of the tunnel was not possible, and the high-enthalpy wind tunnel development effort was discontinued.

Power generation by means of an MHD generator is pursued by two means. The first is to recognize that from a thermodynamic viewpoint, the MHD generator is a turbinelike device, albeit with a very high-temperature inflow. The body force exerted on the fluid is volumetric (rather than acting on the blade surface of a conventional turbine) so that cycles with high "turbine" entry temperatures (T_4) may be contemplated. With the body force volumetric, the flow configuration may be simple and the heat transfer loss to the surface may be made relatively small when large-scale devices are considered: the heat transfer loss increases with surface area (L^2), while the power output increases with volume (L^3). For some L then, the efficiency may be sufficiently high that an interesting machine may be devised. Most important of all is that the cycle with large T_4 can be higher in efficiency than that of other methods of utilizing the fuel heat. To this end, an extensive and continuing effort for the development of coal-burning MHD has been underway in the United States and overseas for more than 30 years. A discussion of the MHD generator as an element of a cycle is found in Chapter 11 of Ref. 1-1. This chapter emphasizes the physics and gasdynamics of the conversion process.

The other MHD generator device under development for a time was the liquid metal MHD generator, which takes advantage of the high conductivity and high density of liquid metals. It suffers from requiring the employment of a mixing process to accelerate the fluid, which results in significant irreversibilities that reduce cycle efficiency.

During a time when high-temperature nuclear reactors were under development, there was a significant effort to develop a suitable MHD generator for use in space for primary electric propulsion. While this effort yielded much useful understanding of *nonequilibrium conductivity* (enhanced conductivity through elevation of the electron temperature above the gas temperature, Ref. 2-1), it was terminated when the reactor development ceased and it became clear that the missions were considered improbable. At the time, reactors with temperatures near 1300 K were in development, with 2000 K considered to be achievable. The nonequilibrium conduction was required because the reactor temperatures were insufficient for adequate conductivity in the thermal plasmas. Such systems were very attractive since the work could be obtained at high temperatures, allowing a high radiator temperature for low system weight (see Section 9.10, Ref. 1-1).

When an electrically conducting liquid needs to be pumped, the MHD interaction may be exploited. Such pumps have no moving parts in contact with the fluid. This may be important for applications where the fluid might be corrosive, radioactive, or needs to be ultraclean, such as sterile body fluids.

Determination of the performance of MHD devices involves the physics necessary to determine the conductivity σ to describe the general Ohm's law and finally to describe the dynamics of the fluid through the bounding duct. These issues are addressed in this and the following chapters.

The successful integration of an MHD device into a power plant requires the system to be tailored to the MHD generator characteristics. These characteristics are such that the integration is complex from the technical, economic, and environmental viewpoints. In spite of decades of development dating back to the early 1960s, the component performance and economic risk has (so far) been sufficiently great that electric power utility systems have not tried to use this technology on a commercial scale.

2.2. GASEOUS WORKING FLUIDS: PLASMA

Fluids that undergo force interactions with electric and magnetic fields must contain charged particles. These are obtained from atoms that undergo the ionization reaction to form either positive and negative ions as in a liquid solution or positive atomic ions and electrons in the gaseous phase. The ionization reaction in gases must take place at high temperature.

In Section 5.10 of Ref. 1-1, the equilibrium chemistry of ionization is described, and it should be evident that substances with low ionization potential most easily undergo the ionization reaction for a chosen temperature. The temperature of interest is necessarily limited by the temperature of the heat source in the case of a generator or by the process of energy losses by various mechanisms (heat transfer, for example) in the case of an accelerator. Typical temperatures reached in gases that result in a small degree of ionization of the gas are termed *low-temperature plasmas*. In practice, temperatures considered for these devices range between 2000 and 5000 K. This is in contrast to high-temperature (and low-density) plasmas occurring in astrophysics and in connection with fusion energy conversion.

The low-temperature plasma consists primarily of neutral atoms and a small fraction of electrons and ions. The plasma is *electrically neutral* in the sense that a finite volume of the plasma will contain an equal number of positive charges on the ions and negatively charged electrons. The plasma is said to be *singly ionized* if all ions carry a +1 charge.

For the discussion to follow, the view adopted for development of the physical description is that a plasma is the fluid medium. A conducting liquid may also be examined by simplification of some of the relations that apply to gases, hence the use of a liquid is a special, and often simpler, case of the more general fluid medium.

2.2.1. Electric Charge Density

On a scale that is large compared to the size of the plasma component atoms and to the mean distance between particles, the plasma is electrically neutral. On a smaller scale, the plasma cannot be electrically neutral: the net charge density, defined as the ratio of charge per unit volume, clearly depends on the number and type of particles in the volume considered. Thus there is a small length scale beyond which electrical neutrality is not an appropriate description. The scale is identified in Section 3.1.

2.2.2. Electric Current

In the absence of force fields on the electric charges, the various kinds of particles travel through an area fixed in space so that the net flux of any one type of particle is zero. Their free particle random motion is isotropic. When a force field whose direction depends on the sign of the charge is applied, electrons will continue their random motion, but superimposed on this motion is a "drift" in the direction of the electric field in the frame of reference of the plasma. Ions will drift in the opposite direction. It will be seen that the drift velocities $\mathbf{V}$ of the very light electrons and the much heavier ions are very different. Thus there arises a net charge flux equal to

$$\mathbf{j} = q_e n_e \mathbf{V}_e + q_i n_i \mathbf{V}_i \qquad (2\text{-}15)$$

where e refers to the electron and i refers to the ions. q is the charge per particle and n is the species number density (m^{-3}). The vector quantity $\mathbf{j}$ is the current density. In a plasma consisting entirely of singly ionized ions ($q_i/e = +1$ and $q_e/e = -1$), the ion and electron densities are equal, so that

$$\mathbf{j} = e\, n_e\left(\mathbf{V}_e - \mathbf{V}_i\right) \qquad (2\text{-}16)$$

In a fluid moving with velocity $\mathbf{U}$, the current is better described by introducing "drift" velocities for the electrons and ions as $(\mathbf{V}_e - \mathbf{U})$ and $(\mathbf{V}_i - \mathbf{U})$, respectively. These drift velocities describe the motion of the charged particles relative to the fluid. The current is then

$$\mathbf{j} = e\, n_e\left[\left(\mathbf{V}_i - \mathbf{U}\right) - \left(\mathbf{V}_e - \mathbf{U}\right)\right] \qquad (2\text{-}17)$$

which is entirely equivalent to eq. 2-16 but gives the current in terms of velocities seen by an observer in the reference frame of the moving fluid.

2.3. ELECTROMAGNETIC FIELDS

Classical electricity and magnetism is based on a number of physical observations, such as the force interactions between stationary and moving charges
(i.e., currents). The mathematical description of these observations can be
manipulated to arrive at definitions for interesting field quantities. From their
definitions, one can develop descriptive relations for these fields. These relations are known as Maxwell's equations for the electromagnetic fields. Forces
and work interactions can be determined and in Section 2.4 are added to the
fluid flow equations to study the dynamics of the fluid in response to the electromagnetic fields.

2.3.1. Faraday's Law and the E Field

Faraday observed and stated that there is a force interaction between two
charged particles that can be stated as

$$F_{1,2} = \frac{q_1 q_2}{4\pi\varepsilon_0} \frac{r_{1,2}}{r^3} = -\frac{q_1 q_2}{4\pi\varepsilon_0} \nabla \frac{1}{r} \qquad (2\text{-}18)$$

where the q_1 and q_2 are two charges separated by distance r_{12}, a vector. The
constant ε_0 is the permittivity of free space, which is (see Appendix B):

$$\varepsilon_0 = \frac{10^7}{4\pi\, c^2} \quad (\text{in SI units}) \qquad (2\text{-}19)$$

and c is the velocity of light. Numerical values for these and other physical
constants are given in the appendix cited. The force is vectorially aligned with
the position vector $r_{1,2}$. Figure 2-6 shows the geometry.

Electric Field

One *defines* an electric field as

$$E = \lim(q_2 \to 0)\frac{F_{1,2}}{q_2} = \frac{q_1}{4\pi\varepsilon_0} \frac{e_r}{r^2} \qquad (2\text{-}20)$$

The electric field for a single point charge is given by the second equality. e_r
is a unit vector in the radial direction (**r**). **E** is therefore that quantity that,

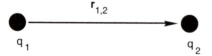

FIGURE 2-6. Force interaction geometry for two charges.

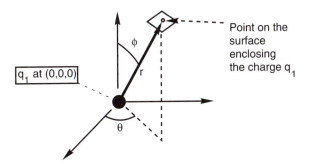

FIGURE 2-7. E field at r due to a charge at the origin.

when multiplied by q_2, gives the force on the charge q_2. The field can thus be visualized as being created or "induced" by q_1.

Determination of $\nabla \cdot E$ and $\nabla \times E$

To determine this quantity, we enclose the charge q_1 by an arbitrary surface and evaluate the surface integral $\int E \cdot dS$. The element of surface area is

$$dS = (rd\theta)(r\sin\theta d\phi)e_r + (a)e_\theta + (b)e_\phi \qquad (2\text{-}21)$$

for the polar coordinate system shown in Fig. 2-7 and where es are unit vectors in the principal directions.

Since the **E** field has only a radial component, the scalar product terms from the θ and ϕ directions are zero, and hence the last two terms for dS in eq. 2-21 are not of interest. The integral is then

$$\int E \cdot dS = \frac{q_1}{4\pi\varepsilon_0} \int r\sin\theta d\theta \int d\phi = \frac{q_1}{\varepsilon_0} \qquad (2\text{-}22)$$

which is independent of position so that the result must be valid for q anywhere inside the surface. The integral is zero when there are no charges inside the enclosing surface. If the charges are distributed with a charge density ρ_c such that

$$q = \int_{volume} \rho_c \, dV \qquad (2\text{-}23)$$

then

$$\int_{surface} E \cdot dS = \frac{1}{\varepsilon_0} \int_{volume} \rho_c \, dV = \int_{volume} (\nabla \cdot E) \, dV \qquad (2\text{-}24)$$

The equality of the first and last terms of eq. 2-24 is a consequence of the Gauss divergence theorem. It follows therefore that

$$\nabla \cdot E = \frac{\rho_c}{\varepsilon_0} \tag{2-25}$$

Further, since from eqs. 2-18 and 2-20

$$E = -\frac{q_1}{4\pi\varepsilon_0} \nabla \frac{1}{r} \tag{2-26}$$

it is evident that

$$\nabla \times E = 0 \tag{2-27}$$

since $\nabla \times \nabla = 0$. Equation 2-27 is valid only when **B** fields are absent.

2.3.2. Ampere's Law and the B Field

Ampere's law is a mathematical statement that a force is experienced between two current-carrying elements (dl_1 and dl_2) of matter. These may be visualized as wires for present purposes. The statement is

$$F_{1,2} = \frac{\mu_0}{4\pi} J_1 J_2 \int \int \frac{dl_2 \times (dl_1 \times r_{1,2})}{r_{1,2}^3} \tag{2-28}$$

where the symbols are identified in Fig. 2-8. J_1 and J_2 are the currents in the loops 1 and 2 that may be associated with a current density j for an element of cross-sectional area **S**. The proportionality constant μ_0 is the permeability of free space, whose magnitude is given in Appendix B.

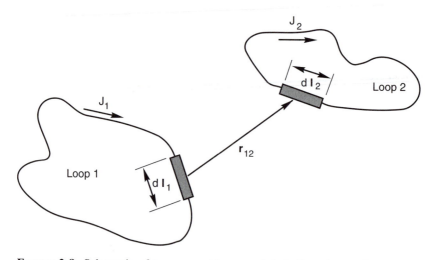

FIGURE 2-8. Schematic of two current loops and their force interaction.

Magnetic Field

Analogous to the electric field, one defines a magnetic field at loop 2 due to the current in loop 1 through

$$B_2 = \frac{\mu_0}{4\pi} J_1 \int \frac{dl_1 \times r_{1,2}}{r_{1,2}^3} = -\frac{\mu_0}{4\pi} J_1 \int dl_1 \times \nabla \frac{1}{r} \tag{2-29}$$

The force on loop 2 is then

$$F_2 = J_2 \int_2 dl_2 \times B_2 \tag{2-30}$$

If the current J_2 is uniform over a differential area dS_2, then

$$J_2 = j_2 \cdot dS_2 \tag{2-31}$$

where j and dS are parallel to each other as well as to dl. The volume of the loop element at 2 is $dS \cdot dl$. For this volume, the force may be written as

$$F_2 = \int_S j_2 \cdot dS_2 \int_2 dl_2 \times B_2 = \int_2 \int_S (dl_2 \cdot dS_2) j_2 \times B_2 = \int_{vol} (j \times B) \; dV \tag{2-32}$$

In other words, the force per unit volume at a point is $j \times B$, where j is the local current density and B is the field induced by all currents flowing elsewhere (in the universe). To summarize (see eq. 2-14):

$$\text{force per unit volume } = f = j \; \text{x} \; B \tag{2-33}$$

and eq. 2-29 can be recast as

$$B = \frac{\mu_0}{4\pi} \int \frac{(j \times r)}{r^3} \, dV \tag{2-34}$$

which is also known as the law of Biot and Savart. It is readily applied for the determination of the B field for simple current flow geometries such as straight wire segments, loops, coils, etc. For such problems, eq. 2-29 is often more convenient.

Determination of $\nabla \cdot B$ and $\nabla \times B$

With B written as in eq. 2-29, it is evident that the divergence of B involves the scalar product of ∇ with a vector normal to ∇, (i.e., $dl \times \nabla$), so that

$$\nabla \cdot B = 0 \tag{2-35}$$

The taking of the curl of **B** (i.e., $\nabla \times \mathbf{B}$) involves some vector calculus. First, it is important to note what this process is in physical terms. Consider an elemental volume (dV') in space where the local current density is **j**. This point is termed the *source point* for our purposes. Also under consideration is another volume (dV) at a *field point* where the magnetic field is **B**. This is illustrated in Fig. 2-9.

The field point is where the derivatives implied by the ∇ operator are applied. In other words, **j** is a constant as far as ∇ operations are concerned. For convenience, one may define

$$-\frac{\mu_0}{4\pi} j dV' = A \qquad (2\text{-}36)$$

and determine

$$d(\nabla \times \mathbf{B}) = -\frac{\mu_0}{4\pi} \nabla \times (j \times \nabla \frac{1}{r}) dV' = \nabla \times (\mathbf{A} \times \nabla \frac{1}{r}) \qquad (2\text{-}37)$$

From an expansion of the last equality, one obtains

$$\nabla \times \left(\mathbf{A} \times \nabla \frac{1}{r} \right) = \left(\nabla \frac{1}{r} \cdot \nabla \right) \mathbf{A} - (\mathbf{A} \cdot \nabla) \nabla \frac{1}{r} + \mathbf{A} \nabla^2 \left(\frac{1}{r} \right) - \nabla \left(\frac{1}{r} \right) (\nabla \cdot \mathbf{A}) \ (2\text{-}38)$$

where the first and last terms are zero because ∇ operations on **A** are zero. Substituting back for **A** and integrating eq. 2-37 results in

$$\nabla \times \mathbf{B} = -\frac{\mu_0}{4\pi} \int_{V'} \left[-(j \cdot \nabla) \nabla \left(\frac{1}{r} \right) + j \nabla^2 \left(\frac{1}{r} \right) \right] dV' \qquad (2\text{-}39)$$

The first volume integral may be carried out through the use of the tensor form of Gauss' divergence theorem, which reads

$$\int_{V'} \left[(j \cdot \nabla) \nabla \left(\frac{1}{r} \right) \right] dV' + \int_{V'} \left[(\nabla \cdot j) \nabla \left(\frac{1}{r} \right) \right] dV' = \int_{S'} \left[\nabla \left(\frac{1}{r} \right) \right] j \cdot dS' \qquad (2\text{-}40)$$

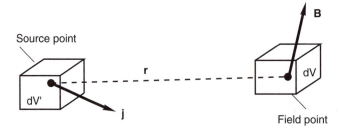

FIGURE 2-9. Differential source and field points in space: **B** is the result of **j**.

Here the second term is zero, again because $\mathbf{j}$ is constant regarding the ∇ operation. The surface integral $d\mathbf{S'}$ is over the outside of the source point wherein the current loops creating $\mathbf{B}$ lie. Since these loops do not penetrate the surface, the scalar product over the surface in eq. 2-40 is zero. This allows one to conclude that the first integral in eq. 2-39 is zero and the equation reduces to

$$\nabla \times \mathbf{B} = -\frac{\mu_0}{4\pi} \mathbf{j} \int_{V'} \left[\nabla^2 \left(\frac{1}{r} \right) \right] dV' = -\frac{\mu_0}{4\pi} \mathbf{j} \int_{S'} \left[\nabla \left(\frac{1}{r} \right) \right] \cdot d\mathbf{S'} \qquad (2\text{-}41)$$

The last equality is through another use of the Gauss divergence theorem. The last integral is

$$\int_{S'} \left[\nabla \left(\frac{1}{r} \right) \right] \cdot d\mathbf{S'} = \int \left[\left(-\frac{1}{r^2} \right) \right] r' \, dr' \, d\Omega = -4\pi \qquad (2\text{-}42)$$

Finally, the last of Maxwell's equations is obtained from eqs. 2-41 and 2-42:

$$\nabla \times \mathbf{B} = \mu_0 \mathbf{j} \qquad (2\text{-}43)$$

This exercise may be summarized physically by stating that the $\mathbf{B}$ field is divergence-free (i.e., source free) which is equivalent to saying that field lines cannot end in space. Further, $\mathbf{j}$ is related to $\mathbf{B}$ in a manner analogous to the relation between the vorticity (ω) in a velocity field ($\mathbf{u}$). This analogy is revisited in Section 3.3.

2.3.3. Electromotive Force

The steady form of Maxwell's equation describing $\nabla \times \mathbf{E}$ may be generalized by incorporating the observation that an open conductor loop will show a voltage when the flux of the $\mathbf{B}$ field through the loop varies in time. Thus consider a loop that encloses magnetic field lines, as shown in Fig. 2-10. The observation, known as Faraday's law of induction, may be stated as

$$\Delta\phi = -\frac{\partial}{\partial t} \int \mathbf{B} \cdot d\mathbf{S} \qquad (2\text{-}44)$$

where the integrand is the differential of the magnetic flux. Since a finite potential exists between the endpoints, the line integral of the electric field ($\mathbf{E}^o$, associated with the changing $\mathbf{B}$) cannot be zero or

$$\Delta\phi = -\int \mathbf{E}^o \cdot d\mathbf{l} = -\int \left(\nabla \times \mathbf{E}^o \right) \cdot d\mathbf{S} \qquad (2\text{-}45)$$

where the divergence theorem has been used again to convert a line integral to a surface integral. Comparing eqs. 2-44 and 2-45,

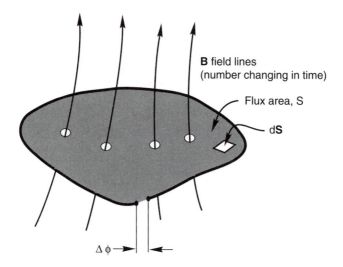

B field lines
(number changing in time)

Flux area, S

d**S**

$\Delta \phi$

FIGURE 2-10. Current loop illustrating Faraday's law of induction: $\Delta \phi$ results from the changing **B**.

$$\nabla \times \boldsymbol{E}^{0} = -\frac{\partial \boldsymbol{B}}{\partial t} \qquad (2\text{-}46)$$

The electrostatic field $\boldsymbol{E}_s$ is curl free so that the total field, $\boldsymbol{E} = \boldsymbol{E}_s + \boldsymbol{E}^{\circ}$, obeys

$$\nabla \times \boldsymbol{E} = -\frac{\partial \boldsymbol{B}}{\partial t} \qquad (2\text{-}47)$$

2.3.4. Maxwell's Equations

The equations resulting from the ∇ operator on **E** and **B** are called the Maxwell's equations. They are summarized here for convenience:

$$\nabla \cdot \boldsymbol{E} = \frac{\rho_c}{\varepsilon_0} \qquad (2\text{-}25)$$

$$\nabla \cdot \boldsymbol{B} = 0 \qquad (2\text{-}35)$$

$$\nabla \times \boldsymbol{B} = \mu_0 \boldsymbol{j} \qquad (2\text{-}43)$$

$$\nabla \times \boldsymbol{E} = -\frac{\partial \boldsymbol{B}}{\partial t} \qquad (2\text{-}47)$$

2.3.5. Work Interactions

From the foregoing, it is evident that work may be done in moving charges through an electromagnetic field. In an **E** field, the work done on a charge moving with velocity **V** is given by

$$\text{work} = \boldsymbol{F} \cdot \boldsymbol{V} = q\boldsymbol{E} \cdot \boldsymbol{V} = \int \rho_c \boldsymbol{E} \cdot \boldsymbol{V} \, dV = \int \boldsymbol{j} \cdot \boldsymbol{E} \, dV \qquad (2\text{-}48)$$

which is generalized over a volume with charge density ρ_c; see eq. 2-23. **V** is either of the velocities in eq. 2-15, and V is the volume. The charge flux constitutes an electrical current.

A charge moving in a **B** field experiences a force that is always orthogonal to the motion (eq. 2-3) so that the work done is zero, physically, because **j** and the charge velocity **V** are parallel:

$$\text{work} = \int \boldsymbol{V} \cdot \boldsymbol{j} \times \boldsymbol{B} \, dV \qquad (2\text{-}49)$$

2.4. FLUID MECHANICAL EQUATIONS

The fluid flow equations with electromagnetic force and energy terms seldom arise in connection with other studies. These terms are, unlike many forces and energy interactions of engineering interest (friction and heat transfer), truly volumetric and are therefore able to be modeled by a differential element approach. As such, they permit unusual and accurate modeling insight into the thermodynamics of fluids. For this reason, they are developed here in detail. In deriving the conservation equations for mass, momentum, and energy, as well as the equation for the generation of entropy, the control volume approach is used. Such control volumes have bounding surface areas through which fluxes of various types will pass.

2.4.1. Fluxes

A flux is an amount of a quantity passing through an area dS per unit time (Fig. 2-11). If the velocity is **U**, the volume flux is

$$\text{volume through } dS \text{ in } dt \ = \ \boldsymbol{U} \cdot d\boldsymbol{S}$$

and the rate of flow of a quantity Q through dS in dt is

$$= (\text{density of Q/volume}) \ \boldsymbol{U} \cdot d\boldsymbol{S} \ = q \, \boldsymbol{U} \cdot d\boldsymbol{S}$$

For example, the mass flux through $d\boldsymbol{S}$ in dt is = (mass density) $\boldsymbol{U} \cdot d\boldsymbol{S} = \rho \, \boldsymbol{U} \cdot d\boldsymbol{S}$.

2.4.2. Mass Conservation

The rate of change of mass in a control volume V must equal the net (in minus out) rate of mass transport into the volume:

$$\frac{\partial}{\partial t}\int_V \rho dV + \int_S \rho\,U \cdot dS = 0 \qquad (2\text{-}50)$$

where the first integral is the time rate of change of the mass in V while the second is the net mass flow *out* if the convention for positive dS is outward. The divergence theorem allows writing a surface integral in the form of a volume integral. With the control volume fixed in time, the time derivative and the integral can be interchanged:

$$\int_V \frac{\partial \rho}{\partial t}dV + \int_V \nabla \cdot (\rho\,U)dV = 0 \quad \text{or} \quad \frac{\partial \rho}{\partial t} + \nabla \cdot (\rho\,U) = 0 \qquad (2\text{-}51)$$

For arbitrary dV, the integrand must be zero as noted. The derivative following a fluid element (total derivative) is given by

$$\frac{D}{Dt} = \frac{\partial}{\partial t} + U \cdot \nabla \qquad (2\text{-}52)$$

so that the continuity equation (eq. 2-51) can be written as

$$\frac{D\rho}{Dt} + \rho \nabla \cdot U = 0 \qquad (2\text{-}53)$$

This form is particularly useful to interpret because it shows that div $U = 0$ when the fluid is incompressible.

2.4.3. Momentum Equation

For the accounting of forces, the term due to viscous effects is neglected. In words, Newton's second law is, when applied to a control volume: the force applied equals the rate of momentum production, or (with neglected viscous forces)

pressure F + electromagnetic F = net rate of momentum out + rate of gain of momentum in V

$$-\int_S pdS + \int_V \left(\rho_c E + j \times B\right)dV = \int_S (\rho U)\,U \cdot dS + \frac{\partial}{\partial t}\int_V (\rho U)\,dV \qquad (2\text{-}54)$$

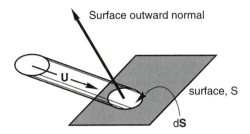

FIGURE 2-11. Flux of a quantity through a surface **S**.

since ρU is the momentum per unit volume. The minus sign on the pressure term is due to the convention for a positive outward normal to a surface element. For an electrically neutral plasma, $\rho_c = 0$. The surface integrals can be converted to volume integrals using the divergence theorem, as

$$\int_S p\,dS = \int_V (\nabla p)\,dV \tag{2-55}$$

$$\int_S (\rho U)\,U \cdot dS = \int_V \left[(\rho U \cdot \nabla)\,U + U\,\nabla \cdot (\rho U)\right] dV \tag{2-56}$$

Thus eq. 2-54 becomes

$$-\nabla p + j \times B = \frac{\partial \rho U}{\partial t} + (\rho U \cdot \nabla)U + U\,\nabla \cdot (\rho U)$$

$$= \rho \left[\frac{\partial U}{\partial t} + (U \cdot \nabla)U\right] + U\left[\frac{\partial \rho}{\partial t} + \nabla \cdot (\rho U)\right] = \rho \frac{DU}{Dt} \tag{2-57}$$

where the second term in large parentheses is zero because of the continuity equation (2-51). The momentum equation is therefore:

$$\rho \frac{DU}{Dt} = -\nabla p + j \times B \tag{2-58}$$

The scalar product of this equation with the velocity (**U**) gives the increase in kinetic energy as the rate of doing mechanical work:

$$\rho \frac{D(U^2/2)}{Dt} = U \cdot (-\nabla p + j \times B) \tag{2-59}$$

2.4.4. Energy Equation

The energy equation is an application of the first law of thermodynamics to a control volume. The heat input (transfer through the control surface is neglected) plus electric power input plus work done by pressure forces equals the net rate of energy transported out of the control volume plus the rate of change of energy in V. Thus

$$\int_V (\mathbf{j} \cdot \mathbf{E})\, dV - \int_S p\mathbf{U} \cdot d\mathbf{S} = \int_S \rho(e + U^2/2)\, \mathbf{U} \cdot d\mathbf{S} + \frac{\partial}{\partial t} \int_V \rho(e + U^2/2)\, dV \quad (2\text{-}60)$$

Here e is the internal energy and $U^2/2$ is the kinetic energy, both per unit mass. One may think of the sum of these two terms as a total internal energy, $e_t = e + U^2/2$. Converting to volume integrals leads to

$$\mathbf{j} \cdot \mathbf{E} - \nabla \cdot (p\mathbf{U}) = \nabla \cdot \left[\rho\mathbf{U}(e + U^2/2)\right] + \frac{\partial}{\partial t}\rho(e + U^2/2)$$

$$= \rho\left(\frac{\partial}{\partial t} + \mathbf{U}\cdot\nabla\right)(e + U^2/2) + (e + U^2/2)\left[\frac{\partial\rho}{\partial t} + \nabla\cdot(\rho\mathbf{U})\right]$$

or with eq. 2-51, one obtains the energy equation in the form:

$$\mathbf{j} \cdot \mathbf{E} - \nabla \cdot (p\mathbf{U}) = \frac{D}{Dt}\left[\rho(e + U^2/2)\right] \quad (2\text{-}61)$$

2.4.5. Entropy Equation

A combination of energy and momentum equations may be obtained by subtracting eq. 2-59 from eq. 2-61,

$$\mathbf{j} \cdot \mathbf{E} - \mathbf{U} \cdot \mathbf{j} \times \mathbf{B} - p\nabla \cdot \mathbf{U} = \rho\frac{De}{Dt} \quad (2\text{-}62)$$

where $\nabla \cdot \mathbf{U}$ may be obtained from the continuity equation, eq. 2-53, which gives

$$\nabla \cdot \mathbf{U} = \frac{1}{\rho}\frac{D\rho}{Dt} = -\rho\frac{D(1/\rho)}{Dt} = -\rho\frac{Dv}{Dt} \quad (2\text{-}63)$$

in the more familiar form using the specific volume, $v = 1/\rho$. The triple scalar product can be rearranged as

$$U \cdot j \times B = -j \cdot (U \times B) \tag{2-64}$$

Thus eq. 2-62 becomes

$$j \cdot (E + U \times B) = \rho \left[\frac{De}{Dt} + p \frac{Dv}{Dt} \right] = \rho T \frac{Ds}{Dt} \tag{2-65}$$

where the last equality stems from the Gibbs equation (eq. 2-10 in Ref. 1-1). This equation shows that the scalar product of **j** and **E′** (see eq. 2-8) gives rise to the production of entropy. This "Ohmic" heat dissipation (or Joule heating) is responsible for the process irreversibility. This is clear when Ohm's law (eq. 2-8) is used to write this product as

$$j \cdot E = \frac{j^2}{\sigma} = \rho T \frac{Ds}{Dt} \tag{2-66}$$

2.4.6. Enthalpy Equation

The div (pU) term in the energy equation (eq. 2-62) can be expanded to read

$$\nabla \cdot pU = U \cdot \nabla p + p\nabla \cdot U \tag{2-67}$$

which, in turn, can be written using the definition of the total derivative (eq. 2-52) and the continuity equation (eq. 2-53) as

$$\nabla \cdot pU = \left(\frac{D}{Dt} - \frac{\partial}{\partial t} \right) p + p\rho \frac{Dv}{Dt} = \rho \frac{Dpv}{Dt} - \frac{\partial p}{\partial t} \tag{2-68}$$

The energy equation then becomes

$$j \cdot E = \rho \left(\frac{D}{Dt} \right) \left(e + pv + \frac{U^2}{2} \right) - \frac{\partial p}{\partial t} = \rho \frac{Dh_t}{Dt} - \frac{\partial p}{\partial t} \tag{2-69}$$

where the total enthalpy is defined as h_t. In steady flow, this equation reduces to

$$j \cdot E = \rho (U \cdot \nabla h_t) \tag{2-70}$$

which states that the total enthalpy responds to work interactions. The result follows directly from the steady form of the first law of thermodynamics (eq. 2-6, Ref. 1-1).

2.4.7. Interaction Parameter and Interaction Length

The equations of fluid mechanics with body force terms, such as the electro-magnetic forces, allow the identification of new parameters which characterize the magnitude of forces relative to the flow parameters. These nondimensional ratios are called *interaction parameters*. In the study of MHD the body force is the $\mathbf{j} \times \mathbf{B}$ force. Using Ohm's law, this force per unit volume is of order $\sigma U B^2$ (see eqs. 2-5 and 2-8), while the pressure force per unit volume is dp/dx, which is of order p/L. One may define an MHD force interaction parameter to be

$$I_{MHD} \equiv \frac{\text{MHD body force/vol}}{\text{pressure force/vol}} = \frac{\sigma U B^2 L}{p}$$

which must not be small if the interaction is to be significant. The Mach number relates dynamic pressure to fluid static pressure

$$\frac{\rho U^2}{p} = \gamma M^2 \tag{2-71}$$

so that for a specified Mach number, an equally valid MHD interaction parameter is

$$I_{MHD} \equiv \frac{\text{MHD body force/vol}}{\text{dynamic pressure force/vol}} = \frac{\sigma U B^2 L}{\rho U} \tag{2-72}$$

Such a parameter definition allows the further identification of a length scale that describes the interaction. For example, depending on preference

$$L_{MHD} = \frac{\rho U}{\sigma B^2} \quad \text{or} \quad \frac{p}{\sigma U B^2} \tag{2-73}$$

Another example from viscous internal flows with which the student may be more familiar may be illustrative in strengthening the concept of an interaction parameter or length. The formation of a ratio of one-dimensional viscous to dynamic forces (per unit volume) from terms in the momentum equation is an interaction parameter

$$I_v = \frac{\dfrac{C_f \rho U^2}{D}}{\dfrac{\rho U^2 \text{ or } p}{L}} = C_f \frac{L}{D} \tag{2-74}$$

Thus, if viscous effects are to play a minor role, the friction coefficient C_f ($\times$ L/D) must be small in the sense given by this interaction parameter. Further, one can show that for a flow with developing boundary layers this parameter can be written in terms of a momentum thickness for the boundary layer θ as

$$I_v = \frac{\theta}{D} \qquad (2\text{-}75)$$

which shows that θ is the interaction length scale for viscous effects, which must be compared to the duct dimension D.

PROBLEMS

1. Use the Biot-Savart law (eq. 2-34) to find the **B** field distributions for a number of simple conductor geometries: infinite straight wire, finite-length straight wire, square loop using the finite-segment result, circular loop.

2. Consider a long column of plasma or a wire that carries a uniform axial current. Show that the **B** field distribution is linearly increasing in the column and then decreases as $1/r$ outside the column. By considering the $\mathbf{j} \times \mathbf{B}$ body force, find the pressure distribution in this static column.

3. Show that the momentum thickness is the proper length scale to measure a viscous force interaction in a developing boundary layer flow in a pipe of diameter D. What is the corresponding scale in a fully developed flow?

BIBLIOGRAPHY

Sutton, G. and Sherman, A., *Engineering Magnetohydrodynamics,* McGraw-Hill, New York, 1965.
Rosa, R. J., *Magnetohydrodynamic Energy Conversion,* McGraw-Hill, New York, 1968.
Jackson, J. D., *Classical Electrodynamics,* John Wiley and Sons, New York, 1962.
Freidberg, J. P., *Ideal Magnetohydrodynamics,* Plenum Press, New York, 1987.

REFERENCES

2-1. Kerrebrock, J. L., "Nonequilibrium Ionization due to Electron Heating, Part I. Theory," *AIAA Journal* (2) 11, 1964, pp. 1072-80.

3

PLASMAS AND ELECTRICAL CONDUCTIVITY OF GASES

A plasma is a homogeneous, electrically neutral, gaseous mixture of atoms, molecules, electrons, and ions. It exists at temperatures sufficiently high so that ionization of a species may take place. This chapter is a description of the plasma conductivity and the vector relation between charge fluxes, and the driving electromagnetic fields: Ohm's law. The conductivity is examined from the viewpoint of individual collisions between electrons and atoms.

3.1. DEBYE LENGTH: NEUTRALITY SCALE

The neutral plasma view necessarily breaks down on a size scale of the individual ions and electrons. It actually breaks down on a larger scale because the plasma components' kinetic energy is sufficient to separate charges against the electrical fields. This scale is of interest, especially in its relation to the physical dimensions of the system wherein the plasma is contained. Maxwell's equation describing the electric field allows one to estimate the magnitude of the field that can be set up by separated charges and thus the work that is required to bring that about. The work must be supplied from the thermal energy of the plasma components. This reasoning allows one to identify a length scale dividing the spectrum of possible charge separation distances into a small-scale regime where one could expect positive and negative charges to be separable and a larger-scale regime where there is insufficient thermal energy for this separation to take place. Consider a plasma that is uniform except that a slab of thickness h, infinite in extent in the other directions, contains no electrons. The charge density is $\rho_c = n_e e$. Figure 3-1 illustrates this situation.

Equation 2-25 specialized to a single dimension gives for the region $0 \leq x \leq h$:

$$\frac{dE_x}{dx} = \frac{n_e e}{\varepsilon_0} \tag{3-1}$$

Since the charge density is assumed uniform, this equation can be integrated, once to find E_x, and a second time to obtain the potential at various locations between 0 and h. Hence with $E_x(0) = 0$,

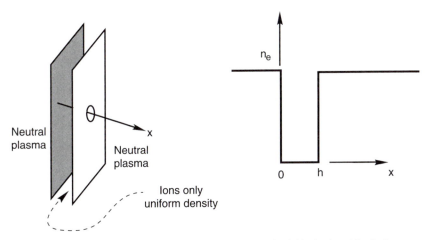

FIGURE 3-1. Sketch of a one-dimensional region of width h, devoid of electrons in an otherwise uniform and neutral plasma.

$$E_x = \frac{n_e e}{\varepsilon_0} x \qquad (3\text{-}2)$$

and with $E = -\nabla \phi$, the (absolute value of the) potential at $x = h$ (relative to that at $x = 0$) is

$$\phi = \frac{n_e e}{\varepsilon_0} \frac{h^2}{2} \qquad (3\text{-}3)$$

This potential times the electronic charge (e) is the work required to bring a charged particle across the gap h. The thermal energy available in one dimension to move this particle is $1/2\ kT$. Equating the energy available and the work required give a length scale h over which one would expect charge separation to be found.

$$e\phi = \frac{n_e e^2}{\varepsilon_0} \frac{h_D^2}{2} = \frac{kT}{2} \qquad (3\text{-}4)$$

The length arising from this argument is the Debye shielding distance, h_D,

$$h_D = \sqrt{\frac{\varepsilon_0 kT}{n_e e^2}} \qquad (3\text{-}5)$$

Typically, this distance is quite small for plasmas of interest in MHD energy conversion. For $T = 2500$ K and $n_e = 10^{19}$ m^{-3}, h_D is of the order 10^{-6} m.

Space charge effects have important consequences near boundaries of the plasma, in the so-called *sheath*.

3.2. OHM'S LAW: MOMENTUM EQUATION FOR THE ELECTRON GAS

Ohm's law as written in eq. 2-8 is a statement regarding forces on charged particles. As such, it is a momentum equation that can be written generally in the form of Newton's second law:

$$F = ma = m\frac{DV}{Dt} \tag{3-6}$$

The forces acting on the ensemble of charged particles are those associated with the electro-magnetic fields, collisions with the other components of the plasma, and, if present, pressure forces. If Z is the atomic mass of the ion, the mass of the ion is 1836 Z times larger than that of the electron. The velocity gain due to forces of the same order for both electrons and ions are very much smaller for the ion so that the drift velocity of the ion is very small compared to that of the electron: $|V_i - U| << |V_e - U|$. The ion contribution to the total current (eq. 2-17) can therefore be neglected for many situations. Since electrons are the principal contributors to the total current, their dynamics are examined first. The electron momentum equation can thus be written as

$$\frac{\text{electric, magnetic, collision forces}}{\text{volume}} - \nabla p_e = \rho_e \frac{DV}{Dt} \tag{3-7}$$

where $\rho_e = n_e m_e$ is the electron mass density. The acceleration term is typically quite small unless the frequency of impressed E fields is high, as high as the other time scale in the problem, namely the mean time between collisions (of order 10^{-11} sec). Excluding the presence of such fields and considering the case of a uniform plasma where gradients in species partial pressure are absent, the Ohm's law written as a momentum equation reduces to

$$\frac{\text{electric f}}{\text{volume}} + \frac{\text{magnetic f}}{\text{volume}} + \frac{\text{collision f}}{\text{volume}} = 0 \tag{3-8}$$

The pressure gradient term must be included when analyzing sheath regions near boundaries where nonuniformities are large. On a unit volume basis, the three forces are: electric: $n_e(-e)\mathbf{E}'$, magnetic: $\mathbf{j} \times \mathbf{B}$, and the collision force, which is the product of:

$$\frac{\text{average momentum lost}}{\text{collision}} \cdot \frac{\text{collisions}}{\text{time, electron}} \cdot \frac{\text{electrons}}{\text{volume}} = \left[m_e (V_e - U) \right] v_c n_e$$

Here v_c is the collision frequency, which can be written in terms of the mean time between collisions, τ_c,

$$v_c = \frac{1}{\tau_e} \tag{3-9}$$

A physical description and first-order calculation of v_c is described in terms of gross parameters in Section 3.2.3. A more general and precise mathematical description is carried out in Section 3.4. The momentum equation now reads

$$-en_e E + j \times B + n_e m_e v_c (V_e - U) = 0 \tag{3-10}$$

Since the electron drift dominates the current vector j, it follows from eq. 2-17 that:

$$j = -en_e (V_e - U) \tag{3-11}$$

or

$$\frac{-e^2 n_e}{m_e v_c} E + \frac{e}{m_e v_c} j \times B + j = 0 \tag{3-12}$$

which is the generalized Ohm's law for electrons. All modeling approximations regarding the collisions during which the electrons lose momentum in the direction of motion are contained in the collision frequency v_c.

3.2.1. Scalar Conductivity

In the absence of a **B** field, this relation provides σ in terms of more fundamental constants. Evidently, the conductivity σ identified in eq. 2-8 is given by:

$$\sigma = \frac{e^2 n_e}{m_e v_c} \tag{3-13}$$

3.2.2. Tensor Conductivity

With a magnetic field present, the relationship between j and E' is a vectorial one rather than a scalar one and depends on the relative orientation between E' and **B**. In order to quantify the importance of this vector relation, eq. 3-12 can be rewritten as

$$\frac{eB}{m_e v_c} j \times e_B + j = \sigma E' \tag{3-14}$$

where the terms on the left-hand side are currents and e_B is a unit vector in the B field direction. A nondimensional ratio of two frequencies appears: v_c is the collision frequency, while $eB/m_e = \omega$ is the cyclotron frequency of an electron around the magnetic field lines, eq. 2-6. This ratio is called the Hall parameter β, which describes the importance of the Hall effect: current flows at an angle to the electric field when a magnetic field is present. The Hall parameter is defined as

$$\beta = \frac{\omega}{v_c} = \frac{eB}{m_e v_c} \tag{3-15}$$

There is also a Hall parameter for ions (β_i), but due to their very large mass, this parameter is usually quite small, and the tendency of ions to follow circular paths between collisions can be neglected in many instances. Note also that a conductivity for ions may also be written, but it is also small compared to the electron conductivity defined in eq. 3-12 again because the ion mass is relatively large. For the following, σ and β are associated with the mobile electrons. Equation 3-12 can also be written in terms of electric fields as

$$E + \frac{1}{en_e} j \times B + \frac{j}{\sigma} = 0 \tag{3-16}$$

where the second term is called the Hall field, that is, the electric field arising from the Hall effect. In order to visualize the relationship between the various vectors, consider a crossed field generator where the critical directions are as shown in Fig. 3-2. The U direction determines $U \times B$. An open circuit electric field opposes $U \times B$. If current flows, it does so in the direction of $U \times B$ while its magnitude (j/σ) is the difference between $U \times B$ and E, as shown. The electron flux is opposite to j (negative electrons). The $(V_e - U) \times B$ is as shown and the resulting (Hall) electric field must be added vectorially to the induced transverse electric field. The sum is as shown, and evidently this vector is not collinear with the current. Thus there is an angle between E and j that is largest when j is a maximum, that is, when $E = 0$ and the electric field consists entirely of the Hall field. With $j < \sigma UB$ as shown in Fig. 3-2, this situation describes that of a generator (note that the $j \times B$ force is antiparallel to U). The conclusion regarding the angle between j and E is not restricted to such a device, but is true in general.

3.2.3. Collision Frequency

Whatever the direction of the charged particle motion, the electrons will encounter neutral particles and ions. These heavy particles will appear to be stationary to the electrons moving in the direction of the applied E field

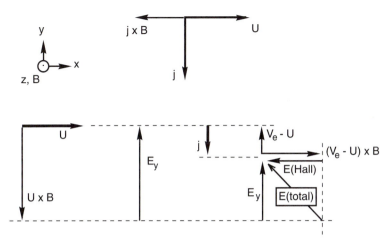

FIGURE 3-2. Summary of vector relationships in a flow situation with orthogonal **B** and **U** showing that with the Hall effect: **E**(total) and **j** are not parallel.

(Fig. 3-3). The interaction between the moving electron and the *stationary* particle may be thought of as a collision with an object of a certain *size*. The momentum lost in the encounter depends on the geometry of the encounter, the electric force interaction, and the velocity of the electron, all of which determine a deflection angle of the electron's path. The details of electron-heavy particle collisions are examined in Section 3.4 where expressions for conductivity are derived for encounters of various types of heavy species.

The size of the encountered particle is characterized by an area that describes the change in electron property such as its momentum. Thus the momentum transfer cross-sectional area is an average quantity that, when swept out by the velocity of the moving electron, gives the number of momentum losing collisions per unit time when the number of point centers are counted in the swept volume. Thus if Q_{es} is the cross section for an electron-s-species encounter and when the number density of species s is n_s, then the collision frequency is given by:

$$\text{Volume swept per unit time by one electron} = c_e Q_{es}$$

$$\text{Number of collision points per unit volume} = n_s$$

therefore

$$\text{Number of collisions per unit time by one electron} = v_c = c_e n_s Q_{es} \quad (3\text{-}17)$$

Since the collision partner number density and average electron speed are well quantifiable, the cross-sectional area hides the details identified with the collision frequency.

The product $n_s\,Q_{es}$ is the *macroscopic* (momentum transfer) cross section for encounters of the s species with units of inverse length, m^{-1}. nQ is a property of the plasma. By contrast, Q itself is a *microscopic* cross-sectional area (m^2), a property of the atom. For a gas mixture, the macroscopic cross section is given by:

$$n_T\,\overline{Q_e} = \sum_s n_s\,Q_{es} \quad \text{with} \quad n_T = \sum_s n_s \tag{3-18}$$

Microscopic cross-sectional areas are generally functions of temperature and the electron energy in particular. For engineering purposes, it is often sufficient to characterize the cross sections by a constant value over the temperature range considered. Table 4-3 in Section 4.5.2 gives a number of values of interest.

3.3. MAGNETIC REYNOLDS NUMBER

The development to this point has established that a magnetic field is set up by the flow of current in space. Equation 2-43 shows how this field is related to the current. The fourth of the Maxwell equations (eq. 2-47) also shows that the magnetic field distribution is related to an unsteady electric field. The existence and variation of that E field determines the current flow through Ohm's law, which implies a coupling of current, E field and B field. The physics of these quantities can be made more clear through a rearrangement of these three equations. Thus if one takes the curl of Ohm's law (eq. 2-8), one obtains:

$$\nabla \times j = \sigma(\nabla \times E + \nabla \times U \times B) \tag{3-19}$$

where $\nabla \times j$ can be obtained from Maxwell's equation (eq. 2-43) as

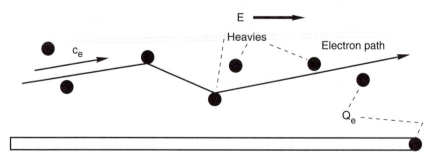

FIGURE 3-3. Collisions between electrons traveling at speed c_e and nearly stationary heavy atoms.

$$\nabla \times \boldsymbol{j} = \frac{1}{\mu_0}(\nabla \times \nabla \times \boldsymbol{B}) \qquad (3\text{-}20)$$

and $\nabla \times \boldsymbol{E}$ from the fourth Maxwell equation, eq. 2-47. Combining these results gives

$$\frac{\partial \boldsymbol{B}}{\partial t} = -\nabla \times \boldsymbol{U} \times \boldsymbol{B} + \frac{1}{\mu_0 \sigma}\nabla \times \nabla \times \boldsymbol{B} \qquad (3\text{-}21)$$

This is a diffusion equation for $\boldsymbol{B}$ with the inertial term on the left and the convective and diffusive terms on the right. Such an equation carries parameters governing the relative importance of the various terms. By dividing the equation through by a velocity, say the magnitude of $\boldsymbol{U}$ ($= U_0$), and a length scale L, this equation becomes nondimensional in terms of operators and variables (primed). The parameter in the denominator of the third term governs the magnitude of the diffusion and is defined as the magnetic Reynolds number, $\sigma\mu_0 U_0 L$:

$$\frac{\partial \boldsymbol{B}}{\partial t'} = -\frac{1}{U_0}\nabla' \times \boldsymbol{U} \times \boldsymbol{B} + \frac{1}{\mu_0 \sigma U_0 L}\nabla' \times \nabla' \times \boldsymbol{B} \qquad (3\text{-}22)$$

Here the prime on the spatial and temporal derivatives is meant to indicate that the operator or quantity is nondimensionalized by U_0 and/or L. The name Reynolds number stems from the analogy to the equation of motion for a viscous fluid. The analogy is developed as follows. Equation 2-59 is the momentum equation which for a viscous force in lieu of the $\boldsymbol{j} \times \boldsymbol{B}$ force reads (see, for example, Ref. 3-1)

$$\rho\left(\frac{\partial \boldsymbol{U}}{\partial t} + \boldsymbol{U} \cdot \nabla \boldsymbol{U}\right) = \nabla p + \mu\nabla^2 \boldsymbol{U} \qquad (3\text{-}23)$$

Here μ is the coefficient of viscosity. This relation can be written as a conservation equation for vorticity defined by

$$\boldsymbol{\omega} = \nabla \times \boldsymbol{U} \qquad (3\text{-}24)$$

as

$$\frac{\partial \boldsymbol{\omega}}{\partial t'} = -\frac{1}{U_0}\nabla' \times (\boldsymbol{U} \times \boldsymbol{\omega}) + \frac{\mu}{\rho U_0 L}\nabla'^2 \boldsymbol{\omega} \qquad (3\text{-}25)$$

The parameter modifying the viscous diffusion term is the reciprocal of the viscous Reynolds number. Equations 3-22 and 3-25 establish that the importance of diffusion of **B** and ω are governed by the magnitudes of the two Reynolds numbers:

$$\frac{\rho\, U_0\, L}{\mu} = Re \text{ (viscous)} \quad \text{and} \quad \sigma\, \mu_0 U_0\, L = Rm \text{ (magnetic)} \tag{3-26}$$

Physically, the magnetic Reynolds number may be interpreted as the ratio of two current densities, the current induced by the existence of the motion through the magnetic field and the current required to set up the magnetic field,

$$Rm = \frac{j_{\text{induced}}}{j_{\text{applied}}} = \frac{\sigma\, U_0\, B \text{ from Ohm's law}}{B/\mu_0\, L \text{ from Maxwell's eq.}} = \sigma\, U_0\, \mu_0\, L \tag{3-27}$$

which shows that the typically small magnetic Reynolds number in MHD plasmas allows one to neglect the induced current as a source of B field in comparison to the current necessary for the externally *applied* B field. In other words, the applied field may be considered constant irrespective of induced current flows.

3.4. LORENTZ THEORY OF THE ELECTRON GAS: ELECTRICAL CONDUCTIVITY OF AN IONIZED GAS

In Section 3.2, a relation between the electric field and the current density was derived from the conservation of momentum for the electron gas. In the absence of a magnetic field, eq. 3-12 gives a balance between acceleration forces due to the electric field and retarding forces resulting from the momentum loss between electrons and the heavy atoms with which they ultimately share their energy. In this form, the equation reads

$$\frac{-e^2 n_e}{m_e v_c} E + j = 0 \tag{3-28}$$

In the following, the expression for the conductivity is derived based on the physics of collisions between the electrons carrying the current and the electric field. By recasting eq. 3-13 as

$$\frac{v_c m_e}{e^2 n_e} = \frac{1}{\sigma} = \frac{m_e (V_e - U) v_c}{e^2 (V_e - U) n_e} = \frac{\text{collision force/electron}}{e j_e} \tag{3-29}$$

it is evident that the conductivity is inversely proportional to the collision force per unit electron flux. If a number of heavy collision species are present, the momentum loss for each must be included in a summation:

$$\frac{1}{\sigma} = \frac{\sum_i (\text{collision force / vol})_i}{e\, n_e\, j_e}$$

(3-30)

By multiplying both numerator and denominator of the right side of eq. 3-29 by n_e, the numerator becomes a force per unit volume as noted.

The physical picture that describes the process of momentum transfer is that of a very light electron approaching a heavy collision partner. The force interaction between these particles is electrical in nature in that the electron sees a radial electric field associated with the heavy particle. The details of its subsequent motion depend strongly on its velocity, the impact parameter, and the force field itself. The impact parameter p is the *miss distance* if there was there no force field and thus no deflection. It may be small in a "head-on" collision or it may be large. The scale of large or small must be judged by comparison with other length scales. One such distance is that an electron would reach were it to convert all its kinetic energy to potential energy in the force field of the heavy atom or molecule.

Evidently, the dynamic parameters control the collision interaction. In a uniform gaseous conductor or plasma, both the electrons and the heavy particles have distributions of velocity. These distributions are described by a so-called distribution function f, which gives a probability that say, an electron group has a certain fraction that has a velocity in a range between u and $u + du$, v and $v + dv$, etc., where u, v, and w are the velocity components in an x-y-z coordinate system. This distribution must be known to obtain averages in quantities such as momentum loss per collision, etc. In particular, the distribution function is defined by

$f\, dx\, dy\, dz\, du\, dv\, dw$ = number of electrons located in volume $dx\, dy\, dz$
that have velocities between
u and $u + du$, v and $v + dv$ and w and $w + dw$

An integral of f over all value of all 3 velocity coordinates gives the electron number density

$$\int_{-\infty}^{+\infty} f\, du\, dv\, dw = n_e$$

(3-31)

In general, the physics of the task ahead is sufficiently complex that analysis cannot be carried out without a number of simplifying approximations. These approximations are excellent in that their use leads to very useful results. These modeling simplifications were first promulgated by Lorentz in connection with his studies of astrophysical phenomena (Ref. 3-2). The development of this material owes its basis in part to the work of Jeans (Ref. 3-3).

3.4.1. The Lorentz Gas Approximation

The simplifying assumptions made by Lorentz are:
1. It is reasonable to assume that the low mass of the electrons compared to that of the heavy particles allows one to state that the approximately same temperatures will lead to very much higher electron velocities. Sufficiently high, in fact, that the typical encounter will involve motion past the heavy particle in such a short time that the heavy atom will not move materially. The heavy particle may thus be assumed to be stationary. This implies that the contribution by very slow electrons interacting with very fast heavy atoms to any calculated quantity is very small.

2. The electrons are describable by a distribution function. This implies that there is a sufficient number of electrons that interact by collisions to enable a temperature to be defined. The degree of ionization must be significant: for engineering devices of interest that rely on current conduction, the existence assumption for an electron distribution is generally valid.

3. The distribution function is assumed known. To avoid having to solve the Boltzmann equation, a Maxwell-Boltzmann distribution with a perturbation to account for net current is assumed.

3.4.2. Force Fields

The atom (or molecule) is assumed to exert a radial force on the electron of the form $F \sim r^{-s}$. The exponent s describes the range of the force field: $s = 2$ is the long-range Coulomb force field, $s = 5$ is a polarizable or Maxwellian field, while $s = \infty$ describes a hard sphere of short-range influence. A constant of proportionality is introduced in connection with the evaluation of the conductivity for the various force law possibilities.

3.4.3. Encounter Geometry

Consider the stationary atom and an approaching electron headed in the direction of the electric field, say, the z direction. Figure 3-4 shows the flight paths for a given force law type and a number of electrons, all having the same far-field velocity (solid lines) but varying impact parameters. Electrons with a small impact parameter suffer a large change in velocity vector, while those with a large one suffer little or no deflection. The figure also shows the dotted path line of an electron with a smaller incoming velocity. This electron is deflected to a greater extent because it spends more time in the vicinity of the atom.

Consider a nominal collision defined by the initial approach velocity vector and the impact parameter p. The velocity is vectorially related to a laboratory reference system. Its magnitude is c, far from the atom. These collision-defining quantities will be allowed to vary over all acceptable values, and their contributions are added by appropriate integrations.

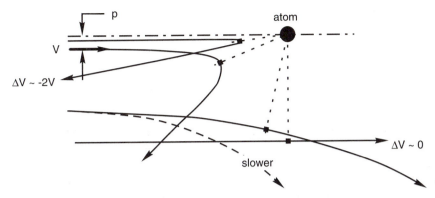

FIGURE 3-4. Effect of impact parameter and initial velocity on collision path. The *speed* (i.e., the kinetic energy) is conserved. The square points are locations of closest approach.

Figure 3-5 shows the path of the electron in the plane of the motion. This path is symmetric about the point of closest approach. The velocity magnitude after the collision is equal to the initial velocity c because the electron energy is conserved. The direction is evidently changed, and thus the electron will experience the momentum change of interest here.

The velocity vector of an electron encountering an atom defines a plane at the center of the atom. This S plane may be visualized as a target with the atom at the center. The electron can arrive from any direction, but the momentum change in the z direction is to be computed because the average current is in this (E field) direction. Figure 3-5 shows the S plane edge on and the laboratory fixed coordinate system, x-y-z. None of these three coordinate directions is in the plane of the figure. The total turning angle experienced through the encounter is $2\phi_0$ as shown.

An angle θ defines the orientation of the particular collision considered with respect to the z direction. This angle will vary over all possibilities. The x-y plane intersects the S plane in a line. The upper part of Fig. 3-6 shows the line as B to A. This figure shows the full view of the S plane from the electron's initial orientation. Note the tail of the c vector. The upper figure also shows a differential element of area (shaded) in the S plane. The angle ε is a polar angle in the S plane measured as shown. The radial location of the projected impact point on S is the impact parameter. The elemental area is $p\, dp\, d\varepsilon$ (shaded) in this "gun sight" view of the atom. Note from the electron view before the collision, the z direction is foreshortened (by the fact that $\theta - 90°$) and is labeled z''. The lower portion of Fig. 3-6 is a perspective view of the rear of the S plane and the x-y-z atom centered coordinate system and shows specifically the angle θ as well as the intersection of the x-y and S planes. Figures 3-7 and 3-8 are photographs of a clear plastic model of the encounter geometry to aid the reader in visualizing the relative orientation of the electron path, the S plane, and the geometric parameters (p and ε) in that plane.

3.4.4. Momentum Changes

Of interest here is the change in z momentum of the electron as a result of this collision. The total momentum change per atom is

$$\text{force} \sim \frac{\Delta \text{ mom}}{\text{particle}} \frac{\text{particles}}{\text{area, time}} \text{ area} \tag{3-32}$$

The momentum change term required is proportional to the change in velocity in the z direction, $w - w'$. The second fraction is the particle flux which depends on the velocity. The differential value of this flux is given by $c\,f\,du\,dv\,dw$. The differential area through which the electron finds its way past the atom is $p\,dp\,d\varepsilon$. Thus the force in the z direction is

$$\text{force} = \iiint \iint m_e (w - w')\, c f p\, dp\, d\varepsilon\, du\, dv\, dw \tag{3-33}$$

This integration is most convenient in a polar coordinate system with the coordinate directions described as in Fig. 3-9. The velocity differential becomes

$$du\,dv\,dw = c^2 \sin\theta\, d\theta\, d\phi\, dc \tag{3-34}$$

or with the number density of heavy atoms of type i, n_i:

$$\frac{\text{force}}{\text{volume}} = n_i m_i \int \int \int \int \int (w - w')\, c^3 f\, pdpd\varepsilon\, \sin\theta\, d\theta\, d\phi \tag{3-35}$$

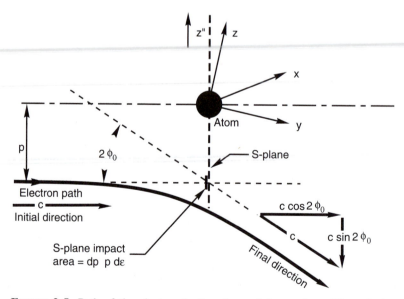

FIGURE 3-5. Path of the electron in the plane of the motion. The velocity vector components before (w) and after (w') the collision used in the calculation of momentum change in the z direction are not shown.

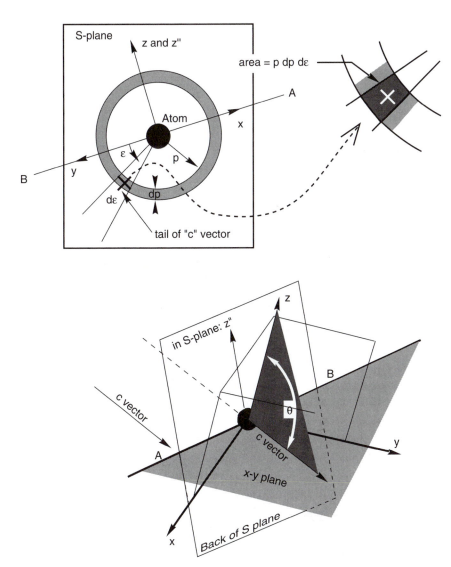

FIGURE 3-6. The S plane and the collision variables. Upper figure is target view of the atom and S plane. Lower shows the rear of the S plane and the x-y-z coordinate system. The **c** vector is of the incoming electron.

The variables have integration ranges as follows:

$$0 \leqslant \theta \leqslant \pi$$

$$0 \leqslant \phi \leqslant 2\pi$$

$$0 \leqslant c \leqslant \infty$$

$$0 \leqslant p \leqslant \infty$$

$$0 \leqslant \varepsilon \leqslant 2\pi$$

The initial velocity in the z direction can be seen from Fig. 3-6 and the lower part of Fig. 3-9:

$$w = c \cos \theta \qquad (3\text{-}36)$$

The final value requires consideration of the collision parameters. Figure 3-5 shows that the final deflection angle is $2\phi_0$. The symmetry of the problem implies that the turning angle is ϕ_0 at the point of closest encounter. The magnitude c is equal to the initial value due to the conservation of electron energy.

The final velocity vector may be described as the sum of two vectors; one

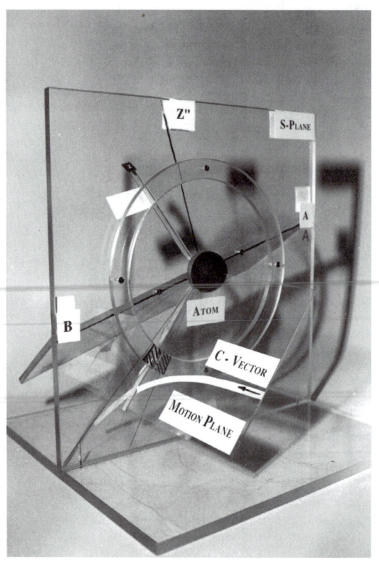

FIGURE 3-7. Photograph of a clear plastic model of the encounter geometry seen from the "front" or incident electron side.

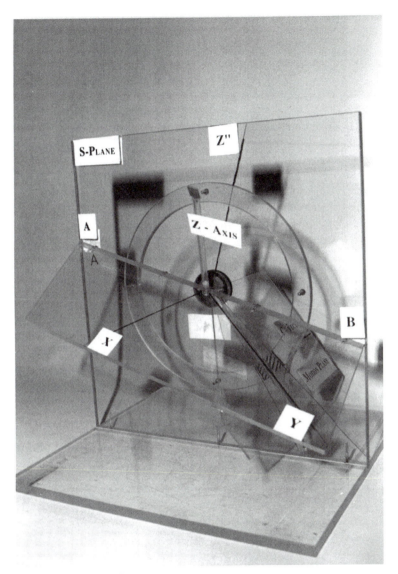

FIGURE 3-8. Photograph of a clear plastic model of the encounter geometry seen from the "rear" or leaving electron side.

is $c \cos 2\phi_0$ parallel to the direction of the initial velocity vector, and another, $c \sin 2\phi_0$ normal to it. These velocities are identified with boxed labels in Fig. 3-10. These two parts of the final velocity are also shown as the hypotenuse(s) of the shaded triangles in the view along A-B. The heavy sides of these two triangles are the components in the z direction. Figure 3-10 shows two views of the S plane and the velocity vectors.

Note that the z direction is at an angle ε to the deflected velocity (gun sight view). Consequently, the component of velocity vector in the direction *normal* to the original motion, $c \sin 2\phi_0$, is $c \sin 2\phi_0 \sin \varepsilon$ in the S plane and, as shown, $c \sin 2\phi_0 \sin \varepsilon \sin \theta$ in the z direction. The velocity *parallel* to the direction of the original motion also has a component in the z direction, which is $c \cos 2\phi_0 \cos \theta$. The velocity in the z direction after the collision is therefore the vector sum of these two components (which are shown as having opposite directions in the illustration):

$$w' = c \cos 2\phi_0 \cos \theta - c \sin 2\phi_0 \sin \varepsilon \sin \theta \qquad (3\text{-}37)$$

and the net momentum change $(w - w')$ suffered by a particle is

$$\frac{\Delta \text{ mom}}{\text{particle}} = m_e c \left[(\cos 2\phi_0 - 1) \cos \theta - \sin 2\phi_0 \sin \varepsilon \sin \theta \right] \qquad (3\text{-}38)$$

At this point it becomes necessary to relate the deflection angle ϕ_0 to the impact geometry–specifically to the impact parameter and the velocity. Here, the force law exponent will play an important role.

3.4.5. Motion in the c Vector and Atom Plane

Figure 3-11 shows the electron at a general position on the trajectory of an encounter. The plane of the motion is defined by the velocity vector and the atom as in Fig. 3-5. The coordinates describing the path are (1) the atom view angle ψ (initially zero when the electron is far from the encounter atom) and (2) the radial coordinate r (initially ∞). Midway through the encounter, the angle is ψ_0 and the distance of closest approach is r_0. The triangle shows that the angle ψ_0 and the deflection angle ϕ_0 are related by

$$\phi_0 + \psi_0 = \frac{\pi}{2} \qquad (3\text{-}39)$$

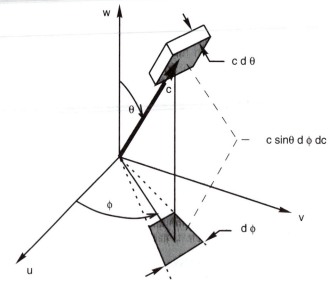

FIGURE 3-9. Schematic of polar velocity coordinates.

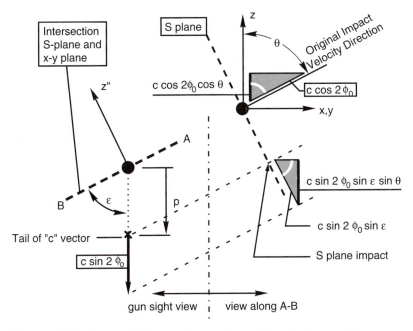

FIGURE 3-10. "Gun sight" and edge-on views of the S plane and the z component contributions by the final velocity vector.

The velocity of the electron at any point on the path is the vector sum of components $\dot{r}$ and $r\psi$ in the radial and angular directions, respectively, so that the equations of motion must be integrated to find ψ_0.

The radial component of the force law describing the atom-electron interaction may be written by specification of a force exponent s as

$$F = -\, m_e \frac{K_s}{r^s} \tag{3-40}$$

where the K_s is identified with a specific force law exponent s, which describes the decrease of the interaction force with distance from the atom. The electron mass, m_e, is introduced to ease the nondimensionalizing of the equations to follow. The potential energy associated with a position r is

$$\int_{\infty}^{r} F\, dr = m_e \frac{K_s}{(s-1)}\, r^{-(s-1)} \tag{3-41}$$

so that the conserved total energy is

$$\frac{1}{2}\left[(\dot{r})^2 + (r\,\dot{\psi})^2\right] + \frac{K_s}{s-1}\frac{1}{r^{s-1}} = \frac{1}{2}c^2 \tag{3-42}$$

The angular momentum of the electron about the atom center of mass is also conserved:

$$r^2 \dot{\psi} = p\,c \tag{3-43}$$

In the energy (and momentum) equation, the form of the constant in the force law allows cancellation of the electron mass. These two equations can be combined by eliminating the time in the formulation. Thus

$$\dot{r} = \frac{dr}{d\psi}\,\dot{\psi} = \frac{p\,c}{r^2}\,\frac{dr}{d\psi} \tag{3-44}$$

The energy equation (eq. 3-42) then becomes, after some manipulation

$$\left(\frac{d\psi}{dr}\right)^{-2} = 2\left(\frac{r^2}{p\,c}\right)^2\left[\frac{1}{2}\,c^2 - \frac{K_s}{s-1}\,\frac{1}{r^{s-1}}\right] - r^2 \tag{3-45}$$

which is an awkward relation between r and ψ. With a change in variable this equation is made easier to manage. Let

$$\zeta \equiv \frac{p}{r} \quad \text{and} \quad \alpha \equiv p\left[\frac{c^2}{K_s}\right]^{1/(s-1)} \tag{3-46}$$

Note α is dependent on s. It follows

$$\frac{dr}{d\psi} = \frac{d\zeta}{d\psi}\,\frac{p}{\zeta} \quad \text{and} \quad \frac{K_s}{c^2} = \left[\frac{p}{\alpha}\right]^{s-1} \tag{3-47}$$

ζ is evidently a nondimensional (inverse) radial position coordinate, while α is a measure of the electron kinetic energy relative to the potential energy associated with approach to a distance p. The equation of motion (eq. 3-45) may be written

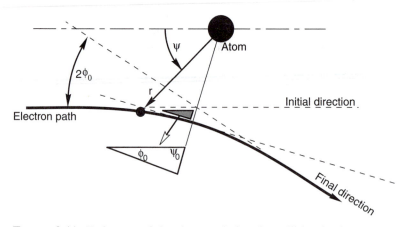

FIGURE 3-11. Trajectory of the electron during the collision in the **c** vector and atom plane.

$$d\psi = \cfrac{d\zeta}{\sqrt{1 - \cfrac{2}{s-1}\left(\cfrac{\zeta}{\alpha}\right)^{s-1} - \zeta^2}}$$

(3-48)

which gives the radial position $r = p/\zeta$ in term of the angular deflection ψ and can be integrated for specific values of s. Of immediate interest is the angular deflection at closest approach, where

$$\frac{dr}{d\psi} \text{ or } \frac{d\zeta}{d\psi} = 0$$

(3-49)

At closest approach, the radial coordinate is given by eq. 3-48 as

$$1 - \frac{2}{s-1}\left(\frac{\zeta_0}{\alpha}\right)^{s-1} - \zeta_0^2 = 0$$

(3-50)

The angular deflection at closest approach is therefore

$$\psi_0 = \int_0^{\zeta_0} \cfrac{d\zeta}{\sqrt{1 - \cfrac{2}{s-1}\left(\cfrac{\zeta}{\alpha}\right)^{s-1} - \zeta^2}}$$

(3-51)

which is a function of only α and s, that is, $\psi_0 = \phi(\alpha, s)$. For a specific choice of the force law exponent s, analytic expressions for ψ_0 may be obtained, and the meaning of a can be made more quantitative.

The Parameter α

Case 1: Collision of an electron with a singly charged ion. Consider the atom to be a singly charged ion for which $s = 2$. The electrostatic force interaction (see eq. 2-20) allows identification of the constant K_2:

$$F_2 = -\frac{e^2}{4\pi\,\varepsilon_0}\frac{1}{r^2} \quad \text{and} \quad K_2 = \frac{e^2}{4\pi\,\varepsilon_0}\frac{1}{m_e}$$

(3-52)

Case 2: Collision of an electron with a neutral, polarizable atom. Another interesting force law is encountered when the atom is electrically neutral with its orbital electrons able to reorganize themselves in response to the charge of a free electron in the vicinity. In this way, the collection of bound electrons are repelled to the far side of the atom, leaving a dipole with a positive charge near the external electron and a negative charge on the far side. The dipole resulting field is said to be induced and the polarizability is a parameter that measures the extent to which such a rearrangement can take place. The force law associated with the dipole field and seen by the electron can be shown to be (Ref. 3-4):

$$F_5 = - \frac{e^2}{4\pi \, \varepsilon_0} \frac{R^3}{r^5} \quad \text{and} \quad K_5 = \frac{e^2}{4\pi \, \varepsilon_0} \frac{R^3}{m_e} \tag{3-53}$$

where the constant R (with length units) is related to the *polarizability*. An electron encounter with this type of heavy particle will allow undisturbed approach much closer to the atom and is therefore is shorter-ranged than a Coulomb ($s = 2$) atom: There is no interaction until the electron approach is close enough for the repulsive field to be set up. The corresponding values of α in these two cases are

$$\alpha_2 = p \left(\frac{4\pi \, \varepsilon_0}{e^2} m_e c^2 \right) \quad \text{and} \quad \alpha_5 = p \left(\frac{4\pi \, \varepsilon_0}{e^2} \frac{m_e c^2}{R^3} \right)^{1/4} \tag{3-54}$$

To illustrate the difference between the laws, one may note that the potential energy acquired in approaching from ∞ to p is

$$PE(p) = - \int_{\infty}^{p} F \, dr \quad \text{or} \quad PE(p) = \frac{e^2}{4\pi \, \varepsilon_0} \frac{1}{p} \quad \text{and} \quad \frac{e^2}{4\pi \, \varepsilon_0} \frac{R^3}{4 \, p^4} \tag{3-55}$$

for $s = 2$ and 5, respectively. This gives α as

$$\alpha_2 = \frac{m_e c^2}{PE(p)} \quad \text{and} \quad \alpha_5 = \left(\frac{m_e c^2}{4 \, PE(p)} \right)^{1/4} \tag{3-56}$$

and may therefore be interpreted as a measure of the kinetic energy, nondimensionalized by the potential energy associated with an approach distance equal to the impact parameter.

The parameter α is descriptive for a specific encounter geometry. Equation 3-54 allows interpretation of an average α when an average kinetic energy is used. Consider the kinetic energy of the electron to be equipartitioned such that $\frac{1}{2} kT$ is associated with each of the three directional degrees of freedom. Thus

$$\frac{1}{2} m_e c^2 = \frac{3}{2} k T \tag{3-57}$$

The electron-ion or electron-electron force law relation (eq. 3-55) gives a distance where the potential energy and the (average) kinetic energy are equal as

$$L_e = \frac{e^2}{12\pi \, \varepsilon_0 kT} = \frac{5.6 x 10^{-6}}{T(K)} \tag{3-58}$$

For a 3000 K plasma, this length is 2×10^{-9} m. This may be viewed as an average approach distance between electrons, as allowed by their kinetic energy. For the electron to be free a large fraction of the time, the product $n_e L_e^3$ should be small (i.e., $\ll 1$). Using the definition of the Debye length, eq. 3-5, it may be shown that

$$\frac{h_D}{L_e} = \sqrt{\frac{1}{12\,\pi\,n_e\,L_e^3}}$$
(3-59)

which shows that the Debye length is typically much larger than the approach distance, especially when the electron density is small. Using this approach distance, the αs may be written

$$\alpha_2 = \frac{p}{L_e} \quad \text{and} \quad \alpha_5 = p\left(\frac{1}{L_e}\frac{1}{R^3}\right)^{1/4}$$

Case 3: Collision of an electron with a neutral, nonpolarizable atom. This last interesting force law case is that for $s = \infty$, the so-called *hard sphere*. This law imparts no effect to the electron until it reaches a certain radius. At this point the repulsion force is extremely large over a very short time resulting in an elastic reflection. The mathematics of this law are special, and, although the model is physically improbable, it does lead to insight regarding the mechanics of current conduction by providing a model that is intuitively simple. The radius of approach where the interaction takes place may be interpreted as the size of the hard sphere.

The definition of dimensionless α (eq. 3-46) implies that the grouping in brackets below must carry units of length:

$$\alpha_\infty = \frac{p}{\left[\left(\dfrac{K_\infty}{c^2}\right)^{1/(s-1)}\right]} = \frac{p}{p_0}$$
(3-60)

p_0 must be the hard sphere radius since there is no interaction until *contact* is made. $\alpha_\infty < 1$ describes a *hit*, while $\alpha_\infty \geq 1$ describes a *miss*.

3.4.6. Collision Force Integral

In eq. 3-33 the momentum change was expressed in terms of integrations over the collision area $p\,dp\,d\varepsilon$. The impact parameter p is therefore best expressed in terms of α:

$$p\,dp = \alpha\,d\alpha\left[\frac{K_s}{c^2}\right]^{2/(s-1)}$$
(3-61)

The collision force per unit volume integral can be written:

$$\frac{\text{force}}{\text{volume}} = n_i m_i \int \int \int \int \left[(\cos 2\phi_0 - 1)\cos\theta - \sin 2\phi_0 \sin\varepsilon \sin\theta \right]$$

$$\text{x } c^4 f \left(\frac{K_s}{c^2} \right) \alpha d\alpha \, d\varepsilon \, \sin\theta \, d\theta \, d\phi \, dc$$

$$(3\text{-}62)$$

The following relations

$$\int d\varepsilon = 2\pi \text{ ; } \int \sin\varepsilon \, d\varepsilon = 0 \text{ ; } \int d\phi = 2\pi \text{ ; and } \cos 2\phi_0 - 1 = -2\cos^2\psi_0$$

$$(3\text{-}63)$$

are useful because they simplify the force integral (eq. 3-35 or 3-62) considerably. From Fig. 3-11, the last equation of eq. 3-63 is an identity. Thus

$$\frac{\text{force}}{\text{vol}} = -2\pi \, n_i \, m_e \, I_s \, (K_s)^{2/(s-1)} \int \int c^{[4(s-2)/(s-1)]} f \sin\theta \cos\theta \, d\theta \, dc$$

$$(3\text{-}64)$$

where the integral

$$I_s \equiv 4\pi \int \cos^2\psi_0 \, \alpha \, d\alpha$$

$$(3\text{-}65)$$

is grouped in this form because it contains only terms involved in the collision mechanics. This integral is subsequently evaluated for various force laws. Further evaluation of the second double integral in eq. 3-64 requires knowledge of the distribution function. A plausible form is a Maxwell-Boltzmann distribution (square brackets) perturbed by a term allowing a flux, that is, a current. An appropriate such form can be shown to be

$$f = \left[n_e \left(\frac{m_e}{2\pi \, k \, T} \right)^{\frac{3}{2}} \exp - \frac{m_e \, c^2}{2 \, k \, T} \right] \left(1 + A \, c^{4/(s-1)} \cos\theta \right)$$

$$(3\text{-}66)$$

The constant A scales the nonisotropic portion of the distribution function and thus is proportional to the current. The velocity dependence of the current term is intuitively resonant with the notion that for a given finite s, the fast electrons are more important than the slow ones in distorting the distribution function because the slow ones are rather easily deflected and thereby randomized. Further, note that the s dependance of the speed integral proportional to A in eq. 3-64 vanishes.

The θ functions in the force expression involves two terms that, when integrated between 0 to π, are

$$\int \sin\theta \cos\theta \, d\theta = 0 \text{ and } \int \sin\theta \cos^2\theta \, d\theta = 2/3$$

and eq. 3-64 becomes:

$$\frac{force}{vol} = -\frac{4\pi}{3} n_e m_e n_i A \left(\frac{m_e}{2\pi k T}\right)^{3/2} I_s (K_s)^{2/(s-1)} \int_0^\infty c^4 \exp\left(-\frac{m_e c^2}{2 k T}\right) dc$$

$$(3-67)$$

The integral is in the form of a gamma function defined by

$$\Gamma(n+1) = \int_0^\infty y^n \exp(-y) dy$$

$$(3-68)$$

This allows the writing of the force term (eq. 3-67) as

$$\frac{force}{vol} = -\frac{4 kT}{3 \sqrt{\pi}} n_e n_i A I_s (K_s)^{2/(s-1)} \Gamma\left(\frac{5}{2}\right)$$

$$(3-69)$$

Electrical Current: Evaluation of A

The electron distribution function allows the current to be determined from

$$j = -e \iiint w f c^2 \sin\theta d\theta d\phi dc$$

$$(3-70)$$

where $w = c \cos\theta$. This expression gives, when integrating over θ (= 2/3) and ϕ (= 2π),

$$j = -\frac{4\pi}{3} e n_e A \left(\frac{m_e}{2\pi k T}\right)^{3/2} \int_0^\infty c^{[3 + 4/(s-1)]} \exp\left(-\frac{m_e c^2}{2 k T}\right) dc$$

$$(3-71)$$

from which A is obtained as:

$$A = -\frac{3\sqrt{\pi}}{2} \frac{j}{e n_e} \left(\frac{m_e}{2 k T}\right)^{[1/2 + 2/(s-1)]} \left[\Gamma\left(2 + \frac{2}{s-1}\right)\right]^{-1}$$

$$(3-72)$$

It follows that the force term (eq. 3-69) can be written in terms of the current j:

$$\left(\frac{force}{vol}\right)_i = -\frac{j}{e} m_e \left(\frac{m_e}{2kT}\right)^{[-1/2 + 2/(s-1)]} \left[n_i I_s (K_s)^{2/(s-1)}\right] \frac{\Gamma\left(\frac{5}{2}\right)}{\Gamma\left(2 + \frac{2}{s-1}\right)}$$

$$(3-73)$$

and the conductivity follows directly from eq. 3-29;

$$\frac{1}{\sigma} = \frac{1}{e \, n_e j} \sum_i \left(\frac{force}{vol}\right)_i$$

$$= \frac{m_e}{e^2 \, n_e} \sum \left(\frac{2kT}{m_e}\right)^{[1/2 \, - \, 2/(s-1)]} \left[n_i \, I_s \, (K_s)^{2/(s-1)}\right] \frac{\Gamma\left(\frac{5}{2}\right)}{\Gamma\left(2 + \frac{2}{s-1}\right)}$$

(3-74)

Here the implication is that for each of the i mixture components, the appropriate value of s is to be used. Γ values of interest are: $\Gamma(1/2) = \sqrt{\pi}$, $\Gamma(1) = 1$, with others given in Table 3-1. Other values may be found using the recursion formula $\Gamma(n+1) = n \, \Gamma(n)$. The role of the force law exponent is summarized in the table by showing the temperature dependence of the conductivity.

Table 3-1. s dependent parameters in expressions for the conductivity.

s	$2/(s-1)$	$\Gamma(2 + 2/(s-1))$	T **exponent in** σ
2	2	6	+3/2
5	1/2	$3\sqrt{\pi}/4$	0
1	0	1	-1/2

The expression for σ can be evaluated for the force law s values cited, and the expression can be transformed into one involving more physically meaningful quantities. To do this, the integral I_s must be evaluated.

Examples for $s = \infty$, 5, and 2: The I_s Integrals and the Conductivity

1. Hard sphere collisions. The simplest model for the I_s integral is for $s = \infty$. ψ_0 is given by eq. 3-51, while α was by eq. 3-60. The ratio ζ/α to a large power divided by that same large number can be shown to approach zero. Thus the expression for the deflection angle becomes

$$\psi_0(s=\infty) = \int_0^{\zeta_0} \frac{d\zeta}{\sqrt{1 - \zeta^2}} = \sin^{-1} \zeta_0 = \sin^{-1}\left(\frac{p}{r_0}\right)$$

(3-75)

which implies that for a collision that is a glancing miss, $\psi_0 = \pi/2$ and the impact parameter cannot be greater than r_0, that is, r_0 is the sphere radius identified in eq. 3-60 as p_0. Figure 3-12 shows the particulars for this collision. In this case,

$$\cos^2 \psi_0 = 1 - \sin^2 \psi_0 = 1 - \left(\frac{p}{r_0}\right)^2$$

(3-76)

The integral is

$$I_\infty = 4\pi \int_0^1 \left[1 - \left(\frac{p}{r_0} \right)^2 \right] \frac{p}{r_0} \, d\left(\frac{p}{r_0} \right) = \pi$$

(3-77)

The radius may be associated with the term $r_0 = (K_s)^{1/(s-1)} = p_0$ so that $\pi \, r_0^2 = Q_{e,\infty}$ is the cross-sectional area and eq. 3-74 for hard spheres becomes

$$\frac{1}{\sigma} = \frac{m_e}{e^2 \, n_e} \sqrt{\frac{2 \, k \, T}{m_e}} \left[n_i \, \pi \, (r_0)^2 \right] \frac{\Gamma\left(\frac{5}{2}\right)}{\Gamma(2)} = \frac{m_e}{e^2 \, n_e} \left\{ \bar{c}_e \, n_i \, Q_{e,\infty} \right\} \frac{3\pi}{8}$$

(3-78)

where the mean thermal speed used is

$$\bar{c}_e = \sqrt{\frac{8 \, k \, T}{\pi \, m_e}}$$

(3-79)

Thus we verify the physical view introduced through Fig. 3-3, that is, that the mean thermal speed $\bar{c}_e$ and the macroscopic cross sectional area, $n_i \, Q_{e,\infty}$, determine the collision frequency (in the parentheses on the right side). The numerical term at the end equals 1.178 and arises from the use of the mean thermal speed. Its magnitude is generally incorporated in the cross section.

2. Maxwellian molecule collisions. Maxwellian and Coulomb force law interactions are algebraically more complex because eq. 3-51 must be solved for ψ_0. For these molecules, the results of numerical calculations are described and compared to similar results for the hard sphere. The solution procedure is as follows:

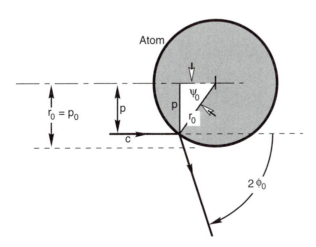

FIGURE 3-12. Hard sphere collision parameters.

α is chosen as the independent variable;

ζ_0, the point of closest approach, is found (eq. 3-50);

The angle ψ_0 is found from integration of eq. 3-51;

ψ_0 is obtained as a function of ζ_0;

A numerical integral for $\cos^2 \psi_0\ \alpha\ d\alpha$ is obtained (eq. 3-65) to find I_s.

The results of such calculations are shown in Figs. 3-13, 3-14, and 3-15. The variation of ζ_0 and ψ_0 are shown in the first two figures, while the third is a cross plot with α eliminated. Note that for small α the $s = 5$ molecule and the hard sphere are quite similar in the distance to which the electrons approach the atom and to a lesser degree to which they are deflected. Grazing encounters for the Maxwellian molecule occur for $1 < \alpha < 2$. On the other hand, the Coulomb force law ($s = 2$, see below) affects much more severely electrons colliding with all as, especially large values corresponding to large impact parameter. A value as large as 10 will give a small deflection, that is, ψ_0 near 90°.

Numerical values for the conductivity for the Maxwellian gas are similarly interpretable as those for the hard sphere. If the mean thermal speed is again used to obtain a cross section, then this cross section is temperature dependent and equal to

$$Q_{e,5} = \frac{1}{4} \sqrt{\frac{e^2}{\varepsilon_0} \frac{R^3}{2kT}} = \frac{\sqrt{6\pi}}{4} \sqrt{L_e R^3} \qquad (3\text{-}80)$$

3. Coulomb collisions. The Coulombic force field is so wide ranging that integration of the terms leading to a cross section becomes singular. This can be seen from the solution for ζ_0 (eq. 3-50):

$$1 - \zeta_0^2 - 2\frac{\zeta_0}{\alpha} = 0 \quad \text{or} \quad \zeta_0 = \frac{1}{\alpha}\left[\sqrt{1 + \alpha^2} - 1\right] \qquad (3\text{-}81)$$

The closest approach azimuth angle ψ_0 follows directly from eq. 3-51:

$$\psi_0 = \frac{\pi}{2} - \sin^{-1}\left(\frac{1}{\sqrt{1 + \alpha^2}}\right) \quad \text{or} \quad \cos \psi_0 = \frac{1}{1 + \alpha^2} \qquad (3\text{-}82)$$

This gives a logarithmic singularity when the I_2 integral is evaluated at the upper a limit:

$$I_2 = 2\pi \left[\ln\left(1 + \alpha^2\right)\right]_0^\infty \qquad (3\text{-}83)$$

Integrating to infinity implies that the $s = 2$ law is so strong that it feels the influence of *all* ions in the universe, which is unrealistic because it leads to

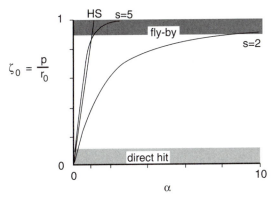

FIGURE 3-13. Plot of ζ_0 with α for various force laws. HS refers to the hard sphere.

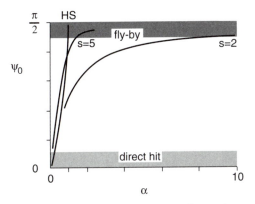

FIGURE 3-14. Plot of ψ_0 with α for various force laws.

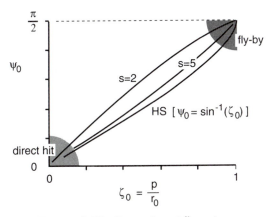

FIGURE 3-15. Cross plot of ζ_0 and ψ_0.

zero conductivity. To make the description more realistic, one can bound the integration to an upper value where the net charge of the plasma is electrically neutral. The length scale over which this is true is the Debye length (Section 3.1). Thus for impact parameters larger than the Debye length h_D, one would expect the electron to be influenced more by the totality of the neutral plasma than the force associated with the single ion under consideration. Substituting into eq. 3-74, and limiting the integral to a maximum, one obtains

$$\frac{1}{\sigma} = \frac{m_e}{e^2 n_e} \sqrt{\frac{2kT}{m_e}} \left[n_i \left(\frac{K_2 m_e}{2kT}\right)^2 \right] \frac{\Gamma\left(\frac{5}{2}\right)}{\Gamma(4)} = \frac{m_e}{e^2 n_e} \left\{ \bar{c}_e\, n_i\, Q_{e,2} \right\}$$

(3-84)

where the electron-ion cross section $Q_{e,2}$ is given by

$$Q_{e,2} = \frac{9\pi^2}{32} L_e^2 \ln\left(1 + \alpha_{2,\,max}^2\right) \approx \frac{9\pi^2}{32} L_e^2 \ln\left(\frac{1}{12\pi n_e L_e^3}\right)$$

(3-85)

The Debye length gives $\alpha_{2,\,max}$ as

$$\alpha_{2,\,max} = h_D\left(\frac{c^2}{K_2}\right) = \frac{h_D}{L_e} = \frac{1}{\sqrt{12\pi n_e L_e^3}}$$

(3-86)

For the 3000 K example under conditions where the electron density of a typical energy conversion plasma is of the order 10^{19} m^{-3}, $\alpha_{2,\,max}$ is about 600 and its square certainly much larger than unity. When the unit term is neglected, the cross section is given by the approximate form in eq. 3-85. For the conditions stated above, this cross section is 1.4×10^{-16} m^2. In comparison to typical neutral molecules which have cross sections of the order 10^{-20} m^2, this large cross section can lead to a significant component of the plasma macroscopic cross section, especially when the degree of ionization is large.

The temperature dependence of $Q_{e,2}$ is strongly influenced by the T^{-2} term (see definition of L_e, eq. 3-58 or 3-84) and the ion density in a slightly ionized plasma. For a fully ionized gas, this conductivity is called the *Spitzer conductivity* (Ref. 3-5), which is weakly dependent on the electron or ion densities. Finally, note that the expression for the conductivity used an order-of-magnitude argument to circumvent a singularity. Differences in the constants will arise depending on how the theory is applied, so that the expression for σ for this component is necessarily approximate.

For a mixture of plasma components, the total conductivity is calculated using the summation indicated in eq. 3-74, and fortunately, in most MHD plasmas the ion contribution is not dominant; see Section 4.5.3.

PROBLEMS

1. The polarizability of a molecule is the constant α_p relating the dipole moment m_{dp} and the electric field E_0, which gives rise to the moment:

$$\alpha_p \equiv \frac{m_{dp}}{E_0} \quad \text{where} \quad m_{dp} = \lim_{(a_x \to 0)} (2\, a_x\, q)$$

a_x is the separation distance for two opposite charges q. Write the field for a dipole and show that the characteristic radius R is given by:

$$\frac{\alpha_p}{4\pi\, \varepsilon_0} \equiv R^3$$

2. Write the expression for the acceleration felt by a colliding electron in the form

$$\frac{dV}{dt} = -\frac{c^2}{p} \left[f(\zeta; \alpha \text{ and } s) \right]$$

and show that for a given s and α, the function increases to a maximum and falls to zero at ζ_0, the point of motion symmetry. Plot this function for various types of encounters.

3. One measure of approach to the atom by an electron is to examine the change in velocity of the electron. Say, for example, that nearness is to be measured by δ given by:

$$-\frac{1}{c} \frac{dr}{dt} = 1 - \delta$$

Find r (i.e., ζ) for a fixed small δ for the $s = 5$ and 2 force laws. Take advantage of δ small so that the resulting equation may be linearized. Show that for $s = 2$

$$r_2 = \frac{1}{\delta} \frac{\text{constant}}{c^2}$$

and for the $s = 5$ force law, the result is much shorter ranged and speed independent:

$$r_5 = \frac{p}{\sqrt{2\,\delta}}$$

4. The impact parameter p and the electron velocity c are constants in a particular collision encounter with a stationary atom. Consider collisions that result in a 90° deflection of the electron. For $s=2$ and 5, what are the relations between p and c such that this condition is satisfied?

REFERENCES

3-1. Batchelor, G., *Introduction to Fluid Dynamics*, Section 4.7 and 5.2, Cambridge University Press, 1967.
3-2. Chapman, S. and Cowling, T. G., *The Mathematical Theory of Non-Uniform Gases*, Cambridge University Press, 1960.
3-3. Jeans, J., *Dynamical Theory of Gases*, 4th edition, Dover Publications, 1954.
3-4. Frank, N. H., *Introduction to Electricity and Optics*, MacGraw-Hill Co., New York, 1950.
3-5. Spitzer, L., *Physics of Fully Ionized Gases*, Interscience Publishers, New York, 1956.

4

MAGNETOHYDRODYNAMICS

The background material developed in Chapters 2 and 3 is exploited to derive the governing equations for bounded flow in ducts where electrically conducting fluids are subjected to electromagnetic fields to provide or absorb electrical power. The emphasis here is on the flow and power output characteristics of the devices where the energy interaction takes place. For a description of the integration of an MHD generator into a power system, see Chapter 11 of Ref. 1-1. A related energy conversion scheme is the so-called *electrohydrodynamic* power generation described in Chapter 5.

The analysis in this chapter is simplified as much as realistically possible to highlight the performance potential and limitations of this method of energy conversion. To that end, a number of simplifications are made in the analyses and their limitations are described.

4.1. CROSSED-FIELD DEVICES

The interactions described above apply well to the design and analysis of flow devices designed to have an interaction between the electromagnetic fields and the flowing medium. Generators and accelerators have already been described as means for extracting from or adding electrical energy to the flow. The interactions of interest for power generation are primarily steady, that is, they involve DC power. The simplest geometry is one where the flow proceeds in the x direction, the electrical connection is in the y direction while the applied **B** field is in the z direction. This is the crossed field arrangement shown in Fig. 2-5.

The flow proceeds in a single direction and is most simply modeled by a steady, one dimensional flow through a duct of flow area A. On the basis of large characteristic dimensions (i.e., small surface-to-volume ratio), the effects of friction and heat transfer are neglected. Thus the equations for the fluid behavior (eqs. 2-53, 2-58, 2-66, and 2-70) become the so-called channel flow equations:

$$\text{mass conservation:} \quad \frac{d}{dx}(\rho\, u\, A) = 0 \qquad (4\text{-}1)$$

$$\text{x momentum:} \quad \rho\, u\, \frac{du}{dx} + \frac{dp}{dx} = j_y\, B \qquad (4\text{-}2)$$

$$\text{enthalpy:} \quad \rho\, u\, \left[\frac{d\left(h + \frac{1}{2} u^2\right)}{dx}\right] = j_y\, E_y + j_x\, E_x \qquad (4\text{-}3)$$

While these equations form the basis of many MHD devices, one additional equation may be important (i.e., the y momentum equation), especially if current flows in the x direction. The principal effect of such a current is to give rise to a transverse pressure gradient, since motion cannot be appreciable due to the presence of the walls:

$$\text{y momentum:} \quad \frac{dp}{dy} = -j_x B \qquad (4\text{-}4)$$

Motion resulting from transverse body forces may be significant in rendering the 1D flow assumption invalid. The enthalpy equation is written to allow for the existence of x- and y-current components and electric fields.

4.1.1. *Current Flow and Electric Field Constraints*

The current of primary interest flows through the x-z, or electrode walls, and parallel to the x-y walls. This latter walls must not present a short circuit path for this current, hence is constructed as an insulator wall. Figure 4-1 shows a portion of the duct and the walls normal to the current flow direction (electrode wall) and normal to the applied uniform magnetic field, **B**.

The design of the walls constrains either the current flow or the electric field. If the electrode wall is a continuous conductor in the x direction, the

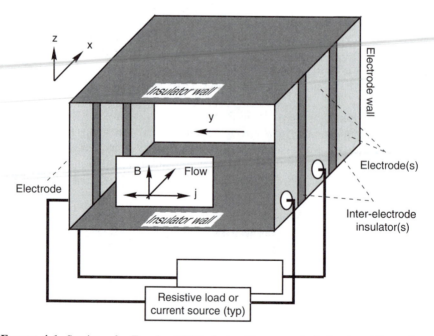

FIGURE 4-1. Section of a Faraday MHD duct with two typical circuits. Electrode and insulator walls are noted.

electric field in that direction is zero, $E_x = 0$. On the other hand, a finite E_x may be sustained if the electrode wall is segmented into short elements, each pair of which is connected to a separate external current circuit. Two such circuits are shown in Fig. 4-1. Such segmentation of the electrode wall allows the various axial pairs to be operated with a voltage level consistent with the Hall field present (E_x). Thus one distinguishes between continuous electrode and segmented electrode devices. Their performance is described in Sections 4.1.3 and 4.1.4.

Devices (such as the one shown in Fig. 4-1) where the load current flows in the y direction is termed a *Faraday device*, while those where the load current arises from an axial (or Hall) current (j_x) flow is a Hall device. The Hall generator is described in Section 4.1.5.

In order to understand the variation of the gas dynamic variables under the influence of the MHD interaction, the governing equations are applied to a simplified situation where the gas is ideal, inviscid, and one dimensional. The electric current flows uniformly from one electrode to another across a uniform plasma.

4.1.2. The MHD Terms in the Dynamical Equations

The interaction terms in the gas dynamic equations are

1. $j_y B$ in the x momentum equation;
2. $j_x B$ in the y momentum equation; and
3. $jE_x + jE_y$ in the energy equation.

The units of the momentum terms are force per unit volume and power per unit volume in the energy equation. Equation 3-14 or 3-16 can be written to give current densities in terms of the electric field components as

$$j_x = \frac{\sigma}{1 + \beta^2}\left[E_x - \beta E'_y\right] \quad \text{and} \quad j_y = \frac{\sigma}{1 + \beta^2}\left[E'_y + \beta E_x\right] \quad (4\text{-}5)$$

where σ is the scalar conductivity given by eq. 3-13 and β is the Hall parameter (eq. 3-15). The electric field E'_y is the field measured in the frame of the moving fluid and is related to the field measured in the stationary laboratory frame (E_y) (see eq. 2-5) by

$$E'_y = E_y - u B \quad (4\text{-}6)$$

External circuits relate the transverse current to the transverse electric field in a Faraday device or the axial current to the axial field in a Hall device. Further discussion is best carried out for three specific examples. Consider the special but most interesting case of the generator. The conditions of interest are the open circuit voltage, that is, the voltage measured when the load resistance is infinite and the short circuit current which flows through a zero resistance 'load'.

4.1.3. *Continuous Electrodes Generator*

For a continuous wall electrode, the field E_x is zero. The Ohm's law components read

$$j_x = \frac{\sigma}{1 + \beta^2}\left[-\beta\left(E_y - u\,B\right)\right] \text{ and } j_y = \frac{\sigma}{1 + \beta^2}\left[E_y - u\,B\right] \qquad (4\text{-}7)$$

from which it follows that

$$j_x = -\beta\,j_y \qquad (4\text{-}8)$$

Under these circumstances, the current flows at an angle across the duct given by the $\tan^{-1}\beta$. The transverse short circuit current is

$$j_{y\,.\,sc} = -\frac{\sigma\,u\,B}{1 + \beta^2} \quad \text{at} \ E_y = 0 \qquad (4\text{-}9)$$

while the open circuit electric field is

$$E_{y,\,oc} = u\,B \quad \text{at} \ j_y = 0 \qquad (4\text{-}10)$$

The variation of the electric field between the values indicated suggests a nondimensional *load factor* defined as

$$k = \frac{E_y}{uB} \begin{array}{l} = 0 \text{ at short circuit} \\ = 1 \text{ at open circuit} \end{array} \qquad (4\text{-}11)$$

The momentum equation terms are:

$$j_y\,B = \frac{\sigma\,uB^2}{1 + \beta^2}(k-1) \text{ and } j_x\,B = -\beta\,\frac{\sigma\,uB^2}{1 + \beta^2}(k-1) \qquad (4\text{-}12)$$

The transverse body force term gives rise to a pressure gradient and/or flow in the y direction that is smallest near open circuit operation.

The energy equation term written in terms of k is:

$$j_y\,E_y = \frac{\sigma u^2 B^2}{1 + \beta^2}\,k\,(k-1) \qquad (4\text{-}13)$$

showing that the rate of energy removal ($k < 1$) is proportional to the *power density* in the generator, $\sigma\,u^2\,B^2$. The load resistance, through k, controls the rate of power removed from the stream with a maximum rate at $k = 0.5$.

It turns out that for most gaseous plasmas of engineering interest, the Hall parameter β is of order 1-10 which has a significant effect on the momentum and energy equation terms by effectively reducing the conductivity, $\sigma_{eff} = \sigma / (1 + \beta^2)$, which in turn reduces the power density and increases the interaction length, eq. 2-73. This disadvantage is eliminated by segmenting the electrodes.

4.1.4. Segmented Electrode Generator

For the segmented electrode generator, the axial current is forced to be zero by allowing an axial (E_x) electric field to be set up. Ohm's law (eq. 4-7) then reads

$$j_x = 0 = \frac{\sigma}{1 + \beta^2}\left[E_x - \beta E'_y\right] \quad \text{or} \quad E_x = \beta E'_y$$

(4-14)

$$j_y = \sigma E'_y = \sigma \left(E_y - u B\right) = \sigma u B (k - 1)$$

which is obtained by substituting for E_x in the equation for j_y (eq. 4-5). The power density is given by

$$j_y E_y = \sigma u^2 B^2 k (k - 1) \qquad (4\text{-}15)$$

which is larger than that for the continuous generator by the factor $(1 + \beta^2)$, eq. 4-13. The axial body force term is similarly larger by the same factor so that a shorter interaction length is realized. Since the axial current is absent, the transverse pressure gradient is absent for this geometry. For this superior electrode configuration, the voltage-current characteristic and the power output are shown in Figs. 4-2 and 4-3, respectively. The V-I characteristic is linear, while the power output is quadratic with a maximum at $k = 0.5$, just as

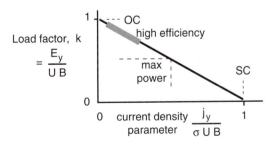

FIGURE 4-2. Voltage-Current (actually non-dimensional **E** field and current density) characteristic of a segment of a Faraday MHD generator. SC, short circuit; OC, open circuit.

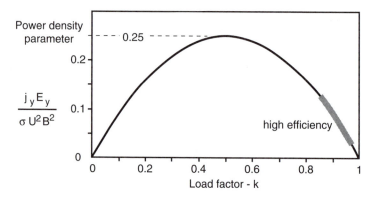

FIGURE 4-3. Power density parameter for a segmented (or continuous, see eq. 4-13) electrode Faraday generator.

for the continuous electrode geometry. The same plot applies to both with the note that the power density parameter is

$$\frac{j_y E_y}{\sigma u^2 B^2} : \text{segmented} \quad \text{or} \quad \frac{j_y E_y}{\sigma u^2 B^2}(1 + \beta^2): \text{continuous electrodes.}$$

Faraday Load Resistance

The relation between load resistance and load factor is established by Ohm's law for the plasma element affected by the electrode pair. Consider the pair to have the dimensions indicated in Fig. 2-3. The current through and the voltage across the electrodes are, respectively,

$$I = j_y h L \quad \text{and} \quad \phi = E_y d \tag{4-16}$$

so that the load resistance R is

$$R = \frac{\phi}{I} = \frac{E_y d}{(-j_y) h L} \quad \text{or} \quad \frac{j_y}{E_y} = -\frac{d}{R h L} \tag{4-17}$$

The minus sign arises from the fact that the negative charges constitute the current flow. Equating this ratio of j/E to that from Ohm's law (eq. 4-14), one obtains a relation between the load factor and the ratio of load to plasma resistance:

$$k = \frac{R \sigma \dfrac{h L}{d}}{1 + R \sigma \dfrac{h L}{d}} \tag{4-18}$$

Evidently k and $R = 0$ correspond to a short circuit condition while infinite R

gives $k = 1$. The magnitude of R is scaled by its relation to the resistance of the plasma,

$$R_{\text{plasma}} = \frac{d}{\sigma \, h \, L} \tag{4-19}$$

Efficiency

In a length Δx or L, the fluid undergoes changes in its thermodynamic state to produce the electric power transferred to the load. The equation of motion states that a force is exerted $(j_y B)$ while the energy equation states that the total enthalpy is decreased. The product of force and velocity is the rate of doing work. In particular, the flow work done (per unit volume) by the fluid is, in general,

$$\text{work done} = j \times B \cdot u$$

while the power to the load is

$$\text{power removed} = j \cdot E$$

The ratio of these is defined as a local or stage efficiency:

$$\eta_s = \frac{j \cdot E}{j \times B \cdot u} = \frac{E_y}{uB} = k \tag{4-20}$$

for a segmented electrode generator. Thus the load factor may be viewed as a measure of the effectiveness of the generator in converting flow work to output power. The portion of the power not converted to output is irreversibly converted to heat deposited in the flow. Equation 2-66, for steady flow, shows the entropy production rate in a segmented electrode generator is given by

$$\rho \, u \, T \frac{d\,s}{d\,x} = \frac{j^2}{\sigma} = \sigma \, (u\,B)^2 \, (1 - k)^2 \tag{4-21}$$

for a segmented electrode generator. Hence operation k close to unity is of greatest interest.

A similar development for the relation between load resistance and k and for the stage efficiency may be carried out for the continuous electrode generator, although the results are not likely to be of interest since that device's power density is relatively low; see Figs. 4-2 and 4-3.

Hall Voltage

Equation 4-14 shows that the electric field in the x direction varies with transverse voltage. In nondimensional terms we have

$$\frac{E_x}{u\,B} = \beta \, (1 - k) \tag{4-22}$$

In practice, this electric field impresses a voltage across the insulator between adjacent electrode pairs, which may cause a local breakdown and shorting. To the extent that such shorting reduces the mean E_x, the performance of the segmented electrode generator power density will approach that of the continuous electrode device. Figure 4-4 shows the mean E_x together with the axial field in the vicinity of the electrode wall. Apparently, the electrode width (L) and the insulator thickness determine the magnification of the far-field E_x near the insulators where the risk of breakdown is largest because of the presence of the thermal and viscous boundary layers as well as the electrical sheath.

To first order, the value of the breakdown voltage for the plasma conditions determines the length of the allowable electrode pitch. In practice, the value is on the order of a few tens of volts (10-50) and depends on the bulk plasma properties and those of the boundary layer on the electrode wall.

$$L \text{ (per electrode)} \approx \frac{\phi_{\text{breakdown}}}{\beta\, u\, B\, (1 - k)}$$

Operation at relatively large values of the load factor k and efficiency also helps keep the axial field to low levels, which can be translated to enabling the use of larger electrode lengths or, equivalently, fewer load electrode circuits.

4.1.5. Hall Generator

Evidently, in a Faraday generator the axial voltage grows with increasing transverse current, that is, decreasing k (eq. 4-22). This suggests that a generator configuration may be devised in which the Hall voltage is applied to a single load while the transverse current is maximized. Figure 4-5 shows such a configuration, which has the advantage over the Faraday configurations

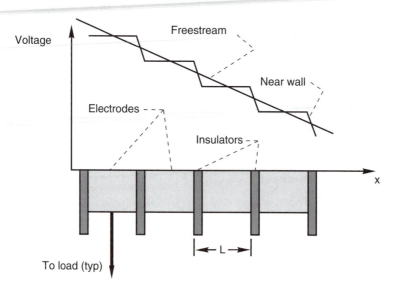

FIGURE 4-4. Axial (Hall) voltage distributions along a Faraday MHD generator: near electrode wall and in the bulk of the plasma.

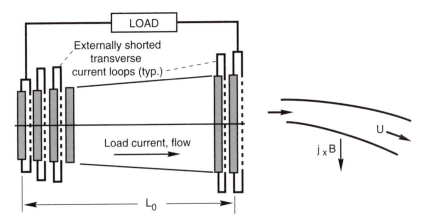

FIGURE 4-5. Hall generator: load current flows parallel to the flow. Side figure shows channel curvature to accommodate the transverse pressure gradient and thus maintain 1 D flow.

enabling use of a single load through electrodes separated by a distance L_0. In this geometry, the load current is axial. To avoid the complications associated with a transverse pressure gradient, the duct may be curved, as shown in Fig. 4-5. The fluid thus may be made to balance $j_x B$ with the centripetal acceleration.

Ohm's law (eq. 4-5) for the Hall generator (for which $E_y = 0$) states:

$$j_x = \frac{\sigma}{1 + \beta^2} [E_x + \beta u B] \quad \text{and} \quad j_y = \frac{\sigma}{1 + \beta^2} [-u B + \beta E_x] \quad (4\text{-}23)$$

The following quantities are obtained for this configuration:

$$\text{open circuit electric field: } -\beta u B \quad (4\text{-}24)$$

$$\text{open circuit voltage: } V_{OC} = -\beta u B L_0 \quad (4\text{-}25)$$

$$\text{short circuit current density: } j_{x, SC} = \frac{\beta}{1 + \beta^2} \sigma u B \quad (4\text{-}26)$$

$$\text{short circuit current: } I_{SC} = \frac{\beta}{1 + \beta^2} \sigma u B (h\, d) \quad (4\text{-}27)$$

where all quantities are appropriate average values. These characteristics suggest the definition of a Hall load factor ($0 \geq k_H \geq 1$) as

$$k_H \equiv \frac{-E_x}{\beta u B} \quad (4\text{-}28)$$

The external load coupling condition is

$$-j_x d h = \frac{E_x L_0}{R} \quad (4\text{-}29)$$

Equations 4-28 and 4-49 allow writing the load factor in terms of resistance:

$$k_H = \left(1 + \frac{L_0 (1 + \beta^2)}{\sigma R h d}\right)^{-1} \tag{4-30}$$

In terms of k_H, Ohm's law reads:

$$j_x = \frac{\sigma u B}{1 + \beta^2} \beta (1 - k_H) \quad \text{and} \quad j_y = \frac{\sigma u B}{1 + \beta^2} \left(1 + \beta^2 k_H\right) \tag{4-31}$$

The power output (per unit volume) is

$$-j_x E_x = \frac{\beta^2}{1 + \beta^2} \sigma u^2 B^2 \left[k_H (1 - k_H)\right] \tag{4-32}$$

Comparing this to the result from the segmented Faraday generator (eq. 4-15), it appears that for Hall parameters larger than about 3, the two power densities are about the same. The load factor for maximum output power is (as for the Faraday generator at $k = 0.5$) at $k_H = 0.5$, that is, at half the open circuit voltage. The voltage-current characteristic for the Hall generator, like that of the Faraday, is linear with maximum value endpoints, as indicated in Fig. 4-6, which may be compared with Fig. 4-2.

The efficiency of the Hall generator is obtained from the ratio of power output to flow work:

$$\text{flow work} = j_y u B = \sigma u^2 B^2 \frac{(1 + \beta^2 k_H)}{(1 + \beta^2)} \tag{4-33}$$

and the power output is given by eq. 4-32. The conversion efficiency

$$\eta_{\text{Hall}} = \frac{\beta^2 k_H (1 - k_H)}{(1 + \beta^2 k_H)} \tag{4-34}$$

is plotted in Fig. 4-7 for various β. Evidently, a large value of β and intermediate values of k_H are desirable for high efficiency.

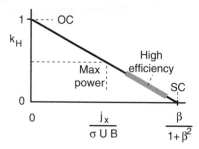

FIGURE 4-6. Voltage-current characteristic for the Hall generator. The Hall load factor is defined in eq. 4-28 or 4-30.

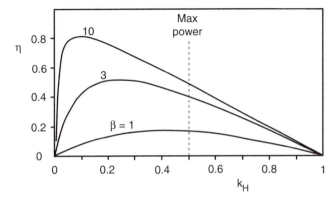

FIGURE 4-7. Hall generator efficiency as a function of load factor and Hall parameter. Power is quadratic (Fig. 4-3, eq. 4-32) with a maximum at $k_H = 0.5$ as noted.

The load factor for maximum efficiency is obtained by differentiation of eq. 4-34 and shown together with the value of the maximum efficiency in Fig. 4-8.

$$k_{H, \max \eta} = \frac{\sqrt{1 + \beta^2} - 1}{\beta^2} \quad \text{and} \quad \eta_{\max} = 1 - 2 \, k_{H, \max \eta} \qquad (4\text{-}35)$$

The Hall generator is of interest for large values of the Hall parameter and must be operated at relatively low values of the load factor, that is, close to *short circuit*. This is in contrast to the Faraday generator, where operation nearer *open circuit* is desirable.

In summary, the performance of the Faraday and Hall generators may be contrasted as shown in Figs. 4-9 and 4-10. Note the power density parameter is $\sigma u^2 B^2$ and that the Faraday results are independent of β. The Hall generator cannot achieve 100% efficiency because the shorted transverse current always leads to joule dissipation.

A plot of the actual load current (rather than current density) versus the voltage would be similar to Fig. 4-9, except that the scale would be more extreme because the Hall voltage for the Hall generator is larger than the corresponding voltage for the Faraday generator by a factor L_0/d, while the current is larger for the Faraday by the same ratio. In general then, the Hall generator is a *high-voltage* device, while the Faraday generator is a *high-current* device.

In a linear Hall generator, the external shorting circuitry may be incorporated into the channel design by constructing the opposing electrode pairs into a metal module that serves as the conductor. No transverse insulator wall is required, although axial insulation between such modules is necessary. Such a module is shown in Fig. 4-11.

The Hall generator is well suited to an axisymmetric radial disc flow geometry (Ref. 4-1) because the shorting current may be contained entirely within a circular annulus of the flow. Under these circumstances, the **j x B**

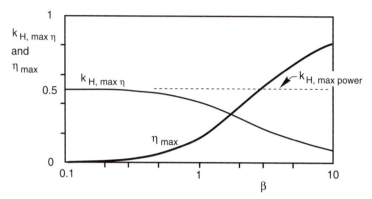

FIGURE 4-8. Maximum-efficiency Hall generator performance. A large β is required for high efficiency, which also requires small k_H.

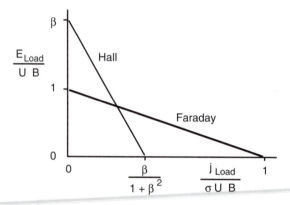

FIGURE 4-9. Comparison of voltage-current characteristics for the Hall and Faraday MHD generators.

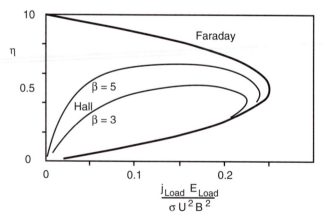

FIGURE 4-10. Power (density)-efficiency characteristics for the Hall and Faraday MHD generators.

body force associated with the load current is tangential and imparts an angular momentum to the fluid, which may be removed by a "stator" external to the generator. The ease with which this may be done has led to serious consideration of such a Hall generator as an alternative to linear Hall generators.

4.1.6. *Diagonal Faraday Generator*

In practice, when a Faraday generator is expected to operate at constant load factor, it is possible to take advantage of this fact to reduce the number of loads whose power must be combined in the subsequent power conditioning equipment. This is done by constructing the generator channel in such a way as to take advantage of planes of constant potential.

In such a Faraday generator, lines of constant potential are as sketched in Fig. 4-12, looking along the z direction (i.e. the **B** field direction). The total electric field is

$$|\mathbf{E}| = \sqrt{E_x^2 + E_y^2} = u B \sqrt{\beta^2(1-k)^2 + k^2} \qquad (4\text{-}36)$$

and planes of constant potential lie at an angle θ to the x axis, as shown in Fig. 4-12. This angle is given by

$$\theta = \tan^{-1}\frac{(-E_y)}{E_x} = \frac{k}{\beta(1-k)} \qquad (4\text{-}37)$$

With this construction technique, the number of loads can be held to a number between 2 and 5, rather than a number that is typically 10 times larger. It can be shown that this load configuration leads to performance with similarity to both the Hall and Faraday generators.

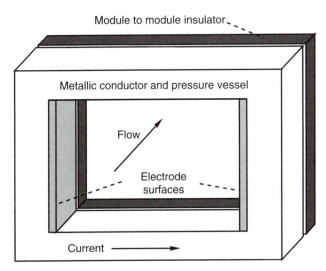

FIGURE 4-11. Linear Hall generator module showing the shorting current flow. Not shown are provisions for cooling and module-to-module connection.

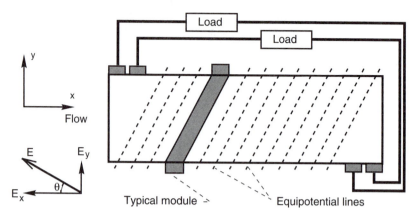

FIGURE 4-12. Diagonally connected Faraday generator showing a typical channel module.

4.2. MHD CHANNEL FLOW GAS DYNAMICS

For the following, the electrical configuration is assumed to be that of a Faraday generator. This assumption allows one to discuss the local or stage performance of a section of the generator. The Hall effect results in establishment of an axial electric field, and ideally does not influence either load voltage or current.

The analysis will admit to the possibility that the resistive load may be made a source of current and thus the generator becomes an accelerator. This situation is obtained when $k > 1$; that is, the sign of the current in Ohm's law is reversed. The following analysis is due, in part, to Sears and Resler (Ref. 4-2) and gives a clear insight into the effects of the MHD interaction on the gas dynamic variables. This approach is also described, to a different degree, in Ref. 4-3.

4.2.1. Characteristic Velocities

Assume that the load condition fixes E (i.e., E_y) and the impressed **B** field is known at all points in the channel. The ratio E/B is a quantity with units of velocity defined as

$$u_3 \equiv \frac{E}{B}, \text{ also let } u_1 \equiv \frac{\gamma - 1}{\gamma} \frac{E}{B} = \frac{\gamma - 1}{\gamma} u_3 \qquad (4\text{-}38)$$

The numbering of characteristic velocities follows the original derivation of Refs. 4-2 and 4-3 should become clearer further on. The ratio u_3/u (= $1/k$) determines the sign of the current and thus whether the device is a generator or an accelerator (i.e., from Ohm's law):

$$\frac{j_y}{\sigma u B} = \frac{u_3}{u} - 1 \qquad (4\text{-}39)$$

The derivatives of the gas dynamic variables indicate whether a quantity increases and on what scale. Hence such derivatives are of interest.

The continuity equation for steady 1D channel (eq. 4-1) flow in differential form is

$$\frac{d \ln \rho}{d x} + \frac{d \ln u}{d x} + \frac{d \ln A}{d x} = 0 \qquad (4\text{-}40)$$

The momentum equation (eq. 4-2) reads

$$\frac{\rho u^2}{p} \frac{d \ln u}{dx} + \frac{d \ln p}{dx} = \frac{j_y\, u\, B}{p} = \frac{\sigma\, u\, B^2}{p} \left(\frac{u_3}{u} - 1 \right)$$

Equation 2-73 gives the interaction length scale, which reappears here. The dimensioned group on the right-hand side can be used to nondimensionalize the physical length x. Thus

$$\xi = \frac{x}{L_{MHD}} \quad ; \quad L_{MHD} \equiv \frac{p}{\sigma\, u\, B^2} \qquad (4\text{-}41)$$

and the momentum equation reads, with the definition of Mach number for a perfect gas:

$$\gamma\, M^2 \frac{d \ln u}{d\xi} + \frac{d \ln p}{d\xi} = \left(\frac{u_3}{u} - 1 \right) \qquad (4\text{-}42)$$

The enthalpy equation (eq. 4-3 with $j_x = 0$) for the perfect gas becomes, with a corresponding manipulation,

$$(\gamma - 1) M^2 \frac{d \ln u}{d\xi} + \frac{d \ln T}{d\xi} = \left(\frac{u_3}{u} - 1 \right) \frac{u_1}{u} \qquad (4\text{-}43)$$

The right side contains the current term and a term characterizing the **E** field; see eq. 4-38. The state equation completes the set of equations required to solve for any one of the state variable derivatives. In differential form,

$$\frac{d \ln p}{d\xi} = \frac{d \ln \rho}{d\xi} + \frac{d \ln T}{d\xi} \qquad (4\text{-}44)$$

The equations 4-40, 4-42, 4-43, and 4-44 can be manipulated to give the variations of u, p, T, ρ as well as the stagnation quantities and the Mach number given by their definitions. From

$$\frac{p_t}{p} = \left(1 + \frac{\gamma-1}{2} M^2 \right)^{\gamma/(\gamma-1)} \quad \text{and} \quad \frac{T_t}{T} = 1 + \frac{\gamma-1}{2} M^2$$

it follows that

$$\frac{d \ln p_t}{d\xi} = \frac{d \ln p}{d\xi} + \frac{\frac{\gamma}{2} M^2}{1 + \frac{\gamma-1}{2} M^2} \frac{d \ln M^2}{d\xi} \tag{4-45}$$

$$\frac{d \ln T_t}{d\xi} = \frac{d \ln T}{d\xi} + \frac{\frac{\gamma-1}{2} M^2}{1 + \frac{\gamma-1}{2} M^2} \frac{d \ln M^2}{d\xi} \tag{4-46}$$

The variation of M is given by

$$\frac{d \ln M}{d\xi} = \frac{d \ln u}{d\xi} - \frac{1}{2} \frac{d \ln T}{d\xi} \tag{4-47}$$

from

$$M = \frac{u}{a} = \frac{u}{\sqrt{\gamma R T}} \tag{4-48}$$

These equations may be manipulated to eliminate all but one of the dependent variables. For example, the variations of u and M are given by:

$$\frac{d \ln u}{d\xi} = \frac{1}{M^2 - 1} \left[\frac{d \ln A}{d\xi} + \left(\frac{u_3}{u} - 1\right)\left(1 - \frac{u_1}{u}\right)\right] \tag{4-49}$$

$$\frac{d \ln M}{d\xi} = \frac{1 + \frac{\gamma-1}{2} M^2}{M^2 - 1} \left[\frac{d \ln A}{d\xi} + \left(\frac{u_3}{u} - 1\right)\left(1 - \frac{u_2}{u}\right)\right] \tag{4-50}$$

$$\text{where} \quad u_2 = \frac{1 + \gamma M^2}{1 + \frac{\gamma-1}{2} M^2} \frac{u_1}{2}$$

These results are complicated by the presence of the area variation term. In the absence of the MHD terms, these relations give the variation of u and M in a duct of varying area, the nozzle being a specific example. For example, $M = 1$ can be obtained only when dA/dx or $d \ln A/dx$ has a minimum. In Section 4.2.2 the flow area is taken to be constant in order to focus attention on the MHD interaction.

4.2.2. Sears-Resler Diagram

The Sears-Resler diagram is a map on the velocity-Mach number plane. With $dA/dx = 0$, the magnitude of u in relation to the electromagnetic field velocities u_1, u_2, and u_3 determines the sign of the u or M derivative. For the purpose of illustrating the changing flow conditions, it is useful to show the variations of the three characteristic velocities (nondimensionalized by u_1) in this plane. Figure 4-13 shows the ratios u_2/u_1 and $u_3/u_1 = 3.5$ for $\gamma = 1.4$ assumed here. For $u > u_3$, the device is a generator, since $\mathbf{j} \times \mathbf{B}$ is antiparallel to the velocity vector, $\mathbf{u}$. Otherwise it is a heater or accelerator. The distinction between these is made clearer by examining the variation of the other flow parameters.

The cross hatching in Fig. 4-13 shows the signs of the u and M derivatives. The resulting process path directions are indicated from examination of the signs of du/dx or dM/dx, and the arrows in the various domains of Fig. 4-14 show the flow evolution direction. The sonic line at $M = 1$ is approached asymptotically under a wide set of conditions with "tunneling" possible at $u = u_1$ or at $u = u_3$. For a discussion of the special tunnel points, see Refs. 4-2 and 4-3.

The variation of static and stagnation pressures as well as temperatures can be written as they have been for the variations of u and M. Additional characteristic velocities arise in connection with each of the flow property variations. The equations for the variation of properties, together with the relevant characteristic velocity definitions, are:

$$\frac{d \ln T}{d\xi} = \frac{(\gamma - 1) M^2}{1 - M^2} \left[\frac{d \ln A}{d\xi} + \left(1 - \frac{u_4}{u}\right)\left(1 - \frac{u_3}{u}\right) \right] \tag{4-51}$$

where
$$u_4 = \frac{\gamma M^2 - 1}{(\gamma - 1) M^2} u_1$$

$$\frac{d \ln p}{d\xi} = \frac{1}{1 - M^2} \left[\gamma M^2 \frac{d \ln A}{d\xi} - \left(1 + (\gamma-1) M^2\right)\left(1 - \frac{u_5}{u}\right)\left(1 - \frac{u_3}{u}\right) \right]$$

$$\tag{4-52}$$

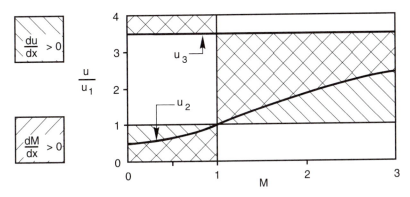

FIGURE 4-13. Sears-Resler diagram showing the sign of the derivatives of u and M.

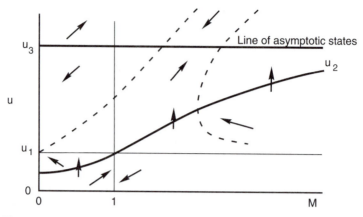

FIGURE 4-14. Processes represented on the Sears-Resler (u-M) diagram. Arrows show process direction. Thin dashed lines are typical processes, while solid lines indicate where sign changes for the derivatives of u or M occur.

where
$$u_5 = \frac{\gamma M^2}{1 + (\gamma-1) M^2} \; u_1 = \frac{(\gamma-1) M^2}{1 + (\gamma-1) M^2} \; u_3$$

$$\frac{d \ln p_t}{d\xi} = - \left(1 - \frac{u_6}{u}\right)\left(1 - \frac{u_3}{u}\right)$$

(4-53)

where
$$u_6 = \frac{\frac{\gamma}{2} M^2}{1 + \frac{\gamma-1}{2} M^2} \; u_1 = \frac{\frac{\gamma-1}{2} M^2}{1 + \frac{\gamma-1}{2} M^2} \; u_3$$

$$\frac{d \ln T_t}{d\xi} = \left(1 + \frac{\gamma-1}{2} M^2\right)^{-1} \left[\frac{u_1}{u} \left(\frac{u_3}{u} - 1\right) \right]$$

(4-54)

Note that for completeness the area variation terms are included where they appear. The combination of eqs. 4-53 and 4-54 allows the calculation of the entropy generation rate as

$$\frac{d\left(\frac{s}{R}\right)}{d\xi} = \left(1 - \frac{u_3}{u}\right)^2 + \frac{\gamma M^2}{2} f \frac{L_{MHD}}{D}$$

(4-55)

where the last term is a friction term, which would arise if it were included on the right side of eq. 4-42 (as a negative term). The first term is the nondimensional joule dissipation of primary interest here.

The resulting characteristic velocities are summarized in Table 4-1 together with the flow variables with which they are associated. These u-M relationships are plotted on the Sears-Resler diagram in Fig. 4-15.

Table 4-1. Characteristic velocities for constant area MHD flow

Variable	Characteristic velocity	Definition (divided by u_1)
u	u_1	$= 1$
M	u_2	$= \dfrac{1 + \gamma M^2}{2 + (\gamma - 1) M^2}$
Tt	u3	$= \dfrac{\gamma}{\gamma - 1}$
T	u_4	$= \dfrac{\gamma M^2 - 1}{(\gamma - 1) M^2}$
p	u_5	$= \dfrac{\gamma M^2}{1 + (\gamma - 1) M^2}$
p_t	u_6	$= \dfrac{\gamma M^2}{2 + (\gamma - 1) M^2}$

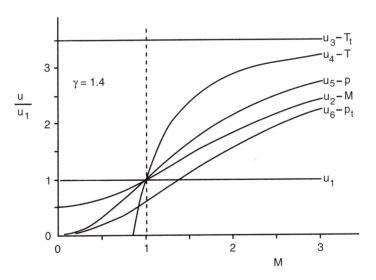

FIGURE 4-15. Characteristic velocities (u_n) on the Sears-Resler diagram.

From the governing equations, it is evident that the static quantities change sign at $M = 1$, at $u = u_3$ and at $u = u_j$ which is the line associated with the particular variable, as shown in Table 4-1. For the stagnation temperature, there is a sign change only at $u = u_3$, while the stagnation pressure changes across $u = u_3$ and across $u = u_6$. The lines describing the characteristic velocities shown in Fig. 4.15 are labeled for the physical quantity to which they are related. Regions of positive derivative in the static temperature (u_4) and in the stagnation pressure (u_6) are shown in Figs. 4-16 and 4-17, respectively. The static temperature is of interest because the conductivity of the plasma is most directly controlled by it, while the stagnation pressure gives a clear idea about the overall processes at play. The condition $u = u_5$ describes an "impulse" generator.

The constant total pressure line differentiates the region where the device is an accelerator (increasing p_t) and that where it is a heating device where p_t falls in the flow direction. Similarly, derivatives for the variations of other parameters such as the interaction length or the power density may be obtained from their definitions.

The equations of motion for the fluid allow one to determine the area variation required to achieve a constant temperature flow, for example. Equation 4-51 gives the area variation required to have $dT/dx = 0$. Finally, note that a line of constant stage efficiency, $\eta_s = k = E/uB$, is a horizontal line. $u = u_3$ corresponds to $k = 1$. Lines representing less efficient operation of a generator lie above this.

4.3. MHD ACCELERATORS

Devices that serve to generate a high-momentum jet with the MHD body force have been investigated. MHD accelerator systems require a heater wherein the gas is raised in temperature to the levels sufficient to reduce the interaction length to a practical value. In the accelerator itself, the MHD body force may be used to exert a force that leads to high fluid velocity and thus to high specific impulse. This method contrasts with the alternative of investing that same

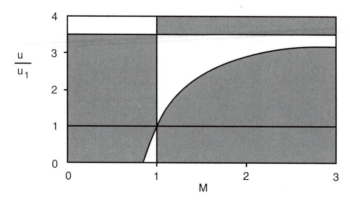

FIGURE 4-16. Zones of increasing *static temperature* (dark) on the Sears-Resler diagram, $\gamma = 1.4$.

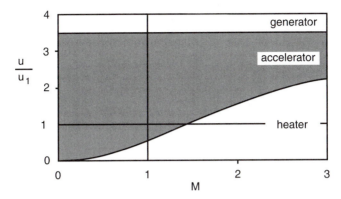

FIGURE 4-17. Zones of increasing *stagnation pressure* on the Sears-Resler diagram, $\gamma=1.4$. A heater is a device wherein the stagnation temperature rises and the stagnation pressure falls.

energy in the gas as thermal energy and expanding the hotter gas through a nozzle. The latter approach has the important disadvantage in that heating a gas to high temperature leads to dissociation and ionization which is only partially recoverable in the short expansion process taking place in the nozzle.

The MHD accelerator may suffer similar losses since the conductivity must be high. The Sears Resler diagram also shows that in order for the MHD effect to be truly accelerating rather than heating, the ratio E/uB (u_3/u) must be close to unity at very high Mach number. The reason is that if it is not, the total temperature rises while the total pressure falls, which is not an efficient way of adding energy. With E/uB close to 1, the interaction length is long and viscous as well as heat transfer effects become relatively important. This makes the MHD accelerator a somewhat difficult device for propulsion.

An issue that tends to dominate the design of such accelerators is that the stagnation conditions are severe, leading to difficulties in the ability to cool the walls. This, together with a shortage of space propulsion missions that might require the use of the MHD accelerator, have resulted in relatively little development effort toward this device.

4.3.1. *MPD Thrusters*

The MHD body force is important in a class of propulsion devices that are finding near-term application. These are the magneto plasma dynamic (MPD) thrusters. These generally small thrusters may be used in satellites for orbit adjustment, station keeping, and as primary propulsion for deep space missions. On satellites, their high performance results in an improved propellant utilization and thus increases satellite life and reduces cost. An MPD thruster is shown in Fig. 4-18, where a constricted arc is struck between a central cathode (electron emitter) and the anode, which resembles a nozzle "skirt." A number of mechanisms are used to obtain a high-velocity jet. These include electromagnetic forces and Joule heating. The geometric arrangment show in the figure is one member of a family of devices (Ref. 4-5) that vary in their

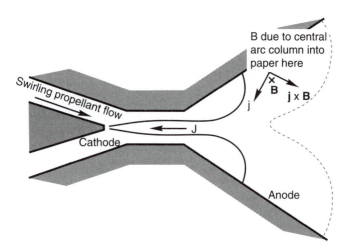

FIGURE 4-18. Schematic of an MPD thruster, showing the radial and axial force components of thrust. The stabilized arc column is kept from proximity to the wall.

physical complexity and consequently in their ease of performance modeling. The factors involved in these devices include the provision for (or lack of) an externally applied magnetic field and use of the Hall effect. Here discussion is limited to the swirling flow accelerator to illustrate the physics of this class of devices. For a physical and analytical description of other devices, the reader may consult Ref. 4-5. The author concludes that in spite of a relatively large number of descriptive parameters, overall performance characteristics can be predicted with a relatively simple model.

The constriction is attained by swirling the propellant so that cool fluid separates the arc from the wall. When the current exits the nozzle, the quasisteady sheet spreads to contact the anode. The figure shows that the arc column induces a cylindrical **B** field which extends to the anode region. The elements of the current in the spreading sheet interact with that **B** field resulting in a body force on the fluid element. In general, a fluid element will experience an axial (thrusting) and a radial force component. The thrust component adds to the thermal expansion through the nozzle, while the radial component raises the mean pressure on the central portion of the flow and thus on the cathode, where a thrust force is realized.

The performance analysis of these devices is complex, owing to the low flow Reynolds number, the multiplicity of heat transfer processes, and the chemical reactivity. The reader is encouraged to examine some of the modeling approaches described by Jahn (Refs. 4-4, 4-5, and the periodic literature, e.g., Refs. 4-6 and 4-7).

4.4. GASEOUS AND LIQUID METAL WORKING FLUIDS

To this point, the conductivity of the working fluid has been assumed known. The physics of the electric conduction in gases is quite complex, although insight into the physical quantities used to calculate conductivity may be exposed by an examination of the collision dynamics as given in Section 3.4. The result is a clarification of the significance of cross-sectional area as an average measure of the microscopic details of the electron-heavy-particle encounters. For the following, simple macroscopic arguments are used to allow insight into the engineering aspects of practical devices.

The important parameters governing the performance of an MHD device are:

1. The power density (proportional to $\sigma u^2 B^2$);
2. The interaction length ($p / \sigma u B^2$); and
3. The efficiency.

The high-power-density requirement dictates the use of a magnet of the highest practical field strength with an appropriate volume sufficient to accommodate the MHD duct. The state of the art in magnet design is that B may be as large as 5 tesla (= 5 webers/m^2 = 50,000 gauss), which allows channels of the order of 1 m in "diameter" and a few meters in length (Ref. 4-8). For steady, long-term power generation, for example, the magnet must be of the superconducting type, since the joule losses in a resistive conductor magnet would be unacceptable.

Given that B is thus fixed, practical devices may be optimized by operation at maximum power density (maximum in the product σu^2), or minimizing the interaction length ($1/\sigma u$), while maintaining the efficiency of conversion to a value near the stage efficiency k of the channel length element. The last objective is achieved by limiting the losses associated with other irreversibilities such as fluid friction and heat transfer.

These fluid flow losses depend on the characteristic channel dimension and are minimized by the use of *large* channels. Quantifying what is meant by large requires examination of parameters like the flow Reynolds number, which determines the thickness of the boundary layers that grow on the channel walls. One may think of the viscous and heat transfer losses as being similar to ordinary boundary layer on a duct wall. Unfortunately, the flow of current along the insulator walls and across the electrode walls alters the velocity and temperature profiles so that the magnitude of the wall friction and heat transfer is altered considerably. The reader is referred to the literature for a discussion of MHD boundary layer effects (Ref. 4-9). Here the scale for MHD generators of interest is assumed to be sufficiently large that the dominant irreversibility is that associated with the Joule dissipation (I^2R) due to operation at $k < 1$ (eq. 4-21). For MHD accelerators, operation at k greater than but close to unity also affords good performance. Figure 4.17, showing the p_t variation on the Sears-Resler diagram, illustrates that operation near $k = 1$ minimizes the entropy production rate.

The product σu^n should thus be large. Two kinds of machinery suggest themselves: liquid metal generators and gaseous plasma generators. The conductivity of liquid metals is very large (10^6 mhos/m) while gaseous plasmas range between 10 and 50 mhos/m. On the other hand, velocities achievable with liquids are low (~10 m/sec) while gases can be accelerated to several thousand meters/sec. Thus with $B = 3$ T, $p = 1$ atm, say, power densities and interaction lengths are as estimated in Table 4-2.

Table 4-2 Parameters of gaseous and liquid metal MHD fluids (B ~ 3 T)

Fluid	σ (mhos/m)	u (m/sec)	$\sigma u^2 B^2$ (W/m^3)	$p/\sigma u B^2$ (m)
Liquid metal	10^6	10	10^9	10^{-3}
Gas	30	2000	10^9	10^{-1}

Liquid metal MHD generators systems consists of a means for forcing a gaseous working fluid to form a high-speed jet. The jet is used to accelerate the liquid metal to high velocity through the MHD duct. Figure 4-19 shows such a system. The efficiencies of the mixing, acceleration, and diffusion processes have a serious limiting impact on the performance of such systems. As a consequence, the liquid metal generator is not considered further.

4.4.1. Pumping of Incompressible, Conducting Fluids

Ionic solutions and liquid metals are capable of carrying an electrical current flow and thus can be pumped in a constant area duct by forcing current to flow through the liquid when a magnetic field is also imposed. The 1D fluid mechanical equations simplify because ρ = constant and ρu = constant, which results in the momentum equation (eq. 4-2), giving

$$\frac{dp}{dx} = jB$$

(4-56)

where j is determined by the resistance of the liquid and the circuit as well as the source voltage. The pressure in an MHD pump rises linearly in the flow direction when j and B are uniform. For a duct of width d in the **E** field direction and length L, an applied voltage (ϕ) results in a pressure rise given by

$$\Delta p = \sigma \phi B \frac{L}{d}$$

(4-57)

4.4.2. The MHD Flow Meter

An application of the ideas developed here is for the measurement of volume or mass flow rate of a viscous fluid in a 2D duct. Consider the channel shown in Fig. 4-20 with a magnetic field as shown aligned with the direction of uniform properties. If two (high-resistance) probes are inserted to contact the liquid, one will rise in voltage above the other by an amount that is the integral of the electric field.

$$\phi = -\int_0^d E \, dy = -\int_0^d uB \, dy$$

(4-58)

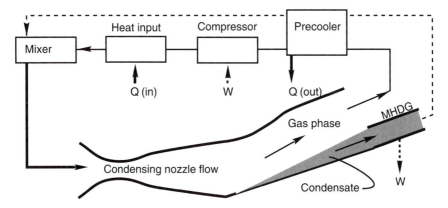

FIGURE 4-19. Liquid metal MHD system showing the collection ramp for the liquid metal.

The second equality follows from Ohm's law (eq. 2-8) for zero (or negligible) current flow. The flow walls may provide a nonuniform velocity distribution of $u(y)$, which when integrated gives the volume flow per unit depth in the z direction. Thus

$$- \frac{\phi}{B} = \int_0^d u(y)\, dy = \frac{1}{\rho} \frac{d\dot{m}}{dz}$$

(4-59)

For round or similar cross sections, the total mass flow rate may be inferred from a number of such measurements obtained through rotation of the **B** field and the measurement probes.

4.5. GAS PHASE POWER SYSTEMS

Gaseous working fluids are attractive because the thermal energy may be converted to kinetic energy with high efficiency and high power density. A system consists of

1. A means to generate a high-temperature gas (2500-3500 K) at a sufficient pressure to enable the conversion to a high speed jet;
2. A nozzle;
3. The MHD generator;
4. A diffuser; and
5. Additional components to utilize the remaining thermal energy.

Figure 4-21 shows the principal components of the power extracting portion of an MHD system using either a closed-cycle working fluid or a combustion energy source. The larger picture is discussed briefly in Section 4.6.

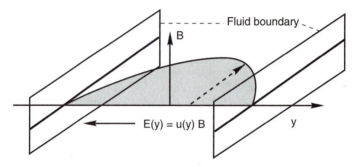

FIGURE 4-20. **E** field required for the volume flow rate measurement in a 2D flow with applied **B** field and nonuniform velocity profile.

4.5.1. *Gaseous MHD Analysis Model Approximations*

The analysis of the combustion gas MHD generator as an energy conversion device deals with temperatures limited by combustion processes with an alkali metal seed as an electron source. The most commonly encountered conditions allow three major approximations made in the analysis of the gas dynamics of such devices. These are:

1. The perfect gas assumption;
2. Viscous flow effects are neglected in favor of the MHD interaction;
3. The degree of ionization is small so that the depletion of neutral seed atoms is neglected; and
4. The macroscopic collision cross section of the ions is neglected in comparison to that of the neutral seed and the carrier gas.

The basis and impact of these assumptions is discussed below, together with the conditions where the use of the assumptions may lead to significant error.

Perfect Gas Model

In order for the relations between gas dynamic flow properties to be easily expressible in terms of state changes, the assumption of constant specific heat ratio is invoked. For temperatures ranging from 2000 to 3500 K, this is an approximate description of reality since the triatomic species such as CO_2 and H_2O experience significant variations in C_p in this range. Higher accuracy is easily obtainable from computer calculations, and these are left to the reader to carry out for the specific conditions of interest. In the discussion of Section 4.4, attention is limited to the investigation of the primary flow parameters influence on design choices and performance. The methodology necessary for including the better description of processes is discussed in Ref. 1-1, Chapter 4.

The MHD generator performance depends on optimal and maximum values of several design parameters. In this section, the choice for several of these variables is discussed.

One-Dimensional Flow

The neglect of viscous effects allows one to speak of uniform flow properties across a flow cross-sectional area. This is because viscous flow effects, together with heat transfer effects, occur at the bounding side walls affecting the fluid near the wall more profoundly than that in the central main stream. This complexity and the performance loss (see Section 4.5.8) associated with friction and heat transfer are ignored when the 1D flow assumption is made. Care must of course be exercised to be certain that pressure gradients are such that the boundary layers that do exist are sufficiently benign to allow the 1D flow assumption. The modeling assumptions (3) and (4) are discussed in Sections 4.5.2 and 4.5.3.

4.5.2. Maximizing Conductivity of a Gaseous Plasma

Equation 3-13, or equivalently 3-74, gives the scalar conductivity of a gas mixture as

$$\sigma = \frac{e^2 \, n_e}{v_c \, m_e} \tag{4-60}$$

where the important variables are the electron density and the collision frequency.

Electron Density

A large value for the number density of the electrons, n_e, is required for large σ. The law of mass action for the ionization reaction (eq. 5-40, Ref. 1-1, or Refs. 4-3 and 4-10) gives n_e in terms of the temperature and pressure. In

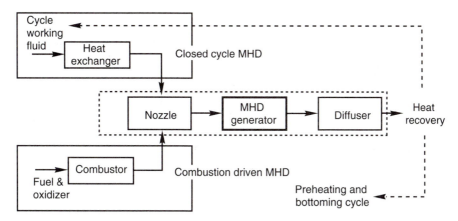

FIGURE 4-21. The component arrangement of a gaseous MHD power system. The combustion system (lower loop) and the closed cycle (upper loop) are two heat source options.

terms of the atomic constants involved, the law of mass action for ionization (or Saha equation) reads

$$\frac{n_e\, n_i}{n_a} = 2\left(\frac{2\pi\, m_e\, k\, T}{h^2}\right)^{3/2} \exp-\left(\frac{\varepsilon_i}{k\,T}\right) \tag{4-61}$$

The ionization energy is lowest for the alkali metals with their single outer electron. The lowest ionization potential is 3.89 eV for cesium. That for far less costly potassium and sodium are 4.32 and 5.12 eV, respectively. Ionization energies for most other atoms and molecules are in excess of 10 eV, which suggests that in a mixture of possible electron donors, the alkali metals alone will contribute the vast majority of the electrons.

This allows one to say that for most MHD plasmas whose temperature is constrained (and therefore sufficiently low) by heat transfer from devices such as nuclear reactors or combustion sources, the electron and the ion densities are equal:

$$n_e = n_i \tag{4-62}$$

The number of ions and un-ionized atoms of the alkali metal must be related to the fractional number density of the alkali metal as a component of the gas mixture:

$$n_{aT} = x_a\, n_T = n_{a,ion} + n_a = n_e + n_a \tag{4-63}$$

which allows n_a to be eliminated from the Saha equation. Thus

$$\frac{n_e^2}{n_{aT} - n_e} \approx \frac{n_e^2}{n_{aT}} = 2\left(\frac{2\pi\, m_e\, k\, T}{h^2}\right)^{3/2} \exp-\left(\frac{\varepsilon_i}{k\,T}\right) \equiv S(T) \equiv n_{aT}\, S_n(T,\, p) \tag{4-64}$$

The approximate form is valid at relatively low temperatures since the magnitude of the $S(T)$ term and the nondimensional S_n is generally small enough as to make the degree of ionization α small:

$$\frac{n_e}{n_{aT}} = \alpha \ll 1 \tag{4-65}$$

In general, the Saha equation (eq. 4-61) may be written (with eq. 4-65) in the form

$$\frac{\alpha^2}{1-\alpha} = S_n\,(T,\, p) \tag{4-66}$$

and in the modeling, the denominator of the fraction on the left was taken as unity so that a simple relation for α can be used (i.e. not requiring the solution of a quadratic). This allows the carrying of algebraic relations for quan-

tities of interest further into the development of an analysis. This approximations is valid when $\sqrt{S_n\ (T,\ p)} \ll 1$.

As will be seen, the typical low-temperature seeded gas plasmas have a
seed fraction of the order 1%. Thus for such a condition and $T = 3000$ K and
$p = 1$ atm pressure, $S_n(T,\ p)$ has a numerical value of 4.8 x 10^{-3}, which
increases to 0.097 (giving a 5% error in α) for $T = 3500$ K. Beyond this condition the assumption of small α becomes difficult to justify. Its use is also jus-
tified at the higher pressure usually used and when a larger seed fraction is
employed. For the analysis described in Section 4.5, the assumption appears
useful.

The seed flow rate of the order 1% is sufficiently large that economic operation requires the recovery and reuse of even low-cost seed such as potassium
compounds. All proposed MHD power plant designs incorporate this process.

Collision Frequency

The collision frequency is given by eq. 3-17 or 3-18 as

$$\nu_c = \bar{c}_e \sum_j n_j\ Q_{e,j} \qquad (4\text{-}67)$$

where c_e is the mean thermal speed, n_js are the component number densities,
and $Q_{e,j}$ is the electron collision cross-sectional areas of component j. The
number densities are given in terms of p and T by the mole fraction and the
state equation by

$$n_j = x_j\ \frac{p}{k\ T} \qquad (4\text{-}68)$$

For a Maxwellian velocity distribution for the electrons (perturbed only slightly
by the fact that a current is flowing), the mean thermal speed is a function of
only the temperature; see eq. 3-79. Combining eqs. 3-79 and 4-67 gives

$$\nu_c = \sqrt{\frac{8}{\pi\ m_e\ k\ T}}\ p \sum_j x_j\ Q_{e,j} \qquad (4\text{-}69)$$

which shows the p and T dependence of the collision frequency. Evidently, for
a given temperature and pressure (which fixes the electron number density n_e),
the gas mixture composition should be such that the weighted cross-sectional
area is a minimum, if σ is to be maximized.

Seed Fraction Optimization

The electron-atom collision cross sections for atoms and molecules of interest are listed in Table 4-3. It should be noted that the gases that may be considered for working fluids have cross sections that are significantly smaller
than those associated with the neutral alkali metal atoms. The electron-heavy

Table 4-3. Electron-atom collision cross-sectional areas (from Ref. 4-3)

Atom or molecule	Approx. cross section area ($\times 10^{-20}$ m^2) at 3000 K
Cs	350
K	400
O_2	3.0
N_2	6.7
He	5.6
CO_2	13
H_2O	50
H_2	8.1

particle collision frequency in the expression for σ is proportional to

$$\nu_c \approx n_g \, Q_{e,g} + n_a \, Q_{e,a} \tag{4-70}$$

if the gas mixture consists of only a carrier gas g, and the neutral alkali metal vapor, a. It is shown in Section 4.5.3 that the density of the ions that accompany the electrons plays a small role in determining collision frequency in most MHD plasmas. The conductivity may thus be written in term of component densities as

$$\sigma \sim \frac{n_e}{\nu_c} \sim \frac{\sqrt{n_{aT}}}{n_g \, Q_{e,g} + n_{aT} \, Q_{e,a}} f(T) \tag{4-71}$$

Here the neutral alkali seed density is taken to equal the total seed density, since $\alpha \ll 1$ may be assumed. The conductivity at any temperature is maximized for

$$\frac{n_{aT}}{n_g} = \frac{Q_{e,g}}{Q_{e,a}} \quad \text{or} \quad n_{aT} \, Q_{e,a} = n_g \, Q_{e,g} \tag{4-72}$$

from a null differentiation of the expression for σ (eq. 4-71) with respect to n_{aT}. The condition states that the macroscopic cross sections of the two gas components must be equal. From the data shown in Table 4-3, the appropriate seed fraction is seen to be of the order of a few percent.

4.5.3. Ion Collisions

The ion cross section is fundamentally different from neutral cross section because the force law is of the long-range Coulomb type (Section 3.4.6). This results in a significant temperature dependence of the macroscopic cross section. At relatively low temperature the contribution is negligible and is therefore neglected. This section is a more detailed discussion of this approximation, including the effect of ion collisions on optimum seed fraction choice.

For a singly ionized ion, the momentum transfer cross section for an electron-ion encounter can be stated in terms of temperature and density as (Ref. 4-3 or Section 3.4.6)

$$Q_{e,i} = \frac{\pi^3 \ln \Lambda}{16} \left(\frac{e^2}{4\pi \varepsilon_0}\right)^2 \frac{1}{(k\,T)^2}$$

(4-73)

where

$$\Lambda = \frac{3\pi^3}{2\,e^3} \sqrt{\frac{2\,(4\pi\,\varepsilon_0\,k\,T)^3}{\pi\,n_e}}$$

This cross section, unlike that for encounters between electrons and neutral particles that are adequately described as constant, depends on the temperature. Since the ion density (which equals the electron density) is also strongly dependent on the temperature, the ion macroscopic cross section is awkward to include in the formulation. In effect, a correction factor must be included in the description of the conductivity that reduces the value calculated using only the cross sections of the neutrals by a factor

$$1 + \frac{n_e\,Q_{e,i}}{\sum_j n_j\,Q_{e,j}} \cong 1 + \frac{n_e\,Q_{e,i}}{2\,n_g\,Q_{e,g}}$$

where the subscript i refers to the ions, j to all the neutral species, and g to the average gas molecule collision partner. The factor of two arises from the usual optimization of seed fraction where the conductivity is maximized by forcing equal macroscopic cross sections for the seed and the carrier gas (see Section 4.5.2). If the seed to gas number density ratio is Sf, then the second term in the correction factor can be obtained from the Saha equation as

$$\text{constant} \sqrt{\frac{Sf}{p}} \frac{1}{Q_{e,g}} T^{-5/4} \exp\left(-\frac{\varepsilon_i}{2\,k\,T}\right)$$

which has the values shown in Fig. 4.22 for the following conditions: T_t as indicated, $p_t = 1$ atm, $M = 1$, $\gamma = 1.4$, $Sf = 0.01$, $Q_{e,g} = 15 \times 10^{-20}$ m^2. The interaction length (which scales as B^{-2}) is also noted for $B = 1$ T. The log Λ term varies weakly with temperature. Evidently, since the macroscopic cross section correction term is of order unity and greater when temperatures exceed 3500 K, the ion cross sections cannot be neglected in an accurate description of the plasma near or above this temperature.

Consideration of the ion cross section on the conductivity leads to the following ratio (see eq. 4-71) to be maximized

$$\frac{\sqrt{n_a}}{n_a\,Q_{e,a} + n_g\,Q_{e,g} + \sqrt{n_a}\,\sqrt{S(T)}\,Q_{e,i}}$$

(4-74)

where $S(T)$ is the right-hand side of the Saha equation as written in eq. 4-64. Differentiating this relation with respect to n_a and setting the result to zero

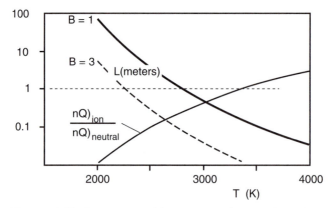

FIGURE 4-22. Importance of ion cross-sections at elevated temperatures. For $p = 1$ atm., $B = 1$ and 3 Tesla, the interaction length L (which scales as B^{-2} is also shown, eq. 4-41).

leads to a maximum independent of $Q_{e,i}$ so that the ion cross section need not be considered in arriving at an optimum seed fraction n_a/n_g.

4.5.4. *Temperature and Pressure Dependence of Conductivity*

For the following, the ions are neglected and the degree of ionization is assumed small ($\alpha \ll 1$). The temperature and pressure dependence of σ for a plasma of specified composition is determined by the right-hand side of the Saha equation as well as the terms brought in through the state equation and the collision frequency. The easiest way of visualizing this dependence is to write σ from eqs. 4-71, 4-64, and 4-69 as

$$\ln \sigma = \frac{1}{2}\left(\frac{3}{2}\ln T - \frac{\varepsilon_i}{k\,T}\right) - \frac{1}{2}(\ln p - \ln T) - \frac{1}{2}(\ln T) \tag{4-75}$$

plus the logarithm of fundamental constants. The first and second terms are associated with the right side of the Saha equation written as eq. 4-64. The last term is associated with the electron thermal speed term (c_e) in the collision frequency. Thus

$$\frac{\partial \ln \sigma}{\partial \ln T} = \frac{3}{4} + \frac{\varepsilon_i}{2\,k\,T} \quad \text{and} \quad \frac{\partial \ln \sigma}{\partial \ln p} = -\frac{1}{2} \tag{4-76}$$

The dependence of σ on T is dominated by the $\varepsilon i / 2\,kT$ term, while the pressure dependence is relatively weak, although it should be noted that higher pressure reduces the degree of ionization. For convenience, the following total temperature parameter is defined

$$E \equiv \frac{\varepsilon_i}{2\,kT_t} \tag{4-77}$$

For cesium and potassium seed, the value of $\varepsilon i / 2k$ is 22,500 and 25,000 K, respectively. For a stagnation temperature range between 2000 and 4000 K, the nondimensional E varies between 6 and 12.

4.5.5. *MHD Generator Flow Mach Number*

The flow entering the MHD generator has fixed values of the stagnation temperature and pressure so that the nozzle's exit Mach number plays a role in determining the flow velocity and static temperature. The velocity and the static temperature and pressure are given in terms of constants of the flow (p_t and T_t) by:

$$u = M a = M \frac{a_t}{\sqrt{1 + \frac{\gamma - 1}{2} M^2}} = \frac{\sqrt{\frac{\gamma - 1}{2} M^2}}{\sqrt{1 + \frac{\gamma - 1}{2} M^2}} \sqrt{(2 C_p T_t)}$$

(4-78)

$$\frac{T_t}{T} = 1 + \frac{\gamma - 1}{2} M^2$$

(4-79)

$$\frac{p_t}{p} = \left(1 + \frac{\gamma - 1}{2} M^2\right)^{\gamma/(\gamma-1)}$$

(4-80)

The conductivity is a function of temperature and pressure and can therefore be calculated for the stagnation temperature and pressure conditions. The resulting σ_t will vary along the MHD generator duct as power is removed. The conductivity normalized to stagnation conditions can be written with eqs. 4-79 and 4-80 as

$$\frac{\sigma}{\sigma_t} = \left[\left(1 + \frac{\gamma - 1}{2} M^2\right)^{-3/4 + \gamma/(2(\gamma-1))}\right] \exp - \left(E \frac{\gamma - 1}{2} M^2\right) \quad \text{where } E \equiv \frac{\varepsilon_i}{2 k T_t}$$

(4-81)

The competition between increasing u and decreasing σ (Fig. 4-23) forces the choice of an optimum Mach number at the generator inlet to be identified. The variations of normalized power density (σu^2) and (inverse) interaction length (σu)

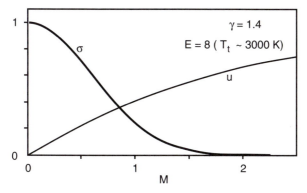

FIGURE 4-23. Variation of conductivity and flow speed with Mach number. The parameter and $\gamma = 1.4$. Indicated stagnation temperature is approximate depending on the seed ionization potential.

are shown in Fig. 4-24. Note that maxima for both parameters are close to one another and near sonic values of the flow Mach number. Higher values of the stagnation temperature or lower values of the ionization energy increase the magnitude of σ and drive the optimum Mach number toward larger values; see Fig. 4-25. These results are quite sensitive to the gas specific heat ratio, as shown in Fig. 4-26.

4.5.6. Enthalpy Extraction

These ideas suggest that the generator ought to be designed to remove as much enthalpy in the shortest length or, almost equivalently, operate at the highest power density. The 1D gas dynamic equations (eqs. 4-53 and 4-54) can be rewritten as

$$\frac{d \ln T_t}{d x} = - \frac{\sigma u B^2}{p} k (1-k) \frac{\gamma -1}{\gamma} \left(1 + \frac{\gamma -1}{2} M^2\right)^{-1} \tag{4-82}$$

$$\frac{d \ln p_t}{d x} = - \frac{\sigma u B^2}{p} (1 - k) \left(1 - k \frac{\frac{\gamma -1}{2} M^2}{1 + \frac{\gamma -1}{2} M^2}\right) \tag{4-83}$$

where the Mach number variation is also controlled by the area variation through a rewritten version of eq. 4-50:

$$\frac{d \ln M}{d x} = \frac{1 + \frac{\gamma -1}{2} M^2}{M^2 - 1} \left[\frac{d \ln A}{d x} - \frac{\sigma u B^2}{p} (1-k) \left(1 - k \frac{\frac{1}{\gamma} + M^2}{\frac{2}{\gamma -1} + M^2}\right)\right] \tag{4-84}$$

The electrical operating condition is specified by the local value of load resistance $(R \, \Delta x)$ (see eq. 4-18) or $k(x)$. Conventional analysis of a given channel

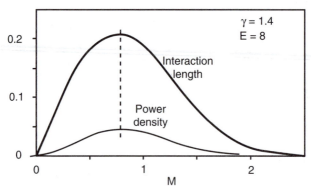

FIGURE 4-24. Plots of σu^2 (power density) and $\sigma u/p$ (the reciprocal interaction length) for $B=1$ (both normalized by stagnation values, see eqs 4-78 to 4-81). The parameter $E = \varepsilon_i / 2 k T_t = 8$ (T_t is approximately 3000 K) and $\gamma = 1.4$.

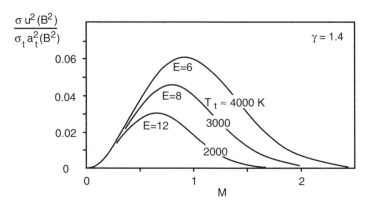

FIGURE 4-25. Power density (normalized to stagnation value) variation for increasing T_t. $\gamma = 1.4$ and calculation is for $E = 6$, 8, and 12, respectively, for which approximate T_t (K) is indicated.

geometry with known entrance conditions is then made directly. The interaction length is a function of p_t, T_t, and M as was shown. With a specification of $A(x)$, $k(x)$, and initial conditions, the calculational procedure reduces to calculating at $x + \Delta x$:

1. A new M with dM/dx from eq. 4-84 using the present value of $\sigma u/p$;
2. New values of p_t and T_t, using eqs. 4-82 and 4-83;
3. New $\sigma u B^2/p$; and
4. Repetition with new $k(x)$ and dA/dx.

The procedure is terminated when $\sigma u B^2/p$ reaches an unacceptably small value, at which point the competitive friction and heat transfer phenomena, neglected to this point, become important. Families of design area variations will result in varying amounts of enthalpy extraction.

For example, a specific area variation may be chosen to hold the static pressure constant, in which case the generator is similar to an impulse turbine. Alternatively, other variables such as velocity, Mach number, etc., may be kept constant in the work extraction process. For this last case, eq. 4-84 shows how the electrical load condition (i.e., specification of k) and the area variation are related. The example with constant k is developed in detail here because it implies that the conversion efficiency remains nearly constant. This may be shown with eqs. 4-82, 4-83, and the definition of the polytropic efficiency (eq. 7-47, Ref. 1-1) :

$$e_E = \frac{\gamma}{\gamma - 1} \frac{d \ln T_t}{d \ln p_t} = \frac{k}{1 + \frac{\gamma - 1}{2} M^2 (1 - k)} \approx k \tag{4-85}$$

The approximate equality to k is for the interesting case of k and M close to 1.

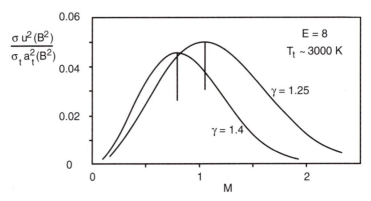

FIGURE 4-26. Power density variation with Mach number for two specific heat ratios.

4.5.7. *Minimum Interaction Length*

A particularly interesting approach to the problem of determining enthalpy extraction is to carry it out in the shortest length. For such a process one must find the Mach number for maximum $\frac{\sigma\, u}{p}\left(1 + \frac{\gamma-1}{2} M^2\right)^{-1}$, as stipulated by the energy equation (eq. 4-82) when the efficiency k is regarded as constant.

The generator entrance conditions determine the *initial* stagnation conductivity, σ_{t0}, a true constant in the expansion description. The velocity is written in terms of the stagnation enthalpy. Thus the energy equation becomes:

$$\frac{d \ln T_t}{dx} = -k\,(1-k)\left(\frac{\gamma-1}{\gamma}\frac{\sigma_{t0}\sqrt{2\,C_p\,T_{t0}}}{p_{t0}}\,B^2\right)\left(\frac{\sigma}{\sigma_t}\frac{u}{\sqrt{2\,C_p\,T_t}}\frac{p_t}{p}\frac{1}{1+\frac{\gamma-1}{2}M^2}\right)$$

$$\times\left(\frac{\sigma_t}{\sigma_{t0}}\sqrt{\frac{T_t}{T_{t0}}}\frac{p_{t0}}{p_t}\right)$$

or

$$\frac{d \ln T_t}{dx} = -k\,(1-k)\left(\frac{1}{L_0}\right)F(\mu,T_t)\,G(T_t,p_t) \tag{4-86}$$

Here $\sigma_{t0} = \sigma(p_{t0}, T_{t0})$ and μ is defined for convenience as

$$\mu = 1 + \frac{\gamma-1}{2} M^2 \tag{4-87}$$

The function F incorporates all Mach number dependence of the right side of eq. 4-86 while G *and* F follow the changing stagnation conditions. The "inlet stagnation interaction length" gathers all dimensioned quantities into a single constant, L_0, defined in eq. 4-86 as

$$L_0 \equiv \frac{\gamma}{\gamma-1}\frac{p_{t0}}{\sigma_{t0}\,B^2\,\sqrt{2\,C_p\,T_{t0}}} \tag{4-88}$$

THE FUNCTION F

Because the Mach number dependence of F exhibits a maximum, operation at this maximum is normally desirable. From eqs. 4-78 to 4-81, one may write:

$$\frac{\sigma}{\sigma_t} = \mu^{-3/4 + \gamma/(2(\gamma-1))} \exp - E (\mu - 1) \tag{4-89}$$

$$\frac{u}{\sqrt{2 C_p T_t}} = \sqrt{1 - \frac{1}{\mu}} \tag{4-90}$$

$$\frac{p}{p_t} = \mu^{-\gamma/(\gamma-1)} \tag{4-91}$$

so that

$$F = \mu^g \sqrt{\mu - 1} \, \exp(- E (\mu - 1)) \tag{4-92}$$

where

$$g \equiv \frac{3}{2} \frac{\gamma}{\gamma-1} - \frac{9}{4} \quad (= 3 \text{ for } \gamma = 1.4)$$

Maximizing the function F is nearly identical to minimizing the interaction length $p/\sigma u$, as shown in Fig. 4-27. The curve with a slightly lower Mach number at the maximum is the function F, while the label L refers to a plot of $\sigma u/p$ alone.

The function F has a maximum at μ_{max} given by

$$\mu_{max}^2 - \mu_{max}\left(1 + \frac{g + 0.5}{E}\right) + \frac{g}{E} = 0 \tag{4-93}$$

The resulting Mach number for maximum F is plotted as a function of $1/E$ (which is proportional to T_t) in Fig. 4-28. For small γ, characteristic of com-

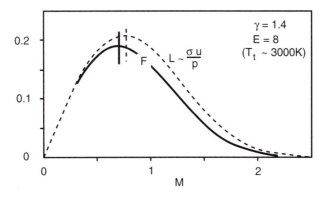

FIGURE 4-27. Plot of the function F (heavy line, eq. 4-92) and the reciprocal interaction length ($\sigma u/p$ is non-dimensionalized by stagnation values, labeled L). The maxima are close as noted.

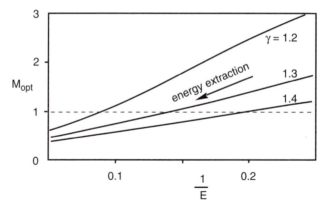

FIGURE 4-28. Variation of Mach number for maximum F with initial stagnation temperature. As energy is extracted, the optimum M falls.

bustion gases, the optimum M lies above unity. Note that as total temperature falls, due to the energy removal, the short interaction condition requires reduction of the Mach number. Figure 4-29 shows the maximum value of the function F (F_{max}) evaluated at μ_{max} using eqs. 4-92 and 4-93. This is a function of the flow total temperature (through $E = \varepsilon_i /(2\ kT_t)$) and γ. For a given γ, a good approximation for F_{max} where "$a(\gamma)$" and "$b(\gamma)$" are constants, is given by $F_{max} \sim \exp\ (a + b\tau/E_0)$.

The Function G

G is expressible in terms of τ, the decreasing total temperature ratioed to its initial value. The changing total pressure for the polytropic process is given by eq. 4-85:

$$\tau \equiv \frac{T_t}{T_{t0}} = \left(\frac{p_t}{p_{t0}}\right)^{k(\gamma - 1)/\gamma} \tag{4-94}$$

Thus

$$G \equiv \frac{\sigma_t}{\sigma_{t0}} \sqrt{\frac{T_t}{T_{t0}}} \left(\frac{p_t}{p_{t0}}\right)^{-1} = \tau^{m-1} \exp\left(- E_0 \left(\frac{1}{\tau} - 1\right)\right) \tag{4-95}$$

where

$$m = \frac{9}{4} - \frac{3}{2}\frac{\gamma}{\gamma -1}\frac{1}{k} \quad \text{and} \quad E_0 = \frac{\varepsilon_i}{2\ kT_{t0}}$$

The constant $m = -4.31$ for $\gamma = 1.4$ and $k = 0.8$. The enthalpy extraction rate is given by

$$\frac{d\tau}{d\left(\frac{x}{L_0}\right)} = k\ (k - 1)\ \tau^m \exp\left[- E_0 \left(\frac{1}{\tau} - 1\right)\right] F_{max} \tag{4-96}$$

The length scale L_0 may be written in terms of the fundamental variables as follows

$$L_0 = \sqrt{\frac{\pi}{16} \frac{\gamma}{\gamma-1} \frac{n_g}{n_e}} \sqrt{\frac{m_g}{m_e}} \frac{\lambda}{\beta^2} \approx O\left(\frac{n_g}{n_e} \sqrt{\frac{m_g}{m_e}} \lambda\right)$$

(4-97)

where λ is the electron mean free path ($= c_e/v_c$), the subscripts g and e refer to the gas molecule and electrons, respectively. A physical interpretation of this length in terms of the fundamental parameters of the plasma is not evident. For representative values of the gas parameters, L_0 is given in Table 4-4.

Equation 4-96 when integrated (numerically) gives the total temperature ratio across the MHD generator:

$$\tau_m = f\left(\frac{x}{L_0}, E_0, \gamma, \text{ and } k\right)$$

(4-98)

where E_0 is a measure of the inlet stagnation temperature for a given seed ionization potential. Figure 4-30 shows the result for a reference case (potassium seed) where these variables are fixed and sequentially varied to show the influence of the parameter. The values are given in Table 4-4.

Evidently, the initial stagnation temperature is very important in determining the length (x) required to extract 20% of the enthalpy (last row of table). At higher temperature, an extraction on the order of 20% is obtained for $x/L_0 = 4$-10 initial stagnation interaction lengths. Beyond this point the interaction becomes weak. The total pressure change that accompanies this power extraction is shown in Fig. 4-31 and is seen to result in a total pressure ratio for the expansion process of the order of 0.25 to 0.4.

This analysis gives the relative sensitivity to the input variables. Also listed in Table 4-4 are a number of parameters of interest for the scaling of the length L_0. For the calculation of L_0, the following plasma properties are used:

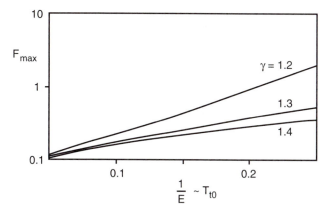

FIGURE 4-29. Plot of maximum F as a function of initial stagnation temperature. μ_m from eq. 4-93 substituted into eq. 4-92.

Table 4-4. Calculated flow parameters for conditions noted in the text; L_0 and x are in meters

Quantity	Value	T_{t0}	γ	k
Reference value		3500 K	1.4	0.7
Sequential variation	Ref.	3000	1.3	0.8
$1/E_0$	0.14	0.12	0.14	0.14
M_0	0.75	0.67	0.98	0.75
$F_{max,0}$	0.21	0.18	0.24	0.21
initial $-d\tau/d\xi$	0.044	0.039	0.050	0.033
x/L_0 ($\tau = 0.8$)	6.70	8.82	4.78	9.88
p_{t0} ($p_{t,ex} = 1$)	3.05	3.05	3.98	2.65
L_0 ($p_{t0} = 3$)	0.064	0.26	0.072	———
x ($\tau = 0.8$)	0.43	2.3	0.34	0.63

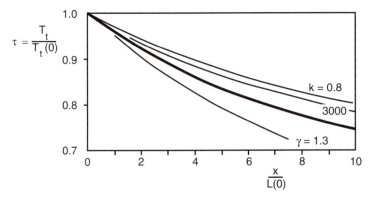

FIGURE 4-30 Variation of total temperature ratio with choice of parameters noted. Heavy line is for the reference case: $T_{t0} = 3500K$, $k = 0.7$ and $\gamma = 1.4$.

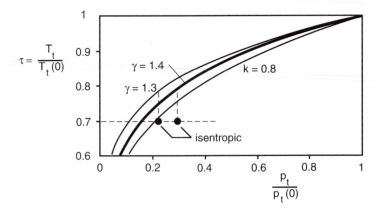

FIGURE 4-31. Plot of eq. 4-94 for total pressure ratio with specified parameters. Heavy line is the reference case $\gamma = 1.4$ and $k = 0.7$. The ref. line varies approximately as $p \sim \tau^{5.1}$. Note that for an isentropic temperature ratio of 0.7, the pressure ratio is .29 and .21 as shown, for $\gamma = 1.4$ and 1.3, respectively.

Q_{eg} = 15 x 10^{-20} m^2 (combustion products), B = 4 T, molecular weight = 30, 1% potassium seed fraction, p_{t0} = 3 atm.

Summary

It may be concluded that the following design choices will maximize the MHD generator performance:

Stagnation temperature:	as large as possible
Seed material:	low ionization potential
Gas working fluid:	desirable is low electron collision cross sec–tion but one may have to accept whatever combustion process dictates
Seed fraction:	minimal total macroscopic cross section for gas and seed
Total pressure:	value required to remove enthalpy fraction desired consistent with efficiency and down-stream pressure
Magnetic field strength:	largest practical value
Flow Mach number:	near sonic as determined by ε_i/kT_{t0} and γ, eq. 4-93
Length:	5-10 initial stagnation interaction lengths given by eq. 4-88
Efficiency:	free to be specified, although it influences the flow length required and cycle perfor–mance, see Section 11.6, Ref. 1-1

These conclusions are generally accepted as necessary for good generator performance (Ref. 4-12) in spite of the simplifications made here to reach them.

4.5.8. *Viscous Effects*

The properties of the boundary layers in an MHD generator are potentially quite different from those in an ordinary duct or even one dominated by the changing pressure. One could examine the pressure gradient to see the devel-opment of the boundary layer and from that infer the point where the com-petition between viscous losses and energy removal affects the polytropic efficiency in a significant way. An alternative is to recognize that the rate of work removal is initially large and the process should be terminated when the marginal contribution becomes small. This could be argued to be where the local T_t rate falls to 10-20% of the initial rate.

Inclusion of viscous flow effects with a volumetric term modifies the momentum equation (eq. 4-42) to

$$\gamma M^2 \frac{d \ln u}{dx} + \frac{d \ln p}{dx} = \left(\frac{u_3}{u} - 1\right)\frac{1}{L} - \frac{\gamma}{2} M^2 \frac{f}{D} \tag{4-99}$$

where L is the interaction length. The viscous force does not affect the energy equation but appears in the equation for the variation of total pressure and consequently in an expression for the entropy production rate (eqs. 2-66 and 4-55):

$$\frac{d\left(\frac{s}{C_p}\right)}{dx} = (1 - k)^2 \frac{F\,G}{L_{t0}} + (\mu - 1)\frac{f}{D} \tag{4-100}$$

where the ratio u_3/u is written as the load factor (k) and the Mach number term as a function of μ; see eq. 4-87. Neglecting the friction term, the interaction was maximized above by finding μ for maximum F. With this new term, this condition can be interpreted as finding the Mach number that minimizes the entropy production rate and leads to

$$\frac{d F}{d\mu} = \frac{f\,L_{t0}}{(1 - k)^2\,G\,D} \tag{4-101}$$

This equation reduces to eq. 4-93 when $f = 0$. The optimum Mach number for finite f is evidently at a value larger than that for $f = 0$. As the interaction proceeds, the function G decreases, that is, $L_{t0}/G = L_t$ increases. For a given friction factor, this suggests that the Mach number should increase or not decrease as rapidly as seen with the frictionless flow.

4.5.9. Flow Area Variation

The variation of the flow area required may be calculated from eq. 4-84, with the result that the variation of M may obtained from the results shown in Fig. 4-28. A rearrangement of eq. 4-84 yields the result

$$\frac{d \ln A}{d x} = (1 - k)\{1 - k\,[f\,(M,\,E_0,\,\tau,\,\text{and } \gamma)]\}\frac{F_{max}\,G}{L_0} \approx (1 - k)\,\frac{F_{max}\,G}{L_0} \tag{4-102}$$

where F_{max} and G are functions of E_0, τ, and γ. When the nearly linear variation of F_{max} with $1/E$ is exploited to evaluate the right-hand side, the plot shown in Fig. 4-32 is obtained for the conditions noted. The figure shows that the area variation is weakly positive, that is, the duct increases in area as the flow and energy removal proceeds, on a scale governed by $L_0/(1-k)$ with an initially minor influence due to changing stagnation conditions (G), which eventually competes with the effect due to changing Mach number (F_{max}).

4.6. CYCLE IMPLEMENTATION

The MHD generator processes a compressible gas, which results in the cycle that utilizes it as having the characteristics of the Brayton cycle. There are important differences that distinguish its performance from cycles like the gas

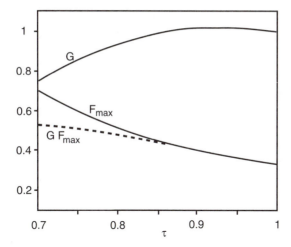

FIGURE 4.32. Variation of the channel divergence parameter on the right-hand side of eq. 4-102. $T_{t0} = 3500$ K, $\gamma = 1.3$.

turbine and its derivatives. The most important features are that the MHD inlet temperature is not fundamentally limiting. Rather, the temperature at the exit of the MHD generator must be high to have the interaction length be sufficiently short, and the temperature at the hot end of any air preheater must be lower than its material limitation. Within the limits of heat transfer load to the walls, the peak cycle temperature can be as high as that allowed by the heat release from the fuel.

An analysis of a combination MHD cycle together with a bottoming Brayton cycle may be carried out (see Chapter 11, Ref. 1-1). The principal result is that the efficiency performance of such dual cycles depends strongly on (1) the enthalpy extraction of the MHD portion of the cycle (because work obtained at high temperature is delivered with a higher efficiency) and (2) the limitations imposed by the heat exchangers, which process the exit stream. They impose the temperature limits on the bottom cycle and thus control the conversion efficiency. Overall, when enthalpy extraction approaching 25% is achieved, the MHD topping cycle can help the overall efficiency reach levels near 50%. Such performance is 25% better than currently available conversion schemes using coal in the Rankine cycle.

4.7. CONCLUDING REMARKS

The fluid mechanics, electrodynamics, and thermodynamics of the MHD inter-action control the first order and limiting performance of this method of energy conversion. The principal development effort in the field of MHD was aimed at generation of electricity in a central station power plant using coal resources because these are abundant in the United States. The successful completion of this effort required a high fraction of enthalpy extraction by means of the MHD generator (Ref. 1-1, Chap. 11) and solution of a number of practical issues. These had to be satisfied in the setting of a utility company's requirement for long and reliable operation. The high-temperature flow environment continues to present demanding challenges.

Even though the interaction is volumetric, the surfaces of the generator channel are exposed to high heat transfer rates, which have the potential of compromising the requirement for long service life. The plasma is composed of chemically reactive species that can, when they encounter a surface, combine and release the recombination energy to the wall. This energy deposition rate is in addition to the ordinary heat transfer associated with a hot gas to cooler wall. While the high heat transfer rate poses difficulties, it is also required because the electrode wall must be at least locally hot enough to emit electrons into the gas.

The general approach to solving design problems associated with these demanding conditions was to recognize that coal will contain oxides and silicates (of Si, Ca, Al, Mg, etc.), which, when heated, become *slag*, a glassy liquid in the gas stream and on the walls unless they are removed. The condensation of such layers on the walls may protect the walls. Because the layers necessarily contain seed material and are therefore electrically conducting, a number of balancing factors need to be addressed in a successful design:

1. The layer on the electrode wall must rise in temperature to a level allowing thermionic emission.
2. The layer must not be so thick as to present a significant low resistance path to current flow in the transverse or Hall field directions, because the heat is deposited in the layer itself and reduces terminal voltage.
3. Control of the slag carryover into the gas stream at the burner end of the power train must be available to achieve these ends. In practice, an effort has been successfully carried out to remove at least a part of this slag during combustion (Refs. 4-15 and 4-16).
4. The glassy slag must be processable at the low-temperature exit end of the train to allow for removal and the transfer of heat to waste recovery heat exchangers. Behind the MHD generator, the gas is cooled and the slag becomes more viscous and thus may solidify.
5. The site where this cleanup operation must be carried out is also where the seed must be removed for recycling. The seed flow rates are typically too large to enable economic and clean open cycle operation.
6. The characteristics of coal are sufficiently variable that these issues have to be addressed for the individual coal types used.

Finally, no real flows are one dimensional. Boundary layers on the electrode walls and on the insulator walls form layers that have different properties than the freestream and thus, like the slag layers, may allow current flows that reduce performance (Refs. 4-17 and 4-18). The regions where the applied magnetic field seen by the moving fluid is changing near the channel entrance and exit represent regions where the induced electric field cannot balance the field associated with the load. Thus here, as through the wall layers, recirculating currents can reduce performance (Ref. 4-19).

The technical papers presented at the Symposium on the Engineering Aspects of MHD over the years after 1960 focused on the design of the practical system to allow these constraints to be met. The effort included design of the plant and the demonstration of long-term channel performance under realistic conditions. A world-wide group of government laboratories, corporations, and universities contributed to and continue the development.

The MHD combustion process must be at a sufficiently high temperature for the interaction to be strong. These conditions are also favorable to the production of nitrogen oxides from the oxidizing air. A sound design for the plant must recognize and deal with this issue.

A number of noteworthy variants of the MHD generator have been investigated. One is the two-terminal Hall generator in a disc configuration (Ref. 4-1), which avoids the problem of the shorted Faraday current having to be emitted through electrodes. The flow proceeds radially while the shorting current flows azimuthally only in the gas.

The other innovative approach to the utilization of MHD in a closed cycle for space application is to use a nuclear power source for heat. Unfortunately, the temperature capability of the reactor is limited to temperatures where the equilibrium electron density of even cesium is too low. Experiments following the suggestion of Kerrebrock (Ref. 2-1) to use a seeded noble gas in which the electron gas is weakly coupled to the heavy gas have shown that the electron temperature can be at a higher, nonequilibrium level and the electron density correspondingly larger. This effect has been successfully demonstrated by researchers in small and generator-sized configurations (Ref. 4-17).

The status today is that much of that work awaits higher energy prices and the concomitant willingness of power utilities to see that the benefits are sufficient to motivate a pilot plant demonstration and development. The effort is very small in the mid 1990s and may be rekindled in the future. The principal competitive scheme for utilizing coal is the gasification process (where cleanup may be carried out) and in Brayton cycle engines, combined cycles, and potentially in fuel cells.

PROBLEMS

1. Determine the magnetic Reynolds numbers (see Section 3.3) for the conditions listed in Table 4-2 if $L \sim 0.1$ m.

2. Show that the friction term incorporated in the 1D equations of motion leads to the equation for the entropy variation given by eq. 4-55:

$$\frac{d\left(\frac{s}{R}\right)}{d\xi} = \left(1 - \frac{u_3}{u}\right)^2 + \frac{\gamma M^2}{2} \frac{fL}{D}$$

3. Write the 1D flow equations for an axisymmetric geometry when $\mathbf{u}$ is radial and $\mathbf{B}$ is in the z direction. Indicate the electrical quantities of interest when a Hall generator is configured this way: $\mathbf{E}$ fields, load voltage, and load current.

4. Obtain expressions for the load voltage characteristic (appropriately nondimensionalized as in Section 4.1.4), maximum power condition

for k, and the efficiency, when a segmented Faraday generator duct is only partially successful at realizing the full Hall potential : $E_x = \eta_H \beta (E_y - UB)$, where $\eta_H < 1$.

BIBLIOGRAPHY

Rosa, R.J., *Magnetohydrodynamics Energy Conversion*, McGraw-Hill, New York, 1968.

Shercliff, J. A., *A Textbook of Magnetohydrodynamics*, Pergamon Press, Oxford, 1965.

Symposium on the Engineering Aspects of MHD, 1960 - 1980.

Louis, J. F., *Open Cycle Coal Burning MHD Power Generation — An Assessment and a Plan for Action*, U.S. Department of the Interior, Office of Coal Research, R&D Report No. 64, 1971.

Parkinson D. H. and Mulhall, B. E., *The Generation of High Magnetic Fields*, Plenum Press, New York, 1967.

REFERENCES

4-1. Louis, J. F., "Disk Generator," *AIAA Journal*, 6, 9, pp. 1674-78, 1968.

4-2. Resler, E. L. and Sears, W. R., "Magneto-Gasdynamic Channel Flow," *ZAMP* 11b, ppg. 509-18, 1958.

4-3. Sutton, G. and Sherman, A., *Engineering Magnetohydrodynamics*, McGraw-Hill, New York, 1965.

4-4. Jahn, R., *Physics of Electric Propulsion*, McGraw-Hill, New York, 1968.

4-5. Sasoh, A., "Simple Formulation of Magnetoplasmadynamic Acceleration," *Physics of Plasmas*, 1 (3), March 1994.

4-6. Nerheim, N. M. and Kelly, A. J., AIAA paper 67-688, 1967.

4-7. *Proceedings of the 22nd International Electric Propulsion Conference*, Pisa, Italy, 1992.

4-8. Stekly, Z. J. J., Thome, R. J., Cooper, R. F., and Pape, R., "Superconducting Saddle Magnet Design Considerations," 12th Symp. on the Engineering Aspects of MHD, Argonne National Laboratory, 1972.

4-9. Moreau, R. J., *Magnetohydrodynamics*, Kluwer Academic Publishers, Dordrecht, Boston, 1990.

4-10. Fay, J. A., *Molecular Thermodynamics*, Addison-Wesley, Reading, Mass., 1965.

4-11. Carter, C. and Heywood, J. B., "Optimization Studies on Open Cycle MHD Generators", *AIAA Journal*, 6 (9), 1968.

4-12. Decher, R., "MHD Generator Characteristics with Insulator Wall Losses," *AIAA Journal* **8** (1), January 1970.

4-13. Hoffman, M. A., "Non-equilibrium MHD Generator Losses due to Wall and Insulator Boundary Layer Leakages," *AIAA Journal* **6** (9), 1968.

4-14. Decher, R., "End Loop Shorting in Non-Equilibrium MHD Generators," *AIAA Journal* **10** (8), August 1972.

4-15. Demirjian, A. M., Petty, S. W., and Solbes, A., "Electrode Development for Coal Fired MHD Generators," 17th Symposium on Engineering Aspects of MHD, Stanford University, March 1978.

4-16. Pian, C. C. P., Sadovnik, I., Petty, S. W., and McClaine, A. W., "Voltage-Current Characteristics of the Insulator Gaps in a Slagging Magnetohydrodynamic Generator," *AIAA J. of Propulsion* **6** (4), p. 482, July-August 1990.

4-17. Decher, R., Hoffman, M. A. and Kerrebrock, J. L., "Behavior of a Large Non-Equilibrium MHD Generator," *AIAA Journal* **9**

5

ELECTROHYDRODYNAMIC POWER GENERATION

Electrohydrodynamic (EHD) power generation is a means of exploiting the voltages generated by forcing the electrons and ions in a gas mixture to separate as a result of gas dynamic action. The process is the inverse of that carried out in an ion engine for space flight. In the ion engine, a large electrostatic field accelerates ions to form a beam that is neutralized by means of thermal electrons emitted by a hot surface. The momentum carried by the electrons in both the ion engine and the EHD generator is negligible because of their low mass relative to the ions.

The development of this chapter follows the general approach developed by Soo (Ref. 5-1). The EHD flow interaction is such as to yield a conversion device with high (DC) output voltage, which limits its utility for practical applications. Nevertheless, the topic is included here because it may be suitable for special applications.

5.1. THE EHD GENERATOR

In an EHD generator, a low-density, low-temperature gas is made to proceed through a corona discharge, where the gas is ionized (Fig. 5-1). The gas may be chosen to optimize its characteristics in the conversion process. The ions in the moving gas are swept downstream toward a collector electrode, which establishes this device as a cell where ions become charge carriers from which (flow) energy can be removed. The following one-dimensional analysis of the generator describes the general characteristics of this device, which takes in fluid mechanical power and transforms it to electrical output. A complete conversion system must include the means to produce the required flow using a fan or compressor. The identification of desirable gas flow properties and related performance characteristics are explored in this chapter.

5.2. ANALYTIC DESCRIPTION

Consider the incompressible flow in a direction x, with a uniform velocity u. The flow proceeds through a constant-area duct, although a duct of varying cross-sectional area is a ready extension of this work. The ions created at the channel entry proceed toward the collector, and their motion is controlled by the electric fields and the neutral gas in which they are embedded. Maxwell's equation relates the charge density (n_c) of the ions to the 1D electric field:

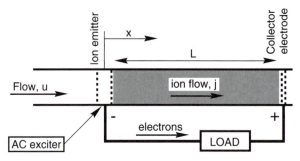

FIGURE 5-1. Schematic of an EHD generator showing the discharge-producing ions, the collector, and the load circuit.

$$\frac{d E_x}{d x} = \frac{e\, n_c}{\varepsilon_0} \tag{5-1}$$

This field results in a potential between the ion generating discharge and the collector electrode:

$$\mathbf{E} = -\nabla V \qquad \text{or} \qquad V = \int_0^L E_x\, d x \tag{5-2}$$

where L is the channel length. Electrons flow externally from the high-voltage corona end $(x = 0)$ to the collector through a load to neutralize the ions. The electron current (proportional to the current density j) therefore flows from the collector to the load, as indicated in Fig. 5-1. In low-density plasmas, the average (steady) velocity of a charged particle in response to an electric field is described by mobility μ. The drift velocity v_d is given by

$$v_d = \mu\, E_x \tag{5-3}$$

The current in a stationary medium $(u = 0)$ is $j_0 = e\, n_c\, v_d$, so that it follows that mobility and conductivity are closely related:

$$j_0 = \sigma\, E_x \qquad \text{or} \qquad \mu = \frac{\sigma}{e\, n_c} \tag{5-4}$$

Mobility may thus be thought of as a conductivity per unit charge carrier.

5.2.1. E Field and Voltage Distributions

The fluid is convected downstream with velocity $u,$ but the ions resist the tendency by drifting against the flow due to the electric field. The net velocity of the ions in the stationary reference frame is:

$$v_c = u - v_d \tag{5-5}$$

and the net electrical current (per unit duct area) along the duct is

$$j_x = e\, n_c\, v_c = e\, n_c\, (u - v_d) = \varepsilon_0 \frac{d\,E_x}{dx}\, (u - \mu\, E_x) \tag{5-6}$$

For a constant-area duct, this current density is conserved along the duct so that j_x = constant. Thus eq. 5-6 may be integrated to yield a distribution for the field E_x at x:

$$j_x\, x = \varepsilon_0\, u\, (E_x - E_0) - \frac{\varepsilon_0\, \mu}{2}\, \left(E_x^2 - E_0^2\right) \tag{5-7}$$

This equation suggests the definition of dimensionless variables. One describes the electric field

$$\gamma = \gamma(x) \equiv \frac{E_x(x)}{E_x(0)} = \frac{E_x}{E_0} \tag{5-8}$$

With $\gamma_L = E_x\, (L)\, /\, E_0$, the nondimensional electric field varies between the limits $1 \le \gamma \le \gamma_L$.

Another parameter is used to describe the drift velocity of the ions relative to the flow, an ion slip parameter:

$$\Lambda \equiv \frac{v_{d0}}{2\, u} = \frac{\mu\, E_0}{2\, u} \tag{5-9}$$

Physically, Λ must lie in the range $0 \le \Lambda \le 0.5$. Substituting these definitions into eq. 5-7 and dividing the resulting equation by itself evaluated at $x = L$ to eliminate j_x yields:

$$\frac{x}{L} = \frac{(1 - \gamma)}{(1 - \gamma_L)}\, \frac{[1 - \Lambda\, (1 + \gamma)]}{[1 - \Lambda\, (1 + \gamma_L)]} \tag{5-10}$$

which describes the nondimensional electric field along the channel $\gamma = f(x/L)$. This distribution is plotted in Fig. 5-2. The magnitude of E_x is largest at the entry and decreases with increasing x to a minimum possible value of zero. Thus the importance of E_0 is evident. For the limiting case of $\Lambda = 1/2$ and $\gamma_L = 0$, the variation of x/L is as $(1 - \gamma)^2$.

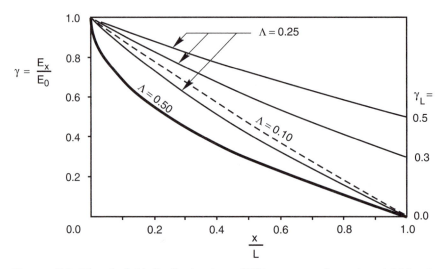

FIGURE 5-2. Electric field distribution in an EHD generator for various initial values and values of the ion slip parameter, $\Lambda \leq .5$.

The voltage along the channel is obtained from

$$V(L) = E_0 L \int_0^1 \gamma \, d\frac{x}{L}$$

(5-11)

and plotted in Fig. 5-3 for the parameters used in Fig. 5-2. The magnitude of the voltage is essentially a fraction of the initial field times the duct length. The larger the field at the exit (i.e., the more uniform the field) the more linear the voltage distribution.

5.2.2. Current

At the exit, the minimum value of γ is zero. This corresponds to a space-charge-limited profile where the current drawn cannot be increased by changing the electric field. In this situation, any current that does flow near the exit does not contribute to power output because the **E** field is locally zero. The space-charge-limited (SCL) current is obtained from eq. 5-7 by setting E_x at $x = L$ to zero:

$$j_{x, \text{SCL}} L = -\varepsilon_0 u E_0 \left(1 - \frac{\mu E_0}{2u}\right)$$

or in equivalent nondimensional forms,

$$\frac{j_{x, \text{SCL}} L}{\varepsilon_0 u E_0} = -\left(1 - \Lambda\right) \quad \text{or} \quad \frac{j_{x, \text{SCL}} L}{\varepsilon_0 \mu E_0^2} = -\left(\frac{1}{\Lambda} - 1\right)$$

(5-12)

The relation between the **E** field and the current follows from eqs. 5-7, 5-8, and 5-12:

$$\Lambda \gamma^2 - \gamma + (1 - \Lambda) \left(1 - \frac{j_x}{j_{SCL}} \frac{x}{L} \right) = 0$$

or

$$\gamma = \frac{1}{2} \left[1 - \sqrt{1 - 4\Lambda(1-\Lambda) \left(1 - \frac{j_x}{j_{SCL}} \frac{x}{L} \right)} \right] \qquad (5\text{-}13)$$

The electric field at the exit γ_L $(x = L)$ equals zero when the current is the space-charge-limited value. Note that the $4\Lambda(1-\Lambda)$ group has a maximum value of unity. The minimum value of this parameter is zero, and the resultant electric field is itself zero. Thus the ion slip must be such that Λ must be > 0 for the situation to be interesting. The overall **E** field at the exit γ_L variation with current is shown in Fig. 5-4. Evidently, a large current requires γ_L to be small.

5.2.3. *Power Density*

The power output per unit volume is given by the product $j_x E_x$ integrated over the channel length

$$\dot{w} = \int_0^1 j_x E_x \, d\frac{x}{L} \qquad (5\text{-}14)$$

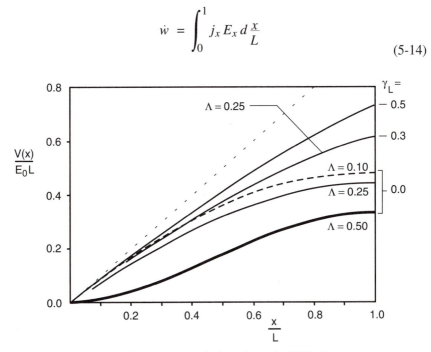

FIGURE 5-3. Voltage variation along the EHD duct.

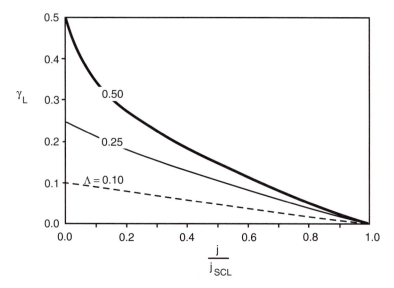

FIGURE 5-4. E field at the channel exit $(E_x(L)/E_x(0))$ variation with current.

In nondimensional form, this is evaluated from a differential form of eq. 5-10 as

$$\dot{w} = \varepsilon_0\, u\, E_0^2 \int_1^{\gamma_L} \gamma\, (2\Lambda\gamma - 1)\, d\gamma \tag{5-15}$$

or in terms of the property μ, in lieu of the velocity u which can be chosen as a matter of design,

$$\dot{w} = \frac{1}{2}\, \varepsilon_0\, \mu\, E_0^3 \left[\frac{4\Lambda}{3}\, (\gamma_L^3 - 1) - (\gamma_L^2 - 1) \right] \frac{1}{2\Lambda} \tag{5-16}$$

This variation of the power density with initial electric field strength is shown in Fig. 5-5. This power density is evidently largest when $\gamma_L = 0$, although a value as large as 0.2 will allow realization of nearly the largest value of power density. The maximum power is a function of only the ion slip, μ, and E_0:

$$\dot{w}_{max} = \frac{1}{2}\, \varepsilon_0\, \mu\, E_0^3 \left(\frac{1}{2\,\Lambda} - \frac{2}{3} \right) \tag{5-17}$$

This result suggests that a low value of the ion slip parameter is desirable for high power density.

5.3. E FIELD LIMIT

Evidently, a larger E_0 leads to larger power density, and so it is appropriate to examine the question: what ultimately limits the electric field one can impose on a gas? In such a field, charged particles, electrons in particular, accelerate to energies that may be large enough to begin of a cascade of events leading to the production of more electrons. The growing number of electrons will allow the conduction of current that then reduces the magnitude of the **E** field. This instability is known as *electrical breakdown*. The maximum field achievable is thus dictated by an equality between the energy gained between collisions and that required to ionize a neutral plasma component. Thus one may write this criterion in terms of a mean free path (λ) and a collision frequency (v_c), which can be written in terms of an ionization collision cross section (Q_{ei}):

$$E_{max} \lambda \approx \varepsilon_i \quad \text{or} \quad E_{max} \approx \varepsilon_i v_c = \left[\varepsilon_i Q_{ei} \left(\frac{\bar{c}}{kT} \right) \right] p \qquad (5\text{-}18)$$

The ionization energy and cross section depend on the nature of the gas used, while the electron mean thermal speed term depends primarily on temperature. Thus the ratio of allowable E_{max}/p tends to be a constant for a given gas at a chosen temperature. The power density for the EHD generator thus scales as

$$\dot{w}_{max} \sim \varepsilon_0 \mu p^3 \left(\frac{E}{p} \right)^3_{breakdown} \sim \varepsilon_0 (\mu p = \text{const.}) p^2 \left(\frac{E}{p} \right)^3_{breakdown}$$

$$(5\text{-}19)$$

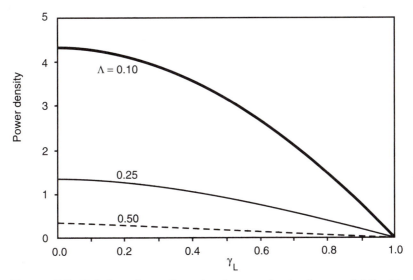

FIGURE 5-5. Variation of non-dimensional power density (see eq. 5-16) with initial E field parameter.

since the mobility varies roughly inversely with pressure. For air at standard atmosphere conditions, the values of the physical parameters are:

$$p = 10^5 \text{ N/m}^2$$

$$\rho = 1.22 \text{ kg/m}^3$$

$$\mu = 1.6 \times 10^{-4} \text{ m}^2/\text{volt-sec (Ref. 5-2)}$$

$$E/p)_{bd} \sim 10^7 \text{ volt/m/atm} \sim 100 \text{ volt m/N (Ref. 5-2)}$$

and with $\varepsilon_0 = 8.85 \times 10^{-12}$ coul/volt-m, the product μp is of the order 10 N/volt-sec. The resulting power density is therefore of the order

$$\dot{w}_{max} \sim 10^{-11} \times 10 \times \left(10^5\right)^2 \left(10^2\right)^3 \sim 10^3 \text{ kW/m}^3$$

which is sufficiently high for the EHD generator to be interesting as an energy conversion device.

5.4. FLUID MECHANICS

For a given maximum **E** field, the flow velocity is, from the definition of Λ:

$$u = \frac{\mu \, E_{max}}{2 \, \Lambda} \tag{5-20}$$

The momentum lost by the fluid is the body force per unit volume integrated over the volume of the duct. If the flow Mach number is low ($M^2 \ll 1$), this momentum loss is primarily a pressure drop resulting from the electrostatic body force per unit volume (see eq. 2-54):

$$\Delta p = \int_0^L e \, n_c \, E_x \, dx = \frac{1}{2}\varepsilon_0 \left(E_x^2(L) - E_0^2\right) = -\frac{1}{2}\varepsilon_0 \, E_0^2 \tag{5-21}$$

assuming $E_x(L) \sim 0$ for maximum power density. The flow work done is the sum of the extractive pressure drop plus any drag associated with the electrodes and the duct. Thus

$$\dot{w}_f = (\Delta p)u \approx \left(\frac{1}{2}\varepsilon_0 \, E_0^2 + C_D \frac{1}{2}\rho \, u^2\right)u \tag{5-22}$$

The drag coefficient C_D characterizes the design. Note that the drag term scales directly with the pressure p.

5.4.1. *Efficiency*

A conversion efficiency may be defined as the ratio of actual work output to flow work:

$$\eta = \frac{\dot{w}}{\dot{w}_f} = \frac{(1 - 4\Lambda/3)}{\left(1 + C_D \dfrac{\rho\, u^2}{\varepsilon_0\, E_0^2}\right)} = \frac{(1 - 4\Lambda/3)}{\left(1 + C_D \dfrac{\rho\, \mu^2}{4\varepsilon_0\, \Lambda^2}\right)} \equiv \frac{(1 - 4\Lambda/3)}{\left(1 + \dfrac{k_1\, C_D}{\Lambda^2}\right)}$$

(5-23)

Here k_1 is the nondimensional grouping of

$$k_1 \equiv \frac{\rho\, \mu^2}{4\varepsilon_0} \sim \frac{\rho\, (\mu\, p)^2}{4\varepsilon_0}\frac{1}{p^2} \sim \frac{(\mu\, p)^2}{4\varepsilon_0}\frac{1}{RT}\frac{1}{p}$$

(5-24)

The efficiency is plotted in Fig. 5-6 for values of the drag loss determining parameter. When $C_D = 0$, then the ion slip is the only loss present. Using the values listed above for atmospheric air, the combination of the physical variables defined as k_1 may be estimated to have a value of 10^3. This factor may be as much as a factor of 10 smaller for other gases. Gas mass effects will influence the gas constant R and μ. Note that k_1 scales with inverse pressure, which favors higher-pressure devices. Operation at higher density for increased power density allows the drag loss to be dominated by the high E fields, which this implies.

The variation of efficiency shows that the ion slip has an optimal value when the finite flow drag is included. The line through the optima is noted. When the drag is large, the ion slip should be correspondingly large and close to the maximum value of 0.5. The maximum efficiency for a system with 1% flow loss is about 60% with an ion slip parameter of 0.2.

5.4.2. *Flow Velocity and Current*

The magnitude of the parameters listed in the previous section allow a general summary of the characteristics of the EHD energy converter. Air has a breakdown E field in excess of 10^6 V/m at standard conditions (Refs. 5-2, 5-3). Then if a field of $10^5 = E_0$ is judged suitable, the velocity may be calculated as

$$\Lambda = \frac{\mu\, E_0}{2\,u} = \frac{(\mu\, p)\left(\dfrac{E}{p}\right)_{bd}}{2\,u} \quad \text{or} \quad 0.2 = \frac{(1.6 \times 10^{-4})\, 10^5}{2\,u}$$

gives $u \sim 40$ m/sec, which is a realistic flow speed for subsonic flow of air.

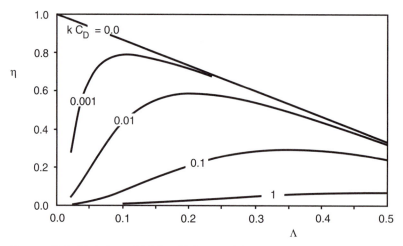

FIGURE 5-6. Variation of EHD efficiency with ion slip parameter and drag. The numerical values noted correspond to the combination $C_D \rho \mu^2 / 4 \varepsilon_0$.

In the space charge limited case, the current density for a duct length of 0.1 m is given by eq. 5-12 as

$$ j_{x,\text{ scl}} \approx \frac{\varepsilon_0 u E_0}{L} = \frac{10^{-11} \; 40 \; 10^5}{0.1} \sim 4 \times 10^{-4} \; \text{A/m}^2 $$

showing the important role of the duct length.

5.5. REMARKS

The EHD generator relies on physics well developed in connection with devices such as the ion space propulsion engine and the Van de Graaf generator using a fluid rather than a moving belt to separate charges. As power generation machinery, EHD devices have the distinct disadvantage of operating with very large voltage and low current. This makes the coupling to realistic loads awkward, a problem that would have been surmouted if the efficiency of practical devices were such as to be clearly superior to competitive devices, such as ordinary rotating machinery or MHD. As a consequence, development of this energy conversion scheme has not been pursued in recent years. Soo (Ref. 5.1) states that power densities of (rather modest) 10^2 to 10^3 kW/m^3 were at one time thought to be possible.

PROBLEMS

1. Equations 5-16 and 5-20 were evaluated for $\gamma_L = 0$ to obtain the efficiency of the EHD generator in Section 5.3.1. Consider the case where

the drag term has a value of 0.01, as in Fig. 5-6, but γ_L is not zero. Calculate and plot the variation of efficiency with γ_L.

2. Develop the nature of the changes to the performance of this device brought about by a linear duct area variation such that the velocity varies as:

$$u = u_0 \left(1 + c\frac{x}{L}\right)$$

where the constant c may be positive or negative. Comment on the relative merits of the c choice options.

3. Describe the nature of dissipative heating that might take place as a result of ion current flow in the duct. How does this affect the efficiency?

REFERENCES

5-1. Soo, S. L., *Direct Energy Conversion*, Prentice-Hall, Inc., Englewood Cliffs, N.J., 1968.

5-2. Cobine, J. D., *Gaseous Conductors*, Dover Publications, Inc., New York, 1958.

5-3. Hirsh, M. N. and Oskam, H. J., *Gaseous Electronics, Vol. 1, Electrical Discharges*, Academic Press, Orlando, Florida, 1978.

6

HEAT TO ELECTRICITY VIA FREE ELECTRONS: THERMIONIC POWER GENERATION

Thermionic power generation depends on the thermal addition of the energy required to remove the electron from a conductor surface. When the freed electron falls to another metal surface with a smaller energy "well," the difference in well depth energies is a potential through which the electron has been elevated by thermal means. A net current will flow through a diode consisting of facing electrodes at different temperatures because emission depends strongly on the surface temperatures. Thus heat is accepted at the hot electrode and rejected at the colder electrode to affect a steady current flow. This is the operational essence of the thermionic converter as DC electrical power source.

Thermionic systems, as well as the photovoltaic (Chapter 8) and the thermoelectric systems (Chapter 9), have the distinctive advantage of working entirely in the solid state (i.e., have no moving parts), which allows the design of potentially very reliable electric power production means over a long service life. To date, these direct conversion methods have found application in limited, special-purpose applications, but their use may become more common in the future. The reader may find Ref. 6-1 to be a useful collection of well-written keystone papers on the physics of energy conversion techniques, thermoelectric and thermionic methods in particular, which were new at the time.

6.1. THE THERMIONIC DIODE

A diode is a pair of parallel plates at different temperatures facing one another. These plates are connected to an external circuit constituting a load. A complete discussion of thermionic energy conversion requires development of the physics of current emission from a hot metal surface. The central Richardson–Dushman equation for current and its dependence on temperature is discussed in detail in Section 6.2. This result is used in Section 6.4 to describe the thermionic converter as a practical device.

6.2. THERMIONIC EMISSION

In a number of engineering devices it is necessary to pass electrons into a vacuum or gaseous fluid in order to have current flow through the medium. Examples are the thermionic diode described in this chapter, the MHD generator (Chapter 4), and devices where arc heating of a fluid takes place, among others. These devices allow electrons to be "boiled" from a high-temperature surface. This section is a development of the physics that controls the thermionic emission current from an electrode.

The Richardson-Dushman equation gives the emitted current density in terms of surface temperature, and the work function, a property of the metal. The need for high temperature for large emission rate generally has important engineering design consequences for the surface and results in a difficult search for good materials that can operate satisfactorily in the high-temperature environments required for practical devices.

6.2.1. *Physics of Metals*

Metals are distinguished from nonmetals through their mobile electrons, which, although bound, on average to the positive nuclei, are free to travel within the metal in response to applied electric fields. The presence of these electrons distinguishes a metal (a conductor) from a nonmetal (or insulator). In the nonmetal, the electrons bind the material atoms into molecules and thus cannot readily move in response to electric fields. The mobile electrons in the metal lie in a *conduction band*, where the energy is lower than the "free" or unbound state (Fig. 6-1). The conduction band is a range of electron energies within the metal where the least energetic electron can just move from one atom to another, and the most energetic has a value consistent with the temperature of the metal. The band of conduction electrons in the metals is sometimes called the "Fermi sea." The energy of the ensemble of electrons is bounded, and the distribution is constrained by the laws of quantum mechanics. The resulting statistical distribution of electron energies allows some to have more energy than that required to hold them to the metal, and thus they escape. It is these electrons that are of interest for the purpose of calculating the emitted current.

Section 3.4 introduced the idea of a *distribution function* to describe the nature of plasma particle collisions. The model described allows determination of such a function for the electrons in a metal (Refs. 6-2 and 6-3).

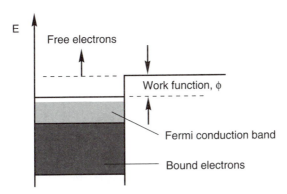

FIGURE 6-1. Energy levels for the electrons in a metal: bound and conduction electrons.

Specifically, the energy distribution function gives the number of electrons per unit volume $f(E)$ with energy in a range between E and $E + dE$. Integration of the distribution function f over all energies gives the number density of electrons:

$$n_e = \int_0^\infty f(E)\, dE \qquad (6\text{-}1)$$

Integration of higher moments of the related *velocity*, rather than energy, distribution function allows calculation of charge and of energy fluxes. Appendix A is a review of the nature of the Maxwell-Boltzmann distribution function and its properties. A distribution function may be thought of as a density in the (unbounded: $-\infty$ to $+\infty$) velocity or (0 to $+\infty$) energy spaces. At zero temperature, the *energy* distribution function varies as the sharply terminated function shown in Fig. 6-2: No electron has an energy greater than a specific value. The energy of the electron with the largest energy level (termed the *Fermi level*) defines the energy required to just remove that electron from the metal. The energy gap is the *work function* ϕ (see Fig. 6-2).

At a finite temperature, the thermal agitation of the atoms in their nominally crystalline structure results in a distribution where a few electrons will have higher energies than the Fermi level as shown. The electrons in the highest-energy "tail" can be liberated from the surface provided they have sufficient energy to overcome the work function. The flux associated with these escaping electrons is small at low temperatures, increases rapidly with increasing temperature, and is larger for a metal with a small work function. This flux of electrons carries charges (an electrical current) and carries energy by virtue of their potential and kinetic energies away from the surface. The resulting current density is derived below and is given by:

$$j = A\, T^2 \exp\left(-\frac{\phi}{k\,T}\right) \qquad (6\text{-}2)$$

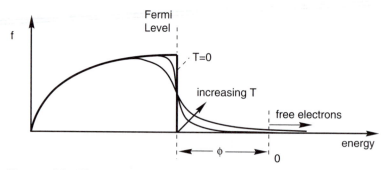

FIGURE 6-2. Electron energy distribution function of the conduction electrons in a metal. f is the number density of electrons with energy between E and $E + dE$.

Table 6-1. Thermionic converter material properties

Material	Work function	A constant
	ϕ (eV)	(10^6 A/m^2 K^2)
Cs	1.89	0.50
C	3.96	0.46
Mo	4.2	0.55
Ni	4.61	0.30
Pt	5.32	0.32
Pt	5.40	1.70
Ta	4.19	0.55
W	4.52	0.60
W	4.54	0.46
W+Ba	1.6	0.015
W+Th	2.7	0.04
BaO	1.5	0.001
SrO	2.2	1.00
ZrC	3.94	1.20
Theoretical value	——	1.23

This Richardson–Dushman equation bears the names of two pioneers for their contribution to its development. The work function ϕ carries units of potential energy. Some authors choose to use volts to measure this energy, and the change requires ϕ to be replaced by $e\phi$, where e is the electronic charge. The constant A is, ideally, a collection of fundamental constants (eq. 6-18) with the magnitude given in Table 6-1. For real materials A may be determined experimentally. The numerical value of the constant often depends on the surface characteristics, which may differ substantially from flat and materially uniform as assumed in ideal surface models. Table 6-1 is a summary of typical work function data for interesting materials from Ref. 6-7 and others. These values are obtained by different experimental means and thus may vary depending on the source.

6.2.2. *The Fermi–Dirac Distribution Function*

Consider Fig. 6-3, showing the atoms of a metal and their attractive fields. Most of the electrons will "rest" at as low an energy level as possible, particularly if the metal temperature is low, that is, when the random excitation by the atoms is minimal or absent. At zero temperature, the highest-energy electron will be at an energy level ϕ below the free state. The experimental evidence for this model is the so-called *photoelectric effect*, where one takes light of a certain wavelength and directs it on the metal and measures if electrons are knocked out of the metal by absorbing the photon to be measured by a current measurement device. If the wavelength of the incident light is such that the photon energy is less than the work function, then no current will be measured, while for larger energies the current is proportional to the light intensity. Further, the kinetic energy of the emitted electrons is equal to the excess energy of the photon over the work function. A summary of this idea is illustrated in Fig. 6-4.

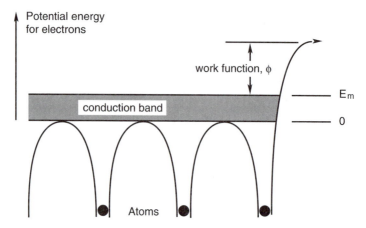

FIGURE 6-3. Potential well for electrons in a metal. Note the bound states, conduction band, and the free states.

This picture has two interesting consequences for a space between an anode and a cathode wherein a current is to be established. First, contact ionization can take place whereby a neutral atom with an ionization potential less than the work function could transfer its electron to the anode surface; see Section 6.6 and Fig. 6-14. Thus a conduction current by means of ions is possible. Second, this ion current is necessarily very small (see eq. 3-7) because the ion thermal speed is very low in comparison to that of the electron. As a result, the electron current is much more interesting.

Within the Fermi sea one has the following:

A collection of energy levels available to the electrons;

The electrons number density of the electrons is high, ideally equal to the atom number density; and

The metal temperature is relatively cool ($kT \ll \phi$), and one would expect the low-lying energy levels to be fully occupied.

The Pauli exclusion principle of quantum mechanics, however, imposes restrictions on the energy distribution through a limitation on the momenta of the electrons. This limitation is that no two identical particles can occupy the same volume of *phase space*, that is, space defined by the three spatial coordinates and the three momentum coordinates:

$$\Delta x \, \Delta y \, \Delta z \quad \Delta p_x \, \Delta p_y \, \Delta p_z \; = \; h^3 \qquad (6\text{-}3)$$

Here p_i is the momentum in the i direction ($m_e V_i$) and h is Planck's constant. For the electron, a spin degeneracy allows two electrons to occupy the same phase-space "volume" element.

At zero temperature, one would therefore expect a distribution function for the electrons in the conduction band to have a form such as shown in

Fig. 6-2. The energy of the highest-energy electron at $T = 0$ K is E_m. It is the sharpness of the cutoff in this distribution function (even at modest temperature) that leads to the results observed in the photoelectric experiment. The area under the curve is the total energy of the electrons in the bound state. The distribution described is the Fermi-Dirac (FD) function to be determined.

Statistical mechanics gives an important clue that the model described here is correct. The specific heat of a substance can be related to the number of particles that share thermal energy. If the electron were indeed free to share such energy by their motion, one would expect the specific heat (per atom or mole) of a metal to be larger than that of a nonmetal, when in fact they are about the same. This implies that the electrons do not share this energy and are, in effect, locked onto the atoms.

Zero Metal Temperature

The FD distribution function is obtained by considering the momentum space with coordinate dimensions, p_x, p_y, and p_z. A particle may be associated with a momentum vector whose components are p_x, etc. The total momentum is $\mathbf{p} = m_e \mathbf{V}$. The number of electrons with momentum magnitude between p and $p + dp$ is given by

$$dN_e = \frac{\text{differential } p \text{-space "volume"}}{p \text{-space "volume" allowed to each electron}} = \frac{4\pi p^2 \, dp}{\Delta p_x \, \Delta p_y \, \Delta p_z} \times 2$$

(6-4)

The 2 is to allow for the spin degeneracy. The numerator is the volume of a spherical shell of radius p. With the exclusion principle (eq. 6-3), this expression becomes

$$dN_e = \frac{8\pi p^2 \, dp}{h^3} (\Delta V) \quad \text{or} \quad dn_e = \frac{8\pi p^2 \, dp}{h^3}$$

(6-5)

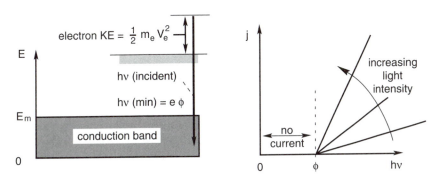

FIGURE 6-4. Photoemission from a metal surface. The incident photon must be sufficiently energetic to liberate an electron.

where dn_e is the number density (electrons/m³) in the range given by the right-hand side (here p and $p + dp$). The energy may be written in terms of momentum as

$$E = \frac{1}{2} m_e V^2 = \frac{p^2}{2 m_e} \quad \text{and} \quad dE = \frac{p \, dp}{m_e} \tag{6-6}$$

so that the differential of n_e may be written in terms of energy. Thus the zero-temperature Fermi-Dirac distribution function, $f_{FD,0}$, is:

$$d n_e = \frac{8\pi \sqrt{2} \, m_e^{3/2} \, \sqrt{E} \, dE}{h^3} = f_{FD,0} \, dE \tag{6-7}$$

The total number of particles follows from an integration over the entire energy range available (0 to E_m):

$$n_e = \int_0^{E_m} d n_e = \frac{16 \pi \sqrt{2} \, m_e^{3/2} \, E_m^{3/2}}{3 \, h^3} \quad \text{or} \quad E_m = h^2 m_e \left(\frac{3 \, n_e}{16 \pi \sqrt{2}}\right)^{2/3} \tag{6-8}$$

This expression gives an estimate of E_m because the number density of electrons in a metal is fixed and approximately equal to the atom number density. For example, tungsten with a density of 19.3 g/cm³ and a molecular weight of 184 has a number density of

$$n = \frac{6.025 \times 10^{26} \ (\text{kg mole})^{-1} \ 1.93 \times 10^4 \ \text{kg/m}^3}{184 \ \text{kg/(kg mole)}} = 6.32 \times 10^{28} \ \text{m}^{-3} \tag{6-9}$$

With $n = n_e$, one obtains $E_m = 9.26 \times 10^{-19}$ J or 5.78 eV or 67,000 K upon substitution into eq. 6-8. The average energy of these electrons is obtained from

$$\bar{E} = \left(\frac{\int E f_{FD,0} \, dE}{\int f_{FD,0} \, dE}\right) = \frac{3}{5} E_m \tag{6-10}$$

which is of the order of 40,000 K. This implies that these electrons are far from rest and are indeed very agitated.

Finite Metal Temperature

The modification to the FD distribution function for finite temperature is not derived here. Instead the result is stated and shown to be physically consistent. The distribution is

$$\frac{d n_e}{d E} = \frac{f_{FD,0}}{1 + \exp\left(\dfrac{E - E_m}{kT}\right)} = f_{FD} = \frac{8 \pi \sqrt{2} \, m_e^{3/2} \, h^{-3} \, \sqrt{E}}{1 + \exp\left(\dfrac{E - E_m}{kT}\right)} \tag{6-11}$$

The new term is such that for $T = 0$, $E < E_m$ the exponential term is zero, while for $E > E_m$ this term is infinite, leading to an absence of any electrons with such energies. This is consistent with the result of eq. 6-7.

Figure 6-2 shows a sketch of the distribution function for finite temperature. The lowest-energy electrons are unaffected by the increased temperature, while a small number have energies in excess of the Fermi level energy, $E > E_m$. Evidently, the electrons with sufficient energy to overcome the work function can escape. The flux of such electrons (i.e., the current) is derived in the following section.

6.2.3. Emission Current

A particle flux (sec^{-1} m^{-2}) is given by a velocity component (u, for example) moment integration of the distribution function, and that quantity is the electric current density (A/m^2) when multiplied by the electronic charge e:

$$j = e \int u f \, dE \qquad (6\text{-}12)$$

Consider the element of the metal surface shown in Fig. 6-5. The normal to the surface from an element of emitter area in the interior of the metal is designated by θ, as shown. All electrons within the solid angle $2\pi \sin \theta \, d\theta$ have the same probability of reaching the surface. The fraction that does reach it is given by

$$\frac{2\pi \sin \theta \, d\theta}{4\pi}$$

When integrated between 0 and $\pi/2$, this fraction is 1/2. In other words, half of the electrons have a chance to reach the surface. Here, however, the electron must have a velocity component normal to the surface that is large

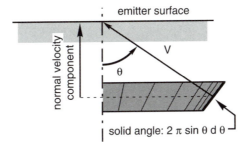

FIGURE 6-5. Electron velocity must have a component normal to the surface with sufficient kinetic energy to leave it.

enough to have $E > E_m + e\,\phi$. Thus the value of θ that allows escape must be such that

$$\frac{1}{2} m_e (V\cos\theta)^2 \geq E_m + e\,\phi \tag{6-13}$$

As a result, there is a *maximum* value of θ beyond which electrons cannot escape the surface. Thus the current may be written

$$\frac{d^2 j}{d E} = e\, f_{FD}\, V\cos\theta\, \frac{\sin\theta\, d\theta}{2}$$

or

$$j = \frac{3}{4}\frac{e\, n_e\, E_m^{-3/2}}{\sqrt{m_e}} \int_{E_m + e\phi}^{\infty} \int_0^{\cos^{-1}\left(\sqrt{\frac{E_m + e\phi}{E}}\right)} \frac{E}{1 + \exp\left(-(E_m - E)/kT\right)}$$

$$\times\ \cos\theta \sin\theta\, d\theta\, dE \tag{6-14}$$

The limits of the integration include only those electrons that have sufficient energy and are correctly oriented to escape. To integrate this, we note the θ integration yields

$$\int_0^{\cos^{-1}\Psi} \cos\theta \sin\theta\, d\theta = -\frac{1}{2}\left(\Psi^2 - 1\right) = \frac{1}{2}\left(1 - \frac{E_m + e\,\phi}{E}\right) = \frac{1}{2}\zeta\frac{kT}{E} \tag{6-15}$$

where Ψ is the square root term is the upper limit of the integral in eq. 6-14. ζ is a new nondimensional variable characterizing the energy defined by

$$E - \left(E_m + e\,\phi\right) \equiv \zeta\,(kT) \tag{6-16}$$

from which it follows

$$-\frac{(E_m - E)}{kT} = \zeta + \frac{e\,\phi}{kT} \tag{6-17}$$

The lowest energy of a free electron is described by $\zeta = 0$, and ζ ranges to very large values. Since $kT \ll e\phi$, the exponential term in the denominator of the distribution function (eq. 6-14) is well approximated by

$$1 + \exp\left(\zeta\right)\exp\left(\frac{e\phi}{kT}\right) \approx \exp\left(\zeta\right)\exp\left(\frac{e\phi}{kT}\right)$$

and with $dE = kT \, d\zeta$, the integral reduces to

$$\frac{1}{2}(kT)^2 \exp\left(-\frac{e\phi}{kT}\right) \int_0^\infty \zeta \exp(-\zeta)d\zeta$$

The integral is unity, and the equation for the current therefore reduces to the Richardson–Dushman equation:

$$j = \frac{4\pi \, e \, m_e}{h^3}(kT)^2 \exp\left(-\frac{e\phi}{kT}\right) = A \, T^2 \exp\left(-\frac{e\phi}{kT}\right)$$

so that

$$A = \frac{4\pi \, e \, m_e \, k^2}{h^3} \qquad (6\text{-}18)$$

after substituting for E_m from eq. 6-8. The theoretical value of A is 1.23×10^6 A m^{-2} T^{-2} (Table 6-1).

6.2.4. Emission Heat Transport

As the electrons leave the surface, they carry with them energy supplied by the metal. This heat flux is an important element of the thermal balance that establishes the temperature of the emitting surface and thus allows the thermionic emission to take place. The energy flux is calculated from the particle flux times the energy per particle. The differential particle flux is $d(j/e)$ and the energy E per electron must be included in the integral given by eq. 6-14. Thus

$$q = \frac{3}{4}\frac{n_e \, E_m^{-3/2}}{\sqrt{m_e}} \int_{E_m + e\phi}^\infty E\left[E - (E_m + e\phi)\right]\exp\left(-\frac{E}{kT}\right) d E \qquad (6\text{-}19)$$

which, when integrated, gives

$$q = \frac{4\pi \, m_e}{h^3}\left[2kT + E_m + e\phi\right](2kT)^2 \exp\left(-\frac{e\phi}{kT}\right) = \frac{j}{e}\left[2kT + E_m + e\phi\right] \qquad (6\text{-}20)$$

The electrons must therefore be supplied with sufficient energy to (1) escape the potential well and (2) carry $2kT$ away as well. Once outside they will equilibrate to $3/2kT$, meaning that they cool the cathode by $1/2kT$ per electron as they leave the surface. Both q and j are vectors with an orientation normal to the surface, although they are written here as scalars.

6.3. SPACE CHARGE EFFECTS

The space into which emitted electrons proceed may be occupied by a large number of other electrons. This is certainly true for devices where the current density is large enough for power density to be of interest. Under such circumstances, the charge of the electron cloud in the space constitutes a repulsive potential barrier that hinders electron emission. The result is that the potential energy required for the electron to enter the space between two plates is elevated above the work function. The theoretical basis for this follows directly from consideration of Maxwell's equations (eqs. 2-10 and 2-26) for the electric field as it is influenced by the charge density. Due to current conservation, the electron density in the space above the emitting surface will not be uniform, and the potential distribution will reflect this distribution. If it were not for these space-charge effects, the energy of the emitted electron could by transformed into electrical potential, which would thus be available for an electrical load. The simplest example of the role of charge distribution arises in connection with the Debye length described in Section 3.1. An example of greater interest in thermionics is developed below. The physical problem is as follows: For a given current emitted from a surface, is there a maximum voltage that can be reached at some level h above the surface? And what fraction of the maximum voltage does this constitute? The inverse problem is the solution for the space-charge-limited current for a given voltage. It follows from this discussion that the effect of the space charge is to raise the voltage barrier above that of the pure work function, which reduces the performance of a thermionic diode.

6.3.1. Emission across a Small Gap

To appreciate the effects of space charges, consider a surface emitting electrons into an evacuated space. The situation is as depicted in Figs. 6-6 and 6-10(c): At the emitting cathode ($x = 0$) the potential is taken as zero. At $x = h$, the electrons have reached constant velocity so that the potential is constant. For the contrasting situation of charges traveling into a space occupied by a gas, see Appendix A. As these electrons decelerate from the emitter, they lose their initial kinetic energy associated with velocity $u_{e,0}$. With $V(0) = 0$, the energy equation for an electron in a space $0 \leq x \leq h$ reads

$$\frac{1}{2} m_e u_{e,0}^2 + e V(0) \, (= 0) = \frac{1}{2} m_e u_e^2 + e V \qquad (6\text{-}21)$$

The problem is to find the value of the potential at $x = h$ given a certain current flow. The continuity equation for electrons is simply that the current is constant:

$$j = e n_e u_e = j_0 \qquad (6\text{-}22)$$

These equations can be combined by eliminating the velocity:

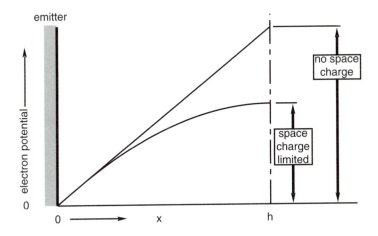

FIGURE 6-6. Schematic of current emission to a collector at $x = h$. Ideal and actual potential distributions are noted.

$$\left(\frac{1}{n_e}\right)^2 = \left(\frac{1}{n_{e,0}}\right)^2 - \frac{2\,e^3}{m_e\,j_0^2}\,V \tag{6-23}$$

Evidently the electron density *increases* as the $x = h$ plane is approached. This equation is solved with the Maxwell's equation (1D combination of eqs. 2-10 and 2-25) for the resulting potential:

$$\frac{d^2 V}{dx^2} = -\frac{e}{\varepsilon_0}\,n_e = -\frac{e}{\varepsilon_0}\left[\left(\frac{1}{n_{e,0}}\right)^2 - \frac{2e^3}{m_e\,j_0^2}V\right]^{-1/2} \tag{6-24}$$

or nondimensionally

$$\frac{d^2 v}{d\xi^2} = \frac{-1}{\sqrt{1 - \alpha\,v}} \tag{6-25}$$

where the following definitions simplify the mathematical problem: $\xi = x/h$ and

$$v \equiv \frac{V}{V_{sc}^*} \quad \text{where } V_{sc}^* \equiv \frac{e\,n_{e,0}\,h^2}{\varepsilon_0} = \frac{h^2}{h_{D,c}^2}\frac{k\,T_c}{e} \tag{6-26}$$

V_{sc}^* is a characteristic space-charge potential, which is the ratio of physical diode width to Debye length (squared; see eq. 3-5 for the definition of h_D) times the energy kT_c/e. The constant α is the ratio of potential energy associated with the emitter to electron kinetic energy at the emitter, defined here in terms of both the characteristic voltage and the constant current:

$$\alpha \equiv \frac{e V_{sc}}{\frac{1}{2} m_e u_{e,0}^2} = j_0 \frac{e h^2}{\frac{1}{2} m_e u_{e,0}^3 \varepsilon_0} = \frac{1}{2} \frac{h^2}{h_{D,c}^2} \tag{6-27}$$

The third relation arises with the use of the fact that the emitted electrons have an energy of $2kT_c$ as they leave the emitter (see eq. 6-20). The nonlinear equation for the potential v can be transformed into

$$2 \frac{dv}{d\xi} \frac{d^2 v}{d\xi^2} = \frac{d}{d\xi}\left(\frac{dv}{d\xi}\right)^2 = \frac{-2}{\sqrt{1 - \alpha v}} \frac{dv}{d\xi} \tag{6-28}$$

from which $d\xi$ may be eliminated and the equation integrated

$$\left(\frac{dv}{d\xi}\right)^2 = \frac{2}{\alpha} \int \frac{1}{\sqrt{1 - \alpha v}} d(-\alpha v) = \frac{4}{\alpha}(\sqrt{1 - \alpha v} - C) = \frac{4}{\alpha}(\sqrt{1 - \alpha v} - \sqrt{1 - \alpha v_1}) \tag{6-29}$$

The constant of integration C is evaluated at $x = h$, where $dV/dx = 0$ and the (unknown, nondimensional) potential is v_1. This equation can be integrated again with a change in variable and carrying the constant C for convenience. Thus define a nondimensional electron velocity u:

$$u = (\sqrt{1 - \alpha v} - C) \quad \text{for which} \quad du = -\frac{\alpha}{2} \frac{1}{u + C} dv \tag{6-30}$$

The values of u at the boundaries are $u(0) = 1 - C$ and $u(1) = 0$.

6.3.2. Space-Charge-Limited Current

With this definition, eq. 6-29 becomes

$$dv = \frac{2}{\sqrt{\alpha}} \sqrt{u} \, d\xi = -\frac{2}{\alpha}(u + C) \, du$$

or

$$\int_0^{1-C} \frac{(u + C)}{\sqrt{u}} du = \sqrt{\alpha} \int_0^1 d\xi \tag{6-31}$$

This gives a cubic equation for C in terms of α as

$$\frac{9}{4}\alpha = (1 - C)(2C + 1)^2 \quad \text{where} \quad C = \sqrt{1 - \alpha v_1} \tag{6-32}$$

For a given temperature, the initial electron velocity $u_{e,0}$ is determined so that it, together with $n_{e,0}$, gives the initial and constant current density, $j = j_0$. The definition of α (eq. 6-27) shows that it is a direct measure of current and the relation given by eq. 6-32 is a space-charge-limited current-voltage relation where the most significant parameter is the gap spacing h. Of particular interest are distributions with C small, because the initial velocity is $1 - C$ and thus large potential can be achieved for large initial velocity.

The relationship between voltage and current plotted in Fig. 6-7 for modest values of C and may be interpreted as follows. If it were not for space-charge effects, the potential an electron could reach is given by eq. 6-21 as $V_{max} = m_e u^2_{e,0}/2e$. Thus the ratio of the potential at $x = h$ to the maximum possible is given by

$$\frac{V(h)}{V_{max}} = \frac{V(h)}{V^*_{sc}} \frac{V^*_{sc}}{V_{max}} = v_1 \frac{e^2 n_{e,0} h^2}{\frac{1}{2} m_e u^2_{e,0}} \frac{1}{\varepsilon_0} = \frac{v_1}{2} \frac{h^2}{h^2_{D,c}} \quad (6\text{-}33)$$

using the definition of the Debye length h_D (eq. 3-5) at the cathode and the fact that the ratio α can also be written as a length ratio as given by eq. 6-27 so that the product αv_1 is V/V_{max}. In terms of the constant C, this may be written as

$$\frac{V(h)}{V_{max}} = \alpha v_1 = 1 - C^2 \quad (6\text{-}34)$$

showing that C near its minimum (zero) is desirable for highest recovery of the electron kinetic energy as potential. The ratio V/V_{max} is also plotted in

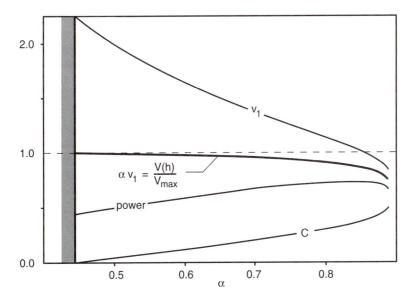

FIGURE 6-7. Variation of the (nondimensional) voltage barrier (v_1) as a function of current parameter α for the vacuum diode. Voltage axis is $v_1 = V(h)/V^*_{sc}$. Also noted are $V(h)/V_{max}$ and the constant C.

Fig. 6-7. This occurs at $\alpha = 4/9$ when $C = 0$ (eq. 6-32). This implies the following relation between current and the voltage rise across the gap h. From the defintion of α and relating the initial electron velocity $u_{e,0}$ to the potential:

$$j_0\, h^2 = \frac{4}{9}\, \sqrt{\frac{2e}{m_e}}\, \varepsilon_0\, V^{3/2} \tag{6-35}$$

This is the maximum, or space-charge-limited, current for a voltage rise equal to the emitted electron kinetic energy. The magnitude of the current (and therefore the power) is evidently maximized through the use of a small gap h.

If the potential to be achieved is less that the theoretical maximum, then the current can be larger to reach the space-charge limit. The power density of the electrons transferred across the gap is the product of voltage times current. This product is given by (eqs. 6-27 and 6-33):

$$j_0 = \alpha\, \frac{m_e\, u_{e,0}^3\, \varepsilon_0}{2\,e\,h^2} \quad ; \quad \frac{V(h)}{V_{\max}} = \alpha v_1 \quad \text{or} \quad j_0\, \frac{V(h)}{V_{\max}} \sim \left(\alpha^2\, v_1\right) \tag{6-36}$$

This product is plotted in Fig. 6-7 and labeled "power." The maximum power density is obtained for $\alpha \sim 0.84$ as noted. Operation near this point approximately doubles the cell power density over the space-charge-limited value at the maximum voltage. The space-charge current limitation places an upper bound on the performance of the vacuum diode.

6.4. THE THERMIONIC DIODE

Thermionic electric power production (Refs. 6-4 and 6-5) takes advantage of the difference in electron fluxes from two facing surfaces at different temperatures. Thus a net current is established, driven by the temperature difference. Figure 6-8 shows a cell consisting of two facing electrodes held at different temperatures. The electrode at higher temperature will generally emit a greater current than the colder electrode so that a net current flows. The hot electrode is the net emitter of electrons into the space between the electrodes. The terms *emitter* and *cathode* are used interchangeably to describe the function of the hot electrode. Since both cold and hot electrodes emit electrons, the reference is to *net* production. A similar comment applies to *collector* and *anode*. The parallel-plate arrangement shown is called a *vacuum diode* when no neutral gas or ions occupy the space between the electrodes.

The energy picture for an electron passing from the (net) emitter to the (net) collector (i.e., cathode to anode) is shown in Fig. 6-9. Consider a cell consisting of two materials, one with a high work function and the other with a lower value. If both materials are in contact and at the same temperature (left), the Fermi levels will differ because of the common free states energy level. The resulting voltage that appears across the open terminal of such a

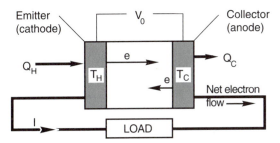

FIGURE 6-8. A thermionic diode as an energy converter. Note hot and cold emission surfaces.

cell or junction equals the difference in work functions and is the (isothermal)
contact potential:

$$V_{ca} = \varphi_c - \phi_a \tag{6-37}$$

When the two surfaces of the cell are maintained at different temperatures,
each electrode will emit a current.

6.4.1. *Open Circuit Voltage*

The current emitted from the electrodes as separate entities depends only on
the temperature and work functions (here in volts) of the electrodes. For the
discussion to follow, the assumption that the A constant for cathode and anode
materials is identical is implicit. Relaxation of that assumption involves more
complex relations and is left to the reader. The currents from the two electrodes are given by

$$j_c = A\, T_c^2 \exp\left(-\frac{e\,\varphi_c}{k\,T_c}\right) \quad \text{and} \quad j_a = A\, T_a^2 \exp\left(-\frac{e\,\phi_a}{k\,T_a}\right) \tag{6-38}$$

and the net current in a cell where these surfaces face one another is

$$j = j_c - j_a \tag{6-39}$$

At open circuit, the net current j must be zero. To enforce this constraint, the
potential of the cathode must rise to such a value to force $j = 0$. This picture
is shown in Fig. 6-9 (right). The cathode potential at open circuit is therefore
given by

$$j = A\, T_c^2 \exp\left(-\frac{e\,(V_c)}{k\,T_c}\right) - A\, T_a^2 \exp\left(-\frac{e\,\phi_a}{k\,T_a}\right) = 0, \quad \text{for } V_c = V_{oc} \tag{6-40}$$

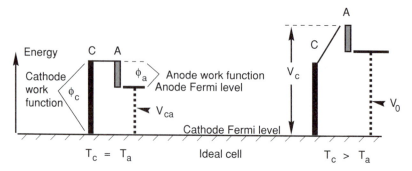

FIGURE 6-9. Energy level diagram for electrons in an isothermal (left) and nonisothermal (right) cell. Note the Fermi levels, the work functions, and the terminal voltage.

Here V_c is the potential cathode-emitted electrons must overcome to escape and balance the anode current. Thus the open circuit voltage is

$$V_{oc} = V_c - \phi_a = \phi_a\left(\frac{T_c}{T_a} - 1\right) + 2\frac{kT_c}{e}\ln\left(\frac{T_c}{T_a}\right) \qquad (6\text{-}41)$$

Evidently, for a chosen set of electrodes (ϕs), the open circuit voltage increases with increasing temperature difference between cathode and anode.

6.4.2. Cell Current

For finite current, the cell operates as a thermodynamic heat engine since the elevated cathode temperature is used to provide the *ionization* energy while *recombination* heat is given up at the anode. The remaining potential energy is the useful electrical potential. The accompanying net heat flux from hot to cold is an element of irreversibility.

The potential distribution in the interelectrode gap is influenced by charges that are present because these present a repulsive force field. Figure 6-10 shows the temperature-driven distribution (a) together with the influence of charges. Figure 6-10(b) shows that the presence of electrons changes the curvature (eq. 6-28: $d^2V/dx^2 < 0$) of the potential distribution as noted. The impact on cell performance may be viewed in either of two ways. If the current is maintained, the output voltage is reduced as shown in the figure. Alternatively, if the output potential is maintained, the effective barrier to electron transport across the cell is raised. Either view leads to the conclusion that power output is reduced.

The electrons in the interelectrode space thus retard the emission of cathode current. This situation persists with decreasing anode voltage until the anode potential is "shielded" by the flowing electrons, which ultimately causes the potential distribution to be "flat" at the anode. Figure 6-10(c) shows a space-charge-limited current may be imposed by the anode when $dV/dx = 0$ at the anode (Section 6.3). Under these circumstances, forcing more current

to the anode can only be accompished by changing the potential of the cathode. Finally, the most current that can be forced through the cell is that limited by the emission of cathode electrons. This limit is established by the
temperature of the cathode [Fig. 6-10(d)].

6.4.3. Saturation Current

The maximum possible current density from the cathode at a given temperature is given by

$$j_c = A \, T_c^2 \, \exp\left(-\frac{e \, \phi_c}{k \, T_c}\right) \equiv j_{sat} \tag{6-42}$$

In the absence of any space-charge effects and negligible anode emission current, that is,

$$J_{a/c} \equiv \frac{j_a}{j_c} = \frac{T_c^2 \, \exp\left(-\dfrac{e \, \phi_c}{k \, T_c}\right)}{T_a^2 \, \exp\left(-\dfrac{e \, \phi_a}{k \, T_a}\right)} = \frac{T_c^2}{T_a^2} \, \exp\left[-\frac{e}{k}\left(\frac{\phi_c}{T_c} - \frac{\phi_a}{T_a}\right)\right] \ll 1 \tag{6-43}$$

the net current is approximately equal to the cathode emission current.

6.4.4. Voltage-Current Characteristic

The cell output voltage V_0 is, in the absence of space-charge effects, equal to
the cathode potential less the anode work function:

$$V_0 = V_c - \phi_a \tag{6-44}$$

Every electron that makes it over the cathode barrier will be transferred to the
anode (provided that the load voltage is sufficiently low, i.e., less than V_{oc}).

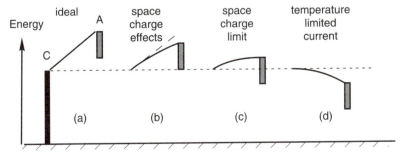

FIGURE 6-10. Energy level diagram for electrons in a thermionic cell under
increasing current conditions. (a) ideal cell, (b) influence of charges in interelectrode space, (c) space-charge-limited current at the anode, and (d) temperature or emission-limited current at the cathode.

This may be expressed mathematically as $j \sim j_c$ or, with eq. 6-44, when V_c is expressed as a load voltage and finally in terms of the saturation current (eq. 6-42):

$$j = A \, T_c^2 \exp\left(-\frac{e\left(\phi_a + V_0\right)}{k \, T_c}\right) = j_{sat} \exp\left[-\frac{e\left(V_0 - \left(\phi_c - \phi_a\right)\right)}{k \, T_c}\right] \quad (6\text{-}45)$$

The typically large magnitude of the ratio eV/kT makes the exponential behave as a sensitive determinant of current. If the argument is negative, the current decreases exponentially with voltage V_0. On the other hand, if the argument is positive, the barrier presented by the load is so low as to allow every emitted electron to be transferred across the gap. Under these circumstances, the diode is emission limited at the saturation value of the current, independent of the load voltage. The critical cell bias voltage (where the load imposes an increase in the barrier height) is the contact potential, $V_{ca} = \phi_c - \phi_a$. For values larger than this, a reduction in the current with increasing voltage is to be expected. Thus

$$j = j_{sat}, \qquad\qquad \text{for} \quad V_0 \le V_{ca}$$

$$j = j_{sat} \exp\left(-\frac{e\left(V_0 - V_{ca}\right)}{k \, T_c}\right), \quad \text{for} \quad V_0 \ge V_{ca}$$

$$(6\text{-}46)$$

This characteristic is plotted in Fig. 6-11. It shows the operating point(s) of primary interest (*) because the power output there is largest, as can be readily ascertained by an examination of

$$\dot{w} = j \, V_0 \qquad\qquad (6\text{-}47)$$

The decreasing current regime is called the Boltzmann or retarding region. The logarithmic scale of j results in the linear plot. Webster (Ref. 6-10) provides a discussion of the incorporation of space-charge effects and the resulting effect on the voltage-current characteristic of these devices.

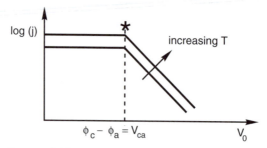

FIGURE 6-11. Voltage-current (density) characteristic (semilog scale) of a thermionic diode. Space-charge effects are neglected. $V_{ca} = \phi_c - \phi_a$.

6.5. PERFORMANCE

Power density and efficiency are the key performance parameters of an energy conversion system. The voltage current characteristic enables the calculation of the power density of a converter operating at a given load condition. For the following, barrier voltage increments due to space-charge effects are included. Their origin and the means employable to minimize them are discussed in Section 6.3. The analysis to follow draws on the work of Houston (Ref. 6-8) and others (Ref. 6-9).

6.5.1. *Efficiency*

Figure 6-12 shows the general variation of the interelectrode potential with a maximum between the electrodes. The potential energy the electrons from the emitter must overcome is V_c, which is the sum of the work function plus the height of the electrostatic barrier voltage. Similarly, electrons emitted from the anode must overcome a potential of V_a. The lower portion of Fig. 6-12 clarifies the definition of the various potentials in relation to the reference state. V_c and V_a may be written

$$V_c = \varphi_c + \Delta V_{bc} = V_{max}$$

$$V_a = \varphi_a + \Delta V_{ba} = V_{max} - V_0$$

(6-48)

where the diode output voltage V_0 is

$$V_0 = \varphi_c - \varphi_a - (\Delta V_{ba} - \Delta V_{bc}) = \varphi_c - \varphi_a - \Delta V_b \qquad (6\text{-}49)$$

The Fermi level of the cathode is taken to be zero as a reference. As shown in Fig. 6-12, the (positive) barrier heights (ΔV_{bc} or ΔV_{ba}) are the additional potentials in excess of the work function the electrons must overcome. ΔV_b is the *net* barrier height, the amount of which the diode potential is reduced from the contact potential V_{ca}. The cathode and anode currents are given by the Richardson-Dushman equations (eq. 6-2 or 6-18) with the appropriate barrier potentials:

$$j_c = A\, T_c^2 \exp\!\left(-\frac{e\, V_c}{k\, T_c}\right) \quad \text{and} \quad j_a = A\, T_a^2 \exp\!\left(-\frac{e\, V_a}{k\, T_a}\right) \qquad (6\text{-}50)$$

The net current density follows from the difference of these competing components:

$$j = j_c - j_a \qquad (6\text{-}51)$$

In the absence of Joule losses associated with current flow through the metal portions of the diode, the output voltage is

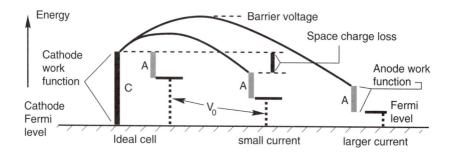

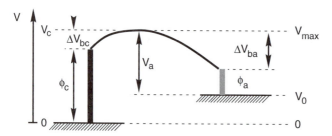

FIGURE 6-12. Energy level diagram for electrons in a thermionic cell under various conditions. The lower part of the figure defines the potentials and potential differences used in the text.

$$V_0 = V_c - V_a = \varphi_c - \varphi_a - (\Delta V_{ba} - \Delta V_{bc}) \qquad (6\text{-}52)$$

An efficiency calculation requires determination of the net heat input to the diode as a system. The hot cathode energy inputs include

1. Potential energy of the cathode electrons required to reach the potential maximum, $j_c V_c$;
2. Thermal energy carried away from the surface, equals particle flux times energy carried per particle [$= (j_c/e)\, 2kT_c$; see eq. 6-20)];
3. Two energy gains that are realized from the collector side: the thermal energy brought by collector emitted electrons at temperature T_a and the fall of collector emitted electrons through the emitter potential V_c; these energy gains are proportional to the current j_a and must be subtracted from the net input to the emitter; and
4. Radiative transfer from the (assumed black) surface ($= \sigma\, T_c^4$). The radiating area can be assumed to equal the emission area, since the small gap in a diode as shown in Fig. 6-8 leads to nearly complete "viewing" of the opposing plates.

If the radiative fluxes are neglected for the present, the net power input to the hot side of the diode is the gross input at the cathode less the transfer from the anode:

$$q_H = j_c \left(V_c + \frac{2 k T_c}{e} \right) - j_a \left(V_c + \frac{2 k T_a}{e} \right) \tag{6-53}$$

This, together with the net power output,

$$w = (V_c - V_a)(j_c - j_a) \tag{6-54}$$

allows calculation of the thermal efficiency of the device. The resulting expression may be written in terms of new nondimensional parameters. The first is a parameter that describes the cathode potential (and indirectly the work function of the emitter) relative to the thermal energy:

$$\beta \equiv \frac{e V_c}{k T_c} = \frac{e \phi_c}{k T_c} + \frac{\Delta V_{bc}}{k T_c} \tag{6-55}$$

The temperature may be parameterized as in a way similar to that used in the cycle analysis (see Chapter 1 and Ref. 1-1, for example) but unlike tradition in this field, where θ is defined as the inverse of the ratio used here

$$\theta = \frac{T_c}{T_a} > 1 \tag{6-56}$$

The physical properties of materials and realistic conditions lead to the conclusion that β is rather large, in the range of 10 to 30. The efficiency of this device, defined as the ratio of the quantities given by eqs. 6-53 and 6-54, cannot exceed the Carnot efficiency, given by

$$\eta = \frac{w}{q_H} \leq \eta_{rev} = 1 - \frac{1}{\theta} \tag{6-57}$$

In the limit of a cell operating with a very low anode temperature so that the emitted current can be neglected, the efficiency is

$$\eta(T_a = 0) = \frac{V_c - V_a}{V_c + \frac{2 k T_c}{e}} = 1 - \frac{\phi_a + \Delta V_{ba} + 2 (k/e) T_c}{\phi_c + \Delta V_{bc} + 2 (k/e) T_c} \tag{6-58}$$

Note that the positive barrier voltages and the temperature factor raise the work function ratio toward unity, decreasing the efficiency. In the absence of the small cathode temperature term(s), this expression reads

$$\eta(T_a = 0) = 1 - \frac{V_a}{V_c} \equiv 1 - y \tag{6-59}$$

or

$$\eta(T_a = 0 \text{ and } \Delta V_b = 0) = 1 - \frac{\phi_a}{\phi_c} \tag{6-60}$$

where the last form is obtained when the barrrier voltages due to space-charge effects are small. Evidently, the efficiency of this limit is not bounded by thermodynamic limits since the very small collector emission limit is equivalent to a 0 K rejection temperature for this heat "engine." The role of the ratio V_a/V_c suggests that it makes a logical nondimensional performance parameter y. Thus from eq. 6-59

$$y = \frac{V_a}{V_c} = 1 - \frac{V_0}{V_{max}} = \frac{\phi_a - \Delta V_{ba}}{\phi_c + \Delta V_{bc}} < 1 \qquad (6\text{-}61)$$

The voltage ratio y incorporates the barrier voltages and thus simplifies the resulting expression for the efficiency obtained by combining eqs. 6-59, 6-53, and 6-54:

$$\eta = \frac{1 - y}{1 + \frac{2}{\beta}\left(1 - \frac{\exp(\beta(1-\theta y))}{\theta^3}\right)\left(1 - \frac{\exp(\beta(1-\theta y))}{\theta^2}\right)^{-1}} \qquad (6\text{-}62)$$

To gain some insight into the dependence of efficiency on the value of the parameters, one notes from eq. 6-54 that this device will not produce work output if the electrode potentials are equal: that is, when $y = 1$. The change to the expression for η brought about by the consideration of the collector emitted current (j_a) is in the collection of parameters in the denominator of eq. 6-62. This term is positive and therefore decreases the efficiency, as one would expect. With normally large β (~20), $2/\beta$ is a small number. When the parameter β is fixed, one may imagine a system where the cathode situation is determined and changes in θ imply changes in the anode temperature so that an optimum may be found. By fixing y, one assumes that the electrode materials are chosen and the barrier voltages are invariant.

Equation 6-53 may be interpreted more easily with the current ratio is given by eq. 6-43 as

$$J_{a/c} = \frac{j_a}{j_c} = \frac{\exp\left[\beta(1 - y\theta)\right]}{\theta^2} \qquad (6\text{-}63)$$

which must be less than unity for this device to be interesting as a power producer; see Fig. 6-13, where this ratio is plotted. Thus one must have $y\theta > 1$. The expression for efficiency becomes

$$\eta = \frac{1 - y}{1 + \frac{2}{\beta}} \approx (1 - y) \qquad (6\text{-}64)$$

In view of the large β, examination of this expression shows that the temperatures (through θ) play a relatively small role in determining the efficiency. Another way of looking at the role of θ is to fix the collector temperature, and this introduces a variation for β of the form

$$\beta^* = \frac{e\,V_c}{k\,T_a} \; ; \; \beta = \frac{e\,V_c}{k\,T_c} = \frac{\beta^*}{\theta} \qquad (6\text{-}65)$$

so that eq. 6-62 becomes

$$\eta = \frac{1 - y}{1 + \dfrac{2}{\beta}\,\dfrac{\theta}{\theta_{ref}}} \qquad (6\text{-}66)$$

Thus here again, because of the large β, it may be concluded that temperature effects play a minor role in the relation between the voltage ratio y and the efficiency. The actual variation of the efficiency is shown in Fig. 6-13. It climbs to a maximum near $y\theta$ equal to unity, which could be determined by differentiation of eq. 6-62, but, since losses have been neglected, it appears unwarranted.

The temperature ratio θ may realistically be limited to the range between 2 and 4. From a Carnot viewpoint, one cannot expect an efficiency larger than $(1 - 1/\theta)$. This can be seen from the case $y\theta = 1$, which is near maximum efficiency. At this condition, the arguments in the current emission exponentials are identical for anode and cathode and equal to unity. The maximum efficiency is approximately given by:

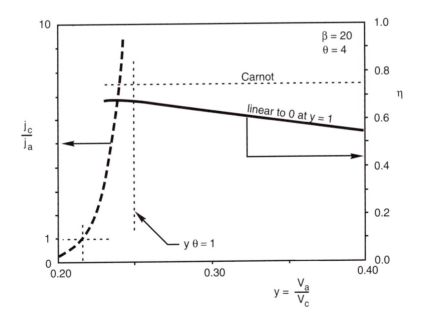

FIGURE 6-13. Variation of efficiency and emitter–collector current ratio near the point $y\theta = 1$. The η curve decreases linearly to 0 at $y = 1$.

$$\eta_{max} \approx \frac{1 - \frac{1}{\theta}}{1 + \frac{2}{\beta} \frac{\theta^2 + \theta + 1}{\theta^2 + \theta}} \tag{6-67}$$

Thus $(1 - y)$ becomes the Carnot term, and the remainder of the expression serves to show how far below this maximum efficiency such devices must operate. The large magnitude of β shows that the efficiency is close to Carnot: The θ grouping in the denominator is 1.17 at $\theta = 2$ and decreases to unity as θ increases. This makes consideration of losses critical, and these are discussed below.

One may summarize the efficiency performance of an ideal vacuum diode by stating that it is limited primarily by the electrode potentials, irrespective of the operating temperatures. The power output, however, is current and thus temperature dependent. A search for candidate materials must therefore consider the work functions for high efficiency. The power output (per unit area) from the ideal diode is therefore of the order

$$j_c V_c = A \, V_c \, T_c^2 \, \exp\left(-\frac{e \, V_c}{k \, T_c}\right) \tag{6-68}$$

At a temperature of 1000 K and $V_c = 1$ V, this power density is about 1.1×10^6 W/m^2 or 110 W/cm^2.

6.5.2. Losses

A more accurate calculation of efficiency requires consideration of irreversibilities. In vacuum diodes the principal losses are (Ref. 6-9):

1. The transport of radiation from the hot cathode to the anode;
2. Conduction by the surrounding structure; and
3. Resistive heating of the current-carrying materials.

The last two are configuration sensitive, and their estimation is straightforward, so that only the radiative loss is considered here. The expression for efficiency is altered by including a net radiative term in the heat input:

$$q_L = \sigma \left(T_c^4 - T_a^4\right) \tag{6-69}$$

which leads to an efficiency expression of the form

$$\eta = (1 - y)\left[1 + \frac{2}{\beta} \frac{\left(1 - \frac{J_{a/c}}{\theta}\right)}{(1 - J_{a/c})} + \frac{\sigma \, T_c^4 \left(1 - \theta^{-4}\right)}{j_c \, V_c \, (1 - J_{a/c})}\right]^{-1} \approx (1 - y)\left[1 + \frac{2}{\beta} + \frac{\sigma \, T_c^4}{j_c \, V_c}\right]^{-1} \tag{6-70}$$

Here J ($<<$ 1) is the ratio of anode to cathode current as given by eq. 6-43. The importance of the radiative loss can be gauged when the operating point is determined so that $j_c V_c$ is available. This approach suggests how the effects of other losses should be included should they be judged important. For the 1 V, 1000 K case considered above, the ratio $\sigma\, T_c^4 \,/\, j_c V_c$ is of the order 0.05.

6.6. PLASMA DIODES

The discussion above showed that space-charge effects could be minimized to obtain good diode performance. Small spacing is useful to reduce these deleterious effects, but in practice, very small plate separation distances must be maintained, of the order 0.1 to 0.01 mm or less. For example, Webster (Ref. 6-10) shows that the peak power density varies as a function of emitter-collector gap, as shown in Fig. 6-14. Such small spacing presents significant manufacturing and operational difficulties, which include degradation due to surface evaporation. The introduction of an easily ionizable vapor into the diode will produce ions by *contact ionization* (see Fig. 6-15) and thereby reduce space-charge effects through reduction of the net electron density. Contact ionization occurs when the ionization potential is less than the work function of the emitter, which increases the probability that the valence electron fall into the conduction band of the conductor. The principal substances of interest for this purpose are the alkali metals. Of these, cesium has the lowest ionization potential in the periodic table, a value of 3.89 eV. A material such as tungsten makes a suitable emitter because of the low work function and the ability to operate at high temperature.

Introduction of the cesium into the interelectrode space thus reduces the space charge at the emitter face where ions are created, which reduces the net space-charge density. This lowers the effective potential barrier the emitted electrons face on their way to the collector. Considerably larger currents and therefore power densities are achievable in contrast to the vacuum diode.

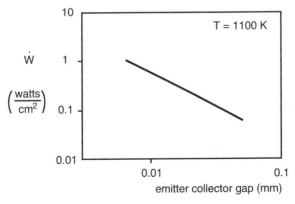

FIGURE 6-14. Effect of gap spacing on power from an energy converter diode. From Ref. 6-10.

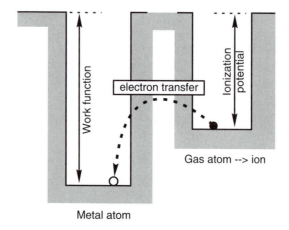

Metal atom

FIGURE 6-15. Contact ionization is the transfer of
an electron from a gaseous element of low ionzation
potential to a solid with a large work function.

The presence of the cesium in the space also serves to help matters at the
collector where the alkali can coat the surface. A high coverage level at low
temperature reduces the work function of tungsten from 4.52 to 1.69 eV. This
increases the output voltage (ϕ_c - ϕ_a, through a smaller ϕ_a), which again
increases power output. The physics of these effects is well described in Refs.
6-10 and 6-11, based on the pioneering work of Langmuir (Ref. 6-12).

6.7. TECHNOLOGY

Thermionic energy conversion is in development for two principal areas of
application: space power generation (Refs. 6-13 and 6-14) and terrestrial
power generation (Ref. 6-15). The power density of practical systems is on
the order 10-50 kW/m^2 or 1-5 W/cm^2. Successful operation for periods of well
over a year have been demonstrated.

In space power systems, the high reliability of such systems related to the
lack of moving parts and the requirements for high "cold"-side temperature
(to minimize radiator area) has brought thermionics close to practice. Such
power systems are well suited for use with nuclear heat sources, and so-called
in-core and *out-of-core* designs have been proposed and developed. Such systems have demonstrated achievement of 12 to 15% thermal efficiency operating between temperatures of 900 and 1750 K, with an additional 10
percentage points thought to be achievable. The successful implementation of
this technology continues to require a significant development of heat pipe
technology to carry heat to and away from the cell.

In terrestrial power generation applications, the use of thermionics is envis-
aged as a topping element because of the high input and rejection temperatures. The critical element in the successful application of this technology
requires protection of the materials that make the thermionics possible from

exposure to high-temperature oxygen or combustion products. To that end, significant progress has been made over the past few decades.

PROBLEMS

1. Obtain an expression for the thrust force experienced by the cathode per unit area as the current j is emitted by calculating the momentum of the electrons leaving the surface.

2. Show that for a space-charge-limited current, the product of current j_0 and barrier voltage is a minimum near the maximum voltage.

BIBLIOGRAPHY

Angrist, S. W., *Direct Energy Conversion*, Allyn & Bacon, 1971.

Kaye, J. and Welsh, J. A., Eds., *Direct Conversion of Heat to Electricity*, John Wiley & Sons, New York, 1960.

Angelo, J. A. and Buden, D., *Space Nuclear Power*, Orbit Book Company, Malabar, Florida, 1985.

REFERENCES

6-1.   Levine, S. N., *Selected Papers on New Techniques for Energy Conversion*, Dover Publishing, New York, 1961.

6-2.   Fermi, E., "Wave Mechanics of Collision", *Zs. Phys.*, 40 (5), 399, 1926.

6-3.   Dirac, P. A. M., "Theory of Quantum Mechanics," *Roy. Soc. Proc. (London)*, **112**, 661, 1926

6-4.   Hatsopoulos, G. N. and Kaye, J., "Analysis and Experimental Results of a Diode Configuration of a Novel Thermoelectron Engine," *Proceedings of the IRE* **46** (9), Sept. 1958.

6-5.   Hatsopoulos, G. N. and Gyftopoulos, E. P., *Thermionic Energy Conversion - Vol. I: Processes and Devices*, MIT Press, Cambridge, Mass., 1973.

6-6.   Kettani, M. A., *Direct Energy Conversion*, Addison Wesley Publishing Co., Reading, Mass. 1970.

6-7.   Culp, A. W., *Principles of Energy Conversion*, McGraw-Hill, New York, 1979.

6-8.   Houston, J. M. "Theoretical performance of the thermionic energy converter," *J. Appl. Phys.* **30** (4), April 1959.

6-9.   Wilson, V. C., "Conversion of Heat to Electricity by Thermionic Emission," *J. Appl. Phys.* **30** (4), 475, April 1959.

6-10. Webster, H. F., "Calculation of the Performance of a High Vacuum Thermionic Energy Converter," *J. Appl. Phys.* **30** (4), 488, April 1959.

6-11. Sutton, G. and Sherman, A., *Engineering Magnetohydrodynamics*, McGraw-Hill, New York, 1965.

6-12. Langmuir, I., *Phys. Rev.* **21**, 426, 1923.

6-13. Huffman, F., Reagan, P., Miskolczy, G., and Merrill, O., "Thermionic Technology Infrastructure for Space Power," IECEC 829316, 1982.

6-14. Kutznetsov, V. A., "The State and Direction of Thermionic Converter Research in the USSR," IECEC, 1976.

6-15. Huffman, F., "Overview of Terrestial Thermionics," IECEC 839027, 1983.

7

CHEMICAL ENERGY TO ELECTRICITY: ELECTROCHEMISTRY

Direct methods of producing electric power from chemical energy are available. In this chapter, the conversion of chemical energy in fuel cells as an alternative to combustion is discussed. The material leads naturally to a discussion of batteries, an important means of storing energy supplied as electrical power. Electrochemical systems may have a significant position in future energy systems because of the potentially attractive economics and their ability to use natural gas (methane) and (reformed) fuels from abundant sources such as coal.

7.1. GALVANIC EFFICIENCY IN ELECTROCHEMICAL REACTIONS

Chemical reactions that result in energy release are molecular rearrangements involving the electrons of the reacting atoms or molecules. By allowing the reaction to proceed in a particular way, it is possible to direct the "energy" change into an electric load. Thus the electrons involved can be made to fall into a potential well of the final configuration by traveling through the load, giving up their energy to it. A chemical reactor that allows this to happen is called a *reaction cell*. Such cells may operate in a steady-flow fashion, accepting reactants, discharging electric power, waste products, and, in some cases, heat. The Gibbs free energy, defined as (Section 4.2, Ref. 1-1):

$$g = h - Ts \qquad (7\text{-}1)$$

is useful in describing the state changes to be considered here. From the combination of the first and second laws of thermodynamics, one may write:

$$dg = v\, dp - s\, dT \qquad (7\text{-}2)$$

For an isobaric and isothermal process involving no chemical reaction, the Gibbs free energy change is zero. For a chemical reaction (with $dp = dT = 0$) the change in the Gibbs free energy is the work required to effect a state change associated with the chemical reconfiguration (see Section 5.7, Ref. 1-1, or Ref. 7-1). Equation 5-18 of Ref. 1-1 states that $-\Delta G$ is the useful work obtainable when the temperature and pressure are constant. This process may involve heat and work interactions between the system and its environment. For constant-pressure and -temperature processes, the chemical state energy change of a given mass (the system) may be written in terms of changes of previously utilized thermochemical properties (eq. 7-1), $\Delta G = \Delta H - T \Delta S$ or in terms of positive quantities

$$-\Delta G(= W' = \text{useful work}) = -\Delta H \text{ (heat evolving from reaction)}$$
$$+ T \Delta S \text{ (from environment)} \tag{7-3}$$

For the chemical reaction cell, eq. 7-3 shows that the magnitude of the change in Gibbs free energy ($-\Delta G$) available is the change in enthalpy ($-\Delta H$, see eq. 5-4, Ref.1-1) plus any heat transferred to the system ($T \Delta S$) from the environment to keep the temperature constant. The properties needed for the state change description are available from thermochemical tables, such as the JANAF tables discussed in Chapters 4 and 5 and Appendix C of Ref. 1-1 .

The ratio $\Delta G/\Delta H$ is a measure of *work* obtainable as a result of a constant p and T process relative to the *heat* available in the irreversible, constant p (isobaric) combustion process. This ratio is called the *ideal* or *Galvanic* efficiency:

$$\eta_{id} \equiv \frac{\Delta G}{\Delta H} \quad \text{in general,} = 1 - \frac{T \Delta S}{\Delta H} \quad \text{for constant } p, T \tag{7-4}$$

If heat is absorbed *from* the environment during the reaction, the galvanic efficiency can be greater than unity. For constant-pressure combustion processes $\Delta G = 0$ and the integral $\int T \, ds$ (not $T \Delta S$) represents the heat transferred between the system and its environment, ΔH. The reader may wish to consult the discussion in Section 5.3 of Ref. 1-1. Evidently, the Galvanic efficiency for the combustion process is zero. It is important to note that the process of harnassing the chemical energy from combustion and obtaining mechanical work could also be very high, *if* a reversible cycle operating at the resulting temperature could be devised. In reality (i.e., for a practical energy conversion device), neither the heat engine nor the electrochemical cell can be operated at their highest efficiencies, albeit for different reasons.

7.2. CELLS

A number of reactant combinations are suitable for the construction of cells whose primary purpose is to store electrical energy, while others are suited for the steady production of electrical power. Cells for the irreversible conversion of fuels or reactants to power are called *primary batteries* or, more commonly, *fuel cells* or *unrechargeable batteries* (dry cell). Fuels cells operate as steady-flow devices. *Secondary batteries* involve reactants packaged in a closed container that undergo a reversible conversion to electrical power. The lead–acid battery is a commonplace example of a secondary battery.

An early, historically important, electrochemical cell is the Daniell cell (1836). Figure 7-1 illustrates the important components of such a cell. They are:

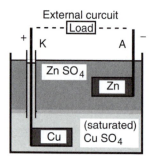

Figure 7-1. The Daniell cell as an example of a migrating ion cell.

1. The container and the *electrolyte* (which may be either a liquid or a solid) containing ions, in this case, a solution of doubly negative sulfate (SO_4^{2-}) ions,

2. *Two electrodes*, one anode (*A*, negative), which *accepts* electrons from the electrolyte and a cathode (*C*, positive), which *emits* negative ions into the electrolyte. (A more general definition of the cathode involves emission of a <u>net</u> flux of negative charges. Thus positive charges moving into the electrode make it a cathode.) In secondary batteries electrodes are typically consumed while they act as catalysts in primary cells.

3. The *external circuit* (not shown), which allows electrons to flow *from the anode to the cathode* through a load. A positive current flows in the opposite direction, that is, from + to -.

The electrolyte in the Daniell cell consists of a saturated $CuSO_4$ solution in water in the lower portion of the cell overlaid with a lower density $ZnSO_4$ solution. A simpler electrolyte consists of a single chemical in solution. The SO_4^{2-} ions are free to migrate in response to electric fields and concentration gradients (i.e., diffusion) and thus serve to transport charges across the cell.

In any cell, the transport of ions across the electrolyte completes the circuit. The ability of the ions to migrate across the cell in response to the electric field as well as the electrode surface reaction rates determine the rate of current flow through the cell to the load. The internal resistance of the cell is thus controlled by the ion transport and is considered in Section 7.4.4.

7.3. CHEMICAL REACTIONS

In the discharge of the Daniell cell a sulfate ion (from the cathode) is made available at the anode because it can cross the solution boundary (the sulfates are on both sides). Thus the reactions at the electrodes are, at the anode:

$$\text{at the anode } SO_4^{2-} + Zn \rightarrow [ZnSO_4]_{aq} + 2\,e^- \qquad (7\text{-}5)$$

Here the $[Zn\,SO_4]_{aq}$ is in actuality an association of Zn^{2+} and SO_4^{2-} in the solution as (Zn^{2+} and SO_4^{2-}). A possibly better way to state eq. 7-5 is as, for the anode:

$$Zn \rightarrow Zn^{2+} + 2\,e^-$$

The anode is therefore consumed while two electrons are liberated to it. At the cathode, the external circuit provides two electrons, which are returned to the electrolyte as a sulfate ion. This requires the formation of a neutral copper atom at the cathode. Again, the $CuSO_4$ may be thought of as (Cu^{2+}, SO_4^{2-}). Thus, at the cathode:

$$2\ e^- + [CuSO_4]_{aq} \rightarrow Cu + SO_4^{2-}$$

or

$$2\ e^- + Cu^{2+} \rightarrow Cu \qquad (7\text{-}6)$$

The sulfate ions are conserved, and electrons do their work in the external circuit and are conserved as well. Ions that flow *toward* the anode are referred to as *anions*, while those flowing toward the cathode are *cations*. Zinc is consumed while copper is deposited on the cathode from the electrolyte. The net cell reaction is

$$Zn + [CuSO_4]_{aq} \rightarrow Cu + [ZnSO_4]_{aq}$$

or

$$Zn + Cu^{2+} \rightarrow Cu + Zn^{2+} \qquad (7\text{-}7)$$

The choice of cell chemicals determines parameters such as energy density and physical properties. Some examples of representative cell reactants are discussed in Section 7.4.1 in connection with cell capacity.

For fuel cells, the principal reactants of interest are the relatively simple combinations of hydrogen and carbon together with an oxidizer. A number of example reactions are listed in Table 7–1 together with their thermochemical characteristics at 298 K. The Galvanic efficiency, η_{id}, is determined from its definition, eq. 7-4.

Table 7–1. Reaction thermochemical data for fuel cell reactions; the first column is the net number of gaseous moles produced (+) or absorbed (-); data of this type are often given in eV: 1 eV = 22.9 kcal/mole, see Ref. 7-2, from which some of these data are taken with permission.

Reaction	ΔH (cal/mole)		ΔS (cal/ mole K)	ΔG (kcal/mole)	η_{id}
$H_2 + 0.5\ O_2 \rightarrow H_2O$ (l)	(-1.5)	-68.14	-39	-56.7	0.83
$H_2 + 0.5\ O_2 \rightarrow H_2O$ (g)	(-0.5)	-57.84	-10.6	-54.6	0.94
$C + 0.5\ O_2 \rightarrow CO$ (g)	(+0.5)	-26.4	21.4	-32.8	1.24
$C + O_2 \rightarrow CO_2$ (g)	(0)	-94.05	0.7	-94.3	1.00
$CO + 0.5\ O_2 \rightarrow CO_2$ (g)	(-0.5)	-67.62	-20.7	-61.4	0.91
$CH_4 + 2O_2 \rightarrow CO_2 + 2\ H_2O$	(-2)	-212.2		-195.0	0.92
$CH_3OH + 1.5\ O_2 \rightarrow CO_2 + 2\ H_2O$	(-0.5)	-173.2		-167.3	0.97
$C_2H_6 + 3.5\ O_2 \rightarrow 2\ CO_2 + 3\ H_2O$	(-2.5)	-372		-349	0.94
$C_2H_5OH + 3\ O_2 \rightarrow 2\ CO_2 + 3\ H_2O$	(-1)	-325		-314	0.97
$NH_3 + 0.75\ O_2 \rightarrow 0.5\ N_2 + 1.5\ H_2O$	(-1.25)	-91.1		-80.5	0.88

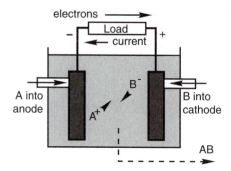

FIGURE 7-2. Production of current through formation of product *AB* in a chemical cell.

Note that the net production of gaseous moles (first column in parentheses in Table 7–1) correlates with the sign and magnitude of ΔS. ($T\,\Delta S = \Delta U$ (~0 for an isothermal process) + $p\,\Delta V$). With galvanic efficiency as a yardstick, it is apparent that the conversion efficiency of chemical to electrical energy is potentially high, and not encumbered by the Carnot limitation imposed on heat engine performance.

7.4. ELEMENTARY CELL PERFORMANCE

Most fundamentally, electrochemical cells are limited by the ability to transfer the ion current through the electrolyte. Other current-limiting factors may be present at the surface at the electrodes; see Section 7.5.3. This current requires a large surface area to be provided by the electrodes. In practice, porous solid spongelike metals are often used. The current limitation establishes the design of the cell configuration and the power density of the cell as a power producer. Larger cells tend to be better than smaller ones because of the favorable surface-to-volume ratio of a given geometry.

7.4.1. *Capacity*

A power production cell may be described as in Fig. 7-2, where reactants *A* and *B* in the form of solid electrodes combine to form the product *AB* in the electrolyte. The cathode reaction is

$$B + e^- \rightarrow B^-$$

while at the anode

$$A - e^- \rightarrow A^+$$

Here both A^+ and B^- ions migrate in the electrolyte. Much more commonly, one of the ions in a fuel cell is much more mobile than the other, and therefore travels to meet the other at the site where it is created. The first ion is therefore the cell's charge carrier. In the example given, a single electron is involved in the formation of a molecule of *AB*. In any cell reaction, the number of electrons that participate in the reaction for each atom of reactant involved is referred to as *n* or the valence change. For example, in the Daniell cell, this number is two. For a reaction involving a monovalent reactant, such as Ag^+ in the reaction

$$Ag^+ (NO_3)^- + e^- --> Ag + (NO_3)^-$$

the valence change *n* =1.

The current, measured in amperes (coulombs per second) determines the production or consumption rate of a solid electrode material. In practical terms, the ampere has been defined as the current flowing to deposit *exactly* 0.001118 g/sec of silver (Ag) from a $AgNO_3$ solution as in the reaction given above. Recently, a more precise standard has now been adopted, but that definition is not important for the purposes of this discussion. Thus, since the molecular mass of Ag is 107.87 g/g mole, one has that

$$\frac{107.87 \text{ g/mole}}{0.001118 \text{ g/sec/A}} = \frac{96493 \text{ coulombs}}{\text{g-mole}} = \frac{9.65 \times 10^7 \text{ C}}{\text{kg-mole}} \qquad (7\text{-}8)$$

are required in the silver (or any other monovalent reactant) depositing process. This unit is of wide utility and is called the faraday, *F*. For reactions of valence change *n*, the number of coulombs required is *nF*. Another way of saying this is that a faraday will deposit a mass equal to

$$\frac{\text{molecular mass}}{n} = \frac{MW}{n} = \text{kilogram equivalent} \qquad (7\text{-}9)$$

The faraday is often expressed in more practical units by converting units from coulombs/g mole to Ah/kg. For a substance with molecular mass *M*,

96,493 coulombs/g (= 1 g mole of electrons) = 26,804/*M* in A h/kg

$$(7\text{-}10)$$

Computing *nF*/(MW) = α, one obtains the so-called *capacity* (with units of Ah/kg), given in Table 7–2 for a number of substances of interest. As an example,

Table 7–2. Cell material capacities α ($C_6H_5NO_2$ is nitrobenzene)

Anode materials	Capacity (Ah/kg)	Cathode materials	Capacity (Ah/kg)
H_2	26,591	O_2	3,351
HC	11,440	$C_6H_5NO_2$	1870
Be	5900	F_2	1408
Li	3850	Cl_2	755
Zn	818	HgO	246
Pb^{2+}	257	Ag Cl	185
		Hg Cl	196

one may determine the mass of a cell using the following reaction

$$Zn + HgO \rightarrow ZnO + Hg \qquad (7-11)$$

for a capacity of, say, 1000 A h. The mass of Zn required is $1000/818 = 1.22$ kg and HgO is $1000/246 = 4.06$ kg for a total mass of 5.28 kg. The capacity of the cell as a whole is $1000/5.28 = 189$ A h/kg. Thus, denoting the capacity of the cell materials by α_A and α_C it follows that the total cell capacity is given by

$$\alpha_{cell} = \left(\frac{1}{\alpha_A} + \frac{1}{\alpha_C}\right)^{-1} \qquad (7-12)$$

7.4.2. *Ideal Cell Potential*

An important quantity interest is the *voltage* (or potential energy of the electrons) of the cell. The voltage is the energy per unit charge. Hence the maximum voltage obtainable (at open circuit) is obtained from the energy per mole of reactant released in the isobaric and isothermal process:

$$E^o = \frac{-\Delta G}{nF} \qquad (7-13)$$

since nF is the number of electron moles per mole reactant involved in the reaction. The symbol E for voltage is common in this field and ϕ will also be used in this chapter. A typical variation of ΔG with temperature is as sketched in Fig. 7-3. Table 7–3 shows the valence change n and the open circuit potential for the reactions listed in Table 7–1. The derivative in the last column follows from the temperature dependence of G and is discussed subsequently.

An operating cell connected to a resistive load has a linearly decreasing voltage with increasing current when the internal cell resistance (R_{int}) is constant. This description is generally valid between open circuit and the condi-

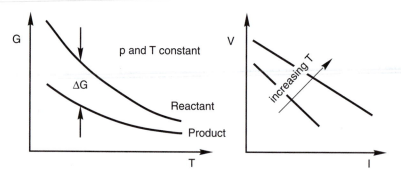

FIGURE 7-3. Typical variation of the Gibbs free energy for fixed pressure and specified temperature. Open circuit voltage decreases with increasing temperature in this example.

Table 7–3. For the reactions of Table 7–1, valence, cell potential, and, for some reactions, the sensitivity to temperature at 298 K; data in part from Ref. 7-2 with permission

Reaction			n	E^o (V)	d E^o/ d T (mV/K)
$H_2 + 0.5\ O_2$	$\rightarrow$	H_2O (l)	2	1.23	-0.85
$H_2 + 0.5\ O_2$	$\rightarrow$	H_2O (g)	2	1.19	-0.23
$C\ + 0.5\ O_2$	$\rightarrow$	CO (g)	2	0.71	+0.47
$C\ +\ O_2$	$\rightarrow$	CO_2 (g)	4	1.02	+0.01
$CO\ + 0.5\ O_2$	$\rightarrow$	CO_2 (g)	2	1.33	-0.45
$CH_4 + 2O_2$	$\rightarrow CO_2 + 2\ H_2O$		8	1.06	
$CH_3OH + 1.5\ O_2$	$\rightarrow CO_2 + 2\ H_2O$		6	1.21	
$C_2H_6 + 3.5\ O_2$	$\rightarrow 2\ CO_2 + 3\ H_2O$		14	1.09	
$C_2H_5OH + 3\ O_2$	$\rightarrow 2\ CO_2 + 3\ H_2O$		12	1.14	
$NH_3 + 0.75\ O_2$	$\rightarrow .5\ N_2 + 1.5\ H_2O$		3	1.17	

tion for maximum power. The product of $(E^o)^2/R_{int}$ is a measure of the power that can be extracted from the cell. By decreasing the load resistance from an infinite value at open circuit, the voltage decreases and the power of a simple cell wherein only ohmic resistance is important increases until the power output maximum value of $(E^o)^2/ 4R_{int}$ is reached. The reasons are identical to those articulated in connection with eq. 9-26 for a thermoelectric generator and eq. 4-15 (Section 4.1.4) for an MHD generator. Note that a given cell operated at various load conditions may or may not operate at constant temperature because the mechanisms that dissipate the Joule heat in the cell may be temperature dependent.

7.4.3. *Temperature Effects on Cell Performance*

At lower temperatures, the mobility of the ions through the cell is hindered by the reduced molecular agitation. This increases the cell internal resistance at lower temperature. The open circuit voltage is also affected by temperature because this quantity is proportional to the temperature-dependent Gibbs free energy. Consider, for example, the variation of reaction potential shown in Fig. 7-3, which increases characteristically with decreasing temperature. From this, one can calculate

$$\left(\frac{\partial E^o}{\partial T}\right)_p = -\frac{1}{nF}\left(\frac{\partial \Delta G}{\partial T}\right)_p \tag{7-14}$$

The result of such a determination for a number of formation reactions is shown in Table 7–3. The design choice for cell temperature is determined by maximizing the cell power $(E^\circ)^2/R_{int}$ subject to practical material limitations. The load condition resistance, which gives, for example, the current for maximum power, is related to the cell resistance at the chosen temperature. Figure 7-3 summarizes the effects of operation at varying temperature.

7.4.4. Cell Internal Resistance

The conductivity of electrolytes (σ) and the cell geometry are the primary parameters that establish the internal resistance of a cell. The geometric details may be important, but for modeling purposes, the cell configuration can often be reduced to a rectangular box of dimensions as given in Fig. 2-3 for the MHD generator. For such a geometry the resistance to current flow is related to the conductivity as given by eq. 2-12. The geometrical factor, with dimensions of length, is the grouping of terms Lh/d, where d is the length in the direction of current flow and the others are normal to it.

To put the magnitude of the conductivity of electrolytes in perspective, it is important to note that the value of ultrapure water was determined by Kohlrausch (Ref. 7-3) as 4.3×10^{-6} mhos/m at 18°C, whereas ordinary distilled water in CO_2 equilibrium with air is about $\sim 70 \times 10^{-6}$ mhos/m. Thus pure water will be seen to be relatively poor as an ionic conductor. The conductivity of aqueous electrolytes such as HCl and NaOH are given by (Ref. 7-3)

$$\sigma = c_{eq} \Lambda = c_{eq}\left(\Lambda_0 + k_c \sqrt{c_{eq}}\right) \tag{7-15}$$

where c_{eq} is the concentration of the ion provider in the water in equivalents (see eq. 7-9 for the definition of equivalents) per cm^3 or per liter, where 1 equivalent/liter = 0.001 equiv./cm^3. For example, the concentration c of a 1 molar solution of Na_2SO_4 (valence = 2) is 2 equivalents per liter. In spite of attempting to adhere to the strict use of SI units, it is sometimes better (here, for example) and conventional (in the field of physical chemistry) to describe quantities in terms of the smaller centimeters, in which the device dimensions under consideration are more likely to be measured. Thus we adopt this length unit here.

In eq. 7-15, Λ is the equivalent conductivity (mhos cm^2 equiv^{-1}) and Λ_0 is the same quantity at infinite dilution ($c_{eq} = 0$). Λ decreases with increasing c, as shown in Fig. 7-4, but the physical conductivity σ increases with increasing concentration of the electrolyte. The constant k_c is an empirically determined constant whose magnitude may be deduced from Fig. 7-4.

The physical conductivity as determined by eq. 7-15 is shown in Fig. 7-5. Note that the magnitude of σ for gases and ionic liquids are of the same order. When salts, rather than acids or bases, are used, the conductivity is lower; hence these are of relatively smaller interest as aqueous electrolytes in fuel cells.

In an ionized solution, both the positive and the negative charge carriers conduct charge currents. Unlike in the gaseous plasma, their relative contributions are of the same order since the mechanism for the transport of these

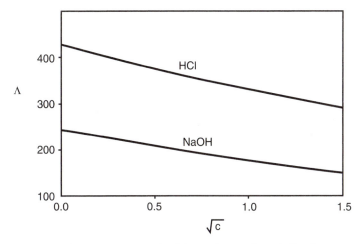

FIGURE 7-4. Equivalent conductivity (mhos cm^2 equiv^{-1}) of aqueous electrolyte solutions: hydrochloric acid and sodium hydroxide at 25°C. The units of c are equivalents per liter. Adapted from Ref. 7-3.

charges is similar. For weak electrolytes, the contributions of the two types of charge carriers to the conductivity are additive according to Kohlrausch's *law of the independent migration of ions* (Ref. 7-3). Thus

$$\Lambda_0 = \lambda_0^+ + \lambda_0^- \tag{7-16}$$

where the λ_0s are the *equivalent ionic conductivities*. The values of these ionic contributions are given in Table 7-4. Note the correspondence of the values given with that for the electrolytes, for which Λ is given in Fig. 7-4. Note also that whatever electrolyte is used must be dissociated at the conditions where used. This is an issue for water, which would appear, according to the data, to be a good electrolyte but is not, in fact.

7.4.5. *Energy Density of Batteries*

The energy density of a cell is proportional to the capacity. In practice, this density is difficult to predict analytically; nevertheless Table 7–5 gives a measure of what is achievable in practice and/or what is thought to be possible. Because such numbers are subject to change due to the development of technology, the reader is encouraged to consult recent literature.

Note that the heating value of a hydrocarbon fuel is of the order 40 MJ/kg, and a direct comparison of this value with the numbers in column 3 of Table 7–5 is not appropriate because the mass of the engine to convert the fuel heat energy to work should be included in a meaningful accounting. Including the engine mass reduces the effective value of fuel energy density to perhaps 10–20 MJ/kg, depending on the mission.

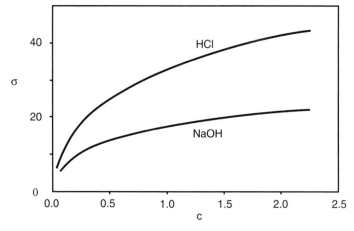

FIGURE 7-5. Physical conductivity (mhos/m, SI units) of aqueous electrolyte solutions: hydrochloric acid and sodium hydroxide at 25°C. The units of c are equivalents per liter. Adapted from Ref. 7-3.

Table 7–4. Equivalent ionic conductivities (mhos cm^2 equiv^{-1}) for a number of ions at 25°C; from Ref. 7-3

Ion	λ_0	Ion	λ_0
H$^+$	349.82	OH$^-$	198.0
Na$^+$	50.11	Cl$^-$	76.34
K$^+$	73.52	$\frac{1}{2}$ SO$_4^{2-}$	79.8
Ag$^+$	61.92		
$\frac{1}{2}$ Ca^{2+}	59.50		

Table 7–5. Practical primary cell energy densities of cells available and under development (1 MJ ~ 277.8 W h)

Reactants	Energy density	
	W h/kg	MJ/kg
Pb–H$_2$SO$_4$	30 – 60	0.1–0.2
Ag–Zn	200	0.6
Ni–Fe (KOH)	45	0.16
Li–F	6000	22
Al–O$_2$	3000	11
Mg–S	1700	6
Na–S	800 – 1500	3–6

7.4.6. *Lead Acid Battery*

By far the most common, well-developed, and successful battery is the lead–acid cell. It is used in many applications ranging from energy storage for starting automotive vehicles (SLI batteries: starting, lighting, ignition) to running industrial vehicles in limited range service and standby power. SLI batteries are commonly constructed in (12 V) sizes ranging from a few to several hundred watt hours capacity. The energy density of lead–acid batteries ranges between 30 and 40 W h/kg and the specific gravity of complete cells is on the order of 2. Industrial batteries have similar characteristics except that they may be larger in capacity and are used to a deeper discharge state (near 80% of capacity is used). Generally, the useful number of charge–discharge cycles exceeds 1000 for a high-performance lead–acid battery.

The lead–acid cell electrodes are porous lead at the negative electrode and PbO_2 at the positive electrode. Dilute sulfuric acid is the electrolyte that varies in specific gravity between 1.3, fully charged, and 1.1 discharged. The discharge and charging reactions are generally given as shown in the following.

At the Positive Electrode

$$PbO_2 \text{ (s)} + 4\,H^+_{aq} + SO_4^{2-} + 2\,e^- \quad \underset{\underset{\xleftarrow{\text{charge}}}{}}{\xrightarrow{\text{discharge}}} \quad 2\,PbSO_4 \text{ (s)} + 2\,H_2O \text{ (l)} \tag{7-17}$$

although the left side is more realistically described by involvement of the bisulfate ion

$$PbO_2 \text{ (s)} + 3\,H^+_{aq} + HSO_4^- + 2\,e^- \; \longleftrightarrow \tag{7-17a}$$

because of the relatively low acid concentration used in practice. Typically the rate-limiting reaction at discharge is the formation of a surface reactant that can produce the water:

$$PbO_2\,(H_2^+) \text{ (surface)} + e^- \longrightarrow Pb\,(OH)_2^+ \text{ (surface)} \tag{7-18}$$

At the Negative Electrode

$$Pb \text{ (s)} + \left(SO_4^{2-}\right)_{aq} \quad \underset{\underset{\xleftarrow{\text{charge}}}{}}{\xrightarrow{\text{discharge}}} \quad PbSO_4 \text{ (s)} + 2\,e^- \tag{7-19}$$

or, more realistically, the complement to eq. 7-17a is

$$Pb \text{ (s)} + \left(HSO_4^-\right)_{aq} \quad \underset{\underset{\xleftarrow{\text{charge}}}{}}{\xrightarrow{\text{discharge}}} \quad PbSO_4 \text{ (s)} + H^+_{aq} + 2\,e^- \tag{7-19a}$$

The *overall reaction* is

$$Pb\ (s)\ +\ PbO_2\ (s)\ +\ 2\,(H_2SO_4)_{aq}\ \underset{\underset{\longleftarrow}{charge}}{\overset{\overset{discharge}{\longrightarrow}}{}}\ 2\,PbSO_4\ (s)\ +\ 2\,H_2O\ (l) \tag{7-20}$$

The lead–acid cell is subject to *self-discharge* according to the reactions

$$PbO_2\ (s)\ +\ H_{aq}^+\ +\ (HSO_4^-)_{aq}\ \longrightarrow\ PbSO_4\ (s)\ +\ H_2O\ (l)\ +\tfrac{1}{2}\,O_2\ (g) \tag{7-21}$$

$$Pb\ (s)\ +\ H_{aq}^+\ +\ (HSO_4^-)_{aq}\ \longrightarrow\ PbSO_4\ (s)\ +\ H_2\ (g) \tag{7-22}$$

where the gases may evolve. These reactions are temperature dependent and catalyzed by impurities.

Operational Capacity

The ideal capacity of a cell or battery is obtained from consideration of the chemical energy content in the battery. This capacity decreases with increasing power or current demand in a manner that is modelable as an exponential decrease of capacity with current draw, or its inverse, the time to decrease the capacity to a small value. The characteristic exponential decrease parameter depends on the design of the cell (Ref. 7-4) and can be used for system modeling purposes. Furthermore, the peak power demand that might be placed on a battery system depends on the depth of discharge (dod). Typically, the peak power available decreases from a value at 10% dod to about 0.8 and 0.65 of that value at dod's of 50 and 75%, respectively. These values are dependent on the kind of chemical system under consideration and its physical design (Ref. 7-5).

7.5. FUEL CELLS AS ENERGY CONVERTERS

Fuel cells are steady-flow devices that accept fuel and oxidizer and therewith produce the reaction products as well as direct current (DC) electric power. A typical system of components is as shown in Fig. 7-6: fuel processing to reduce the molecular weight and remove reaction-inhibiting compounds, the cell, and the electrical conversion to the more useful and standard alternating current (AC).

Some of the advantages of fuel cell systems, as cited in the literature, are:

1. High efficiency: no Carnot limitation; within the limits of capacity, efficiency is insensitive to fuel feed rate: high part power efficiency;

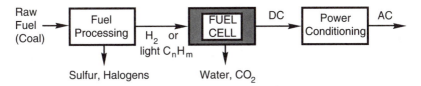

FIGURE 7-6. Fuel cell power system. The power conditioning includes inversion to AC power.

2. Performance is insensitive to plant scale, which means that plants can be built incrementally, which, in turn, implies reduced cost of capital investment required during construction;

3. Responsive to load by means of change in fuel feed rate;

4. Modular siting — can be located near users for waste heat utilization;

5. Modular construction in factory setting — avoids quality control problems associated with field assembly;

6. Low noise emissions; and

7. Low emissions of chemical pollutants.

Some of the possible design issues are:

1. Low cell voltage (0.6 – 0.85 V): a significant number of cell connected in series must be used; this may have implications for the reliability of the system;

2. Makeup water is required if cell temperature exceeds about 35°C (95°F);

3. Fuel reformation may be required since reactions are most practical with low-molecular-weight fuels;

4. Halogens and sulfur must be removed from fuel; and

5. Electrode life may be a concern, although very long life has been demonstrated.

The best operating temperature is derived from a balance between electrode corrosion at high temperature and low ion conductivity (mobility) at low temperature. Candidate fuel cell plants currently are envisioned to be operated at 150–200°C with phosphoric acid or 600–700°C with molten carbonates (Na_2CO_3, K_2CO_3, or Li_2CO_2)(Ref. 7-6).

7.5.1. *The Hydrogen-Oxygen Cell*

A typical fuel cell is illustrated schematically in Fig. 7-7. Shown is an input of H_2 on the left of a porous metal anode and of O_2 on the right side of a cathode. The electrolyte may be basic (such as KOH in this example), or it may be acidic. For the acidic electrolyte case, the reactions below are in square brackets.

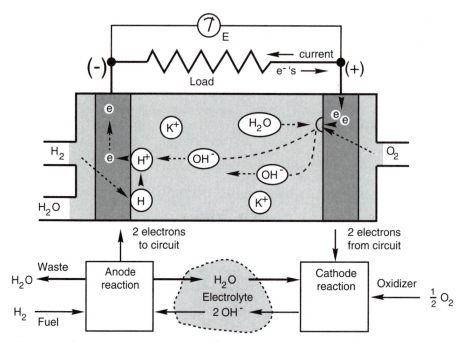

FIGURE 7-7. Hydrogen-oxygen fuel cell connected to a load showing the generation of the hydroxyl ion from oxygen reduction at the cathode and the water generation from hydrogen oxidation by the OH ion at the anode. For an acid cell, the water is produced at the cathode. The positive ion in the electrolyte is not involved in the process of charge transfer.

The reactions at the anode are:

1. Dissociative adsorption of hydrogen;
2. Reaction of adsorbed hydrogen with OH⁻ from solution to make water; the minus charge of the hydroxide ion then appears as an electron in the metal (m), or, in the acid cell, H⁺ ion generation from the adsorbed H.

Anode

$$H_2 \longrightarrow 2\,H_{ads} \tag{7-23}$$

$$\text{basic: } H_{ads} + OH^-_{aq} \longrightarrow H_2O + e^-_m \tag{7-24}$$

$$[\text{acid: } H_{ads} \longrightarrow H^+_{aq} + e^-_m] \tag{7-24a}$$

where the subscript ads indicates an adsorbed species, aq indicates aqueous species, and m signifies that the electron is in the metal. Suitable metals to carry out this task include platinum, palladium, and nickel.

The reactions at the cathode are:

3. Dissociative adsorption of oxygen;
4. Hydroxide ion formation by dissociation of electrolyte (water), or, in the acid cell, water formation with the H^+ ions and the adsorbed O.

Cathode

$$O_2 \longrightarrow 2 O_{ads} \tag{7-25}$$

$$\text{basic: } O_{ads} + H_2O + 2 e^-_m \longrightarrow 2 OH^-_{aq} \tag{7-26}$$

$$[\text{acid: } O_{ads} + 2H^+_{aq} + 2 e^-_m \longrightarrow H_2O] \tag{7-26a}$$

Cathode materials used in practice include gold, silver, nickel, and platinum which resist oxidation by the atomic oxygen. Note that the doubly negative O^{2-} radical is not involved in the $H_2–O_2$ reaction because it is not stable in the presence of water. The entire sequence of reactions 7-23 through 7-26 must occur in order to realize energy from the fuel cell. In fact, the anode reactions (eqs. 7-23 and 7-24) must occur twice as often as those of the cathode (eqs. 7-25 and 7-26) in order to balance the production and consumption of electrons. The overall reaction in the fuel cell is

$$H_2 + \tfrac{1}{2} O_2 \longrightarrow H_2O \tag{7-27}$$

in which two electrons travel through the wire for every molecule of water formed. The fuel cell converts the free energy of this reaction ΔG to electrical energy according to eq. 7-13, where n is the number of electrons transferred (two), F is Faraday's constant, and E is the potential difference between cathode and anode when the cell is in thermodynamic equilibrium. In other words, molecular hydrogen and oxygen represent stored chemical energy, which the fuel cell converts to electrical energy.

How does the fuel cell accomplish this task? Using the example of an alkaline fuel cell, one may examine the cathode first. The cathode, usually a metal like platinum, facilitates dissociate adsorption of oxygen through reaction (eq. 7-25). (This is an example of catalytic behavior; electrodes that function also as catalysts, as do both cathode and anode in a fuel cell, are called *electrocatalysts*.) Adsorbed oxygen then reacts with water to form hydroxide ions, withdrawing two electrons from the cathode (and thereby allowing electrical work) in the process. The ability of the water to react with adsorbed, atomic oxygen through reaction 7-26 again depends on the catalytic properties of the cathode. This reaction creates a local excess of hydroxide ions, however, which can only be removed by diffusion of hydroxide ions to the anode. There, reaction with adsorbed, atomic hydrogen removes the excess hydroxide ions to form water along with an electron in the anode, according to reaction given by eq. 7-24. The adsorbed hydrogen is present on the anode by virtue of its catalytic ability towards reaction (eq. 7-23).

Summarizing this process, one can say that the fuel cell converts chemical to electrical energy by a combination of "pushing and pulling" at its two electrodes. Oxygen reduction at the cathode "pushes" hydroxide ions to the anode, while at the same time "pulling" electrons through the wire, whereas hydrogen oxidation at the anode "pulls" hydroxide ions through solution and "pushes" electrons through the wire. It is clear that both processes must occur, simultaneously and in balance, in order for the fuel cell to function. Figure 7-7 summarizes the process in a cell from which current is drawn.

In a pragmatic sense, one need not care how pushing and pulling ions through solution generates electricity. When a fuel cell is used to drive an electrical load, one desires only that a certain *potential* difference exist between the positive and negative terminals of the fuel cell, and that this potential difference not decrease appreciably when a load is placed on the cell. Thus one seeks the same performance of a fuel cell as one would from a battery.

7.5.2. Chemical and Electrochemical Potentials

Systems with chemical reactions are not simple in the sense that properties of components depend not only on specification of independent state variables such as T and p, but on the composition as well. Thus state changes of a two-component (1 and 2) system will involve, for example,

$$dH = \left(\frac{\partial H}{\partial p}\right)_{S, n_1, n_2} dp + \left(\frac{\partial H}{\partial S}\right)_{p, n_1, n_2} dS + \left(\frac{\partial H}{\partial n_1}\right)_{S, p, n_2} dn_1 + \left(\frac{\partial H}{\partial n_2}\right)_{S, p, n_1} dn_2$$

(7-28)

where n_i is the number of moles of species i. Note that here H, S, and n are extensive. The first two derivatives may be evaluated at constant composition as (eq. 7-2):

$$\left(\frac{\partial H}{\partial p}\right)_{S, n_1, n_2} = V \quad \text{and} \quad \left(\frac{\partial H}{\partial S}\right)_{p, n_1, n_2} = T$$

(7-29)

while the last two are the *chemical potentials* defined as

$$(\mu_1)_{S, p} \equiv \left(\frac{\partial H}{\partial n_1}\right)_{S, p, n_2} \quad \text{and} \quad (\mu_2)_{S, p} \equiv \left(\frac{\partial H}{\partial n_2}\right)_{S, p, n_1}$$

(7-30)

Thus

$$dH = V \, dp + T \, dS + (\mu_1)_{S, p} \, dn_1 + (\mu_2)_{S, p} \, dn_2$$

(7-31)

A similar statement may be derived for a change in the Gibbs free energy:

$$dG = V\,dp \ - \ S\,dT \ + \ (\mu_1)_{T,p}\,dn_1 \ + \ (\mu_2)_{T,p}\,dn_2 \qquad (7\text{-}32)$$

The chemical potentials $[(\mu_1)_{T,p}$ and $(\mu_1)_{S,p}$, for example] in eqs. 7-31 and 7-32 may be shown to be identical by the following argument. From the definitions of H and G, it may be shown that (Section 4.2, Ref. 1-1, or Ref. 7-6)

$$dG + S\,dT - V\,dp \ = \ dH \ - \ T\,dS \ - \ V\,dp \qquad (7\text{-}33)$$

From these last three equations, it follows

$$(\mu_i)_{T,p} \ = \ (\mu_i)_{S,p} \ \text{and furthermore} = (\mu_i)_{T,V} \ = \ \mu_i \qquad (7\text{-}34)$$

where the T,V case is connected with the Helmholtz free energy. In other words, the chemical potential is independent of the state variables held constant.

From eq. 7-32, it also follows that minimizing the Gibbs free energy ($dG = 0$) to find an equilibrium state (with specified T and p) requires

$$\sum_{i=1}^{N} \mu_i\,dn_i \ = 0 \qquad (7\text{-}35)$$

for N components. Since dn_1 is arbitrary, this equation gives a relation between μ_1 and μ_2 for the two-component case. dn_1 is a negative multiple of dn_2 according to the stoichiometry. This statement is equivalent to the statement embodied as the law of mass action (Chapter 5, Ref. 1-1).

In the case of reactions with charged reactants, the *electrochemical potential* comes into play because of the energy involved in the creation of the electrostatic field associated with the charged reactants in a given phase (solid electrode or liquid electrolyte). This electrochemical potential is defined as the work required to transfer 1 mole of species i into a phase from an infinitely dilute gaseous state, infinitely far away. It is the free energy change associated with such a transfer process. For a specific phase, this potential is given by (Ref. 7-7)

$$\bar{\mu}_i \ = \ \mu_i \ + \ (n_i\,e)\,F\,\phi_i \qquad (7\text{-}36)$$

Here μ_i is the chemical potential, $\bar{\mu}_i$ is the electrochemical potential, and ϕ_i is the electrostatic potential in the phase considered. $(n_i e)$ is the charge transferred per mole of reactant. Thus when a charged particle can move between two phases in contact, $\bar{\mu}_i$ must be the same for both. The chemical and electrochemical potentials of uncharged species are identical.

7.5.3. *Half-Cell Potential*

How does the fuel cell obtain its potential difference? Again, the cathode is examined first. Combining reactions 7-25 and 7-26 and assuming reversibility, one may write eq. 7-35 as

$$O_2 + 2\ H_2O + 4\ e^-_m \longleftrightarrow 4\ OH^-_{aq} \tag{7-37}$$

This *equilibrium* reaction may be expressed in mathematical (and thermodynamic) terms according to eq. 7-36 as

$$\mu_{O_2} + 2\ \mu_{H_2O} + 4\ \bar{\mu}_{e^-_m} = 4\ \bar{\mu}_{OH^-} \tag{7-38}$$

It shows the relationship among the processes undergone by the reactants and products, namely, that a given (electro-)chemical potential of oxygen, water, and hydroxide ion determines the electrochemical potential of the electron in the (solid phase of the) cathode. The chemical potential of oxygen is controlled by its concentration (i.e., pressure), that of water is a constant, and the electrochemical potential of hydroxide ion is controlled by the *pH* of the electrolyte. These quantities determine the electrochemical potential of the electron in the cathode, or in equivalent terms, the Fermi level of the cathode.

Because eq. 7-37 represents a half-cell reaction (an electrochemical reaction written for just one electrode), we must exercise some caution in its interpretation. Equation 7-38 suggests that one can know the absolute position of the Fermi level of the cathode, but, of course, this is impossible because energy is not an absolute quantity. The position of the Fermi level may be known against a suitably chosen reference, and a number of possibilities exist, but the values of those references are a subject of current research (and controversy) and beyond the scope of this book. Fortunately, when one combines the description of cathode and anode reactions to make a complete electrochemical cell, the choice of reference cancels out. The important point here is to see that the potential of the cathode is determined by the reaction occurring at its surface and how the reactants and products are controlled by externally adjustable parameters.

One may develop a similar discussion of the anode. The overall reaction at the anode is

$$H_2 + 2\ OH^-_{aq} \longleftrightarrow 2\ H_2O + 2\ e^-_m \tag{7-39}$$

and the corresponding representation of (electro)chemical potentials is

$$\mu_{H_2} + 2\ \mu_{OH^-} = 2\ \bar{\mu}_{H_2O} + 2\ \bar{\mu}_{e^-_m} \tag{7-40}$$

The potential difference that appears at the terminals of a fuel cell in thermodynamic equilibrium is, then, with eq. 7-13,

$$E = \frac{\bar{\mu}^C_{e^-_m} - \bar{\mu}^A_{e^-_m}}{-e} \tag{7-41}$$

where e is the charge of an electron. Note that the cathode and anode have been designated by superscripts. From eq. 7-13 and Table 7–1, the equilibrium potenial of a H_2–O_2 cell is 1.23 V. This is the maximum potential difference available in a single fuel cell. Figure 7-8(a) shows the variation of electron energy (which is the negative of the elecrostatic potential) distribution at open circuit. To obtain higher voltages, fuel cells are often "stacked" in series in the same manner that batteries may be connected in series.

To obtain a more complete understanding of the fuel cell operating in a nonequilibrium situation, one must examine the individual reactions occurring at the cathode and anode and follow the electrostatic potential difference from cathode to electrolyte, through the electrolyte, and from electrolyte to anode. This is illustrated in Fig. 7-8(a–c), in which the relative positions of electron energy levels is shown in (a) and those of electrostatic potentials for equilibrium and nonequilibrium situations are shown in (b) and (c). The electrochemical potential of species i in phase P can be separated into chemical and electrostatic components according to eq. 7-36. The chemical potential of electrons depends primarily on their concentration, and it is a relatively straightforward exercise to show that, under typical conditions, the electronic concentration changes by only a trivial amount (less than ppm levels) when the electrostatic potential of the metal changes by a volt. For practical purposes, one may regard the chemical potential of electrons in phase P as a constant. If both cathode and anode are of the same material (for example, platinum), combination of eqs. 7-36 and 7-41 shows that the measured potential difference of the fuel cell is equivalent to the difference in electrostatic potentials,

$$E^0 = \phi^C - \phi^A \qquad (7\text{-}42)$$

since the chemical potentials of electrons in the two electrodes cancel each other. (A footnote: If cathode and anode are of different materials, eq. 7-42 must be modified slightly as the chemical potentials no longer cancel. In this case, one can always attach a common material, namely, a copper wire, to each electrode so that eq. 7-42 represents the difference between the electrostatic potential of the copper wire attached to the cathode and that of the copper wire attached to the anode.) This electrostatic potential difference is depicted in Fig. 7-8(b). Note that the ordinate has been reversed to account for the difference in sign between electrostatic potential and electron energy.

The functions of cathode, electrolyte, and anode may now be examined in more detail by splitting the overall electrostatic potential difference of the cell into a series of differences across the respective portions of the cell,

$$E^0 = \phi^C - \phi^A = \left(\phi^C - \phi^{S,C}\right) + \left(\phi^{S,C} - \phi^{S,A}\right) + \left(\phi^{S,A} - \phi^A\right) \quad (7\text{-}43)$$

Here $\phi^{S,C}$ and $\phi^{S,A}$ are the electrostatic potentials in the electrolyte near the cathode and anode, respectively. The three terms on the right-hand side of

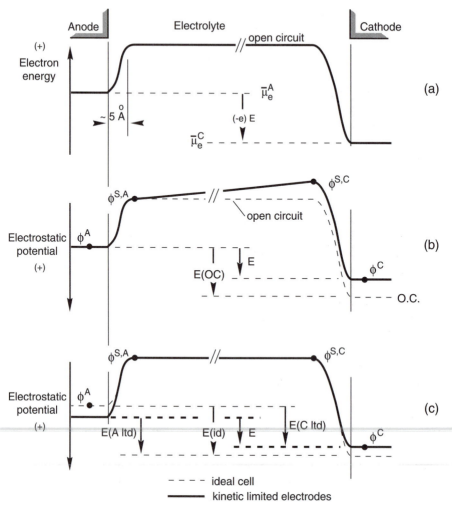

FIGURE 7-8. Electron energy and electrostatic potential distributions in a fuel cell. At open circuit (a) the ideal distribution of energy is shown. $1 \text{ Å} = 10^{-10}$ m. The potential distribution in an ideal cell carrying current (electrolyte resistance loss only) is shown in (b). Here the anode potential is arbitrarily set at zero. When anode and cathode (kinetic) limitation losses are present (c), the potential distribution is such that output voltage is further reduced. E = actual output, $E(\text{id})$ = no kinetic losses, and $E(\text{ltd})$ refers to output with only the electrode noted presenting a current limitation.

eq. 7-43 represent electrostatic potential differences from cathode to electrolyte, across the electrolyte itself, and from electrolyte to anode.

Capitalizing on these ideas, the operation of cells as a power system are considered further in Section 7.6.

7.5.4. Hydrocarbon Fuel Cells

Hydrocarbon fuels are processed in so-called *redox cells* which use the carbonate ion (CO_3^{2-}) in the electrolyte (Fig. 7-9). Near the anode, where fuel is introduced, a reforming reaction takes place to produce simple fuel molecules from the more complex ones introduced. Consider a fuel with a H:C ratio of n and balanced to produce no oxygen. The result is the production of H_2 and CO:

$$(CH_n) + a\,CO_2 + (1-a)\,H_2O \longrightarrow (1+a)\,CO + \left(\frac{n}{2} + 1 - a\right) H_2 \qquad (7\text{-}44)$$

At the anode, these products are further oxidized with the electrolyte ions. Anode:

$$H_2 + CO + 2\,CO_3^{2-} \longrightarrow H_2O + 3\,CO_2 + 4\,e^- \qquad (7\text{-}45)$$

Part of the CO_2 produced at the anode must be brought to the cathode, where it is oxidized to produce the carbonate ion. Cathode:

$$4\,e^- + 2\,CO_2 + O_2 \longrightarrow 2\,CO_3^{2-} \qquad (7\text{-}46)$$

At the anode, the remaining CO_2 is waste to be removed with the water also produced there.

An alternative and more direct method to the use of a hydrocarbon is reforming the fuel ahead of processes in the fuel cell (Ref. 7-8). Here a fuel, such as methane or a light petroleum fuel, is made to undergo a series of reactions to produce hydrogen for use in the fuel cell. The process includes halogen and sulfur removal followed by the high-temperature endothermic steam reaction:

$$CH_4 + H_2O \dashrightarrow 3\,H_2 + CO \qquad (7\text{-}47)$$

This is followed by the exothermic *water gas shift* reaction

$$CO + H_2O \dashrightarrow H_2 + CO_2 \qquad (7\text{-}48)$$

The resulting gas is high (~75%) in hydrogen is fed to the fuel cell, and the carryover can be burned to generate the heat for the endothermic reaction and drive the necessary air feed machinery (Ref. 7-8). This is also being tried in

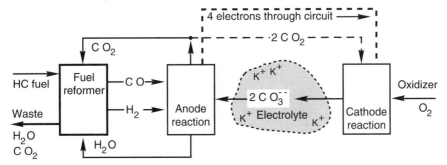

FIGURE 7-9. Charge transfer process in an operating carbonate cell.

low-temperature fuel cells, but the CO removal must be very good in these cases to reduce the poisoning caused by the presence of CO at low temperature.

7.5.5. *Solid Electrolyte Cells*

Fuel cells must provide a medium for the ionic transfer of charges between the reactants. In the cells described above, the ions are mobile by virtue of their presence in a liquid state substance, the acidic or basic solution, or the molten electrolyte itself, as in the case of the carbonate cell. Solid materials may also be made carriers of ions. Two solid electrolyte systems are promising. These are the *solid oxide* and the *solid polymer* electrolyte systems.

Solid Oxide

The oxygen ion (O^{2-}) is of interest because of its role as oxidizer in air–fuel reactions. This motivates the search for chemical oxides (and oxide mixtures) to find those with a high ionic conductivity. Specifically of interest are substances with high diffusivity of the oxygen as an ion. Fortunately, such oxides exist, and an important compound (mixture) is zirconium oxide (zirconia) mixed with other materials such as yttrium oxide (yttria) or calcium oxide (calcia). Such compounds and mixtures are in the solid state. The mixtures were developed to prevent phase transitions (which were accompanied by significant density changes) as these materials were subjected to temperature changes. The density changes usually led to failure of the structural integrity of the oxide. To avoid this, the ZrO_2 is stabilized by the oxides under scrutiny here, which results in substances with both structural stability and ionic conductivity.

The typical mixture forms an oxygen lattice with half the sites available occupied by Zr with a valence +4. The presence of a metal with a lower valence (Y= +3, or Ca= +2) in the Zr pattern leads to oxygen vacancies in the array. An oxygen ion can be readily made to occupy this "hole" and thereby move across the oxide mixture in response to concentration gradients or electric fields. In effect, the oxygen ion is transported across a thickness of oxide carrying its mass and its charge by introduction at one edge and the removal of another ion at the other edge. The ionic conductivity of oxides is very temperature dependent because of the increased mobility of the chemical compounds and the migrating ions. At a practical level, relatively high temperatures [1000°C or $1/T(kK) = .78$] are required to permit effective migration of the oxygen ion toward a fuel so that chemical union can take place to form either CO_2 or H_2O via an electrochemical reaction. An increase to 2000 K increases σ by about 2 orders of magnitude. Figure 7-10 shows the variation of σ for a solid electrolyte such as a mixture of 0.85 Zr $O_2 + 0.15$ CaO. The conductivities of other mixtures of this type are similar. Note σ is of the order of 1 mho/m, which requires the characteristic dimension d/Lh to be small (eq. 2-12) for a low internal resistance. Hence the thin sandwich cell construction is characterized especially well in Fig. 7-12.

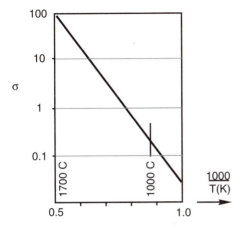

FIGURE 7-10. Ionic conductivity of .85 ZrO_2 + .15 CaO as a function of temperature. From ref. 7-9.

In oxide electrolytes, the reaction takes place in the *fuel* side of the electrolyte, and the products of the reaction are discharged into the *fuel flow stream*. This has important consequences for the discharge of waste products into the environment, and steps must be taken to minimize the discharge of unreacted fuel elements (CO and hydrocarbons, in particular) with the exhaust.

The high temperature required for the effective diffusion of ions has practical consequences for the design of the cell. The maintenance of fuel and air in their passageways without leaking is a challenge. The output voltage (or Gibbs free energy; see Table 7–3) of an electrochemical cell decreases with increasing temperature, and a lower temperature is therefore more desirable. The behavior of the cell materials and the impact of operating temperature on the economic lifetime of the cell are consequently important to the successful design and use of such the cell.

The high temperature has a secondary benefit for the utilization of simple hydrocarbon fuels such as methane. For example, if water (steam using waste heat) is introduced with the fuel, the reforming reaction takes place in the gas phase (see Section 7.5.2). The completion (equilibrium composition; see Chapter 5 of Ref. 1-1) of this reaction depends on the temperature, but the products of this reaction are removed at the cell boundary by inducing more of the reactants (the original fuel and water) to be consumed. Consequently, the oxidation reaction is that of the very simplest molecules, which gives *rates* of conversion that are as fast as one can hope. In practice, this results in interestingly large power densities for the cell. Development work, currently underway, will result in the identification of acceptable operating temperatures, optimistically as low as 600-700°C considering the constraints cited above.

Geometrical Arrangements

The art of successful design centers around the configuration. The possibilities are many, and just a few will be cited to provide a perspective. Consider the planar design in Fig. 7-11. Here the electrolyte is sandwiched between two porous materials designed to distribute air to one side of the electrolyte and fuel to the other. These porous elements also carry the current to the outside

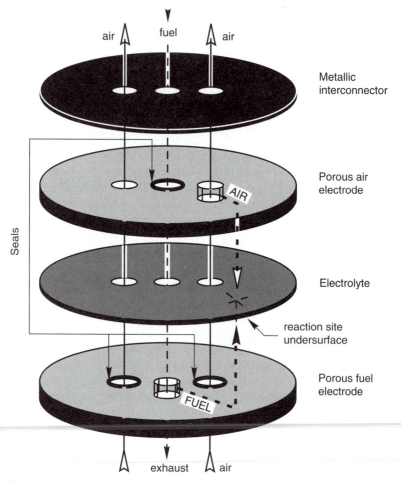

air   fuel   air

Metallic
interconnector

Porous air
electrode

AIR

Seals

Electrolyte

reaction site
undersurface

Porous fuel
electrode

FUEL

exhaust   air

FIGURE 7-11. A planar fuel cell (courtesy Technology Management, Inc., adapted from Ref. 7-10).

world. If the cell is arranged as part of a stack of a multiplicity of cells, the electrical connection can be made for the cells to operate in series and the fuel and air feed can be provided through alternate arrangements of seals that channel the gases to their intended reaction sites.

Figure 7-12 shows an arrangement where the electrolyte material is a split open cylinder. The split is to allow electrical contact with the air electrode (cathode), which is also cylindrical, with air flowing in axially from one or both ends. The split fuel electrode (anode) surrounds the electrolyte. By suitable arrangement of the connectors through the split electrolyte and anode, the current is collected.

Another cell configuration is an array structured like a cross-flow heat exchanger (Chapter 6, Ref. 1-1), with the reactants entering at right angles to each other. Finally, thin film devices are also under study.

In summary, the major types of fuels cells each have characteristics that make them more or less useful than alternatives. Table 7–6, obtained from

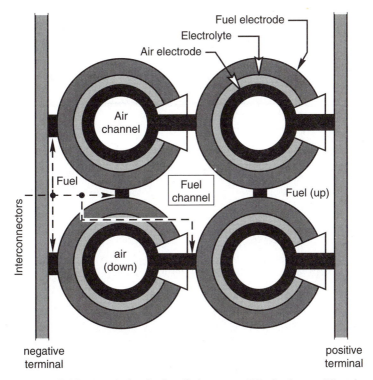

FIGURE 7-12. A tubular fuel cell (courtesy Westinghouse Electric Corp. adapted from Ref. 7-10).

Ref. 7-2 (with permission), summarizes the major issues and development status of fuel cells in the mid-1990s.

7.6. CELL SYSTEM PERFORMANCE

7.6.1. *Voltage–Current Characteristic*

The voltage–current characteristic of a fuel cell as a power producer is described by a number of "voltage drops" associated with various processes. The open circuit voltage is always less than the ideal (thermodynamic) cell voltage by an amount termed rest overvoltage. A typical single fuel cell has an open circuit voltage of 0.8 to 1.1 V. Thus typical fuel cell efficiencies vary from 50% to 70% (compared with 83% at 25°C from Table 7–1). This implies that the actual voltage of a cell with current flow is even lower. The most important voltage drop is associated with current flow (I) through the load resistance R_L:

$$\phi(\text{load}) = IR_L \qquad (7\text{-}49)$$

Here ϕ is used to denote voltage or potential, in contrast to E used in the fuel cell community. A major goal in fuel cell design is to keep the potential

Table 7–6. Characteristics of fuel cell types

Electrolyte	Temperature (°C)	Advantages	Drawbacks	Status (1994)
Alkaline	70-200	high curent and power density; high efficiency	CO_2 intolerance	Extensive field testing
Proton exchange membrane*	80-110	high current and power density; long operating life	CO intolerance water management; noble metal catalyst	Field testing (automotive)
Phosphoric acid	150-210	well advanced	efficiency; lifetime; noble metal catalyst	Commercially available
Molten carbonate	550-650	high efficiency internal fuel processing, high-grade waste heat	electrolyte instability; lifetime	Field testing (2 MW scale)
Solid oxide ceramic	1000-1100	internal fuel processing; high-grade waste heat; lifetime; potentially inexpensive	high temperature; efficiency; low ionic conductivity	Laboratory testing (kW scale)

* The proton exchange membrane (PEM) fuel cell uses solid material as a proton conductor in a way that is similar to an acid electrolyte cell. It was initially used in the aerospace industry but developments have led to its strong candidacy for automotive applications; Refs. 7-11 and 7-12.

difference high, to at least 0.6 V, for a current level consistent with operation near maximum power output. The ϕ-I characteristic of a specific cell might be as shown in Fig. 7-13.

In practice, a number of mechanisms are at play to complicate this characteristic further, as shown at the bottom of Fig. 7-13. Near open circuit, a voltage drop associated with an "activation" process reduces the output. This drop is associated with finite energies required to overcome barriers to initiate the reactions at finite rates.

With increasing current flow, the decrease in potential from ideal thermodynamic values is due to nonidealities associated with the processes described above. These nonidealities lead to resistances inside the fuel cell that limit the available terminal voltage. Resistances (or output voltage reductions) may be classified according to:

1. Supply of gas to the electrodes (external mass transfer limitation);
2. Transport of ions through the electrolyte (internal mass transfer limitation); and
3. Catalytic reactions occurring at the electrode surface (kinetic limitation).

External mass transfer (1) limitations may be circumvented by appropriate design of the fuel cell. When ion transport through the electrolyte becomes limiting, an electrostatic potential gradient will exist across the electrolyte, as shown by the dashed line in Fig. 7-8(b). If the reaction kinetics at the cathode and an-ode remain unaffected, the potential differences in eq. 7-43, $\left(\phi^{C} - \phi^{S,C}\right)$ and $\left(\phi^{S,A} - \phi^{A}\right)$, remain fixed. The result is that the overall potential difference decreases to a value given by $E < E(OC)$. In the situation where kinetics limits the potential difference at the corresponding electrode, $\left(\phi^{C} - \phi^{S,C}\right)$ or $\left(\phi^{S,A} - \phi^{A}\right)$, will change in a manner that also reduces the overall fuel cell potential difference, $E < E_{id}$. For a kinetic limitation at the cathode, the cathode must become more reducing, which is accomplished by a decrease in electrostatic potential. Similarly, kinetic limitation at the anode requires a more oxidizing electrode; so the electrostatic potential must increase to realize the same current. Figure 7-8(c) shows both effects with the corresponding overall potential differences of $E(C$ ltd) for cathode limitation and $E(A$ ltd) for anode limitation.

The internal mass transfer (2) limitation may be encountered at a high current level, a potential is required to counter the reactant depletion at a reaction site due to the high rate of processing. In effect, diffusion may not be sufficient to maintain the process rate.

Kinetic limitations (3) can be reduced through appropriate design of an electrocatalyst to maximize catalytic activity, while minimizing undesirable side reactions that may poison the electrode or other processes that cause long-term deactivation. Both of these are active applied and fundamental

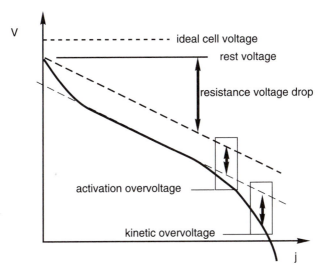

FIGURE 7-13. Voltage-current characteristic of an ideal and a real fuel cell showing the various loss voltage drops.

research topics, and hold good promise for some exciting advances in the near future.

The maximum power point is typically in the linear section of the characteristic.

7.6.2. Efficiency

The efficiency of transforming fuel energy to electrical output is associated with a number of processes:

1. The ideal efficiency of the electrochemical process;
2. Cell efficiency ($= \phi/\phi_{oc}$) as described above, which depends on current and the irreversibilities caused by current flow, such as Joule heating, heating due to activation, and concentration voltage gradients, all of which are related to materials and geometry; and
3. The utilization of reactants (as measured by carryover to the waste stream or reaction to undesirable products).

Thus overall efficiency is therefore

$$\text{overall } \eta = (\text{galvanic } \eta) \times \left(\text{cell } \eta = \frac{\phi}{\phi_{oc}} \right) \times (\text{utilization } \eta\text{'s})$$

or

$$\eta_0 = \eta_{id}\, \eta_{cell}\, \eta_f \qquad (7\text{-}50)$$

The reactant utilization efficiency may be important when the process rate (i.e., current) is high. The utilization efficiency is sometimes referred to as a *faradaic* or *current efficiency*, defined by

$$\eta_f = \frac{j}{n\, F\, \dot{n}_{fuel}} \qquad (7\text{-}51)$$

where $\dot{n}_{fuel}$ is the molar fuel feed rate per unit cell area. The combination of efficiencies gives an overall conversion efficiency, η_0. In sum, for realistic efficiencies of these processes, realistic fuel cell plants are projected to have overall conversion efficiencies between 40 and 75%, depending on the type of fuel.

The supply of fuel and air to the reaction site requires the gases to be pressurized, especially if the system is to be compact. The work associated with compression represents a performance penalty. In addition, there are flow pressure losses because the fuel, air, and waste stream flows are typically through passages of large length-to-diameter ratio, L/D. Some of the remaining pressure and the heat generated can, if the system cost justifies it, be recovered. Thus a complete accounting involves

1. - Compression work of fluids;
2. - Flow losses;
3. + Heat recovery; and
4. + Work recovery from waste stream;

in a calculation of overall efficiency. The losses listed above are very design specific so that estimates are not given here.

7.6.3. *Other Issues*

Research in the field of fuel cells is motivated by the high conversion efficiency of the fuel energy to electric power. It is realistically possible to seek a level of 60% efficiency and perhaps as high as 80% if the waste heat is utilized. An attractive feature of the fuel cell is that, within limits, the fuel feed rate determines power output. Thus its *scalability* to small size (watts to MW) and the potentially very low emissions make it possible to install in close proximity to the user, who might be able to utilize the output of electrical power and the "waste" heat.

The economic utility of energy conversion devices is strongly influenced by the cost per unit capacity ($/kW). From the viewpoint of materials required to construct a cell, the cost is a few percent of the cost to build a fossil combustion central station power plant. Researchers in this field are optimistic that fuel cell *plant* costs will be significantly less than coal combustion plant costs, perhaps less than one-half. It is worthy of note that a proper comparison between fuel cells and coal-fired central power generation must include the fuel cell system cost of converting coal to lower-molecular-weight fuel gas.

A central aspect of performance is the *power density* of the cell as a power producer. This is contrasted to *energy density* of a battery, as discussed in Section 7.4.5. Because the voltages are fixed by the energetics of the chemical changes, power output is determined by the current density that the electrolyte and the electrodes themselves are able to carry. These currents are on the order of 1 A/cm^2 of electrode area, so that two of the dimensions required to establish a volume for a specified power output are fixed. The third dimension is the thickness of the electrolyte layer. These physical lengths, potentially altered by effects associated with surface roughness, are geometrical considerations that combine to determine power density and, to some extent, cost. The reader should be aware that this aspect of fuel cell development evolves rapidly in response to opportunities in the marketplace. As a matter of interest, power densities of complete systems for building-scale power generation are of the order 10 kW/m^3. For automotive and similar applications, practical systems must be about an order of magnitude larger.

PROBLEMS

1. A cell has a linear voltage-current characteristic. For a linear load, determine the voltage for maximum power output in terms of the other relevant parameters. How does any "rest overvoltage" affect the maximum power condition?

2. A cell has the characteristics given in the table. The parasitic losses are given as Q in units of the product IV.

V	I	Q
1.0	0.0	0.0
0.9	0.1	0.01
0.5	0.8	0.06
0.0	1.0	0.14

Curve fit the data to allow determination of the current and voltrage at maximum power.

3. A reaction cell has an open circuit voltage and a cell internal resistance that decrease linearly with temperature as it changes away from a reference value, though not at the same rate. For maximum cell power output, how is the temperature to be chosen and what are the consequences of this temperature choice on the optimum load resistance?

4. Determine the energy density of a cell using the reactants AgCl and Zn.

5. A nearly reversible cell operates at a voltage of 1.2 V. This cell is discharged at a voltage of 1.0 V and recharged at a voltage of 1.4 V. Estimate the efficiency of one charge–discharge cycle for this cell.

BIBLIOGRAPHY

Hart, A. B. and Womack G. J., *Fuel Cells*, Chapman & Hall, London 1967.

Sutton, G. W., *Direct Energy Conversion*, McGraw-Hill, New York, 1966.

Vielstich, W., *Fuel Cells*, Wiley-Interscience, New York, 1965.

Vincent, C. A., *Modern Batteries*, Edward Arnold Publishers, Ltd., London, 1984.

Levine, S. N., *Selected Papers on New Techniques for Energy Conversion*, Dover, New York, 1961.

REFERENCES

7-1.   Denbigh, K., *The Principles of Chemical Equilibrium*, Cambridge University Press, Cambridge, 1961.

7-2.   Kartha, S., and Grimes, P., "Fuel Cells: Energy Conversion for the Next Century," *Physics Today*, November 1994.

7-3.   Moore, W. J., *Physical Chemistry*, 3rd printing, Prentice Hall, Englewood Cliffs, N.J., 1963.

7-4. Manwell, J. F., and McGowan, J. G., "Lead Acid Battery Storage Model for Hybrid Energy Systems," *Energy* **50** (5), 399-405, 1993.

7-5. DeLuca, W. H., et al., "Performance Evaluation of Advanced Battery Technologies for Electric Vehicles," 25th Intersociety Energy Conversion Engineering Conference, 1990.

7-6. Daubert, T. E., *Chemical Engineering Thermodynamics*, McGraw-Hill Book Company, New York, 1985.

7-7. Goodisman, J., *Electrochemistry: Theoretical Foundations*, John Wiley and Sons, New York, 1987.

7-8. Cannon, C. A., Handley, L. M., Oestrich, L. C., and May, G. W., "Leveraging the Fuel Cell Power Plant's Benefits," ASME Joint Power Generation Conference, Portland, Oregon, 1986.

7-9. Moulson, A. J., and Herbert, J. M., *Electroceramics*, Chapman and Hall, London, 1990.

7-10. Douglas, J., "Solid Futures in Fuel Cells," *EPRI Journal* **19** (2), March 1994.

7-11. DeLucchi, M. A., "Hydrogen Fuel Cell Vehicles," Research Report UCD-ITS-RR-92-14, Institute of Transportation Studies, University of California, Davis, 1992.

7-12. Srinivasan, S., Velev, A., Parthasarathy, D., and Manko, A., *J. Power Sources* **36**, 299, 1991.

8

SEMICONDUCTORS: PHOTOELECTRICITY

Photons carry energy as wave packets. This energy may be transferred to charges in a static electric field, which causes the charges to move against the field and thus to a higher potential. This is the function of the photoelectric cell: provide an electron current at an elevated voltage brought about by the interaction between radiant power and a semiconductor constructed to establish the necessary electrostatic field. This chapter is a description of the physics of photocells and of systems whose objective is to generate electric power from sunlight and from radiant thermal sources. The characteristics of electric power systems utilizing thermal sources and the technology described here are discussed so that their role as competitors to other methods may be assessed. For a more complete discussion of solar power systems, the reader may consult Refs. 1-1, 8-1, 8-2, among many others, some of which are noted in the references for specific points in the discussion to follow.

8.1. THE PHOTOELECTRIC EFFECT AND CELLS

In Chapter 6, the configuration of the electronic structure in a metal is described. It may be characterized by the energy levels of the valence electrons in the metal, which fully occupy the lowest energies available. Some of these electrons have large energies because of the thermal transfer from the agitation of the atoms. This model is useful for a derivation of the electron emission current from a heated surface; see Section 6.1.2 and eq. 6-2 in particular.

An extension of this model permits a description of the so-called *photoelectric effect*. Consider a surface to be illuminated with a stream of monoenergetic photons. These photons collide with (or equivalently, are absorbed by) the electrons in the metal. If the energy involved is sufficiently large (i.e., $h\nu \geq e\phi$, where ϕ is the work function), these photons may cause the liberation of the affected electrons from the metal surface. An externally established electric field may be present to capture the freed electrons in a circuit that counts them by measurement of the current. This effect is the basis for the photomultiplier, a light intensity measurement instrument wherein a number of amplification stages are used to allow measurement of small photon fluxes by means of currents large enough to be processable.

Figure 8-1 shows the elements of the photoelectric experiment. The result from such an experiment is as shown in the right side of Fig. 6-8. For low-frequency light input, no current is observed, and for higher frequencies (i.e., energies), a current proportional to the photon flux is seen. This experiment

194

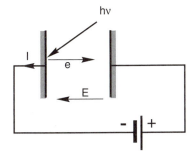

FIGURE 8-1. The classical photoelectric experiment with an applied electric field. A current flow (I) depends on the incident light frequency.

is not a useful conversion scheme for converting photon energy to electrical energy because of the requirement for an external electric field. For an energy conversion device, a practical means (i.e., without external energy input) for establishing an **E** field must be available. Semiconductors allow this possibility.

Solid materials are composed of atoms or molecules. These solids can be structured as a periodic lattice or randomly organized. The regular organization is termed *crystalline,* while the alternative is termed *amorphous.* Crystalline solids may also be regular on various length scales: a large distance between grain boundaries or no grain boundaries at all characterize the single crystal, whereas smaller distances that of the polycrystalline solid. The following discussion emphasizes the single crystal solid. Solids are also differentiated on the basis of their electrical conductivity: thus metals and nonmetals or dielectrics form extremes in the range of possibilities.

Metals are distinguished from nonmetals or insulators by the fact that the most energetic electrons are relatively free to travel within the conduction band of the metal structure. A description of electrons in these materials requires a discussion of the energy states available to electrons. In the lowest energy levels are the electrons, which fill orbits for the individual atoms in the lattice. These electrons are tightly bound to the atoms and cannot be involved in current conduction. These electrons are not free to accept energy because they occupy quantized energy states within the atom. The outermost electrons associated with an atom are the *valence* electrons (in the valence band). These electrons can participate in chemical bonding by filling orbitals of other atoms so that the two or more atoms together form a molecule or compound. When they do form molecules from atoms, the energy states of the electron *acceptor* are filled by those of the *donor.* The valence electrons are thus in filled orbitals where they, like the lowest-energy electrons, must also conform to the laws of quantum mechanics, which restricts the energies to specific levels. The shared electrons are therefore also unable to respond to forces such as those provided by an applied electric field. This restriction prevents the electrons from acquiring kinetic energy and consequently the freedom to move. A lattice of a molecular compound is therefore a nonconductor because the somewhat higher energy levels for the electrons are forbidden. This is termed the *forbidden band.* More precisely, the band refers to the aggregate collection of energy levels of the ensemble of atoms in a macrostructure. The next higher available band is associated with a higher quantum state(s), which typically are much higher in energy so that the energy provided by electric fields or radiation quanta is normally insufficient to reach that state. The energy required to bring an electron from the valence band to the largely unfilled conduction band is called the *band gap energy*, V_g, normally measured in volts.

In a metallic conductor, the valence-band states are unfilled, and the electrons can be easily elevated in energy and thereby move. This freedom distinguishes conductors from nonconductors. Figure 8-2 shows the energy levels available to conductors (metals) and contrasts this picture to nonmetals. Note the valence, forbidden, and conduction bands in the two material types.

8.1.1. *Doped Semiconductors*

When a substance consists of elements in the middle of the periodic table, notably silicon (Si) and germanium (Ge), the structure of the array is controlled by a sharing of equal (or nearly equal) numbers of electrons from the atoms bound in the array. Substances with such *covalent* bonding are termed *semiconductors* because they are neither metals nor nonmetals. For such material crystals, the band gap energy is relatively small (of order 1–2 electron volts) compared to that in a nonconductor. In other words, the forbidden band is relatively narrow in energy: modest energy inputs can cause electrons to be transported in the material. A pure array of a such a material is called an *intrinsic* semiconductor. The electrical conduction characteristics of semiconductors can be significantly influenced by impurities in the crystal to obtain specific characteristics. Thus semiconductors are deliberately *doped* by the addition of other atom types in the array.

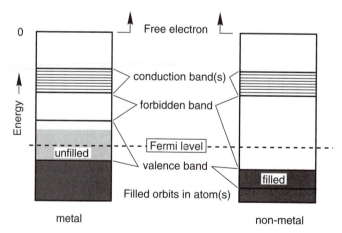

FIGURE 8-2. Energy level diagram for a metal and a nonmetal. The filled states' electrons cannot accept energy and therefore cannot move.

Consider the crystal lattice of silicon shown in Fig. 8-3. A pure Si (valence +4) array of atoms is uniform in its electron structure. Only the electrons that are thermally excited above the band gap are mobile and respond to an applied electric field. The result is an electrical conductivity that is much smaller than that of a metal, but larger than that of an insulator. Specifically, the electrical conductivities of copper and fused silica (SiO_2) as examples are 5×10^6 and 10^{-12} (ohm cm)$^{-1}$, respectively. High-performance insulators may achieve conductivities of 10^{-18}. By contrast, the conductivity of Si varies between 10^2 and 10^{-5}, depending on the doping. Note that the units of inverse ohm cm or (ohm cm)$^{-1}$ are sometimes called mhos/cm, or Siemens, depending on the tradition in the field. Note further the use of centimeters (rather than SI system meters), which is also customary in this field. The range of resistivity or conductivity of over 32 orders of magnitude is probably the broadest of any common physical properties of solids (Ref. 8-3).

On the left side of Fig. 8-3, phosphorus atoms (P, valence +5) are introduced to replace a relatively small number of Si atoms. This impurity introduces one (=5-4) excess electron per dopant atom so that the crystal array now has electrons that are comparatively mobile. This doping make the silicon an *n-type* semiconductor. Other dopants are available to achieve a similar electron excess. If, on the other hand, a +3 valence atom is used, the electronic array will have an electron deficit, or *hole* (which an electron can occupy). For this purpose, Fig. 8-3 shows a boron (B) atom in a Si lattice, making it a *p-type* semiconductor. Under all circumstances, the pure and the doped material is electrically neutral on a macroscopic scale: there is a positive nuclear charge for every electron.

An electric field applied to doped semiconductors gives rise to a net migration of these loosely bound electrons or holes in response to the field.

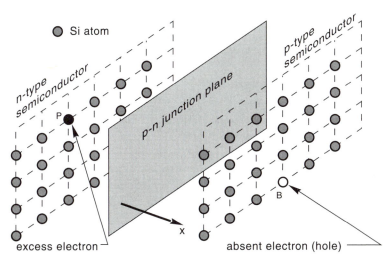

FIGURE 8-3. *p*-doped (here with boron, B) and *n*-doped (here with phosphorus, P) in a crystal lattice of silicon. Shown is the first layer of the atom lattice on each side of the *p-n* junction.

Since the hole behaves like a positive ion, the motion of holes is necessarily in the opposite direction from that of an electron. Figure 8-4 shows the energy levels of the semiconductor and the dopant atoms. Note that the excess electron in the P dopant (n-type) is quite close to the conduction band of the Si, in this case. A modest energy input from thermal agitation or a photon can move the electron into the conduction band. The P is thus an electron *donor*. Similarly the B atom is an electron *acceptor*.

8.1.2. *The p-n Junction*

Consider a surface formed by a *p*-type and an *n*-type semiconductor in contact with one another as shown in Fig. 8-3. This surface is a *p-n* junction, which is an abrupt discontinuity in the atomic concentration of atomic species of dopants. This junction establishes a potential difference for charged particles in the two semiconductor materials, far from the junction. The physical establishment of the associated electric field is examined in this section.

Since the excess electrons are free to move, the electrons (on the *n* side) diffuse to the *p* side. They diffuse over to that region, leaving an excess positive charge on the *n* side. This diffusion extends as far from the *p-n* junction as the resultant electric field that counters this diffusion allows. The net charge density along an axis normal to the *p-n* junction will take on a shape shown in Fig. 8-5: positive in the *n* region and negative in the *p* region. Far from the junction (at $x = \pm \infty$), the charge density is zero. The charge density is also zero at the interface, because there, one has an electron for every hole. The antisymmetric distribution of charge density is controlled primarily by the diffusivity of the holes and electrons in the lattice.

A charge density distribution of this type leads to the establishment of an electric field through the establishment of the two oppositely charged regions.

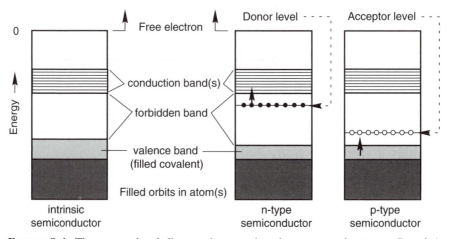

FIGURE 8-4. The energy level diagram in a semiconductor, *p*- and *n*-types. *D* and *A* illustrate the donor and acceptor roles of the dopant atoms, which serve to reduce the band gap.

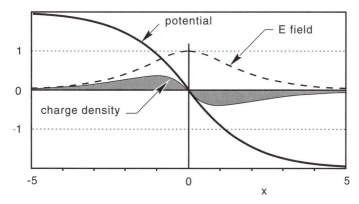

FIGURE 8-5. The spatial distribution of charge density, electric field, and potential for charge carriers near a *p-n* junction.

Maxwell's equation, eq. 2-25 (here in one dimension) allows the calculation of the field strength:

$$\frac{d E_x}{d x} = \frac{\rho_c(x)}{\varepsilon_0} \tag{8-1}$$

For the purpose of illustrating the charge density distribution, the variation in Fig. 8-5 is assumed to vary with a nondimensional x as

$$\rho_c(x) = \rho_{c0}\, x \exp(-x) \tag{8-2}$$

This antisymmetric function is assumed to be a solution determined by the electron diffusion equation, which is not solved here, although the physical parameters involved are discussed below. The integration of eq. 8-1 with eq. 8-2 gives E_x. The potential V is also obtained from its definition (again in one dimension):

$$E_x = -\frac{d V}{d x} \tag{8-3}$$

The resulting variations of E_x and V are shown in Fig. 8-5. The algebraic result of the integrations is not of direct interest because the charge distribution is of an assumed form. Nevertheless, the form of the integrated functions is critical. Note that E_x is symmetric and V is antisymmetric. From this integration, the potential difference between the two sides of the junction is determined and is of the order

$$V = V_{max} \approx \frac{e\, n_c}{\varepsilon_0} L^2 \tag{8-4}$$

where ($\rho_c = e\, n_c$) is the charge density and L is a diffusion distance that may be thought of as the distance from $x = 0$ to the point of maximum charge

density. This diffusion distance is established by a balance between the diffusivity of the *minority* charge carriers and the average length of survival of
these carriers. The minority carriers are either holes or electrons, holes in the
negative charge density region established by the absence of holes (i.e., *n*-
type) and vice versa, electrons in the *p*-type. In the *n* region, electrons are the
majority carriers. The sparseness of the minority carriers establishes the rate
at which they can be annihilated by recombination with a majority carrier.
Thus a carrier conservation (diffusion) equation establishes the length scales
as the product of *diffusion* coefficient (*D*) and a survival *lifetime* (*t**):

$$L = \sqrt{D\, t^*} \tag{8-5}$$

where *D* for the minority carriers is related to the *mobility* (μ, defined as the
ratio of drift velocity to electric field causing the motion) given by the
Einstein relation:

$$D = \mu \frac{kT}{q}, \quad \text{where} \quad q = \pm e, \quad \mu = \frac{e}{m^* v_c} \tag{8-6}$$

This equation connects the motion of species in response to a concentration
gradient and of charges in response to a potential (energy) gradient (**E** field).
The mass *m** is the effective (i.e., the reduced) mass of the charge carrier in
the crystal lattice and v_c is the collision frequency of the charge carrier as it
encounters lattice elements in its drift in the direction of the electric field. The
reader should note the correspondence between the mobility and the conductivity that is developed in connection with free electrons drifting through a
plasma; see Chapter 3. Specifically, the last equation and the conductivity (eq.
3-13) can be combined to show the charge density n_c

$$\mu = \frac{\sigma}{e\, n_c} \tag{8-7}$$

The lifetime is given by the inverse of the collision frequency (see the similar eq. 3-17) for annihilation collisions characterized by a cross-sectional area
Q_r:

$$t^* = \frac{1}{u_c\, n_r\, Q_r} \tag{8-8}$$

Here u_c is the carrier drift velocity and n_r is the density of recombination sites.
As an estimate, the carrier drift velocity is of the order of the mean thermal
speed of the electron, 10^5 m/sec = 10^7 cm/sec. Within the estimates of the various physical quantities cited (Q_r ~ atom size ~ 10^{-14} cm^2) and specification
of the length scale *L*, the relation for *L* may be used to estimate the density
of recombination sites n_r (Ref. 8-4):

$$n_r = \frac{D}{u_c\, Q_r\, L^2} \tag{8-9}$$

In practice, the length scale L is of the order 10^{-6} m ($= 1$ μm). Consideration of this distance is also important in the design of cells because of its impact on the resistive loss for current conduction and absorption in the first semiconductor layer, which thermalizes the radiation. This topic is revisited in Section 8.3.3.

As a consequence of the need for photons to reach the vicinity of the p-n junction, the thickness of the n-type material is approximately 1 μm.

8.1.3. *Photon Energy and Voltage*

When two materials are brought in contact under no external light conditions, they must share a common Fermi level because this is the energy level associated with the two materials as a system with no external energy input (Refs. 8-5 and 8-6). Thus a sketch of the energy level picture for a p-n junction is as shown in Fig. 8-6. The diffusion of electrons and holes establishes an electric field and therefore a potential between the two materials. This energy level diagram is shown for electrons and is similar, but inverted, for holes. Thus energy accepted by an electron moves it "up" to the level of the conduction band, and that same energy moves the holes "down" in energy, that is, "up" in negative energy. These charge carriers are then able to flow to the far-field level of their respective conduction bands (electrons to the right in Fig. 8-6, n region, and holes to the left). The electrons are thus at an elevated energy level relative to the hole and can give up that energy by flowing through a resistive load. Thus one may envisage an energy conversion scheme whereby a single photon is delivered to a p-n junction, an electron-hole pair is created by the absorption of its energy, and the electron can be forced to return to

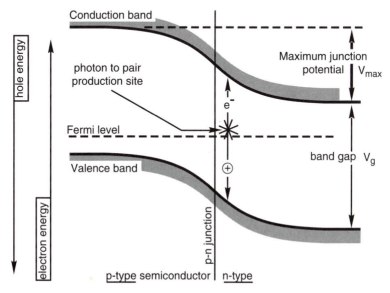

FIGURE 8-6. The energy level diagram for a p-n semiconductor junction. Note the gap potential, V_g, and maximum energy rise of the created electron, V_{max}.

"fill" the hole by traveling through a circuit where it gives up its energy. Such a circuit is illustrated in Fig. 8-7. The maximum voltage at which such a photon-generated electron can be delivered is V_{max}, identified in Fig. 8-6 and in eq. 8-4.

When an external stream of photons is added to the *p-n* junction, the picture is altered. Specifically, the voltage introduced by the load through which the electrons flow changes the Fermi level and thus the potential to which the photon generated electrons is raised. This is discussed in Section 8.3.3. The separation of electron-hole pairs can also be accomplished by transferring phonon or lattice wave energy (i.e., heat) to the *p-n* junction. This is thermoelectric energy conversion and is discussed more completely in Chapter 9.

Figure 8-6 summarizes the various energies described in this section and the consequences of energy input by means of incident photons. The voltage that must be supplied to the electron is the band gap energy, V_g. Table 8-1 gives a partial listing of the band gap energies associated with specific semiconductors. Also noted is the maximum wavelength (minimum energy) of the light required (λ_0 = cutoff wavelength) to transfer the electron across the gap, and a number of temperatures characterizing the spectral maxima of blackbody radiation.

8.1.4. *Dark Current*

In the absence of light input, the charge migration across the junction establishes a static electric field. The local charge density is determined by the majority charge carriers, but the minority carriers diffuse to neutralize their counterparts by thermal motion into the majority carrier region. Thus the diffusion of minority carriers to recombination sites establishes a current (j_0 is

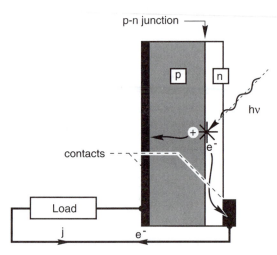

FIGURE 8-7. The cell and the photon-electron hole interaction at the *p-n* junction. Also shown is the external load circuit.

Table 8–1. Band gap energy for a number of semiconductors and the cutoff wavelength of photon energy $[\lambda_0$ (in μm) $= 1.24/V_g(eV)$, $T(\max \lambda_0) = 2985\ V_g(eV)$, $T_{\max\ x} = 5256/\lambda_0]$; the temperatures are discussed in Section 8.2.1

Chemical (compound)	Symbol	Band gap V_g (eV)	λ_0 (μm)	Temperatures (K)	
				$B(\lambda_m)$ peak	$B(v_m)$ peak
Germanium	Ge	0.68	1.82	1650	2900
Gallium antimonide	GaSb	0.69	1.80	1650	2900
Silicon	Si	1.1	1.13	2650	4650
Indium phosphide	InP	1.27	0.98	3050	5400
Gallium arsenide	GaAs	1.35	0.92	3250	5700
Aluminum antimonide	AlSb	1.49	0.83	3600	6300
Cadmium telluride	CdTe	1.5	0.83	3600	6350
Zinc telluride	ZnTe	2.1	0.59	5050	8900
Aluminum arsenide	AlAs	2.16	0.57	5200	9150
Gallium phosphide	GaP	2.24	0.55	5400	9500
Cadmium sulfide	CdS	2.37	0.52	5700	10050

the dark current) that depends primarily on the temperature, the diffusivity of the minority carriers, and the lifetime of the minority carrier.

For the purpose of obtaining an estimate of the magnitude of the dark current, the following is a brief summary of the argument made by Angrist (Ref. 8-5). The goal is to display the large temperature dependence of this quantity, which plays a significant part in determining the performance characteristics of a photocell.

The physical picture is of a cell configured with

1. A heavily doped p region;
2. A moderately doped n region; and
3. A junction thickness thin compared to the diffusion length so that diffusion is negligible in the junction field region.

Items 1 and 2 together are equivalent to assuming that the total current is carried by the holes (subscript h) generated in the n region, which diffuse over to the p region. The absolute value of this current is approximately the product of hole number density and diffusion velocity:

$$j_h = e\,n_h\,u_h \qquad (8\text{-}10)$$

where the diffusion velocity is given by (eqs. 8-5 and 8-6):

$$u_h = \frac{D_h}{L_h} = \frac{\mu_h}{L_h}\frac{k\,T}{e} \qquad (8\text{-}11)$$

using eq. 8-7. From equilibrium arguments the distribution of charge carriers in a semiconductor can be written as (see development of Chap. 3 in Ref. 8-5)

$$n_h \, n_e = n_c^2 = 4 \left(\frac{2\pi m_e kT}{h^2} \right)^3 \exp\left(-\frac{e \, V_g}{kT} \right) \tag{8-12}$$

where n_c is the equilibrium charge carrier number density in the intrinsic semiconductor and n_e is the electron density in the n region. This expression is very similar to the ionization law of mass action, except that here, the upper state is the conduction band. These relations can be combined by eliminating u_h and n_h to give

$$j_h = \frac{\mu_h}{L_h} \frac{kT}{n_e} \, 4 \left(\frac{2\pi \, m_e kT}{h^2} \right)^3 \exp\left(-\frac{e \, V_g}{kT} \right) \tag{8-13}$$

This expression can be simplified by introducing the electrical conductivity for the electrons

$$\sigma_e = \mu_e \, e \, n_e \tag{8-14}$$

Finally, the dark current can be written in terms of properties and the temperature:

$$j_0 = j_h = \left[4 \left(\frac{2\pi \, e \, m_e}{h^2} \right)^3 \right] \left[\frac{\mu_h \, \mu_e}{L_h \, \sigma_e} \right] \left[(kT/e)^4 \exp\left(-\frac{e \, V_g}{kT} \right) \right] \tag{8-15}$$

The product of the values of μ for electrons and holes ranges from 10^4 to 3×10^5 (cm^2/ V sec)^2 or, in SI units, 1 to 30 (m^2/ V sec)^2. From the properties of the semiconductor(s), the constants may be determined. The most important aspect of this estimate is the strong temperature dependence:

$$\frac{\partial \ln j_0}{\partial \ln T} = 4 + \frac{e \, V_g}{kT} \approx 4 + 40 \, ! \tag{8-16}$$

for a 1 V gap at the reference temperature. This implies that the cell performance is sensitive to operating temperature, although its control to under 100°C is rather straightforward with proper design. Before the dark current's role in determining cell performance is discussed, it is appropriate to review the nature of the incident photons.

8.2. REVIEW OF RADIATION PHYSICS

Thermal radiation is due to the acceleration of electrical charges at the atomic level. Classical physics describes, in statistical terms, the motion of atoms within the lattices of solid materials. The atomic nuclei and their electrons are excited when a material is at an elevated temperature. As a consequence, they vibrate about mean positions, and the frequency of the vibration is directly related to the energy carried by the photons emitted under the circumstances. The relation between the energy and the frequency is given by

$$E(\text{photon}) = h\nu \tag{8-17}$$

where h is Planck's constant.

8.2.1. *Blackbody Cavity, Emissivity from Solids*

Consideration of the atomic motion of a lattice at temperature T allows (Ref. 8-7) a determination of the equilibrium energy distribution of the photons within a cavity (Hohlraum) where the walls are at T. An opening in such a cavity allows this photon flux to escape and the flux remains a close approximation of the equilibrium flux inside if the cavity dimensions are such that the opening is small (Fig. 8-8).

The energy flux carried by the photons that escape the opening is given by the integration of the energy per photon over all photon energies. The energy distribution function of photons from a blackbody is given by (Ref. 8-5)

$$B(x) = \frac{15}{\pi^4}\, \sigma T^4\, \frac{x^3}{e^x - 1}\; ;\; x \equiv \frac{h\nu}{kT} \tag{8-18}$$

The function $B(x)$ is the spectral power density in terms of a nondimensional or reduced frequency x, and its units are W/m^2. The integral of $B(x)\, dx$ gives the (blackbody) radiant power

$$\dot{w} = \int_0^\infty B(x)\, dx = \sigma T^4 \quad \text{since} \quad \int_0^\infty \frac{x^3}{e^x - 1}\, dx = \frac{\pi^4}{15} \tag{8-19}$$

σ is the Stefan-Boltzmann constant, which is also a collection of fundamental constants (Ref. 1-1). The function $B(x)$ is plotted in Fig. 8-9. Note the

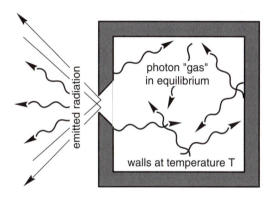

FIGURE 8-8. Blackbody cavity and the (blackbody) flux emitted from a small opening.

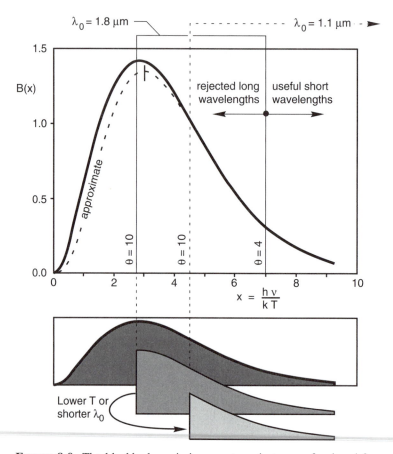

FIGURE 8-9. The blackbody emission spectrum in terms of reduced frequency x, heavy line. The dashed line is an approximate form of the energy distribution described in Section 8.3, θ is a nondimensional temperature $= T/288$ K, and the lines indicated are associated with a cutoff frequency corresponding to $\lambda_0 = 1.8$ μm. For lower cutoff wavelengths (1.1 μm in the example), the vertical lines are shifted to the right (dashed).

maximum at $x_m = 2.82$. A related maximum, expressed in terms of wavelength rather than frequency distribution function, is the Wien displacement law (Ref. 1-1). In Table 8-1 and Fig. 8-10 the temperatures corresponding to the peak in the blackbody distribution function expressed in terms of wavelength and the frequency maximum (eq. 8-18) are noted. Note that all semiconductors except Ge and GaSb (gallium antimonide) require sources with high emission temperatures. These two exceptions permit consideration of radiant power collection from practical material sources as radiators. The semiconductors labeled between Si and CdTe are relatively well matched to the power peak frequency associated with solar radiation at about 5800 K.

On the high-frequency side of the $B(x)$ distribution, the unity in the denominator of eq. 8-18 or 8-19 may be neglected for sufficiently large $x > x_m$. For the purposes of clarifying the role of the spectral energy distribution

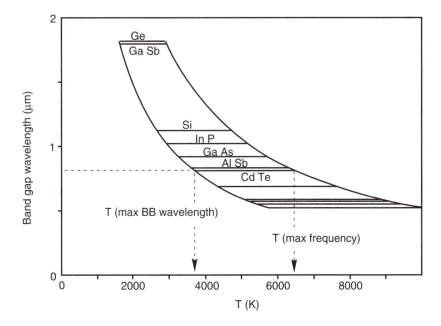

FIGURE 8-10. The cutoff energy may be expressed the longest wavelength absorbable in the photocell. This plot, for various semiconductor materials, shows the cutoff wavelengths and relates them to the temperatures a blackbody would have to have for the maxima in the blackbody functions $B(\lambda)$ and $B(\nu)$ to be at the cutoff wavelength.

of photons from a radiating body, the description of a surface as a blackbody radiator is often adequate. This approximation is examined in Section 8.2.3.

In connection with radiant energy transfer, a number of technical terms are used. To avoid associated confusion, one may note that surfaces emit power (W/m^2) into the half-space "above" the surface. This power is termed *radiant emittance*. It is called *irradiance* when the radiation is *to* the surface. A point or differential element of surface radiates with a *radiant* or *luminous intensity* into a unit solid angle, watts/steradian or watts/steradian/m^2. The radiant intensity integrated over the 2π steradian half-space is the radiant emittance.

8.2.2. *Emission Spectra of Real Surfaces*

The characteristics of real surfaces are generally determined experimentally. When the surface emits a spectrally uniform fraction (ε) of the blackbody radiation, the surface is described as a *gray* body. Real materials have an emissivity that is spectrally nonuniform because of the physical structure of the material lattice configuration. Figure 8-11 shows the spectral emission of silicon carbide (SiC) as an example of a material suitable as a high-temperature radiator. Other materials that may be considered are refractory oxides, ytterbium oxide, in particular. Tabulated values of the (temperature-dependent)

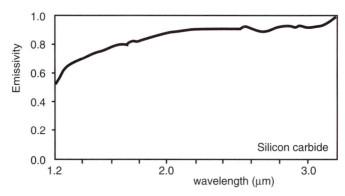

FIGURE 8-11. Emission characteristics of a high-temperature solid (SiC); from Ref. 8-8.

emissivity available in the literature for various materials are *integrated* values of the spectral emissivity, as shown in the figure. These values should therefore be used with care when calculating the performance of photocells.

8.2.3. *Physics of Radiation Interacting with Matter*

The determination of the performance of practical devices involving radiative power transfer requires consideration of the fact that radiation may encounter matter. If the matter is solid, the radiation may be *reflected*. The fraction reflected and the remainder that is admitted to the material's interior depends primarily on the change in the *index of refraction, n*. The fraction of the light reflected is given by the reflectivity r_2 given by

$$r = \frac{\text{reflected } \dot{w}}{\text{incident } \dot{w}} = \left(\frac{n_{\text{cell}} - n_{\text{ext}}}{n_{\text{cell}} + n_{\text{ext}}}\right)^2 \tag{8-20}$$

For example, for Si and air, the refractive indices are 3.4 and 1.0, respectively, and the reflectivity of this combination is consequently ~ 0.30. Intermediate layers of low-n materials can significantly reduce the reflection and are called antireflection coatings. Filters, consisting of a sandwich of materials with specific optical properties, may be designed to pass photons of a certain frequency range and reflect or absorb others (Fig. 8-12). Such filters will be seen to be useful in the construction of power systems using thermal radiation by their ability to reduce reflectivity to a few percent (Ref. 8-8).

Once inside a material, photons of a specific energy can interact with energy modes characteristic of the material. That is, absorption, the inverse process of emission, can take place. The interaction is on an atomic or crystal lattice structure level. It depends primarily on the coupling with the available degrees of freedom of the atom or molecule encountered and on their density.

The light proceeding through the matter may be absorbed by an available energy mode and reemitted with a very short "lifetime." This photon is said to undergo a *scattering* reaction. Alternatively, it may be absorbed (and converted to heat) if the time leading to reemission is so long that the energy is lost to the photon stream. The absorption mechanisms are effective where the degrees of freedom are resonant with the particular frequency of the light. Thus absorption is light frequency dependent. The light frequency couples to those material elements that can accept the energy within the rules of quantum mechanics. These elements can be electrons, molecules, or atoms. Electrons are elevated from a level E_1 to a new level E_2 by interaction with a photon (see eq. 8-17 and Fig. 8-11) whose energy is given by the difference in energy levels

$$hv = E_2 - E_1 \qquad (8\text{-}21)$$

Such absorption leads primarily to (broadened) *gaps* in the spectrum of the emitted radiation. As an example, the sun emits radiation that is approximately but well modeled as being that of a body at 5800 K, except that a close examination will reveal absorption line gaps in this spectrum as the sun's as well as the earth's atmospheres absorb specific energies. This is referred to as an *absorption spectrum*. Typically, line radiation is rather ineffective at transferring heat from a radiant source at modest (i.e., realistic) temperatures to a gas. The pathways in the energy absorption process through solid materials are summarized in Fig. 8-13. The process of photon-induced production of electron-hole pairs of interest here is significant only in semiconductors.

The absorption of photon energy by atoms and molecules takes place most efficiently by a coupling to the wide range of lattice wave motion possibilities in a solid. The energy is thus transferred to phonons, which share their energy with the atoms and molecules. It is the absorption of photons by electrons in a semiconductor lattice that allows the *p-n* junction to serve as a mechanism for creating charge carriers (electrons and holes) at an elevated energy (potential).

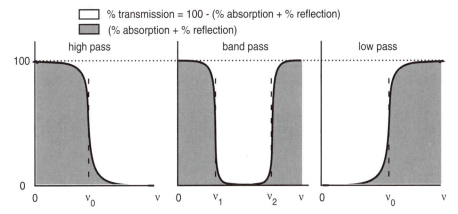

FIGURE 8-12. Variation of transmission of high pass, low pass, and band pass filters.

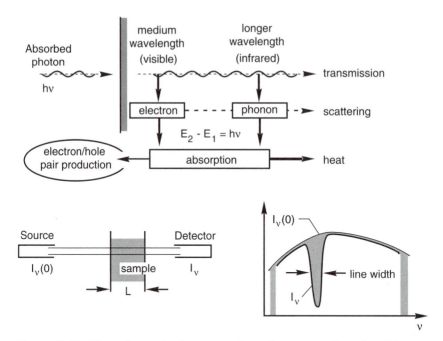

FIGURE 8-13. The pathways in the energy absorption process through solid materials. Electron–hole pair production is limited to semiconductors. In the lower figure, absorption in a cell of material of width L by a single mode characterized by a (broadened) line.

Macroscopically, one speaks of energy transfer between radiation and matter in terms of a frequency-dependent absorption coefficient (k_ν), which describes the exponential attenuation of a monochromatic light beam as a function of distance in the medium.

$$\frac{I_\nu}{I_\nu(0)} = \exp\left(- k_\nu L\right) \qquad (8\text{-}22)$$

This process is of considerable importance to solar energy conversion and its relation to sunlight attenuation through the earth's and, to a lesser extent, through the sun's gaseous atmospheres (Section 1.11, Ref. 1-1). Absorption is also important in the design of photocells since the photons must be able to traverse the n-type semiconductor to reach the p-n junction. Thus absorption controls the allowable thickness of the n layer (Section 8.3.3).

8.3. SPECTRAL ASPECTS OF ELECTRIC POWER FROM PHOTOCELLS

Not all photons from a radiation source are capable of elevating the energy of electrons in the p-n junction of a semiconductor into the conduction band. Two aspects of radiative energy conversion into electric current must be considered in the design of a system. The first is that the photons from a thermal source with energies below the cutoff energy (V_g) are not usable by the photocell. The other consideration is that photon energy in excess of that required for the process of creating electron-hole pairs is "wasted" by reduction to heat, which may have to be actively removed to keep the cell from overheating.

The reference literature is replete with data describing the performance characteristics of semiconductors, in particular their spectral sensitivity related to the associated band gap; see Table 8-1. These particular characteristics govern the performance of the photovoltaic cell. In this section, the goal is to describe an analysis approach that can be applied to any semiconductor by specializing it to the spectral energy distribution available and to the characteristics of the cell. The starting point is the theoretical maximum performance of a unit area of cell. As an example, the numerical parameters to be used for illustrative purposes reflect an interest in converting the photon power in the infrared spectrum through the use of a germanium cell (λ_0 = 1.8 µm) and in the visible range through the silicon solar cell (λ_0 = 1.1 µm). The challenge of converting solar power (i.e., visible spectrum thermal radiation from a blackbody $T \sim 5800$ K) to electrical power is covered in an extensive literature ranging from physics to manufacturing to system analysis (including, for example, Refs. 8-10, 8-11, and in Section 1.11 of Ref. 1-1).

8.3.1. *Photon Flux and Current*

For the purposes of describing the current from a photocell, it is useful to obtain the electron flux generated assuming that each photon with an energy greater than $h\nu_0$ can be converted to an electron in the conduction band. For the work to follow, it is convenient to nondimensionalize the temperature by a reference value as:

$$\theta \equiv \frac{T}{T_0} \tag{8-23}$$

where T_0 is taken as 288 K. The frequency (see eq. 8-18) is also nondimensionalized as

$$x \equiv \frac{h\nu}{kT} = \frac{h\nu}{kT_0}\frac{1}{\theta} \left(= \frac{hc}{kT}\frac{1}{\lambda} \right) \tag{8-24}$$

λ is the wavelength corresponding to ν. The frequency cutoff at ν_0 allows identification of x_0 as

$$x_0 \equiv \frac{h\nu_0}{kT} = \frac{h\nu_0}{kT_0}\frac{1}{\theta} = \left(\frac{hc}{kT_0}\right)\frac{1}{\lambda_0}\frac{1}{\theta} \tag{8-25}$$

Note that the zero subscript is used to denote the arbitrary reference temperature state and the cutoff wavelength or frequency of the photocell, which is not arbitrary in that it depends on the specific materials used in the construction of the cell. This should not cause confusion and is maintained to keep consistency with other aspects of this text.

The number of useful photons incident on the surface of the cell is the energy flux divided by the energy per photon. Equation 8-18 gives this photon flux as

$$\dot{n}_\phi = \frac{15}{\pi^4} \, \sigma \, T_0^4 \, \theta^4 \int_{x_0}^{\infty} \frac{1}{h\nu} \frac{x^3}{e^x - 1} \, dx \tag{8-26}$$

or, after conversion of $h\nu$ to x using eq. 8-24,

$$\dot{n}_\phi = \frac{15}{\pi^4} \frac{\sigma \, T_0^3}{k} \, \theta^3 \int_{x_0}^{\infty} \frac{x^2}{e^x - 1} \, dx \approx \frac{15}{\pi^4} \frac{\sigma \, T_0^3}{k} \, \theta^3 \int_{x_0}^{\infty} x^2 \, e^{-x} \, dx \tag{8-27}$$

for large x_0. When x_0 is sufficiently far to the high side of the maximum shown in Fig. 8-9 (i.e., $x_0 > x_m = 2.82$), the integrand may be approximated by neglecting the unity in the denominator. This approximation is valid for relatively low temperatures, low as measured by the cutoff frequency through eq. 8-25. The simplification allows a direct integration to arrive at an expression for the photon flux in terms of temperature and the cutoff frequency as given by x_0. The approximate form of the energy distribution function is plotted in Fig. 8-9 together with the exact form.

The integral allows definition of a photon flux parameter given by

$$\Phi \equiv \frac{\dot{n}_\phi \, k}{\sigma \, T_0^3} \frac{1}{\theta^3} = \frac{15}{\pi^4} \int_{x_0}^{\infty} x^2 \exp(-x) \, dx = \frac{15}{\pi^4} \left(x_0^2 + 2\,x_0 + 2\right) \exp(-x_0) \tag{8-28}$$

which is shown as a function of θ in Fig. 8-14. The data in Fig. 8-14 are carried out for two cases representative of Ge and Si with $\lambda_0 = 1.8 \ \mu m$ or $x_0 = 27.8/\theta$ and $\lambda_0 = 1.1 \ \mu m$ or $x_0 = 45.5/\theta$, respectively. Note that θ for the solar spectrum is about 20 and the approximate form of eq. 8-27 and a similar result given by eq. 8-36 are not valid. The *quantum efficiency parameter* Φ is a direct measure of the effectiveness of the cell with a specific cutoff frequency to generate electrons.

Note that fewer electrons can be generated with a lower cutoff wavelength, that is, a higher cutoff frequency. Combining eq. 8-27 and the definition of Φ gives the photon flux capable of creating an electron (as an electron-hole pair) as

$$\dot{n}_\phi = \left(\frac{\sigma \, T_0^3}{k}\right) \theta^3 \, \Phi \tag{8-29}$$

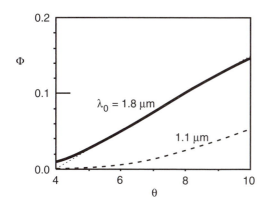

FIGURE 8-14. Variation of quantum efficiency parameter Φ given by eq. 8-27 for two values of the cutoff frequency, labeled here in terms of wavelength. For $\lambda_0 = 1.8$ μm, $\Phi \approx 0.025\,(\theta - 4)$.

The group of constants $\sigma T_0^3/k$ in this equation constitutes the reference value of the photon flux $= 0.98 \times 10^{23}$ m^{-2} sec^{-1} for $T_0 = 288$ K. Multiplying this value by the electron charge gives the current density associated with the photon flux, assuming one charge pair is produced per photon (with sufficient energy). This current is obtained for a cell operating at *short circuit*, j_s, because at this condition, the electron production rate is not hindered by the potential imposed by a load. The reference short circuit current density $(j_{s,\,0})$ is 1.57×10^4 A m^{-2} or 1.57 A/cm^2. The actual current (and power) density depends on the emitter temperature and is

$$j_s = \dot{n}_\phi\, q = \frac{\sigma T_0^3}{k}\, q\, \theta^3\, \Phi = j_{s,0}\, \theta^3\, \Phi \qquad (8\text{-}30)$$

The product $\theta^3\, \Phi$ is plotted in Fig. 8-15 and shows how rapidly current increases with increasing radiation source temperature.

Incident Energy Fluxes

The total energy brought in by <u>all</u> photons is given by the blackbody radiant emittance, eq. 8-19. The energy brought in by all photons with energy in excess of the cutoff energy (x_0) is given by

$$\dot{w}_0 = \frac{15}{\pi^4}\, \sigma T_0^4\, \theta^4 \int_{x_0}^{\infty} \frac{x^3}{e^x - 1}\, dx \qquad (8\text{-}31)$$

The energy brought in with each of these photons is greater than that required to create each pair. That useful portion of the energy (actually power density) is the number of photons times the band gap energy required:

$$\dot{w}_u = \dot{n}_\phi\, h\nu_0 = \frac{h\nu_0}{k\,T_0}\left(\sigma T_0^4\right) \theta^3\, \Phi = x_0 \left(\sigma T_0^4\right) \theta^4\, \Phi \qquad (8\text{-}32)$$

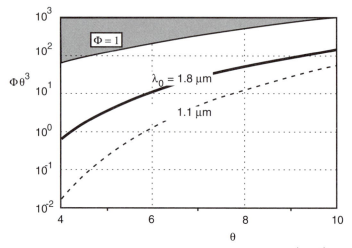

FIGURE 8-15. Plot of the current density multiplier $(\Phi \, \theta^3)$ as given by eq. 8-30.

x_0 is introduced though eq. 8-25. Alternatively eq. 8-32 may be written

$$\dot{w}_{\mathrm{u}} = \frac{15}{\pi^4} \, \sigma \, T_0^4 \, \theta^4 \int_{x_0}^{\infty} \frac{x_0 \, x^2}{e^x - 1} \, dx \qquad (8\text{-}33)$$

Effective Source Emissivity

These power densities allow the definition of a number of dimensionless parameters to characterize the performance of a radiator and a cell as an energy conversion system. For this purpose, it is convenient to assume that the radiator has a spectrally uniform *(gray)* body) emissivity. The thermal power of a radiator is reduced by a factor that may be termed an *effective emissivity* of the radiator. It is defined as the ratio of the power emitted by the radiator (at *T*) up to the wavelength that can be received by the cells to the total power emitted (Ref. 8-1). Thus from eqs. 8-19 and 8-31

$$\varepsilon(x_0) = \frac{\dot{w}_0}{\dot{w}_B} = \int_{x_0}^{\infty} \frac{x^3}{\exp(x) - 1} \, dx \Bigg/ \int_{0}^{\infty} \frac{x^3}{\exp(x) - 1} \, dx \qquad (8\text{-}34)$$

Here $x_0 = $ (constant x v_0/θ) and the constant intrinsic emissivity cancel out of the expression. This effective emissivity is the fraction of a radiator's power that is potentially useful to a cell with a cutoff wavelength given by λ_0. Figure 8-9 shows the frequency variation of the spectral radiance (radiant emittance) and identifies the areas on the plot from which the effective emissivity is formed. The wavelength limits shown are $\lambda_0 = 1.8$ and 1.1 μm as well as the noted values of θ. The lower portion of the figure illustrates the areas under $B(x)$ used in forming the emissivity ratio. Note that for $\lambda_0 = 1.8$ μm and θ less than about 9, the difference between the blackbody function integrand and its approximation is small (and neglected). Thus the emissivity is well approximated by

$$\varepsilon(x_0) \approx \frac{15}{\pi^4} \int_{x_0}^{\infty} x^3 \exp(-x)\, dx \approx \frac{15}{\pi^4} \left(x_0^3 + 3\,x_0^2 + 6\,x_0 + 6\right) \exp(-x_0)$$

$$(8\text{-}35)$$

Figure 8-16 shows the variations of $\varepsilon(x_0)$ in the temperature range of interest. θ less than about 4 is probably uninteresting from a power density viewpoint.

The second parameter of interest accounts for energy utilization. A realistic system would be designed to utilize the power $\dot{w}_0$ as the net input, with the remainder from the blackbody source being recycled to the source (see Section 8.5). The energy conversion efficiency for such a system (from usable radiant heat at T to electric power) may be defined as:

$$\eta_q = \frac{\dot{w}_u}{\dot{w}_0} = \frac{x_0 \left(\sigma T_0^4\right) \theta^4\, \Phi}{\varepsilon(\theta) \left(\sigma T_0^4\right) \theta^4} = \frac{x_0\, \Phi}{\varepsilon}$$

$$(8\text{-}36)$$

for a particular value of the cutoff wavelength. Here x_0, Φ, and ε are all functions of the temperature θ. This energy efficiency is plotted in Fig. 8-17 and is valid for θ less than ~10 because of the use of the simplified $B(x)$. The λ_0 value is noted. The approximate form of η_q is algebraic and reads

$$\eta_q \approx \frac{x_0^3 + 2\,x_0^2 + 2\,x_0}{x_0^3 + 3\,x_0^2 + 6\,x_0 + 6}$$

$$(8\text{-}37)$$

A comparison of Figs. 8-15 and 8-17 illustrates the desirability of high radiator temperature for high power and a lower temperature for high efficiency.

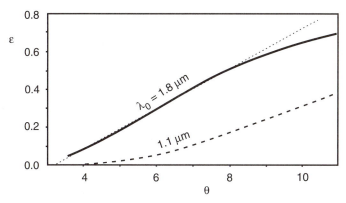

FIGURE 8-16. Effective emissivity given by eqs. 8-34 and 8-35 of a blackbody radiator with a cutoff wavelengths $\lambda_0 = 1.1$ and 1.8 μm. For $\lambda_0 = 1.8$ μm, $\varepsilon(\theta) \approx 0.1\,(\theta - 3.3)$.

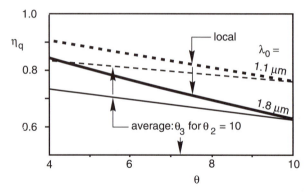

FIGURE 8-17. Variation of the energy conversion efficiency for a photocell with specific cutoff wavelengths, x_0 > x_m. The heavy curves are local values at temperature θ, while the lighter lines are averages between θ_3 and θ_2 = 10; see section 8.5.3.

It is important to remember that the heat deposited to the cell varies as $1 - \eta_q$. This heat must be removed to maintain a satisfactory operating temperature.

A last efficiency may be calculated using the ratio of useful to total blackbody power *input* ($\dot{w}_B$). This efficiency is the product x_0 and Φ ($< \eta_q$) and is normally not of great interest.

8.3.2. *Photovoltaic Cells*

Figure 8-7 shows the basic functional elements of a photocell. The cell must evidently consist of a structural and conductive backing (substrate) on which is built a *p*-type semiconductor. The *n*-type serves as the first active surface. The pairs produced at the junctions result in electron flow in the *n*-type layer and holes in the *p*-type. The hole charge carriers are collected at the contact with the conducting substrate, which constitutes the positive side of the cell. The *p*-type semiconductor can be made thin so that the holes reach the substrate with a minimum of loss and resistance.

The electrons, on the other hand, must travel along the *n*-type semiconductor to a collection network element above the first surface (Fig. 8-18, top). The network is required because the *n*-type layer is required to be thin and thus may present a high internal resistance. The collection element may also be a point connection often made through the junction to the rear of the cell as shown in Fig. 8-18 (bottom). Linear first surface connection elements are typically located where they may occlude some of the cell area. This loss in availability is a design aspect of the cell that is ideally optimized for a minimum of cell area occlusion with acceptable resistance to electron flow. Good design minimizes the shading loss by surface conductors. For example, an option available is to cover the cell with a transparent layer into which grooves are cut (Fig. 8-19, Refs. 8-5 and 8-11) above the surface collector elements. These grooves deflect rays about to impact the conductors sideways onto the cell surface.

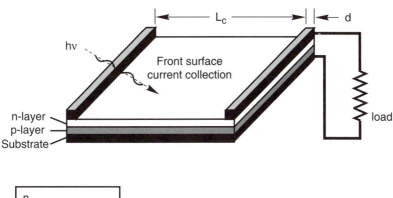

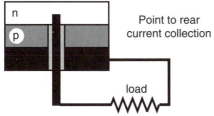

FIGURE 8-18. Sketch of a photocell showing the electrical current collection network.

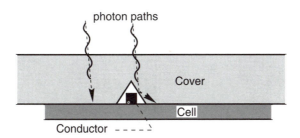

FIGURE 8-19. Grooved surface layer to minimize shading losses.

8.3.3. *Losses in Cells*

The critical design issue is the cell resistance, which is strongly affected by the thickness of the *n*-type semiconductor. This value must be kept small so that photon absorption takes place in the active region between the first surface of the cell and the *p-n* junction. In practice, the absorption coefficient for photons in semiconductor is very strongly wavelength dependent (Fig. 8-20). For low-energy photons, the absorption is very small, and the material is essentially transparent. At the wavelength or frequency corresponding to the band gap, the absorption coefficient (α) rises rapidly to values of the order 10^3 cm^{-1} or more. Thus to capture the photons at the *p–n* junction, it must be very close to the surface. In practice, the *n*-layer thickness is typically measured in micrometers. Following eq. 8-22, the fraction of the power absorbed in a layer of *n*-type semiconductor of thickness L_n is given by

$$\frac{\text{absorbed } \dot{w}}{\text{incident } \dot{w}} = \exp\left(-\alpha\, L_n\right) \qquad (8\text{-}38)$$

Here it is assumed that the radiation enters normal to the cell surface. For a finite resistivity of the *n* layer, the thickness of the layer dictates the characteristic spacing (L_c, Fig. 8-20) that must be employed between the point or linear element collection sites. Commonly this length is most practical to be a few millimeters. In addition, the shape and cross sectional area of the conductors (dimension *d*, Fig. 8-18) on the front surface are an integral aspect of the design problem. The resistance of these conductors, which are in series with the load, depends on the current flow area, and the cell shading depends on the surface width of the conductor. The joule or ohmic heating losses are

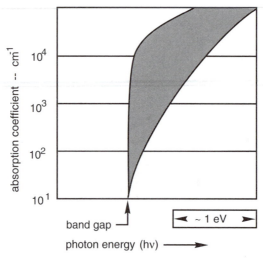

FIGURE 8-20. Variation of absorption coefficient for a generic semiconductor. A specific curve will typically lie within the shaded area.

essentially those associated with finite resistance associated with the n layer and the collector grid as

$$R_{internal} \sim \rho_{n\text{-layer}} \frac{1}{L_n} + \rho_{conductor} \frac{L_c}{d^2} \qquad (8\text{-}39)$$

where ρs are the electrical resistivities (= $1/\sigma$). The characteristic spacing between collection wires of diameter d is L_c; see Fig. 8-18. These elements constitute a major portion of the internal cell resistance identified in Fig. 8-20. A detailed study of these design issues is beyond the scope of this text, and the reader should consult the specialist literature. For example, Ref. 8-5 devotes more space to this issue.

Figure 8-21 shows a cross-sectional view of a cell and the mechanisms that are involved in the processing of energy. Reduction from ideal performance is experienced through the following phenomena: photons do not reach the region near the p-n junction, pairs produced do not reach the circuit, and losses by joule heating occur in the circuits, particularly those associated with the collection system described in the section above. The charge pairs created at the p-n junction that do not contribute to cell output current may be lost by recombination in the p layer. This is due to the finite probability that a hole and electron can diffuse toward one another and combine, resulting in local heat deposition. All mechanisms that result in heat deposition in the cell potentially reduce performance.

To illustrate the magnitude of the various losses in a silicon cell system for the conversion of solar radiation, Table 8-2 shows the magnitude of the loss elements and thus the level of performance obtainable for such a process. As technology is improved, some of these factors noted may be expected to lead to higher conversion efficiency.

8.3.4. *The Equivalent Circuit*

As an energy production device, the cell may be visualized as an element in a power circuit (Fig. 8-22). The p–n junction is a current source whose output depends on the photon flux. The recombining pairs constitute a current through a diode, reducing the net output and the resistance in series with the load is the internal cell resistance. The shunt in parallel with the junction is the intrinsic self-shorting of the cell, which is small and may often be neglected.

The first focus of attention is the junction itself. The photons converted to higher-energy electrons are the source of the current. Section 8.1.2 described the physics of the photon-electron interaction at the p–n junction. The flow of current is seen to be very sensitive to the cell potential, so that one should expect a nonlinear voltage-current characteristic.

In the absence of any radiation, the p–n junction develops a contact potential, which is that potential (V_{max}) required to prevent further diffusion of charge carriers, and the steady energy picture shown in Fig. 8-6 is obtained. This contact potential cannot be used to cause current to flow because the

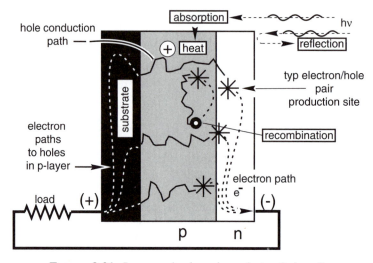

FIGURE 8-21. Loss mechanisms in a photovoltaic cell.

Table 8–2. Estimated performance of a Si cell in sunlight; adapted from data in Refs. 8-1, 8-12, 8-13, and 8-14

Mechanism	% Energy lost in remaining stream	% Energy remaining
First surface shading	4	96
Reflectance	10	86
Long-wavelength photons not absorbable	23	67
Photon energy to heat	43	38
Junction loss, V_{oc}/V_g	38	24
Fill factor, $\dot{w}_w/\dot{w}^*$	18	19
Recombination/leakage	12	17
Series resistance, useful power	3	16

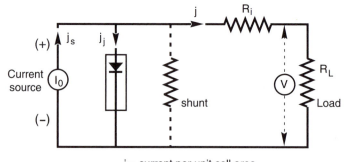

j = current per unit cell area

FIGURE 8-22. Equivalent circuit for a power-producing photovoltaic cell showing the important reverse current junction flow.

connection of leads to the contacts would introduce new contact potentials and the circuit thus formed reestablishes a new equilibrium. From a thermodynamic viewpoint, one could argue that if the junction *were* able to provide a current, it would be equivalent to creating (electrical) work at the expense of properties of a single thermal reservoir, a violation of the second law.

The distribution of electron energies in the p and n regions of the semiconductor are related to energies relative to the Fermi level, taken here as the zero energy reference. The electrons in the conduction band of the p region have a greater energy than those in the conduction band of the n region. As a consequence they can move to the n region. This electron flow constitutes a current whose energy source is the heat in the semiconductor material at temperature T. This current flows from p to n and is termed a "thermal" current density, j_0, p–n. The current density, rather than the current, is used here because it, the power, and a number of other quantities scale with cell area. The thermal current toward lower energy is proportional to the number density of electrons in the p region:

$$j_{0,\,p\text{-}n} \quad \alpha \quad n_{e,p} \quad \alpha \quad \exp\left(-\frac{\varepsilon_p}{kT}\right) \tag{8-40}$$

where ε_p is the electron energy in the p region above the Fermi level. The Boltzmann factor describes the decreasing likelihood that, for a given temperature, an electron will be found at a higher energy level. Similarly, the number of electrons in the conduction band of the n region is given by a similar equation, and the necessary recombination current (from n to p) is

$$j_{r,\,n\text{-}p} \quad \alpha \quad n_{e,n} \quad \alpha \quad \exp\left(-\frac{\varepsilon_n + eV_{\max}}{kT}\right) = \exp\left(-\frac{\varepsilon_p}{kT}\right) \tag{8-41}$$

Here $V_{\max}$ is the height of the potential barrier the electrons traveling from n to p must overcome. The equilibrium condition requires

$$j_{0,\,p\text{-}n} = j_{r,\,n\text{-}p} \tag{8-42}$$

When the contacts of the cell are connected to a potential, this balance of currents is disrupted. The potential may be generated by a voltage source, such as a battery. For example, if the voltage applied increases the magnitude of the contact potential (reverse bias), the recombination current is decreased, while the thermally generated remains constant. Similarly, when the bias direction is changed (to a forward bias), the recombination current is increased and the net current therefore changes sign. The potential distributions and the response of thermal, recombination, and net currents (under a no-photon input condition) are illustrated in Fig. 8-23. The holes respond similarly to the bias voltage. The cell as a whole therefore produces a recombination current that is related to the thermal current according to

$$j_r = j_0 \exp\left(\frac{eV}{kT}\right) \tag{8-43}$$

where the barrier height V is related to the bias voltage V_b through:

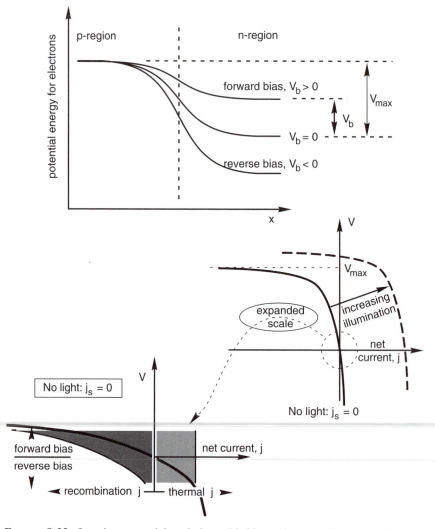

FIGURE 8-23. Junction potential variation with bias voltage and corresponding V-j characteristic. Also noted is the effect of light illumination on the cell.

$$V = V_{max} - V_b \qquad (8\text{-}44)$$

Equation 8-43 shows the equality of these currents when the bias voltage $V_b = 0$. Note that an electrical load biases the cell to reduce the cell voltage V to a value less than V_{max}:

The *dark* current, j_0, includes of the contribution of the holes. The *net* current across the junction (j_j), in the direction against the desired output current, is

$$j_j = j_r - j_0 = j_0 \left[\exp\left(\frac{eV}{kT}\right) - 1 \right] \qquad (8\text{-}45)$$

Figure 8-23 shows the variation of the net current density with voltage. This variation is characteristic of a rectifier, which effectively allows current in one direction only, and eq. 8-45 is referred to as a diode equation.

The difference between V_{max} and the bias voltage V_b is the voltage seen by a load, V. When the cell is short circuited, $V = 0$, all photoelectrons are converted to current and the net current from the cell (j, see Fig. 8-22) is j_s. At a finite bias voltage V, established by the combination of load and internal resistance, the net cell current is

$$j = j_s - j_j = j_s - j_0 \left[\exp \left(\frac{eV}{kT} \right) - 1 \right] \tag{8-46}$$

or, rearranging to obtain V in terms of j

$$\frac{V}{V_{oc}} = \frac{\ln \left[1 + \left(1 - \frac{j}{j_s} \right) \frac{j_s}{j_0} \right]}{\ln \left(1 + \frac{j_s}{j_0} \right)} = \frac{\ln \left[1 + (1 - J)A \right]}{\ln (1 + A)} \; ; \; \text{where} \quad J \equiv \frac{j}{j_s} \; \text{and} \; A \equiv \frac{j_s}{j_0} \tag{8-47}$$

J is a nondimensional output current and A is the ratio of short circuit to dark current densities. Note that the ideally large A is the principal performance parameter of the voltage-current characteristic. Recall the strong temperature dependence of the dark current, eq. 8-16.

Open Circuit Voltage

In terms of A, the open circuit voltage is given by a rearrangement of eq. 8-46 with $j = 0$ as

$$V_{oc} = \frac{kT}{e} \ln \left(1 + \frac{j_s}{j_0} \right) = \frac{kT}{e} \ln (1 + A) \tag{8-48}$$

An important deduction from eq. 8-48 is that the open circuit voltage depends on the incident photon flux, which determines j_s. The open circuit voltage realized by a cell is an important measure of the efficiency of the cell as an energy converter. Consider that the photons must have an energy at least as large as the band gap, $V_g = 1.1$ V for Si. Such a cell might have a maximum open circuit voltage given by eq. 8-48. For $V_{max} = 0.6$ V, eq. 8-48 gives the required $A \sim 3 \times 10^{10}$. Under full sunlight conditions, the actual open circuit voltage is about 0.5 V. Thus it is apparent that for a silicon solar cell in sunlight, only about 1/3 [0.4 (= $V_{max\ power}$) /1.1] of the energy required to create a pair is realized as potential energy for the electron generated.

A plot of eq. 8-47 is shown in Figs. 8-23 and 8-24. In Fig. 8-23, the direct effect of the photon stream is shown on the V–j characteristic established by

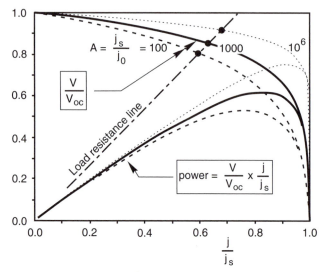

FIGURE 8-24. The nondimensionalized voltage current characteristic of a photocell. The intersection of the load resistance line (here units of resistance are ohm cm^2) and the *V-j* characteristic is the operating point. Also shown is the power output (per cm^2).

the dark current. This effect is quantified by the magnitude of the current ratio, A, as shown in Fig. 8-24. For large A, as is typically the case, the equations simplify somewhat, but the physical current scales directly with A, whereas V_{oc} scales as its logarithm. Clearly, large values of A are desirable because the absolute output increases, as does the power fraction of the cell, as Fig. 8-24 shows.

On the plot of voltage versus current, a representative, *linear* line of constant load resistance (units of resistance are ohm-cm^2) is shown. Higher resistance lines have steeper slopes, and the operating point lies at the intersection of the resistance and cell *V–j* characteristic, as shown in Fig. 8-24.

Short Circuit Current

The short circuit current is obtained from eq. 8-46 with $V = 0$ or

$$J_{sc} = 1 \qquad (8\text{-}49)$$

Under these conditions, there is no potential barrier for electrons to climb, so that every photon of sufficient energy can create a pair. As an example shown in Fig. 8-25, a silicon cell has a short circuit current proportional to illumination. For this cell the current is about 28 mA/cm^2 (280 A/m^2) at a solar illumination intensity of 100 mW/cm^2 = 1 kW/m^2.

To characterize the quality of the cell as an electron producer, one may define a *collection efficiency* as

$$\eta_{coll} = \frac{j_s}{(1 - r)[1 - \exp(-\alpha L_n)] e \dot{n}_\phi} \tag{8-50}$$

where $e\dot{n}_\phi$ is the electron current if all photons with sufficient energies produced a charge carrier pair. r is the reflected fraction of the incident beam, and the term in brackets represents that portion not absorbed in traversing the thickness (L_n) of the n layer; see eq. 8-38.

8.3.5. *Cell Performance*

The extremal voltage (V_{oc}) and current (j_s) characteristics for a specific silicon cell are shown in Fig. 8-25. For these data, the dark current j_0 lies between 10^{-8} and 10^{-9} mA/cm². The calculated curves (dashed) are for values of A corresponding to these values of j_0.

The product of j_s and V_{oc} is a power density parameter for the cell. Thus one may define

$$\dot{w}^* = j_s V_{oc} = j_s \frac{kT}{e} \ln\left(1 + \frac{j_s}{j_0}\right) \approx \frac{kT}{e} j_s \ln\left(\frac{j_s}{j_0}\right) \tag{8-51}$$

as a measure of the power density capability of the cell. Evidently the power obtainable from a cell is a strong function of the illumination, which gives j_s. The fraction of this power obtainable is calculated from

$$\text{fill factor} = \frac{\dot{w}}{\dot{w}^*} = \frac{jV}{j_s V_{oc}} = J\frac{\ln[1 + (1 - J)A]}{\ln(1 + A)} \tag{8-52}$$

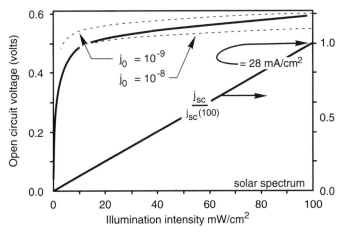

FIGURE 8-25. Short circuit current and open circuit voltage of a Si solar cell illuminated with a solar spectrum of the power level noted (Refs. 8-5, 8-15).

This ratio is called a *curve factor* or *fill factor*, which is plotted as a function of current drawn in Fig. 8-24 for three values of A. Note that the maximum power point is relatively close to the short circuit current and open circuit voltage. The voltage-current characteristic becomes "fuller" at larger values of A.

The operating point for maximum power is obtained by differentiating eq. 8-52 with respect to J and setting the resulting expression to zero. The result is an implicit expression for J_w calculated from

$$\ln\left(1 + A\left(1 - J_w\right)\right) = \frac{A\, J_w}{1 + A\left(1 - J_w\right)} \tag{8-53}$$

Figure 8-26 shows J_w together with the resulting ratio V_w/V_{oc} and the fill factor as these vary with the current ratio A. The lower part of the figure shows the maximum power fill factor and its relation to the V–j characteristic.

8.3.6. Temperature Effects

Increased temperature operation gives rise to an increase in the magnitude of the dark current. This current increases very rapidly with increasing temperature; see eqs. 8-15 and 8-16. As far as the cell performance is concerned, this leads to a decrease in A for a given illumination intensity which in turn decreases the nondimensional maximum V and thus the fill factor. The effect on J is relatively small and is typically positive. The actual voltage will change due to a change in temperature (see eq. 8-51) as well as the decreas-

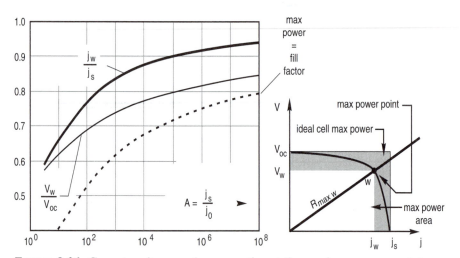

FIGURE 8-26. Current, voltage, and power ratios at the maximum power point as a function of short circuit current to dark current ratio or, equivalently, illumination intensity for cell at a constant temperature. The lower part of the figure shows the maximum power point and the areas used in the definition of the fill factor.

ing A, as seen from eq. 8-48. In practice, the open circuit voltage decreases with increasing cell temperature. Over a temperature increase from 40°C to a readily reached 150°C, the power output from a silicon solar cell can fall to 60% of its low-temperature power level. The efficiency falls to roughly from ~20% at 300 K to ~10% at 400 K (Ref. 8-2). Reference 8-1 and others gives for a crystalline silicon (10 ohm-cm) cell at room temperature the following values for the temperature derivatives:

Short circuit current $dj/dT = 10^{-4}$ A/m²/K

Open circuit voltage $dV_{OC}/dT = -2.2 \times 10^{-3}$ V/K

Power (expressed as a percentage) $= -0.5\%$ K⁻¹

In examining the performance of a given cell at various illumination intensities, the increasing photon power input raises not only the flux of convertible photons and thus the power, but also the flux of photons, which ultimately end up as heat. Thus the subjugation of a cell to increasing illumination also affects its temperature and thus its performance as the decreasing value of A in Fig. 8-26 shows.

8.4. RADIANT CONVERSION POWER SYSTEMS

8.4.1. *Solar Power*

Solar power is readily available, especially in regions within 30 degrees of the equator with desertlike climates. Solar power availability has been an important motivation for the development of silicon-based solar cells because these cells have the potential for low unit cost and are reasonably well matched to the solar spectrum, where most of the power is transmitted in the visible light spectral region. Approaches for solar cell development include attempts to lower the manufacturing cost of single crystals, the use of lower-cost amorphous thin films, which, unfortunately, have a lower performance, and the use of concentrating systems to decrease cell area requirements for a given level of electric power (Ref. 8-4). To varying degrees, the performance of solar cells can be increased through the use of multilayer cells, which incorporate p-n junctions with varying band gap energies to capture a greater fraction of the solar spectral power.

The reader may refer to Chapter 1 of Ref. 1-1 for a more thorough discussion of the challenge to the exploitation of solar energy and to Ref. 8-11 for a discussion of the more general range of possibilities regarding solar energy in space and related power transmission aspects. In summary, solar power is dilute, at best of the order 1 kW/m², and conversion efficiency is relatively low (~10-20% on average), so that a large collection area is required for a significant power output for the user. The amortized cost of whatever collection means is employed is currently high compared with that of engines using low-cost fossil fuels.

The use of solar energy requires the ability to store it in some usable form. This storage is required on daily as well as annual time scales. On the daily time scale, losses may be manageable, but on a yearly scale they constitute a serious economic challenge. Methods for energy storage are available, but they always place an additional cost burden on the system and therefore on the power delivered to the user. Exploitation of solar power is particularly difficult for people living in midlatitude regions of the earth where the power required for industry is large and the availability is rather low due to the solar orientation in the sky and the related climate at these latitudes.

There are thermal (i.e., nonelectric) applications that have been economically very successful in the use of solar power. Among these are rooftop hot water heating systems, especially in hotter climates, and architectural design for passive solar heating of living spaces.

8.4.2. *Nuclear Radiation and Heat*

Nuclear processes in reactors or decay masses involve emission of very energetic photons. These are not convertible to electric power by means of cells described in this chapter because of the energy mismatch between these photons (γ rays) and practical band gaps available. However, the heat from a reactor can be applied to a thermally radiating surface and thereby generate photoelectric power, much like the combustion system described in Section 8.5. The design of the reactor fuel element would have to be adapted to higher-temperature operation than conventional or even gas-cooled reactors. Nuclear rocket propulsion reactors exceed the requirements of this application and may well point the way to reactor power used with radiative transfer.

8.4.3. *Thermal Radiation*

The economics of power conversion from photons to electricity is significantly more favorable for cells that operate in the infrared spectral region with larger λ_0 (Ref. 8-4) than for solar cells operating with visible light. The principal reason for this is that the radiation power density may be increased to levels approaching 100 suns (~100 kW/m^2) to reduce the area required by the cell and thereby the cost of the cell. The thermal sources available for converting infrared energy include fuel-generated thermal radiation and solar thermal power collected in a variety of concentration devices, including those that track the sun. An example of a high-concentration-ratio solar collector is the "power tower" built by the U.S. Department of Energy in Barstow, California. This concept uses a central collector mounted above an array of steerable mirrors that direct and concentrate the solar power into a receiver cavity to heat a working fluid. The energy collected may be used as heat either (1) directly or (2) stored in a medium for later use by a heat engine or as a radiation source. The working or storage medium is most practically a liquid at a temperature consistent with handleability and heat loss. Thus it is possible to envisage systems where materials may be heated to high temperatures for storage or direct use using solar power. The cost of the first surface area (mirrors and tracking means, lenses, etc.) for capturing solar power will be an important component of the system cost, although there is optimism that these costs can be reduced in the future (Ref. 8-16). Until such breakthroughs are realized, solar concentration systems utilizing the free solar power may continue to be costlier than fossil-fuel systems for some time to come.

If fossil-fuel systems are considered, then radiation temperatures up to those consistent with the steady stoichiometric combustion of the fuel with air are practical. Such temperatures may reach 3000 K and are encountered only in the burner itself and the radiator of a system, which minimizes losses and problems in handling.

8.5. INFRARED PHOTOVOLTAIC SYSTEMS

An infrared photovoltaic system (IRV) consists of a surface (a tube, for example) heated by combustion gas to a temperature where the emission spectrum is such that a significant fraction of the photons can be absorbed by a photocell array (Fig. 8-27). Photons with wavelengths longer than λ_0 should be reflected to the emission surface, where they are reabsorbed, and thus the energy has another opportunity to be sent as a more energetic photon.

From a radiation viewpoint, temperatures in the range $\theta \sim 4$ to 10 are of interest. At $\theta = 4$ (1000 K), the radiant power density (eq. 8-19) is relatively low, while $\theta = 10$ (3000 K) is near the limit possible by combustion of the fuel and air. The radiation travels from the radiator through a long-wavelength reflector (or at least a high-pass filter, Fig. 8-14, to minimize the heat load on the cell), through the optics, whose performance may be assumed ideal, and finally to the cell generating electric power and dealing with waste heat. Figure 8-28 shows the energy fluxes identified in Section 8.3.1.

Ideally, the temperature of the emission tube should be high for high power density. The limited chemical energy of fuel combustion with air therefore requires preheating of the combustion air. The heat supply system thus logically consists of an air preheat heat exchanger and a constant-pressure burner (Fig. 8-25). The pumping power of the atmospheric pressure air and

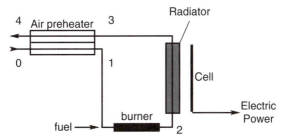

FIGURE 8-27. Schematic of the IRV conversion system. Noted are station numbers for the thermodynamic analysis of the heating process in Section 8.5.1.

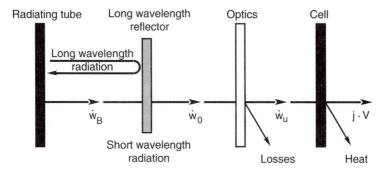

FIGURE 8-28. Schematic energy flow from radiator tube to photocell converter.

combustion gas is small and hence negligible from an energy accounting viewpoint. The temperature of the cold end of the radiator must be sufficiently high to make the power density there sufficiently high. The states of the gas are numbered in the sketch. The following is an analysis of the system shown to determine its characteristics as an electric power producer. Other system configurations are discussed in Ref. 8-17, together with a greater emphasis on the performance-determining engineering details.

8.5.1. *Thermodynamics of Heat Generation by Combustion*

The principal design and performance parameters are the radiation tube entry and exit temperatures, θ_2 and θ_3, whose difference is a measure of the heat given up by the flow. For analysis purposes, the properties of air and light hydrocarbon combustion gas are taken to have constant specific heats (C_p) at values that depend on the chemical composition (i.e., whether the gas is air or combustion gas) and are constant with temperature. Thus one may define the ratio

$$\delta \equiv \frac{C_{p,2}}{C_{p,0}} - 1 = \left(\frac{\text{combustion gas } C_p}{\text{air } C_p} - 1\right) \sim \text{ of order 0.2} \qquad (8\text{-}54)$$

The mass flow of the stream after combustion is larger than that of air by the amount of fuel added. The fuel mass fraction f_f is

$$f_f \equiv \frac{\dot{m}_{\text{fuel}}}{\dot{m}_{\text{air}}} \qquad (8\text{-}55)$$

This fraction is maximally of the order 0.07, depending on the fuel-air stoichiometry (see Chapter 1 and Section 8.5.2 in Ref. 1-1).

The thermal balance on the preheater determines the temperature changes. For a counterflow heat exchanger with a capacity rate mismatch ($\alpha \neq 1$), this reads (Ref. 1-1, Section 6.2):

$$(1 + f_f)(1 + \delta)(\theta_4 - \theta_3) = \theta_1 - 1 \quad \text{or} \quad \alpha(\theta_3 - \theta_4) = \theta_1 - 1 \qquad (8\text{-}56)$$

Here α is the capacity rate ratio and is defined by this relation as $\alpha \equiv (1 + f_f)(1 + \delta)$. A heat exchanger with $\alpha > 1$ can at best be designed to have equal temperatures at the hot end (Section 6.2.1, Ref. 1-1) and the conventional modeling approach is to define a *heat exchanger effectiveness* (η_x) as a parameter to describe the proximity to this ideal design possibility:

$$\eta_x = \frac{\text{heat transferred}}{\text{heat transferrable}} = \frac{\theta_1 - 1}{\theta_3 - 1} \tag{8-57}$$

In general, therefore, the preheater outlet temperature is given by

$$\theta_1 = 1 + \eta_x(\theta_3 - 1) \tag{8-58}$$

From eq. 8-56, the temperature of the spent combustion gas is given by

$$\theta_4 = \theta_3 - \frac{\eta_x}{\alpha}(\theta_3 - 1) = 1 + (\theta_1 - 1)\left(\frac{1}{\eta_x} - \frac{1}{\alpha}\right) \tag{8-59}$$

The form given in terms of the preheat temperature (θ_1) shows clearly that heat waste is necessarily involved, because $\theta_4 > 1$. In a system where high efficiency is required, this heat may be used for other useful purposes. For an ideal heat exchanger and $\alpha = 1.25$, the waste gas temperature is approximately $\theta_4 \sim 0.8 + 0.2\,\theta_1$, which is greater than 1 for the interesting cases with an elevated preheater temperature, $\theta_1 > 1$.

Burner Heat Balance

The fuel energy determines the final temperature of the combustion gas, θ_2. An enthalpy balance on the combustion process reads:

$$q_{in} = \alpha\,\theta_2 - \theta_1 \tag{8-60}$$

or in terms of θ_2 and the more interesting radiator tube exit temperature θ_3:

$$q_{in} = \alpha\,\theta_2 - 1 - \eta_x\left(\theta_3 - 1\right) \tag{8-61}$$

The heat delivered to the IRV system is lost by radiation between the temperatures θ_2 and θ_3. In the IRV, the heat loss from the gas is

$$q_{out} = \alpha\left(\theta_2 - \theta_3\right) \tag{8-62}$$

Thermal Conversion Efficiency

The ratio of heat output through the tube to fuel heat input may be used as a basis for a definition of the thermal efficiency of the heating system. Thus we define

$$\eta_{th} = \frac{q_{out}}{q_{in}} = \frac{\alpha\left(\theta_2 - \theta_3\right)}{\alpha\,\theta_2 - 1 - \eta_x\left(\theta_3 - 1\right)} = \frac{\theta_2 - \theta_3}{\theta_2 - \theta_3/\alpha} \quad \text{when } \eta_x = 1 \tag{8-63}$$

For the ideal and realistic cases of η_x = 1.0 and 0.90, respectively, this thermal efficiency is shown in Fig. 8-29. The decreasing thermal efficiency at the higher tube outlet temperature θ_3 is essentially a reflection of the higher waste gas temperature θ_4. Operating at high values of θ_3 would generally force utilization of the waste heat by additional means to raise the effective thermal efficiency.

8.5.2. Radiative Transfer to Cells

The optimal geometric arrangement of radiator and cell is that in which the radiation emitter area and the receiving cell area are parallel and facing one another. If these areas are closely spaced, the view angle from any element in either area to the other is very close to 2π steradians. In this case, the only loss of photons is that emitted from near the edges of the radiator. This transfer inefficiency is related to the ratio of spacing (s) to characteristic size dimension (D). By design with small s/D and/or manipulation of the characteristic size ratio for emitter and cell, the photon transfer loss can be made suitably small. Further consideration of view aspects of radiative transfer is therefore neglected here but may be included by applying the basics of radiative heat transfer. A detailed performance of this transfer process also requires consideration of the conductive transfer from emitter to cell by the material used to separate them. Further, any gaseous substance between these surfaces may cause convective transfer of heat.

The simple practical form for a thermal radiator is a cylindrical one with fuel and air entering from one end and reacted combustion products leaving from the other. Alternatively, a heated fluid could surrender its sensible heat to the walls as it travels along a tubular flow element. In any case, the cylindrical geometry is well adapted to providing thermal radiation, which can be manipulated for processing by a infrared photocell array. Figure 8-30 shows

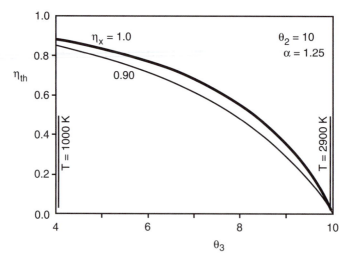

FIGURE 8-29. Thermal efficiency of the heating system. α = 1.25 and the heat exchanger effectiveness (η_x) is as noted.

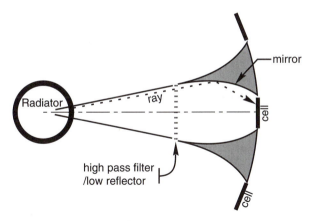

FIGURE 8-30. View of a sector of a cylindrical radiator, the high pass filter, the reflection surface, and the cell.

an implementation of the elements shown in Fig. 8-28 as an end view of a cylinder with a high-pass filter and a concentrating lens.

The inclusion of reflecting surfaces (see Fig. 8-30) to concentrate emitted light to the cell involves losses associated with the reflection process. These losses are angle and wavelength dependent. An accurate determination of performance of IRV conversion systems must consider such losses, although the associated efficiency should be expected to be high.

8.5.3. *Radiator Tube Length*

The final temperature of the emission tube determines the length of the radiator tube required to transfer a given amount of power per unit area by thermal means. One may estimate the length of this tube by examining the power balance on the tube. For this purpose, one may assume that a long-wavelength reflector is used for the cell band gap energy, assumed here to be 1.8 μm so that the problem is definite. With such a reflector, the tube emits with an effective emissivity given by eq. 8-34. If the tube is long and thin, one may as a first approximation neglect axial heat conduction so that a power balance between loss of heat from the gas by radiation applies locally. The heat balance along the tube ($0 \leq z \leq L$) gives:

$$\dot{m}\, C_p\, dT \;=\; \varepsilon\,(T)\, \sigma\, T^4\, \pi\, D\, dz \tag{8-64}$$

On a nondimensional basis,

$$\frac{d\,z}{L_{RT}} \;=\; -3\, \frac{d\theta}{\varepsilon(\theta)\, \theta^4}, \quad \text{where } L_{RT} \;=\; \frac{\dot{m}\, C_p}{3\, \pi\, D\, \sigma\, T_0^3} \tag{8-65}$$

L_{RT} is a characteristic radiative transfer length, which incorporates the 3 as an integration factor. This characteristic radiative transfer length (in meters) may be written in terms of the flow parameters as

$$L_{RT} = \frac{\dot{m}\, C_p}{3\pi\, D\sigma\, T_0^3} = D\,\frac{\gamma}{\gamma\text{-}1}\,\frac{1}{12}\,\frac{p_0\, u(z{=}0)}{\sigma T_0^4} \approx D\, M(z{=}0)\, 2.5\times 10^4 \quad (8\text{-}66)$$

for T_0 =288 K. D is the tube diameter, γ (~1.4) is the specific heat ratio, p (~ 1 atm) is the fluid pressure, u is the flow speed, and M is the corresponding Mach number at the radiator entrance. Nominal values substituted give this length as noted. The lengths L and L_{RT} are directly proportional to M and D. This is since M is a direct measure of the rate at which enthalpy is introduced into the tube. This rate is also proportional to D^2, but the loss varies as D so that the net effect of D on L is direct proportionality.

The equation for the θ variation (eq. 8-65) may be integrated (between θ_2 and θ_3) for ε =1 as a reference case to yield

$$\frac{L}{L_{RT}} = F(\theta_3) - F(\theta_2) \quad \text{where} \quad F(\theta_i) = \frac{1}{\theta_i^3} \quad (8\text{-}67)$$

This quantity is plotted in Fig. 8-31 for θ_2= 10 (2900 K) and labeled "blackbody." Of greater interest is the role of the emissivity. With an approximate model of the effective emissivity, (see Fig. 8-16), the length integral is given by a similar equation, except that F is given by

$$F(\theta) = \frac{3}{\varepsilon_1}\int \frac{d\theta}{(\theta - c)\,\theta^4} = \frac{3}{\varepsilon_1}\left[\frac{1}{c^4}\ln\left(\frac{\theta - c}{\theta}\right) + \frac{1}{c^3\theta} + \frac{2}{c^2\theta^2} + \frac{3}{c\theta^3}\right] \quad (8\text{-}68)$$

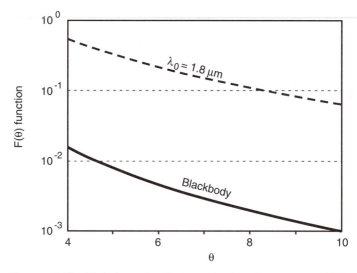

FIGURE 8-31. Variation of radiation tube length parameter $F(\theta)$ required to transfer energy from all photons (a true blackbody, labeled blackbody) and from only the photons with a wavelength shorter than 1.8 μm.

where $c \sim 3$ and ε_1 is ~0.1. This description using c and ε_1 should be adequate in the interval $4 < \theta < 10$. This plot is a determination of the $F(\theta)$ function for the calculation of the required length between any two temperatures.

Figure 8-31 shows the importance of the temperature-dependent emissivity, which serves to lengthen the tube to emit the power, by about an order of magnitude. For a temperature variation from $\theta = 10$ to 5, the lengths required are 0.007 (blackbody) and 0.27 ($\lambda_0 = 1.8$ μm), a factor of about 40. An obvious conclusion to be drawn from this analysis is that the lower the exit temperature, the longer the radiation tube required and the higher the efficiency of heat utilization by the heat supply system. To some extent, the logarithmic ordinate hides the steepness of this relation.

Further, the flow length is about 0.01 or 0.3 times the characteristic L_{RT}, where

$$L_{RT} \approx D(=0.01) \frac{M(=0.01)}{\sqrt{\theta(=10)}} \times 2.5 \times 10^4 \cong 1 \text{ m} \tag{8-69}$$

meaning that the physical length required to radiate the available heat is quite short under these modeling assumptions, even for the limited emissivity. The square root of the temperature dependence arises from the competitive variations of the density (mass flow rate at constant pressure) and speed of sound with temperature.

Conversion Efficiency

The conversion of radiant power to electric power may be estimated by considering the radiator elements of length dz to operate at a temperature θ, and this section of the cell array converts the power with a local efficiency related to θ. Thus the electric power produced is given by an integration of an energy balance similar to eq. 8-64

$$d\dot{W}_e = \eta_q \dot{m} C_p dT \tag{8-70}$$

where η_q varies with temperature and is given by eq. 8-36. An average efficiency may be defined to describe the total electric power conversion from the enthalpy change:

$$\dot{W}_e \equiv \overline{\eta_q} \dot{m} C_p T_0 (\theta_2 - \theta_3) \tag{8-71}$$

or

$$\overline{\eta_q} = \frac{-1}{(\theta_2 - \theta_3)} \int_{\theta_2}^{\theta_3} \eta_q d\theta \tag{8-72}$$

This efficiency accounts for the varying temperature as the radiator tube decreases in local power density. This efficiency may be interpreted as a generalization of the local definition given in eq. 8-36. For $\lambda_0 = 1.1$ and 1.8 μm η_q is plotted in Fig. 8-18 together with the integrated value given by eq. 8-72 for the specific value of $\theta_2 = 10$ and variable θ_3. This average efficiency is relatively high, somewhat higher for lower cutoff wavelength, λ_0.

8.5.4. *System Characteristics*

The infrared photovoltaic (IRV, sometimes called TPV for thermal photo-voltaic) converter provides DC electric power with a minimum of moving parts. It is intrinsically quiet, modular, and can be built in relatively small sizes. It may be ideally suited for applications calling for distributed needs for both electric and thermal power, such as homes. The critical components may be designed to have long design life. An important design issue must be the inclusion of a cooling system to keep the cell at an appropriate temperature. The cost of a system is determined primarily by the cell area required. The power density from a source at 2500 K ($\theta = 8.5$) is about 2200 kW/m^2 at the source of the emitter. This falls to about 280 kW/m^2 at 1500 K. Thus the emissive power is the first parameter required to determine the cell area required. This, in turn, requires the identification of the peak source tempera-ture θ_2 as well as the lowest source temperature θ_3. Additionally one needs to consider the conversion efficiency and the concentration ratio of the optical system (Ref. 8-18). The optics of a central tube radiator such as that shown in Fig. 8-30 shows that increasing the ratio of radiator to cell areas above a factor of ten is a significant challenge.

The efficiency of the IR photovoltaic conversion system includes the fol-lowing components:

1. Fuel heat content to sensible heat and thermal radiation. This efficiency η_{th} is given by eq. 8-63 and shown in Fig. 8-29. It shows that, in addi-tion to the peak temperature, the radiator exit temperature through the radiator is also important. If this temperature drop is large (to a rela-tively low value of θ_2), the efficiency is high, but the power density is small in the section where the last of the radiant energy is transferred to the cell. Conversely, for θ_2 close to θ_3, the efficiency is low, unless means are used to recover the wasted heat.

2. Radiant heat not utilizable: this fraction is given by the actual (ϵ) to effective emissivity ϵ_{eff} given by eq. 8-34. This may be made close to ideal by providing a perfect reflector of long-wavelength radiation.

3. Excess energy in short-wavelength photons: the local efficiency is given by η_q (eq. 8-37) and global average by $\overline{\eta}_q$ (eq. 8-72 and Fig. 8-17). It shows that the efficiency is generally high and better for lower emitter temperatures. It is also better for cells with a shorter band gap wave-length.

4. Photon to electron-hole pair production: This aspect of the cell perfor-mance is intimately associated with the cell materials: reflection and pair recombination. This efficiency, η_{coll}, is given by eq. 8-50.

5. Cell power to load power: Joule dissipation in cell and associated circuitry is an unavoidable aspect of operation at any operating point. The ratio of power output to $\dot{w}^*$ gives the useful fraction. This ratio is shown in Fig. 8-24.

Using the nomenclature developed above, the overall efficiency (neglecting minor loss mechanisms such as internal reflection) is

$$\eta_{\text{overall}} = \eta_{\text{th}} \left(\frac{\varepsilon}{\varepsilon_{\text{eff}}} \right) \overline{\eta_q}\; \eta_{\text{cell}}\; \frac{\dot{w}}{\dot{w}^*} \qquad (8\text{-}73)$$

The magnitude of this efficiency requires analysis of design optimization of the system for a particular application. It is realistic to speculate that it may be sufficiently large to be interesting as a competitor to other energy conversion schemes. Particularly worthy of note is that the combination of efficiencies given in eq. 8-73 tends to favor temperatures that are relatively low, as indicated by their decreasing tendency with temperature. On the other hand, high power density requires high temperature. Thus this converter, like most others, must be designed to strike a balance between power (system cost) and efficiency (fuel cost). The optimal temperature has to be identified in connection with a specific performance requirement. Figure 8-32 qualitatively summarizes these ideas and specific experimental results that underscore them are described in Ref. 8-19.

Other aspects of the system characteristics are important. The cell operates at voltage levels less than 1 V, DC. Practical devices require minimal voltages in the range 10-100 V. This requires the cell array to be structured so that, say, sets of 20 to 200 cells are connected in series and these sets are then connected in parallel. The large number of connections is a design issue relating to reliability: the failure of one cell or connection in a set removes the set from the circuit as a power producer unless special matrix intertie connections are provided. The critical characteristic that renders an all-solid-state device less than perfectly reliable is the low cycle thermal movement associated with startup and shutdown.

The IRV converter is likely to be point designed for operation at a fixed (i.e., constant) power level. Even a small reduction of fuel input rate will reduce combustion temperatures and thereby reduce operating temperatures to much lower levels. This decreases the cell power density and probably decreases performance rapidly. As a consequence, this converter may be best suited for continuous power supply with modest modulation.

This discussion does not address an important set of design considerations that dictate performance level because it is outside the scope of this chapter: the gas dynamic and heat transfer considerations required for a successful design.

The cost and weight of a conversion device are typically related. The state of development of IRV devices is at present not sufficiently mature to judge weight accurately, but indications are that from the nature of the device, the weight could be low in comparison to that of competitive systems.

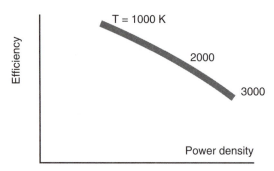

FIGURE 8-32. Qualitative relation between efficiency and power density of thermophotovoltaic converters as radiator temperature is varied.

Fuel-driven energy conversion systems all share similar environmental impact issues: emissions of H_2O and CO_2 (unavoidable), of CO and unburned hydrocarbons (relatively easy to control in surface-dominated processes where residence time is relatively long), and of elements in the fuel.

REFERENCES

8-1. Treble, F. C., Ed., *Generating Electricity from the Sun*, Pergamon Press, Oxford, 1991.

8-2. Lasnier, F. and Ang, T. G., *Photovoltaic Engineering Handbook*, Adam Hilger, Bristol, 1990.

8-3. Kittel, C., *Introduction to Solid State Physics*, John Wiley and Sons, New York, 1966

8-4. Fraas, L. M., Chapter 4 in *Current Topics in Photovoltaics*, Academic Press, New York, 1985.

8-5. Angrist, S. W., *Direct Energy Conversion*, 2nd edition, Allyn and Bacon, Boston, 1971.

8-6. Tauc, J., *Photo and Thermoelectric Phenomena in Semiconductors*, Pergamon Press, New York, 1972.

8-7. Fay, J. A., *Molecular Thermodynamics*, Addison-Wesley, Reading, Mass., 1965.

8-8. Möller, H. J., *Semiconductors for Solar Cells*, Artech House, Boston, 1993.

8-9. Pernisz, U. C. and Saha, C. K, "Silicon Carbide Emitter and Burner Elements for a TPV Converter," First NREL Conference on Thermophotovoltaics, Copper Mountain, Colorado, July 1994.

8-10. Kreith, F. and Kreider, J. F., *Principles of Solar Engineering*, Hemisphere Publishing Corp., Washington, 1978.

8-11. Billman, K. W., ed., *Radiation Energy Conversion in Space*, Volume 61, Progress in Astronautics and Aeronautics Series, M. Summerfield, Ed., AIAA, Washington, D.C., 1978.

8-12. Merrigan, J. A., *Sunlight to Electricity: Prospects for Solar Energy Conversion by Photovoltaics*, M.I.T. Press, Cambridge, Mass., 1975.

8-13. Wolf, M. J., "The Fundamentals of Improved Silicon Solar Cell Performance," Chapter 4 of Ad Hoc Panel on Solar Cell Efficiency, P. Rappaport, Chairman,

"Solar Cells; Outlook for Improved Efficiency," National Academy of Sciences, Washington, D.C., 1972.

8-14.   Hu, C. and White, R.M., *Solar Cells: From Basic to Advanced Systems*, McGraw-Hill Book Company, New York, 1983.

8-15.   Rappaport, P., RCA Review, *20*, 373, 1959

8-16.   Luque, A., "Photovoltaic Concentration," Chapter 12 of Treble, F. C., Ed., *Generating Electricity from the Sun*, Pergamon Press, Oxford, 1991.

8-17.   Hottel, H. C. and White, D. C., "Important Factors in Determining the Efficiency of TPC Systems, Part I, Exploratory Investigation of TPV Systems," First NREL Conference on Thermophotovoltaics, Copper Mountain, Colorado, July 1994.

8-18.   Hottel, H. C., "Important Factors in Determining the Efficiency of TPC Systems, Part II, Radiative Transfer Efficiency of a flat TPV System: Analytical Model and Numerical Results," First NREL Conference on Thermophotovoltaics, Copper Mountain, Colorado, July 1994.

8-19.   Fraas, L. M., Ballantine R., Samaras, J.and Seal, M., "Electric Power Production Using New GaSb Photovoltaic Cells with Extended Infrared Response," First NREL Conference on Thermophotovoltaics, Copper Mountain, Colorado, July 1994.

9

HEAT TO ELECTRICITY VIA BOUND ELECTRONS: THERMOELECTRICITY

Direct methods of producing electric power from thermal energy using the bound electrons in a solid are available and are termed *thermoelectric*. This chapter is a discussion of the physics and design parameters of systems where heat is used to elevate the energy of bound electrons. Since semiconductors are superior for taking advantage of this conversion scheme, this chapter is grounded in the discussion of the material found in Chapter 8.

9.1. PHYSICAL PHENOMENA IN THERMOELECTRIC INTERACTIONS

In metals and semiconductors, electrons (and holes, i.e., electron deficiencies, in the latter case) are free to move in the conduction band. These electrons respond to electric fields, which establish a flux of charges, or current. They can also respond to a gradient in temperature so as to accommodate a flow of heat. In either case, the motion of the electrons transports both their charge and their energy. Interesting physical effects can be observed in the limit of pure heat transfer or the application of an electric field because these phenomena are accompanied by interrelated manifestations, particularly at junctions of dissimilar materials where the electrons flow across a discontinuity in the energy levels of the conduction bands.

Consider first a conductor of material a that is connected to a voltage measurement device by means of two wires of material b, as shown on the left side of Fig. 9-1. When the two ends of the bar a are maintained at differing temperatures, say, $\Delta T = T_1 - T_2$, Seebeck (1822) observed that a voltage V (which varies with ΔT) can be measured when the current is zero. The limiting value of the proportionality constant is the Seebeck coefficient for the junction a-b:

$$\alpha_{ab} \equiv \lim_{\Delta T \to 0} \left(\frac{\Delta V}{\Delta T} \right) \quad \text{or} \quad V = \int_{T_1}^{T_2} \alpha_{ab}\, dT \qquad (9\text{-}1)$$

The integral form of this equation states that electrons will acquire an electric potential as electrons are transported from a region of varying thermal energies as measured by their temperatures.

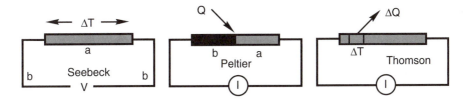

FIGURE 9-1. Fundamental thermoelectric effect experiments.

Consider next two bars of material a and b that are joined as shown in the center of Fig. 9-1. A current source is connected as shown. Peltier observed (in 1844) that the current flow results in the evolution of heat in an amount proportional to the current and that heat is absorbed when the direction of the current is reversed. Today this is known as the *Peltier effect* and is quantified through a proportionality constant associated with a particular junction of materials. The Peltier coefficient is defined as the ratio of heat evolved to current flowing:

$$\pi_{ab} \equiv \left(\frac{Q}{I}\right) \tag{9-2}$$

A related observation of Thomson (Lord Kelvin, 1854) is that a unit length of bar with a temperature gradient (right side of Fig. 9-1) evolves heat (in excess of the joule dissipation $= I^2R$) when current flows. The Thomson coefficient characterizes this phenomenon through the formation of the ratio:

$$\gamma \equiv \lim_{\Delta T \to 0} \frac{1}{I}\left(\frac{\Delta Q}{\Delta T}\right) \quad \text{or} \quad Q = \int_{T_1}^{T_2} \gamma I\, dT \tag{9-3}$$

These three effects and the phenomenological constants (α, π, and γ) that describe them are related through an energy balance that must apply around a circuit such as that shown in Fig. 9-2. The balance states that the electrical power generated as a result of a temperature difference maintained across a junction equals the heat dissipated at the two junctions and through the two bars. Thus

$$\int_{T_1}^{T_2} \alpha_{ab} I\, dT = (\pi_{ab\,2} - \pi_{ab\,1}) I + \int_{T_1}^{T_2} (\gamma_a - \gamma_b) I\, dT \tag{9-4}$$

or, in differential form,

$$\alpha_{ab} = \frac{d\,\pi_{ab}}{dT} + (\gamma_a - \gamma_b) \tag{9-5}$$

An additional relation may be invoked to relate the three coefficients if the process of conversion between heat and electric power in the electrothermal device is reversible. This assumption is borne out experimentally and results in the requirement that the entropy production rate for the system in Fig. 9-2 be zero. The entropy generated at the two junctions, where the temperatures differ, gives the entropy generated as

$$\Delta s = \left(\frac{\pi_{ab\,2}}{T_2} - \frac{\pi_{ab\,1}}{T_1} \right) I \qquad \text{or} \qquad ds = I\, d\left(\frac{\pi_{ab}}{T} \right) \tag{9-6}$$

Thus

$$\int_{T_1}^{T_2} I\, d\left(\frac{\pi_{ab}}{T} \right) + \int_{T_1}^{T_2} I \frac{(\gamma_a - \gamma_b)}{T}\, dT = 0 \tag{9-7}$$

where the second term is the dq/T term from the a and b legs of the circuit. The differential form of eq. 9-7 is

$$\frac{d\,\pi_{ab}}{dT} - \frac{\pi_{ab}}{T} + (\gamma_a - \gamma_b) = 0 \tag{9-8}$$

Inspection of eqs. 9-5 and 9-8 reveals that the Peltier and Seebeck coefficients are related through:

$$\frac{\pi_{ab}}{T} = \alpha_{ab} \tag{9-9}$$

This result is generally substantiated through experimental evidence so that the assumption of reversibility appears valid. Additional manipulation of these equations yields a relation for the Thomson coefficient in terms of either of the other two. In generators of practical interest, the effects of phenomena controlled by the Thomson coefficient are generally small (because the temperature gradients are small) so that they are not considered further.

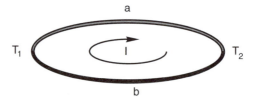

FIGURE 9-2. A simple, isolated thermoelectric circuit of two dissimilar materials, a and b.

9.2. THERMOELECTRIC POWER GENERATION

The convertibility of thermal power to electric power has led to the development of thermoelectric generators, whose principal advantage is simplicity and reliability due to a lack of moving parts. Any heat source is suitable and many have been used or proposed, including nuclear reactors, masses undergoing isotope decay, as well as combustion sources.

It turns out that the Seebeck effect and its related phenomena are minimal in metals. Its usefulness lies primarily in temperature measurement by means of the thermocouple. The use of semiconductors is more appropriate because the Seebeck coefficient is one to two orders of magnitude larger. Table 9-1 (from Ref. 9-1) gives the values in microvolts per K for a number of elements and of an alloy used in thermocouples.

Table 9–1. Seebeck coefficients at 100°C

Material	α (μV/K)
Al	-0.2
Constantan	-47.0
Cu	+3.5
Fe	+13.6
Pt	-5.2
Ge	+375.0
Si	-455.0

The Seebeck coefficient is not the sole measure of the adequacy of junction materials suitable for thermoelectric power generation. The thermal (k) and electrical conductivities (σ) are also important because they control the flow of heat and current. As a result of the generator analysis to follow, it will turn out that the ratio $\alpha^2 \sigma/k$ is critical. Jeaumotte (Ref. 9-2) makes the argument that semiconductor materials are optimal because the Seebeck coefficient decreases with increasing material electron density as one proceeds from insulator to semiconductor to metal, while the electrical conductivity increases in this progression. This leads to a maximum in the product of these properties. The role of thermal conductivity is minor because the increasing contribution of electronic thermal transport is relatively small compared to that associated with phonon (lattice wave) motion, which is independent of the electron density.

Figure 9-3 shows a representative configuration for a thermoelectric generator where m series units are coupled to yield a practical output voltage to the load resistance R_L. The legs connecting the hot and cold junctions are taken to be p and n doped semiconductor materials, as noted.

The p and n legs have thermal and electrical conductivities k_i and σ_i, respectively. For either conduction phenomenon, the conductance (K) of a bar of length L and cross-sectional area A is given by

$$K_i = k_i \frac{A_i}{L_i} \tag{9-10}$$

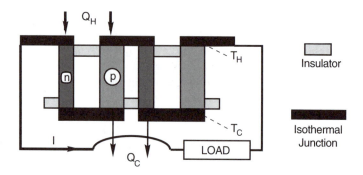

FIGURE 9-3. Segment of two series-connected thermoelectric
generator units.

where the i refers to either p or n. The thermal conduction paths for the two
conductor types are in *parallel*, so that the total thermal conductance for m
elements is

$$K = K_p + K_n = m\left(k_p \frac{A_p}{L_p} + k_n \frac{A_n}{L_n}\right) \qquad (9\text{-}11)$$

The electrical resistance is calculated in a similar way except that the m elements are in *series*. Thus the electrical resistance of the generator R, rather
than its inverse, the conductance, is more relevant. The resistance of the
power-generating portion of the circuit, as viewed by the load, is

$$R = R_p + R_n = m\left[\left(\sigma_p \frac{A_p}{L_p}\right)^{-1} + \left(\sigma_n \frac{A_n}{L_n}\right)^{-1}\right] \qquad (9\text{-}12)$$

9.2.1. *Efficiency and Power*

The energy conservation statement applied to the hot and cold junctions
involves four quantities associated with the various energy transport mechanisms. These are, for the hot junction:

1. Thermal input (Q);
2. Input from the resistive heating (Joule heating);
3. Output from thermoelectric effect (TE); and
4. Output by conduction (COND) away from the hot junction toward the
   cold one.

For the cold junction, the contributions are:

1. Thermal output;
2. Input from resistive heating;

3. Input of thermoelectric power; and

4. Input from conduction.

The direction of these terms is summarized in Fig. 9-4, and no significance should be attached to the magnitude of the vectors.

Since the Seebeck coefficient varies with temperature, the coefficient for the two junctions must be computed from

$$\bar{\alpha} = \frac{1}{T_H - T_C} \int_{T_C}^{T_H} (\alpha_p - \alpha_n)\, dT \qquad (9\text{-}13)$$

in order for the reversibility argument to be valid. This allows the writing of the hot and cold junction thermoelectric power terms as $m\,\bar{\alpha}\,T_H\,I$ and $m\,\bar{\alpha}\,T_C\,I$, respectively. The magnitudes of the heat input and output are:

$$Q_H = m\,\bar{\alpha}\,T_H\,I + K\,\Delta T - \frac{1}{2}\,I^2 R$$

$$Q_L = m\,\bar{\alpha}\,T_L\,I + K\,\Delta T + \frac{1}{2}\,I^2 R \qquad (9\text{-}14)$$

For the materials of interest, it may be assumed (see, for example, Ref. 9-3, p. 157) that the temperature profile is nearly linear and therefore the joule heating is equal to both cold and hot junctions.

The conversion efficiency is the ratio of electrical power delivered to the load of resistance R_L relative to thermal power input:

$$\eta = \frac{I^2 R_L}{Q_H} = \frac{I^2 R_L}{m\,\bar{\alpha}T_H\,I + K\,\Delta T - \frac{1}{2}\,I^2 R} \qquad (9\text{-}15)$$

This expression may be simplified by eliminating the current:

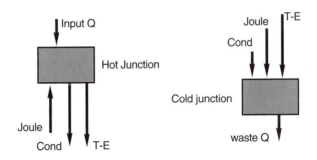

FIGURE 9-4. Energy balances on thermoelectric junctions.

$$I = \frac{m\,\overline{\alpha}\,\Delta T}{R + R_L} = \frac{m\,\overline{\alpha}\,\Delta T}{R\,(1+\mu)} \ ; \ \mu \equiv \frac{R_L}{R} \qquad (9\text{-}16)$$

where μ is a parametric measure of the load resistance relative to the generator resistance, R_L/R. This parameter is similar to the load factor described in Chapter 4. The efficiency expression then becomes

$$\eta = \frac{\mu\,\Delta T}{(1+\mu)\,T_H + (1+\mu)^2/Z - \Delta T/2} \qquad (9\text{-}17)$$

Here Z is a figure of merit for the thermoelectric generator materials defined by

$$Z = \frac{m^2\,\overline{\alpha}^2}{K\,R} \qquad (9\text{-}18)$$

which is equivalent to the reciprocal of a characteristic temperature for the materials. That this quantity represents a temperature may be deduced from the units or from the expression for η. Note that both K and R are proportional to m, so that Z is independent of it. This product may be written as

$$K\,R = m^2 \left(\frac{\kappa_p}{\sigma_p}\right)\left(1 + \frac{1}{x\,k_{pn}} + x\,\sigma_{pn} + \frac{\sigma_{pn}}{k_{pn}}\right) \qquad (9\text{-}19)$$

where

$$\sigma_{pn} \equiv \frac{\sigma_p}{\sigma_n}, \ k_{pn} \equiv \frac{k_p}{k_n}, \text{ and } x \equiv \frac{A_p\,L_n}{L_p\,A_n} \qquad (9\text{-}20)$$

The x parameter is a geometric factor, which can be chosen to maximize Z. From eq. 9-19, the value of x for minimum KR is

$$x_{\min\,KR} = \frac{1}{\sqrt{k_{pn}\,\sigma_{pn}}} \text{ and } (K\,R)_{\min} = m^2\,\frac{k_p}{\sigma_p}\left(1 + \sqrt{\frac{\sigma_{pn}}{k_{pn}}}\right)^2 \qquad (9\text{-}21)$$

From this, the maximum value of Z follows:

$$Z_{\max} = \left[\frac{\frac{1}{T_H - T_C}\int_{T_C}^{T_H}\alpha_{pn}\,dT}{\left(\sqrt{\frac{k_p}{\sigma_p}} + \sqrt{\frac{k_n}{\sigma_n}}\right)}\right]^2 = \frac{1}{T^*} \qquad (9\text{-}22)$$

Here Z_{max} is written in terms of a characteristic temperature because of its units. In order to see the variation of η with load resistance (μ), one may treat Z_{max} parametrically, noting that its inverse (i.e., T^*) varies between 200 and 1000 K (Ref. 9-3). Figure 9-5 shows this variation for the temperatures noted. The plot is for "nominal" values, $T_H = 900$ K, $T_C = 300$ K, and $T^* = 400$ K. Individual changes from these values are given as indicated. The Carnot efficiency of a heat engine operating between the temperatures of the nominal case is 0.67.

For a fixed set of temperatures and choice of p and n materials, the efficiency depends only on the load resistance through μ. The load factor for maximum efficiency is given by

$$\frac{\partial \eta}{\partial \mu} = 0 \quad \text{or} \quad \mu_{max\,\eta} = \left(\frac{R_L}{R}\right)_{max\,\eta} = \sqrt{1 + Z_{max}\frac{(T_C + T_H)}{2}} \qquad (9\text{-}23)$$

from which the maximum efficiency may be determined using eq. 9-17. Although one could, it is not appropriate to plot η as a function of reservoir temperatures (T_H and/or T_C) because the Seebeck coefficient is strongly temperature dependent, as is Z_{max} (or T^*). Kettani (Ref. 9-3) shows that the product ZT is of order unity or less and strongly peaked between 400 and 1000 K for a variety of materials. Figure 9-6 shows a sketch of a typical variation of Z.

Since the current is determined by a fixed maximum voltage (once the operating temperatures are established) and resistances, the voltage-current characteristic is linear with an open circuit voltage (V_{oc}) and short-circuit current (I_{sc}) given by:

$$V_{oc} = m\,\bar{\alpha}_{pn}\,\Delta T \quad \text{and} \quad I_{sc} = \frac{m\,\bar{\alpha}_{pn}\,\Delta T}{R} \qquad (9\text{-}24)$$

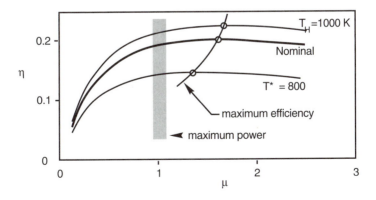

FIGURE 9-5. Thermal efficiency variation with load resistance. Nominal case is $T_H = 900$ K, $T_C = 300$ K, and $T^* = 1/Z_{max} = 400$ K. Other cases with changes are indicated.

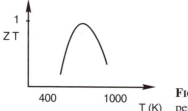

FIGURE 9-6. Variation of Z with temperature for a typical material.

where R is the generator internal resistance, given by eq. 9-12. The linear voltage–current characteristic and resulting power output are sketched in Fig. 9-7. The ratio I/I_{sc} is related to the resistance parameter μ through

$$\frac{I}{I_{sc}} = \frac{1}{1 + \mu} \tag{9-25}$$

The peak power point is at half-open-circuit voltage and half-short-circuit current. The peak power is

$$\text{maximum power} = \frac{\left(m\,\bar{\alpha}_{pn}\,\Delta T\right)^2}{4\,R} \tag{9-26}$$

and from eq. 9-25, the load resistance at this point is R so that $\mu_{max}W = 1$.

One may conclude that the advantage of simple and potentially very reliable thermoelectric systems must be balanced with relatively low thermal efficiency. The load resistances for maximum power and maximum efficiency are not far from one another. The efficiency at maximum power is not much less than its absolute maximum. The power output is scaled directly by the magnitude of the Seebeck effect voltage (squared), which can be established for chosen materials. A small electrical resistance of the semiconductor helps to increase power, although this is not a property that can be readily manipulated.

The development of successful system designs for thermoelectric energy conversion will continue to involve development of materials with superior properties and a better understanding of the nature of solid materials (Ref. 9-4). A review of the property development of silicon–germanium as a thermoelectric material, for example, is given in Ref. 9-5. Energy conversion using solid electrolytes has been investigated (Ref. 9-6) and appears to be interesting for a number of applications that range from commercial electric power to space power generation. The following section is an introduction to the physics of one kind of solid electrolyte converter.

9.3.   ALKALI METAL THERMOELECTRIC CONVERSION

Heat may be used to drive a current of ions, rather than neutral atoms, across a barrier. In this way, the flow of a hot material and its energy to a state of lower energy is realized and the thermodynamic consequence is that the elec-

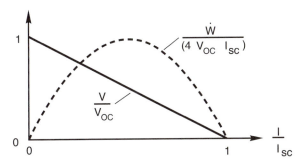

FIGURE 9-7. Voltage-current and power characteristics
of the thermoelectric generator.

trons that are created in the process carry the energy to a load. This section
is a brief summary of the physics of such an energy conversion process, called
by its acronym AMTEC (alkali metal thermoelectric conversion), as given by
Cole (in Ref. 9-6 and the citations noted there).

The possibility of this energy conversion arose from the development of
the sodium sulfur battery and the *sodium heat engine*. It centers on the fact
that beta"-alumina solid electrolyte (BASE) has a much larger ionic conductivity for Na^+ ions than for electrons. Thus this material is a selective barrier.
The BASE has a nominal composition of $Na_{5/3}Li_{1/3}Al_{32/3}O_{17}$ and is usually
fabricated as a dense microcrystalline ceramic. It is chemically unreactive to
temperatures near 1300 K, where it needs to operate in an energy conversion
process.

An AMTEC system configuration is shown in Fig. 9-8 with a heat source
(to 1300 K) and a sink in the 400–800 K range. From a Carnot viewpoint,
this heat engine realizes 70 to 40% thermal efficiency based on these temperatures. These values are sufficiently high that real devices may be interesting. The vapor pressure of sodium establishes the pressures in the system.
It varies from 10^{-9} atm at 400 K, 10^{-2} at 800 K, and 2.5 atm at 1300 K. The
pressure downstream of the electrode is therefore quite low, especially at low
temperatures.

A flow of sodium is established by an MHD pump (Section 4.4.1) acting
on the liquid phase, which raises the pressure from p_1 to p_2. The liquid
sodium is then heated isobarically to T_2. At this high temperature and pressure, the sodium liquid is forced into a section of the beta"-alumina, where
the adsorption reaction yields an electron on the liquid side of the alumina,
which is conducted to the load.

$$Na(liquid) \longrightarrow [Na^+]_{ads} + e^-_m \qquad (9\text{-}27)$$

The Na^+ ion is forced to a porous electrode downstream of the alumina, where
it is neutralized by the low-energy electrons from the load (Fig. 9-8) by the
above chemical reaction in reverse. An internal short circuit electron path
through the alumina is prevented by the high resistance to that charge carrier.

A low-pressure Na vapor is thus generated at this electrode. The free molecule flow of vapor then condenses upon exposure to the low-temperature reservoir at T_1. The power production part of the thermodynamic cycle is, in effect, an isothermal expansion from state 2 to state 3 at T_2.

9.3.1. *Voltage and Current*

The open circuit voltage generated by the chemical reaction is given by the Gibbs free energy change (eq. 7-13), which, in this isothermal process, is given by the Nernst equation:

$$\phi_0 = \frac{RT_2}{F} \ln\left(\frac{p_2}{p_3}\right) \tag{9-28}$$

The zero subscript on ϕ is to indicated zero current flow. Additional consideration of current flow changes a voltage-current relation somewhat into a nonlinear one. Equation 9-28 is, nevertheless, sufficient to establish the cell voltage as about 1 V.

The current density of this cell is determined by the flux of sodium vapor that can be created at the downstream side of the electrode by the combination of sodium ions and electrons from the load. If the electrode is modeled as "ideal" in the sense that it offers zero resistance to the flow of sodium, then $p_4 = p_3$, and the rate of molecular emission ($\dot{n}$, moles/sec/unit area) into a (near) vacuum is given by the random flux at temperature T for which the random thermal speed, $<c>$, is :

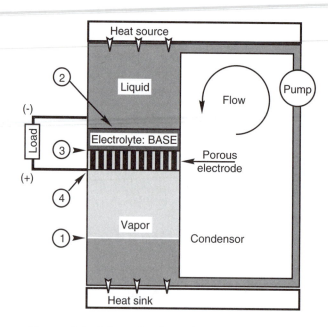

FIGURE 9-8. Schematic of an AMTEC power system.

$$\tilde{n} = \frac{n <c>}{4 N_0} = \frac{p}{N_0 \, k \, T} \frac{1}{4} \sqrt{\frac{8 \, k \, T}{\pi \, m_{Na}}} = \frac{p}{\sqrt{2\pi \, R \, T \, (MW)_{Na}}} \qquad (9\text{-}29)$$

Here n is the number density of the vapor, m_{Na} is the Na atom mass, m_1 is the unit atomic mass, [so that m_{Na}/m_1 is the molecular weight of Na, $(MW)_{Na}$], N_0 is Avagadro's number, and R is the gas constant for sodium vapor. The sodium emitter is the electrode at T_2, where the pressure is approximately that of the condenser. Since each mole carries a faraday's worth of charges, the current density is

$$j = \tilde{n} \, F = \frac{p_1 \, F}{\sqrt{2\pi \, R \, T_2 \, (MW)_{Na}}} \qquad (9\text{-}30)$$

Thus for conditions of interest, current densities of the order 1 A/cm^2 are practical, which establishes an interesting power density for this device. The reader is encouraged to consult Ref. 9-6 and the current periodical literature for a more complete discussion of this device as an energy converter. Efficiencies obtained for practical devices are about 15% at this stage of development.

PROBLEM

1. Show the validity of eq. 9-23.

BIBLIOGRAPHY

Angrist, S.W., *Direct Energy Conversion*, Allyn & Bacon, 1971.
Egli, P.H., *Thermoelectricity*, John Wiley, New York, 1958.
Goldsmid, H.J., *Applications of Thermoelectricity*, Methuen, London, 1960.
Gray, P.E., *The Dynamic Behavior of Thermoelectric Devices*, John Wiley and MIT Press, 1960.
Kaye, J. and Welsh, J.A., Eds., *Direct Conversion of Heat to Electricity*, John Wiley & Sons, New York, 1960.

REFERENCES

9-1.   Culp, A.W., *Principles of Energy Conversion*, McGraw-Hill, New York, 1979.
9-2.   Jaumotte, F.E., "Thermoelectric Effects," *Proceedings of the IRE*, **46** (3), March 1958.
9-3.   Kettani, M.A., *Direct Energy Conversion*, Addison Wesley Publishing Co., Reading, Mass., 1970.
9-4.   Wood, C. *Thermoelectric Energy Conversion*, Jet Propulsion Laboratory, California Institute of Technology, Pasadena, Calif., 1986.

9-5. Vining, C.B. and Fleurial, J.-P., "Silicon-Germanium: An Overview of Recent Developments," *International Conference on Thermoelectric Energy Conversion,* Cardiff, UK, 1991.

9-6. Cole, T., "Thermoelectric Energy Conversion with Solid Electrolytes," *Science,* **221**, 4614, 915, 2 September 1983.

APPENDIX A
MAXWELL-BOLTZMANN DISTRIBUTION FUNCTION

The distribution of velocities for a low-density gas is given by the Maxwell-Boltzmann (MB) function. For the criterion to ensure that the density is sufficiently low, see Chapter 4, Ref. 1.1. Any distribution function may be written in terms of a number of coordinates that characterize the velocity. These may be the speed, the velocity components, or the energy. The MB function gives the number of particles with speed between c and $c + dc$ as

$$dn = f(c) \ dc \qquad \text{(A-1)}$$

where the distribution function is

$$f(c) = 4\pi \ n \left(\frac{m}{2\pi \ k \ T}\right)^{3/2} c^2 \exp\left(-\frac{\frac{1}{2} \ m \ c^2}{kT}\right) \qquad \text{(A-2)}$$

In order to calculate gas particle fluxes, this distribution must be written in term of velocity components. In an x-y-z coordinate system, the velocity components (see Fig. 3-7) are

$$u = c \sin \theta \cos \phi$$
$$v = c \sin \theta \sin \phi$$
$$w = c \cos \theta \qquad \text{(A-3)}$$
$$c^2 = u^2 + v^2 + w^2$$

The differential of the velocity-space volume is

$$du \ dv \ dw \ = \ \sin \theta \ d\theta \ d\phi \ c^2 \ dc \ = \ 4\pi \ c^2 \ dc \qquad \text{(A-4)}$$

The last form of the differential is obtained from an integration over the allowable angular space variables. In terms of the Cartesian coordinate system velocities, the MB distribution function is

$$f(u, v, w) \ du \ dv \ dw = n \left(\frac{m}{2\pi \ k \ T}\right)^{3/2} \exp\left(-\frac{m \left(u^2 + v^2 + w^2\right)}{2 \ k \ T}\right) du \ dv \ dw \qquad \text{(A-5)}$$

The *average speed* in the ensemble of gas molecules is:

$$\bar{c} = \frac{1}{n} \int_0^\infty c\, f(c)\ dc = \sqrt{\frac{8\,k\,T}{\pi\,m}} \qquad \text{(A-6)}$$

For an area defined in space, the number of particles traveling through it per unit time *in one direction* (cancelling the flow in the other) is the particle flux given by

$$\int_{\theta=0}^{\pi} \int_{\phi=0}^{\pi} \int_{c=0}^{\infty} c\, f(c)\ dc\ d\phi\ \sin\theta\ d\theta = n\sqrt{\frac{kT}{2\pi\,m}} = \frac{n\,\bar{c}}{4} \quad \text{(A-7)}$$

where θ and ϕ (both equal to $\pi/2$) define the direction defining the normal to the area through which the flux is counted. The average (kinetic) energy per particle is

$$\bar{E} = \frac{1}{n} \int_0^\infty c^2\,(c)\ dc = \frac{1}{2}\, m\,\bar{c}^2 = \frac{3}{2}\, kT \qquad \text{(A-8)}$$

The distribution function is often desired to be written in terms of energy. Thus substituting eq. A-4 in to eq. A-2, one obtains a form equivalent to eq. A-1:

$$dn = n\,\frac{2}{\sqrt{\pi}}\sqrt{\frac{E}{kT}}\ \exp\left(-\frac{E}{kT}\right)\, d\left(\frac{E}{kT}\right) \qquad \text{(A-9)}$$

the number of particles with energies between E and $E + dE$.

Appendix B

FUNDAMENTAL PHYSICAL CONSTANTS

Table B–1. Values of fundamental physical constants (SI or MKS units)

Symbol	Value	Units	Name
m_e	9.109×10^{-31}	kg	electron mass
m_g (1 amu)	1.661×10^{-27}	kg	mass of atom of unit molecular "weight"
m_p	1.672×10^{-27}	kg	proton rest mass
m_n	1.675×10^{-27}	kg	neuton rest mass
h	6.626×10^{-34}	J-sec	Planck's constant
k	1.381×10^{-23}	J/K	Boltzmann's constant
e	1.602×10^{-19}	Coulomb	electronic charge
ε_0	8.8543×10^{-12}	$F\ m^{-1}$	permittivity of free space
μ_0	$4\pi \times 10^{-7}$	$H\ m^{-1}$	permeability of free space
c	2.998×10^8	$m\ sec^{-1}$	speed of light
N_0	6.022×10^{-26}	$(kg\text{-}mole)^{-1}$	Avogadro's number
F	9.649×10^{-7}	$C\ (kg\text{-}mole)^{-1}$	Faraday constant
R_u	8.314×10^3 1.987	$J\ (kg\text{-}mole)^{-1}\ K^{-1}$ $cal\ (mole)^{-1}\ K^{-1}$	universal gas constant
σ	5.669×10^{-8}	$W\ m^{-2}\ K^{-4}$	Stefan-Boltzmann constant
m_p/m_e	1836.1		proton-to-electron mass ratio
G	6.673×10^{-11}	$N\ m^2/kg^2$	gravitational constant

Source: *Rev. Mod. Phys.* **41** (375), 1969, American Institute of Physics.

INDEX